KATE CHOPIN

Also by Emily Toth

Regionalism and the Female Imagination, editor (1985)

Daughters of New Orleans (1983)

Inside Peyton Place: The Life of Grace Metalious (1981)

A *Kate Chopin Miscellany,* co-editor with Per Seyersted (1979)

The Curse: A Cultural History of Menstruation,
with Janice Delaney and Mary Jane Lupton (1976 and 1988)

KATE CHOPIN

EMILY TOTH

WILLIAM MORROW AND COMPANY, INC.

New York

Frontispiece photograph courtesy of J. A. Scholten/Missouri Historical Society, St. Louis.

Grateful acknowledgment is here given for permission to quote from the following materials:

Kate Chopin's published and unpublished works: David Chopin; Kate Chopin's papers, including her "Leaves of Affection," Commonplace Book, 1894 diary, poems, and correspondence with Marie Breazeale, Eliza O'Flaherty, Cornelia Maury, George S. Johns, R. E. Lee Gibson, Lewis Ely, Lizzie L., Sue V. Moore, L., Anna L. Moss, unknown correspondent, Janet Scammon Young, Dr. Dunrobin Thomson, *Youth's Companion*, Alexander DeMenil: Missouri Historical Society; Kate Chopin materials first published in *A Kate Chopin Miscellany*: Northwestern State University Press of Louisiana; J. H. Tighe letter to James Murrin: Jeannine Cook and Mary Nowicke; Oscar Chopin's letters: Jean Bardot; Albert Sampite's correspondence and papers: Leona Sampite; Kate Chopin's letter to Marion A. Baker: American Antiquarian Society, Miscellaneous Manuscripts "M"; Kate Chopin letter to Stone & Kimball: Kate Chopin Collection (no. 9442), Manuscripts Division, Special Collections Department, University of Virginia Library; Kate Chopin's correspondence with Stone & Kimball and Herbert S. Stone (1894–1899): Herbert S. Stone papers and Stone & Kimball papers, The Newberry Library, Chicago, Illinois; Kate Chopin's correspondence with the *Century*: Century Company Records, and Richard Watson Gilder: Richard Watson Gilder Papers—both in Rare Books and Manuscripts Division, The New York Public Library, Astor, Lenox and Tilden Foundations; Kate Chopin's correspondence with Houghton, Mifflin, H. E. Scudder, and Walter Hines Page: The Houghton Library of Harvard University; Kate Chopin's letter to Waitman Barbe: Waitman Barbe Papers, West Virginia and Regional History Collection, West Virginia University Libraries; Kate Chopin's "live oaks" version of the poem called "White Oaks": Barbara Sims; "To Carrie B.," "If Some Day," "To 'Billy' with a Box of Cigars," "The Haunted Chamber": Louisiana State University Press; Kate Chopin's autograph to Ruth McEnery Stuart: Howard-Tilton Memorial Library, Tulane University; Madison Cawein letter to R. E. Lee Gibson: Cawein Collection Manuscript Department, The Filson Club, Louisville, Kentucky; Kate Chopin letter to Lydia Ward: Lydia Ward Collection (no. 5672-a), Manuscripts Division, Special Collections Department, University of Virginia Library; Kate Chopin's letter to Richard B. Shepard, November 8, 1899: Harry Ransom Humanities Research Center, The University of Texas at Austin; Gustine Weaver letter to Cammie Henry and Florian Flanner letter: Melrose Collection, Cammie G. Henry Research Center, Eugene P. Watson Memorial Library, Northwestern State University of Louisiana.

Library of Congress Cataloging-in-Publication Data

Toth, Emily.
Kate Chopin / Emily Toth.
p.   cm.
Includes bibliographical references and index.
ISBN 0-688-09707-3
1. Chopin, Kate, 1851–1904.   2. Authors, American—19th century—Biography.   I. Title.
PS1294.C63T68   1990
813'.4—dc20
[B]   90-37894
                                                   CIP

Printed in the United States of America

First Edition

1 2 3 4 5 6 7 8 9 10

BOOK DESIGN BY MANUELA PAUL

To those who aided and sheltered and inspired me:

Lucille Tinker Carnahan

Dorothy Ginsberg Fitzgibbons

Susan Koppelman

Bruce Toth

PREFACE

I HAVE BEEN WORKING ON
Kate Chopin's literary career longer than she did.

She published for only fourteen years, yet produced over a hundred tales of
promise and passion, humor and melancholy and richness—and I had never
heard of her in 1970. Then a friend at an antiwar march handed me a copy of
The Awakening and said, "You have to read this." I did, and was astonished
that a woman in 1899 had asked the same questions that we, in the newly
revived women's movement, were asking seventy years later.

My friend, Annette Stadd, eventually took off for Denver to find herself (a
pursuit that Kate Chopin would have approved of)—while I, a graduate student
at Johns Hopkins University, had found a dissertation topic and a lifelong
pursuit.

When I began writing *That Outward Existence Which Conforms: Kate Chopin and Literary Convention*, only one other dissertation had been written on
Chopin. By the time I finished mine, there were nearly a dozen. I was part of
a wave of enthusiasm for a rediscovered writer: Her forgotten novel, *The Awakening*, was on its way to becoming a classic. Women readers were stunned by
the book; students were enthralled; professors embraced and dissected it.

Still, no one had answered the questions gnawing at me. How *had* Kate
Chopin known all that in 1899? What impelled her to write such pointed
observations about women and men? Was she indeed a pious widow who confined her romantic imaginings to her husband's memory—or an independent

woman who made untraditional choices? And was she truly silenced when *The Awakening* was condemned?

I finished my dissertation in 1975; I edited *The Kate Chopin Newsletter* (1975–1977) and co-edited *A Kate Chopin Miscellany* (1979)—and then, in 1983, I began trying to find answers to my questions. Per Seyersted, Chopin's editor and biographer, had generously shared his discoveries, and I retraced his trails and opened others. Squinting over long-unread manuscripts and blurry microfilms, I unearthed hitherto-unknown Kate Chopin writings. I interviewed Kate Chopin's family, a talented, engaging, and generous group of descendants she would have been delighted to know—and I sought out the historians and genealogists in St. Louis, New Orleans, and Cloutierville, Louisiana, the three places where Kate Chopin had lived.

In Cloutierville, the tiny French village where so many traditions remained, including the wisdom of a community of women, I found answers—surprising facts that gave a very different picture of Kate Chopin's marriage, widowhood, and passionate life. From what had been remembered and passed down in that small town, I learned that Kate Chopin had been playing a game of you-can't-catch-what-I'm-really-saying with her readers. Embedded in her Louisiana short stories, and in *The Awakening*, was the romance of her life—the man she loved, then left behind, in pursuit of something that mattered much more. At a critical moment in her life, Kate Chopin had made the same choice that Edna Pontellier makes: She chose herself.

This biography is the record of my own quest after the elusive Kate Chopin; it is also the first Chopin biography to be published in more than twenty years. But in the story of her life there are still gaps, and opportunities for speculation and reinterpretation. So much about Kate Chopin remains unknown, and perhaps unknowable—and so she remains, for me, what one of her contemporaries called her: a woman of "mysterious fascination."

—Emily Toth
Baton Rouge, Louisiana
January 1990

ACKNOWLEDGMENTS

I HAVE BEEN PREPARING TO write a biography of Kate Chopin for more than a third of my life. Virtually everyone I've met in the last twenty years has contributed in some way to my knowledge of Kate Chopin—by being amusing, or boring, or outrageous, or intriguing. Everyone has taught me a little bit about human peculiarities—and those, of course, are the subject of any biography.

Living in South Louisiana has taught me to appreciate the culture that inspired Kate Chopin, with its spicy food, gallows humor, sprightly and bluesy music, tropical beauty, and unique blend of goofiness and exoticism, corruption and ingenuity. Living in New Orleans in the 1970s changed me forever, as living in New Orleans in the 1870s did Kate Chopin: We met Louisiana at an impressionable age, and it stamped us forever.

I am also glad to have taught Kate Chopin's writings to thousands of college students over the past two decades, for their comments have been eye-opening. In the 1970s, my students wanted to know whether Kate Chopin had been involved with another man; by the 1980s, they cared most about whether she'd been able to make a living as a writer. Finance has replaced romance in American life.

As for my specific debts: All writers about Kate Chopin owe particular gratitude to Per Seyersted, who rediscovered her and made her works and her life story available to us. Seyersted has also been a generous collaborator with me, both on A Kate Chopin Miscellany (1979) and its forthcoming successor, Kate Chopin's Private Papers.

11 ❖

I am grateful to Annette Stadd for introducing me to *The Awakening*, and to the late Laurence B. Holland of Johns Hopkins University for encouraging me to write a dissertation on Kate Chopin. Along with my committee members, Susan O'Malley and Richard Macksey, Dr. Holland taught me about writing, thinking, and being a humane academic. Later colleagues, especially Sabrina Chapman, Lynne Goodstein, Audrey Rodgers, Susan and Michael Radis, and Daniel and Beatrice Walden, reinforced those ideas.

I have also benefited from former colleagues and associates who share my love of biography and gossip: from Morgan State University, Mary Jane Lupton; from the University of New Orleans, Carol Gelderman, William Rose, and Thomas Schlunz; from the University of North Dakota, Elizabeth Hampsten; from Pennsylvania State University, Philip and Fruma Klass and Stanley and Rodelle Weintraub. At Louisiana State University, where I moved after completing most of this manuscript, I have enjoyed biographical speculations with Veronica Makowsky and with my graduate students in a seminar on Gossip and American Writers.

The library staffs at all these universities have been energetic far beyond the call of duty, and I owe particular thanks to Charles Mann and Sandra Stelts at the Rare Books Collection at the Fred Lewis Pattee Library, Pennsylvania State University, and to Noelene Martin and Ruth Senior of Penn State's Interlibrary Loan Office. The present and former librarians at the Missouri Historical Society in St. Louis have been invaluable helpers in my research, especially Beverly Bishop, Martha Clevenger, Janice Fox, Peter Michel, Frances Hurd Stadler, and Carol Verble. I have also been aided by the staffs at the Library of Congress; at the Louisiana Collection, Howard-Tilton Library of Tulane University, especially Jane Stevens and Gay Craft; at the Historic New Orleans Collection, especially Jessica Travis; at the St. Louis Mercantile Library, especially Robert Behra, Charles Brown, and John Neal Hoover; at the Rare Books Collection, St. Louis Public Library, especially Erik Stocker; at the Rare Books Collection, Olin Library of Washington University, St. Louis; at the Cammie G. Henry Research Center, Eugene Watson Memorial Library, Northwestern State University of Louisiana; and at the Hill Memorial Library, Louisiana State University. At the National Archives of the Society of the Sacred Heart, Villa Duchesne, St. Louis, Sisters Marie Louise Martinez and Mary Cecelia Wheeler added immeasurably to my picture of Kate O'Flaherty's schoolgirl years. At the Watson Library at Northwestern State University of Louisiana, archivist Carol Wells has been a biographer's dream, and her energy and insights inform much of what I know about Kate Chopin's Natchitoches Parish years.

Financially, I have been aided by research grants over the years from the University of North Dakota; from Penn State (College of Liberal Arts, English

Department, sabbatical); and from Louisiana State University (Manship Research Fellowship). A National Endowment for the Humanities Travel to Collections Grant enabled me to do much of the St. Louis reading for this book, and a Research and Publication Grant from the Louisiana Endowment for the Humanities helped with final expenses.

Two research assistants—Marilyn Bonnell at Penn State and Judith Stafford at Louisiana State University—have done much to find lost footnotes and save me from my own follies. Marilyn Bonnell's transcriptions of Kate O'Flaherty's schoolgirl diaries and manuscript account books have been invaluable.

For assistance with photographs, thanks go to Mary Linn Bandaries, Don Sepulvado, Jill Sherman, and Duane Snedekker.

My greatest debt is to the countless people who shared their knowledge, encouragement, and often their hospitality in the two decades I've worked on Kate Chopin, and in the seven years I've devoted specifically to this biography. (And I apologize in advance for any I neglect to mention.)

My mother and father, Dorothy and John Fitzgibbons, taught me to read and love literature, and my mother has been a model and inspiration to me as a writer, thinker, and feminist activist. My aunt, Sara Ruffner, and my brother, Dennis Fitzgibbons, continue family traditions, to which Ellen Boyle and Theresa and Frank Toth also contribute.

My longtime friend Susan Koppelman has been my finest colleague, sounding board, and fellow yenta for gossip about dead people. I have also enjoyed the unique contributions of SKMSI, the best network imaginable for feminist writers and scholars: Cathy Davidson, Annette Kolodny, Dale Spender, and Linda Wagner-Martin should be particularly mentioned. Vickie Leonard provides both enthusiasm and skepticism, as needed. Linda Gardiner, editor of *Women's Review of Books,* has taught me about punctuation: I now use colons as well as dashes. Mindy Werner, Viking Penguin editor, has been a strong supporter. Havi Shafer served as feline muse for much of this project: Her Meow Mix is made at the Ralston Purina plant, on the site of Kate O'Flaherty's first home.

For my delving into Kate Chopin's hidden life, Lucille Tinker Carnahan of Cloutierville is the one who has made this book possible, for she knows more about the Cane River country than anyone else I've ever met. She has generously shared her knowledge, her insights, her memories, and her guest bedroom in ways I can never repay. The women of Cloutierville, Louisiana, have also made my research visits a delight—especially Leona Sampite, Emma Richter Masson, and the late Mildred McCoy, as well as many others who've shared tidbits with me. In Natchitoches, Louisiana, Gene Watson and the late Arthur Watson (Kate Chopin's great-nephew) have encouraged this project for years. Genealogists Elizabeth Shown Mills and Maryhelen Wilson have piqued my curiosity and tirelessly answered my nitpicking questions.

Other Kate Chopin scholars have formed a generous community that has nurtured this biography. Barbara Ewell has been a retriever of good things from New Orleans archives and collections, as well as a willing ear, a constant co-panelist, and friend: Her deep knowledge of Chopin's work has enriched mine. Thomas Bonner, Jr., has been generous with his research and ideas, particularly with the Guy de Maupassant translations and with less-apparent aspects of Chopin's Catholicism, and his *Kate Chopin Companion* has saved me from many a mistake. Bernard J. Koloski, another early discoverer of Kate Chopin, keeps alive the Chopin spirit in central Pennsylvania. His work shows us new ways to teach—and see—*The Awakening*. Jean Bardot, a newer Chopinist, has provided unique and fascinating information on Kate and Oscar Chopin's French roots, and he has finally solved the mystery of Kate Chopin's birthdate. I have also gleaned insights about Kate Chopin and Louisiana lore from (among others) Lynda Boren, Sara deSaussure Davis, W. Kenneth Holditch, Rosan Jordan, and Pamela Parker.

Kate Chopin's family has been cheerful and helpful: She would have liked her descendants. The St. Louis Chopins (David, Ann, George, Marie, Kate) have shared genealogical information and family reminiscences, as have Thomas and Rose Chopin of Florida. I have also benefited from the memories of those who knew Kate Chopin: the late July Breazeale Waters of New Orleans; the late Carmen Breazeale of Natchitoches; and Julie Chopin Cusachs of Baton Rouge.

My literary agent, Geri Thoma of the Elaine Markson Agency, first nudged me to do a Chopin biography, and she has been a clever adviser, valued friend, and smooth handler of countless obstacles. Susan Leon, the rare and intelligent and supportive editor who stays with projects until they come to fruition, has been with me and Kate Chopin since the beginning, for a much longer project than either of us ever anticipated. Deirdre Mullane did the first editing of a monstrous manuscript; Kate Christensen assisted in the last throes.

My husband, Bruce Toth, has always been a source of good humor, thoughtful questions, culinary treats, and irreverent pleasures. Kate Chopin and I are grateful.

CONTENTS

KATE CHOPIN

PROLOGUE

"PROVIDE YOURSELF WITH ammonia salts, brandy, etc," Lewis Ely warned Kate Chopin in a quickly scrawled note on May 13, 1899. "You have had or will have hysterics, I'm sure." He enclosed a review of her just-published novel, *The Awakening*. It was, her friends knew, her most daring and ambitious work.

Lewis Ely, an attorney, was one of many young admirers who swarmed about Kate Chopin in St. Louis in the 1890s. She had always been popular with men: Thirty years earlier, as a postwar belle, Kate O'Flaherty had been a famous "Irish Beauty." A man who met her only once called her the epitome of "female loveliness"; both sexes praised her "amiability" and "cleverness."

Now, nearing fifty, Kate Chopin was a nationally acclaimed writer, a stately woman with magnificent white hair and the air of a marquise. Contemporaries still praised her wit and admired her beauty, but also sought her literary advice—and wondered what she really thought. Her faint half-smile made her "a woman of mysterious fascination"; one friend called her "a rogue in porcelain." Even visitors to her literary salon—people who read her short stories and delighted in her sparkling conversation—felt they did not truly know her.

Kate Chopin had always had her secrets.

Even as a child, Kate O'Flaherty had not been sweet and submissive. She grimaced in family portraits; she asked impertinent questions; she stayed home from school to read romantic novels. In her teens, she preferred reading and writing to "general spreeing" or dancing until dawn with men "whose only talent lies in their feet." She despised mindless social chitchat, but knew exactly how to be a successful flirt: she revealed her secrets in her diary.

As a young wife in Louisiana, Kate Chopin gave birth to six children in nine years, but refused to be a conventional wife and mother. She smoked Cuban cigarettes, promenaded in her extravagantly fashionable clothes, lifted her skirts too high when she crossed the street, and scandalized the neighbors—especially after the sudden death of her husband, when she was thirty-two.

A resourceful and ambitious widow, Kate Chopin took over her husband's business with a flair. She also took an interest in another man. But when she returned to St. Louis to be with her mother, she left that man (and his wife) behind in Louisiana—and for the rest of her life, Kate Chopin wondered if she had made the right choice.

Then, within a year after the death of her pious Catholic mother, Kate O'Flaherty Chopin abandoned the church. Within four years, she had embarked on a literary career, writing stories set in the sensual atmosphere of the Louisiana she remembered. At first she published love poems, children's stories, and local-color sketches, mostly in daily newspapers. But her real interest was in examining independent women and not-so-happy marriages—and soon her realistic portrayals of passionate, discontented women were appearing in the most distinguished national magazines.

Her friends tended to be iconoclasts, among them bohemian newspaper editors who railed against censorship, plutocrats, and "society swells." Kate Chopin's friends were, her son Felix said, "a pink-red group of intellectuals" who "often expressed their independence by wearing eccentric clothing." They praised anarchy and nonconformity, encouraged Kate Chopin's writing and abetted her eccentricities, and agreed with her assessment of book reviewers: The ones with "a worthy critical faculty," she said, "might be counted upon the fingers of one hand."

At the center of such an avant-garde coterie, Kate Chopin evidently did not think that reviewers would be shocked by *The Awakening*—a novel about a Louisiana wife and mother who loses interest in her husband and children, falls in love with another man, devotes herself to her painting, and has an affair. Chopin's heroine Edna finds that men admire her, and desire her, but that is not enough; nor is it enough that women offer her sympathetic understanding. Edna cannot have what she most wants, an independent self, and in the end she eludes everyone, alone.

In *The Awakening*, Kate Chopin wrote about friendship, love, desire, fulfillment, and disillusionment. Through creating the roué who inspires her heroine's sexual awakening, Chopin relived her own memories of warm Louisiana nights and the "seductive entreaties" of another man: She transformed the passion of her Louisiana days into the sensual rhythms of prose. But *The Awak-*

ening is also about Edna's search for herself. Chopin originally called her novel *A Solitary Soul*, and she made it a hymn to aloneness as a source of strength and power.

To her contemporaries, though, *The Awakening* was a dangerous specimen of "sex fiction." It was "not a healthy book," the *St. Louis Globe-Democrat*'s reviewer wrote in the clipping Ely sent Kate Chopin. "It is a morbid book," the same critic concluded, "and the thought suggests itself that the author herself would probably like nothing better than to 'tear it to pieces' by criticism if only some other person had written it."

"I didn't know there was such a fool in the world as the writer of that article," Lewis Ely exclaimed, adding that the critic "drivels and drools along over the page just as though words were solely intended for idiots' tongues to splash in like a frolicsome infant in the soap suds." Ely was one of very few male friends who remained loyal to Kate Chopin.

The *Globe-Democrat*'s was only one of many vicious reviews condemning *The Awakening* for "coarseness" and immorality. The *St. Louis Mirror* reviewer, Frances Porcher, wrote that she would prefer "sleep unending" to what Kate Chopin revealed in *The Awakening*: "what an ugly, cruel, loathsome monster Passion can be when, like a tiger, it slowly stretches its graceful length and yawns and finally awakens." The *Pittsburgh Leader*'s young reviewer, Willa Cather, condemned *The Awakening*'s theme as "trite and sordid"; the *Providence Sunday Journal* said that "the purport of the story can hardly be described in language fit for publication." Even the *St. Louis Post-Dispatch* called the novel "Too strong drink for moral babes—should be labeled 'poison.' "

Still, women readers admired the book, and sent Chopin loyal and warm letters of praise for "the artist with the courageous soul that dares and defies." Seven months after *The Awakening* was published to an overwhelming chorus of male disapproval, the Wednesday Club—representing the women's intellectual elite of St. Louis—put on a special program honoring Kate Chopin.

Those who loved *The Awakening*—like those who hated it—recognized that Kate Chopin had written a deeply radical book, delving into the soul of a woman who yearned for passionate connection and deep solitude, and for "more wisdom than the Holy Ghost is usually pleased to vouchsafe to any woman." It was a soul very much like her own.

Chapter 1

A CURIOUS CHILD

KATIE O'FLAHERTY WAS A lively, inquisitive child—and something of a brat. Although her first portrait reveals the round, chubby, dimpled darling favored by baby lovers everywhere, she quickly developed a pugnacious streak. A photograph taken in 1855, when she was five, shows her wearing a mismatched vest and checkered dress, and sporting disordered ringlets in a wild variety of lengths. Despite her rigid pose—neck clamps were used for fidgety subjects—Katie O'Flaherty has rebellion in her eye.

By that time, Kate was no longer the baby of the family. One little sister, Marie Therese, had already died in infancy, as countless children did in St. Louis's unhealthy and dangerous climate: In 1849, over eight thousand St. Louisans, a third of them children, had died in a devastating cholera epidemic. It was not until two years later, a year after Kate O'Flaherty was born, that city authorities finally drained Chouteau's Pond, a stagnant sewer stuffed with butchers' offal and factory waste, only ten blocks from the O'Flahertys' home.

Nor was disease the only hazard in St. Louis. In May of the cholera year, St. Louis's worst fire destroyed four hundred buildings, including most of the warehouse district by the levee, where Thomas O'Flaherty, Kate's father, had his business. Almost every spring the Mississippi threatened to flood both sides of the river, and St. Louis was notorious for grime: The burning of soft coal for winter fuel blackened the city with a pall so dense that citizens used candles at noon—and everyone coughed incessantly. Every summer people sickened and died in the sultry, brick-baking heat.

Infants who survived their second summer were said to be safe—but by the fall of 1855, Katie O'Flaherty had another baby sister, Jane, who would be too fragile to survive. The crowded O'Flaherty household also included Kate and Jane's seven-year-old brother, Tom; their parents; their grandmother, Athénaïs Charleville Faris; five very young aunts and uncles; Ed. O'Flaherty, a surveyor; and slaves—four in 1855 and six in 1860, ranging in age from six months to sixty-four years. There was also George, Kate's winsome fifteen-year-old half-brother from Thomas's first marriage—but George was boarding at St. Louis University, where in 1855 he won honorable mentions in arithmetic and elocution. Noted for his kindness, George was popular with everyone, and his half-sister Katie adored him. That September 25, he sent her a letter that she treasured for the rest of her life.

> Dear Sister
>   I write to you this little letter because I love you so much & do
> not know what to do to show it. I hope your own dear little self
> and your sweet little sister Jane are both very well your brother
> George is well and hopes that you & your sweet little brother are
> going to school & learning fast. You must tell your Ma I hope
> She and my pa are well & tell her to come & see me & bring me
> some more clothes. I am Glad to call
>
>   Myself your Brother
>   George

According to most biographers, Kate O'Flaherty came into the world on February 8, 1851, but according to the United States Census, taken in August 1850, Katherine O'Flaherty had already made her appearance a year earlier. (She would have been born at home, and February 8, 1850, was a "wet, disagreeable day," according to the newspapers.) The census lists husband, wife, sons George and Thomas, and a seven-month-old baby whose name is given as "Cath."

Birth certificates were not systematically kept in St. Louis until two decades later, and the women in Kate O'Flaherty's family often fibbed about their ages, making themselves a year or two younger. Nevertheless, the St. Louis Cathedral registry does list, in a very misspelled record, the baptism of little Katherine O'Flaherty on May 12, 1850. According to the records signed by Father O. Renaud, Catherine O'Flaherty had been born the previous February 8, and her godparents were Jane and Charles Sanguinet. Kate may have been named for Saint Catherine of Siena—or for Thomas O'Flaherty's first wife.

Years later, the mature Kate Chopin claimed to believe that birthdays were meaningless: In her diary for June 2, 1894, she wrote, "I am younger today *at*

13 than I was at 23. What does it matter." (Emphasis added.) But the "Cath." of the 1850 census and the "Catherine" of the 1850 baptismal record was actually forty-four when she wrote that entry. She was lying to her diary.

It may be that Katie O'Flaherty's first, and longest-lasting, work of fiction was her own age.

Katie O'Flaherty's father left the house very early every day: She had spied on the huge black horses, the colorfully clad black footman, and the black-and-gold family carriage that came each morning to take Thomas O'Flaherty away. She was intrigued. "Where do you go?" Kate finally asked her father—and one day, over her mother's and grandmother's mild protests, he took her with him.

First they went to mass, at the old cathedral: Her father went to church every morning. Kate was somewhat disappointed—and (according to her son Felix) in later life she could never tell why. The weekday mass did lack the splendor of high mass on Sunday, with very few people, lights, or decorations, and even the holy pictures were hard to see. Only two pale candles burned while the priest said mass and her father knelt by her side, praying.

Then her father took her to the levee, a mile-long scene of excitement, with steamboats belching smoke and mule-driven drays, wagons, and carriages racing by, as men jostled and cursed at each other. The steamboats with their gaudy gingerbread trim resembled huge white animals, looming over hogsheads of sugar, bags of coffee, bales of cotton, and barrels from all over the world. Part of the wharf was paved with lumpy bricks, but the rest was steaming black mud, a hazard to a child's tiny slippers.

Kate smelled the Mississippi River, and the fish, the mud, the hay, the hides, and the stinking "fur rows" of pelts brought by trappers. She gawked at the Indians in their colorful clothes, and listened to the organ-grinders and bagpipers, and the musical cries of cigar vendors, apple and orange girls, boiler cleaners, and bootblacks. Everything fascinated her—although she would have been too young to understand some of the sights: the drunkards, confidence men, and pickpockets, the homeless, begging children, and the young girls who survived by selling their bodies to steamboatmen.

The outing created a special bond between Kate and her father, who encouraged her curiosity. The trip also inspired Kate O'Flaherty with a lifelong interest in the world that respectable young ladies did not see—and she connected being outdoors with freedom from social restraints. Twenty years later, as a young wife in New Orleans, she described riverfront scenes in her diary, including a cotton "pickery"; more than forty years later, she wrote *The Awakening* about a woman who swims out "where no woman had swum before."

In September 1855, Katie O'Flaherty started school, as a boarder at the Sacred Heart Academy on Fifth and Market Streets. (Day pupils were not yet admitted.) All the girls lived at the City House (*Maison de Ville*), a stern gray building with high walls, and Kate was separated from her mother for the first time.

Eliza Faris O'Flaherty was a quiet, self-possessed young woman: pretty, charming, gentle, and soft-voiced, she spoke English with a French lilt. She had led a sheltered life, was not greatly educated, and could not truly be called aristocracy—especially on her father's side, which had its share of Virginia rogues and renegade Protestants. Her grandfather Aaron Faris had been a state representative, but he was better known as the flashy proprietor of a boarding-house. Her father, Wilson Faris, was a well-educated man who, although he was a Protestant, was married in the Catholic Church. But Wilson Faris was also an incompetent businessman whose chronic failures enraged his shrewd and practical father-in-law, Joseph Charleville.

Joseph Charleville had never forgiven his daughter Marie Anne Athénaïs (Kate O'Flaherty's grandmother) for marrying an "American"—and although he gave special favors to other sons-in-law, Charleville did nothing to improve the lives of Athanaise and Wilson Faris. At one point, the hapless young Faris even signed over all his worldly goods to his father-in-law, including his furniture and his horse, to repay a debt owed for "rent of a house and boarding." Eventually Wilson Faris abandoned his wife and seven children, leaving them with very little money. He died within a year of his daughter Eliza's marriage to an Irishman old enough to be her father.

In his only surviving portrait, taken with his second wife, Eliza, Thomas O'Flaherty looks rigid and unbending—with regular features set in a stern, unsmiling face. He wears a starched white shirtfront and the high, tight collar and cravat and black coat worn by all respectable businessmen of his day. Eliza Faris O'Flaherty looks livelier, with bright dark eyes and glossy black hair parted in the middle, a striking contrast with her husband's sparse gray hair. On their wedding day, Thomas was thirty-nine, four years older than his mother-in-law. Eliza had just turned sixteen.

In the eyes of the old French of St. Louis—including his own grandmother-in-law, who spoke only French and never could pronounce "O'Flaherty"— Thomas was an upstart, without background. He was Irish at a time when Irishmen were widely assumed to be drunkards, thieves, loafers, and rowdies. (The St. Louis newspapers regularly identified some miscreants as "Irishmen.") But Thomas O'Flaherty had made a complete break with his past.

According to Daniel Rankin, who published the first biography of Kate Chopin in 1932, Thomas O'Flaherty was an educated and ambitious youth, born in Galway in 1805. According to Rankin, Thomas learned French and ematics from a parish priest; he liked to tramp about the Irish countryside; and "the varied activities of outdoor life were the diversions of his boyhood." At eighteen, Thomas, "dissatisfied with his father's occupation" as "land agent," left Ireland for America. In St. Louis, Thomas made his fortune, courted and married a young woman from an old French Creole family, and so achieved the Irish-American dream.

But the true story of Thomas O'Flaherty has much more heartache—and mystery—than Rankin admits into his sunny narrative. County Galway in 1823, when Thomas left, was one of the most blighted portions of that "most distressful country," Ireland—and most of the Irish emigrants to America were from Galway or the adjoining counties (Limerick, Cork, Mayo, Tipperary, and Kerry). The people of Galway, like their gray, rocky land, had never been willing to bend.

When the English first invaded Ireland, six centuries before Thomas O'Flaherty departed for the New World, the O'Flahertys had been among the most courageous defenders of Irish freedom. When the invaders barricaded themselves in a walled city in Galway, they inscribed on the West Gate their greatest fear: "From the fury of the O'Flahertys good Lord protect us."

Yet even the fierce O'Flahertys were powerless against oppression, illiteracy, poverty, and starvation. Rankin's description suggests that Thomas O'Flaherty, the son of Bridget and James O'Flaherty of Galway, chose to leave an idyllic life in Ireland—but that was not the lot of Catholics in the early nineteenth century. "The law does not suppose any such person to exist as an Irish Roman Catholic," British Lord Chancellor Bowen had declared. Irish Catholics could not vote or teach or carry guns; they could not make or sell books, or inherit large pieces of land—unless they converted to Protestantism. Their churches could not have steeples, and their public crosses were destroyed. Irish women were brutally raped by the British overlords.

Thomas O'Flaherty "enjoyed sailing boats," Rankin claims about Kate's father's early life, but virtually the only Irish boats around Galway were the rough *currachs* of the fishermen of the Aran islands. The typical Irish family owned only the clothes on their backs and the cramped hut they lived in— with mud walls and a turf roof barely five feet above the ground. In the winter, the Irish huddled with their animals, for warmth, and only the potato kept them all from starvation.

The O'Flahertys, Rankin suggests, were rather better off, as "land agents" in Galway for generations. But under British law, Irish Catholics could not buy land from Protestants, who owned almost all of it—and a land agent would have been a collaborator with the British oppressors. Thomas O'Flaherty left, Rankin writes, because he was "dissatisfied with his father's occupation," but he may also have been dissatisfied with his father's principles. Thomas O'Fla-

herty may have had a driving spirit of adventure—but he was also refusing a
life of poverty, or collaboration with the British enemies, or both. Instead, he
spent weeks at sea in the fetid, dangerous hold of a British ship—the only way
the Irish could reach America.

Thomas arrived in New York, according to Rankin, with "small means,
without undue family pride and all the futile snobberies it frequently fosters."
He joined the parade and cheered the dignitaries who gathered to celebrate the
opening of the Erie Canal. What work he did in New York is not recorded—
but there were plenty of risky jobs for Irishmen: unloading ships, digging canals
and ditches, constructing new buildings. (In slave states, bosses preferred Irishmen to slaves for the most dangerous jobs—because if a slave were killed, his
owner had to be reimbursed. As many as twenty thousand Irishmen died building the canals in New Orleans.)

Whatever New York offered was not enough. By 1825, two years after leaving Galway, Thomas O'Flaherty was heading west with his friend Roger
McAllister, who had arrived the year before from Belfast, and Thomas's "brother
Edmund O'Flaherty" (according to Rankin). The three trekked across the Al-
leghenies by stagecoach, traveled down the Ohio River by steamboat, and finally rode the ferry across the Mississippi River to the frontier city of St. Louis.

Roger McAllister eventually became Kate O'Flaherty's uncle: He and Thomas
married sisters. "Ed. O'Flaherty," listed as just twenty-five in the 1850 census,
may have been Thomas's son instead of his brother—perhaps the son of one
of the "Bridgets," the young Irish women who left home to be domestic servants in the New World, and lived and died in the squalid tenements of New
York. The presence of Edmund may have been what impelled Thomas
O'Flaherty to go west again. For every step Thomas made toward his goal, he
left behind losses, and mysteries.

In St. Louis, though, Thomas had a chance to try again—to be an indepen-
dent businessman, in a city that was the jumping-off point to the West. The
Irish of St. Louis were not so mired in poverty as those in New York—and
"Kerry Patch," the famous Irish ghetto, did not take shape until the 1840s,
twenty years after the first celebration of St. Patrick's Day in the city. By then
Thomas O'Flaherty had enough money to donate funds to the Erin Benevolent
Society for the half-starved squatters living in shanties in "The Patch." And a
half-century later, Thomas's daughter, Kate, perhaps inspired by her father's
memory, wrote a story about Kerry Patch, "A Vocation and a Voice."

At first, new to the city, Thomas went to work for the Irish-born merchant
Edward Walsh. Within a decade, Thomas O'Flaherty and Roger McAllister
had established a boat store, and the 1842 city directory lists Thomas at Seventh Street between Franklin Avenue and Washington, where he bought land
that was still providing income to his daughter half a century later. Thomas

cultivated a close friendship with Archbishop Peter Richard Kenrick of St. Louis, became secretary of the Catholic Orphan Association, and joined the Catholic Institute. He obviously valued reading: He contributed generously to the Institute's library and newspaper, and was an early subscriber to the St. Louis Mercantile Library.

Thomas O'Flaherty helped to bring the telegraph to Missouri; he sold supplies to pioneers traveling west; and he helped equip soldiers going off to the Mexican War—an effort that gained him an honorary title: captain. Captain O'Flaherty also joined a group of volunteer "gentlemen firemen," Union Fire Company No. 2, and he wore the crew's ceremonial uniform: colorful blue hats, blue shirts with a large number 2 displayed in gold, red silk neckties, and red patent-leather belts.

Captain O'Flaherty also married well. In November 1839, in the French village of Portage des Sioux in St. Charles County, he married Catherine Reilhe, the nineteen-year-old daughter of a French-Canadian merchant. She was related to the first American governor of Missouri, and her mother's family had founded Portage des Sioux. The marriage gave thirty-four-year-old Thomas O'Flaherty a new social status. A year later, their son, George, was born, but four years after that, Catherine Reilhe O'Flaherty died in childbirth.

Within six months, Thomas O'Flaherty would marry again, to another daughter of an old French family.

Whether Eliza Faris chafed at marrying a man just a year younger than her father, and a bare half-year after the man's first wife died, is not recorded. Nor was it common in Eliza's family to marry at sixteen: Her mother had been a bride at eighteen, and her sisters later married at nineteen, twenty-five, and twenty-eight.

Why Eliza married a man twenty-three years her senior, a widower and an Irishman, is obvious: As the eldest child, she did it to provide for her family. After her father's desertion, Eliza's marriage solved the Farises' desperate need for money. Her new husband handled the family debts, and paid the school bills for Eliza's six younger sisters and brothers. Eliza's little sister Josephine Faris was able to attend the Sacred Heart Academy, with Kate; Eliza's brother Charles Faris eventually married Clémence Benoist, daughter of the financier Louis A. Benoist, who left $5 million when he died.

For Thomas O'Flaherty, his marriage cemented his standing in St. Louis society—for on her mother's side, Eliza Faris's Charleville ancestry could be traced back to the earliest days of St. Louis. Her great-grandmother's guardian had been the powerful Auguste Chouteau, one of the founders of the city, and the Charlevilles still owned an estate—a reconstructed homestead originally built of logs—in St. Louis County.

If Eliza ever regretted her marriage, she left no record—but her daughter Kate Chopin included more than a few hints in her novels and short stories. Chopin's fictional wives are often discontented, and attracted to other men; some of them yearn for the freedom of their single days, as does the heroine in "Athénaïse," a story named for Kate's grandmother. Kate Chopin may also have been thinking of her mother's marriage when she wrote *The Awakening*— in which Edna, after several youthful infatuations, marries an older man who is safe, secure, and rich, thereby "closing the portals forever behind her upon the realm of romance and dreams."

Eliza Faris and Thomas O'Flaherty were married on August 1, 1844, in St. Francis Xavier Church, and four years later their first child, Thomas, Jr., was born. The family settled in a large, handsome, two-story southern-style home on Eighth Street, between Chouteau and Gratiot. The house, sketched for a *St. Louis Post-Dispatch* article on Kate Chopin in 1899, had a high flight of stone steps, tall columns, and a wide southern gallery extending the length of the house. The large dining room overlooked a lush garden of flower beds, paths, and a stone column with a sundial—but, most important, there was an attic, where, later, Katie O'Flaherty could read and be alone.

The O'Flahertys did own four slaves in 1855, but only one name has been passed down: Louise, who may have been Kate's mammy. A male slave used to hold Kate's pony while she rode. The neighbors, also slaveholders, were members of the upper class that Thomas O'Flaherty wanted to join. On Chouteau Avenue was the home of Juliette McLane Garesché, an ambassador's daughter, and Peter Bauduy Garesché, whose daughter Kitty became Katie O'Flaherty's lifelong friend. Mrs. Sophie Chouteau, from St. Louis's founding family, lived on Eighth Street, as did James Harrison, of the banking firm of Chouteau, Harrison & Valle; and George Knapp of the *Missouri Republican* later lived on the same street.

By the fall of 1855, Captain Thomas O'Flaherty had a daughter at the Sacred Heart Academy and a son at St. Louis University—something he could scarcely have dreamed of in Ireland, where no Catholic could attend a university. He had a young wife who was noted for her charm and lavish hospitality, and his net financial worth qualified him as one of the "solid men of St. Louis."

His business was also certain to improve with the opening of railroad connections to Jefferson City over the new Gasconade Bridge. On All Saints' Day, November 1, 1855, St. Louis would become the gateway to the West.

The first train over the Gasconade Bridge on November 1 was full of solid men, including the mayor and city council. Crowds cheered, bands played, soldiers paraded, and over six hundred invited guests jammed the gaily bedecked railroad cars for the historic journey. Among them were Captain Thomas O'Flaherty, the ministers Artemus Bullard and John Teasdale, and the banker Louis A. Benoist, the richest and most powerful man in St. Louis and owner of a magnificent country estate called Oakland. (It was at Oakland, over a decade later, that Kate O'Flaherty met a handsome Benoist grandnephew from Louisiana named Oscar Chopin.)

There was a driving rain as the ceremonial train approached the Gasconade Bridge. The locomotive had just reached the edge of the first pier when the floor timbers suddenly cracked under the impact, and the wooden trestle work of the bridge gave way. The locomotive fell backward and downward. Ten of the cars plunged thirty feet, into the river.

Some cars fell on the ones before them; others hung precariously on the edge of the cliff; two or three turned upside down. Only the last car stayed on the rail, while below it was a mass of twisted metal. Just before his car went down, Reverend Teasdale was heard to exclaim, "Great God! how terrible are thy judgments!"

"As soon as the crash was over," the *Missouri Republican* reported, "a moment of painful silence ensued, and then issued from the wreck the groans of the wounded, the supplications of the imprisoned, the screams of the agonized, while here and there might be observed the upturned face of the dead, mangled and clotted with blood, or the half-buried forms of others whose spirits had passed away forever. To add to the horror of the scene, a storm of lightning, thunder and rain arose of the severest description."

Thirty men died, including the ministers Artemus Bullard and John Teasdale. The financier Louis A. Benoist escaped with only a small cut in his leg, although his trousers were torn from his ankle to his thigh. On Sundays in later years, he sometimes wanted to skip going to mass—whereupon his wife, who had given birth to their daughter Clémence just a month after the disaster, would fetch Louis's torn and bloody trousers from the closet and wave them over his head, crying, "Remember the Gasconade!"

The telegraph first brought the news to St. Louis, and then the newspapers. Later, the *Missouri Republican* retracted the reports of two deaths. A Mr. Moore from Cape Girardeau was injured, not killed, and a Mr. Bryan, a St. Louis lumber merchant, had not been on the train at all.

But Captain Thomas O'Flaherty had indeed been on the train—and he was dead.

Thomas O'Flaherty's funeral took place at nine o'clock on Sunday morning, November 4, 1855, in the old St. Louis Cathedral, where he had first taken his daughter, Katie, to mass before their outing to the levee. The funeral was Kate's first encounter with the finality of death.

At the solemn mass of requiem for the repose of her father's soul, the five-year-old Katie O'Flaherty heard her father's Irish friend, the stern and gray-haired Archbishop Peter Richard Kenrick, give "a beautiful and touching address." Kate kept, and later gave to her own children, the expression of sympathy from the Catholic Institute, praising Captain O'Flaherty for his "urbanity of deport-ment," "purity of heart," and zeal for Catholic enterprises. The Institute's loss was small, the members wrote, "compared with that of those who, in his de-cease, mourn for a husband, and a father, but to whom he leaves the priceless heritage of an unsullied name."

"The remains of Capt. Thomas O'Flaherty were accompanied to the grave," the *Missouri Republican* reported, "by an immense number of his personal friends and those who respected him for his many virtues, and also by the Washington Guards, of which he was an honorary member." He was buried in the Calvary Cemetery plot that he had bought two years earlier, along the Way of the Sorrowful Mother, and a stone pillar was erected in his memory.

All the next week was devoted to mourning. Businesses were closed; repre-sentatives urged the legislature to aid the railroads; pulpit sermons called the disaster the will of God. Funds were set up to aid the wives and families of indigent victims—but Eliza O'Flaherty's husband had provided well for her, and Kate's tuition at the Sacred Heart Academy had been paid through No-vember 20.

But by then Kate had left school, and for the next two years she would be at home.

Eliza O'Flaherty seemed to be a pious widow, devoted to her husband's memory. Kitty Garesché, Kate's friend, recalled that Mrs. O'Flaherty was "sad and beautiful. . . . This I explain to myself by knowing that her soul must have been shrouded in grief at her dear husband's untimely death."

Thomas O'Flaherty had died without a will, but Eliza O'Flaherty and the children (George, Thomas, Kate, and Jane) were declared his heirs, according to the affidavit of heirs filed on November 10. The widowed Eliza, just twenty-seven, now controlled a large estate, valued at $24,160 in 1861. She had not married for romantic reasons, and she had already buried at least one infant— and a widow mourning the loss of her husband was always respected in society (as Kate Chopin later showed in "A Lady of Bayou St. John"). There were many reasons for a widow to remain single, and Eliza never remarried.

As for her daughter, Katie O'Flaherty evidently brooded over her father's death and her mother's life. Thirty-nine years after the Gasconade, in "The Story of an Hour," Kate Chopin used a husband's reported death in a train accident as a catalyst for a wife's "monstrous joy": The new widow revels in being "Free! body and soul free!" But when her husband walks in, having been nowhere near the crash, the wife, Louise, has a sudden attack, and the doctors say she died of "heart disease—of joy that kills."

In real life, Eliza O'Flaherty's French-speaking relatives called her "Elisa," pronounced "Eleeza"—a name that would sound very much like *Louise* to a frightened, eavesdropping child. Eliza's sister was named Josephine—and so is the fictional Louise's. Chopin even gave the husband a name similar to one of the Gasconade dead, Artemus *Bullard*: Brently Mallard. And Mallard's initials are those of Bryan and Moore, the two men falsely reported dead at the Gasconade Bridge. Through "The Story of an Hour," Kate Chopin rewrote a childhood grief.

And when Thomas O'Flaherty died, one member of the household found in his death an opportunity—to mold a young girl's mind.

Chapter 2

TALES AT AN
IMPRESSIONABLE
AGE

WHEN SHE EMBARKED ON HER life's great work, the education of her great-granddaughter Katie O'Flaherty, Madame Victoire Verdon Charleville was already in her seventies. Four years earlier, in May 1851, Madame Charleville had carefully divided her property among her children, to assure their "temporal prosperity"—and then she proceeded to live for another dozen years.

In her only surviving portrait, painted around the time Katie O'Flaherty was born, Madame Charleville looks stern, but with hints of unconventionality. A trace of a smile lurks in one corner of her mouth; her bonnet is tied coquettishly in a side bow; her gaudy brooch is pinned in the middle of her chest instead of at the neckline. She does not wear the traditional crucifix: Victoire Charleville was no blind follower of patterns.

Madame Charleville, named Victoire Verdon after her mother, was probably born in 1784, although she may have been born as early as 1780, known as "*L'Année du Grand Coup*"—the year of the last sustained British and Indian attack on St. Louis. As many as sixty St. Louisans were killed in the raid, launched while the *habitants* were gathering strawberries for Corpus Christi Day. Among the fiercest defenders of the small French village was Madame Rigauche, founder of the first school for girls in St. Louis. If the future Madame Charleville attended school at all—few girls did—the heroic Madame Rigauche, who lived to be ninety-five, would have been her teacher.

The young Victoire Verdon had, at most, very little formal education: Even in the generation after hers, half the heads of households in St. Louis signed legal documents with an X. Still, more women than men could sign their own names, and some had definite intellectual pursuits: Village women read the memoirs of duchesses and the letters of Madame de Sévigné to her daughter. At least one of Victoire Verdon's female contemporaries, Catherine Condé Benoist, was a self-educated, avid reader of French philosophy and drama, who according to her obituary "was one of the few women who know how to mingle the literary, the domestic and the religious elements." Victoire Verdon Charleville seems to have been another.

Madame Charleville began teaching her great-granddaughter at an impressionable age—and her influence would endure for the rest of Kate's life. Unlike other "Americans," Madame decided, Kate would learn to speak and write French well. Madame spoke the soft Creole patois, less sharp than the French of Paris, and her conversation was full of colorful and picturesque imagery. Kate and her great-grandmother had daily conversations in French, and in later life Kate was always at home in French: She wrote it in her diary, spoke it when she lived in Louisiana, and used it to translate Guy de Maupassant's stories in the 1890s.

Madame Charleville's curriculum included a daily music lesson at the piano (whether she began the lessons secretly, before the year of mourning for Thomas O'Flaherty was over, cannot be known). Music had long been an appropriate accomplishment for young ladies, but Kate was no dilettante: Years later, she paid for extra piano lessons at school, and described in her diary the almost sensual pleasure she took in beautiful music. In her first published short story, "Wiser Than a God," Kate Chopin wrote about a pianist who prefers her art to the love of a young man; and in *The Awakening*, she described the magnificent piano playing of Mademoiselle Reisz, especially when she does "Chopin."

Madame Charleville liked to teach through storytelling. Kate learned early St. Louis history, and learned that she should not trust appearances: She should be clear-sighted and fearless. Madame Charleville's refusal to judge others nurtured the realism of Kate Chopin's later fiction—and Madame's stories also gave Katie O'Flaherty unusual insight into human peculiarities and possibilities. Before her father's death, Kate had seen that the world of men—the world at the levee—was very different from the domestic lives of ladies. But when Madame Charleville taught Kate about women's values and women's culture, she gave her the most exciting stories of all.

From her great-grandmother's stories, Kate O'Flaherty discovered that she came from a long line of determined maternal ancestors. The Charleville family had been in the New World for nearly two centuries, ever since Marthe

L'hauteux Chauvin forsook home and family in 1658 to be a "frontier bride" in Montreal.

The Charlevilles evidently came from Château d'Oléron, a seaport on L'Île d'Oléron, an island of fishermen and vineyards off the coast of La Rochelle, in northern France. La Rochelle was a center for hat making, and for Protestantism in France: In Alexandre Dumas's *The Three Musketeers*, La Rochelle appears as a nest of Huguenot subversives. Possibly religious nonconformity— as well as a spirit of adventure—motivated those Charlevilles who sailed to the New World and settled in the wilds of Canada.

Half a century later, in 1704, when the first boatload of unmarried French-women arrived in the Louisiana colony, another Charleville ancestress was among these "Pelican Girls," named for the ship that brought them. Marie Briard Rivard, an adventurous Parisienne, soon rebelled: She and her ship-mates could not cook—or eat—the peculiar roots and leaves and corn they found in the tiny Louisiana colony. In the "Petticoat Rebellion of Mobile," Marie and the others marched on Governor Bienville's house, threatening to leave on the next boat if conditions did not improve.

They were saved by a woman. The governor's Choctaw cook showed them how to transform Indian corn into hominy and grits, and how to dry and crush sassafras leaves to make *filé*—the spicy, tingling powder that was the soul of the soup they called "gumbo." And so Marie Briard Rivard and her friends were among the first white people to appreciate—and then to create—the piquant flavors that have made Louisiana cookery famous around the world. Marie herself married a farmer, one of the first on the Bayou St. John in New Orleans.

Then, some eighty years later, Katie O'Flaherty's great-great-grandmother had marital misadventures that made St. Louis history.

Like most French Catholic girls, Kate's great-great-grandmother was christened with the name Marie. Born on the Île d'Oléron between 1745 and 1751, Marieanne Victoire Richelet immigrated with her parents to the Louisiana colony. She was married, gave birth to two daughters, was abruptly widowed— and then married again.

Victoire's second husband, Joseph Verdon, was a carpenter some twenty years her senior. They prospered, and she gave birth to four more children, but according to the historian Frederick Billon, their tempers were not congenial, and "they kept matters pretty lively at home with continual bickering and quar-rels for a period of twelve years." Eventually they held "a council of war and decided that 'for the salvation of their souls' they had better live apart the balance of their days."

Since divorce was not possible for Roman Catholics, the Verdons in 1785 obtained a legal separation, the first one ever granted in St. Louis. Madame Verdon was given all the property, except for Joseph's gun, bed, clothes, and tools. She agreed to pay all debts, and "Old Joe" Verdon agreed "not to trouble her nor make any demand."

Then, four-and-a-half years later, Victoire Verdon gave birth to a son, duly registered as the child of Joseph Verdon—but it is unlikely that the feuding Verdons had reconciled. More likely, Victoire had a lover. And although early St. Louisans were quick to sue one another for slander, usually over a lady's virtue, no lawsuits were filed about Victoire Verdon and her son of questionable parentage—perhaps because Victoire had become a powerful person in the community.

At the time of the legal separation, Victoire Verdon could neither read nor write, but she had a spirit of enterprise. She began to take short trips downriver, trading small household items of particular value to women—buttons, pins, utensils—for furs and salts. Her business grew and expanded, until she was operating an entire line of very profitable trading vessels between New Orleans and St. Louis. She had a keen business sense, and learned to sign her name with a flourish: not a simple "Victoire Verdon," but a grand "La Verdon" (*the* Verdon). When she died in 1796, she left a sizable fortune, and the guardian of her minor children (including Kate's great-grandmother) was the great Auguste Chouteau, one of the founding fathers of St. Louis.

La Verdon also, apparently, bequeathed to her children a taste for feuding. The founder Auguste Chouteau died thinking he had long ago discharged his legal obligations toward the Verdon children—but in 1852, some twenty-three years after his death, La Verdon's daughter, Victoire Verdon Charleville, sued his estate, claiming he had defrauded her of land. The court ruled that the whole matter had been settled in 1799, that the land was worthless anyway, and that it would set a very bad precedent if people were allowed to bring up "old and stale demands" and sue individuals who had been dead for more than twenty years. Madame Charleville seems to have been motivated more by malice than by legal right—although she may have given Katie O'Flaherty a different version of the story.

Madame Charleville's own story of married life began a year after "La Verdon" died—when the younger Victoire married Joseph Charleville on July 17, 1797. (The bride may have been as young as thirteen.) The customary banns had not been read for three consecutive Sundays before Victoire married Joseph—and the young Madame Charleville's first child was born only five months after the ceremony.

Eventually Madame Charleville gave birth to fifteen children, eight of whom lived to adulthood. She outlived her husband by eighteen years, and she had a great deal to tell her little great-granddaughter about early St. Louis and the changes she had seen.

Colonial St. Louis had been famous for its fragrant gardens and gossipy inhabitants, among whom a conversational talent (*repartie*) was considered a great blessing. But life was also primitive by the standards of the 1850s: Most women split wood, carried water, milked cows, sewed their own clothes, and went barefoot in the summer. Most families lived in whitewashed log cabins, and social standing seemed to derive, as in Voltaire's *Candide*, from the number of windows and doors.

In fact, Voltaire was one of the authors whose works appeared in the libraries of Auguste Chouteau and Pierre Laclède Liguest, the other founder of St. Louis: Fully a quarter of Chouteau's library consisted of books by Voltaire, Descartes, Locke, and others who were on the church's Index, the list of books Catholics were forbidden to read. From the earliest days, St. Louisans had been nominal Catholics—but actual freethinkers. (A Baptist minister who visited St. Louis in 1818, when Madame Charleville was in her thirties, was astonished to note that mass was attended only by "females and illiterate Frenchmen," and that the French leadership, influenced by Voltaire, considered religion a superstitious form of "priestcraft.")

Many St. Louisans were freethinkers in morals as well as faith. Madame Charleville knew—and told Kate—about the most famous scandal of early St. Louis: Madame Marie Thérèse Bourgeois Chouteau, the mother of the founder, had left her brutal husband and gone to live with Pierre Laclède Liguest, the elegant, brave, and well-read Frenchman who founded the city, with her young son Auguste. Madame Chouteau stayed with Laclède for the rest of his life, but their four children were given her husband's last name—so that most of the grand Chouteaus of St. Louis were really Laclèdes. Madame herself never took Laclède's name, and never married him, although she could have: Her husband died two years before Laclède did.

It was a tale that always troubled moralistic minds in St. Louis. Genteel historians (including Kate Chopin's contemporary Alexander DeMenil) never gave up claiming that Madame Chouteau had really been faithful to her husband—or that she and Laclède had a secret common-law marriage. According to Rankin, Madame Charleville told Kate the tale of Madame Chouteau and Laclède "with sad and sordid explanations"—but in fact, Madame may have told the story with great relish.

Indeed, Kate's later attitudes toward adultery suggest a realistic, if not amoral, attitude on the part of her great-grandmother: The famed Madame Chouteau, like the Charleville women, did not follow duty blindly. She outlived Laclède by thirty-six years, never remarried, and was a tough businesswoman who drove a hard bargain. She made herself one of the wealthiest fur traders in St. Louis history, and social-climbing St. Louisans always claimed kinship to Madame Chouteau.

There were other notorious tales for Victoire Charleville to share with Katie O'Flaherty. There was Madame Elizabeth de Volsay, for instance, whose husband had denounced her for "open and shameless debauchery" with another man, and convinced the governor to dissolve their marriage in 1779, in St. Louis's first divorce. According to her neighbors, Madame de Volsay had flagrantly lived with her lover during her husband's absence on business, and the two had squandered Monsieur de Volsay's wealth. Madame de Volsay was condemned by the men of her day—but her husband was hardly a faithful spouse: In his will, he left most of his property to his illegitimate mixed-blood daughter.

There were also the sins of Madame Charleville's own uncles. One fathered two half-Indian children by an Osage woman he never married; another, in a liaison with a mixed-blood woman, fathered the quadroon Louis Dunois, who called himself Louis Charleville and became a successful cattle dealer and part of "The Colored Aristocracy of St. Louis." He was buried in Calvary Cemetery, a stone's throw away from his white relatives.

So much had changed, though, since Madame Charleville's youth. When the Americans took over in 1804, after the Louisiana Purchase, the French-speaking population believed that moral decay had immediately set in. As the French viewed them, American men were a churlish, drunken, brawling lot, with none of the French respect for manners and breeding. Half a century later, Katie O'Flaherty's St. Louis was no longer a village, but a brick and stone metropolis, with gaslight, steamboats, and streetcars pulled by mules—but adventure was still possible for the intrepid.

Madame Charleville's youngest son, Fred ("F. A.," Kate's great uncle), was among thousands of forty-niners who rushed to California in search of gold. With his bride, Gabrielle, he left St. Louis two years before Katie was born, and their firstborn child, Joseph, was born and died as their wagon train stopped at Carson's Gap, now the California-Nevada border. F. A. and Gaby buried the child under a crude marker, and pressed on—but never found gold.

The adventures for women in St. Louis were of a different sort: Madame Charleville's heroines were women torn between morality and freedom, convention and desire. Madame Charleville was a Frenchwoman, not a Victorian; she was a worldly woman, not a pious *précieuse*. She showed Kate that the bragging oratory of men was not the only way to tell a story: that women, with a trained eye for details and hidden meanings and ironic twists, could be the best storytellers.

Madame Charleville was a superb teacher—and her lessons meant that throughout the rest of her life, Kate O'Flaherty would be out of step with her society, for she would see its contradictions and its restrictions and its hypocrisies. She would know that truth has many faces—and she would try to write about what she saw.

Madame Charleville provided her great-granddaughter with her first great awakening, and Kate reciprocated: She always wrote affectionately about the wit and wisdom and fighting spirit of old women, both white and black. In such stories as "Odalie Misses Mass" and "Old Aunt Peggy," she showed that young girls could appreciate old women as storytellers—as rich storehouses of information about the past.

Kate Chopin never wrote directly about her ancestors, but the spirit of Madame Charleville permeates much of her writing. In "The Maid of St. Phillippe," her only foray into historical fiction, Chopin created a free-spirited character who wears boy's clothes, carries a gun, loves the outdoor life, and resists the English takeover of her village. The images of the simple French village are the ones Kate remembered from Madame Charleville's stories, including the log cabins and the tavern where the men gather to share the day's news.

But the story is truest to the spirit of Madame Charleville in the main character's choice, which she makes alone—as all of Kate Chopin's characters do. The maid's suitor, a captain, wants to marry her, take her back to La Rochelle, and give her jewels and silks and soft velvet carpets, but she refuses to "be the mother of slaves." (St. Phillippe was the first village in the "Illinois country" in which slavery was instituted.) The maid chooses independence, "the free air of forest and stream," and the Cherokees.

"The Maid of St. Phillippe" takes place in 1764, a generation before Madame Charleville. It is the era of "La Verdon," Marieanne Victoire Richelet Verdon, Kate's spirited great-great-grandmother, the steamboat entrepreneur. With her heroine, Kate Chopin paid tribute to "La Verdon," the most daring of her female ancestors—for the maid bears La Verdon's first name: Marianne.

Deep mourning for Thomas O'Flaherty lasted a year, until November 1856. By then little Jane had also died, and within another year Madame Charleville—who had been staying with her daughter Henriette and her husband, Captain Daniel Hunt—moved permanently to the O'Flaherty-Faris home.

Formal, away-from-home education for young girls was not yet a tradition, and the early deaths of her two young sisters had made Katie the much-petted baby of the family. The household on Eighth Street still included Kate's young Faris aunts and uncles, Zuma and Josephine and Charley and Wilson, as well as her half-brother, George, at St. Louis University, and her brother,

Tom. Before Kate was ten, her young uncle Wilson Faris was killed in a steamboat explosion, and Ed. O'Flaherty departed, replaced by Michael Garney, a twenty-eight-year-old clerk, according to the 1860 census. (He was presumably a boarder.)

Finally, in the fall of 1857, two years after her father's death, seven-year-old Katie O'Flaherty was registered again at the Sacred Heart Academy on Fifth Street. She would be a day pupil, not subject to the school's fixed routine: She did not have to wear a uniform or live in a dormitory room with twenty other girls. She could also develop close friendships outside of school.

"Kate and I first knew each other when, as wee tots, we went as Day Scholars to our old Convent on 5th Street, founded by our Venerable Mother Duchesne," Kitty Garesché wrote to Daniel Rankin in 1930, more than seventy years after she and Kate O'Flaherty became intimate friends and sometime schoolmates.

Catherine Milligan Garesché and Katherine O'Flaherty were both children of somewhat mixed marriages, with branches of Huguenots in their family trees, and one parent from outside the world of upper-class St. Louis. Kitty's father, Peter Bauduy Garesché, had even married a Protestant: Juliette McLane, daughter of the American ambassador to England under Andrew Jackson. Juliette Garesché, a Catholic convert, was still an oddity in St. Louis social circles.

Kitty's family lived on the north side of Ninth Street and Chouteau Avenue, just a block from the O'Flahertys'. "As our homes were very near one another," Kitty wrote, "we were constantly together, sharing all our pleasures. These were climbing trees in summer, skating in winter, an occasional party with other children, riding a pony that Kate owned, always in the care of a faithful negro servant, but principally, and certainly first in our affection, music and reading—veritable passions."

Kitty, six months younger than Kate, was the dark-haired, dark-eyed oldest child in her family: She was round-faced, with earnest eyes and finely chiseled French features. In her portraits, she looks more docile than the impudent Katie O'Flaherty. Like most of the Sacred Heart girls, Kitty was descended from one of the old, aristocratic French families of St. Louis. Her uncle Alexander J. P. Garesché was a judge whose wife organized the first Sacred Heart Sodality in St. Louis; her uncle Ferdinand, a businessman, had been one of the founders and moving spirits in the Union Fire Company No. 2, along with Thomas O'Flaherty.

Kate and Kitty became inseparable chums who also enjoyed the chatter and gossip of other people. Kate's young aunts and uncles were too old to be playmates: By the time Kate returned to school in 1857, the youngest, Josephine, was already fourteen. Only Kate's brother Tom, at nine, was even close to Kate and Kitty's age—and so, "Instead of my going as much to her house," Kitty recalled in 1930, "she came more often to ours where there was a band of little ones to make it noisy. *Indeed, she was my only friend ever allowed to stay overnight*; and my dear parents found their delight in making our evenings very pleasant. Charades, generally acted, games, and as we grew older, my father would read aloud." In the garden, Kate "could play with a little fawn and feed it, or help bury and write an epitaph for a pet bird."

The Gareschés, like the O'Flahertys, had servants and slaves to do cooking, cleaning, and laundry, and the mistress of the house supervised them—but there was little more for an intelligent woman to do with her talents in the secular world.

There were no women's clubs to promote social reform; there were no Female Anti-Slavery Societies in St. Louis, as there were in the East (and few women of St. Louis's upper class would have dared come out against slavery). Some Sacred Heart graduates joined the convent, where a world of rich possibilities opened: teaching, administration, and scholarship, with real responsibility and power. But that choice also meant a retreat from the world: Nuns were cloistered.

The Sacred Heart Academy was dedicated to producing better Catholic wives and mothers, but for most women there was no formal education after high school. Only a handful of American colleges admitted women, and only one proper profession was open to married women: writing.

There were many restless women in Kate and Kitty's world, and they found different ways to fill their time. Kate's neighbor Mariquitta Garesché, the wife of Kitty's handsomest uncle, Julius, spent all her time shopping. ("Mariquitta hunts up auctions with her habitual energy," Julius wrote to his mother-in-law in 1857.) But that was preferable, he said, to his beloved Mariquitta's filling her head with impossible notions gleaned from romantic novels—and then reproaching him for not being attentive enough, for not having "the heart for loving her."

Mariquitta Garesché was just twenty-seven, nine years younger than her husband, in 1857—and everyone knew their story. Marie Louise Charlotte Coudroy de Lauréal was the daughter of emigrés from the exotic Caribbean island of Guadeloupe, and her tall and elegant husband was so handsome that strangers used to stare at him, and unknown women would send him suggestive invitations—but he had eyes only for his pretty wife.

Then war intervened—and in 1862, while Kate and Kitty were still schoolgirls, Julius Garesché would be one of the first West Point graduates killed in the Civil War, his horse shot out from under him at the battle of Murfreesboro. His beloved Mariquitta, who saved all his adoring letters and passed them on to their son, died nine years later, the year Kate Chopin gave birth to her own first son.

Kate never forgot this romantic couple. In *The Awakening*, Edna's first schoolgirl crush is on a man like Julius Garesché, "a dignified and sad-eyed cavalry officer" whose face is "something like Napoleon's." Years later, as the book ends, her mind reverts to that childhood memory: "The spurs of the cavalry officer clanged as he walked across the porch."

Nor did Kate Chopin forget Mariquitta Garesché: In *The Awakening*, Chopin also created an earthy shrimp girl who is given to flirtatious exaggerations, like those in romantic novels. Only a very romantic name would suit such a character, and so the mature Kate Chopin named the shrimp girl for the passionate young wife she remembered from her childhood: Mariequita.

Kate and Kitty, creative children with vivid imaginations, could climb trees while they were young, wearing little girls' pantalettes. Later, that was impossible, in the tight-laced corsets and voluminous hoopskirts that came into fashion during the 1860s, just as Kate and Kitty reached their teens.

But in the 1850s, before the rules of ladylike propriety hedged them in, the two girls had favorite trees. In the center of the O'Flahertys' garden, there was a stone column with a sundial, Kitty recalled, and "[a]t the end of the Garden were some large trees—some of those we used to climb—and going recklessly high perhaps—each trying to out-top the other." The two girls, Kate wrote years later, "divided our 'picayune's' worth of candy—climbed together the highest cherry trees; wept in company over the 'Days of Bruce,' and later, exchanged our heart secrets."

From the top of a tree, on clear days when the city was not covered with a black pall from burning coal, one could see most of St. Louis. A sharp-eyed little girl could see her way to the river, and the frenetic activity at the levee; or she could peer in the direction of South St. Louis, where the Germans lived, with their sharp, tangy sausage and pumpernickel and küchen and sauerkraut; or she could gaze at the sedate mansions of her neighbors, where slaves scrubbed the steps and washed the clothes and raised the children of their white families.

For Kate and Kitty, climbing trees was like swimming out beyond where other women dared to go, and decades later, when Kate Chopin wrote stories protesting restrictions on women, she remembered what she and Kitty had seen.

When the heroine in "The Story of an Hour" abandons herself to startling thoughts about life without her husband, she looks out her window. Her first image of freedom, "all aquiver with the new spring life," is from Kate O'Flaherty and Kitty Garesché's childhood: the newly widowed Louise sees "the tops of trees."

*   *   *

Kate O'Flaherty had an erratic Sacred Heart school record through the 1850s and early 1860s. Sometimes she was a boarder and sometimes a day student, but she usually left school by the end of February: Until she was ten, Kate never spent an entire year in school. Besides tuition, board, books, and school supplies, Eliza O'Flaherty also paid extra each term for Kate's "use of piano" ($1.20 to $2.00) and sometimes for "music book" ($1.50).

Whenever Kate boarded at the academy, she was required to furnish her own bedding, eating utensils, sewing materials, and underwear, as well as gloves, sunbonnet, and a white muslin veil. Girls were forbidden to bring anything not on the official list of provisions—including unapproved books, dolls, and toys.

The boarders shared one large dormitory room, with twenty or thirty beds arranged in long neat rows. Each girl had her own alcove, with a cross on the wall, a desk, a washstand, and one drawer for her possessions. Her iron bed would be surrounded by white muslin curtains, closed at night to keep out mosquitoes and night damp.

For boarding pupils, school days began with the six o'clock wake-up bell (*sonnette*) and prayers intoned by a supervising nun. Kate and Kitty learned the dressing ritual: Forbidden to be entirely nude, or to show any bare part of their bodies to one another, Sacred Heart girls carefully tied the sleeves of their nightgowns around their waists while they dressed.

Although Katie O'Flaherty resisted most rituals, she remembered the dressing and undressing routine in the story "Lilacs," which she wrote almost forty years after she entered convent school. In Kate's story, Sister Agathe "disrobed noiselessly behind her curtains and glided into bed without having revealed, in the faint candlelight, as much as a shadow of herself." Meanwhile her worldly friend Adrienne shakes and folds her own clothes "with great care, placing them on the back of a chair as she had been taught to do when a child at the convent. It secretly pleased Sister Agathe to feel that her dear Adrienne clung to the habits acquired in her youth."

Since looking glasses were forbidden, Sacred Heart boarders checked each other for grooming—especially making sure that each girl's hair was parted neatly. Hair was pulled back tightly or plaited: Curls were frowned upon. Since inessential speech was not permitted, the girls nodded or signed to each other that all was in order.

Each day the girls went to mass, and then to breakfast—always in neat lines and phalanxes, or in groups of three (*two* girls might form a particular friendship that unfairly excluded others). But especially close friends like Katie O'Flaherty and Kitty Garesché might contrive to gossip secretly, or smile meaningfully, or slip each other notes—and Sacred Heart schools were full of intrigue, rivalry, and revolt.

After breakfast, study hall began with morning prayers ("*Veni Sancte*" and "*Ave Maria*"). Students had exactly five minutes to gather their books, pens, and writing materials. When the *surveillante* (supervising nun) rang a bell, the children closed their desks, and were not allowed to open them again during that study session. The *surveillante* would mark down anyone who was idle, or who disobediently opened her desk, or who talked or laughed. If a child got three marks against her, she would not be eligible for the ribbons and prizes awarded for study or good conduct—and she might not be permitted to enroll as a boarder for the following term.

Every hour was scheduled, including a Wednesday promenade (the week's exercise), study and quiet times and *Prîmes* ("Preems"), the weekly merit assembly. At three in the afternoon there was *goûter*—the French equivalent of high tea—and on special occasions, such as the feast of the foundress, Madeleine-Sophie Barat, there might be pink cupcakes. Classes were taught by the "Mesdames of the Sacred Heart"—who, unlike the nuns in other orders, retained their original names.

Even at night, there was a prescribed routine. Sleeping in a curled-up position was frowned upon: The proper pose was to lie on one's back "like a Christian," with hands crossed on one's chest. In case a girl should die in the night, that would be a more becoming posture in which to meet the Lord. The pupils' first and last words of the day were supposed to be "Wash away my sins"— although there were some who lulled themselves to sleep by pondering the Agony in the Garden, or the ecstasy of Saint Teresa of Avila.

Years later, Kate Chopin poked gentle fun at the instructions of her youth. In the story "Lilacs," Sister Agathe advises her sleepless worldly friend Adrienne to say Hail Marys over and over again—but if that fails, "Then lie quite still on your side and think of nothing but your own respiration. I have heard that such inducement to sleep seldom fails." Yet even that perfectly secular cure does not succeed for Adrienne.

In her Sacred Heart school, Kate learned to be skeptical about remedies of all kinds. Katie O'Flaherty and Kitty Garesché were taught according to the prescribed Plan of Studies for 1852, a uniform curriculum for Sacred Heart schools all over the world. The Sacred Heart order, founded in France after the Revolution, stressed rigorous standards. The nuns dedicated themselves to teaching young Catholic girls "of good family" to be pious wives and mothers—but also to be knowledgeable, clear, and independent thinkers, to "meet with adequacy the demands of time and eternity."

The girls were usually taught in English, but the values they learned were often French: The Society of the Sacred Heart continued the traditions of French intellectual women, especially Madame de Sévigné, whose letters represented the finest examples of "epistolary art." The 1852 Plan of Studies specified goals for the "children of the Sacred Heart," including spelling and penmanship, literature, history, oral reading, "formation of the reasoning power and judgment," "fieldwork in botany as well as gardening," and knowledge of current events and scientific discoveries, "that they may take part intelligently in conversation when at home or in social gatherings."

Writing was essential: "The mistresses of the higher classes will assign each week two themes, or essays; one of these will always be a letter, the other alternately an essay, narrative or descriptive, and a literary analysis."

As boarders in 1858, Kate and Kitty were in the elementary department, where the lower-division subjects included reading, writing, Bible stories, arithmetic ("counting"), geography ("some fundamental ideas"), and Little Catechism. As they grew, their studies began to include Bible history, dictation (French or English), world geography ("taught by wall maps"), arithmetic ("counting, addition, subtraction, mental work daily"), and memory work. Later, as older girls, they were supposed to study the histories of nations, great literature, ancient and modern geography, fables and poetry for the formation of style, geometry—and, always, religion.

The Sacred Heart children were also required to learn fine needlework, because women were believed to need the "stabilising effect of responsibility such as comes with the homely realities of life, or the direct fulfilment of their apostolic vocation." Kate and Kitty learned plain sewing and embroidery, and they made clothes for the poor and altar linen and vestments. The sewing courses ran through all the years of schooling—which may explain Kate Chopin's characters' dislike for needlework.

Mademoiselle Salambre, the seamstress in "Miss McEnders," sews solely to earn a living, and Calixta in "The Storm" is seen "sewing furiously" on a cotton sheet, with her sewing machine—but when a former lover presents himself, she races to abandon her work.

Sewing for Sacred Heart girls was a sign of docility, and purity, and domesticity. Few characters in Kate Chopin's stories ever sew if they can help it.

For Sacred Heart girls, the Virgin Mary, the saints, and guardian angels were looked to as real people who could aid girls in distress. A child who lost a hair ribbon or a pencil learned to pray to Saint Anthony (who was also useful for avoiding temptation). Our Lady of Good Success was said to help exam-takers, and Saint Cecilia was the patron saint of music—the one who got young girls into the choir. And, of course, a girl's guardian angel occupied a place next to her in her chair in class, and on her pillow at night.

Sacred Heart students were supposed to think of the community, rather than of themselves—and they were allowed very little that was theirs alone. Letters, except from parents, were read and could be censored; deep pockets and work-boxes and desks could be searched at any time. And all nuns were to be greeted with deep curtsies—even if the children were weighted down with armloads of books. The girls spent hours practicing, so that when they curtsied in rows for distinguished visitors or for the Reverend Mother at *Prîmes*, they sank and rose like the crest of a wave.

There were a few treats: Besides *goûter*, there was a Thursday afternoon "bazaar" in which the children could buy writing paper, pencils, sewing materials, notebooks, and pious pictures—small French prints, ornamented with lace paper, which the children gave each other as gifts. (One of Kate O'Flaherty's pious pictures is in the Missouri Historical Society in St. Louis.) The pictures were very popular in Sacred Heart schools: they were the ideal vehicle for passing notes from one prayer book to another, during mass.

Years later Kitty Garesché looked back on her childhood, and Kate's, as a time full of innocent entertainment and intellectual pleasures. By then, Kitty had been a teacher for many years, and had thought about what young girls ought to know.

Writing to Daniel Rankin from Grosse Pointe, Michigan, where she was living in 1930, Kitty described the frontier St. Louis of her youth, where "[g]entlemen could hunt deer and grouse within a short distance, and Kate could stand on the sidewalk to watch the 'Indians come to town,' riding on horseback in procession, every month, from some nearby Reservation."

Kitty yearned for the good old days: "The entertainments provided for children were of a much more elevated order, and of more educational value than those of the present day. At school we little ones were allowed to assist at the Solar Microscope views, thrown on the wall; and Kate and I must have been seated side by side as the monsters in a drop of water were shown."

Of her girlhood outings with Kate, Kitty wrote, "We were taken to such as taught good lessons. I remember a trained dog, who went through the alphabet, putting his paw as called for on each letter printed on one-foot square cards." There were also "[b]ird shows, where they were harnessed to wagons, and shot off guns as mimic soldiers," and sleight-of-hand exhibits, "as a novelty."

The two girls were enlightened about other countries and cultures, Kitty remembered: "In the late 50's Dr. Kane gave an illustrated lecture with magic lantern slides of his Arctic Explorations, with one of his sledge dogs by his side." Dr. Kane's Arctic Expedition was actually a "Grand Panorama," produced at Wyman's Hall and Museum for those who wanted educational uplift as well as thrilling sights. According to the *Missouri Republican* on Kate's eleventh birthday—February 8, 1861—the Grand Panorama was "attracting large audiences nightly, and we would advise all lovers of science and art to pay it a visit. The painting is magnificent, and the lecture accompanying it a fund of information."

There was also "a fine Museum in the city," Kitty remembered, "to which we often went to examine fossils of extinct animals, rare coins, and reproductions of famous statues." Kitty must have meant the "beautiful and rare collection of natural curiosities" at the St. Louis Museum, owned by Edward Wyman. According to the *Missouri Republican*, it was "the most perfect collection in the United States."

A typical exhibit might contain as many as two thousand specimens, including stuffed "quadrupeds" and huge reptiles, one of them a prehistoric alligator found in stone in Alabama. The "fine Museum" also showed a "very large fine specimen of the rib-nosed babboon," kangaroos, armadilloes, serpents, and innumerable varieties of birds: swans, snipes, eagles, vultures, parrots, and an exquisite collection of many-colored hummingbirds, "clustered jewels fit to grace the brow of a queen." There was even a "cock strutting and paying delicate attention to his mate." Edward Wyman, a skilled taxidermist, did much of the mounting himself, and prided himself on placing his beloved stuffed birds in lifelike settings and natural positions.

Although Katie O'Flaherty learned a great deal about animals and birds, she found people far more entertaining. Later, in her writings, she used birds mostly as symbols, and she particularly detested parrots (in "Athénaïse" and *The Awakening*)—but she did appreciate fat, sleek cats. Often in her stories they prance or preen or sun themselves on windowsills—enjoying their independence and solitude, communing with themselves, and owing nothing to anyone else.

Kate O'Flaherty and Kitty Garesché also got to see one of the world's most-loved performers: General Tom Thumb, P.T. Barnum's three-foot-tall star, who appeared at Wyman's Hall and Museum.

By the early 1860s, Tom Thumb had been on exhibit for more than a decade—touring Europe, serenading Queen Victoria, dancing Highland flings, impersonating Napoleon, and coming out victorious in David-and-Goliath skits with the circus giants. Audiences always roared their delight at his patter, and at Barnum's announcement: "It is only by placing the General in contrast with a very small child that the audience can form a right conception of his real height. Will some little boy step on the stage for a moment?"

Tom Thumb would always interrupt angrily, "I would rather have a little miss!"

The chosen child would get to compare sizes with General Thumb—and see that the famous midget's hand was the size of a half-dollar, and his foot only three inches long. Seventy years later, what Kitty Garesché remembered most about the tiny gentleman was, "A child of three years old was as tall when placed by his side."

There was also much of St. Louis that Katie O'Flaherty and Kitty Garesché did not see: The "Local News" section of the *Missouri Republican* was full of crimes committed against women. Young girls were assaulted; servants were seduced and abandoned, often by their employers—and at least one desperate seventeen-year-old killed her baby. The newspaper reported crimes by men, but condemned those by women: "Mary Kennedy, a besotted, sinful wretch who has long been on the highway of degradation and ruin, was yesterday fined . . ." Nor were women's political rights given serious coverage. Although women at the Seneca Falls convention for women's rights had met in 1848 and published their call for the vote, St. Louis newspapers in the 1850s tended to see the subject as trivial: An advertisement headlined WOMEN VOTING declared that women had already voted—on where to buy their "gaiters," shoes, and slippers.

Nor was politics much on the minds of young girls. Kitty Garesché shared Katie O'Flaherty's passion for reading and writing—and that passion impelled Kate to illicit actions at home.

She used to snoop in bureau drawers for forbidden reading.

Chapter 3

SECRETS
AND A SPECIAL
FRIENDSHIP

"I ONCE KNEW A VERY YOUNG person who, while rummaging in a bureau drawer discovered a volume secreted in its disordered profundity," Kate Chopin wrote in the St. Louis Criterion in March 1897. Chopin was writing about censorship, and its effect on Thomas Hardy's Jude the Obscure—a book she considered dreary and obvious. To her, Jude was important only because it was banned, and she did not approve of banning books. As for her own girlhood sin:

> The book was obviously in hiding, and no other than she herself was the important personage from whom it was being hidden! She at once locked the door, abstracted the volume, and sat herself down to its perusal. Expectation was rampant within her. She had been scenting mysteries in the air, and the hour of illumination was at hand! The book was something obscure, metaphysical, hysterical. It was dull reading, but she persevered. She would greatly rather have been up in the attic reading Ivanhoe. But no one had hidden Ivanhoe in the far depths of a bureau drawer—Voilà!

The mature Kate Chopin was parodying the Gothic and adventure novels of her youth, with phrases like "Expectation was rampant," and "Illumination was at hand!" The young Katie O'Flaherty had always preferred a rip-roaring story like Ivanhoe to anything metaphysical or obscure—but occasionally she and Kitty were motivated to self-improvement.

"Our story books were read together, often 'mid laughter and tears," Kitty recalled. "It was the perusal of—I think—*Blind Agnes* that determined us to learn Italian." *Blind Agnese; or the Little Spouse of the Blessed Sacrament*, by Cecilia Mary Caddell, was the kind of book recommended for Catholic school-girls: First published in 1853, it was dedicated to "the Sacred Heart," because "none are too young to love Jesus."

Blind Agnese, an Italian beggar girl who lives with her adopted grandmother and faithful dog, is so pious that other children make fun of her. When a wealthy lady (who proves to be Agnese's grandmother) takes her away to Ireland and tries to convert her to Protestantism, another girl, Grace, takes it upon herself to protect Agnese (Grace proves to be Agnese's sister). Finally, after many frightening events and demonstrations of the evils of Protestantism, Agnese is allowed to return to Italy, where she consecrates herself to God, and dies on the Feast of the Sacred Heart.

Kate and Kitty may have been encouraged to read *Blind Agnese* before their First Communions, since Agnese makes her First Communion just before her death: On the feast of Corpus Christi, "He Himself, in her first communion, had allowed her, by her own experience, 'to taste and see that the Lord is sweet.' "

Blind Agnese also makes Italy seem warm and sensuous, a land of charity, generosity, beauty, and flowers—all of which evidently inspired Katie O'Fla-herty and Kitty Garesché to learn Italian. And so, Kitty told Daniel Rankin, "*Ollendorf's Method* was bought unknown to anyone, and we began the study all by ourselves, as a great secret. I must confess that we soon reached a point which seemed to say to our puzzled brains, 'Thus far shall you go and no farther.' "

But they remained undaunted in their reading. Before the summer of 1863, when they were separated by war, Kate and Kitty's most memorable readings were, according to Kitty:

> Grimm's *Fairy Tales, Blind Agnes, Paul and Virginia, Orphans of Moscow, Dickens for Little Folks*, a series: *Little Nell, Little Dorrit*, etc., *Queechy, The Wide Wide World, Scottish Chiefs, Days of Bruce, Pilgrims Progress*. We particularly loved *Zaidee*— a beautiful, old-fashioned romance; and *John Halifax, Gentleman*.
>
> Of poetry we read the metrical romances of Scott, with his *Talisman* and *Ivanhoe*, with some of the chosen poems of Pope, Collins, and Gray.

Some books had special meanings in their families. *Paul and Virginia*, the romantic story of two children of nature by Bernardin de Saint-Pierre, was first

published in 1797, the year Madame Charleville was married. The novel created a sensation in colonial St. Louis and made "Virginia" a favorite name
among French families: Madame Charleville had named one of her daughters
Virginia; that daughter named her daughter Virginia; and even Kitty Garesché
had a sister Virginia. Kate and Kitty probably read—and wept over—Madame
Charleville's copy of *Paul and Virginia* from the well-stocked library in the
O'Flaherty household.

The story also stayed with Kate. Decades later, in *The Awakening*, Kate
Chopin described Grand Isle as a tropical paradise like Paul and Virginia's,
with warmly scented air, flowers, and birds. In Chopin's story "Ripe Figs,"
characters tell time in the sugarcane country just as Virginia does in *Paul and
Virginia*, by the rhythms of the seasons. And on two occasions, Chopin even
used a variant of the character Virginia's last name—de la Tour—as her own
pen name: for "Miss McEnders" and "The Falling in Love of Fedora," the
author was originally listed as "La Tour."

Most of the books on the girls' reading list—their best-remembered, best-
loved books—were popular novels by English and American women: Susan
Warner (*Queechy, The Wide Wide World*), Jane Porter (*Scottish Chiefs*), Grace
Aguilar (*Days of Bruce*), Margaret Oliphant (*Zaidee*), and Dinah Mulock (*John
Halifax, Gentleman*). *Orphans of Moscow; or, the Young Governess*, by Catherine Thérèse Woillez, was translated from the French. Through novel-reading, Kate and Kitty learned about women's lives and women writers, few of
whom they read in school.

Zaidee, for instance, is about an orphan girl, "a quick-growing, strange, out-
of-the-way girl, whom everybody wondered at." Parts of *Zaidee* lingered in
Kate's mind: Zaidee's "startling alertness of motion . . . her quick, keen, vivid
perceptions, and those wild visionary moods" strongly resemble the characteristics Kate Chopin gave to her similarly named Zaida, the central character in
the story "A Night in Acadie."

Other books Kate O'Flaherty and Kitty Garesché read were about indubitably
virtuous characters. In *The Wide Wide World* and *Queechy*, women work to
create perfect homes for their husbands and children, and young girls are dainty,
Christian, and always obedient. Kate's family was different: The only adult
men in her household were her brother George and her uncle Charley Faris,
both in their late teens, and one slave. Nor were the women in Kate's family
apt to be sentimental: Her mother, grandmother, and great-grandmother did
not spend time dwelling on the Christian virtues of their departed husbands.
Madame Charleville, in particular, might have seemed to Protestant American
writers to have an unseemly zest for life.

Later in life, Kate Chopin read Ralph Waldo Emerson, who—like many of
his contemporaries—believed deeply in separate, complementary spheres for

the sexes. Emerson wrote that "women are strong by sentiment"; that "the same mental height which their husbands attain by toil, they attain by sympathy with their husbands. Man is the will, and Woman the sentiment . . . Will is the rudder, and Sentiment the sail." But Kate Chopin, with a sly cynicism, showed Edna in *The Awakening* using Emerson not for wisdom but as a soporific: One night Edna "read Emerson until she grew sleepy."

Emerson's was not the worldview Madame Charleville had given Katie O'Flaherty, for in Madame's pre-Victorian youth, women had much more control over their own destinies. Women worked hard in the frontier village of St. Louis, but they also had their rights—to gossip, to be eccentric, to dance and flirt, to inherit and control money and land, and even to take lovers if they were not too flagrant about it. (Madame Chouteau, after all, was always respected—as was "La Verdon.")

Although in later life Kate Chopin did write sentimental short stories, especially for children, she kept a skeptical eye. The only Chopin character who reads domestic novels is Fanny in *At Fault*, and the narrator calls such books "unwholesome intellectual sweets"—because they do not give young women enough truths about life. Katie O'Flaherty's early encounters with *The Wide Wide World* and *Queechy* helped teach her an important lesson that she carried through the rest of her life: not to believe everything she read.

Kate had also been reading Sir Walter Scott's novels since she was six years old, and in *Ivanhoe* she and Kitty read about noble men in action. The heroic Ivanhoe, in disguise, vanquishes corrupt aristocrats, restores the rightful king to the throne, and marries the insipid Rowena: fair, blue-eyed, Anglo-Saxon, "mild, timid, and gentle." But the dark, exotically beautiful "Jewess" Rebecca is a far more interesting character.

Similarly in Grace Aguilar's *Days of Bruce: A Story from Scottish History*—a book that Kate O'Flaherty and Kitty Garesché wept over—there is a romantic heroine named Agnes, who is golden-haired, meek, and mild, too innocent and pure to live. Agnes's mother, the queenly Isabella, falls in love with Robert Bruce, a man she cannot have—while a third woman, Isoline, is "too confident and self-reliant" ever to be contented.

Three decades later, when Kate Chopin came to write *The Awakening*, she drew on her early immersion in *Ivanhoe* and *Days of Bruce*. Chopin's disagreeable pianist Mademoiselle Reisz resembles Aguilar's Isoline in her confidence, self-reliance, and isolation; the madonna Madame Ratignolle, with her golden hair, sapphire-blue eyes, and cherry lips, is a descendant of Scott's Rowena and Aguilar's Agnes. (Chopin even wrote knowingly, "There are no words to describe her save the old ones that have served so often to picture the bygone heroine of romance and the fair lady of our dreams.")

For Edna, Kate Chopin also remembered *Days of Bruce*: Like Isabella, Edna is tall, with "splendid poses" and "noble beauty." Edna, like Isabella, has given up youthful infatuations and married a man unsuited to her—and both heroines fall desperately in love later, with a man named Robert.

Kate and Kitty read *Days of Bruce* over and over, absorbing ideas that Kate echoed years later in *The Awakening*. To Aguilar's tormented Isabella, "What could be now the past, save as a vision of the night; the present, a stern reality with all its duties—duties not alone to others, but to herself." For Chopin's Edna: "The past was nothing to her; offered no lesson which she was willing to heed. . . . The present alone was significant. . . ." For Aguilar's Isabella, "Memory had awakened dreams and visions"; Chopin's Edna has her own "impassioned, newly awakened being."

Kate and Kitty evidently did not read *Uncle Tom's Cabin*: Harriet Beecher Stowe's antislavery novel would not have been popular in their slaveholding households. Although Missouri was a slave state, few St. Louisans actually owned slaves: In the 1860 census there were only 1,542 slaves in St. Louis, along with 1,755 "free colored" and 157,476 white people. But the city was a center for slave trading, and slaveholders like Eliza O'Flaherty lived only blocks away from radical German immigrants who detested slavery with all their souls.

On Locust Street, midway between Fourth and Fifth Streets, Bernard Lynch kept his slave pen, just a short walk from the Sacred Heart Academy on Fifth Street. The pursuit of runaway slaves occupied much newspaper space, and the most famous abolitionist lawsuit, initiated by a St. Louis slave, had been decided by the Supreme Court in 1857. According to the Dred Scott decision, slaves were not entitled to the rights of citizens, and blacks had "no rights which the white man was bound to respect."

Slave auctions in *Uncle Tom's Cabin* and other abolitionist novels created pity and horror in the reading public; slave auctions in real life were frequently held in downtown St. Louis, near the slave pens in which, it was advertised, there were "Negroes available at all times." Although young girls were curious, "I never went to slave sales, nor do I think Kate ever did," Kitty Garesché told Daniel Rankin, "though we wanted to."

In the winter of 1860–61, Kate O'Flaherty and Kitty Garesché had a new parish church, the Church of the Annunciation, commissioned by the Irish-born Father Patrick J. Ryan, famed for his "eloquent soul-stirring sermons." The church, bounded by Chouteau Avenue, Labadie, and Seventh Streets, was dedicated on Sunday, December 16, 1860, with exercises conducted by Archbishop Kenrick, the late Thomas O'Flaherty's close friend. The new building was a massive and imposing structure with Corinthian columns, three altars of the purest Italian marble, a large statue of the Virgin Mary, and rich frescoes and costly paintings: According to Kitty, it was "an artistic gem, everything in it calculated to foster piety and educate our minds to spiritual realities."

But the excitement at the new parish church was overshadowed by political events. Over the summer, the men of St. Louis had campaigned fiercely, and sometimes violently, for their presidential candidates. There were raucous torchlight parades, and after the election of Abraham Lincoln, slaveholding voters—the most influential men in St. Louis—began muttering even more about insurrection and secession and states' rights.

The day after the Church of the Annunciation was dedicated, a month after the election, the pro-southern *Missouri Republican* printed a speech exhorting all slave states, including border states such as Missouri, to secede together. Three days later, when South Carolina voted to leave the union, there were prayers and the ringing of bells all over St. Louis, and men sorted themselves into various political groupings: secessionists, conditional Unionists, unconditional Unionists.

If Thomas O'Flaherty had lived, he might have been a conditional Unionist: In the late 1840s, he was one of thirty-eight signers of an "Address to the Democracy of Missouri" calling slavery "an acknowledged evil" but urging that "the Democracy of the North" respect the rights of slaveholders. Most of the other signers supported the Union when war began—but by the end of 1860, young men's political clubs of all persuasions had begun drilling, not very secretly.

For Christmas in 1860, Kate O'Flaherty received a special gift from her great-aunt Pelagie Charleville Boyer: a tan copybook, with LEAVES OF AFFECTION stamped in gold on the cover. It was inscribed "To Katie, from her affectionate aunt Boyer, December the 25th, 1860."

The frontispiece of the notebook bore a picture of a gloomy thatched castle, labeled "Oakland" (not in Kate's handwriting). Inside were paintings of flowers and proud ladies, and sentimental printed inscriptions, including, "Let this album be dedicated to friendship."

At first, Kate pasted in magazine pictures: a mother and a chubby child; extravagantly gowned ladies; another chubby child playing with a toy and leaning on a half-sleeping dog; and two close sweethearts in a pose much like the lovers Kate Chopin later described in *The Awakening*: "leaning toward each other as the water-oaks bent from the sea. There was not a particle of earth beneath their feet. Their heads might have been turned upside-down, so absolutely did they tread upon blue ether."

Kate also copied a favorite poem into her notebook:

I love to linger on my track
Wherever I have dwelt,
In after years to loiter back,
And feel as once I felt;
My foot-falls lightly on the sward,
Yet leaves a deathless dint—
With tenderness I still regard
Its unforgotten print.

Old places have a charm for me
The new can ne'er attain.
Old faces—how I long to see
Their kindly looks again!
Yes, these are gone:—while all around
Is changeable as air,
I'll anchor in the solid ground
And root my memories there!

"I love to linger on my track . . ." was the first expression, in writing, of ideas Katie O'Flaherty held throughout her life: She appreciated the pleasures of loitering and loafing; she like to let the past catch up with the present. And the resolution at the end sounds like the mature Kate Chopin, who took a level-headed and realistic view of life and its possibilities.

The poem also inspired Kate O'Flaherty's own first work of literary criticism. Below the poem, in pencil, in a later handwriting style, an older Kate wrote snidely, "very pretty but where's the point?"

Before the old year ended, Kitty Garesché contributed a favorite poem to Kate's copybook: "We Have Been Friends Together," by the English poet Caroline Elizabeth Sarah Norton. Kitty dedicated it "To Katie" and Kate wrote above it, "My sweet friend Kitty."

After the poem, Kate pasted in another picture, entitled "Visit of Charity," showing a society lady carrying a food basket for the poor. That was Kate's last contribution to the album until 1863, in the middle of wartime.

Throughout the winter of 1860–61, everyone in St. Louis seemed to be anticipating something. Business was slow, no one bought real estate, and merchants "seemed to have an abundance of leisure," according to James Thomas, one of the few free blacks in the city at the time. People who "had a little money" hid it away indefinitely, Thomas remembered—and even when summer came, many people continued to wear their old, threadbare winter clothes.

Meanwhile young men were eager for the adventure of their generation.

Kate O'Flaherty's brother, Tom, thirteen in 1861, was too young to fight—but her half-brother, George, was twenty-one. An 1858 graduate of St. Louis University (but without any honors or prizes), George was a clerk with the Union Insurance Company.

Young men like him were everywhere, studying *Hardee's Rifle and Infantry Tactics*, written by a veteran of the Seminole War. Whenever a young man took a seat, the barber James Thomas recalled, "he would reach for his pocket and get out Hardee and try to get into his head how to parry and thrust."

"Old St. Louis"—the aristocrats, many of French descent like George O'Flaherty—favored the South and supported secession. But the Germans, the city's largest immigrant group, wanted to end slavery and preserve the Union. Many of the Germans were educated, idealistic young men who had left Germany after the failed revolution of 1848, and they identified the "Slavocratic interest" in St. Louis with the ruling class they had left behind. They were unmoved by old French claims that Catholics treated slaves better than non-Catholics did; that Catholics faithfully taught religion to slave children (whom they called "*les négrillons*"); and that every French family had stories about the loyalty and sacrifices of slaves for their white owners.

Still, slaves had become rebellious, and many employers had quietly replaced them with Irish servants. By 1860, most of the slaves remaining in St. Louis were domestics; the majority were women. Many prominent men had freed their slaves, and in 1859 even the impoverished owner of "Hardscrabble Farm" outside the city—a West Point graduate, down on his luck, named Ulysses S. Grant—freed his one slave.

In 1860, the widowed Eliza O'Flaherty owned six slaves: a male, sixty-four years old; four females aged twenty-eight, seventeen, nine, and six; and a male baby, six months old. The three oldest were recorded by the census as "Blacks," while the three youngest, the baby and the nine- and six-year-old girls, were designated as "mulattoes," raising the possibility that their mother was the twenty-eight-year-old and their father a white man in the neighborhood—and maybe even in their own household.

The first two "mulattoes" were born while the elder Thomas O'Flaherty was still alive (George O'Flaherty and his uncle Charles Faris would have been too young to be their fathers). But when the baby was born, George and Charley were twenty and nineteen, working as clerks and living in the family home on Eighth Street.

The fatherhood of the "mulattoes" cannot be determined, since the census did not record their names, but the mature Kate Chopin was well aware of white men who used their slaves sexually: In "Désirée's Baby," Désirée's husband, Armand, has a relationship with the slave La Blanche. Interracial relationships were also not unknown in Kate's mother's family: Madame Charleville's uncles included men who had fathered at least two half-Indian children and the well-known quadroon Louis Charleville.

Kate may just have imagined men like Désirée's Armand—or she may have known them.

After the New Year, 1861, other states began seceding from the Union: Mississippi, Florida, Alabama. On January 12, Archbishop Kenrick published an announcement in the *Democrat*, advising the Catholics of St. Louis that because of the disturbed conditions, they should avoid public excitements, for "the indiscretion of a word, or the impetuosity of momentary passion might endanger public tranquility." The Sacred Heart convent was briefly threatened by "Black Republicans" (fierce abolitionists)—but the nuns recorded in their journal that "the day said to have been appointed by them for an attack on us passed tranquilly."

Secessions continued: Georgia; Louisiana (where Eliza O'Flaherty's Charleville cousins would fight for the Confederacy); Texas. In early February, delegates met in Alabama to create the Confederate States of America.

By February, everyone in St. Louis was on edge. On Kate's eleventh birthday, February 8, a fire alarm sounded on Market Street. Suddenly, three or four "German horsemen, fully armed and equipped," were seen dashing down the street, until they realized that the sound was not a call to arms. The Germans had organized themselves into Union clubs; the secessionists had the Minute Men, with headquarters at the Berthold mansion on Fifth Street and Pine. The Bertholds, an old St. Louis family, had daughters who had gone to school with Kate O'Flaherty and Kitty Garesché. When a Confederate flag appeared over the Berthold mansion in March, a crowd gathered to protest, boo, and hiss.

In April, the war began—a "tragedy whose unfolding kept the civilized world in suspense," Kate Chopin wrote thirty-two years later in "A Lady of Bayou St. John." After the Confederate guns fired on Fort Sumter and forced the Union commander to surrender, President Lincoln called for soldiers. When the news came to St. Louis over the telegraph, Union supporters were generally silent—but "Seceshes" held noisy street demonstrations, and "blew and blasphemed, and hurrahed for Jeff Davis."

The Sacred Heart nuns were warned to hide all their valuable objects, important papers, and sacred vessels. "The First Communion ceremony was advanced," the nuns recorded in their journal, "as the parents of many of the children are leaving the city which, they say, will be burnt or pillaged by the soldiers." The sisters' friends begged them to evacuate, but Reverend Mother Tucker wanted to remain in St. Louis as long as possible. "We are not so exposed, and we have no money to pay the expenses of a flight, as the tuitions are most inexactly paid." (One of the unpaid tuitions was Kate's: Eliza O'Flaherty still owed $30.60 on Kate's tuition for the term.)

Two weeks after Fort Sumter, while both sides were recruiting soldiers in St. Louis, Kate and Kitty made their First Holy Communion.

The girls had been drilled in their catechism for months, and Kate placed an appropriate picture in her "Leaves of Affection" book: A young girl wearing a garland is looking up at the Virgin Mary, while a female angel with protective wings hovers over the girl. Kate wrote underneath it, "May 1st, 1861, My First Communion Picture."

Kate and Kitty were confirmed by Archbishop Kenrick in their "dear old convent chapel," Kitty recalled much later. "We had been prepared most carefully and fervently and I remember how we talked over together the secret emotions of that Day."

Kitty remained a devout practicing Catholic all her life; Kate, once she left her mother's home, fell away from the church. But in their little white dresses, on May 1—May being the month dedicated to the Blessed Virgin Mary—the two friends could not have known that they had just two more years together.

"Then came the Civil War with all its thrilling and very sad events for Missouri," Kitty Garesché wrote to Daniel Rankin. Ordinarily the days after First Communion were happy ones, filled with more presents and congratulations and celebration as the young ones were welcomed to the community of Catholic believers. But St. Louisans were preoccupied with war, and the Missouri state legislature passed a bill requiring every able-bodied man in the state to join a militia—but it was not clear who or what the militia was supposed to defend. (Since Missouri did not secede, it was officially a Union state.)

Kate's brother George joined the Confederate troops, enlisting as a private in Company A, Boone's Regiment of Missouri Mounted Infantry. At first, young men joined the rebel troops openly, but later they had to sneak away in the night, to avoid Yankee patrols.

Two days after Kate and Kitty's First Communion, on May 3, Confederate sympathizers began drilling at Lindell Grove, at Olive Street and Grand Avenue, on the western edge of the city. They dubbed their spot "Camp Jackson," after the secessionist Missouri governor Claiborne Jackson.

Exactly a week later, on Friday, May 10, 1861, the Sacred Heart girls were having a typical school day, studying French and composition and sewing, and making bouquets and garlands for Mary month. Trees and flowers bloomed outside the peaceful convent walls on Fifth Street, but the building was still threatened, the nuns recorded in their journal: "The Republicans want our house and property for barracks and parade grounds."

While the Sacred Heart students gently recited their lessons, some twenty blocks away, the Union captain Nathaniel Lyon and his German-American soldiers attacked the Confederate Camp Jackson. The secessionists, outnumbered, surrendered without a struggle—although the O'Flahertys' neighbor John Knapp broke his sword into pieces rather than surrender it. But a crowd gathered and cursed the Germans as "damned Dutch" and "Hessians"—and then, somehow, someone fired. There were more shots, and within a few minutes twenty-eight people were dead, including a woman with a baby in her arms.

The Sacred Heart school was only a brisk march away from Camp Jackson. The terrified nuns, under orders from Archbishop Kenrick, closed their school. City girls, like Kate O'Flaherty and Kitty Garesché, were bundled home. After a weekend under convent windows barricaded by mattresses, orphan girls were sent to the country.

In St. Louis, frightened citizens were fleeing the "damned Dutch," the hotheaded "Seceshes," or both. Every boat that could cross the river to Alton, Illinois, was full; carriages and wagons were commandeered.

The next day, Saturday morning, four Germans were found dead in various parts of the city—one on Seventh Street and Franklin, where Eliza O'Flaherty owned land. At Ninth and Market, a German man had been severely beaten and dragged with a rope about his leg. On Fifth Street, not far from the Sacred Heart convent, a German regiment was attacked, and six people were killed in the firing.

The mayor issued a stern proclamation: All drinking places were closed, all good citizens would remain indoors after nightfall as much as possible, and all minors would stay within doors for the next three days.

Just ten days after their First Communion, Kate O'Flaherty and Kitty Garesché were prisoners in their own homes.

In June, the Yankees and Confederates had their first skirmish in Missouri, at Boonville. In St. Louis, jumpy Home Guards again fired on civilians, this time into buildings on Seventh Street between Olive and Pine—ten blocks from the O'Flahertys'. Seventy-five bullets raked the houses, and four people were killed instantly.

By late July, the O'Flaherty household had a new, and thoroughly unwelcome, neighbor: General John C. Frémont, the newly appointed Union commander for the West. The famous "Pathfinder" who had mapped the Pacific West had also run for president in 1856 and was married to the daughter of Missouri's most famous and powerful senator, the late Thomas Hart Benton.

Frémont set up his Union headquarters in the Brant mansion, an elegant three-story marble-fronted house on the southeast side of Chouteau Avenue near Eighth Street. It was just three doors away from the O'Flaherty home.

Frémont loved ceremony: With his extravagant three-hundred-man entourage of heel-clicking dandies, he affected the style of a grand monarch. But Jessie Benton Frémont, the general's wife, would have been far more interesting to Katie O'Flaherty and Kitty Garesché. At thirty-seven, "General Jessie" Frémont was just four years older than Eliza O'Flaherty—but she had been her husband's confidential secretary, press representative, unofficial chief of staff, and emissary to Washington for nearly twenty years. She had published five books, and was energetic and self-confident: The neighbors saw Jessie commanding as the Frémonts moved in, telling soldiers where to install the printing press and telegraph office. She also recruited women for hospital work—the first time St. Louis women had ever worked as professional nurses.

Then, exactly one hundred days after their arrival, the Frémonts were gone. General Frémont had, on his own authority, placed the whole state under martial law and drafted an emancipation proclamation for Missouri—which an infuriated President Lincoln rescinded. Not long afterward, Frémont's lavish spending, incompetent management, and unsavory friends cost him his job.

The Convent of the Sacred Heart had always held elaborate graduate ceremonies in late June or early July, with songs, plays, and musical performances accompanying the awards and ribbons and prizes. But in the spring of 1861 the school year ended on May 10, with the assault on Camp Jackson.

The school did reopen in September, although many people advised the nuns against doing so: "Reverend Mother Tucker thinks it best to make every effort to maintain it," the sisters wrote in the convent journal. "The *rentrée* was far better than we expected, with thirty-eight boarders and thirty-four day pupils. . . . It had taken all our courage to set to work, for we fear that classes will just be organized when our convent will be confiscated and we ourselves driven from the city."

By the fall of 1861, St. Louis was inundated by refugees from other parts of Missouri—people driven from their homes by bushwhackers, jayhawkers and guerrillas who seized on the war as an excuse to pillage and plunder helpless civilians. General Henry W. Halleck, Frémont's replacement as Union commander, hit upon a scheme to punish St. Louis "Seceshes": He would tax them to feed and clothe the refugees. Halleck proceeded to assess sixty-four of the most outspoken Confederate sympathizers, for amounts ranging from $50 to $500. Roger McAllister, the husband of Eliza O'Flaherty's sister Amanda, was on the list of the "disloyal."

Louis A. Benoist, the millionaire, immediately paid his assessment; others were excused after they took a loyalty oath—but twenty-five refused, and sent a letter of protest. Among them was Juliette B. Garesché, Kitty's mother, an obvious target because her husband had already gone south. The O'Flaherty household was not assessed, and Eliza's property was not confiscated, although George O'Flaherty's Confederate service was well known.

Still, arbitrary searches and seizures were commonplace. Even a hint of pro-southern sympathies might land the sympathizer in the Gratiot Street Prison, the large, gray stone octagonal building that used to be Dr. McDowell's Medical College, on the northwest corner of Eighth and Gratiot Streets. The O'Flahertys' house, in the middle of Eighth Street, lay halfway between the prison and Union headquarters: from their porch, Kate could see the prison's looming cupola and its arched, square openings, more like portholes than windows. Dr. McDowell had gone south to join the Confederacy, and now his fortress, built to withstand attacks from Know-Nothings and antivivisectionists, housed rebel prisoners.

Meanwhile Katie O'Flaherty, her mother, brother, grandmother, great-grandmother, young uncle, and aunts, lived in constant fear: In the skirmishing that made up the war in Missouri, George O'Flaherty was never out of danger. Perhaps for his own safety, the family enrolled fourteen-year-old Tom O'Flaherty in the commercial course at St. Louis University from 1862 to 1864 (he was not a distinguished student).

During the war years, young people were often reckless—and not just the young men. On at least one occasion, Kate O'Flaherty took the law into her own hands.

Chapter 4

REBELLION AND SILENCE

ONE DAY, DURING THE WAR, a Union flag suddenly appeared on the O'Flahertys' porch—fastened there, Kitty Garesché wrote, by "an unknown hand."

Katie O'Flaherty was outraged.

By 1863, two years into the war, the Union authorities were taking seriously every threat and hostile gesture. Soldiers swarmed all over the O'Flahertys' neighborhood, marching to and from the Gratiot Street Prison, warily eying the houses of the "disloyal." A German-American soldier had denounced his landlord as a secessionist and then shot him; a merchant who declared that "Jefferson Davis is a great man" was sentenced to prison for sixty-three days.

Young ladies were frequently seized for wearing secessionist colors, red and white, and in July 1863 three young women were charged with "the utterance of treasonable and disloyal sentiments." They were put in the Female Military Prison, on the Eighth Street side of Gratiot Street Prison, and not released until two days later, when they signed an oath of allegiance.

The flag that mysteriously appeared on the O'Flahertys' porch was intended as an insult, for "[no] Unionist ever displayed the old flag without the knowledge of the fact that it was an unwelcome sight to those who had ceased to love and honor it," Mrs. Hannah Isabella Stagg of St. Louis remembered vividly, forty-two years after the war had ended. When Unionists displayed the flag in churches—as they did for the first time during the war—their southern friends walked out. Even children were instructed to walk around, not under, a displayed Union flag.

When Kate O'Flaherty saw the hated flag on the O'Flahertys' porch, she tore it down.

"The Yanks" were instantly at the door, demanding their flag and wanting to search the house. Kate undoubtedly taunted them, as other young secessionists did: "The children of '61–'65 were veritable little warriors with their tongues, if not with more deadly weapons," Mrs. Stagg recalled.

"The Yanks" never found their flag (which Kate had hidden in a bundle of scraps)—but the Yankees could see that the rebel Katie O'Flaherty had something to do with the crime. They decided to arrest her.

But a powerful and persuasive neighbor intervened. Dr. Charles W. Stevens, a Union supporter, said he would vouch for Kate—that she was not a dangerous person who needed to be locked up for the safety of the Union. Kate was released.

The flag incident made Kate O'Flaherty famous among southern sympathizers, as one who'd stood up to the Yankees—and the O'Flahertys' Fourth Street neighbor Anne Ewing Lane mentioned the escapade in a letter to her sister Sarah in Europe. Kate became known as St. Louis's "Littlest Rebel."

Meanwhile, her soldier-brother George, with his charm, handsome face, and gift for making himself well liked, had spent only a short time with the mounted infantry—whose cumbersome duty it was to ride about in the thick of battle, dismount to fire cannons, and then get back on their horses. George was unusually well educated, at a time when half the Confederate soldiers were illiterate, and he soon became secretary to General Thomas C. Hindman, commander of the trans-Mississippi district of the Confederate Army and an eager recruiter of rebel soldiers.

Then, on August 18, 1862, George and a friend from Arkansas (whose name has been lost to history) were among forty-nine prisoners captured at a rebel guerrilla camp on the Meramec River in Jefferson County, Missouri.

George and his companion were taken to Gratiot Street Prison, that gloomy, forbidding building within sight of his family home. The O'Flahertys' priest, Father Ryan, was spiritual adviser at the prison, where "necessities" were brought by the women of St. Louis, and watching "the ladies" from the window was the prisoners' main sport. Sometimes Kate and Kitty picked bouquets of flowers from Kate's garden and took them to the sentinel for the Confederate prisoners—but George was there only two days before he was sent to the military prison across the river in Alton, Illinois.

Meanwhile George's companion had become critically ill from exposure and tuberculosis—and Eliza O'Flaherty evidently appealed to Dr. Stevens, Kate's rescuer in the flag escapade. Dr. Stevens got the soldier paroled in his care, then sent him to live in the O'Flaherty household, for food and rest and enthusiastic attention. But the Arkansas soldier had been there only a week when he suddenly died.

George remained in the Alton prison until September 23, when he was sent to Vicksburg, Mississippi, as part of a prisoner exchange at Aiken's Landing on November 11, 1862. Although he was free to go home, he chose to stop in Little Rock for a condolence visit with his friend's family. He missed the Christmas holidays in St. Louis, and the lively New Year's Day visits, and the sudden early January thaw—soft, unseasonable weather, followed abruptly by severe cold spells and six inches of snow. That meant good sleighing and skating on Chouteau's Pond for the young folks—but it was deadly for elderly St. Louisans.

On January 16, at the O'Flahertys' house at seven o'clock in the evening, Victoire Verdon Charleville died.

According to her obituary, Madame Charleville "died a true Christian, and was universally beloved." She was almost eighty-three, and had lived in St. Louis all her life, "witnessing strange mutations in the city, and great change in its social aspects and in the governments to which it has been subjected." She had lived under three flags—of France, Spain, and the United States— and "was a lady of estimable character." When she was buried in Calvary Cemetery, in the section next to Thomas O'Flaherty's, it was only a month before Kate's thirteenth birthday. She had lost her mentor and first teacher— and George still had not returned from Arkansas.

When there were no letters from a Confederate soldier, his relatives in Union cities had no way of knowing whether he was dead or alive. On March 15, 1863, George appeared in the *Missouri Republican*:

DIED:

> At Little Rock, Arkansas, February 17th, 1863,
> GEORGE O'FLAHERTY,
> of typhoid fever, in the 23rd year of his age.

George, who had died on Mardi Gras day, was called a "brave, kind, and gentle young man" who "had the very brightest and best of prospects only for this unfortunate war. Many a sacred and sincere tear will be shed for poor George. The Professors and Teachers at all the different schools, colleges and universities, and the clergymen who instructed this pious, good and really religious and most excellent young man, as well as his young male and female friends, will sincerely regret the death of a bright specimen of humanity in the very early dawn of manhood."

George was also buried in Calvary Cemetery, under the large stone pillar that marked his father's grave. Years later, Kate Chopin named one of her sons George, and she used the name George in her first published story: George Brainerd is the handsome, rich, but full-of-himself suitor in "Wiser than a God" (1889). Kate does not mention her brother George in her surviving diaries, but in a school composition called "The Early Dead," she asked, "How then express the grief with which we follow the young, the gifted, the beautiful to the silent tomb."

She never found the words.

Despite her losses, Katie O'Flaherty apparently attended school during the spring and summer of 1863: She passed around her "Leaves of Affection" book for autographs in July, at the end of the school year. One Mary Elder contributed a sixteen-line poem celebrating "The Little Flower Forget-me-not"; someone signed "H. P." inscribed a five-line Spanish poem called "A *una Flor*," about lost illusions of the heart. Annie Shore, apparently a closer friend, addressed her contribution directly, but wrote "the" for "thee":

To Katie.

This little emblem of respect.
My youthful friend I gave to the
Treat not this motto with neglect
It is, dear Katie, remember me.
And if on native shores I dwell.
And yet am absent still from the
Let hallowed friendship deign to tell.
If Katie will remember me.

After Annie Shore's poem, Kate copied verses from Chateaubriand and Robert Burns, and then someone else contributed a romantic, unsigned entry:

Yes Loving is a painful thrill,
And not to love more painful still,
But oh! it is the worst of pain,
To love, & not be loved again!

Kate wrote after the poem her opinion of it: "foolishness"—a comment she may have meant not only for the poem, but also for the drawing on the other side of the page: a butterfly with a head resembling a carrot, and flowers growing out of the head.

Kate's autograph collection ended with "My name shall be last in your album," signed "Jennie"—but a secret admirer apparently seized the book and wrote after Jennie's name: "and ought to be forever in your heart miss Katrine guess who I am for I cannot place my name after the above sweet injunction."

One well-known name was missing from Katie O'Flaherty's autograph book: There is no inscription from "my sweet friend Kitty"—for Kitty Garesché had been forced to leave St. Louis.

Kitty's father, Bauduy Garesché, had always sympathized with the South, and he also knew how to make gunpowder. Early in the war, when he refused to take the Union oath of allegiance, Bauduy Garesché was expelled from St. Louis. Leaving his wife and children, Garesché enlisted in the Confederate Army and went to run the powder works at Columbia, South Carolina.

The Gareschés had been separated for two years by 1863, when Juliette Garesché decided to join her husband—but when her plans became known, her home and household goods were confiscated, and she and her children were officially banished from St. Louis. Kitty and the three younger children went to live with Juliette's sister in New York, while Juliette Garesché embarked on another perilous journey, to South Carolina.

After the war, the Gareschés moved to New York, because in St. Louis they would have been required to swear that they had "never been in armed hostility to the United States." Kitty finished her schooling at Manhattanville in New York, and did not return to St. Louis until 1868. At the time they were abruptly separated, Katie O'Flaherty and Kitty Garesché were thirteen-year-old schoolgirls—but when they saw each other again, they were eighteen, young ladies out of school, on the brink of society.

Kate and Kitty considered each other lifelong friends—but the five-year break in their friendship made them, in some ways, always strangers. Still, Kate honored Kitty, who by then had been a Sacred Heart nun for thirty years, in a passage in *The Awakening*: Edna's "most intimate friend at school had been one of rather exceptional intellectual gifts, who wrote fine-sounding essays, which Edna admired and strove to imitate; and with her she talked and glowed over the English classics, and sometimes held religious and political controversies." But Edna, like Kate, is reserved: She likes to be alone.

Kate O'Flaherty stayed home during much of the war—writing, reading, thinking. Her school was thriving: When the Sacred Heart Academy opened in September 1863, over a hundred boarding students and twenty-five day pupils were registered—sixty more pupils than there had been two years before. St. Louis parents evidently wanted to shelter their daughters from the war.

During the war years, a stepladder in the attic at home became Kate O'Flaherty's own refuge. There, with a big shawl around her in winter or in "airy dishabille in the dog days," she pored over the attic's stacks of fiction and poetry (the formal library had "solid and pretentious cyclopaedias and Roman Catholic religious works"). Kate much preferred reading Sir Walter Scott and Edmund Spenser "to doing any sums or parsing stupid sentences," and for the first time she was truly alone with her reading: without Madame Charleville, without Kitty. The losses of 1863 taught her to depend on herself alone.

Outside the house, St. Louis was also a terrifying place: After the bloodiest battles, the streets were filled with the wounded. One O'Flaherty neighbor wrote that the refugees from the battle of Shiloh were "creatures looking as if they had been stolen out of a graveyard." That was the face of war Kate O'Flaherty saw—and for her mother, the Union victory at Vicksburg meant a day of terror.

News about the siege had filtered back for weeks: how the southern defenders dug in on the bluffs, how the natives lived in actual holes in the ground. The constant shelling drove people mad—and between the trenches the dead and dying lay untouched and rotting for days in the blazing sun. Vultures circled constantly. The siege lasted for forty-five days, and when the Confederates finally surrendered on July 4, they were starving, diseased, naked. Even their horses—the ones they had not yet eaten for food—were animated skeletons.

Eliza O'Flaherty also heard that the Charleville boys—her Louisiana cousins Azenor Wilson, Julien, and Joseph—had been killed at Vicksburg. She knew them all, for they had been educated in St. Louis: Joseph was just two years ahead of George O'Flaherty at St. Louis University. But the report was wrong: Later Eliza wrote to her uncle that the young men "have been wounded, but are now well, the poor fellows, they have fought like *heros* for their freedom, & I hope they will be rewarded."

The three cousins had indeed been captured at Vicksburg, and so had a nineteen-year-old neighbor of theirs, a handsome planter named Albert Sampite, who had enlisted with them and also fought on the Confederate side until the bitter end. Nearly two decades later, he would change Kate Chopin's life—but at the time of Vicksburg, Katie O'Flaherty was just a frightened young girl, and still in mourning.

After the Vicksburg victory, Union supporters in St. Louis rejoiced—sporting cockades and rosettes, illuminating all the houses, hanging flags everywhere, screaming and whistling and shouting and firing guns and firecrackers into the air. In residential areas, the O'Flahertys' neighbor Anne Ewing Lane reported to her sister in Europe, the houses were "resplendent" on Union row, although one "outrage" was committed: "the soldiers going in to Mrs. O'Flaherty's on 8 Street near Chouteau Ave. breaking the vases in her yard and the shrubbery & hoisting a flag over her house."

Eliza O'Flaherty wrote about it to her uncle F. A. Charleville in California: "I was forced by a compy of dutch devils at the point of the bayonet to illuminate my house & to hoist a flag, it was to celebrat[e] the taking of Vicksburg, they threatened to burn the house over our heads—"

Years later, when she visited her daughter in Cloutierville, Louisiana, Eliza O'Flaherty still talked about her terror when the German soldiers invaded her home. She also showed curious youngsters how she had worn her apron backward, to hide her valuables from the hated Yankees: She had had to hide everything herself, because she had lost her slaves. "These are strange times we are living in," Eliza had written to her uncle during the war. "My negroes are leaving me[,] old Louise ran off a few days ago, I suppose the rest will follow soon. God's will be done."

Kate evidently forgot—or chose not to remember—that the slaves had run off. Kate had known "the faithful love of her negro 'mammy,' " her friend William Schuyler wrote some thirty years later, and she had seen the "devotion of which the well-treated slaves were capable during the hard times of the war, when the men of the family were either dead or fighting in the ranks of the 'lost cause.' "

By then, the war years had taken on a certain nostalgic glow, and Schuyler did not mention how many men had not fought in the war—buying substitutes, suddenly claiming British citizenship, sitting out the war years in Canada or Europe. Even Kate's uncle, Charles Faris, twenty-one the year the war began, was not a soldier, but "one of the best clerck of his age on the River, he is geting two hundred dollars a month," according to Eliza O'Flaherty's often-misspelled letter to her uncle. After the war, Charley Faris married the millionaire's daughter Clémence Benoist.

During the war, there was one family romance: Kate's aunt Zuma (Eliza and Charles's sister "Puss") had been engaged for four years to John Tatum, one of the most daring rebels in the South (according to Eliza). In early February of 1864, Tatum sneaked into St. Louis in disguise, and on the seventeenth, "was married in our parish Church," Eliza wrote to her uncle F. A. It was at seven in the evening, with only the immediate family: "[I]t had to be very secret, had he been discovered, it would have cost him his life." The wedding was so secret that Zuma did not even mention it in a letter to California relatives: She said only that she was going to see "Tom Thump" and his wife at the circus. "The beauty of it all," Eliza O'Flaherty wrote, "is it was done under the nose of two or three Regiments, that are stationed in our neighbourhood."

But there was little romance in what Kate Chopin remembered from the war: The lost cause had little bright sheen for those who lived through it. Although Kate was proud of tearing down the Yankees' flag from her front porch, and later gave the small torn flag to one of her sons, she resisted writing about the escapade. Stealing the flag had been an outburst of rage, not a childish prank. She made fun of it later—irony was a way of keeping her real thoughts to herself—but the war years touched her in ways too deep for humor, or boasting, or dreams of glory.

In her short stories, a quarter-century later, Kate Chopin did not consider the war a Glorious Cause. In "A Lady of Bayou St. John," Chopin describes a young, childlike wife who spends her life mourning the death of her soldier husband: As her distraught suitor says, she has wedded her young existence to the dead. In "Ma'ame Pélagie," the heroine lives on tortured memories of the dashing young men who rode off to glory and never returned—while the Yankees set fire to the only home she had ever known. Nor were white women the only female victims of the war: In "Beyond the Bayou," a black woman known as "La Folle" cannot cross the bayou near her cabin because during the war "she had been frightened literally 'out of her senses.' "

Chopin wrote other stories alluding to the war: In "A Wizard from Gettysburg," a soldier who lost his memory in "the black desolation of war" finally wanders home; in "The Return of Alcibiade," an old gentleman, failing in body and mind, waits futilely for his long-dead son to return from the war. Chopin gave both stories conventional happy endings, but her real interest was more somber: showing men who had given their youths to war.

Kate Chopin described the scene of battle only once, in an unpublished story called "The Locket" that she wrote in 1897, the year before her son Fred joined the Spanish-American War for the patriotic adventure of his generation. In "The Locket," Chopin describes a lonely Confederate soldier, in his shabby gray uniform, longing for the young woman he left behind. A battle takes place, a clergyman ministers to the dead, and the great black vultures circle the plain, waiting to feast on the bodies. When the soldier's sweetheart hears (falsely, it turns out) that he is dead, "[a] spasm of resistance and rebellion seized and swept over her. Why was the spring here with its flowers and its seductive breath if he was dead! . . . The soul of her youth clamored for its rights; for a share in the world's glory and exultation."

In her Civil War stories, Kate O'Flaherty Chopin described what she remembered from the war: Young people dreamed of bravery and romance but got only ashes and bitter memories, and a lifetime of mourning. So many young men, like her half-brother George, had ridden off for fame and glory— and so few had returned with minds and bodies intact. So many had not returned at all.

For the crucial years between eleven and fifteen, Kate O'Flaherty had lived in the midst of street violence, constant fear, and sudden death. She had lost her great-grandmother, her brother, and her dearest friend. For Kate, the war years brought bitter memories and never-ending grief.

Chapter 5

"A TELLER
OF MARVELLOUS
STORIES"

"SHE WAS NOT DISTINGUISHED as a scholar during her rather irregular attendance at the convent school," her friend William Schuyler claimed in an 1894 profile of Kate Chopin for a national magazine. Only during the last two years of her schooling did young Katie O'Flaherty "ever do any serious work."

Kate reappeared on the Sacred Heart ledgers in the fall of 1864, a tumultuous term—for Confederate General Sterling Price's armies were poised to invade St. Louis. Schools and businesses closed; many citizens fled; others barricaded themselves in their homes until the threat passed. During Kate's spring term, the battered Confederate armies finally surrendered in Virginia. Southern sympathizers in St. Louis accepted their defeat stoically; Catholics pointed out that General Robert E. Lee had surrendered on Palm Sunday, April 9.

Then, on Good Friday, April 15, President Abraham Lincoln was shot by John Wilkes Booth, an actor who had sometimes performed in St. Louis. (Seeing Booth's wild histrionics, many St. Louisans had thought him either drunk or demented.)

By Easter Sunday, the president was dead.

When Madeleine-Sophie Barat, the founder of the Society of the Sacred Heart, died in Paris only five weeks later, all the Sacred Heart schools around the world were shrouded in mourning. Masses were said, and the good deeds and achievements of Madeleine-Sophie were constantly recited.

For Katie O'Flaherty, whose father had died on All Saints' Day, whose great-

71 ❖

grandmother had died three weeks after Christmas, and whose brother had died on Mardi Gras, religious holidays became overwhelmingly associated with silence, black crepe, mourning, and moralizing.

At least outwardly, Katie O'Flaherty had become more sedate. In her first young-adult portrait, taken in 1866, she stands against a classical backdrop, one hand gracefully draped over the ornate back of a chair. In the other hand, she carries the belle's indispensable implement: a fan. She wears a fashionable flounced bell skirt over a hoop—and her face looks serious, pensive. With her close-set dark eyes, her small mouth, and her dark hair parted in the middle (only a few rebellious curls escaping), Kate resembles her mother—except for her less-stern chin, which suggests the possibility of humor.

Kate still did not attend school in an orderly sequence. She was a Sacred Heart day student during the 1864–65 and 1866–67 school terms, and during the spring of 1868, but she was a special student at the Academy of the Visitation for 1865–66, the year she was sixteen. Usually young women's schooling ended at sixteen, but Kate prolonged her studies—possibly to compensate for lost semesters, or (more likely) to continue her music education. From 1866 on, Eliza O'Flaherty paid an extra thirty dollars per semester for Kate's music lessons.

Sometime between 1865 and 1866, Kate O'Flaherty and her family moved to 1118 St. Ange Avenue, half a dozen blocks southwest of the house on Eighth Street. Eliza O'Flaherty, thirty-seven in 1865, had already been a widow for a decade, and with a picture she sent to her uncle F. A. Charleville in California, she wrote, "I am not old in years, but old in looks, tell the Children that it is a cousin that loves them well."

In the new house, Kate, her mother, grandmother, and brother, Tom, joined Eliza's younger sister Amanda, her husband Roger McAllister, and their children Nina, Andrew, and Marie, all younger than Kate. Kate was no longer the cherished youngest member of the household, and little Nina McAllister, with her insatiable appetite, was a particular irritant.

Eliza's sister and brother, Josephine and Charley, were also still living at home, as were Eliza's married sister "Puss" (Zuma) Tatum and her husband, John (the former Confederate soldier who'd married her on that sudden, secret trip into St. Louis in early 1864). John Tatum became a steamboatman after the war, and by June of 1866, he and Puss had already buried two children.

The O'Flaherty-McAllister-Faris-Tatum household was crowded (in the 1870 census it included twelve people), and it gave the inquisitive Katie O'Flaherty her first opportunity to observe the lives of married couples. Amanda McAllister had made a sensible marriage to her brother-in-law's business partner: Roger McAllister, prosperous and middle-aged, was one of St. Louis's solid men. But

Puss Tatum had made a romantic marriage, to a man whose economic prospects were not promising, and whose occupation kept him away for long periods. Aunt Amanda was thirty-three and Aunt Puss was in her late twenties— the ages of young and discontented wives in Kate Chopin's fiction—and Kate was already, unconsciously, gathering material for stories about women and men, marriage and its discontents.

Possibly the dislocations of moving provoked Kate O'Flaherty to enroll at the Academy of the Visitation in the fall of 1865. The Visitandines, the Sacred Heart nuns' friendly rivals, also taught girls from old French-Catholic families, including Kate's future aunt Clémence Benoist. The Visitation school in north-central St. Louis abutted sawmills, breweries, and "Kerry Patch," the Irish ghetto notorious for crime and squalor.

Sometimes called "the Castle of Kerry Patch," the academy was at Cass Avenue and Twenty-second Street, prettily set inside a stone wall and iron carriage gates, with shady walks, sage hedges, and pink and white rosebushes. Its attractions were the beauty of the grounds, its quiet removal from the outside world, and its greater allowance for individual idiosyncrasies. Visitation girls were required to wear their black uniforms only on Thursday and Sunday; for the rest of the week, they could wear any dresses they chose. The discipline was much less strict than at the Sacred Heart school, and the curriculum less academically rigorous.

Yet even at the Visitation Academy, Kate O'Flaherty was an oddity. She is not listed in any records of classes attended, or prizes awarded. She was not one of the year's graduates (although she is now called "the greatest public achiever among Academy students"), nor did she receive the crescent, the symbolic gold brooch awarded to all Visitation graduates. Kate seems to have been solely a "Special"—a student who enrolled to pursue a particular subject.

Most likely, Kate devoted herself to music, especially the piano. She was famous among friends for her musical memory: She could attend the opera one evening and the next morning reproduce by ear the parts she liked best. The Visitandines had long been known for their musical programs (theirs was the first piano ever seen in French-settled Kaskaskia, Illinois, in the 1840s), and their school offered "Music, on the Harp, Piano Forte, Melodeon, Guitar, and Vocal Music." For their practice sessions, the girls even had special lamps, designed to extinguish themselves automatically if they were knocked over.

The "Viz" year gave Kate a chance to concentrate on her music—and, perhaps, to decide that she wanted a more rounded intellectual education.

In the fall of 1866, Kate returned to the Academy of the Sacred Heart, where the curriculum for older girls was intended to create "intelligent, active, unselfish women, with minds and hands trained for the sphere in which God had placed them, whether it be home-life or some wider social field"—an unusual admission that the place of Sacred Heart women might be outside the home. The students were to "take part intelligently in conversation when at home or in social gatherings"; they learned to write interesting and correct letters; they discussed scientific discoveries and current events; and they made judgments. (Of Isabella II of Spain, Kate O'Flaherty wrote in her notebook that the queen "is beloved by her subjects, but her character is not stainless.")

Sacred Heart pupils also competed vigorously for honors and prizes, including colored ribbons, medals, and crowns. But the greatest honor was to be one of the Children of Mary—elected by students and teachers for their leadership, piety, popularity, and hard work. Children of Mary were supposed to be capable, studious, stable, and well rounded; they were expected to show scrupulous kindness to younger girls (which often meant tactfully handling the little ones' intense crushes on pretty and popular big girls). The Children of Mary were everyone's favorites.

On November 21, 1866, "Katie O'Flaherty, Day Scholar, St. L., Mo." was inducted into the Children of Mary, along with her friend "Frank" Blakely (a day student from Liverpool, Ohio), and another girl named Mary Farrell.

The new members were to follow the "Rules of the Congregation of the Blessed Virgin Mary," mostly religious duties: celebrating holy days, taking communion, and saying daily prayers. The Children of Mary were also warned against bad practices, and specific "occasions of sin," among them "evil Companions, Quarrels, Contentions, murmurings." In honor of the Blessed Virgin Mary, they were to "strenuously endeavour to imitate her Virginal and more than Angelic Purity, and always cherish an inconsiliable [sic] hatred and aversion for the opposite degrading vice."

Children of Mary received a special medal, which many of them (including Kitty Garesché in far-off New York) wore on their belts. They also had the right to flaunt their high status by signing their names with a special flourish:

> Katherine O'Flaherty, E. de M.
> ("*Enfant de Marie*," or Child of Mary.)

When they left school, the Children of Mary were expected to join adult sodalities and devote themselves to charity work: visiting the sick, volunteering at hospitals, operating lending libraries. As an adult, Kate Chopin paid dues to the St. Louis Children of Mary Sodality for most of her life, but does not seem to have been involved in good works. (The St. Louis Congregation of the Children of Mary sewed altar linens and vestments and supplied equipment for liturgical services.)

Eventually Kate fell away from most of the Children of Mary precepts, notably "Angelic Purity"—and at times she seemed to welcome "occasions of sin."

The Sacred Heart nuns had taught Kate to think, but after she left their care, she had less and less to do with religion of any kind. Still, one gifted and sympathetic Sacred Heart nun changed Katie O'Flaherty's life—by encouraging her to write.

The Sacred Heart nun whom Kate called "our much loved teacher, Madam O'Meara" evidently saw in Kate a talented young woman who needed discipline. Madam O'Meara, Kitty Garesché remembered, "was one of our nuns most gifted for composition in both verse and prose; it was she who doubtless developed Kate's talent for writing, because as children we never attempted anything in that line, so far as I can remember." Madam O'Meara assigned Kate to copy long extracts from other authors, and to write on sometimes dull and even morbid subjects—but she also encouraged Kate to develop her own voice as a writer.

Mary Philomena O'Meara was an inspiring teacher whose influence lasted far beyond the classroom. Her parents, like Thomas O'Flaherty, had fled Ireland to escape starvation and religious oppression. As a child, Mary O'Meara had been much like Katie O'Flaherty: precocious and willful, curious, and imaginative. (A lonely child, she sometimes took a statue of the Virgin Mary to bed with her for companionship.) In her childhood, Mary O'Meara loved reading and climbing trees, and the only complaint against her in school was that she was "too studious" and "loves her books too much." Then, at fourteen, after a hopelessly ill sister was miraculously cured, Mary O'Meara dedicated her own life to "love and service" in religion. In December 1861, she took the habit as a Sacred Heart nun; two years later, on Christmas Eve, 1863, she took her vows.

Mary O'Meara, with her broad brow and gray eyes, had "a richly dowered character, a penetrating mind, an affectionate heart," according to her Sacred Heart biographical notice. She especially enjoyed working with the Children of Mary and making them into "valiant women." She was young, just six years older than Katie O'Flaherty, but she was no easy mark for obstreperous or lazy students. Her classes were always exciting: "[J]ust to see her at her desk, erect, alert, her beautiful, strong face turned toward her class was a challenge to all the faculties to be alive."

In class Madam O'Meara would fire rapid questions at students; she had no tolerance for "slouchy English," snap judgments, or "resting on oars." She loved history, and told vivid and colorful stories of monks and queens and heroes. Her other love was literature, which she insisted was much closer to real life than science could ever be—and better at character formation. She considered the writing of good English "the best all round test of culture" and had a special gift for composition herself.

Madam O'Meara possessed a lively imagination and a gift for repartee, a long memory, a great intellect, exquisite tact—and an appreciation for "the interior life," the growth that might take place within a child long before others might see the results. In Katie O'Flaherty, she found a gifted girl scarred by losses. Madam O'Meara encouraged Kate to confront her grief by writing about death—but she also helped develop Kate's keen sense of humor, her precious "habit of looking on the amusing side of everything."

Kate O'Flaherty's commonplace book, which she began in 1867, was a plain notebook with lined pages and a green and black mottled cover, on which was printed "Katie O'Flaherty, St. Louis." The notebook had no lock, and clearly it was intended for Madam O'Meara's eyes as well as Katie O'Flaherty's.

Kate inaugurated her notebook with due solemnity, as if consciously writing for an adult audience. Later, she alternated between stiff pomposities (presum- ably expected by a grown-up teacher), and lively and fresh observations that she wrote for herself. But within a year Kate had recognized the true value of her journal, and she wrote one day, "What a dear good confident my book is. If it does not clear my doubts it at least does not contradict and oppose my opinions—You are the only one, my book, with whom I take the liberty of talking about myself."

At first, though, she began with a stern extract from Edward George Bulwer's *My Novel*:

> To many minds at the commencement of one grave and earnest pilgrimage, I am vandal enough to think that the indulgence of poetic taste and reverie does great and lasting injury; that it serves to enervate the character; give false ideas of life, impart the sem- blance of drudgery to the noble toils and duties of the active man.

Not all poetry would have this dreadful effect, Bulwer conceded, "But the poetry which youth usually loves and appreciates the best—the poetry of mere sentiments—does so in minds already over-predisposed to the sentimental, and which require bracing to grow into the healthful manhood."

Kate also copied from Bulwer a criticism of his age for not appreciating its writers, and then a statement with more personal relevance: "Oh! it is such a joy in youth to be alone with one's day dreams." But Bulwer assumed that such a youth was male, a potential statesman or a "prince of arts and letters" or an adventurer who "goes on with kingly step to the future." He was not really talking to young women.

From T. B. Macaulay's *Ranke's History of the Popes*, Kate copied an extract and then commented on it, showing that she had learned to see history the Sacred Heart way, as a ceaseless combat between Catholic and non-Catholic forces. "It is to me a subject of wonder," seventeen-year-old Kate wrote judiciously, "that a mind such as Macaulay's, so enlightened and free from bigotry, should have considered the Catholic Church a mere work of 'human policy.' He yields however to this politic work a superiority and primacy, in which we Catholics see every evidence of a divine Institution."

Kate also made less judicious-sounding judgments. In her opinion, *The Life and Letters of Madame Swetchine* by the Count de Falloux was "a queer book—which did not interest me much." She had her reasons: "In fact translations from the French and German rarely interest me; because French and German notions and ideas are so different from the English—that they lose all their naive zest by being translated into that [most] practical of tongues."

Nevertheless, probably aware that Madam O'Meara would be reading her notebook, Kate attempted a balanced assessment: "That 'portrait of Fontenelle' is given in a piquant manner;—I should have preferred reading it in French, but was unable to procure the book. I like it because I can glance over it as an occasional reminder that a monster once lived upon earth."

Monsieur de Fontenelle, a complete misanthrope, appeared in one of Madame Swetchine's most scathing sketches: He never laughed, felt emotions, or responded to anything, including music—and that reminded sixteen-year-old Kate O'Flaherty of "a joke told at my expense":

> Mama one afternoon sent me in the parlor to entertain a gentleman, who, though deemed bashful has never yet succeeded in making that ingredient in his composition known to myself. I immediately took to the piano as the most pleasing way both to himself and me of filling my mission of entertainer. Wishing to suit his taste whatever it might be—I played pieces of every variety: operas—Sonatas—Meditations—Galops—Nocturnes—Waltzes & Jigs—after accomplishing which I turned to him expecting approbation if not praise and admiration; when to my utmost dismay, he cooly informed me that there was nothing on earth he disliked more than music—at any time—in any place—and of any kind from a brass band to a jew's harp.

Kate copied other passages that seemed to be the choices of Madam O'Meara, including a short history of the Rothschild banking family, in which Kate noted that Nathan Rothschild of London was the first "adhearant" of the "Jewish religion, that ever held seat in Parliament." She included character sketches of noted leaders (Louis XIV, the Duke of Marlborough and Prince Eugene of Savoy); she copied, in French, Chateaubriand's poem "*Le Montagnard Emigré*"; and she wrote descriptions of unusual historical events—among them the Venetian "Espousals of the Adriatic" and "Sicilian Vespers" ("a famous massacre").

With few exceptions, Kate O'Flaherty was learning about the historical doings of great men, although her sketches of "Reigning Sovereigns of Europe" did include Queen Isabella II of Spain and Queen Victoria. In her section on "Last words of celebrated Personages," Kate included just two women: the empress Josephine, who said, "Isle of Elba—Napoleon," and Catherine Macaulay ("O, if I knew—death could be so sweet I had never feared it so much.")

In her commonplace book, Kate O'Flaherty refined her tastes, decided what subjects interested her as a writer, and insisted on clarity in other writers, as well as herself. When famous authors were not so forthright as she liked, she edited them—as she did with Longfellow's romantic novel *Hyperion*.

She gave fifteen pages of her notebook to quoting the novel, and commented, "What a subtle charm exists in each line of Longfellow's." She liked his peasants' song: "The Rhine! the Rhine! a blessing on the Rhine!" and his passages of self-doubt; she also copied disputes over whether one can learn more from books or real life. But when Longfellow grew too long-winded, Kate cut passages to make his story move faster. In his description of spring, she deleted children's singing; and where the famous poet called spring "the rising of the broad green curtain," Kate O'Flaherty changed it matter-of-factly to "the opening of the scene."

Nevertheless, Longfellow "is a poet and a true one," Kate O'Flaherty concluded (since Sacred Heart students were supposed to make judgments),

> and prose and poetry bear alike the stamp of his soft poetic genius. His Hyperion from beginning to end might be compared to a "river of flowing gold" so rich is it in real and imaginative beauties. I read and reread with the keenest enjoyment his exquisite descriptions of German scenes and scenery; for my passion has always been to travel in that land—that cradle and repository of genius. And even while longing, I still fear to visit it lest my long cherished dreams fail of accomplishment and prove but the baseless fabric of a vision. "Hyperion" would implant in any heart an aching after Germania's beauties as it has long since implanted in mine.

Then, as if conscious that such high-flown rhetoric did not really suit her, Kate concluded: "Heigh Ho! Il faut espérer."

In her original compositions, Katie O'Flaherty was struggling to express her own meaning exactly. Sometimes her writing wavered wildly, as in her first composition, "The Early Dead."

Kate dedicated the essay "To the mem of Minnie Enninger, 1866," possibly a schoolmate who died in the cholera epidemic that year: Her "visions of future womanly happiness" would never come true. At first, Kate filled some lines with conventional phrases about death and sorrow—but soon she grew enthusiastically morbid, throwing in Gothic touches like those in the novels she and Kitty had read together: "Lift one of those marble hands, which clasps so confidingly the jeweled cross; how cold it is—its chill sends a shiver through the frame; drop it,—hear how heavily it falls against the alabaster bosom." Kate concluded that those who die young must be singularly blessed, for they escape sin, sorrow, and disease.

Kate was preoccupied with death—but she was also working on silly as well as solemn ways to write about it. In "Memories," a fourteen-stanza poem about an old man's regrets and losses, she wrote seriously about a stone monument like the one in Calvary Cemetery that marked the graves of her father and brother George: "Proud manhoods course was sadly traced/By many a gleaming shaft of stone. . . ." But Kate also wrote much of the poem with silly misspellings ("braided heir"), a singsong rhythm, and Gothic or sentimental phrases: "nerveless hand," "memories of yore," "his mother's knee." After a while, she began to pile on clichés to the point of nonsense:

> His cottage home in his jasmine frame,
> Still smiled beneath the linden shade,
> When the south-wind an early pilgrim came,
> And the wild flowers a rich mosaic made.

Whether Madam O'Meara recognized "Memories" as a parody of mawkish poetry is not recorded: She may have been pleased with a pupil clever enough to make fun of her own assignment (or she may have recognized a gesture of defiance when she saw it). In any case, Kate continued to write as if producing for two audiences: an academic, adult one, which expected seriousness and pomposities; and a direct, down-to-earth one, which appreciated wit and originality.

Often she could not resist sabotaging her own apparent seriousness. In the longest prose composition in her book, "Christian Art," Kate began loftily, "Great indeed were the mighty empires of long ago that could lay their hold upon nations and call them theirs." She then discoursed on the superiority of modern art because it comes from Christianity—but she betrayed her lack of interest with misspellings and incoherent sentences. Religion, she wrote, provides "beauties celestion and terrestrial"; for the Christian, "faith and genius lead him advisingly within the penetralia of Omnipotence itself." In the next paragraph, she praised Michelangelo's "Moses" for its "sturn dignity."

Kate seemed truly interested only when she wrote about music: Already she was struggling to describe the ineffable and overwhelming emotional effect of music on susceptible minds. In her commonplace book, the adolescent Kate O'Flaherty described "the harmony of that wondrous 'Miserera,' now, now stealing forth from the darkness like the first wail of a broken heart, growing fainter and fainter till it dies away in silence as if the grief were too great for the strain; then leaping forth, not like the voice of song, but of agony—floating and swelling with irresistable [sic] power till it sinks again into the low broken tones of intense anguish."

Evidently the students shared each others' work, for Kate O'Flaherty's "essays and poetic exercises were thought to be quite remarkable, not only by the scholars, but even by the sisters." Her classmates praised her "gifts as a teller of marvellous stories, most of them the promptings of childhood imagination"—and she portrayed those classmates in an original poem called "The 'Congé,' " about the lively female community at the Sacred Heart school. Her verses poke gentle fun at friends and relatives, and demonstrate the wit and curiosity that would mark her professional writing a quarter-century later.

Beneath her title, Kate explained that the "congé" was a Sacred Heart tradition, the last day "at which the day scholars are permitted to mingle with the boarders." This congé was "given in honor of Mother Galwey's feast. The 'Madam' alluded to was our much loved teacher Madam O'Meara. The day following, for a class-exercise, we were given the subject of the past day's amusement."

Kate wrote about real people: not just her odious little cousin Nina McAllister, but also her own contemporaries Frank (Francis Blakely) and Lizzie (Lizzie Thornton or Lizzie Bulte). In the Children of Mary elections, held October 14, 1866, the Under Sacristans chosen had been Lizzie Thornton and Aurore Charleville (Kate's Louisiana cousin, known as "Lovy"); the librarian was Lizzie Bulte; and two "Other members" were Katie O'Flaherty and Frank Blakely.

For their congé, the Children of Mary (the "Brights") had been assigned to clean up the laboratory—and one "Katie O'F" was a troublemaker. (During the next year, Eliza O'Flaherty paid another five dollars for "Chemical Apparatus"—perhaps to atone for Kate's misconduct.)

The "Congé"—1867

The Congé is past and the frolic and fun
Was over, before it seemed scarcely begun;

For with playing and romping and teasing away,
The quick fleeting hours soon filled up the day.
But the morning was not to amusement devoted
For *Madam* to all of her "Brights" had allotted
The task (this displayed a heart ever trusting)
Of arranging and breaking and mending and dusting,
Her chemical tools, which of delicate make
We could easily handle and—easily break.
There was Lizzie who thought with importance of air
That we could do nothing if she was not there,
And Frank—thinking much, and speaking but little
Who handled with safety tools e'en the most brittle
While Katie O'F, poor unfortunate lass
Broke Implements stoutest as though they were glass.
But this war of destruction, thanks, soon was to cease
And the room and its contents left happily in peace.
For kind Madam Hamilton, with due form and state,
Announced the dinner no longer could wait,
And arranging the girls with artistical taste,
Led the way to the hall without trouble or haste.

The rest of the *"congé,"* Kate wrote, provided much drama and humor:

But ye Fates! On arriving I found 'twas my doom
For want I presume of more benches or room,
To sit between Lizzie and Nina my cousin
Who seemed to have appetites due to a dozen,
And gave me scarce time to breathe or to think
With asking for butter—the bread—or a drink.
But between these demands which indeed were not few,
I found time to admire an arrangement or two
Of the garlands of flowers and pigs à la fry
Which in every direction were greeting the eye.
But all these howe'er beautiful sink into nought,
In considering the fun which the afternoon brought;
For through cellar and basement and garret so high,
We tumbled and tossed in the game of "I spy."
Now into the barn yard—the loft or the stable,
Hiding in every place—any place that we were able;
And thrown into ecstasies of foolish delight
At not being found or at seeking aright.
But at length Madam M. with mysterious air,
Comes whispering that the girls must prepare

To enter a room, shut out from all light,
To see a strange thing—a most wonderful sight:
Which sight we soon found was a new source of pleasure
Got up by "our Madam" whose mind is a treasure,
Ever teeming with jewels of science and fun,
And in whom we all think sets and rises the sun.
'Twas a strange magic lantern which displayed a queer sight
Of devils in every conceivable plight.
Of hills and volcanoes; St. Peter's at Rome;
Of Pantheons at Paris—or a neat cottage home.
Of monkeys and tigers and elephants rare—
All displayed with precision and mentioned with care.
But my keen disappointment one cannot conceive.
When, at the best part we are told we must leave;
For fear that the already fast fading light
Would leave us in fear at the coming of night.
And as I reluctantly arose to obey,
Though my reason said "homeward" my heart bade me stay.
So greatly put out—nearly ready to cry,
I kissed my companions—bade Madam good bye—
And secretly knowing I'd no time to waste
Turned my steps towards home with all possible haste.

Eventually, as she approached the end of her schooling, Kate began collecting passages about women. Her beloved Madam O'Meara believed that Sacred Heart graduates should be "companions intellectually of their husbands, Mothers fit for their sublime trust, women able to bear life's responsibilities and courageous to meet them." Literature, as always, would be their way to learn about "the nobility and beauty of the life before them."

From Anna Brownell Jameson's *Sketches of Art*, Kate copied two passages emphasizing women's power. The Medusa at Cologne, according to Mrs. Jameson, had "full rich lips curled with disdain . . . the extreme of loveliness and terror." Dannecker's Ariadne was not the usual forlorn, forsaken Ariadne, but a noble and strong woman: "immortal and triumphant, as the bride of Bacchus."

Kate also noted Mrs. Jameson's discussion of German women: "I thought the German women, of a certain rank, more *natural* than we are," Kate copied—herself underlining the word *natural*. According to Mrs. Jameson, an English girl's education too often consisted of "You must not do this" and "You must not say that"—and if a girl asked, "Why?," her mother or governess would invariably tell her, "It is not the custom—it is not lady-like—it is ridiculous!," and "My dear, you must not argue—young ladies never argue."

But in Germany, Mrs. Jameson wrote, the situation was much better: Young ladies' affections and impulses were not "so habitually crushed or disguised" and "more of the poetry of existence is brought to bear on the common realities of life." Specifically, she wrote, German women—even of the upper classes—involved themselves with housekeeping—which the English considered vulgar. Goethe's "description of Werther's Charlotte, cutting bread and butter, has been an eternal subject of laughter among the English, among whom fine sentiment must be garnished out in something finer than itself; and no princess can be suffered to go mad, or even be in love except in white satin. . . . To any one who has lived in Germany, the union of sentiment and bread and butter, or of poetry with household cares, excites no laughter."

To Kate O'Flaherty, a lady's doing her own housework was something of a foreign notion, for her family had always had servants, if not slaves. (In the 1870 census, the O'Flaherty-McAllister-Faris household had three servants, all Irish-born: Mary Gibson, twenty-five; Margaret Bradley, twenty-two; and Mary Ann King, thirteen.) But the idea of being *natural*—of being truly oneself—was most appealing, for Katie O'Flaherty was already conscious of what Edna Pontellier also recognizes at an early age: "the dual life—that outward existence which conforms, the inward life which questions."

Kate returned to the subject of women and men with her extracts from *Lady Blessington's Conversations with Byron*. Kate copied the description of the handsome and notorious poet, and the comment that when he discussed Sir Walter Scott, "his eyes became humid." Kate, at eighteen, copied the description of Lady Blessington at the same age: "a just matured woman, full of loveliness and love, the kind of creature with whose divine sweetness the gazer's heart aches. . . ." And the half-Irish Katie O'Flaherty duly wrote down the description of Lady Blessington's mouth, with its "ripe fullness and freedom of play peculiar to the Irish physiognomy."

But with Lady Blessington, Kate was most intrigued by the discussion of Madame de Staël's novels of strong passionate women, *Corinne* and *Delphine*. Byron had told Madame de Staël that both books were "very dangerous productions to be put into the hands of young women"—and she never forgave him for it. Nevertheless, he insisted that in *Corinne* the virtuous characters were all dull, and that this was "a most insidious blow aimed at virtue." It was "dangerous," Byron argued, to "inculcate the belief that genius, talent, acquirements, and accomplishments, such as Corinne was represented to possess could not preserve a woman from becoming a victim to an unrequited passion, and that reason, absence, and female pride were unavailing."

They had a fierce argument, Byron said, about which of them was more immoral—he in his life, or Madame de Staël in her writing. She took the quarrel seriously; he laughed much of the time—but for Katie O'Flaherty, the question of what a talented woman could do with her life was pressing, incessant, and very serious.

Kate O'Flaherty graduated from the Sacred Heart Academy on June 29, 1868, leaving behind the gray brick convent building with its brick walk and its tall lilac bushes, whose sweet fragrance scented the air after late spring rains.

At the graduation ceremonies, Kate O'Flaherty played an "Instrumental— duo de Norma, Charles Wells" with her classmate Kate Saltonstall, and also read her own essay, a composition called "National Peculiarities." (In her notebook, Kate had copied Charles Lamb's observation that "I have been trying all my life to like Scotchmen, and am obliged to desist from the experiment in despair.")

Kate also won a first blue ribbon, the highest honor for day scholars. Then "the highest honors of the institution, with the gold medal, the award of excellence of conduct and proficiency in studies" were presented to the four best Sacred Heart students: Kate Saltonstall, Frank Blakely, Sarah McKee—and Kate O'Flaherty.

By the fall of 1868, Kate O'Flaherty was in society, as "one of the acknowledged belles of St. Louis," praised for her beauty, "cleverness," and "amiability of character." There were countless concerts and operas and parties, and Kitty Garesché had returned from New York, but she was in mourning. Her father had died suddenly, just as workmen were completing a new home, from which Kitty would make her debut.

During the debutante round in the season of 1868, Kate O'Flaherty began using her commonplace book as an actual diary, a place to record her thoughts. She was "already fast acquiring that knowledge of human nature which her stories show," her friend William Schuyler wrote years later—but for the moment, her discoveries were her own secrets.

Her diary became her confidante and accomplice.

Chapter 6

POPULARITY AND ITS PRICE

WHEN KATE O'FLAHERTY ENtered St. Louis society, she was an "Irish Beauty," according to Kitty Garesché. Kate resembled her father more than her mother, she was not tall, and she had winsome features: "Her very abundant dark hair drooped in a wave, lower on one side than on the other, which gave her a very arch, sprightly expression. Her eyes were brown, and looked right at you." She was about five feet five inches tall.

Kate O'Flaherty in 1868 was not unlike her own Edna in *The Awakening*: "Mrs. Pontellier's eyes were quick and bright. . . . She had a way of turning them swiftly upon an object and holding them there as if lost in some inward maze of contemplation or thought. . . . Her face was captivating by reason of a certain frankness of expression and a contradictory subtle play of features. Her manner was engaging."

At eighteen, Kate O'Flaherty also had "a droll gift of mimicry" and an air of reserve, which Kitty said was mingled with a healthy realism:

> Though she was the object of great admiration, she accepted it in a matter-of-fact way and did not seem a bit vain. She had remarkable self-possession, a certain poise of manner, though very sweet and simple. Her laugh was quiet; her voice gentle and low. It seems to me that in her, intellect predominated and kept the passions cool.

Kate did remain passionate about music, and St. Louis offered an endless variety of philharmonic societies, German bands, and formal and informal concerts. For several weeks each year, the touring Grand Italian Opera Company performed the standard repertory (*Ernani, La Favorita*) as well as newer pieces: Theirs was the first St. Louis production of Gounod's *Faust*. But it was the performance of the legendary Norwegian violinist Ole Bull that inspired Kate O'Flaherty to use her commonplace book as a diary, a record of her thoughts.

> *Dec. 1868.* Last evening I enjoyed the pleasure of hearing the famous violinist Ole Bull; never having heard him before, I was at once delighted and surprised. He came forward upon the stage, and was greeted with the most enthusiastic applause. His age I should judge to be between sixty and seventy; but though old he is still handsome—tall straight and robust. His countenance is excessively pleasing; his hair of an iron gray; and his whole appearance that of a gentleman of the old school. He handles his instrument, as I thought, tenderly, as though it were something he loved, and in his performance is perfectly at ease—displaying nothing of that exaggerated style most usually seen in fine violinists. His selections were mostly those of his own composition, and these I preferred to his borrowed pieces.

Kate also attempted to capture in words the power of music (an effort she continued throughout her writing life):

> To describe the effect his music had upon me would be impossible. It seemed the very perfection of the art, and while listening to him, I for the first time longed to be blind, that I might drink it all in undisturbed and undistracted by surrounding objects.

Although she was attractive and popular, Kate O'Flaherty did not relish every moment of her "season." The life of a belle was frantic and all-consuming: the fittings of new gowns, the trying and buying of new hats, the carriage rides from place to place, the descent each time with the utmost care so as not to disarrange one's ensemble or tumble into the sea of mud that was St. Louis's streets during much of the year.

Moving nimbly was impossible, for ladies of the 1860s wore whalebone corsets, tightly laced up the back so as not to disturb the smooth line in the front. The corsets enforced good posture and encouraged elegant poses—but precluded healthy breathing. By the late 1860s, young belles no longer wore hoops of wood or steel: The current fashion, set by the empress Eugénie and her couturier Monsieur Worth in Paris, was the bustle—yards of fabric gathered in a pillowlike shape to form an artificial protrusion behind a woman's body. Below the bustle, fashionable ladies wore tight, tubular skirts that forced them into stately, mincing steps; behind the bustle, long trains dragged along the ground.

In a portrait from 1869, Kate O'Flaherty is dressed in a lady's walking costume, including a high feathered headdress, a gown with elaborate flouncings and ruchings, and an overskirt with bustle trailing behind her. She looks distinctly uncomfortable.

There was very little encouragement for a young belle who liked to read and write and think, as Kate complained to her diary on New Year's Eve Day, December 31, 1868:

> Rain! Rain! Rain! I am going to receive calls tomorrow—My first winter I expect a great many visits. I trust the weather will change— this rain is intolerable.—What a nuisance all this is—I wish it were over. I write in my book to day the first time for months; parties, operas, concerts, skating and amusements ad infinitum have so taken up all my time that my dear reading and writing that I love so well have suffered much neglect.

Kate did try to develop self-discipline: She continued copying passages into her diary, as she had done in school—and during Lent, a time for determination and self-sacrifice, she attended her first meeting of the German Reading Club. ". . . And from this day," she wrote in her diary after the February 24 gathering, "I hope to be able to speak the language more and more fluently." She practiced her German script with stories and poems by Goethe, Hans Christian Andersen, and others; she wrote biographical sketches and copied extracts from Schiller, Ludwig Uhland, and Gottfried August Bürger. She was also keenly aware of women in the lives of great authors: With Bürger she mentioned his three marriages; with Goethe she listed the significant women in his life, and praised his Mignon as "one of the most interesting characters in Wilhelm Meister."

Kate was sometimes subject to moods and tensions, which she recorded in her diary: "Heigh ho! This is one of my blue days; Reading, music, German, walking, skating—all of which are this morning within the range of my ability—have no attractions for me." Perhaps to sort out her feelings, she sometimes copied passages with opposing messages—such as Boucher de Perthes's *"La Petite Mendiante,"* the sad story of a six-year-old motherless girl begging for food, followed by *"Espoir"* by Victor Hugo, a call to hope for a better tomorrow.

Kate also used her diary to gather literary impressions, some of which stayed with her for decades: Nathaniel Parker Willis's "Healing of the Daughter of Jairus," a sensuous poem about light and night, musical sounds and the sea, anticipates *The Awakening*. When she copied Alphonse de Lamartine's romantic poem *"Le Lac,"* Kate O'Flaherty also summarized a plot similar to her own "At Chênière Caminada," nearly a quarter-century later: "Lamartine having passed a happy summer with a friend who resided near the lake of Geneva, and with whose daughter—a beautiful girl—he was accustomed to walking on the banks—wrote the above piece, on finding, when he returned the next summer—that the girl had died."

The spring of 1869 was not only Kate O'Flaherty's "season," but also a time of activism for St. Louis women. American women had been petitioning for the right to vote since before Kate was born: In 1848, the Seneca Falls Women's Rights Convention had passed a resolution calling for women's "sacred right to the elective franchise." But American suffragists had agreed to put aside their cause until slavery was ended, and during the Civil War, St. Louis women had organized relief organizations, served as nurses, sewn uniforms, picked lint for bandages, and sat with the wounded and dying men.

After the war, St. Louis was full of energetic women who questioned the conventional bourgeois path from academy to marriage to motherhood to the grave. Many involved themselves in philanthropy, and some pursued very untraditional professions: Kate Field became a New York journalist; Phoebe Couzins, a belle once praised for her beauty, became in 1869 the first woman ever admitted to law school at Washington University. In Kate O'Flaherty's own generation, there would be women like Mary Foote Henderson, an art collector and president of the Woman-Suffrage Association, and eventually the author of two books on hygienic and scientific cooking. There was also Adele Sarpy Morrison, another Sacred Heart graduate, who traveled and studied in Europe, married a diplomat, and devoted herself to organizing crèches (day care) for the children of poor women in St. Louis.

After the Civil War, however, women had not been rewarded for their wartime sacrifices. Once Congress passed the Fourteenth and Fifteenth Amendments, making black men citizens and giving "all male citizens" the right to be represented in Congress, states promptly passed voting laws making it clear that only males could legally vote. In 1867, while Kate O'Flaherty was a Sacred Heart student, Virginia Minor of St. Louis had called a meeting at the Mercantile Library, to start the Woman-Suffrage Association of Missouri. It was the only organization in the world devoted solely to getting voting rights for women.

By early February of 1869, St. Louis suffragists had grown impatient, and a delegation of ten women's rights women traveled to Jefferson City to lobby the legislators (all male). But the State House tabled the idea of women's votes as "premature," and one outraged House member declared that the women had "unsexed themselves by coming here with their demands."

It was also in early February that Kate O'Flaherty, apparently wondering whether intellectual and political women had to be misfits, defined "Blue Stockings" in her diary:

> A title which originated in England in the time of Dr. Johnson for ladies who cultivated learned conversation. Boswell relates that in 1781 it was fashionable for ladies to form evening assemblies where they might converse with literary and ingenious men. One of the most eminent talkers on these occasions was a Mr. Stillingfleet who always wore blue stockings, and whose absence at any time was so much regretted that it used to be said—"One can do nothing without Blue Stockings." "Blue Stockings" soon became a title for pedantic or ridiculous literary ladies.

In her diary a few weeks later, Kate returned to the subject of women's roles, this time with a quotation from Dinah Mulock, a popular English novelist whose *John Halifax, Gentleman* she and Kitty had read together. (Kate had continued reading women authors: The list in her diary includes Jane Austen, Madame de Staël, Maria Jane McIntosh, Catherine Gray Frances Gore, and Charlotte Brontë.) The passage Kate copied from Mulock's *The Woman's Kingdom* expressed very traditional ideas—much like those of the Missouri lawmakers who opposed voting rights for women.

> What is it makes a house bright? pleasant to go to—to stay in—even to think about, so that even if fate totally annihilates it we recall tenderly for years its atmosphere of peace, cheerfulness, loving-kindness—nay, its outside features—down to the very pictures on the walls, the patterns of the papering, the position of the furniture? While other houses—we shiver at the remembrance of them, and the dreary days we spent in them—days of dullness, misery, or strife—these houses we would not revisit for the world!

> Why? If a house with fair possibilities of home comfort is thoroughly comfortless—if there is within it a reckless impossibility of getting things done in the right way or at the right time—or if, on the contrary, it is conducted with a terrible regularity, so that an uninvited guest or an extempore meal sends a shock throughout the whole abode—if the servants never keep their places long—and

the gentlemen of the family are prone to be "out of evenings"—
who is to blame?

Almost invariably, the women of the family. The men make or
mar its outside fortunes; but its internal comfort lies in the women's
hands alone. And until women feel that—recognize at once their
power and their duties—*it is idle for them to chatter about their
rights.*—Men may be bad enough out of doors; but their influence
is limited and external. It is women who are in reality either the
salvation or the destruction of a household.

Kate O'Flaherty underlined the sentence about rights, and underlined *rights*
twice—but did not indicate whether she agreed or disagreed with the words.
(Years later, though, she used similar ideas: Léonce Pontellier's litany of household complaints in *The Awakening* strongly resembles Mulock's second paragraph.)

Kate O'Flaherty did share with the suffragists the common problem of intellectual women: Her ideas were not taken seriously. Often she was melancholy
in her diary entries:

Thursday, March 25th, 1869—Holy Thursday,—and no sun—no
warmth—no patch of blue sky, nothing to make one's heart feel
glad; nothing but mud in the streets, and an incessant rain pattering
against the pavements making the passers-by look blue and cold,
and miserable. I feel in a very idle humor to day—and a little cross
at thinking that my proposed visit to the churches by moonlight,
has been so disagreeably interrupted.

In three more days Lent will be over—and then commence again
with renewed vigor—parties—theatres, and general spreeing. I feel
as though I should like to run away and hide myself; but there is
no escaping—

Kate did escape at least once, however—from a soiree at the home of Julia
Chouteau Maffitt, a powerful society leader given to long-winded reminiscences about the great General Lafayette. (Years later, Kate Chopin quoted a
friend's suggestion for a memoir: "It'd be kind of funny, though, to tell about
the night you went to Mrs. Maffitt's party on Sixth and Olive, and slipped
down the stone steps trying to get away from—")

But in 1869 Kate O'Flaherty mostly did what was expected of her—and
sometimes despised herself for it.

I am invited to a ball and I go.—I dance with people I despise; amuse myself with men whose only talent lies in their feet; gain the disapprobation of people I honor and respect; return home at day break with my brain in a state which was never intended for it; and arise in the middle of the next day feeling infinitely more, in spirit and flesh like a Liliputian, than a woman with body and soul.—I am diametrically opposed to parties and balls; and yet when I broach the subject—they either laugh at me—imagining that I wish to perpetrate a joke; or look very serious, shake their heads and tell me not to encourage such silly notions.

I am a creature who loves amusements; I love brightness and gaiety and life and sunshine. But is it a rational amusement, I ask myself, to destroy one's health, and turn night into day? I look about me, though, and see persons *so* much better than myself, and *so* much more pious engaging in the self same pleasures—however I fancy it cannot have the same effect upon them as it does upon me. Heigh ho! I wish this were the *only* subject I have doubts upon. One does become so tired—reasoning, reasoning, reasoning, from morning till night and coming to no conclusions—it is to say the least slightly unsatisfactory.

Still, Kate O'Flaherty recognized that her own reserved character had much to do with other people's reactions to her.

A friend who knows me as well as anyone is capable of knowing me—a gentleman of course—told me that I had a way in conversation of discovering a person's characteristics—opinions—and private feelings—while they knew no more about me at the end than they knew at the beginning of the conversation. Is this laudable? Bah! I'll not reason it, for whatever my conclusion I'll be sure to follow my inclination.

She did have one trusted confidante, her diary—and in her diary, she confided a somewhat jaundiced view of flirting as a social art.

You are the only one, my book, with whom I take the liberty of talking about myself. I must tell you a discovery I have made—the art of making oneself agreeable in conversation. Strange as it may appear it is not necessary to possess the faculty of speech; dumb persons, provided they be not deaf, can practice it as well as the most voluable. All required of you is to have control over the muscles of your face—to look pleased and chagrined, surprised indignant and under *every* circumstance—interested and entertained. Lead your antagonist to talk about himself—he will not enter reluctantly upon the subject I assure you—and twenty to one—he will report you as one of the most entertaining and intelligent persons,—although the whole extent of *your* conversation was but an occasional "What did *you* say?"—"What did *you* do?"—"What do *you* think?"— On that principal you see, my friend you are very entertaining; but I must admit that for want of a sympathetic countenance *tu es non peu unnuyant* (what I would never dare tell a mortal).

Then, sometime during her entrance into St. Louis society, Kate O'Flaherty met Oscar Chopin of Louisiana.

Oscar's mother was a Benoist, and he had come to St. Louis to study banking with Louis A. Benoist's banking firm in 1866, four months before Monsieur Benoist died suddenly of cholera, during a trip to Cuba in January of 1867. (Benoist's widow, Sarah, soon married her husband's business partner, and after a decent interval continued the lavish entertainments at the Oakland estate. Sarah's brother, George Wilson, eventually married Kate's aunt Josephine Faris.)

Oscar Chopin—whose full name, in the grandiose fashion of the day, was Aurelian Roselius Oscar Chopin—had been born on September 30, 1844, and raised on the family plantations in Natchitoches Parish in northwest Louisiana. The Chopins pronounced their name "SHOW-pan," just as the composer did, and most of their neighbors in and around the quiet village of Cloutierville were from France themselves or descended from French immigrants.

But Oscar had had the bad luck to turn seventeen—a soldier's age—in the fall of 1861, half a year after the war began in far-off South Carolina. Oscar's father, a French-born physician who had always hated everything American, abruptly packed the family off to France, where they stayed until the Americans finished fighting one another.

In France, the Chopins lived at Château-Thierry, about twenty miles from the family's ancestral estate, and Oscar finished school as a day scholar at the Collège de la Madeleine. In 1863, he (and the other five Château-Thierry candidates for literature degrees) all failed their *baccalauréats*, the examination for the French General Certificate of Education. Their priest called it a "massacre." Whether Oscar tried again the following year is unknown, but by the end of 1865, with the war over, he was back in Louisiana with his father.

In some ways, Oscar resembled Wallace Offdean, as Kate Chopin described him some two decades later, in "A No-Account Creole": Offdean had done "the usual things which young men do who happen to belong to good society."

He had gone to college, traveled, "frequented society and the clubs," and "worked in his uncle's commission-house" with "a modicum of energy" and a yearning to do more.

When he met Kate O'Flaherty of St. Louis, Oscar Chopin had a European air and a cosmopolitan background, as well as a gentlemanly profession: He was learning to be a cotton factor, the middleman between the cotton growers and the cotton buyers. Oscar spoke French perfectly; he was from the right social circles; and he was handsome, with a dark, wavy mustache.

From the start, Oscar appreciated St. Louis's romantic possibilities: To his cousin Louis Chopin in France, Oscar wrote in 1866 that "St. Louis is really a charming place . . . its delights are as great as those of the Rivoli in Paris . . . the women here are more beautiful than our lovely ladies in Paris. It is charming. It is interesting. There is indeed a vast opportunity for love and I can assure you that the god Eros is not forgotten here."

Oscar had long admired many kinds of women: At nineteen, just after failing his *baccalauréat*, he had written to his cousin Louis from Paris, about going to

> the Boum Magenta, where the girls were kind enough to make us punch and give our pipes a bashing. Mine is no longer in good condition, poor thing. But we can forgive them for that, dear little wenches; they are so nice; they have such big fascinating eyes, charming sighs, smiles, which get you, right there in the heart, little feet you can't forget, heady perfumes . . . and then . . . well you know the rest.

Oscar had claimed to dislike aristocratic women ("confounded prudes") and to prefer "working girls" who were "much nicer with their noisy and natural laughter and their bold looks which do not pretend to be affected by shyness."

Later, from St. Louis, Oscar wrote more to his cousin about his past:

> But, talking of love, I always remember my first steps in this connection and the first object of my affection. Do you remember the lovely blue-eyed blonde of the railway? and also my other love, the brunette from the Faubourg Montmartre in Paris? These love affairs, however, have long since been replaced in my heart by many other more and more pleasant ones.

> I can't help sympathizing with these two tender creatures and, as I remember them, my heart (which is not very tender) melts.

There are no surviving letters from Oscar Chopin about Kate O'Flaherty—
nor did Kate, who prided herself on her discretion, record their meeting in her
diary. But she had been attending parties at Oakland, the Benoist estate,
throughout the winter of 1869, and she had made a strong impression on at
least one other eligible male: J. H. Tighe from New York wrote in a glowing
letter to a St. Louis friend that "I wish to be kindly remembered to Mrs.
O'Flaherty, Miss Josephine, and Miss Katie O'F—:—the latter is a charming
specimen of female loveliness."

During the spring of 1869, Kate made her first long visit outside St. Louis—
but if she met Oscar's parents, who had recently moved to New Orleans because of his mother's ill health, she did not mention the meeting in her diary.
Instead, when she sat down to record her New Orleans trip, Kate started with
chitchat—a writer's technique for loosening the pen.

> *Saturday May 8th, 1869.* What a bore it is to begin a story—
> become interested in it and have to wait a week—a full round week
> before you can resume it. Thus have I devoured in Appleton's Jour-
> nal (a new paper by the way) "The Man Who Laughs" by V. Hugo,
> devoured it to the very last word of the last number and must wait
> till next Saturday to satisfy in a small degree my ravenous appetite.

She complained about the spidery "hairs and such rubbish" on her pen, but
then turned to her trip:

> March 25th and May 8th quite a span. Let me see what have I
> been doing with myself. Three weeks were consumed in going to
> New Orleans and coming back again, and what a trip it was! Mother
> Miss Rosie (poor Rosie), Mrs. Sloan, Mamie, Nina—and myself
> formed the party. Not remarkably gay for me when one reflects that
> Mother is a few years older than myself—Rosie an invalid—Mrs.
> Sloan a walking breathing nonentity—Mamie a jovial giggler and
> Nina a child.

The trip down and up the river would have been by boat, possibly on one
of the famous "floating palaces," decorated with white and gold curlicues, European carpets, and luxuriously appointed staterooms, and supplied with magnificent feasts and serenading musicians. But Kate O'Flaherty recorded only a
note about her destination: "N. Orleans I liked immensely; it is so clean—so
white and green. Although in April, we had profusions of flowers—strawberries
and even black berries."

By St. Louis standards, New Orleans was clean: It lacked the ever-present smoky pall from burning coal, and its unhealthy aspects (the mosquitoes, the open drains) were not so evident in April—although everyone slept under mosquito netting, which descended in a white cloud from the high tester beds. The humid air of New Orleans had a sensuality that was altogether new, and the fruits and flowers were signs of a lush climate in which everything grew profusely.

New Orleans was also exotic, French, and colorful. On the streets the *calas* vendors, wearing high bandana *tignons,* sang the praises of their sweet rice cakes; amateur musicians danced, sang, and begged for pennies. The savory aromas of gumbo and fresh shrimp were wafted from the open courtyards—and everywhere Kate could hear the soft patois, the Creole French with its sliding New Orleans intonations. There were still Union soldiers in the city, but the grand opera companies were again performing, and the dainty French Quarter homes, with their white and green shutters and their iron-lace balconies, impressed all visitors. After the war, the Creoles of New Orleans, who prided themselves on their pure French or Spanish descent, remained in the Vieux Carré (the French Quarter) and avoided "the Americans" on the other side of Canal Street. The Creoles—Oscar Chopin's people—still spoke more French than English.

On one memorable occasion, Kate O'Flaherty and Mamie Sloan, who was her age, attended a social gathering away from their elders.

> One evening I passed in N. O. which I shall never forget—it was so delightful and so noval. Mamie and myself were invited to dine and spend the evening with a Mrs. Bader—a [G]erman lady. She, her husband and two brothers in law lived in a dear little house near Esplanade St. a house with an immensity of garden. One of the brothers was a gay, stylish and very interesting fellow—with whom Mamie fell very much inamorata. I quaffed all sorts of ales and ices—talked French and German—listened enchanted to Mrs. Bader's exquisite singing and for two or three hours was as gay and happy as I ever had been in my life. Mrs. Bader had been but a year married, she was the famous Miss Ferringer—Singer and Schauspielerin, who in order to support indigent parents went upon the stage, thereby not only retaining respect, but gaining it from every quarter. Her talents and womanly attractions won her a kind and loving husband—Mr. Bader—one of the first merchants of New Orleans and a man worth $600,000.

But Kate evidently wanted to catch up on her reading, and she wrote nothing more about her New Orleans trip. Between May 8 and May 24, 1869, she devoted herself to her diary, rapidly copying long and short extracts from authors both romantic and realistic.

Her first entries were long quotations from Alphonse de Lamartine's romantic novel *Graziella*—another sad story of a young woman the poet loved and lost (the hero Lamartine even reads *Paul and Virginia* to Graziella in installments). Kate copied quotations showing Lamartine's youthful idealism; she wrote, in full, his description of the beautiful, passionate Italian peasant Graziella; and she copied his lament for *"Pauvre* Graziella," after he has left her and she has died. Kate O'Flaherty also added her own opinion:

> "Poor Graziella"?—No rich Graziella! happy Graziella! To have won not only the tears—the remembrance of Lamartine, but an offering of his rich and rare talents at the shrine of her memory.— The story is doubly enhanced when we think that it is really an episode, and a cherished one in the life of the gifted writer. What tears of grief and indignation does one not shed over its pages— tears all ending in forgiveness. For at the end we feel an assurance that Graziella has conquered—since her heart's idol—years after her death—weeps at her remembrance.

Kate also headed a page in her diary for extracts from Björnstjerne Björnson's *The Fisher Maiden*, a Norwegian novel just a year old, about a woman artist's liberation from a stifling and conventional life.

Reading Lamartine and Björnson at the same time, Kate was obviously still "reasoning, reasoning, reasoning"—conducting the internal dialogue that continued throughout her life, asking herself whether it was better for a woman to be passionately loved (and dead), or to be a courageous artist with a soul that dares and defies. But Kate never copied the *Fisher Maiden* extracts, and crossed out the page heading.

Instead she copied the first stanzas of Byron's "The Siege of Corinth," and then began a large section (fourteen pages) of "Short Extracts from different authors," alphabetically organized under such headings as Adversity, Affection, Atheism, Beauty (the largest group of quotations, most of them from Byron), Books, Conduct, Death, Happiness, and Life. She was writing very swiftly— her handwriting crackles across the pages—and she began with a quotation appropriate for one who saw through the surface of society conversation:

> A man who knows the world, will not only make the most of every thing he does know, but of many things he does not know, and will gain more credit from his adroit mode of hiding his Ignorance, than the Pedant by his awkward attempt to exhibit his Erudition. Cotton.

Kate quoted from Shakespeare, Swift, "Anon," and many others, including Madame de Staël: "It is difficult to grow old gracefully." Some of Kate's chosen quotations were pointed: "It is shameful for man to live in ignorance of the structure of his own body, especially when the knowledge of it mainly conduces to his welfare, and directs his application of his own powers." (Melancthon). She contrasted definitions of beauty, and compared sentiments about reading—but commented only on a quotation from Seneca on Conduct. Seneca had said, "I will govern my life and my thoughts, as if the whole world were to see the one and read the other; for what does it signify to make anything a secret to my neighbor, when to God (who is the searcher of our Hearts) all our privacies are open." Kate wrote: "Quite laudable in Mr. Seneca—but not as practicable as possible."

Then, on May 24, 1869, after finishing her quotations on "Life," Kate stopped writing in her diary for a year.

She did not stop writing altogether. On separate sheets of lined school paper, she wrote a full-blown short story, "Emancipation. A Life Fable," about a will to freedom, a curiosity about life, and a hunger for sensuous experiences. In "Emancipation," her earliest surviving story, Kate O'Flaherty's hero is an animal, of unknown species, with sleek and handsome flanks, who is born in a cage. Air and light come to him only through iron bars—but he has food and drink whenever he wants it, and a fine bed of straw to lie on, and the sun beam, he thinks, exists "but to lighten his home."

One day, the door of his cage accidentally stands open. In fear and wonder he approaches the door, backs away, approaches again, "seeing each time more Light." Finally he bounds from his cage, in a "mad flight," eagerly "seeing, smelling, touching of all things." No longer is everything provided for him, but he lives "seeking, finding, joying and suffering." The cage door stays open, Kate concluded, "but the cage remains forever empty!"

The animal in "Emancipation" was apparently inspired by Hugo's *The Man Who Laughs*, in which the central characters are a man and a wolf who perform at fairs: The man, Ursus, is misanthropic, while the wolf, Homo, is sweet-tempered, polite, and well-read. Kate soon lost interest in animal stories, but not in the subject of accidental emancipation, which she used much later in "The Story of an Hour" and *The Awakening*.

In 1869, "Emancipation" also expressed Kate O'Flaherty's thoughts about the life of a society belle—caged by conventions, kept from experiencing all of life. In Louisiana, she had learned to smoke cigarettes—a daring departure for young ladies—and in Louisiana she had known the sensuality of life outdoors. She valued being away from home, and being alone—and during the winter of 1869–70, she was thinking more and more about passion.

She was being courted, at Oakland.

✳   ✳   ✳

The Oakland estate was vast, with a springhouse, smokehouse, stable, and landscaped gardens. The elegant rooms at the main house included chandeliers and ceiling medallions, marble bathtubs and washbasins. The most romantic spot of all was the stone watchtower, four stories high, with balconies all around, from which visitors could gaze out over the entire estate, including a four-acre lake. Also, climbing the narrow winding walnut staircase to the tower was a romantic adventure: Two people could negotiate it only by squeezing very tightly together.

Kitty Garesché was not part of the world of romances and balls and parties at Oakland, having joined the Sisters of the Sacred Heart in January of 1870. The first phase of her new life was a time for silence and prayer, wide reading, and "the training in manners at an age when youth most desires to shake off control." (A quarter-century later, in a tantalizing story called "Two Portraits" or "The Nun and the Wanton," Kate Chopin described the religious and worldly paths for the same imaginative young woman—and in that story, the nun has the happier life.)

But in February of 1870 Kate O'Flaherty had just turned twenty, and her vision of emancipation meant seeing, tasting, touching, sampling all of life—which at Oakland meant a world of splendor. At the Oakland balls, ladies wore pearls and low-necked velvet gowns trimmed with elaborate laces, and dinner tables were laden with dainty suckling pigs, juicy cuts of venison, and plump game birds. The guests danced, and played games, and—always—flirted with one another.

Yet the most famous match made at Oakland was the most secret one. Nothing is known about when Kate O'Flaherty and Oscar Chopin met, or what they talked about. They may have danced together, and climbed the tower at Oakland; they may have discovered a common love for music or literature; they may—or may not—have flirted passionately in English or argued intellectually in French. Their decision to marry may have been passionate, or practical, or both. According to Kate's son Felix half a century after his mother's death, Kate always treasured the memory of the time at Oakland when "love came to her heart"—but she did not confide anything about that time to her diary.

Instead she resumed writing on May 24, 1870, with a brusque announcement:

> Exactly one year has elapsed since my book and I held intercourse, and what changes have occurred! not so much outwardly as within. My book has been shut up in a great immense chest buried under

huge folios through which I could never penetrate, and I—have not missed it. Pardon me my friend, but I never flatter you.

All that has transpired between then and now vanishes before this one consideration—in two weeks I am going to be married; married to the right man. It does not seem strange as I thought it would— I feel perfectly calm, perfectly collected. And how surprised every one was, for I had kept it so secret!

In fact, Kate O'Flaherty was still being secretive: She did not even mention Oscar Chopin's name in her diary.

June 8th Wednesday Tomorrow I will be married. It seems to me so strange that I am not excited—I feel as quiet and calm as if I had one or two years of maiden meditation still before me. I am contented—a

Kate was evidently interrupted. Her next entry, under the heading "Three Months Abroad," begins with *"June 9th* My wedding day!"

Chapter 7

A WRITER'S
HONEYMOON

⌒ "MY WEDDING DAY! HOW SIM-
ple it is to say and how hard to realize that I am married, no longer a young
lady with nothing to think of but myself and nothing to do," Kate O'Flaherty
Chopin wrote in her diary for June 9, 1870.

> We went to holy communion this morning, my mother with us,
> and it gave me a double happiness to see so many of my friends at
> mass for I knew they prayed for me on this happiest day of my life.
> The whole day seems now like a dream to me; how I awoke early
> in the morning before the household was stirring and looked out of
> the window to see whether the sun would shine or not; how I went
> to mass and could not read the prayers in my book; afterwards how
> I dressed for my marriage—went to church and found myself mar-
> ried before I could think what I was doing.

The wedding took place at Holy Angels Church, the parish church for the
O'Flaherty-Faris-McAllister household, on St. Ange Avenue between Chouteau Avenue and LaSalle Street. Holy Angels was a neat brick Gothic church,
just three years old, and Kate and Oscar were married by the Irish-born Father
Francis M. Kielty, noted for his playful sense of humor, "a most keen sense of
the ridiculous," and "a trenchant pen," with which he contributed letters and
articles to St. Louis periodicals.

Her wedding day was full of joyous hugs and some regrets, Kate O'Flaherty
Chopin wrote in her diary:

What kissing of old and young! I never expect to receive as many embraces during the remainder of my life. Oscar has since confessed that he did not know it was customary to kiss and that he conferred that favor on only a very few—I will have to make a most sacred apology for him when I get home. It was very painful to leave my mother and all at home; and it was only at starting that I discovered how much I would miss them and how much I would be missed.

Although Kate and Oscar left immediately on their honeymoon, they were not long alone:

We met several acquaintances on the cars who congratulated us very extensively, and who could not be brought to realize that they must call me Mrs. Chopin and not Miss Katy. They joined us however in consuming a few champagne bottles that had escaped the dire destruction of their companions to meet with a more honorable consummation by the bride and groom.

Evidently Kate and Oscar spent their wedding night on the train, for they arrived in Cincinnati at six o'clock the following morning, Friday, June 10. Kate recorded that they would "leave with quite a pleasing impression of the 'Queen City,' " which was "a nice cheerful place" with a "handsome bridge over the Ohio" and interesting dietary habits:

. . . the sole life sustaining article of the inhabitants is *Beer*, simply Beer; without it they would cease to live—"vanish into thin air." In saying so I do not speak from my own observation, mind, although it was extensive enough to warrant my saying; but from private information received from a gentleman—native of the city, whose name it would be treason to disclose.

During an afternoon walk in Cincinnati, Kate and Oscar met an acquaintance, a "Mr. Dobmeyer, who was very much surprised and seemingly pleased to see us." He took them to an amateur concert, which, Kate wrote, "did not amount to a row of pins." But afterward they went to the rehearsal of the "great 'Saenger Fest,' " which, Kate wrote, "I believe and hope will prove a success. Farewell to Cincinnati and a fond farewell to its Beer Gardens—may their number never grow less!"

By Sunday afternoon, June 12, after "a long, dusty, tedious, trip," the newlyweds were in Philadelphia: "[W]hat a gloomy puritanical looking city!" she wrote.

> Perhaps it is owing to the Sabbath that every thing should look so miserable, for posatively the people all look like Quakers—the streets look like Quakers—and the very houses resemble them with their odious red brick fronts, and those everlasting white shutters! Oh! those white shutters; what rows and rows and miles of them! Why will not *some one*, out of spite, out of anything, put up a black blind, or a blue blind, or a yellow blind—any thing but a white blind.

But Kate, wanting to appear fair, added that Philadelphia did have its attractions:

> Fairmount is pretty though, a very pretty park, and I hardly think we will see any lovelier view in Europe than we had from the rising ground of the park, of the Schuylkill river, bright and sparkling— with its picturesque little boat houses—the city—like Campbell's mountain looking more *enchanting* in the *distance*, and the full round moon staying the departure of twilight.

In Philadelphia, Kate and Oscar stayed at the Continental Hotel, famous for its green velvet furnishings and marble mantels. It was their first honeymoon night not on a train, and their first opportunity for complete privacy and intimacy. Kate may have been discreetly alluding to the consummation of her marriage when she wrote about that evening in Philadelphia, in the most romantic passage in her entire honeymoon diary: "It was a *lovely* night! and I thought of how the moonlight looked at Oakland. The moon knew better how to honor the sunday than did the people—for it filled us with—happiness and love."

The next day, Philadelphia looked "a little less gloomy," with the stores open and "a great many people on the streets. We saw a few pretty girls on Chestnut St. whose chief beauty consisted in the lovely complexions. We were not sorry to take the 6 P.M. train for New York"—and on the way, they also had "the honor and pleasure of making the acquaintance of Miss Clafflin, the notorious 'female broker' of New York."

"Miss Clafflin" would have been either Victoria Woodhull or Tennessee Claflin, the adventurous sisters who had started as clairvoyants and mediums in small-town Ohio, then gone east to make their fortunes. They published their own women's rights newspaper, *Woodhull & Claflin's Weekly*, and advocated free love, spiritualism, magnetic healing, and women's suffrage—and their beauty, charm, and evident shrewdness captivated Cornelius Vanderbilt, the eighty-four-year-old Great Commodore, in New York. He set them up as the first women stockbrokers in the United States, and later Victoria Woodhull would be the first woman to run for the American presidency (1872).

Although Kate did not indicate which of the Claflin sisters they met, either could fit her description: "a fussy, pretty, talkative little woman." Miss Claflin "discussed business extensively with Oscar," and then turned to Kate and "entreated me not to fall into the useless degrading life of most married ladies— but to elevate my mind and turn my attention to politics, commerce, questions of state, etc. etc. I assured her I would do so—which assurance satisfied her quite."

The newlywed Chopins spent two weeks in New York, waiting for a ship to Europe, "without amusing ourselves to any great extent," Kate wrote in her diary. "Oscar thinks it is a great den of swindlers, and I have only to follow his opinion." Still, Kate did like some features of New York. She and Oscar visited Central Park, the green oasis recently designed by the famous architect Frederick Law Olmsted, and they went "several times to hear Theo. Thomas's Orchestra—how I *did* enjoy it! It has been my chief pleasure in New York." Kate also seized the opportunity to poke fun at men of business: "I have heard the 'Bulls and Bears of Wall St.' bellowing and grunting in the Stock and Gold Boards—proceedings which interested me very much, though I was to some extent incapable of understanding their purport."

Overall, New York was "dull, dull!" With great relief, she and Oscar finally managed to book a good cabin on the German vessel, "the Rhein." "Now I can only hope that we will have a fortunate passage and no sea sickness," Kate wrote in her diary.

The journey from New York to Bremen took twelve days, giving travelers ample opportunity to admire the broad sweep of the Atlantic Ocean, and to attune themselves to the ship's seesaw motion in the dark blue rolling waves. On ship, passengers played cards and shuffleboard, when the ship's motion permitted it; women sewed, while men played dominoes and smoked cigars. Both sexes gossiped and made sure that the flag was dipped three times whenever a strange ship passed. Imaginative travelers took their opera glasses on deck, hoping to see monsters of the deep.

The Chopins were among the lucky few: Their passage was "agreeable," with "no sickness whatever and the sea has been as a lake," Kate wrote in her diary. "It is indeed a great pleasure to be on the ocean when one feels well and comfortable."

Unlike many amateur author-travelers, who carted along lap desks, blocks of paper, collections of pen nibs, and even watercolors to illustrate their effusions, Kate Chopin traveled light. She did write to her mother and to her cousin Nina McAllister, and recorded in her diary in August that she had not forgotten Kitty Garesché's birthday—but her only literary equipment seems to have been her well-worn commonplace book, where she kept her honeymoon diary, making short comments and no attempts at drawing picturesque scenes.

She wrote in her notebook only once on shipboard: on July 6, the day before the ship reached Bremen. Like Mark Twain in *Innocents Abroad*, published just the year before, Kate sometimes looked on her fellow Americans with a satiric eye, as when she wrote about American Independence Day celebrations at sea:

> Day before yesterday a faint effort was made to celebrate our na-
> tional festival, but I am forced to admit that enthusiasm was want-
> ing. The Dutch band scraped out "Hail Columbia" and a few other
> martial strains, whilst we were occupied in dining, and some, more
> patriotic than their companions, laid aside knife and fork to give
> vent to a feeble "bravo"—after which "order was restored."

Oscar, of course, had grown up in French-speaking Louisiana and spent his early manhood in France, so that raucous demonstrations of American patrio-tism would have seemed quite odd to him. Memories of the Civil War, and of the martial "Dutch" (Germans) who invaded her home to celebrate the July 4 taking of Vicksburg seven years earlier, no doubt contributed to Kate's own lack of patriotic fervor.

Several passengers had left the ship at Southampton, having "thought they had been long enough on the 'briny deep,' " Kate wrote, but they had missed "the most beautiful part of the trip, for to night we are on the North Sea. I had studied at school about the atmosphere of these northern regions but I had not till now realized what it meant. At ten o'clock it was still twilight, and a clear twilight."

She grew romantic: "The moon is out again, full and round like in Phila-delphia, but how many thousands of miles closer it looks! it seems so immense too, and the stars appear so huge that one can scarcely imagine them so very, *very* far off."

Meanwhile the happiness was contagious on board ship: "No more sick com-plaining people; every one is gay and happy with the prospect of reaching land tomorrow; and with this calm sea, and this magnificent sky, it seemed sinful to leave the deck. But tomorrow—Terra Firma!"

Within the next week, the newlywed Chopins visited Bremen, Cologne, and Bonn, and by July 14, Kate was quoting *Hyperion* again: " 'The Rhine! The Rhine! A blessing on the Rhine' so says Longfellow & so say I." They visited Mayence, Wiesbaden, Frankfurt, Heidelberg, Stuttgart, and Ulm, and by July

28 they were in Switzerland, where they traveled for almost a month before going on to Paris.

The newlyweds were rarely truly alone. Steamer trunks had to be carted about by servants and stevedores (no gentleman carried his own luggage). Guidebooks always urged travelers to pack only a single small trunk (the English called it a "portmanteau")—but only bachelors with a fanatic dedication to austerity did so. Everyone else, especially Americans in Europe for months at a time, endured constant packing and unpacking, and continual weighing and charging for baggage. All continental travelers also coped with the same petty annoyance: No two scales ever gave the same reading for the same luggage.

Meanwhile, ladies simply could not travel light, if they were to dress properly for dinner. On ship, old clothes were recommended, and since it was cold at sea even during the summer, travelers were advised to bring overcoats, warm underclothing, shawls and railway rugs. Tipping, a universal nuisance, was no doubt handled by Oscar, who had made the trans-Atlantic crossing before, but for Kate, ladies' maids had to be engaged for hairdressing and mending; laundry had to be attended to by washerwomen. On July 20, in Stuttgart, Kate wrote despairingly, "Rose late—feeling not well & staggered at the amount of unpacking and washing to be given out; which interesting occupation engaged my time till 5 in the afternoon."

The Chopins met acquaintances virtually everywhere. In their first stop, at "the free and independent city of Bremen," they met Mr. and Mrs. Griesinger, friends from New Orleans, and visited with them for much of the time in Germany.

Kate wrote that Bremen "pleases me immensely: The private residences are the most exquisite little gems, and the people all look so amiable and happy." She watched everything with great interest ("the houses were all thatched and the cows all black") and enjoyment ("a lovely place . . . so white so neat and so ornamented with flowers. The people are exceedingly polite and obliging").

With the Griesingers, the Chopins stayed at the Hillman Hotel ("a very lovely house"), went shopping and sightseeing, heard a famous Viennese comedian, Knack, at the Summer Theatre, and afterward finished the evening in the notorious "Rathskeller," the most celebrated wine cellar in the world.

With the Griesingers and two more friends, Mr. Bechtel and Mr. Brantlet, the Chopins visited a Mr. Knoop, "the wealthiest merchant of Bremen," in "the princliest private residence that I have ever seen—a miracle of costliness and exquisite taste." There, the Chopins, Griesingers, and the other gentlemen "took tea, a regular *German* tea in the *loveliest* spot—in a sort of bower-nook— summer retreat—I know not what to call it—and all grew merry on cheese and fresh milk."

When Kate and Oscar took their first trek alone in Bremen, they followed their guidebook, and "gracefully wended our way towards the Cathedral, an old edifice founded by Charlemagne in 800—now a Protestant temple. The chief interesting object was the Blei Keller—Lead celler—which possesses the power of preserving bodies from total decay."

Evidently the newlyweds expressed some skepticism. "In order to convince us that there was no hoax in the story, an old woman—fit keeper for such treasures, displayed to us several dried up remains—the mummies they call them—ghastly old things that would have been infinitely more discreet in crumbling away hundreds of years ago."

Meanwhile, travel was not always easy or pleasant: "[W]hat wild unheard of things we do in travelling that at home we would shudder to think of," Kate wrote at one point. It took a small bribe for the Chopins and Griesingers to "get a coupe all to ourselves" on the overnight train from Bremen to Cologne—and even then, they went without sleep: "Is there any greater agony than waiting for a connection in the middle of the night? I know of none, & prefer passing over those two hours in silence," Kate wrote.

Still, she kept her sense of humor. "I hate Zoological Gardens of a hot Sunday afternoon," she noted—and so it was "under a broiling sun" when the Chopins and Griesingers visited the Cologne zoo. Kate admired the "girls in white waists and variegated skirts" looking longingly at a house "set aside every sabbath evening for the pious purpose of dancing." As for the zoo itself, Kate thought it "a very fine one, and we saw any number of wild beasts that showed their teeth in the most wonderful manner—but we weren't at all frightened, which I set down as an instance of bravery on our part." Finally, "[a]t sunset we tore ourselves away, not from the animals, from the scene."

Kate and Oscar rarely went long without meeting someone they knew. They had been strolling through the Cologne Cathedral ("a marvelous conception and exquisite piece of work"), when "whom should we come suddenly upon but Bunnie Knapp. To say he was surprised to see us would be using a very feeble term—he was astounded."

Vernon ("Bunnie") Knapp's family had been Kate's neighbors on Eighth Street; they owned and edited the conservative *Missouri Republican*. Vernon Knapp, twenty-three in 1870, was evidently on a Grand Tour, sampling the pleasures of Europe. (Half a century later, after a career as a St. Louis attorney, he would write an article calling Kate Chopin "the most brilliant, distinguished and interesting woman that has ever graced St. Louis.")

The newlywed Chopins eagerly agreed to meet Bunnie Knapp again in Bonn, where he was taking a course of lectures. In Cologne, they also "invested in sundry bottles of its famous water" and went to the Bellevue Gardens on the river "and were caught in a drenching rain for our pains"—only the first of many such dampenings during their honeymoon.

Unlike other Americans abroad, Kate O'Flaherty Chopin never used her honeymoon diary as an educational travelogue, replete with dates and facts and figures about everything she saw. She was far more interested in down-to-earth details: Beyond her admiration for the cathedral at Cologne, she wrote only that "it is still incomplete, and they say will not be finished for ten years." Unimpressed with Cologne's "narrow ugly streets," which wound along the river, the Chopins were happy to take the Rhine Boat to Bonn, where Kate was also unimpressed with the birthplace of "the great Beethoven": It "resembled very much all the other houses in the neighborhood."

Despite her studies at the German Reading Club in St. Louis, Kate Chopin never succeeded in speaking German well, and Oscar apparently was little better. Their Bonn tour driver "rejoiced in a very amiable disposition, and endeavored to explain all the objects of interest which we encountered; we understood one half of his communications and guessed at the other." Nor did they do any better in Heidelberg: They "started off like true mountaineers" toward the famous castle, but found "It was rather hard at first with our rather imperfect knowledge of German to get into the right path."

Occasionally, though, they were linguistically lucky—as on the day in Bonn when they "took into our heads that we should like to visit the University" and found "an amiable sprightly woman who spoke French and offered to 'show us around.' " But:

> The good dame would not take us through the hall in which the students were gathered, "for," she said, "the young gentlemen are not sorry when a young lady passes through their room." I ventured to suggest that my being married might in a manner abate the interest with which they might otherwise regard me: but my argument proved weak, and failed utterly.

Instead, Kate and Oscar again met Bunnie Knapp, who had been "diligently occupied in playing cards in a 'Bier Hall,' " yet insisted on accompanying them on the train up the Rhine. "It was indeed lovely!" Kate wrote: "The Drachenfels—black and in bold relief against the sky; below it and nearer us the island of Nonnenwerth, half buried in the Rhine waters—with Rollensecke keeping guard in the distance."

This was a story Kate could not resist recording: "The legend attached to the spot is romantic, & I have no doubt perfectly true." The first part would have reminded Kate of the Civil War, and her brother George:

> It is related that during the first Crusade, Rollen, a brave and generous youth, fired with holy enthusiasm, took himself off to fight

in the good cause, leaving behind him disconsolate friends, and a
weeping sweetheart.

But time passed,

> and in an evil hour a report reached the quiet neighborhood that
> Rollen had met his death in Palestine. Fancy the wild grief of the
> maiden! In her utter despair she fled from friends and family &
> entered the convent still to be seen on the island of Nonnenwerth,
> intending there to bear with her grief, and in the course of human
> events, to die. But listen! On a warm summer's day a solitary horse-
> man entered the small town which has since been demolished, and
> the lone traveller was none other than Rollen. He hastens to the
> home of his beloved filled with expectant happiness.

Kate continued writing in the present tense, caught up in the urgency of her
story:

> He enters—"Where is Gretchen?" he cries. "Mein Gott, we thought
> you were dead—she has gone to the convent." Grief and rage min-
> gle in the bosom of the hero to render the scene terrible. Moved
> by contending emotions, he flies to the top of a distant mountain
> and builds himself the castle of Rollensecke, from the windows of
> which he watches the convent night and day, catching occasional
> glimpses of a form which he loved alas! too well. Thus ended his
> life—a wreck—the fruits of a false report.

The Chopins and Bunnie feasted on "a delightful beverage composed of
Rhine wine and strawberries and known as 'Endeberren-Boule,' " and during
their train ride back to Bonn ("I am enchanted with Bonn," Kate wrote), they
caught a glimpse of the famous queen of Prussia. But once they reunited with
the Griesingers and formed "a nice little party at once," the Chopins managed—for the first time—to behave with the boorishness that Europeans expected from Americans abroad.

By the 1870s "American girls" in Europe were known for their high spirits
and unrefined manners. (Four years later, Jennie Jerome of New York would
marry Lord Randolph Churchill—setting the fashion for American debutantes
to marry into Old World aristocracies.) During their evening in Bonn, the
Chopins, the Griesingers, and Bunnie Knapp grew rowdy:

> What quantities of that maddening Rhine wine I have drunk today.
> The music—the scenery—the bright waters—the wine—have made

me excessively gay. In fact we all gave play to our spirits more or less, and I fear these phlegmatic Germans will consider our American sociability as somewhat too loud.

But the German behavior was even worse: A citizen-student encounter over "a fancied slight" was leading up to a duel.

Kate preferred serene moments, such as "the exquisite panorama" on a Rhine boat ride the next day: "Shall I ever forget the beauties of the beautiful Rhine? The gray & stately ruins,—the churches peeping out of the dense foliage, & those vineyards upon vineyards sloping to the water's edge."

Although it was their honeymoon, Kate and Oscar did not spend every moment together. Oscar was sometimes absent when Kate wrote in her diary: "— Dear me! I feel like smoking a cigarette—think I will satisfy my desire and open that sweet little box which I bought in Bremen. Oscar has gone to some Halle to witness these Germans' interpretation of a galop—a waltz etc."

Kate rarely wrote about Oscar, although she sometimes joshed affectionately when she did mention him. In Wiesbaden on July 16, when they went to the famous boiling springs, Kate tasted the water "and thought it shocking," but "Oscar of course found it delicious."

Something unfortunate had happened the day before: "What an unpleasant souvenir I retain of Mayence. Let it dwell only in my memory—and I trust even there, not too long." Instead she shifted to a description of activity in the elegant gaming house, the Cursaal: "It is all as I had pictured—the sang froid of the croupier—the eager, greedy, and in some instances fiendish look upon the faces of the players. I was tempted to put down a silver piece myself—but had not the courage." She was not feeling well.

The next day, in Wiesbaden, she walked around "rather listlessly," dined with Oscar, and heard "the incomparable Wachtel in Wm. Tell"—but her diary finally gives a clue as to the unpleasantness that took place in Mayence: "How I could and how I would have enjoyed it, had I felt better, but have been feeling badly all day."

"Feeling badly" was a common euphemism for menstrual cramps—and in fact, exactly twenty-eight days later, Kate recorded "one of my fearful head aches" in her diary (August 13). What happened in Mayence may have been an accident connected with her menstrual period. There may have been an unexpected stain on sheets or clothes—an offense against the German hotels' spotless cleanliness; she may have had trouble explaining, in German, her need for menstrual rags. Such a problem could easily be an "unpleasant souvenir."

In any case, Kate had recovered her spirits the following day, Sunday, July 17—when the whole direction of the Chopins' honeymoon changed. "What an uproar! What an excitement!" Kate wrote in her diary. "I do not see how we got out of Wiesbaden alive."

The news was shocking: France and Germany were at war.

Unlike Oscar, Kate had lived through war in a beleaguered city. Her school had been closed; her best friend had been banished; her brother had died. Now, Kate, who had expected leisurely visits to Wiesbaden and Frankfurt, was caught up, again, in wartime panic. As soon as the war was declared, Kate wrote in her diary for July 17:

> . . . all the hotels emptied their human contents into the various depots. French women with their maids, their few children, their laces and velvets hastening to get started on their homeward jour-ney—every other nationality equally anxious to get back to their respective domiciles. The depot from whence we took the train for Frankfurt, presented a scene of fashionable excitement, that I shall never forget.

Kate evidently resolved to be calm: For the rest of her diary entry for July 17, she described a typical tourist day.

> We reached Frankfurt at 10 o'clock. I was struck by the familiarity of an otherwise very refined German lady, with her maid. They seemed more like sisters, than mistress and maid. Remained in F. only four hours. Took a good dinner & then started out to see the objects of interest. It seems to be a city of statues: Gottenberg is remembered in a magnificent representation, nor are Goethe & Schiller forgotten.

Despite the war, the Chopins doggedly pursued a typical travelers' itinerary. In Frankfurt, they visited the houses belonging to Goethe, Luther, and the founder of the Rothschild financial family (whose achievements Kate had stud-ied in school). In Heidelberg, they climbed up to the famous castle, a con-glomeration of facades and towers, statues and dungeons, decorations and moats and turrets.

Kate was fascinated: "I have thought and talked a great deal of Heidelberg, and for once in my life have not been disappointed by the real versus the ideal. It is a magnificent old ruin: the scenery surrounding it being well worth walk-ing miles to see." Everything was a delight: "And what a glorious day! And glorious walk to the very top of the Berg where we dined with hungry appetites on eel and necker wine, enjoying at the same time, the exquisite view through the soft summer landscape."

Nevertheless, there was always a shadow over the Chopins' honeymoon:

How unfortunate is this war! We cannot go as was our intention to Baden and it is even probable we may not visit France. That would indeed be deplorable; for what is Europe outside of Paris? So say tourists. Tomorrow we see a little more of Heidelberg, then leave for Stuttgart where, heaven be praised, our tents shall be pitched for a breathing space.

Before they left Heidelberg the next day, Kate and Oscar "strolled about town all morning making a few purchases of books and music" in the university town. If they saw any roistering Heidelberg students (Kate had read about them in William Howitt's *Student Life in Germany*), she did not record the encounters. Nor did she say anything about the students' famous romantic duels (but thirty years later, in *The Awakening*, she gave the roué Alcée Arobin a grotesque and fascinating dueling scar).

Kate and Oscar's trip to Stuttgart was also dogged by war: "difficulty in securing comfortable railway accommodations owing to the large number of soldiers in movement. Passed through a lovely country, picturesque in the extreme and reached Stuttgart at 10 p.m. Have come to the Marquart Hotel." At Stuttgart, she and Oscar met up again with the Griesingers, and relaxed: "Read and went to bed late after an uneventful day," Kate wrote on July 20; on the 21st, "Have done nothing but lounge—took a ride in the afternoon and retired early."

Inspired by the chance to stay in one place for a while, Kate became determinedly domestic. She and Lina Griesinger embarked on a shopping excursion with Lina's mother-in-law, who was German and "speaking neither french nor english, does not converse much with me; unless when Lina acts as interpreter. A delightful lady." (Whether Kate was being sincere or sarcastic cannot be determined.) In any case, she "[b]ought a black lace shawl—some brussels and valenciennes lace—table and bed linnen &c in anticipation of that house keeping which awaits me on the 'other side.' " But she did not like Stuttgart: " 'The reason why I cannot tell' but the blame must rest with me & not with the no doubt charming city."

And always, there were reminders: the hotel was filled with troops milling about, and Kate even "met the commander in chief Von Moltke face to face on the stair way. What an iron countenance; the French I fancy will meet their equal when they encounter the rugged old general and his troops."

After five more days in Stuttgart, the Chopins left on July 27 for Ulm, where they visited "the handsome Cathedral and fine fortifications." They reached Friedrichschafen late at night, slept there, and "started early in the morning for Constanz." As might be expected with a war spreading across Europe, "We are anxious to get into Switzerland."

❊   ❊   ❊

Kate and Oscar Chopin spent a month in Switzerland—evidently hoping for an opportunity to enter France, while ominous war tidings reached them every day. They also had a month of almost constant rain, which Kate noted with great exasperation, from July 29 ("Rain! All the day rain") through August 23: (". . . were far from the shelter of a hotel, when the rain commenced to fall in torrents").

One morning, after several days of amusing themselves by "making mental photographes of the falls" at Schaffhausen, the hardy Chopins woke up to sunshine. After they cheerfully descended the steep path to "the Rhein falls (the largest in Europe)," and "drank some 'bier' to the delicious accompaniment of a zither"—the rain and hail descended. "We scrambled as best we could up the slippery path which a moment before had seemed so idyllic—drenched to the skin. My gabardine I fear is ruined." Later Kate comforted herself with "the perusal of Dickens," and still later, at Lauffen Castle she and Oscar had their finest view of the falls: "So closely did we approach them that the spray fell upon us like rain—such a delicious, indescribable feeling of moistness."

Their ability to make friends kept the Chopins amused. In Schaffhausen, one day when everything was "stupidly quiet a l'ordinaire," they met "a Russian family, consisting of husband wife & little boy, to whom we have taken a great fancy." She characterized the Kendenskys in just a few words: "The lady is a lovely blond, full of spirits and speaks charming French: what linguists are the Russians! The husband seems delicate and the boy very pleased with us; he calls me *die schöne Dame*, not being able to master the intricacies of Chopin." Evidently delighted with their new acquaintances, Kate also recorded a long French story Mrs. Kendensky told one day at dinner (the joke hinged on a French pun: "*bonté*" and "*bon thé*").

The Chopins were in Schaffhausen long enough for mail to reach them: On August 9, Kate received a letter, dated June 29, from her St. Louis friend Lil Chouteau. Two days later, and for the first time, Kate recorded some irritation with her new husband:

> I wish to leave at all events on the 2:30 train. It is 10 o'clock and Oscar is still asleep. I woke him a moment ago and said something about going—but he turned over mumbling "weather too bad—go tomorrow." Up at last, changes his mind—thinks we will go.

Finally they reached Zurich, still in the rain, and the next day, evidently for the first time on their honeymoon, Kate set out as a tourist alone. She tried rowing on the lake: "I find myself handling the oars quite like an expert." That emboldened her to do more on her own:

Oscar took a nap in the afternoon and I took a walk alone. How very far I *did* go. Visited a panorama which showed the Rigi Kulm in all its grandeur—the only audience being myself and *two* soldiers. I wonder what people thought of me—a young woman strolling about alone. I even took a glass of beer at a friendly little beer garden quite on the edge of the lake; and amused myself for some time feeding the importunate little fish who came up to the surface as tame as chickens to receive their crumbs.

Then the Chopins went, by boat on Lake Zurich, to Hugan, and the following morning, "got into a delightful little stage, with no one but a delightful old lady, who did not in the least object to smoking—on the contrary, rather liked it, and gave us to understand that she indulged herself in an occasional weed." But on the boat to Guda, Kate and Oscar met a group of Americans—some of whom were the sort every American dreaded: "gent and wife, two young men and a young German, the last of whom was very nice, the rest perfect Yankees."

With the "perfect Yankees," Kate and Oscar tried real Swiss mountain-climbing. When they "commenced the ascent of the Rigi"—Righi, the mountains between the Swiss lakes of Zug, Lucerne, and Lowerz—Kate, the "gent," his wife, and the young German rode on horseback. Oscar and the other two Yankees walked, presumably with the traditional alpenstocks—stout staffs, about six feet long, with an iron spike at one end and a goat horn, blackened and polished, at the other. Along the way, climbers traditionally stopped for bread, cheese, wine, and honey before pushing on; American climbers were wont to burst into song, to the amusement and astonishment of Swiss guides. It was also commonplace for Americans to overestimate their own climbing abilities, and to reach the summit breathless and exhausted.

"What views we had coming up the mountain!" Kate wrote. "Can there be anything finer in Switzerland! Reached the summit at 6, but too cloudy to see much." She was also in no mood to write much (it was exactly twenty-eight days after her last "feeling badly" day): "Had one of my fearful head aches, which took me directly to bed—knowing that sleep alone would come to my relief."

Then it was another day of travel, exhausting enough to be recorded in bursts: "started down at 8 for Küssnach—pretty much in a fog—breakfasted and took a hack for Lucerne. En route visited Tell's chapel: the spot where Tell is said to have killed Gesler. Hot ride—reached Lucerne at 3. Have taken rooms at the Kelbe Veen—parted with our Yankee acquaintances."

Kate's last sentence in her entry suggests a sly smile at her groom for his brave and righteous climbing: "Oscar is very tired from his walk up and down the mountain."

✻   ✻   ✻

Throughout their honeymoon, Kate and Oscar paid little attention to religion. Sometimes they blithely skipped mass—and even when they attended, religious devotion was not Kate's primary thought.

Twice they missed mass entirely. On July 31, in Schaffhausen, Kate wrote, "Sunday! *Intended* to go to church—but what is it they say of the paving stones of the lower realm? Did not rise till ten and the church is three quarters of an hour from here." Instead, she and Oscar took their hike to the falls and were drenched with rain and hail (which Kate evidently did not interpret as a sign of divine wrath).

Two weeks later, Kate noted that it was the "feast of the Assumption, which fact I discovered when it was too late to attend Mass." Instead the Chopins and Kendenskys went to see the famous dying Lion of Lucerne: "It impressed me as a grand piece of art," Kate decided. She spent the rest of that day rowing on Lake Lucerne (handling the oars "with marked improvement"), eating ices with Oscar, reading a letter from her cousin Nina McAllister ("Nothing unusual has occurred since my absence"), and recording an apt anecdote told by Mrs. Kendensky about

> an old priest who made such an impressive sermon to his congre
> gation of the sufferings of Christ, as to excite them all to tears.
> Seeing the affliction into which he had thrown his good people, he
> exclaimed: "Do not cry thus my good children, for after all, it may
> not be true."

When the Chopins did go to church, in Lucerne, the day after the feast of the Assumption, they heard a performance of the incomparable cathedral organ. The organist began with simple hymns, and then Mendelssohn's "Wedding March," and finally the thunderstorm—a musical rendition of distant thunder, rising wind, rushing mountain streams, and trickling rain drops. The tempestuous music grew and grew, until it seemed to shake the great cathedral, while the wind howled and the waters roared—but then, gradually, the storm ceased, and a babbling brook could be heard. The performance ended with the sweet singing of an invisible choir—and the entire performance, including the "vox humana," was done by one man, playing one organ.

Kate Chopin jotted down only cryptic comments on the performance—"Heard the great organ play—beautiful music—wonderful imitation of the human voice—and a storm"—but years later she described the effect of such unearthly music on Edna Pontellier in *The Awakening:* "The very first chords which Mademoiselle Reisz struck upon the piano sent a keen tremor down Mrs. Pontellier's spinal column . . . the very passions themselves were aroused within her soul, swaying it, lashing it, as the waves daily beat upon her splendid body. She trembled, she was choking, and the tears blinded her."

There were still a few more places that every American tourist had to see in Switzerland. After a last rowing on the lake at Lucerne and a brief trip to Interlaken's "pretty shops, which seem to be filled with curious wood carving," the Chopins spent one afternoon "contemplating the rain fall," while Kate wrote a letter to her cousin Nina. They viewed the glaciers on the lake of Thun, visited Berne ("so quaint and old") and its public bear pit ("enjoying their curious antics for a moment")—and then finally broke the language barrier. On August 20, Kate wrote with delight, she and Oscar "found ourselves in Fribourg, where at last! 'on parle le français.' What a rest it will be! Not that we ever *succeeded* in talking German; but what excrutiating efforts have we not made."

At Fribourg, the Chopins did attend mass at the cathedral, but not from religious impulses: there they heard, Kate wrote, "what is considered, the finest organ in the world."

Their travel was no longer so foreign: In French Switzerland, at the hotel Beau Rivage in Ouchy, "Americans seem to have bodily possession," Kate wrote. She and Oscar met three more American friends, Mrs. Hoyle, Ella, and Charlie, "whom we tried to induce or to inveigle into a row on the lake, but Sunday, taken into connection with some rather menacing looking waves, was enough to deter them"—although the Lake of Geneva was "indescribably lovely."

Kate Chopin was also impressed by seeing "in the distance the castle of Chillon." Like most nineteenth-century girls, she knew all about the one poet who was more dashing, handsome, and wicked than any other. She paid the usual tribute: "a tender thought to Byron, en passant."

But French Switzerland was not all romantic pleasure. "What a dull place is this Martigny," Kate was complaining on August 21—and by August 23, both Chopins were freezing at Argentière: "Although the middle of August, I am sitting at a country hotel, before a blazing wood fire, trying to thaw my frozen corporosity." Caught in yet another freezing, torrential rain, "Oscar's southern blood felt it more keenly than I, and he would alternately walk in hopes of stirring up a little warmth. We arrived an hour ago—with hands and feet almost frozen—and our persons beautifully festooned with icicles."

The freezing rain, which had begun while they were on horseback from Martigny to Chamounix, did force the Chopins to take refuge in a nearby peasant's hut—where Kate found herself gathering story material:

. . . the place & people, formed quite an interesting study to me. Oscar conversed with them freely. The family consisted of the old man, aged 82 years—the old grandfather, who had never in his life been farther than Geneva, a distance of 9 miles; the father, a handsome man, mother and four daughters, the eldest but fourteen. What surprised me was that in a cabin where there was barely a chair to sit on, the eldest girl was going to school (in winter only when she did not work) and showed us her exercises which were written correctly, and in one of the most beautiful hands I have ever seen. . . . The peasants were catholics; the only ornaments in their house being holy pictures. Oscar presented the delighted children with small coin. And when about to leave, the mother called them all to look and feel of my dress (an old black silk) something they had never seen before.

It was the kind of local color scene that Kate Chopin would create so skillfully, years later, with her Louisiana stories: the few but revealing bits of furniture in the house; the quick defining of character; and the fascination with people's values and choices, especially those of young girls.

At Chamounix on August 24, Kate recorded an important milestone: "Kitty Garesché's birthday. I had not forgotten her."

After a brief reencounter with Bunnie Knapp and yet another set of Americans (Mr. and Mrs. Knapp, Miss Harrison, Miss Belsonver, and Andy), the Chopins took "a lumbering old coach and six, which had every appearance of being a relic of the days of Louis XIV." At Geneva (the "loveliest we have visited yet"), Kate complained: "Face burned again—great nuisance." But she consoled herself by buying "a cute, diminutive little watch" on August 26. By eleven o'clock that evening she and Oscar were at Neufchâtel, having taken their last view of the Alps at Lausanne: "How grand they were in the deepening twilight."

But Kate had her worries: "It is very hard to get to Paris: tomorrow, let us hope we start."

For six weeks, Kate had been writing down all the war news she could get. Soldiers had settled in some hotels; domestics were discharged from others; and many were empty because the war "frightened off all visitors. I trust the landlord will not attempt to make his accounts balance at our expense," Kate had written at Schaffhausen. By August, the French war losses were terrible: Wissenbourg, a small Alsatian town, had been set on fire; at Metz the French troops were cut to pieces. At Wörth, four thousand French soldiers were taken prisoner. On August 9, the emperor sent home a clear, and terrifying message: "Hasten preparations for the defence of Paris."

Still, as Kate knew, no tour of Europe would be complete without a visit to Paris—which had become a city of splendor under Napoleon III, the nephew of the great Napoleon. With the skills of the architect Baron Haussman, the emperor and his empress Eugénie had transformed Paris into a symbol of imperial dreams, the city of light and center of civilization and culture.

But by the time the Chopins reached Paris, sometime between August 27 and September 4, the city was in chaos. Virtually all foreigners had fled, even the diplomats: The only ambassador still remaining was the American, Elihu Washburne. Paris was fortifying itself against the Prussian armies, who were sacking and burning French villages along the route of their march.

The tap of drums was incessant, and so were the rumors. Provisions poured into Paris so long as the railroads stayed open: Kate and Oscar Chopin no doubt shared train space with grain, salt, preserved meats, and hay. Possibly only Oscar's knowledge of France and French customs enabled them to go to Paris at all—or made them foolhardy enough to try.

When they reached Paris at last, the beautiful boulevards were filled with cows being driven to the Bois de Boulogne to be pastured there. The Louvre Museum had become a huge armaments workshop, and the streets were clogged with fleeing Parisians and their household goods.

"What an eventful day for France, may I not say for the world? And that I should be here in the midst of it," Kate Chopin wrote in her diary on Sunday, September 4.

"This morning my husband and myself rose at about eleven and after taking our coffee, started of in the direction of the Madeleine for mass." Evidently they were staying in the fashionable *quartier* near the newly completed Opera House, a short walk from the Madeleine, with its lofty ornamented dome, Corinthian pillars, and beautiful statuary and paintings. But other matters claimed Kate and Oscar's attention:

> Very sad and very important news had reached Paris during the previous night, from the seat of war. The Emperor was prisoner in the hands of the Prussians—McMahon either wounded or dead, and forty thousand armed men had surrendered! What did it mean? The people on the streets looked sad and preoccupied.

The truth was actually much worse than first reported: The emperor Napoleon III had had eighty thousand men with him when he surrendered to the German General Von Moltke, whose "iron countenance" had so frightened Kate in Stuttgart. She wrote down everything:

It was now nearly one & we entered church where mass had not yet commenced. It was also the hour when the Corps Législatif was going to meet to decide on an important affair of state, and already there were determined looking people marching towards the Chambre. The short mass was soon over.

We hastened out and stationed ourselves on the Church steps, from which position we commanded a splendid view of the entire length of the street up to the Chamber of the Corps Législatif. There were thousands of people forming one great human mass. In the Chamber was an all important question being decided, and without, was an impatient populace waiting to learn the result.

Then events tumbled, one after another, as the French representatives declared that the Second Empire was dead, and a new Republic was born.

Scarcely an hour passed, when down they came, when down they came, the whole great body, and at once it seemed to pass like an electric flash from one end of Paris to the other—the cry "Vive la République!"

I have seen a French Revolution! And astonishing—no drop of blood has been shed—unless I take into account the blood that has paid sad tribute to the Prussian.

The Gens' D'armes have been dispersed, and the Garde National has taken under its care the public buildings and places of the city.

While Kate scribbled:

Oscar has gone tonight on the Boulevards, where men, women and children are shouting the Marseilles with an abandon and recklessness purely *french*. Now, whilst I write, comes to me that strain from the martial air "Aux Armes, Citoyens! Formons nos Batallions!"

If now they will form their batallions against the Prussian & cease their cry of "A bas l'Empereur."

But the revolution was not without its violent moments:

All day they have been tearing down and casting in the dust the Imperial eagles that have spread their wings so proudly over Paris.

> It cannot but make one sad. We have seen the rude populace run-
> ning & strutting through the private grounds of the Tuileries: places
> that 24 hours ago were looked upon as almost sacred ground. What
> a nation.

Amid a revolution, with the empress Eugénie secretly escaping to England
and the emperor a German prisoner, and with the French populace gleefully
defacing all monuments bearing the royal N—there was little opportunity for
tourists to take in the usual sights.

On the evening of September 5, Victor Hugo—the grand man of letters
exiled under the emperor—returned triumphantly to Paris. Crowds greeted him
deliriously, singing *"La Marseillaise"*—but Kate did not record seeing the famous author. Nor did she see George Sand, the most famous woman writer in
France: Sand had settled permanently at her country house in Nohant. Meanwhile, everywhere, atrocity stories circulated about the Prussian invaders, who
were portrayed as barbarians, rapists, and savages.

"Our stay in Paris was short and of course offered none of those attractions—
fascinations—usually held out to visitors," Kate wrote sadly. If they visited Notre
Dame or Versailles, she did not record it, and the Chopins missed the sumptuous meals Mark Twain had enjoyed in Paris, just two years earlier. Nor was
there, amid revolution, a leisure class of the kind he described in *The Innocents
Abroad:* "the coming and departing company so moustached, so frisky, so aff-
able, so fearfully and wonderfully Frenchy!"

On September 10, the day that Parisians began cutting down and burning
the trees in the Bois de Boulogne, the Chopins left Paris for Brest,

> from which point we took the steamer "Ville de Paris" for New
> York, where we arrived after a very stormy & threatening passage;
> nor did we tarry on our way to St. Louis—where once again I have
> embraced those dear ones left behind.

They had barely escaped being left behind themselves, marooned in a city
under siege. Eight days after their departure, the last mail train left Paris; on
the following day, the last remaining telegraph lines were severed, the gates of
Paris were closed, and the railroad entrances were walled up. With the Prussian
armies encircling the city, the Parisians were left to their own resources and
their own courage. The siege lasted for four-and-a-half months, and sixty-five-
thousand people died of starvation and disease.

But by then Kate and Oscar Chopin were living on Magazine Street in New
Orleans.

On her honeymoon, Kate had lived with a man for the first time, and now knew about sexual passion—although she could not write about it in her diary. Instead she wrote about the things that would reappear two decades later in her fiction: the beauty of nature; the power of music; the pleasures of solitude; and the joys of loafing, eating, drinking, and observing the endless quirks and peculiarities of other members of the human species.

Once the Chopins returned to the United States in 1870, however, Kate was engulfed in domesticity. She was expecting her first child.

Chapter 8

NEW ORLEANS
AND
MOTHERHOOD

IN *THE AWAKENING*, WHICH she began twenty-seven years after moving to New Orleans with her new husband, Kate Chopin gave Edna and her husband "a very charming house on Esplanade Street": a large double cottage with a veranda, round, fluted columns, and green shutters. According to Daniel Rankin, that description "is a picture of Kate Chopin's own home in New Orleans"—but Rankin, as usual, was presenting Kate and Oscar Chopin as much wealthier than they actually were.

Esplanade Street, the home of the fictional Pontelliers, is on the broad, tree-shaded boulevard at the edge of the Vieux Carré (French Quarter), the home of the Creole elite—including Oscar Chopin's father. Those old French families whose fortunes had survived the war still tended their insular mansions in the Quarter. But Kate and Oscar Chopin never lived in the French Quarter—and, in fact, each of their three New Orleans homes was further uptown from Canal Street, the boundary between the French Quarter and the expanding "American" section of the city.

The Chopins' first home, at 443 Magazine Street, was indeed a double cottage, like the Pontelliers'—but the Chopins lived in only one side of the side-by-side duplex. Another family, at 445 Magazine, shared the balcony in front and the long gallery in back, which formed a servants' wing. (Most middle-class white families kept servants, and the Chopins seem to have had a cook and a laundress throughout their married life.) There was also at least one outbuilding, either a kitchen or an outhouse.

The Chopins' block, between Terpsichore and Robin (now Euterpe) Streets, was not a prestigious address: It was not in the Garden District, home of the wealthy "American" merchants. Their parish church was St. Patrick's on Camp Street and Girod, in the neighborhood known as "the Irish Channel." Yet it was there that the Chopins would receive many visitors—including Oscar's father.

Dr. Jean Baptiste Chopin reportedly did not like anyone very much.

By the time Kate and Oscar set up housekeeping in New Orleans, Dr. Chopin was alone and ailing, and all his life had been bitterly critical of Americans. (Years later, when Kate Chopin created Madame Carambeau in "A Matter of Prejudice," she was said to be drawing on her father-in-law's hatreds: "Americans, Germans and all people of a different faith from her own. Anything not French had, in her opinion, little right to existence." Madame even has "an original theory that the Irish voice is distressing to the sick.")

Kate Chopin did not have an Irish brogue—but she had begun life as an O'Flaherty, which was bad enough in Dr. Chopin's eyes.

Victor Jean Baptiste Chopin (who eventually dropped the Victor) was born in 1818 in Jouaignes, in the department of Aisne (the old province of Champagne, not far from the Belgian border and Château-Thierry). Deciding early in life that he would not be a farmer like his father, he set out for Mexico, but settled in Louisiana, one of very few places in the United States where he might make his way without having to speak English. He got his medical training there, and learned enough English to understand what others were saying about him—but he spoke it only when forced to. He purchased land in Natchitoches ("NACK-i-tush") Parish in northwest Louisiana, bought slaves to plant and pick his cotton and corn, and then went looking for the perfect wife: an attractive young woman who owned a great deal of land and had an impeccable French lineage.

He found her in Julie Benoist, the niece of the St. Louis financier Louis A. Benoist. When Mademoiselle Marie Julie Benoist and Dr. Victor Jean Baptiste Chopin were married on July 18, 1842, the bride was fifteen and the groom twenty-four. In the next few years, Dr. Chopin bought considerably more land with his mother-in-law, Suzette Rachal Benoist, whose husband died in the yellow fever epidemic of 1853. The doctor ran his Red River plantations with an iron hand and became famous for brutality toward his slaves. Local folklore confused him with Robert McAlpin, who had owned the land before him and who was sometimes said to be the model for Simon Legree in *Uncle Tom's Cabin*.

Dr. Chopin also abused his wife. (Years later, Kate Chopin wrote about such a man, cruel to his wife and slaves, in "Désirée's Baby.") Dr. Chopin isolated his young wife from all her friends and family and would not let her drive her own surrey, even to church. When she wanted to visit her mother, he locked her in her room, and when Madame Benoist sent her own carriage for her daughter, Dr. Chopin ordered the coachman away. Under Louisiana law, everything his wife brought to the marriage belonged to Dr. Chopin, and he was viciously stingy with money, spoiling even her solitary enjoyments. When their few visitors asked Julie Benoist Chopin to play on the "old styled" piano that she loved, she would say sadly that the piano was old and out of order. In the late 1850s, she tried to have it repaired, but "there were too many things wrong with it, and missing from it," according to a neighbor.

Julie Benoist Chopin gave birth to five children who lived to adulthood: Oscar, born 1844; Eugénie, 1848; J. B. Lamy, 1850; Victor, 1855; and Marie, 1861. Another child, Jules, died before the war. Julie Benoist left Dr. Chopin for several years in the 1850s, but divorce was impossible among Catholics, and she returned before the birth of her last child.

Dr. Chopin had bought a very large plantation, with 4,367 acres and 94 slaves. Because of his cruelty, slaves continually ran away, and overseers refused to work for him. When the doctor forced his eldest son, Oscar, to be his overseer, young Oscar toiled in the fields with the chained slaves, but refused to mistreat them. Dr. Chopin flew into violent rages—and by the time Oscar was fourteen, he had run away to live with relatives.

In the fall of 1861, while military companies were being raised all over Natchitoches Parish, Dr. J. B. Chopin placed his French-born friend Charles Bertrand in charge of the Chopin properties, and took his own family back to Château-Thierry. Dr. Chopin alone returned to Louisiana during 1862 and 1863 and part of 1864 "to protect his interests," according to the land claims he made afterward.

When the invading U.S. cavalry raided the Chopin plantation, they helped themselves to the Chopin horses, mules, and provisions, and turned the house into a hospital. The invaders smashed Julie Chopin's beloved piano, and threw the pieces into the yard. (After Dr. Chopin's death, the inventory of his property included one damaged piano, sold at auction for ten dollars.)

After the Union raid—during which, some witnesses said, Dr. Chopin had fled to the woods—he returned to France. He was living at the Hôtel du Presil in Paris when he applied for a return passport on April 21, 1865, just twelve days after General Robert E. Lee's surrender at Appomattox. Later, the rest of the family joined him.

Thus the Chopin children had French educations, and Dr. Chopin himself had prospered by investing in French railroad stocks. After the war, in which so many Natchitoches Parish men had been maimed or killed, there was much anger against those who did not serve. (For his own damaged property, Dr. Chopin filed suit against the Yankees with the French and American Claims Commission—but by the time his claim was settled, he had been dead for a dozen years.)

The resentment of the local people may have encouraged Dr. Chopin to move to New Orleans with his wife. Their son Victor had died; their children Lamy and Marie stayed with relatives in Natchitoches Parish; and their elder daughter, Eugénie—perhaps to escape tensions at home, and to spite her father's prejudices—married an Irishman, the Natchitoches Parish planter Joseph Henry, twenty years her senior.

Julie and J. B. Chopin were evidently living in New Orleans in the spring of 1870, when Oscar Chopin, who had gone to study finance with the Benoist firm in St. Louis, made plans to marry Kate O'Flaherty. But Julie Benoist Chopin, "a fragile person" according to those who knew her, died suddenly on April 15, 1870 (according to family tradition, both older Chopins died of typhoid). Dr. Chopin, now even more embittered, moved into the St. Louis Hotel, at Royal and St. Louis Streets in the French Quarter.

Less than two months later, Oscar Chopin married Kate O'Flaherty in St. Louis: Evidently his mother's death did not affect his wedding plans.

When the newlywed Chopins returned to New York from Europe on September 21, 1870, they went immediately to St. Louis, but the journey would have taken at least a week, and visits with the relatives at least another. Kate would have begun to suspect her own pregnancy, a fact to be confided to her mother and grandmother—who could be expected to offer all kinds of advice.

Thus it must have been mid-October by the time Kate and Oscar Chopin arrived in New Orleans to set up housekeeping on Magazine Street and receive Oscar's father. General Robert E. Lee had just died, an event mourned throughout the South; New Orleanians were worried about a severe drought, and the beginnings of a yellow fever panic. According to Rankin, the mean-spirited Dr. J. B. Chopin

> was unable to make sarcastic remarks to his son's vivacious young wife. Her brown eyes looked too calmly at him; her clear fluency of French speech, her perfect accent astounded him. Her fair young loveliness won his admiration. Always at ease, her quick change from vivacity to quizzical seriousness baffled him. He detested music. She made him listen to her as she played the piano and soothed his irritability with French melodies heard in his youth and now almost forgotten.

But the truth is that Kate Chopin had scarcely a month in which to charm her father-in-law—or even to become acquainted with him. Dr. Chopin was already suffering from a "long and painful malady," which induced him to make a will on October 14. Exactly a month later, he died. The funeral mass was celebrated on November 15, in the St. Louis Cathedral in the French Quarter, and he was buried next to his wife, in St. Louis Cemetery Number 3.

Old Creole custom required a six-month period of full mourning, during which time it was improper to wear jewelry, or anything white or with colors. If the young Chopins followed the custom, Kate would have worn black for most of her first pregnancy.

In 1870, no other Chopin family members lived in New Orleans, but it was an easy boat trip from Natchitoches Parish. Prosperous merchants and planters, with servants to pack their trunks and carry them to the landing, often visited back and forth for weeks at a time, especially after the cotton season ended in October or November. Natchitoches Parish ladies liked to buy the latest fashions in New Orleans, and everyone was eager to meet Oscar Chopin's new bride.

Not everyone approved of her. Oscar's relatives, according to Daniel Rankin, "shook their heads in wonder or sternly advised him about his duty." To allow Kate to "go on, always in her own way" was "more than unusual, it was horrible. All of this indignation, expressed or suppressed, gave Oscar and Kate genial occasions of merriment. Kate had a fatal gift of mimicry that was not unemployed when Oscar told of a new outburst of advice"—and Oscar found her stories hilarious.

One of Kate's "ways" was to take long, solitary walks around New Orleans, smoking her Cuban cigarettes whenever she could. (Women were not supposed to smoke in public—and ladies were not supposed to smoke at all). During her walks, Kate jotted down descriptions of what she saw, and she was especially intrigued by riverfront scenes and by the colorfully painted mule cars running on Canal Street.

Her solitary walks were a declaration of independence. One day she took a "green car" out to City Park and the Metairie cemeteries—a favorite strolling place for New Orleanians—and stopped for refreshments in a private garden at the "Half-Way House" on the shell road, midway between the city and Lake Pontchartrain. Years later, in Chapter XXXVI of *The Awakening*, Edna would meet Robert in just such a garden and tell him, "I don't mind walking. I always feel so sorry for women who don't like to walk; they miss so much—so many rare little glimpses of life; and we women learn so little of life on the whole."

Most of Kate Chopin's life during the New Orleans years (1870–79) is mysterious, unknown.

New Orleans in those years was an exciting city. Mardi Gras grew more elaborate each year, with more krewes and floats and displays and performers. "The city that care forgot" offered horse racing at the Fairgrounds; drama and music at the St. Charles Theatre and the Academy of Music; and operas at the French Opera House, the first in the United States to stage *Lohengrin* and *Tannhäuser*. But what Kate Chopin attended is not recorded.

She did listen to stories: Older New Orleanians talked about the slaves' famous dances in Congo Square, at Orleans and Rampart Streets, before the war. On Sundays, on the dirt ground, the slaves would perform the Calinda and the Bamboula to intricate African rhythms pounded out on drums. It was a release of tension and a powerful sexual display—and in "La Belle Zoraïde," some two decades later, Kate Chopin wrote about that dancing. Zoraïde, a light-skinned slave, falls desperately in love with a black man for his tenderness and the beauty of his body—like a column of ebony—when he dances the Bamboula: "That was a sight to hold one rooted to the ground."

In New Orleans, Kate seems to have freed herself from some expectations: She apparently had nothing to do with the local Children of Mary Sodality, established in December 1869. Yet moving to New Orleans also meant loneliness, for Kate had been accustomed all her life to a houseful of female relatives. Oscar's orphaned nine-year-old sister Marie, who came to stay with the Chopins, was Kate's only female relative in New Orleans, and the name of only one woman friend (Mrs. L. Tyler) is known. A woman who was both in mourning and obviously *enceinte* (pregnant) was not to be seen in public—and loose, comfortable maternity clothes, street garments for the mother-to-be, did not exist. Unless Kate committed extraordinary violations of decorum, her beloved long walks would have been impossible for many months.

During the New Orleans years, Kate remained close with her mother: They spent months together at a time, in New Orleans or St. Louis. Eliza O'Flaherty came to visit her daughter for Mardi Gras in 1871, the first year a Queen of Carnival was chosen, and the first time that the names of female guests at balls and parade viewings were published in the newspapers. The Krewe of Comus also mounted a magnificent thirteen-float procession with scenes from Spenser's *Faerie Queene*. But by late February (Mardi Gras day was February 21), Kate Chopin was six months pregnant—which would have kept her safely indoors, with her mother, during most of the street spreeing.

Eliza O'Flaherty remained in New Orleans for Kate's first childbirth, attended by Dr. Charles Jean Faget, M.D.P. ("medical doctor, Paris"), a French Quarter physician who lived at the corner of St. Peter and Burgundy Streets and had attended Dr. Chopin in his last illness. (Dr. Faget's bedside manner could be disheartening: In grave cases, he would always ask if the patient had

had the last rites, and then observe, "Ah, well, if he's made his peace with God, just think how much better off he would be if he were dead.")

Dr. Faget was a renowned medical researcher, decorated as a Chevalier of the Legion of Honor for discovering the sign (a falling pulse) used to distinguish yellow fever from malaria. He was also tall, thin, and odd-looking: unbearded, with a hooked nose, a high, receding forehead and "long wavy black grizzly hair, brushed backward." His deliberately unstylish clothes included a low-crown silk or beaver hat, with the broad brim rolled up, in imitation of European priests. He in fact wore a priest's cape, cultivated the soft, gentle voice of a priest, and was financially impractical and "intensely religious."

He also evidently made a strong impression on Kate Chopin: Twenty years later, when she wrote her first short story about a doctor, she gave him Dr. Faget's discretion and generosity—and she named her hero for the doctor's greatest honor, calling him Dr. Chevalier. In "Dr. Chevalier's Lie," the doctor conceals the truth about an innocent Arkansas girl who dies in sordid circumstances in New Orleans. But by the time Kate wrote the story in St. Louis in 1891, Dr. Faget had already been dead for seven years.

In the 1870s, most middle-class white women had doctors for their deliveries: Midwives, who had much more practical experience, had been losing ground to male physicians for generations. The presence of a male physician—even one whose major interest was yellow fever, not babies—was supposed to bring prestige and extra skill. Dr. Faget also brought chloroform, a controversial drug that many men opposed. Although Queen Victoria's taking chloroform for the birth of her eighth child in 1853 had made the drug more respectable, many women were still exhorted to "bring forth children in sorrow," as the Bible told them to do. But Dr. Faget evidently did not believe that women in labor would love their children more because of greater suffering in bringing them into the world.

May was very humid, and Dr. Faget would have worn his summer outfit—his black straw hat—when he came to the little house on Magazine Street for the birth of Kate Chopin's first child.

Twenty-three years later, on May 22, 1894, Kate Chopin recalled her son Jean's birth in her diary:

> I can remember yet that hot southern day on Magazine street in New Orleans. The noises of the street coming through the open windows; that heaviness with which I dragged myself about; my husband's and mother's solicitude; old Alexandrine the quadroon nurse with her high bandana tignon, her hoop-earrings and placid

> smile; old Dr. Faget; the smell of chloroform, and then waking at 6 in the evening from out of a stupor to see in my mothers arms a little piece of humanity all dressed in white which they told me was my little son! The sensation with which I touched my lips and my fingertips to his soft flesh only comes once to a mother. It must be the pure animal sensation: nothing spiritual could be so real—so poignant.

Few of Chopin's contemporaries recorded childbirth so directly in their diaries. Sometimes they wrote, with delicate restraint, that "a little stranger" had arrived; rarely did they talk about the sensuous, primal pleasure in touching a newborn baby. But by 1894 Kate had overcome whatever reticence she once possessed; and a few years later, Edna in *The Awakening* would recall her own childbirths: "an ecstasy of pain, the heavy odor of chloroform, a stupor which had deadened sensation, and an awakening to find a little new life to which she had given being added to the great unnumbered multitude of souls that come and go."

Kate and Oscar Chopin named their little son after his late grandfather—Jean Baptiste—and registered his birth with the civil authorities. Three weeks later, Oscar departed for Paris, where he stayed at the Grand Hôtel Bergère through July 26, selling stocks and settling his father's business affairs. (Hotel records show that Oscar liked treats: He frequently ordered oranges and chocolate, and now and then a cigar.)

He did not return to New Orleans until August 25, but he may have stopped first in St. Louis, where young Jean Baptiste Chopin was baptized on August 15, 1871.

Kate Chopin was now a mother, and entered a new phase of her life with the ecstasies, doubts, and fears that she described many times in her fiction—from Athénaïse's delight in her pregnancy ("Athénaïse"), to Mrs. Mobry's terror of hereditary madness ("Mrs. Mobry's Reason"), to Mamzelle Aurélie's discovering the pleasure of sleeping with a child's "hot, plump body pressed close against her, and the little one's warm breath beating her cheek like the fanning of a bird's wing" ("Regret").

But having a child meant that Kate Chopin herself was no longer a child, her time and creative energies all her own. For the rest of her life, she would do first what Edna Pontellier finally refuses to do: "Remember the children."

During the first ten years of her marriage, Kate Chopin gave birth to five sons and one daughter:

> Jean Baptiste, born May 22, 1871, in New Orleans
> Oscar Charles, born September 24, 1873, in St. Louis
> George Francis, born October 28, 1874, in St. Louis

Frederick, born January 26, 1876, in New Orleans
Felix Andrew, born January 8, 1878, in New Orleans
Lélia (baptized Marie Laïza), born December 31, 1879, in Cloutierville,
  Louisiana

Only one portrait survives from those years. Kate sent the photograph to
Fiddletown, California, to her great-uncle F. A. Charleville, whom she'd never
met, in September of 1876, apparently to show him her growing family. The
picture shows Kate with Frederick, her youngest, cuddled in her lap, wearing
a baby bonnet and sucking his thumb; George, able to stand on his own but
still wearing a child's short dress, clings to his mother's skirt. Young Oscar, his
hair in bangs, wears a scalloped-collar dress with a broad sash and sits uncom-
fortably next to a low pillar, his mouth pursed exactly like his mother's. Only
Jean, dressed in a boy's suit, with shirt and tie and trousers, has been allowed
to put away childish things. He stares fixedly at the camera, his eyes dark and
intense like his father's.

Kate, sitting with the children, looks plump and matronly. She wears a cross
over a high-collared, full dress with a ruffled skirt and her dark hair pulled back
tightly, piled on her head, with just a few curls dangling on her forehead. She
looks tired and harassed, without the animation or the slight smile that plays
around her lips in earlier and later pictures. At twenty-six, she looks closer to
forty.

Oscar Chopin does not appear in the picture, but two years earlier, at Wash-
burn Studios on Canal Street, Oscar was photographed with Jean—the boy
wearing a bow tie, knickers, and long stockings, the man wearing a suit and
vest with watch chain. Oscar's hair was receding slightly, and he still sported a
mustache and well-trimmed beard. He had also grown quite portly, with the
cheerful, large-bellied look of a successful businessman—but what Oscar Chopin did for a living during the first years of his marriage to Kate O'Flaherty is
not clear.

He first appears in the New Orleans city directory in 1872, as a cotton factor
on 26 Union Street, a block with other factors and brokers. Before the war, the
cotton factors, the middlemen who sold cotton for the planters, had been important and powerful men who loaned money and procured supplies—anything
from paper to steam engines—for the planters. The factors charged interest and
commissions that were paid back at the end of the cotton season, and before
the war—which disrupted everything—theirs was a very lucrative profession.

At first, Oscar's business prospered. (An office like his, staffed with well-
dressed gentlemen of leisure, appears in Edgar Degas's *"Bureau de Coton"* (the
Cotton Office), which Degas painted in New Orleans in 1873.) By late 1873,
Oscar had moved his offices from dingy Union Street to a much better address

on 65 Carondelet Street. He advertised himself as a cotton factor and commission merchant whose clerks kept track of market prices on "brooms and brushes, blacking, tumblers, bottles, hermetically sealed fruit, playing cards, candles, whiskey, tobacco, segars, soap, starch, nuts, sugar, molasses, corn."

Oscar also shared his business with his wife—a very untraditional thing to do in the 1870s. The last entry in Kate's New Orleans diary (now lost) described her "journey with Oscar through the district of warehouses where cotton is stored and when sold passes under presses of immense power, reducing bales to half their size for better storage aboard ship." With Oscar, Kate visited the "pickeries where damaged cotton is bleached and otherwise repaired. The whole process of weighing, sampling, storing, compressing, boring to detect fraud, and the treatment of damaged bales is open to public view." But throughout her visit, Kate kept hearing ominous news: "too much rain for cotton" and "the cotton was shedding"—and the cotton trade would never be what it was before the war.

Still, the cotton business did well enough, through the 1870s, for the Chopins to move twice, each time to a somewhat better address. By 1874, Oscar Chopin, "cotton factor and com. mer." was listed as residing at the northeast corner of Constantinople Street and Pitt Avenue; by 1876, the Chopins had moved again, to 209 Louisiana Avenue, between Coliseum and Prytania Streets. No trace remains of the Constantinople Street house, in uptown New Orleans, where Kate and Oscar lived with their three sons. But the pretty Louisiana Avenue double house, which they rented from the sugar dealer Edward Bebee, is now numbered 1413–1415, and is still surrounded by gardens. The Chopins lived in the side now numbered 1413, and their ceiling medallions and fireplaces still survive.

The Louisiana Avenue house was in the Garden District, where well-to-do "Americans" had built their houses to rival the finest in the French Quarter. The house that Kate and Oscar Chopin and their sons inhabited was a simple frame building with a slate roof and galleries along the front and sides and a one-story service building in the back. (Two servants lived there, according to the 1880 census.)

The Chopins occupied only one side of the two-story double, and their downstairs area included front and back parlors with elaborate acanthus-leaves ceiling medallions and two fireplaces, one of blackened stone and the other of reddish brick. Behind the parlors were a dining room or kitchen, and stairs leading to three or four large bedrooms. Kate and Oscar moved in with four sons; their fifth, Felix, was born in that house.

The Chopins' new home was surrounded by a lush profusion of shrubs, trees, and flowers that perfumed the air on warm evenings. Kate and Oscar often entertained friends, and Mrs. Tyler, a frequent visitor, later told Rankin that "Oscar, ever jovial and cheerful and fun-loving and really very stout, liked to romp with the children through the house and about the gardens. 'I like disorder when it is clean' was his favorite saying."

Mrs. Tyler also remembered Kate Chopin as a distinctive personality who "enjoyed smoking cigarettes, but if friends who did not approve of smoking came to visit her, she would never offend them. She was individual in the style of her clothes as in everything else. She loved music and dancing, and the children were always allowed to enjoy themselves." As for the Chopins' marriage, according to Mrs. Tyler: "Kate was devoted to Oscar and thought him perfect."

According to another informant, Mrs. John S. Tritle, "Kate was very much in love with her Oscar," and although she was a social favorite, she and her husband always preferred each other's company to anyone else's.

Years later, Kate Chopin described an apparently perfect married couple in *The Awakening*: The Ratignolles "understood each other perfectly. If ever the fusion of two human beings into one has been accomplished on this sphere it was surely in their union." Rankin believes that Chopin was describing her married life with Oscar—but in fact, the Ratignolles fill Edna with depression and boredom and pity, for the "blind contentment" that strikes her as unthinking, even bovine.

No one told Kate Chopin's first two biographers about any marital discord in the Chopin household—but the sunny picture of Kate and Oscar's New Orleans years is not the whole story. Kate O'Flaherty Chopin, a spirited young woman who enjoyed solitude and reading and writing but found herself engulfed by the demands of children, was already gathering material for a very different kind of tale, and a different set of truths.

Whenever Kate Chopin returned to St. Louis to visit her mother, she rejoined the comfortable world of her childhood. The house was still full of people: Eliza O'Flaherty, forty-three when Kate made her a grandmother in 1871, remained with her mother, Athénaïse Faris, her son, Tom, and her sister and brother-in-law, Amanda and Roger McAllister, at 1217 St. Ange Avenue. By 1875, they had moved to 1125 St. Ange, where their household also included Amanda's children, Andrew and the pesky Nina, who never married. Even Eliza's brother Charles, who married Clémence Benoist, lived just a block away.

In St. Louis, where Kate Chopin went to wait for the birth of her second child during the summer of 1873, there was no one quite like old Dr. Faget— but for her second confinement, Kate chose another eccentric European physician. Dr. Frederick Kolbenheyer, an Austrian with Viennese medical training, was famous for his radical political views—especially a fierce hatred for the Hapsburg monarchy. He had finally "received a hint to leave the country," and arrived in St. Louis in 1871—where he became part of Joseph Pulitzer's newspaper circle, and was known for his outspokenness, quick temper, charm, and fascinating talk. Black-bearded and fierce-looking, he lived in south St. Louis among the German immigrants—but he was also an old and trusted friend of Eliza O'Flaherty's (according to Daniel Rankin).

Attended by Dr. Kolbenheyer, Kate Chopin gave birth to Oscar Charles in September, 1873, and the baby's godparents were Oscar's sister Eugénie Henry and Kate's uncle Charles Faris. As a militant agnostic, Dr. Kolbenheyer almost certainly stayed away from the baptism.

Kate's brother, Thomas, had been the godfather for her first son, Jean (the godmother, listed as "Mary Chopin," was Oscar's ten-year-old sister Marie). Tom O'Flaherty, who had finished just two years of the four-year commercial course at St. Louis University, was employed as a clerk. Like Kate, he was a subscriber-member of the St. Louis Mercantile Library; but he also had something of a wild streak—just three months after Kate gave birth to young Oscar, her twenty-five-year-old brother Tom was dead, in circumstances described by Tom's companion J. S. Berthold in the *St. Louis Daily Times* of December 29, 1873:

O'FLAHERTY'S FATAL RIDE

Between two and three o'clock Saturday afternoon, I started to take Tom O'Flaherty from the stable, 918 Pine Street, to his home at 1217 St. Ange avenue; Eugene Benoist started out of the stable at the same time with his team, accompanied by Andy McAllister; we got as far as Fourteenth Street, where I intended to turn towards St. Ange avenue, but Tom told me to follow the boys, referring to Benoist and McAllister, as he did not want to go home right away; we followed them and my mare acted so badly that I used the whip on her three or four times; she commenced to run and when we reached the crossing at Sixteenth street the front spring broke; I told Tom that the spring was broken; he became very much excited and, without any warning, jerked the lines out of my hands; as he did this he leaned towards me and threw me out of the buggy; this occurred on Pine street between Sixteenth and Seventeenth; when I fell I struck on my head and side, but received no injuries beyond some slight bruises on my right hand, and was on my feet in a minute; I ran in the direction of the buggy, which was now out of sight; [then] on Pine street, between Seventeenth and Eighteenth, near the corner of the Sisters of the Good Shepherd, and about four feet from the curbstone, I found Tom lying on his back in the street; standing over him was a German and an Irishman, whose names I do not know; I asked him to help me carry him to some doctor's; we took him to Doctor Rogers, on the south side of Pine, two or three doors from Seventeenth street; the doctor was not at home, and we then carried him to the drug store at the corner of Seventeenth and Market; I told Captain Dickson to go for Dr. Hodgen, who came, felt Tom's pulse and said nothing could be done, as he was dead, his neck having been broken by the fall.

Tom was buried in the same plot as his father and half-brother, George, beneath the obelisk in Calvary Cemetery.

And so, when Kate Chopin visited St. Louis again in the spring of 1874 for the grand opening of the Eads Bridge—the first to span the Mississippi River at St. Louis—she was Eliza O'Flaherty's only remaining child.

Kate brought Oscar with her, and presumably their sons Jean and Oscar. The first walkers crossed the bridge on May 24 (ticket buyers paid five cents a person); the official ceremonies took place on July 4, 1874, with fireworks, decorations, and triumphal arches. Most likely, Kate did not attend the July 4 ceremonies, for she was visibly pregnant again. She stayed on in St. Louis over the summer and gave birth to her third son, George Francis, on October 28, assisted by Dr. Kolbenheyer. The godparents for the baptism on November 2 were Francis and Virginia Donovan (whose mother was Virginia Charleville Lynch, Kate's grandmother's sister).

But Oscar had returned to New Orleans long before Kate did—and once he was alone, he got himself into trouble.

Reconstruction in Louisiana was a violent time, and New Orleans was full of bribery, corruption, bitter memories, and hatred for the current Yankee occupiers. New Orleans had surrendered early in the war, in April of 1862, and the conquering Yankees had looted the city, harassing and banishing Confederate women, and threatening them with sexual abuse. By the time Kate Chopin arrived in 1870, Louisiana had been readmitted to the Union, but New Orleans was still an occupied city, part of the fifth military district of the United States. Black men were voting, while most former Confederate soldiers were disfranchised.

Louisiana's white men seemed—to one Northern writer—absurdly fearful of conspiracies among black men to "murder the whites and outrage their women." But the result was that white men committed "barbarous and heart-rending murders and outrages" against blacks. Not far from Natchitoches Parish, in Colfax, Louisiana, in April of 1873, whites massacred 105 blacks.

Southern Democrats of New Orleans—like Oscar Chopin—were outraged at the conduct of "radical Republicans" who voted black men into power. Moreover, the 1872 election for governor was obviously corrupt: John McEnery (Democrat) seemed to have the majority of votes, but a Republican-controlled elections board declared that their candidate, the carpetbagger William Pitt Kellogg, had won. In January of 1873, with a singular lack of harmony, both Louisiana governors—McEnery and Kellogg—were inaugurated. And both sides were ready for confrontation.

There may have been a hint of nostalgia for war in the New Orleans men who began not-very-secret military drills in the summer of 1874, after Oscar Chopin returned alone from St. Louis. Most were Confederate veterans who did not need military instruction—but there were also men who had not served in the war, for whom fighting back against the Yankee oppressors was a form of atonement.

That may have motivated Oscar Chopin to enlist.

The Crescent City White League was formed in New Orleans in June 1874, just after Oscar's return, and its nucleus was "the best people," members of the elite Boston Club. On Kate and Oscar Chopin's fourth wedding anniversary, June 9, 1874, the *New Orleans Daily Picayune* wrote that current racial antagonisms should be blamed on "the African race." And so "the white race" would make no more "appeals to this misguided people . . . crazed with the pride and ambition to lord it over their superiors in civilization, in virtue, and intelligence." The White League would change that, the newspaper declared.

The league was a military organization that soon spawned a motley host of allied companies, including "The First Louisiana Regiment"—which Oscar Chopin joined. The regiment, known affectionately as "Louisiana's Own," was organized by Colonel John G. Angell, a handsome, English-born, dark-bearded Confederate veteran and dentist who shared a clinic at 152 Julia Street with his brothers Samuel M., a physician, and James, an apothecary who manufactured and sold "Angell's Cough Remedy."

Oscar Chopin joined Company B, commanded by Captain Frank McGloin, a twenty-eight-year-old sandy-haired lawyer and sometime neighbor (at 388 Magazine Street). McGloin was also an Irish-born Catholic, and the author of poems and articles in the newspapers. In April of 1873, McGloin had published in the *Daily Picayune* a "Satire," taking up fully two columns, headlined THE ORIGIN OF MAY (a misprint: His subject was the origin of *man*.) McGloin wrote with energy and a somewhat ragged meter, and discoursed on subjects dear to the hearts of southern white men: the supposed superiority of whites over blacks, and the gloomy possibilities for all humanity.

As of the summer of 1874, McGloin's Company B had enlisted some sixty men, but could not easily procure weapons: The Metropolitan Police, suspecting trouble, kept a careful watch on arms shipments. Oscar Chopin, living alone with the servants that summer, worked in his office during the day and drilled with the First Louisiana Regiment at night. When the steamboat the *Mississippi* arrived on September 10 with a large shipment of arms for the White League and associated companies, some of the military clubs began drilling openly, in vacant lots and public streets. Then, on Monday, the fourteenth, the long-awaited confrontation took place.

While a crowd of five thousand men listened to fiery speeches at the Henry Clay statue on Canal Street, Colonel Angell and his colleagues sent their troops into the streets. By 10:00 A.M., McGloin's Company B—Oscar Chopin's company—had occupied the Crescent Billiard Hall.

By early afternoon, McGloin's troops, at City Hall, demanded that the mayor surrender. When Mayor Louis A. Wiltz refused, McGloin ordered eleven of his men into the building; his lieutenant followed with forty men carrying long weapons and sidearms; and the rest of the company stationed themselves near the Clay statue. The Metropolitan Police were ordered onto Canal Street, to defend New Orleans from the White League invaders and rebels—who were making barricades of iron street crossings, sewer covers, wagons, and mattresses.

Late that afternoon, the White Leaguers and associated companies attacked the Metropolitan Police, who opened fire with their cannons. Although they fought fiercely, McGloin's Company was not well-equipped. Most had only small pistols; some used old army rifles and muzzle-loaders.

The Battle of Canal Street—which came to be known as the "Battle of Liberty Place"—was only a fifteen-minute shooting match. The Metropolitan Police fled in confusion and terror, and the White League and associated companies won the battle, but at great cost: at least sixteen men killed and forty-five wounded. (The Metropolitans had eleven killed and sixty wounded.) Some of the dead were bystanders, but newspaper notices nonetheless lauded the dead White Leaguers for being "killed in defense of the people's rights."

That evening, and into the early morning, there were more skirmishes and negotiations—and on Tuesday, Company B and two others took over the State House. The Third Precinct police station also surrendered. The insurrection had been a complete success, and Governor Kellogg of Louisiana had been overthrown—briefly.

On the day after the battle, Oscar and the other members of Colonel Angell's companies wore pieces of black ribbon in their buttonholes, to honor the dead. Blood and bullets could be seen on the street, and the Cotton Exchange was closed out of sympathy for the rebels. The dead were eulogized as "the life-blood of our best people poured out upon the altar of their country," and the *Daily Picayune* cheered the rebel "patriots and warriors."

But their success lasted scarcely a week. With federal troops and warships with guns trained on the city, the hated Governor Kellogg was restored to office. The rebels still had sympathizers all over the country: In St. Louis, where Kate Chopin was soon to give birth, U.S. senator Carl Schurz gave a speech denouncing the usurper Kellogg and his government. By the time Kate returned to New Orleans, the "White League Waltz" and the "People's Rights Quick Step" had been published and acclaimed.

But Oscar Chopin and the other rebels were not heroes to everyone. To Kellogg and his officials, the White League companies were revolutionists and traitors who had attacked a duly constituted government—and the penalty for treason was hanging. In January 1875, General Philip Sheridan, the fiery commander of the New Orleans district, proposed that President Grant declare the White League participants "banditti," allowing Sheridan to put them all on trial for murder. Grant did not give the order—and so Oscar, like Kate during the Civil War, escaped being punished for rebellion.

Whether Kate Chopin shared Oscar's prejudices—whether she cheered on the White League—cannot be known. In her fiction, she never depicts social equality between blacks and whites, but such equality existed rarely, if at all, in real life.

Her short story "In and Out of Old Natchitoches" includes a brief incident of school integration, the focus of fierce white resistance in New Orleans in the 1870s—but the white hero's effort to send an unwilling mulatto boy to a rural school is just the start of a budding romance. Likewise, Grégoire in *At Fault*, Chopin's first novel, attempts to do what black men themselves were trying to do on Decoration Day in 1874, while Kate lived in New Orleans: integrate saloons by forcing saloon-keepers to serve blacks. But Grégoire is drunk at the time, and the scene shows more about his ill temper than about Chopin's attitude toward social integration. Like most white southern sympathizers, Kate apparently thought blacks and mulattoes preferred to be with their own: In "A Little Free-Mulatto," a young mixed-blood girl is desperately lonely until her father takes her to "L'Isle des Mulâtres," the colony of free people of color in Natchitoches Parish, where she is "the happiest little Free-Mulatto in all Louisiana."

As a writer, Kate Chopin was not interested in men's political battles over race, but she portrayed black women, especially mothers, with sympathy and deep feeling. Her Zoraïde ("La Belle Zoraïde") goes mad when she believes her child has died; her La Folle in "Beyond the Bayou" surmounts a thirty-year terror of the world beyond the nearby bayou to save a white child. Motherhood, not race, dominated Kate's years in New Orleans, and linked women with one another, across the color line.

※   ※   ※

During the social season—October to May, roughly—the Chopins lived in New Orleans, but according to her friend Mrs. Tyler, Kate's "long summer vacation times were spent with the children at Grand Isle." In the city, the Chopins evidently associated mainly with English speakers and Anglo-Saxons, among them Mrs. Tyler and Mrs. Tritle, Frank McGloin and John Angell. But at Grand Isle, most people were Creoles, and Kate Chopin—like Edna Pontellier in *The Awakening*—was a foreigner.

Whether Kate was astonished, like Edna, to read racy books passed around and discussed freely; and whether she blushed when childbirth was described in harrowing detail; and whether Creole gentlemen stopped telling risqué stories because she was present, cannot be known—but Kate, though she spoke French and was a Catholic, was not a Creole descended from generations of New Orleans Creoles. She was a northerner and an outsider (*étrangère*).

Grand Isle itself had become the quintessential Creole resort after the Civil War, when middle class people—imitating the wealthy who summered at Saratoga and Newport—began to patronize home resorts. Grand Isle was easily reached by boat from New Orleans, and a mule-drawn tramway carried guests from the dock to the *pensions* and the sandy beaches on the Gulf of Mexico. (In *The Awakening*, Edna's husband takes a rockaway—a light, horse-drawn carriage—from the guest houses to the dock.)

The approach to Grand Isle was romantic, through mazes of swamp forest and sea marsh, and at Grand Isle, birds were everywhere, as in *The Awakening*: mockingbirds, gulls with broken wings, and, at midnight, "the hooting of an old owl in the top of a water-oak," with its eternal accompaniment, "the everlasting voice of the sea, that was not uplifted at that soft hour. It broke like a mournful lullaby upon the night."

As early as 1870, the entrepreneur George Willoz had opened a Grand Isle *pension* resembling the Lebruns' place in *The Awakening*: a big house surrounded by smaller cottages connected by bridges, within easy walking distance of the beach. At the Lebruns', each family has its own bathhouse, of "rough but solid construction," with "small, protecting galleries facing the water." Grand Isle also catered to urban tastes: By the 1870s, it had a dining and dancing parlor, gambling tables, billiard rooms, and quarters for a hundred servants. The best hotel was the Grand Isle or Krantz Hotel, under the management of John F. Krantz, Jr. ("Klein's" in *The Awakening*).

For Kate Chopin, and other young mothers, Grand Isle was a wholesome escape from a city that was mercilessly hot and disease-ridden in the summer. In New Orleans, epidemics flourished in the festering open canals and cisterns; mosquitoes swarmed everywhere; and foreign ships brought in diseases with their cargoes. (Yellow fever was called "the strangers' disease.") In 1878, twenty-five thousand people in New Orleans were infected by yellow fever, and four thousand died. New Orleans was also notorious for street crime, but at Grand Isle children could romp freely, and guests left their rooms unlocked: In *The Awakening*, Edna brings down her key only "through force of habit."

Grand Isle was a tropical paradise, with palm trees and vines, orange and lemon trees, acres of yellow camomile, and no streets—only grassy green or sandy paths. Everywhere, there were the "strange, rare odors" Edna Pontellier notices: the smell of damp, new-plowed earth, the "heavy perfume of a field of white blossoms," and always, "the seductive odor of the sea."

For imaginative souls like Kate Chopin, Grand Isle also had the romantic aura of Barataria Bay, the old haunt of the pirate Jean Lafitte. (As a Sacred Heart student, she had read Byron, who praised Lafitte's courage at the Battle of New Orleans in "The Corsair.") At Grand Isle, tales of shipwrecks and lost pirate gold were recited on warm summer nights—just as in *The Awakening*, Robert entrances Edna with tales of hidden treasures and strange spirits abroad on the Gulf at midnight. (When Edna recklessly promises to give Robert all her treasure, he blushes.)

During the week, Grand Isle was the domain of women and children, with long, languorous afternoons like those in *The Awakening*. Sometimes children played croquet, and everyone swam: According to the *New Orleans Daily Picayune*, fashionable women's bathing suits were made of cumbersome wool or flannel; they also covered arms and legs completely.

Husbands worked all week in the city (Edna's husband works on Carondelet Street, as Oscar Chopin did). On weekends, the men took the steamer to Grand Isle for card parties, poker, billiards, recitations, dancing, and music—and they were expected to feign enthusiasm for amateur musical performances, such as the Farival twins' incessant playing of the duet from "Zampa" and the overture to "The Poet and the Peasant."

The Gulf Coast also offered possible excursions. On Grande Terre, an island with an abandoned sugar plantation, visitors could climb the old fort and watch the lizards and wriggling gold snakes, as Robert invites Edna to do. Fort Livingston, its walls made mostly of clam shells and brick in the 1840s, was still intact when Kate Chopin stayed at Grand Isle three decades later: Its guns, placed there for the Civil War, were not removed until April 1872.

There were decorous flirtations at Grand Isle, but if Kate Chopin indulged in them, she left no traces. The atmosphere encouraged indolence and drifting—and some obligations were impossible to perform: There was no regular priest to say mass. Although the Gulf Coast was only a few hours from New Orleans, its year-round residents were mostly independent fishermen and trappers whose spiritual needs were handled, irregularly, by Roman Catholic missionaries—just as if they lived in a foreign country.

The lazy days at Grand Isle gave Kate Chopin an opportunity to listen to the soft, baby-sounding Creole patois, which she used later in such stories as "La Belle Zoraïde." She also listened to tales of life and love and death—some of which she probably included in an 1889 novella, "Unfinished Story—Grand Isle—30,000 words," which she destroyed.

But by the time Kate Chopin was writing about Grand Isle for publication, the resort she remembered was gone. On October 1, 1893, the hurricane of Chênière Caminada devastated the lower coast, killing two thousand people and destroying the cabins. John Krantz, owner of the Grand Isle Hotel ("Klein's"), barely escaped alive.

Three weeks later, on October 21–23, Kate Chopin wrote "At Chênière Caminada" (published under the title "Tonie"), about the kind of romance that would have been gossiped about at Grand Isle: the passion of a poor, illiterate fisherman for a frivolous young society woman from New Orleans. The story was a preliminary sketch for *The Awakening*, with many of the same local characters and much of the sensuous atmosphere: the sea and the sky, the power of love and the power of music, birds and water, love and death and the magical atmosphere of the island.

But the Grand Isle Kate Chopin had known was no more—and *The Awakening*, like "At Chênière Caminada," was an elegy for a lost way of life.

In 1878, a fierce yellow fever epidemic cut off even postal service with the world outside New Orleans: It was believed that the deadly disease might come through the mails. The 1878 cotton crop was poor, and 1879 was little better. Oscar, who as a cotton factor lent money to cotton growers, was going deeper into debt: In June 1878, June 1879, and December 1879, there were three judgments against him for city taxes. He was losing the mortgage on the C. F. Benoist estate (his grandmother's property), and his suit against the federal government for Civil War damages to the Chopin properties had been dragging on since 1864, without any restitution. But Oscar had bought land in Natchitoches Parish, in northwest Louisiana, in 1876 and 1879, in addition to the land his father had owned.

Kate was pregnant again in the fall of 1879 when the Chopins, to save expenses, moved to Natchitoches Parish. Kate and Oscar and their five sons left the busy, crowded, raffish city with all its cultural excitements, for the clean and quiet village of Cloutierville. As a newlywed, Kate Chopin had mimicked Oscar's country relatives behind their backs—and now they would be her neighbors.

For the first time in her life, Kate Chopin would be living in a small town.

* * *

Oscar Chopin had not been in good health for some time. Too, he had worries enough to weaken any man: He had six children to support, a mound of bills he could not pay, and a restless wife who seemed to be the center of village flirting and gossip. He may also have had malaria for some time: It was not uncommon for a patient to have recurrent infections for two or three years.

In late summer, 1881, Oscar had gone to Hot Springs, Arkansas, to "recuperate his health," according to the *Natchitoches People's Vindicator*, which added on September 3, "He is looking well, and is enthusiastic in his praises of the healing qualities of this great resort for the ailing of humanity." But the regimen of baths, wholesome food, and rest apparently did not solve all his difficulties. He had been home barely a month when Kate left for St. Louis, where "she expects to remain several months," the *People's Vindicator* reported on October 8.

Since Louisiana residents did not commonly go north for the winter, such a trip, so soon after Oscar's return, could be taken as a sign of marital troubles.

By late 1882, Oscar had another attack of the fever, and then another. Much later, Kate would describe the deathly chills of malaria in her story "A Sentimental Soul": The character Lacodie shakes "with a chill till the very window panes rattle," and another chill sends "incipient shudders through his frame . . . making his teeth claque."

Oscar was in better health after November 1, the first day that Dr. Scruggs gave him medication ("med." on the doctor's bill). The "med." was probably calamine, commonly prescribed by country doctors for "thin blood" (general weakness) and "gorged" liver (easily confused with the enlarged spleen caused by malaria). Still, rural practitioners did stock quinine, and Dr. Scruggs could have given it to Oscar Chopin at the first sign of intermittent, raging fever— but he did not do so.

Possibly Dr. Scruggs did not take Oscar's pulse and temperature: In rural Louisiana in the 1880s, the clinical thermometer was not a common medical device. Dr. Scruggs may not have seen that Oscar had the deadliest of swamp fevers: malaria.

Dr. Scruggs visited again on November 16, when Oscar suffered a relapse, and again on November 28. In the meantime, bills kept coming in: On November 17, Oscar was billed for testimonies and depositions in his late father's unsettled lawsuit against the United States for war damages. At some point, too, Kate returned from St. Louis. Dr. Scruggs visited Oscar again on December 3, 4, 5, 6, and 7; on the seventh he also treated three Chopin children.

Chapter 9

THE GOSSIP IN CLOUTIERVILLE

"... THIS LITTLE FRENCH village, which was simply two long rows of very old frame houses, facing each other closely across a dusty roadway" ... was Cloutierville, Louisiana, as Kate Chopin described it in her 1891 story "For Marse Chouchoute." Pronounced "Cloochyville," it was a world all by itself, with heart-stopping drama, devoted love, and delicious gossip—but to Kate Chopin in the fall of 1879, the tiny French town seemed empty after the splendors of New Orleans.

Cloutierville natives sometimes went to New Orleans after the cotton harvest: They shopped for clothes, sent each other delicacies and treats, and stayed for weeks. In the winter, steamboats from New Orleans would bring barrels of oysters and ice—a rare commodity—to Natchitoches Parish.

Cloutiervillians also frequently visited Natchitoches, the parish's largest city and the oldest settlement in Louisiana, founded in 1714. The old French outpost, a charming and busy town, was still sometimes called "La Poste," and Cloutierville natives traveling to "the Post" might stay at the Natchitoches hotel described in Kate Chopin's story "the Bênitous' Slave": "The quaintest old stuccoed house, too absurdly unlike a 'hotel' for anything."

Still, Kate Chopin seems to have spent most of her Cloutierville years in Cloutierville: observing, gossiping, and experimenting with new ways of life.

For country people who appreciated natural beauty, autumn in Natchitoches Parish was a delight. Beyond the town stretched miles of rich plantations of cotton and corn, and the sugarcane glittered like green silver. A violet haze trembled over the forests of beech and pine, and the grass was thick and deep and green. But Cloutierville itself was just one long dusty street, dotted with one- and two-story wooden cottages with high, sharp roofs, along the winding Cane River.

Kate Chopin did adapt, somewhat: She substituted horseback riding for solitary walks, and grew to appreciate the docile Cloutierville horses. But when she was in a hurry, Kate would head next door to Oscar's general store, where his horse was tied. And there, in full view of the neighbors, the young matron from New Orleans would unceremoniously leap onto the horse's back and take off down the road, riding astride—an unladylike sight that never failed to scandalize everyone.

Cloutierville, Louisiana, was the site of a failed dream. When the Frenchman Alexis Cloutier founded it in 1822, he hoped to make it the center of a new parish (county)—but it remained a tiny village, inhabited mostly by French immigrants and their descendants, who Anglicized the town's name.

In Cloutierville, Kate Chopin's "tight-fitting clothes, her chic hats and a good deal of lavender colors in all her costumes" were a source of wonder. Half a century later, one villager could still describe Kate's "favorite costume": "a fantastic affair—a close-fitting riding habit of blue cloth, the train fastened up at the side to disclose an embroidered skirt, and the little feet encased in pretty boots with high heels. A jaunty little jockey hat and feather, and buff gloves rendered her charming." When she rode sidesaddle, the elderly ladies of the town agreed that Kate was "lovely"—and youngsters were fascinated.

Emma Perrier, the blacksmith's daughter who sometimes cared for the Chopin children, said that Kate "rode a horse well," and was always "beautifully dressed," favoring "shades of orchid and purple," with a rose at her throat. Lise DeLouche Charleville, the same age as Kate's son Oscar, most remembered "the little hat with the plume."

Still, Kate did not please everyone: "Her love of horseback riding they never understood," one informant told Daniel Rankin. Neighbors also thought her improper: While most Cloutierville women were at home with household chores, Kate Chopin would stroll slowly up and down the street, carrying "her little umbrella" (a fashionable parasol). And virtually every afternoon, at the same time, the beautiful Madame Chopin, in her modish riding habit, would take her "promenade on horseback," down Cloutierville's one street. Every man sweeping or working outside would suddenly drop everything—to gawk.

Kate was also deliberately provocative: Crossing the street, she would lift her skirts higher than was necessary, displaying her "pretty ankles." Some charitable souls explained that Madame Chopin was just keeping her skirts from trailing in the mud, but others harrumphed disapprovingly—and nothing went unnoticed.

In some ways, Kate Chopin did belong in Cloutierville: She spoke French, the everyday language in town, and her mother's Charleville relatives were among the most important local people. Eliza O'Flaherty's cousin Joseph Charleville, a schoolmate of Kate's half-brother, George, had fought with the Confederate Army and was now a notary and retail grocer. Joseph's brother Landry was a very successful dry-goods merchant and saloonkeeper, known for his irascible temper—which he would eventually direct toward Kate Chopin.

Oscar, too, was part of the web of kinship in Cloutierville. His mother had belonged to the Benoist and Rachal families, two of the largest and most influential white families in the area, and his brother Lamy, who ran their father's Red River plantation, was famous for his hospitality. A little man with a small mustache, pink cheeks, bright eyes, and a round face, Lamy was twenty-nine in 1879: Kate and Oscar arrived in Natchitoches Parish around the time that Lamy's first child, Eugénie ("Nini"), was born, in October. Lamy had been married for almost two years to Cora Henry, his sister Eugénie's stepdaughter, and Lamy worked throughout the 1880s to improve the plantation and make "a beautiful and comfortable home" for his wife and daughter.

Although the Chopin brothers were well liked, resentment still lingered against those who had sat out the war. Dr. Chopin's plantation had been plundered, but others suffered much more after the Battle of Mansfield in 1864. The retreating Union soldiers had taken revenge all along Cane River—burning the store belonging to Dr. Chopin's friend Charles Bertrand, looting the church and prancing around in the holy vestments, and slaughtering every chicken they could find. After they destroyed property all over Isle Brevelle, the home of the free people of color, they burned every house on "La Côte Joyeuse" (the Joyous Coast), including Magnolia Plantation (the site of Kate Chopin's most eloquent lament for the losses of war, "Ma'ame Pélagie").

Afterward, devastated fields had to be reclaimed, houses rebuilt, and field workers paid. Most slaves had gone off with the Yankees: In 1862, Dr. Chopin had owned forty-two slaves, but two years later only three—all women—remained. After the war, some whites worked their own fields, while free blacks, now sharecroppers living in cabins instead of quarters, worked the same land they had always worked.

By the time the Chopins moved to Cloutierville, the cotton season was over, and Kate was soon to give birth to her sixth child and only daughter. Eliza O'Flaherty had again come from St. Louis to be with her daughter, who would have a new physician: Samuel Oglesby Scruggs, a wealthy Virginia-born doctor who had married into an old French Cloutierville family, the Deslouches (or DeLouches). During the war, Dr. Scruggs's loyalty to the Confederacy had been under suspicion—but afterward he showed his support for the lost cause in classic Louisiana style: He was indicted for fixing an election. (He was acquitted and acclaimed as a hero.)

When the Chopins arrived in Cloutierville, Dr. Scruggs was fifty-eight years old and respected for his wide education, his travels, his home remedies, and his colorful storytelling. (He claimed that during a visit to his house, Harriet Beecher Stowe had been inspired to write *Uncle Tom's Cabin*—but the proof had somehow disappeared.) Dr. Scruggs was also a Mason, and virtually the only Protestant in town.

In Cloutierville, Kate and Oscar conformed to religious expectations. They owned a bedside prie dieu, a prayer stand with velvet knee cushions, and they had Lélia promptly baptized by Father Jean Marie Beaulieu, on February 29, 1880. Her godparents were Eliza O'Flaherty and Oscar's brother-in-law Joseph Henry. (Kate and Oscar had not been so quick before: Three of their five sons were baptized in St. Louis, but there are no baptismal records for Fred or Felix in St. Louis or New Orleans. Nor is there any record of Oscar and Kate's church membership or activities during their New Orleans years.)

As a boy in the Cane River country, Oscar had grown up in a distinctly unpious environment. According to the French nuns and priests who traveled to northwest Louisiana in the 1850s, the local people were "still part pagan in their ideas of morality," and God "is unknown to these people! Their God is GOLD, PLEASURE, AND GOOD FOOD!" Oscar's family had waited nearly a year to baptize him, and his mother may not have been baptized at all—or at least she was passed over when the traveling priest did visit.

Not much had changed by 1861, the year Oscar turned seventeen: A French missionary priest in northwest Louisiana inveighed against "the immoral custom of leaving little children stay unbaptized for a good length of time." He also found other local fashions deplorable—among them indecently low-necked dresses, public breast-feeding, and "the custom of the boys and the girls running around in the summer time in their homes as naked as worms." Nevertheless, the same priest, Yves-Marie Le Conniat, wrote to his parents that some progress had been made: Five years before that, the bishop had been hanged in effigy.

Oscar's sister Marie, born in 1861, was baptized quickly, but not for religious reasons: Three days after her birth on April 9, Confederate soldiers began firing on Fort Sumter. By April 15, President Lincoln was calling for volunteers, and by April 19 he had blockaded southern ports. The Civil War was well under way by May 21, Marie's baptismal day—and Dr. Chopin had already decided to take his family to France, where people were also very casual about Catholic observances.

By naming their daughter "Marie Laïza," Kate and Oscar conformed to the church's insistence that every child be given a saint's first name, but they always called her Lélia. It was a popular Cane River country name and a well-known literary name: George Sand's novel *Lélia* is the story of a passionate, ambitious woman who finds most men wanting. The name Lélia also honored "Lil" (Lélia) Chouteau, Kate's academic rival at the Academy of the Visitation and one of her correspondents during her honeymoon.

Nearly a decade later, Kate Chopin's first publication would be an 1888 polka called "Lilia," a common misspelling of Lil Chouteau's name—and much later, as an adult, Lélia Chopin, like her Chouteau predecessor, would be known as "Lil." But even in infancy, young Lélia Chopin was considered a personage of importance. A packet boat called *The Lilia*, operated by Captain Teal between the mouth of the Cane River and the town of Natchitoches, was said to be named for the newest Chopin baby.

Kate and Oscar Chopin lived at the very end of Cloutierville's one street, on the road heading toward Derry. Their house, built sometime before 1813 (and put together with handmade square nails) by the slaves of Alexis Cloutier, was one of the largest and most comfortable in town. When Oscar bought it in a sheriff's sale in May 1876, it was known as "the old Fontenot place": The previous owner, Gervais Fontenot, had been in the Union Club with Dr. Scruggs, opposing the war.

The house was a bright and cheery white "Louisiana type" raised cottage, with gate and gardens, a brick walkway, and brick pillars in front. The lower story was brick, and the upper one was heart cypress, built on a framework of heavy cypress timbers, their interstices filled with bricks (*"briqueté entre poteux"*). The upper inside walls were made from *"bousillage,"* mud and Spanish moss reinforced with wooden pegs, and the house included wainscoting, French doors opening onto an upstairs porch, and four fireplaces with a common chimney. A high, pitched roof sheltered the front and rear verandas from sudden thunderstorms, and an outside staircase, on the right front side, led to the upper story.

Although the house had four rooms on each floor—two big ones in front and two smaller ones in back—the Chopins lived only on the second floor, where the breezes were cooler and the mosquitoes less energetic (even so, everyone slept under a mosquito bar). One large bedroom was the boys', and the other was for Kate and Oscar and the baby, the same room that they used as a sitting room for parties and entertainments. Mrs. O'Flaherty, a frequent visitor, stayed in one of the upstairs rooms, probably a small back bedroom.

The rest of the house was devoted to practicalities: The lower story, built of handmade brick with a dirt floor, was used for storage. The kitchen, with its huge fireplace, was in a separate brick building, to keep heat away from the house and prevent fires. The land behind the house was farmed by an overseer, and other outbuildings included a carriage house and a stable, a storage building, and quarters for two live-in servants, both widows according to the 1880 census: Martha Field, fifty-five years old, "Black," was a cook; and Cora William, "Mulatto," forty-five, was a washerwoman. (Cooks usually had at least one helper, and both servants probably also assisted with child care. Most middle-class white people also hired a maid, a yard man, and someone to milk the cows.)

On one memorable occasion when no servants were around, the city-bred Kate Chopin found herself alone with a cow that desperately needed milking. Aided only by her adolescent neighbor Emma Perrier, Kate spent most of the day pushing and pulling at the hapless cow. The two of them finally managed to milk the cow themselves—a comical scene that townspeople laughed about for generations afterward.

In calmer moments, Kate Chopin liked to stand, gazing, at the back of the house at sundown. She could see, according to Rankin, "lonely fields and tracts of forest land leading into a small swamp, and in the distance beautiful Shallow Lake, and Bayou Derbonne." Afterward, when she had become a famous writer in St. Louis, people said that Kate must have been gathering material: watching, thinking, pondering her place in the universe.

She was also never fully reconciled to living in a small town.

Cloutierville had rustic charm, but it lacked the lush prettiness of New Orleans. Although roses were everywhere, there were pines instead of palms, and over the small buildings the sky seemed overarching, and endless. Sometimes the rutted local paths were too muddy or icy for long rides on horseback, and on the worst days, Kate could see little beyond the lonely forests.

Just beyond the Chopins' house, toward the church, was Oscar's general store, bought with the little money he had salvaged from financial ruin in New Orleans. After the agricultural depression of the 1870s, most cotton factors, like Oscar, had become proprietors of general stores—but unlike Kate's Charleville relatives or his own brother Lamy, Oscar was never a business success. Although his two clerks dutifully recorded all purchases in their dingy daybooks, from which pencils dangled from soiled strings, Oscar never expected his customers to pay cash—nor did he push them to pay for what he'd sold them on credit.

His store was very popular, for general stores sold everything: salt meat, flour, cornmeal, and kerosene; saddles, harnesses, and plow points; ladies' dresses, men's hats, shiny shoes, and bolts of fabric. To particularly good customers, a store owner might give *lagniappe* ("lan-yap"—the Louisiana expression for "a little something extra.") Oscar was famous for giving lagniappe.

On Saturday, the traditional day for special sales, Kate sometimes worked in the store, where she met everyone: the Texans passing through, the blacks, the whites, the people of color from Isle Brevelle. There were even a few Chinese, for after the war the adventurous merchant Jules Normand had imported Chinese field workers from Cuba. His experiment—which astonished Cloutiervillians—was a failure, but many of the Chinese men stayed and intermarried with local blacks and whites. In Oscar's store, Kate met the colorful Normand family; she listened to the yarns of people who owed Oscar money; she overheard choice gossip. Small-town general stores were favorite places for loafers, lovers, and busybodies—as Kate showed a decade later in the story "Azélie."

Her hero 'Polyte keeps a store key like Oscar's in his back pocket ("as large as the pistol that he sometimes carried in the same place"). His dimly lighted store is enticing, with its "strong, pungent odor of the varied wares and provisions massed within," and the hungry Azélie "seemed to like the odor, and, lifting her head, snuffed the air as people sometimes do upon entering a conservatory filled with fragrant flowers." 'Polyte falls helplessly in love with Azélie, and tries to bribe her with goodies that he charges to his own store account.

For an imaginative soul like Kate Chopin, Oscar's business was a way to earn a living—but local people were far more interesting than the merchandise.

In 1907, twenty-three years after leaving Cloutierville, Kate Chopin's daughter, Lélia, wrote to a literary critic that her mother had been "the Lady Bountiful of the neighborhood, dispensing advice and counsel, medicines, and, when necessary, food to the simple people around her, and in this way learning to know them and to love them too."

Lélia's contemporaries, descendants of the Cloutierville "simple people" who knew Kate Chopin, also heard that she was beautiful and charitable—but they questioned whether she was truly beloved by all. She was young for a maternal figure (twenty-nine when the Chopins moved to Cloutierville); she was a fashionably dressed city matron in a tiny country town; and she was too busy, with her own six children, to devote much attention to solving the problems of others.

Had she been a Lady Bountiful, Kate would have been sought after as a *marraine* (godmother) to numerous Cloutierville children—but she was a godmother only once. On the day that Lélia was baptized, Father Beaulieu—or someone—designated Kate and Oscar as godparents (*marraine* and *parrain*) for Céline Bussy, also baptized that day. The Chopins were an incongruous choice:

They were a generation younger than the Bussys, and from a different social class (Bussy was a carpenter). If Kate and Oscar Chopin ever paid any particular spiritual attention to Céline Bussy, no evidence has survived.

Kate Chopin was not apt to be thoroughly popular in Cloutierville. She was outspoken, and often (at least with Oscar) she performed excruciatingly accurate imitations of animals, birds, and priests. Still, Lélia Chopin claimed that her mother had loved "the simple people around her . . . for no matter how keenly they appealed to her wonderful sense of humor, she always touched on their weaknesses fondly and tolerantly, never unkindly."

But once Kate Chopin began writing stories based on her Cloutierville days, people she had known in the area doubted her tolerance, her kindness, and her discretion. Local people were recognizable in her stories—among them the village priest, Father Jean Marie Beaulieu (pronounced "Bole-yay" in Cloutierville).

Like many of his parishioners, Father Beaulieu was a transplanted Frenchman who spoke French all his life. After receiving his literary and theological education from St. Meen and Rennes, he was just twenty-two in 1854, when he sailed for the United States. First he settled in Avoyelles Parish, southeast of Natchitoches—where the Daughters of the Cross, struggling against local "pagan" customs, praised the generous and "good little priest." In 1856, he became Cloutierville's first pastor, a position he kept for the rest of his life. When Father Beaulieu died in 1897, Kate had already preserved his memory in her character Père Antoine.

Father Beaulieu's "sympathy, kindness, and patient understanding are reflected lovingly in many of her stories," Daniel Rankin says of Kate Chopin's writing—but Rankin, himself a Marist priest, exaggerates the importance and the heroic qualities of "Père Antoine," who appears only in the novel *At Fault* (1890) and two short stories from 1891. Nor is Père Antoine a very sympathetic character.

In real life, Father Beaulieu was said to make sick calls in any weather—but only if the summoning party would first catch and saddle one of the priest's horses, preferably his favorite red one, Lapin (rabbit). Catching Lapin meant clambering through the adjoining overgrown pasture, which was also the cemetery. Since superstitious Cane River people were reluctant to do that at night, Father Beaulieu was rarely asked to make house calls after dark.

In Kate Chopin's stories, Père Antoine does make house calls, but only if the house is not too far away: He goes to Madame Verchette's cottage in "For Marse Chouchoute," but she lives just at the end of Cloutierville's long street. Madame Verchette is very frail and weak, with sympathetic neighbors who help her with housework, and "often the good priest, Père Antoine, came to sit with her and talk innocent gossip." The priest entertains her, but the neighbors and the United States Post Office (which gives her troubled son a job) do much more to make her life easier.

Nor is Père Antoine of much use to Cane River country people in *At Fault*. Sometime after he blesses the precariously built cabin of the trusting old nurse Marie Louise, both the cabin and Marie Louise are swept away in a flood. When Père Antoine tries to calm the drunken hothead Grégoire Santien, Grégoire calls him a liar, and then goes off to be killed in a brawl.

Kate Chopin made Père Antoine most recognizable as Father Beaulieu in "Love and Easter" (1891), published the following year as "Love on the Bon-Dieu." The Cloutierville priest, who usually wore a cassock, was a short man with a large head, a small, thin mouth, and sad eyes—and in "Love and Easter," Père Antoine's "long, flapping cassock added something of height to his under-sized, middle-aged figure, as did the skullcap which rested securely back on his head."

"Love and Easter" centers around the need for Père Antoine: When Lalie, a poor country girl, goes to see the priest to write an IOU for her, Père Antoine writes the paper—but also disparages Lalie's grandmother as so "cross and crabbed" that "neither God nor the Devil" wants her. He browbeats the grandmother into sending Lalie to mass, and marvels that "no power on earth" can make Lalie "utter a word against her grandmother." He seems to have little understanding of childish fears or family loyalties. Most damning, though, is Père Antoine's attitude when Lalie misses mass, and the young carpenter Azenor goes to the priest for help. She is ill, the priest admits to Azenor, and "I shall go out to-morrow to see about her. I would go to-day, if I could—" but Père Antoine is too busy, the narrator points out, "picking the slugs from his roses." And so Azenor decides that only he will be able to take care of Lalie—by marrying her.

Kate Chopin may have believed in and admired Father Beaulieu when she lived in Cloutierville. No doubt she appreciated his kindness and generosity when he demonstrated them, and his efficiency in performing spiritual duties. But Père Antoine in "Love on the Bon-Dieu" is callous; in *At Fault* and "For Marse Chouchoute" he is likable—but ineffective. Oscar Chopin, whose store was always full of customers because he gave everyone credit, did more to aid the poor than most priests did—and even when he blessed marriages, Father Beaulieu did not seem optimistic about human possibilities.

Among the intricately linked French families of Cloutierville, weddings were constantly being celebrated—and kinship connections made every wedding joyous, spirited, and potentially contentious. Father Beaulieu's typical marriage sermon struck a doleful note:

The little amount of happiness that one enjoys in marriage, the usual dissensions that prevail therein; the terrible scandals which too often burst into the open; all these things should open the eyes of those who wish to undertake it and make them seek the root of the evil. Did God institute marriage to be the torment and torture of humanity?

"No, certainly," Father Beaulieu continued, declaring that "In the plans of God, marriage must be the binding tie of the family; it was established to give to the State good citizens, to the Church children." Moreover: "It unites inseparably the destiny of man to woman and is for them a cure for concupiscence"—the traditional view of St. Paul. Father Beaulieu exhorted the young couple to purify their souls rather than contracting their marriage "in the state of mortal sin, which is sacrilegious"; he reminded them that they had "promised each other a fidelity, an attachment, a love which death alone can break." Then he described the role that each should have toward the other:

> Monsieur, remember always to love your wife as Jesus Christ loved the Church, be her support, her protector, her strength so that the torrent of evil which exists in society can never force you to break your obligations.

> And you, madame, be submissive to your husband; be for him full of tenderness and love, but remember above all that you belong to God and that nothing in the world can authorize you to do what the law forbids you.

Father Beaulieu's conclusion emphasized obedience over pleasure:

> Walk both of you in the way of the Lord and remember that—You no longer belong to yourself—that there is no real happiness on earth except in virtue and that there is no possible way to reach Heaven except by observing the law of God and being obedient to the Church.

When she wrote *At Fault*, using Père Antoine as the priest who marries the central characters, Kate Chopin evidently thought Father Beaulieu's sermon too somber to be reproduced. Her Thérèse and David are married by the Cloutierville priest—but without a sermon at all.

There were things in real life, too, that no prayers and sermons could save— such as the life of Lovy Charleville, Kate's cousin and friend. Lovy's father,

Landry Charleville, a Cloutierville merchant and farmer, was Eliza O'Flaherty's cousin, and had known Kate O'Flaherty since she was a baby in St. Louis. Only one of his and his wife Pauline's five children had lived to adulthood: Aurore Victoria, "Lovy," was twenty-eight, still single and living at home, when Kate and Oscar Chopin moved to Cloutierville.

Kate and Lovy had been Children of Mary together at the Sacred Heart Academy, but Lovy, an untraditional young woman, had dedicated herself to a teaching career. She did not marry until the summer of 1880, a dozen years after her graduation from the Sacred Heart school, and her husband was her first cousin, Louis Abel "Chouchoute" Sers (Kate Chopin's first Cloutierville story would be called "For Marse Chouchoute.") A year after the wedding, Lovy became pregnant—and in July of 1882 she died in childbirth.

Lovy was thirty when she died—a year older than *The Awakening*'s Edna Pontellier when she takes her life into her own hands. During Kate Chopin's own childbearing years, Lovy was not the only one of Kate's friends to die in childbirth: Sarah Wilson Benoist Murrin, the widow of the financier Louis A. Benoist and the hostess for the lavish parties at Oakland plantation, had died that way in 1872.

When Lovy died, Kate was thirty-two and healthy, and she was no longer pregnant every year: Lélia was two and a half. Like Edna in *The Awakening*, Kate was able to see a life for herself beyond the role of mother-woman—but as she showed seventeen years later in *The Awakening*, women could not be absolutely freed from their bodies. In the last pages of the novel, when Madame Ratignolle gives birth in agony, Edna feels a "flaming, outspoken revolt against the ways of Nature"—a rebellion that must owe something to the last moments of Lovy Charleville.

.

As Kate Chopin discovered, Cane River country people were passionate in their loves and hatreds. Romance and marriage were subjects of intense interest; amorous glances were always noted; and the behavior of young people was scrutinized and clucked over.

After the war, which left many aristocrats penniless, quiet social evenings had replaced balls and duels and grand gestures—but moderation in thought and action was not always a Cane River trait. Like Armand in Kate Chopin's story "Désirée's Baby," set on a Louisiana plantation, some Cane River people were wont to fall in love at first sight, "like a pistol shot, or an avalanche, or a prairie fire rolling over all obstacles." (A Cane River country man named William Robinson claimed to have fallen in love at first sight with Eliza O'Flaherty's cousin Aurore Charleville, a St. Louis Sacred Heart graduate—while she was on her way to marry another man. Twenty years later, William Robinson finally convinced the widowed Aurore to marry him.)

Other Cloutiervillians were apt to marry unwisely, condemning themselves to a lifetime of regrets. Mrs. Scruggs's son from her first marriage, Sylvère DeLouche, had married the beautiful, Cuban-educated Maria Normand over the violent opposition of her mother. (Sylvère was known as a "sodden drunk": When Maria, a superb seamstress, made him a fine white linen suit, he drank too much and fell into the river, ruining her handiwork.) Maria's mother refused to attend the wedding; her father bravely gave a small reception at home, with cakes and champagne from New Orleans—and all of this took place on Kate Chopin's thirty-first birthday, February 8, 1881.

The DeLouche-Normand marriage proved to be unhappy, and Maria Normand's marital troubles reverberated throughout Cloutierville. She turned to another man—and both of them left their mark in Kate Chopin's stories of discontented wives and willing lovers.

But even in 1881, Kate Chopin was restless.

Chapter 10

"A CERTAIN LIGHT WAS BEGINNING TO DAWN"

MOTHERHOOD WAS MORE CA-
sual in Cloutierville than in New Orleans. Not expected to walk at an early age, children were carried about until they were fourteen or fifteen months old, and everyone watched everyone else's children. Stores were playlands for little ones, and even dances provided a *parc aux petits* for young children (as described in Kate Chopin's "At the 'Cadian Ball"). Babies might be swaddled in blankets, or spend their days rocking in *branles*, tiny cotton hammocks suspended from hooks in the ceiling. As described in Chopin's "Loka," a *branle* needed only a slight push to send it circling in "slow, sleep-inducing undulations," so that "[t]he baby who has not swung in a branle does not know the quintessence of baby luxury."

Most children began school when they were eight, and by 1882 Jean, Oscar, and George Chopin were all of age to attend the small village school across the street from their house. Mrs. Blanche Prudhomme had started the school in 1875, succeeded by her sister, Miss Sallie Griffin, and both taught geography, grammar, history, spelling, reading, arithmetic, philosophy, and "Scholars Companion."

Kate herself remained a voracious reader, with a growing interest in biology and anthropology. She kept the works of Charles Darwin, Thomas Huxley, and Herbert Spencer as "her daily companions," a St. Louis friend wrote later, "for the study of the human species, both general and particular, has always been her constant delight." Her new reading may also have been to aid her children: No science was taught in the village school. Still, her friend said,

Kate's duties in Louisiana "together with her reading, were not sufficient to occupy her mind."

She loved to play cards, and could play them anywhere in Cloutierville: They were a local obsession. (In Chopin's "A Night in Acadie," a justice of the peace, supposed to be at a wedding, is found playing cards instead.) Women rarely played for money, but they had a strict code of honor. Card playing had to stop when it grew late, and the players would leave their cards face-down, returning to them undisturbed the next day.

A few public entertainments were available for Cane River country citizens: Circuses played at Natchitoches (as in Chopin's story "A Little Country Girl"), and showboats occasionally rolled up the river to Cloutierville. The first electric lights ever seen in Cloutierville were on a showboat.

Cloutierville also had its own dance hall, above Landry Charleville's store. On Saturdays, Cane River people danced all night, accompanied by a squeaky fiddle or two and an accordion, with square-dance calls in French and English. At one such dance, Kate Chopin's character Chouchoute is especially acclaimed for "his pointing of toes; his pigeon-wings in which his feet seemed hardly to touch the floor." For young people, the dances throbbed with romantic possibilities: In Chopin's "At the 'Cadian Ball," couples flirt, change partners, and reminisce seductively, until pistol shots announce that *"le bal est fini."*

Most often, people met for parties in each other's homes, with gossip and card playing and a pot of gumbo and meat pies, which in Cloutierville were always baked. (In Natchitoches and Isle Brevelle, meat pies were fried in pork grease, and there was a heated rivalry as to whose pies were superior). Kate and Oscar's social circle included the Benoists, Charlevilles, and Rachals—all relatives—together with the Scruggses, Normands, DeLouches, and Sampites, all related to one another by marriage.

The Scruggses were known for their feasts at Lisa Anne DeLouche Scruggs's enormous dining-room table. Dr. Scruggs's favorite dinner was game birds—quail, snipe, or robins cooked with the berries they had eaten—but even an ordinary Scruggs dinner party included baked chicken, fried chicken, and pork patties, as well as eggs, ham, potatoes, and Louisiana rice.

Kate and Oscar Chopin also gave their own *veillées*, informal, spontaneous parties with word-of-mouth invitations: "We are goin' to have *veillée* at the house." When guests were invited to "pass *veillée*" at the Chopins', there would be card playing, and sometimes an "evening of music"—with guests taking turns at playing the piano, singing, and dancing. Although the Chopins could give formal dinners (Kate had monogrammed heavy silver forks, engraved *KO'F*), she and Oscar particularly enjoyed board games. They owned a very long and inviting gaming table, with three large drawers on each long side and a green velveteen surface.

Kate amused herself in other ways. She ordered her expensive and modish clothes from New Orleans; she rode and visited everywhere, soaking up atmosphere and listening to people's stories. She continued to shock people (and embarrass Oscar's relatives) by smoking Cuban cigarettes—which had to be rolled, with a booklet of cigarette papers and an adroitly applied bit of saliva.

The ladies' pastimes—visiting all day, sleeping all afternoon—were not enough for Kate's vigorous energies and imagination. She may have toyed with being younger than she was: In the census in 1880, she is listed as twenty-seven instead of thirty. Oscar is listed as thirty-seven, a year older than his actual age, but the children's ages are correct.

By 1880, Kate's childbearing years were over, almost certainly by choice: According to her niece July Waters, Kate "would never have had children she didn't want." Women of her era did limit their families, and not just by closing the bedroom door to their husbands: Although promoting contraception by mail was illegal under the Comstock Laws of 1873, most women did know at least part of "the secret" of contraception. There were douches, condoms, abortions, and abortifacients (and in Philadelphia, a Dr. Foote had invented a diaphragm called the "womb veil"—but he was eventually sent to jail for promoting it). When Kate went to St. Louis for several months in October 1881, she was visiting her mother—but also practicing a most effective form of contraception.

Meanwhile men were rarely absent from Kate Chopin's life in Cloutierville: "She was the prettiest thing around," she dressed up in the evenings, and young men flocked about her. She was not domestic, she was powerful socially, and she was considered rather aggressive for a woman. She was much more popular with men than with women—and for a woman her age there were temptations.

As she showed later in *The Awakening*, it was very possible for a woman in her late twenties, who had married without passion, to discover her own deep desires in the sensual atmosphere of Louisiana. With Edna, "[a] certain light was beginning to dawn dimly within her,—the light which, showing the way, forbids it." At first, that dangerous consciousness "served but to bewilder her. It moved her to dreams, to thoughtfulness, to the shadowy anguish which had overcome her the midnight when she had abandoned herself to tears."

In Cloutierville, Kate was given to long rides after dark, and to seeing the night as her own time.

By 1881, Kate O'Flaherty Chopin had been married for eleven years. Oscar Chopin had grown stout and predictable, gentle and lovable and comfortable. He was a good husband, and Kate no doubt recorded the general view of Oscar when the Creoles in *The Awakening* agree that Léonce Pontellier is "the best husband in the world," and Edna Pontellier is "forced to admit that she knew of none better." The Chopins' daughter, Lélia, always expressed a "warm feeling" about her father.

Still, Oscar would have retained little mystery for a wife who was still young and curious. As a store clerk, Oscar did not know the world of the more raffish men in the Cane River area—a world of whiskey and gambling and swift, violent attacks and brutal loves. There was little that Oscar knew that Kate did not also know—and there was another world beyond the civilized amusements of the town and the sedate expectations of marriage.

In Cloutierville, Kate—like Edna—was given to questioning "her position in the universe." But "the beginning of things, of a world especially, is necessarily vague, tangled, chaotic, and exceedingly disturbing. How few of us ever emerge from such beginning! How many souls perish in its tumult!"

In rural Louisiana there was no particular winter of discontent: Everything moved to a slow, lingering rhythm of the seasons. Kate grew to appreciate the changing sights of the woods and fields: lazy rivers choked with purple water lilies, riverbanks covered with trees and vines, lizards and turtles sunning themselves, birds singing joyously in the morning, mockingly at night.

Kate Chopin's Cane River characters love the colors of spring as she did, the season when the cotton plants send out their first green shoots against the red-brown soil. Her characters drink in the life-giving scents of country life: sassafras, and pungent camomile. La Folle in "Beyond the Bayou" welcomes the beauty of the country: "[T]he white, bursting cotton, with the dew upon it, gleamed for acres and acres like frosted silver in the early dawn," while the violets, magnolias, and roses bring "enchantment beneath the sparkling sheen of dew."

In summer, there were swift and sudden storms almost every day, followed by moist, shimmering sunshine (as in Kate Chopin's story "The Storm"). In the long, hot, dusty days of August, even the leaves hung limply, and chickens dragged their wings—while the scent of decay, ripening and rotting fruit, perfumed the air. But in September, with warm rains, yellow flowers bloomed in the ditches. China trees began turning yellow, pecans waited for the first frost to fall, and there was a kind of death in the air. In late cotton season, the Cane River seemed to turn a deeper blue, and in the clear water, dead trees looked like skeletons.

But Kate Chopin loved best the warm dark nights, filled with the songs of insects and the croaks of frogs. Among her favorite flowers were the "four o'clocks," which opened at four in the afternoon and bloomed all night. She described the nights over and over, with their grim and vibrant beauty, and in one of her few first-person stories, she expressed a restless wish: "[A]ll the same

I could not help thinking that it must be good to prowl sometimes; to get close to the black night and lose oneself in its silence and mystery."

Halloween in Cloutierville was a frolicsome time, with much cavorting and wearing of masks and scaring of the young and the superstitious. In Kate Chopin's *At Fault*, Halloween is "[p]erhaps the only night in the year that some or other of the negroes did not lurk in fence corners, or make exchange of nocturnal visits." Nor are whites any braver: According to the otherwise reckless Grégoire, Halloween or "Tous 'saint' eve" is the time "w'en the dead git out o' their graves an' walk about."

In the Cane River country, Mardi Gras was unimportant, but Halloween was a holiday to frighten and thrill children. In the Chopin household in late 1882, with half a dozen children ranging in age from two and a half to eleven, there were enough to make teams of tormentors. But Halloween in 1882 would not have been a raucous time—because Papa was very ill.

Oscar had had a violent attack of "swamp fever"—the Cane River country term for any lingering fever believed to arise from foul air, decaying vegetation, and swamp miasma. Natchitoches Parish in the 1880s was still crisscrossed with bayous, and out of the swamps came mosquitoes and mysterious, deadly fevers.

Whenever anyone took sick, the first fear was yellow fever, the "saffron scourge" that Kate and Oscar Chopin had lived through in 1878 in New Orleans. From that epidemic, they remembered the stench and fumes of carbolic acid, the endless funeral processions, and the piles of unburied bodies; there had been a quarantine, and anyone who could had fled the city. The Chopins had had particular reason for fear: Little Felix Chopin had just been born in January of 1878, and children were especially susceptible to overmedication and dangerous fumes.

Devastating yellow fever outbreaks, against which victims were helpless, were also not uncommon in the Cane River country. When Oscar Chopin was just nine years old, his grandfather, Charles F. Benoist, had died in the epidemic of 1853.

But when Oscar Chopin took sick in 1882, it was close to the end of the yellow fever season, which stopped with the first hard frost. Nevertheless, a person could develop the deadly symptoms overnight: the fever that turned the skin yellow, the excruciating back and head pains, a sore tongue and mouth and palate, infected eyes, and hemorrhages of the nose and gums. There might also be internal hemorrhaging, which was nearly always fatal, ending with black vomit.

During the first days of Oscar's fever, the Cloutierville doctors, Samuel O. Scruggs and J. F. Griffin, were very concerned. On October 29, Dr. Scruggs visited once; then twice on October 30, and then four times on October 31 (he charged two dollars for each visit). On November 1, he made just one call on Oscar, and then did not see him again until November 16.

Oscar's intermittent fever may have begun long before October of 1882. He had an unpaid bill for his own illness six months earlier, and on that same date, April 16, the doctors had also visited six-year-old Fred Chopin. They visited Fred again on August 20, and sold "crude petroleum" to the Chopins on that date and again on September 15. (Petroleum was placed in puddles and stagnant bodies of water, to keep mosquitoes from breeding.) Oscar had not paid that bill, either.

By November 6, Oscar was well enough to summon Dr. Scruggs to treat another patient, identified in the doctor's bill as "Morgan's son," apparently an employee or tenant. Morgan's son was treated for five days, an average duration for yellow fever—but Oscar had not recovered.

In New Orleans, Kate Chopin could have summoned Dr. Faget, the obstetrician who had discovered how to distinguish yellow fever from malaria. ("Faget's sign" is still used to diagnose yellow fever.) But in Natchitoches Parish a country doctor like Sam Scruggs, who had had his training forty years earlier, was the best available.

Dr. Faget would have begun by taking Oscar Chopin's temperature and pulse: The unique symptom of yellow fever was a slowing pulse rate despite a high or rising fever. The diagnosis could be made in the first few hours of the disease, and yellow fever, according to Dr. Faget, had "one single effervescence—only one paroxysm," with no remission. Doctors sometimes prescribed unproven remedies (calomel, mustard plasters, bloodletting, homoeopathic massages of the kidney region with spirits of turpentine)—but most advised simple purgatives, mild tonics, and bed rest.

But if the patient's pulse rate did not decrease while the temperature kept rising, then the fever might be malaria, the treacherous "swamp poison" characterized by false recoveries. Malaria was an ever-present threat in swampy, moist Louisiana: Between spring and winter, most people had a bout of chills and fever. Malaria's symptoms included a very high fever, which might peak at 107 degrees and last an hour, a day, or more. Afterward, the patient might seem to be healthy—as Oscar Chopin was—for another twelve to sixty hours, before another attack. Other symptoms were chills, anemia, a coated and moist tongue, and an enlarged spleen—so swollen that it could be felt with the fingers.

A remedy did exist: Quinine, derived from the bark of the cinchona tree, had been used for two centuries as a weapon against malaria. Without quinine, a patient might have attack after attack, grow progressively weaker, and finally die of respiratory or other ailments. Still, most people, especially in rural areas, believed that, if left alone, "swamp fever" would run its course, as yellow fever did.

It was not until December 8, nearly six weeks after Oscar's first recorded attack, that Dr. Scruggs finally gave him quinine. Quinine was not considered dangerous, nor was it expensive, but an overdose might cause nausea, vomiting, and diarrhea—and with a severely weakened patient, an overdose of quinine could kill.

The standard dose for malaria patients was ten grains—but Dr. Scruggs and his partner Dr. Griffin, who visited twice on December 8, gave Oscar forty grains of quinine, or four times the usual dosage.

On December 9, Dr. Scruggs visited again, this time performing a "distention"—for which he charged five dollars. The bill for December 10 lists "Last nights vis." for Dr. Scruggs, and records another distention that night, performed by Dr. Griffin—and there the medical record ends.

Oscar Chopin was dead.

Oscar's death was not recorded in the church register in Cloutierville. Father Beaulieu may have been too busy attending to other sick people, or he may have had a fever himself. But Oscar's death was reported in the St. Louis newspaper ("On the 10th inst., after a short illness"). Kate ordered a coffin, for eighty dollars, from Samuel Parson.

It was just fifteen days before Christmas, and Kate Chopin was a widow, with six children. She would never again have Oscar to play with their children, to egg on her imitations and share her laughter, and to lie beside her at night, in the warm intimacy of marriage.

His funeral had to be held quickly, because bodies were not embalmed. Before burial, ice was placed in glass jars and put in the coffin, to keep the body cool. For Oscar's wake, mourners would be assigned shifts to sit in a circle around the open casket and guard the body—lest cats or dogs jump up on it and begin gnawing.

Cloutierville funerals were social events, with the wake held in the home of the deceased, and everyone in town was expected to go. White people visited in the house, while plantation hands (blacks and people of color) came in the back door to pay their respects. For those not in mourning, a Cloutierville wake was a grand party. People brought food to share and ate with great gusto; children dashed around the house, whooping and hollering.

Oscar was buried in Cloutierville, in the little cemetery next to St. John the Baptist Church. Kate—like her mother twenty-seven years earlier—was faced with explaining the death of a father to his young children.

Christmas in Cloutierville was a family holiday, with midnight mass and games and toys. The Chopin children still had their village playmates, but there was no more Papa to romp with them, and Mama was alone in the big master bedroom.

Later, Kate drew on her own life for the beginning of At *Fault*, her first story of widowhood:

> When Jérôme Lafirme died, the neighbors awaited the results of his sudden taking off with indolent watchfulness. It was a matter of unusual interest to them that a plantation of four thousand acres had been left unincumbered to the disposal of a handsome, inconsolable, childless Creole widow of thirty. A *bêtise* of some sort might safely be looked for.

Thérèse Lafirme both was and was not Kate Chopin: Kate was also suddenly widowed, and handsome, and definitely the target for curious and concerned neighbors who hoped for some mischief. But she was hardly childless, nor had she inherited an unencumbered plantation guaranteeing her support for the rest of her life.

Possibly Kate described herself when she wrote about Thérèse's grief:

> Of course Thérèse had wanted to die with her Jérôme, feeling that life without him held nothing that could reconcile her to its further endurance. For days she lived alone with her grief; shutting out the appeals that came to her from the demoralized "hands," and unmindful of the disorder that gathered about her.

But Kate did not need any of the "hands" to point out that she would have to take on new responsibilities. Not only was she now both mother and father to young children—Lélia would be just three years old on New Year's Eve—but she had also inherited an estate that was deeply, even hopelessly, in debt.

"She felt at once the weight and sacredness of a trust, whose acceptance brought consolation and awakened unsuspected powers of doing," Kate Chopin wrote of Thérèse Lafirme—but the responsibilities Kate inherited were more painful than sacred. Most urgently, Oscar's poor management and his generosity to his customers had left Kate over twelve thousand dollars in debt.

She had real estate debts for Oscar's property on 71 Decatur Street in the French Quarter. Oscar had long been slow to pay taxes on this land (known as "Square 29"): As early as 1875, he had been receiving threatening letters about unpaid back taxes. In 1878 and 1879, there were judgments against him for New Orleans city taxes, and in August of 1881 there was a letter threatening foreclosure. From February to May of 1882, Oscar received letters about possible mortgage arrangements, and in September 1882 he sold or rented the building to one Jean Cadillon.

Oscar's estate also owed taxes on five scattered parcels of land in Natchitoches Parish—one on Little River and four at different points on the Cane River known as the Benoist Place, the Pierson Place, the Rachal Place, and the Fontenot Place (the Chopins' home). Oscar had owned or rented livestock, vehicles, and merchandise, and the total tax assessment was $229.60.

There were other debts. Oscar owed money to a Mess. O'Brien and Co., from whom he had been borrowing since 1880 to finance his farm and store operations, at an 8 percent interest rate, and he had been unable to repay them. There were also the bills from F. J. Quinlan of "Boss" Hat House on 27 Magazine Street in New Orleans. Oscar may have ordered the hats to sell— or to please the fashionable Madame Chopin.

Some of Oscar's creditors tried to be considerate of the young widow. H. C. Goodwin, editor and proprietor of the weekly Colfax Chronicle, wrote to the estate on February 7, 1883, about two dollars still owed to him, but added that if Mr. Chopin "leaves a wife and children who need it, I do not want my pay." Kate settled that debt immediately, then continued struggling with the financial morass Oscar had left her.

In January 1883, after she received a letter threatening to seize the property, she paid overdue state and parish taxes for the previous year ($32); she also paid off a $262 debt to R. M. Walsley & Co., New Orleans, probably one of Oscar's suppliers. She paid the doctors' bill on March 8, 1883, and gradually paid family members their share of the succession (the Louisiana term for inheritance): $561.52 to Oscar's brother Lamy, $520.53 to their sister Marie, $462.73 to brother-in-law Joseph Henry, $125.06 to his wife, Oscar's sister Eugénie.

Through much of 1883, Kate whittled away at her debts: fifteen dollars on April 20 to Joseph Charleville (the Cloutierville notary, her mother's cousin), for doing the inventory of her goods; forty dollars on May 5 to Father Beaulieu for the funeral; and ninety-four dollars on May 18 for the New Orleans hats.

Kate also had to establish herself as legal guardian of her children: On March 31, 1883, she petitioned to be appointed "Tutrix" of her children. Her petition was granted, and she took the "natural tutrix's oath" on April 6. On April 19, Oscar's brother Lamy took an oath as "Under Tutor" of the Chopin children.

Although she paid the smaller bills, Kate could not pay off all the debts she inherited. Finally she petitioned to sell some of her property, but her petition (filed on September 8, 1883) was not granted by Judge David Pierson, of the Eleventh District of Louisiana, until October 30.

At the public sale of property from Oscar's estate on December 11, 1883—a year and a day after his death—Kate sold eighty-one hundred dollars' worth of land, and all the property, real and personal, that she could spare, but that was still not enough to pay all her debts. She still owed five hundred dollars in attorneys' fees to Watkins and Scarborough for handling the succession, and she had many other, smaller debts to individuals. The final accounting was signed and concluded on March 15, 1884, fifteen months after Oscar Chopin's death.

In the meantime, Kate had decided to keep Oscar's businesses—the store and some of the plantations—and run them herself. In those months, Kate had discovered more about the pleasures of being an independent woman—and that there were many men willing and eager to console a young widow.

Chapter 11

SCANDAL

~~~~~ FEW OF KATE CHOPIN'S WID-
owhood stories are portraits of grief. Chopin's widows are more apt to find
themselves in "early spring . . . a languor in the air; an odor of jasmine in
every passing breeze" or amid "[s]oft air . . . laden with a hundred subtle
sounds and scents of the springtime." Chopin's widowhood stories emphasize
hope, not bereavement: spring, not winter; possibility, not loss.

And so it was with the widowed Kate Chopin. The shock of loss came in
the winter, but there was no time for long grieving. After Oscar died "in the
midst of the cotton harvest," Kate's St. Louis friend William Schuyler wrote,
"It was then that Mrs. Chopin, having rejected all offers of assistance from
kindly relatives, undertook the management of her plantations and developed
much ability as a business woman."

Besides her brother-in-law Lamy, the "kindly relatives" would have included
Oscar's sister Eugénie and her husband, "old Joe" Henry, on their Grand Ecore
plantation, and Eliza O'Flaherty's cousin, Joseph Charleville, the town notary
who inventoried Kate's property. But unlike many widows, Kate Chopin did
not put her late husband's finances into the hands of the most capable or eager
male relative. She had grown up in a house full of widows who managed their
own lives and their own money—and her decision to run Oscar's businesses
was not an unusual step for the great-great-granddaughter of the steamboat
entrepreneur "La Verdon."

It was challenging work, requiring a clear head, firm hand, and organiza-
tional ability. She worked in the store; she corresponded with New Orleans

cotton factors; she met with local planters, farmers, and sharecroppers and drew up contracts. She stocked the store; she convinced many of Oscar's debtors to pay their bills; and she kept careful financial records (a habit she continued, later on, when she began to sell her stories). She became an accomplished entrepreneur.

Kate also still remained an eager gatherer of others' stories. Much later, in the first-person sketch called "Vagabonds," she described her own encounter with a local tramp—who had also had run-ins with her children Lélia and Jean. That "l'le girl o' yo's," Chopin's tramp says, "—some the darkies tole 'er I was her cousin, an' she cry an' bellow like she want to take a fit. An' that bigges' boy o' yo's he say' I want keep clear o' that plantation, I know w'at's good fo' me."

"They're a proud lot," Kate had herself say.

When she sent out "Vagabonds" for publication, she crossed out her children, and also omitted two significant words. "I could not help thinking that it must be good to prowl sometimes," the narrator says, "to get close to the black night and lose oneself in its silence and mystery and sin." With heavy strokes, Kate crossed out "and sin."

She was a brisk businesswoman during the day, with servants, relatives, and at least one accommodating neighbor—Emma Perrier—for child care. But the dark night was her own, with its prospects for silence and mystery and sin.

In Cloutierville in 1883, men flocked to aid the handsome widow, Madame Chopin. Later, Cloutierville neighbors told their children and grandchildren, "There were many young ladies and young matrons who were sometimes a little jealous of the lovely Kate. When Oscar died, some of the wives felt that their husbands' sympathy for the young widow prompted them to be a little more solicitous in helping her to solve her problems in the store and on the plantation than was necessary."

Emma Perrier, too, told youngsters years later that Kate Chopin was not only "snooty toward children," but was also "a *dirty* lady. You don't know *all* that she did."

When villagers gossiped, generations later, about who was "sweet on Kate," one name kept recurring.

It was no secret to anyone—including his wife—that Albert Sampite was pursuing Kate Chopin.

When Kate Chopin first arrived in Cloutierville, Albert Sampite had been married for eleven years. The handsome planter wrote his name as "J. Albert Sampite" (Joseph was his first name), but he was always known as Albert, with the French pronunciation: "Al-bear." The last name, which used to be written with an accent mark—Sampité—was pronounced "Sam-pi-TAY."

Albert was twenty-four and his bride, Lodoiska DeLouche, twenty-five when they were married by Father Beaulieu on November 7, 1868. Lodoiska ("Loca") Sampite was a tiny woman who gave birth to six children, but only two lived. Marie was the age of Kate Chopin's son Frederick; Joseph Alphonse was the age of Lélia.

Albert Sampite was the son of French immigrants who by the 1850s were well settled in the Cane River country: As late as 1862, the Sampites paid taxes on sixteen slaves. Albert's mother had died during the war; his father's second wife was another Charleville cousin of Eliza O'Flaherty's. Albert Sampite spoke French as readily as he did English, and it was said that he had some education in France, as Oscar Chopin did. Albert, born March 16, 1844, was just six months older than Oscar.

But Albert Sampite had fought in the war, enlisting at seventeen as a private in Company G of the Twenty-Sixth Louisiana Infantry. Captured at Vicksburg, he was paroled and released, and then he walked, barefoot, all the way back to Cloutierville—over a hundred miles, in the scorching summer sun. Soon he was back in the army, and nine months later he was taken prisoner again and exchanged at Alexandria, Louisiana. He did not leave the army officially until June 6, 1865.

Albert knew the violence and the blood and the smoke of war, and he had seen vultures circling the battlefield (as in Kate Chopin's story "The Locket"). He knew the horrors of Vicksburg—where the embattled civilians dug in like moles in caves, and the entrenched Confederate soldiers and civilians alike ate mules and rats and were grateful to have them. Albert had been nineteen at the time, staring death in the face.

After the war, while other planters struggled, Albert Sampite enriched himself. He owned three cotton plantations and commissaries, and Oscar Chopin had been his factor in New Orleans. By the time the Chopins arrived in Cloutierville, Albert Sampite's enormous plantations employed forty-two blacks and "mulattoes," according to the 1880 census. In the 1880s, the taxed value of Albert Sampite's property tripled (and by the 1890s he was buying land in Washington County, Colorado, evidently as an investment). He was one of the wealthiest men in the Cane River country.

At thirty-five, Albert was also lean and vigorous, with a well-trimmed mustache and long goatee, pointed eyebrows, and dark eyes. Depending on the light, he could look devilishly handsome, or just devilish—and he also had a streak of cruelty toward the "hands" working for him. As Kate Chopin would have noticed, Albert Sampite was the image of the wealthy Creole planter in popular novels: sun-bronzed, steel-eyed, strong, at home on horseback as well as in the fields.

Albert Sampite had a French charm and an undeniable way with women ("ladies' men run in the Sampite family" was a Cloutierville saying). According to one of his descendants, "He was what some might call a womanizer. Even when married, he demonstrated an unflagging interest in women"—especially in a certain restless and fashionable young widow who shared his love of fine horses.

By the 1880s, Albert Sampite was also restless and unhappy at home, although much of that unhappiness may have been of his own making. He and his wife, Loca, proved to have little in common: She was interested in home and family and children, while he preferred hunting, gambling, drinking, and riding about at night. Albert liked to roam—traveling to Natchitoches for a day or two, or going to New Orleans to check the cotton markets. Even in Cloutierville, he was rarely home. Many legal documents bear his name as witness: He was around town, available to sign documents. He also frequently sued his neighbors for money owed.

Loca Sampite, meanwhile, was a plain country woman who, like other planters' wives, liked to order expensive black taffeta dresses from New Orleans—but she could not compete with Kate Chopin's glamour and sophisticated airs.

Loca was never called by her exotic first name, the fruit of her father's momentous meeting with a Russian duke in New Orleans (hearing that his new friend's wife was about give birth, the duke had reportedly said, "If it's a girl, name her Lodoiska"). Loca's name was Marie Lodoiska, but people were apt to mangle her name: Lodovasha, Locadie. Mostly the younger generation called her by the plainest of names: "Tante Loca."

Loca could be stubborn and steadfast in her distrust of the flirtatious widow Kate Chopin. They moved in the same social circles—Mrs. Scruggs was Loca's mother—but Kate and Loca approached each other warily, and both could be unkind. Knowing the gossip, people in Cloutierville would have understood why Kate Chopin, a decade later, gave the name "Loka" to one of her most unpleasant characters, whose "coarse, black, unkempt hair framed a broad, swarthy face without a redeeming feature, except eyes that were not bad; slow in their movements, but frank eyes enough. She was big-boned and clumsy." The same Loka also longs for the woods, where "Choctaw Joe and Sambite played dice every night by the campfire" and "fought and slashed each other when wild with drink."

Albert Sampite was a violent, angry man who gambled and drank too much— but he was also dangerously attractive.

* * *

Loca did have a romantic past. As a young girl before the war, she had been sent to school in Bardstown, Kentucky, where many southern planters sent their children. (Loca's half-brother, the younger Samuel Scruggs, went to Bardstown for medical training.) According to family legend, Loca's father, J. B. Sylvère DeLouche, sent her to Kentucky with her own slave, a little black girl, to take care of her needs. Loca and her slave traveled back and forth by steamboat between Bardstown and the Cane River country, and on one trip Loca—in her teens at the time—met a Yankee general, who fell passionately in love with her and wrote her letters while she was in school. That was her one romance—but it ended.

Loca, eighteen the year the fighting began, lived at home in Cloutierville during the war, with her mother and stepfather, Dr. Scruggs. When the rampaging Yankees tore through the Cane River country, Loca hid the silverware in her hoopskirt, then later daringly slipped it past the Union soldiers on the local ferry.

Three years after the war's end, Loca made what appeared to be a fine marriage: Albert Sampite's wealth, good looks, charm, and social position made him highly eligible. Apparently as a dowry, Loca's mother gave her two parcels of land on August 22, 1868, three months before her marriage. But Loca never forgot her earlier romance—and later on, she would never forgive Kate Chopin.

Albert Sampite liked to ride around the Cane River country, consulting with fellow landowners about boundaries and crops, horses and overseers and field hands—and the Chopins happened to own a parcel of land that adjoined his. It was not unseemly, or even odd, for Monsieur Sampite to meet with Madame Chopin at the point where their lands intersected: They might even need to discuss where her property ended and his began. Nor was it odd that they discovered a mutual interest in land and farming and horseflesh.

Kate sold that parcel of land at auction to pay her debts, but there were still many opportunities for meetings—chance or otherwise—in and around Cloutierville. The young widow continued her explorations of Cloutierville, on horseback and on foot: "Vagabonds" shows that she knew the woods, the muddy banks, and the treacherously slimy spring turf.

When merchandise arrived for Kate's store, by boat from New Orleans, she had to go down to the landing to get her goods. It was not uncommon for a local planter like Albert Sampite to be at the landing at the same time—and he might also help carry the widow Chopin's goods back to the store, and help her sort and shelve them in a back room or out-of-the-way cellar.

Somehow, too, Albert Sampite became involved in Kate Chopin's money matters. Among the papers he saved are letters to his children, deeds to land,

and five IOUs, all dated 1883, from Cloutierville residents promising to pay Kate Chopin a total of $301.08, at 8 percent interest. Albert was apparently helping Kate to collect money owed her—and he also valued her financial records enough to keep them with his own personal papers.

There were still other ways in which a willing couple could make connections. While the village dances were unseemly for a widow, there were always weddings and wakes and christenings to attend. (Virtually every wedding created more links of kinship, making Kate and Albert distant cousins by marriage many times over.) Every meeting was an opportunity for talking, and exchanging glances, many of which were duly noted by interested villagers.

And in a sudden storm, it was not impossible for two people to take refuge alone together in a house, or a barn—a sensual scenario Kate Chopin sketched out, years later, in her most explicit short story, "The Storm." Its hero is the planter Alcée—the name for all her heroes based on Albert Sampite.

Kate Chopin knew about women's longings for men who were not their husbands: She wrote about them in *The Awakening* and many other short stories, among them "A Respectable Woman" and "Madame Célestin's Divorce"—in which a polite, respectful man does not own the keys to a woman's heart. Kate also knew how to arrange a clandestine affair. Her Cane River country characters meet while shopping at the local store ("Azélie"); they catch glimpses in church ("Love on the Bon-Dieu"); they hold business meetings in the woods ("A No-Account Creole"); or they just happen to be in the same place, far from home ("At the 'Cadian Ball").

Cloutierville wives and mothers and widows were supposed to stay at home, as Loca Sampite did—but Kate Chopin's Cane River stories show an extraordinary knowledge of outdoor life at night, including the silvery mists in which no one could see clearly, and the snakes and owls and uncanny night creatures. Kate had a particular love for the warm dark country nights, which could conceal a multitude of mysteries.

No one knows whether Kate Chopin and Albert Sampite had begun their romance before Oscar Chopin died.

At least one of Albert's descendants heard that he and Kate were lovers while she was still married—which might explain Kate's restlessness, her escape trip to St. Louis alone, and Oscar's stay at Hot Springs alone. But everyone agrees that after Oscar's death, the affair blossomed.

Kate and Albert were discreet about their romance, by the standards of a century later. If anyone wrote down dates and places and eyewitness descriptions, none of those survive—although Cloutierville residents would certainly have been able to recognize him in her writings. But an affair in the 1880s was not simply a matter of physical consummation. Much less than that could be called "making love": flirting, significant glances, stolen kisses, secret silences.

Kate Chopin, in her diary eleven years after the first spring of her widowhood, suggested that more than flirting had gone on in her life: "I had loved—lovers who were not divine," she wrote, and "And then, there are so many ways of saying good night!" And even in her published writings, Kate left proof that her relationship with Albert Sampite was much more than a casual friendship. It shaped what she wrote about women and men, and love and lust and forbidden desires.

According to Lise DeLouche Charleville, who had been a playmate of the Chopin children, Kate Chopin and Albert Sampite were very "fond" of each other, and "admired each other." But Lise DeLouche Charleville was reluctant to be pinned down: "Kate was a beautiful woman, and every man admired her," Miss Lise used to tell her younger friend, Lucille Tinker Carnahan.

Other Cloutierville residents were more specific when they gossiped with the younger generation: Ivy DeLouche, Albert Sampite's great-niece, heard throughout her childhood that Albert (whom she called "Nonky") had had an affair with Kate Chopin. Albert Sampite's grandchildren heard that "Pépé Albert" had been infatuated with Kate Chopin. Some believed that she was also very much in love with him; others thought that he just "chased her down."

Kate's other Natchitoches Parish relatives evidently did not know about the affair—or at least, they did not speak about it to the younger generation. Still, Kate's niece July Waters, born in 1895, thought it not unlikely that Kate would become involved with the handsomest man in town, wife notwithstanding. Aunt Katie, everyone knew, was "very advanced in her thinking."

Loca Sampite definitely knew about the affair: The Sampites' daughter Marie always said that Kate Chopin destroyed her parents' marriage.

When Kate Chopin came to write about men who kindle desire, and who devote themselves to sexual pleasure, she named them all Alcée, an abbreviated form of Albert Sampité: Al. S-----é and Alcée are both pronounced "Al-say."

Alcée Laballière in "At the 'Cadian Ball" and "The Storm" is "a handsome young planter" who plays cards and enjoys "talking crops and politics"—unless "[a] drink or two could put the devil in his head." Albert Sampite drank continuously, although he rarely seemed drunk—but he had a violent and brutal side that alcohol encouraged.

The character Alcée Laballière in "At the 'Cadian Ball" is, like Albert Sampite, a sensual son of the soil, who works stripped to the waist and pants "a volley of hot, blistering love-words" into the face of his prissy cousin Clarisse. He marries Clarisse—but he desires the "Spanish vixen" Calixta. Then, five years later, in Chopin's sequel "The Storm," Alcée and Calixta have each married others, but they have not forgotten an earlier rendezvous, with its secrecy and mystery and sin: "[H]e had kissed her and kissed her and kissed her; until his senses would well nigh fail. . . . Now—well, now—her lips seemed in a manner free to be tasted, as well as her round, white throat and her whiter breasts."

Kate wrote "The Storm" in 1898, long after leaving Cloutierville: By then, she was a famous St. Louis author. Still, she never attempted to publish "The Storm," which contains the most passionate scene in all of her writing. When Alcée is with Calixta, "[h]er firm, elastic flesh . . . was knowing for the first time its birthright. . . . When he touched her breasts they gave themselves up in quivering ecstasy, inviting his lips. Her mouth was a fountain of delight. And when he possessed her, they seemed to swoon together at the very border-land of life's mystery."

Kate's last published Alcée, the roué Alcée Arobin in *The Awakening*, also has more than a little of Albert Sampite. He has "a good figure, a pleasing face," and his manner is "quiet and at times a little insolent." He admires horses; he flourishes at night; and his wooing of Edna Pontellier is practiced, and almost sincere. Edna feels "like a woman who in a moment of passion is betrayed into an act of infidelity, and realizes the significance of the act without being wholly awakened from its glamour." Arobin's charm and "animalism" appeal to Edna, and with him she shares "the first kiss of her life to which her nature had really responded. It was a flaming torch that kindled desire."

In *The Awakening*, Kate even divided the name *Albert* between Edna's two lovers: *ALcée* and *RoBERT*.

Albert Sampite filled Kate Chopin's imagination for the rest of her life—but she left him.

When the accounting of Oscar Chopin's estate was officially completed on March 15, 1884, all Kate's financial affairs were in order. Oscar's father's lawsuit against the United States government had also been settled at last, with an "award of $2,111 plus 5% interest from 4-1-1864."

Kate was running the store and supervising Oscar's plantations, raising her children and learning to control her own finances—but she was also intimately linked with another woman's husband, and that made her distinctly unwelcome in some Cloutierville circles. Among Catholics there was no divorce, and even under Louisiana civil law, in case of divorce for infidelity, "the offender may not marry his or her accomplice." If Kate Chopin had wanted to marry Albert Sampite, she could never do so, not so long as Loca Sampite was still alive.

The subject of divorce did make Kate bitter—bitter enough to write about it in her first novel, *At Fault*. The main character, the Catholic widow Thérèse, renounces the man she loves because he has been divorced—but Thérèse cannot control her imagination. She wonders, as Kate Chopin must have wondered: What if she *had* married the man she loved, defying the church and the world?

> Here she smiled to think of the storm of indignation that such a marriage would have roused in the parish. Yet, even facing the impossibility of such contingency, it pleased her to indulge in a short dream of what might have been.

> If it were her right instead of another's to watch for his coming and rejoice at it! Hers to call him husband and lavish on him the love that awoke so strongly when she permitted herself, as she was doing now, to invoke it! She felt what capability lay within her of rousing the man to new interests in life. She pictured the dawn of an unsuspected happiness coming to him: broadening; illuminating; growing in him to answer to her own big-heartedness.

If she had wanted it, Kate Chopin would have had no lack of advice. Father Beaulieu would have been more than willing to remind her of the sacredness of marriage vows, and Eliza O'Flaherty was urging her daughter to come home to St. Louis. And in Cloutierville, Eliza's irascible cousin Landry Charleville had strong opinions about wives and mothers who refused to behave properly. On one occasion, clucked over by villagers for years afterward, Landry Charleville took it upon himself to berate Kate Chopin in the middle of Cloutierville's one street, during one of her promenades on horseback. He had grabbed the bridle of her horse and was shaking his finger furiously—when Kate decided that she had heard quite enough. She grabbed her little whip, and she whipped him.

But Albert Sampite, for all his charm, had another, darker side to his character. He had a violent temper and treated his wife cruelly—and he would beat her with a leather strap.

Wife beating was not uncommon in Cloutierville: Some villagers claimed that it was the French custom for men to beat their wives and chase other women. (Alexis Cloutier, the village founder, had beaten his wife to make her wash his feet every night.) But Kate Chopin did not regard wife beating as customary or forgivable. Raised in a household without adult men, she had not seen the domestic violence or heavy drinking that often accompanied marriage—and in the first Chopin story of a wife beater, "In Sabine," the long-suffering wife escapes.

Like many wife beaters, Albert Sampite was irresistible when he was sober, but haughty and cutting when he drank. Whether he was violent toward Kate Chopin cannot be determined—nor is it known whether she sent him back to his wife in a spirit of self-sacrifice, as Thérèse does in *At Fault*.

Kate's romance with Albert was no secret in Cloutierville. According to descendants of those who knew them, "The general talk was that he was in love with the pretty widow, and there were those who believed that she, too, was in love with him. And that may be why she suddenly gave up the store and the plantation and went back to St. Louis."

Kate decided to return home to her mother, choosing a mother's love over a man's uncertain passions. Kate made the same choice that Edna makes in *The Awakening*, when she leaves her lover Robert to be with the mother-woman Madame Ratignolle. Kate chose friendship over passion, mother-love over romance—and then spent the rest of her life wondering about that decision.

When she left Cloutierville, Kate left behind some of her boys with Oscar's brother Lamy. It was not uncommon for a widow's sons to be raised by relatives, if she couldn't "do for the boys." After a certain age, boys in large Louisiana homes were often exiled in their own wing, the *garçonnière*, where their uncivilized behavior would be less damaging to the rest of the household.

Kate left behind a walnut dresser, a handsome piece of furniture, with her neighbor Emma Perrier. A pair of crystal filigree perfume bottles that had belonged to Kate eventually passed to Lodoiska Grandchamp, another Cloutierville resident.

But there were two items that Kate particularly wanted Albert Sampite to have. One was the gaming table, the long green-topped one with the three drawers on each side—probably because of his love for gambling. The other was an oil lamp, clear glass with a slight amethyst tinge—suitable for someone who rode around at night. (Late in life, his grandchildren used to watch Albert Sampite go out to feed his horse at night, carrying a lantern.)

Kate left Albert and Loca Sampite, but took away memories—which she recorded in poems about dark nights, walks in the woods, regrets and unspoken secrets from the past. One of her earliest poems, "Psyche's Lament," is named for the mythical nymph whose lamp drops wax on her sleeping lover, Cupid, driving him away forever. The poem concludes, "O Love, O God, O Night come back to me!"

Many of Kate Chopin's short stories also take place at night, and Robert's farewell note to Edna in *The Awakening*—"Good-by—because I love you"—catches her eye because the paper lies in the light of a lamp.

Sometime in mid-1884, Kate Chopin returned to St. Louis, to the house on 1125 St. Ange Avenue. Kate had left St. Louis as a bride of twenty; she returned as a widow of thirty-four, with her youngest boy, Felix, barely old enough for trousers.

Kate's uncle Roger McAllister had died while Kate was in Louisiana, and his widow, Amanda, still lived with Eliza O'Flaherty. The two sisters, married to business partners, had shared the same household for most of their lives, and they may have inspired Kate Chopin's description of the intimate, confiding friendship between Edna and Adèle in *The Awakening*. (The names are similar: Edna and Eliza, Adèle and Amanda.) Eliza and Amanda had outlived their husbands, but not their loyalty to each other.

When Kate returned to the household where she had grown up, Eliza O'Flaherty was fifty-six, and her dark hair had turned gray. Married at sixteen, Eliza had been a widow for almost thirty years. According to Rankin, Kate Chopin's children admired their grandmother:

> Mrs. O'Flaherty had, together with her poise and her gentility, an assured way of saying gently very positive things to her grandchildren. The Creole way of speaking English, as Mrs. O'Flaherty used it, with her half lost *r*'s and a certain precision in the use of words, delighted Kate Chopin, whose children remember their mother's pride in her mother's speech, and in her indescribable air of caste and good breeding.

At first, Kate moved in with her mother, her aunt Amanda, and the other McAllisters, but the house at 1125 St. Ange was evidently too small. Soon Kate, Eliza, and Kate's children moved across the street, to 1122 St. Ange.

For the children, St. Louis had many advantages. Cloutierville had a catch-as-catch-can village school that existed only when there was a dedicated teacher to run it. After elementary school, Cloutierville pupils had to be sent to boarding school for further education: The Sampites' daughter, Marie, attended Grand Coteau, the Sacred Heart school in central Louisiana. Kate herself had gone to the Sacred Heart boarding school when she was five, Lélia's age when Oscar's estate was settled—but boarding schools were expensive, and Kate liked having her children around her. Moving back to St. Louis solved the problem of the Chopin children's education—for St. Louis, by the 1880s, had developed one of the finest free public-school systems in the United States.

Thanks to the efforts of the energetic philosopher Susan Blow, St. Louis was

the first city in the nation to open kindergartens. The best and brightest thinkers flocked to teach in the city schools, where their superintendent was William
Torrey Harris, editor of the *Journal of Speculative Philosophy* and spearhead of
the "St. Louis Movement," a circle of internationally known Hegelian philosophers. At Central High School, the curriculum was more rigorous than in
most small colleges: ancient and modern history, English history and literature,
geography, mathematics, natural science, and Greek and Latin language and
literature.

In St. Louis, Kate's daughter would not have to be sent away to school, and
her sons' school curriculum would include sports as well as academic subjects
(Felix Chopin became a 140-pound quarterback). Catholics who went to public
school were not, apparently, disapproved of: Kate's distant relative Condé Nast,
later the editor of *Vogue* and *Vanity Fair*, was the age of her son Oscar, and
young Condé attended the St. Louis public schools before a rich aunt sent him
to Georgetown University.

Kate Chopin moved back to St. Louis in time for the 1884–85 school year,
which began the first week in September. It would be her first northern winter
with children, with leggings and boots and winter hats and scarves and mittens—but she would be sharing all that with her mother. Leaving Cloutierville
meant abandoning the seductions of a secret romance, but Kate's departure
would not close that chapter of her life.

Nor did her coming to St. Louis mean that she would always be cherished
and protected again, in the bosom of her family, for on June 29, 1885, the *St.
Louis Post-Dispatch* printed somber news:

DIED

O'FLAHERTY—At noon, on Sunday, June 28, at the residence of her
daughter, Mrs. Kate Chopin, 1122 St. Ange avenue, ELIZA O'FLA-
HERTY, aged 56 years.

Funeral from the Church of the Holy Angels, on St. Ange Avenue
near Chouteau avenue, on Tuesday, June 30, at 8:30 a.m., thence
to Calvary Cemetery. Friends are invited to attend.

According to Rankin, Kate was "literally prostrate with grief."

After the war, writing had been Kate's salvation and consolation: It had restored her to life. Now, shattered by her mother's death, Kate was rescued by
a friend's suggestion that she write.

Dr. Frederick Kolbenheyer, the obstetrician who assisted at the births of her
sons Oscar and George, had read Kate's letters home from Louisiana. He had

admired her writing, and, as reported by Rankin, Kolbenheyer became "a constant visitor. He began bringing letters descriptive of Louisiana that she had written from Cloutierville or Grand Isle, and read them to her. He used the manifestations of talent in these letters to persuade and encourage her to write for publication." Kolbenheyer, as a family friend, also knew that Kate needed money: Most of Eliza O'Flaherty's estate had been swindled away by a trusted friend who preyed on widows, and then disappeared with their property and money.

The Austrian-born Kolbenheyer was a radical thinker, and he had a fascinating circle of literary and intellectual friends—people who did not exist in Cloutierville. St. Louis was a center for freethinking philosophy, women's rights, journalism, and artistic and musical experiments of all kinds—and a spirited widow with a sense of humor and a way with words was always welcome. Writing was also one of the few careers open to women on equal terms with men.

Nudged by Dr. Kolbenheyer, and possibly by other friends as well, Kate Chopin began writing with a professional career in mind. Exactly four years after Eliza O'Flaherty's death, Kate started the story "Wiser than a God," about a young woman deprived "for the second time of a loved parent," who throws "all her energies into work." The character's calling is music, and she tells a suitor that she will not marry him, because "it doesn't enter into the purpose of my life."

Within a few years after her mother's death, Kate Chopin had found her own calling—and it was not to be a wife again or the mistress of a Louisiana planter. When the *Philadelphia Musical Journal* accepted "Wiser than a God" for publication, Kate Chopin had turned in another direction. And although she continued to look back, to draw on her Louisiana years for passion and inspiration, she had found a new purpose in her life, with goals all her own.

Chapter 12

AT FAULT

WITHIN A YEAR AFTER HER mother's death, Kate Chopin had bought a house at 3317 Morgan Street (now Delmar) between Grand and Jefferson, in a newer part of St. Louis. (The St. Louis city directory lists her as "Katie Choplin.") Morgan Street meant a new beginning for Kate and her children, half a city away from the old neighborhood and the scrutiny of relatives like Aunt Amanda, who would surely notice that Kate no longer attended church.

The following year, Kate revisited Natchitoches Parish for the first time.

It had been three years since her sudden move to St. Louis, and much had happened—including a shocking and romantic adventure for Oscar's sister Marie. With her wedding date already set, Marie Chopin had abruptly jilted the man her family wanted her to marry, the well-bred Buddy Henry. She preferred Phanor Breazeale, a fast-talking would-be lawyer who was penniless: He had grown up milking cows and working in the fields. By the age of fourteen, Phanor had made himself notorious for stuffing ballot boxes—and later, caught in a shooting fray between blacks and whites, he had had to flee to Texas. And when he decided to give the sweet, reserved Marie an engagement ring, he did it in a way calculated to enrage her relatives: He won the ring in a poker game.

Nevertheless, Marie was twenty-three, old enough to make up her own mind, when she married twenty-six-year-old Phanor Breazeale on July 15, 1884, at her sister Eugénie's place near Grand Ecore. The wedding was sudden, and Kate Chopin—who had moved back to St. Louis—missed it.

For their visit three years later, Kate and her children stayed with Oscar's

brother Lamy, his wife Cora Henry, and daughter Nini at Chopin, Louisiana,
where on June 21, 1887, Kate wrote to Marie Chopin Breazeale:

> Your kind sweet letter, I received yesterday; and I assure you, we
> shall certainly pay you a visit before returning home: that is as
> many of us as you can accommodate, for I cannot believe that your
> house has such unlimited capacity as to receive the whole family.
> We left St. Louis wednesday morning, and got here thursday night,
> after rather a tiresome trip. The children are not looking well, &
> Petsy has been sick since we got here: though he is better now. You
> know they all had measels lately. I hope they will soon get real
> strong and well.
>
> We are so anxious to see you. I want to see Phanor and the baby,
> because I have never seen them, and I want to see you for I hear
> you have grown extremely stout.
>
> Cora would have written, she says, if I had not been writing. She
> is looking so well. Nini, I think rather thin, but I suppose it is due
> to her recent illness.
>
> With love to yourself & Phanor and a kiss for baby.
>
> Your loving sister,
Katie

Once they did meet, Kate got along famously with Phanor Breazeale. They
liked to roll and smoke cigarettes, play cards, tell stories, and make fun of
religious and other hypocrisies. (Phanor, raised a Catholic, had run away from
home three times to escape being confirmed. Later, out of orneriness, he joined
the Masons, but proclaimed himself a militant atheist.)

A year later, in 1888, Kate Chopin started her first short story, in which the
demure Euphrasie, like Marie Chopin, has two very different suitors. Kate tried
various titles ("Euphrasie," "A Maid and Her Lovers," "Euphrasie's Lovers"),
and wrote them all in her manuscript account notebook, apparently purloined
from her eldest son: The name "J. B. Chopin" appears on the cover. Kate's
first version of "Euphrasie" was a thirty-thousand-word novella that she asked
her friend to read ("Gave to Dr. Kolbenheyer-April," she wrote in her account
book). He returned it in June of 1890, and she revised it, paring it down to ten
thousand words.

The "Euphrasie" story was about a love triangle: Euphrasie is torn between
a penniless Creole planter and an ambitious New Orleans businessman. (There
is a bit of Phanor Breazeale in each of them.) Kate struggled with the story

through the summer of 1891, when it was accepted by the prestigious *Century* magazine. By the time the story was published in 1894, under the title "A No-Account Creole," Kate Chopin was already a nationally famous author, the first to use the Cane River country as a literary world.

In Cloutierville, the dramatic loves and bitter hatreds that inspired Kate Chopin's fiction continued. Eleven months after Kate's return visit and the year she would begin writing "Euphrasie," Loca Sampite left her husband's house— and four months after that, on September 24, 1888, she filed for a legal separation.

Madame Lodoiska Sampite, her petition said, had resided with her husband from the date of their marriage, November 17, 1868,

> until about the 24th of May of the present year, 1888, when she left the matrimonial domicil and returned to her mother's, Mrs. S. O. Scruggs, on account of the habitual violent temper, cruel treatment & outrages of her said husband towards her, carried by him to such excess, that, on several occasions, he has inflicted, upon your Petr [Petitioner], severe blows & injuries with the hand & a leather strap, without provocation on the part of Petr, to justify such abuse. She avers that in a moment of despair she returned to her mother's, and after living there for several weeks, she made up her mind to return and did return to her husband and to try whether further patience and forebearance would have the effect of bringing about a permanent reconciliation & harmony between them. They have proved of no avail. The ill-treatment, outrages & violent words & conduct of her said husband towards her were repeated recently, & were of such a brutal character, as to drive her back to her mother's, where she now resides; to render their living together insupportable; and to necessitate a separation from bed & board from her said husband, and the dissolution of the community of acquets and gains existing between them.

Loca Sampite asked that all their property be inventoried and appraised, and that her husband be enjoined from disposing of any of it until that was done

> for the reason that she fears he will, during that time, dispose of the property held in community, to her prejudice & irreparable injury. She also alleges that a definitive partition of the effects owned & held in community between them is necessary.

Loca remained with her mother (Dr. Scruggs had died in 1886)—and Loca, her petition said, "has been an invalid for about a year; at times, unable even to rise from her bed, and has to pay for everything she needs or wants done." She had no income, she said, and "no clothing but the little she took with her when she left her house, the balance being in the possession of her husband, as well as her furniture which is her individual & separate property, all of which she is in actual & pressing need." She asked for a monthly allowance, and for her clothing and furniture, and said that the community assets amounted to more than fifteen thousand dollars. She also petitioned for custody of the Sampite children, twelve-year-old Marie and nine-year-old Alphonse, and for a monthly sum to support them.

Although she knew about her husband's eye for other women, Loca Sampite did not mention that in her petition. That would have been both embarrassing and useless—since infidelity in men was often winked at.

Judge David Pierson ruled that an inventory and appraisal should be made of the Sampites' goods, that Mrs. Scruggs's home should be designated as Loca's "domicil," and that Loca should be awarded twenty-five dollars per month by her husband, until the termination of the suit, "unless there should exist strong reasons to deprive her of it."

Yet the legal separation was not granted. On the outside of Loca Sampite's petition is written, "In this case on motion of plffs. [plaintiff's] counsel in open court, this case is dismissed on plffs costs. D. Pierson, Eleventh District Judge." That notation is dated April 30, 1889.

Evidently Loca Sampite withdrew her suit—or possibly Judge Pierson advised her that he would not grant a legal separation, for reasons of his own. If Judge Pierson himself refused the separation, that may explain Kate Chopin's use of the name Pierson in *At Fault*, the novel she began on July 5, nine weeks after the dismissal. Chopin's Pierson is a comical, party-loving storyteller who enjoys recounting the humiliations of others. He is also black—and because of heated racial animosities, almost any white southerner in the 1890s would have taken offense at the use of his name for such a character.

In any case, Loca Sampite may have had other reasons for changing her mind about a legal separation. Between September 1888, when she filed her petition, and April 1889, when she withdrew it, several things had happened.

Albert Sampite had gone to see their daughter, Marie, at the Sacred Heart boarding school at Grand Coteau, possibly as a gesture of reconciliation. The girls loved visitors: "Marie is expecting her Papa every day, for her mama wrote to her he was coming," Marie's friend Clémence Benoist wrote home to Cloutierville in November 1888. Later, Clémence reported happily, "Marie's Papa was here a few days ago, he gave us the money you sent."

Then, two months later, in January 1889, Kate Chopin became a published author, when the Chicago magazine *America* printed her poem, "If It Might Be"—with its hint that Kate might still be available for someone who wanted her:

> If it might be that thou didst need my life;
> Now on the instant would I end this strife
> 'Twixt hope and fear, and glad the end I'd meet
> With wonder only, to find death so sweet.

> If it might be that thou didst need my love;
> To love thee dear, my life's fond work would prove.
> All time, to tender watchfulness I'd give;
> And count it happiness, indeed, to live.

America was an impressive literary and political journal for Kate's debut: Its contributors included Algernon Swinburne, James Russell Lowell, Ella Wheeler Wilcox, and Theodore Roosevelt. Word of that publication no doubt reached Cloutierville—and Loca Sampite may have assumed that Kate Chopin would remain with her literary friends in St. Louis, and not trouble the peace of people in Cloutierville.

Kate also did something else in the spring of 1889 that would have fanned Loca's hopes for her own marriage: Kate returned to Cloutierville to have Oscar's body shipped back to St. Louis. The blacksmith Casimir Perrier made the box for the casket, sealing it with resin, and sent it by train from Derry (the railroad station at Chopin, Louisiana) to St. Louis.

Oscar was buried in Calvary Cemetery in St. Louis on April 26, 1889, in the O'Flaherty plot, just behind Eliza O'Flaherty (she was buried between her husband and son Tom). The elder Thomas and his son George were honored by a large obelisk, but Oscar's grave has no marker. Possibly Kate, who was eking out a living for herself and six children on income from land and rental properties, could not afford a gravestone.

Just four days after Oscar Chopin's burial in St. Louis, Loca Sampite withdrew her petition for a separation from her husband.

"To love and be wise is scarcely granted even to a god," Kate wrote above the short story "Wiser than a God," which she began a month after the Sampites' reconciliation. The character Paula chooses her professional career as a pianist over marriage to a rich young man who says that her life's work should be to make him happy. Years later, he appears as a sad domestic fellow whose wife no longer amuses him—while Paula has become famous, and is pursued by a professor determined to win her.

Kate was also working on two novellas, "Grand Isle" and "A Poor Girl" (both destroyed), but in her next short story she experimented with describing another kind of marriage. In "A Point at Issue!," a couple, thinking themselves avant garde, decide to live apart for a while, pursuing their separate intellectual interests. But jealousy (which Kate described with gentle satire) puts an end to that marital experiment—and perhaps to Kate's own wondering about the possibilities of a long-distance romance.

By the end of 1889, "Wiser than a God" had been published in the *Philadelphia Musical Journal* (for five dollars), and "A Point at Issue!" had appeared in the *St. Louis Post-Dispatch* (for sixteen dollars). Both were the usual short-story length—2,500 to 3,000 words—and both were accepted for publication by the first journals Kate tried. She had also written two more short stories, "Miss Witherwell's Mistake" and "With the Violin," but they were rejected half a dozen times each before they appeared in print. In 1888, the sheet music for Kate's piano polka, "Lilia," had also been published by H. Rollman & Sons of St. Louis.

As the 1880s ended, the Sampites in Cloutierville were momentarily reconciled, and Kate Chopin in St. Louis was a published author. She had turned away from the past—her life as wife, mother, and scandalous woman in Louisiana—and was also rejecting the future that might be expected of her, as a widow in an upper-middle-class and well-respected family. Instead, the late 1880s for Kate Chopin became a time of spiritual change and renewal. For the first time in her life, she had a room of her own, and enjoyed the blessings of solitude.

After her mother's death and her move to Morgan Street, Kate Chopin began to make a new community of friends. They were people who read Guy de Maupassant and the latest fiction writers, who questioned established religions, and who devoted themselves to intellectual clubs and social reform. Some were New Women, of the kind Kate described in her earliest short stories: professional women like Paula the pianist in "Wiser than a God," or dedicated intellectual women like Eleanor Faraday in "A Point at Issue!" (although Kate could not resist poking gentle fun at Eleanor for her lofty philosophy).

In "A Point at Issue!" Kate also portrayed a women's rights activist: Margaret, "owing to a timid leaning in the direction of Woman's Suffrage," is "looked upon as slightly erratic." She corresponds with "a certain society of protest" and wears "garments of mysterious shape, which, while stamping their wearer with the distinction of a quasi-emancipation, defeated the ultimate purpose of their construction by inflicting a personal discomfort that extended beyond the powers of long endurance."

Chopin was evidently alluding to bloomers, an emancipated style that had come (and gone) several decades earlier—but she had her own original styles, as her son Felix once recalled: "She was not interested in the woman's suffrage movement. But she belonged to a liberal, almost pink-red group of intellectuals, people who believed in intellectual freedom and often expressed their independence by wearing eccentric clothing." (Kate Chopin's descendants do not know what the "eccentric clothing" consisted of.)

Kate Chopin was not an activist, but her earliest stories were about women who created their own destinies. In "Miss Witherwell's Mistake," written three months after "A Point at Issue!," Chopin created still another career woman: Miss Frances Witherwell, columnist for the *Boredomville Battery*.

Kate knew several newspaperwomen. Her St. Louis circle eventually included Florence Hayward, the columnist and London correspondent for the *St. Louis Globe-Democrat*; Sue V. Moore, editor of *St. Louis Life*; Grace Davidson, who took over *St. Louis Life* from Mrs. Moore and retitled it *The Criterion*; Rosa Sonneschein, creator of *The American Jewess*; and Frances Porcher, the short-story writer and reviewer for William Marion Reedy's *St. Louis Mirror*. In Louisiana, the *Natchitoches Enterprise*, from 1893 on, was edited by Kate's friend Camilla Lachs Breazeale, the widow of Phanor Breazeale's brother.

But even early in her career, with the character of Miss Frances Witherwell, Kate Chopin was making fun of old fashioned notions about fiction writing. Miss Witherwell's lovelorn niece asks advice for a story she claims to be writing, about a young couple who are deeply in love, but are kept apart "by an unjust fate or by a sordid parent." Miss Witherwell eagerly advises, "Your hero must now perform some act to ingratiate himself with the obdurate parent . . . Let him save the father from some imminent peril—a railroad accident—a shipwreck. Let him, by some clever combination, avert a business catastrophe—"The niece's response—that such a story is unrealistic—leaves Miss Witherwell "aghast." She has only one solution: "Marry them, most certainly, or let them die."

For "Miss Witherwell's Mistake," Kate Chopin received her first rejections, from *Harper's*, *Scribner's*, and *Drake's Magazine*—but *Drake's* did send a personal criticism: "Letter—too spun out—clever story—excellent character sketching." Then the *Century* and *Home Magazine* also rejected the story, and it was not published until February of 1891, in *Fashion and Fancy*, a St. Louis periodical.

Kate continued to write. A month after "Miss Witherwell's Mistake," she wrote her first Christmas story on December 11, 1889. "With the Violin" was also rejected by four national magazines, without comment, before it appeared in the *St. Louis Spectator* on December 6, 1890. The story of a hungry orphan whose life is saved by a generous violinist, "With the Violin" inaugurated Kate Chopin's career as an author of children's stories.

Her own children were already too old for her stories—Lélia was eleven that winter—but in the 1890s writing children's stories was one of the best roads to professional literary success.

Victoire Verdon, her great-great-grandmother the keelboat entrepreneur, was the last of Kate Chopin's female ancestors to have a profession. Lovy Charleville Sers, the second cousin who died in childbirth, was the only one of Kate's contemporary relatives to have a career outside the home, and hers was one traditionally open to women: teaching.

By the 1890s, wealthy husbands were supporting a growing class of idle women, like Lou Dawson and Belle Worthington in Kate Chopin's *At Fault*: "two ladies of elegant leisure, the conditions of whose lives, and the amiability of whose husbands, had enabled them to develop into finished and professional time-killers." Mrs. Dawson and Mrs. Worthington are *nouveau riche* targets of satire, who spend their afternoons with cards, matinees, and scandals.

Until the last part of the nineteenth century, single working women were rarely paid enough to support themselves at more than a poverty level—but in the 1890s there were New Women making their own way in St. Louis. Thekla Bernays, one of Kate Chopin's contemporaries, knew five languages, translated German plays and operas into English, published articles describing "Currents of Literature" in six different nations, studied Russian drama, admired Emma Goldman, aided the St. Louis Negro Self-Culture Association, and worked for women's suffrage. She was a thoroughly cosmopolitan intellectual, Jewish, and European-educated (one of her European relatives married Sigmund Freud). But Thekla Bernays was still most often described in St. Louis newspapers as the sister of Dr. Augustus Charles Bernays, a surgeon who in 1894 performed the first cesarean section for placenta previa.

Most St. Louis New Women supported suffrage, and most—like Thekla Bernays and the journalist Florence Hayward, the attorney Phoebe Couzins, and the educator Susan Blow—chose not to marry, but to direct their efforts to improving society. The 1890s was the decade of the single woman: A greater percentage of American women remained single than in any other decade before or since. American women's life expectancy already surpassed men's, and single women with a purpose—like the women's rights advocate Susan B. Anthony—were often exceptionally long-lived.

The campaign for the vote occupied St. Louis women throughout the last part of the nineteenth century. In Missouri, Virginia Minor, founder and guiding spirit of the state's Woman-Suffrage Association, was the plaintiff in *Minor*

v. *Happersett*, called "the Dred Scott decision for women." In that 1875 case, the Supreme Court ruled unanimously that women did not have the right to vote under the Fourteenth Amendment. (On her death in 1894, Virginia Minor left money to Susan B. Anthony, but left her dining-room furniture, vases, pictures, and silverware to William V. Byars, a poet friend of Kate Chopin's.).

The rights of women were constantly discussed in intellectual circles of the 1890s. Kate Chopin's women friends all supported suffrage, as did William Marion Reedy, editor of the *St. Louis Mirror*. Being antisuffrage was seen as reactionary (although the Missouri General Assembly would not give women the right to vote until 1919). Still, Kate Chopin never directly recorded her opinion of women's suffrage: According to her son Felix, "She was, in many ways, a lone wolf."

Also, as early as 1890, Kate had begun making enemies among St. Louis women—with a novel that seemed calculated to offend.

At Fault, a novel set in Louisiana and St. Louis, was Kate Chopin's first book, and it was partly autobiographical—about a Cane River country widow's passionate conflicts and wrenching choices.

Kate began *At Fault* with Thérèse Lafirme, a "handsome, inconsolable, childless Creole widow of thirty." Thérèse is blond and blue-eyed, but otherwise resembles Kate Chopin in her "roundness of figure suggesting a future of excessive fullness if not judiciously guarded." (American beauty standards were in flux in the 1890s, between the athletic Gibson girl and the voluptuous Lillian Russell, celebrated for her extravagant appetite. Ever since the Civil War, when millions of southern women had gone hungry, plump flesh had been considered a prime womanly attraction and a sign of health. When Fanny in *At Fault* gains ten pounds, she is told that she looks the best she has ever looked in her life—and Kate Chopin was often praised for her majestic figure.)

The action in *At Fault* starts with the arrival of David Hosmer at Thérèse's Cane River country plantation. He is a St. Louis businessman and an earnest Yankee type, tall, thin, and sallow, "a man who has never learned to laugh." Nevertheless, Thérèse agrees to his building a sawmill on her land, and that decision changes her life forever.

At Fault is the story of love almost denied. After Thérèse and David fall in love, she learns that he is divorced. She believes that divorce is wrong, and so is desertion: David should have been more loving and forgiving to his alcoholic wife, Fanny, and divorcing her, Thérèse says, was "the act of a coward." (David did, honorably, allow his wife to get the divorce, and he also doubled her alimony without being asked.) David dutifully remarries Fanny, but she proves to be a hopeless alcoholic (one of the first female alcoholics in American fiction). After Fanny drowns in a flood—despite David's heroic efforts to rescue her—Thérèse and David are finally married.

Kate Chopin described in detail Thérèse's principles and David's yearnings, but she gave much less space and sympathy to Fanny—whose role was not unlike Loca Sampite's. Fanny was the suffering wife whose husband no longer loved her, and who was no match for a glamorous widow. Although Kate wrote *At Fault* six years after her own departure from Cloutierville, she still could not afford to sympathize with someone like Fanny.

Kate also made Fanny an outsider, from St. Louis, and much of *At Fault* is a satire on the St. Louis that Kate knew. Compared with Louisiana, St. Louis is cold and gray; Missouri accents are unpleasant; and Fanny is a whiny, weak character who kills time with matinees and "reading morbid literature." Her friends Lou Dawson and Belle Worthington have more vitality but more artificiality: Belle wears suffocating perfume, dyes her hair, and pins on false blond curls.

(Kate Chopin herself was not above using artificial means to enhance her attractiveness: On one visit to Natchitoches, she apparently wore a black short-haired wig—or at least her young relative Carmen Breazeale, a child then, remembered her with short dark hair at a time when Kate's photographs show that her natural hair was abundant, gray, and usually worn in an upswept twist. But Kate Chopin, after all, was a visiting writer who also smoked cigarettes publicly—and was therefore not bound by the restrictions on ordinary women who would be considered irredeemably "fast" if they used hairpieces.)

With the character of Belle Worthington, Kate also directed her satire against certain individuals: A Mrs. Harriet Worthington was the partner of her sister, Mrs. Anna Sneed Cairns, in St. Louis reform activities. The Sneed family had been Kentucky Presbyterians (the background Edna Pontellier runs from in *The Awakening*), and they were known for their Christian principles, their campaign for temperance, and their founding the United States' first university chartered solely for women, Forest Park University for Women.

Harriet Worthington was one of the main contributors to the university, for which Anna Sneed Cairns was collecting funds in 1889 and 1890, while Kate Chopin was writing *At Fault*. Harriet Worthington shared her sister's militant Protestantism and hatred of alcohol—and Kate Chopin found such stances amusing and irritating. In *At Fault*, Belle Worthington's last name is no accident: She enjoys drinking, and her only religion is a clearly faked Catholicism that she foists upon her daughter in a transparent effort at social climbing.

In *At Fault*, Kate Chopin also made fun of women's clubs (although she belonged to them herself). In St. Louis, David's sister Melicent attends a "progressive euchre party" which she describes as "three hundred cackling women," one of whom goes to card parties "only to show her hands and rings." Melicent also detests a clubwoman who has written an original paper on "An Hour with Hegel" and another (a "dry mystical affair") on "Light on the Inscrutable in Dante"—yet does not notice her opponent's trickery with cards.

In *At Fault*, Kate did not limit herself to satirizing local women. Mr. Lorenzo Worthington, an absentminded pedant, strongly resembles the off-in-the-clouds intellectuals of the St. Louis Movement, with their *Journal of Speculative Philosophy* and their Hegelian jargon. In fact, Denton Snider, a professor in the movement, was engaged in the 1890s in a grandiose synthesis: a sixteen-volume analysis of the psychological basis of all knowledge. Snider and his ponderous colleagues were gleefully lampooned by William Marion Reedy in the *St. Louis Mirror*—and Reedy may have abetted Kate Chopin's portrayal of Lorenzo Worthington, who had his own wildly ambitious project: a chronicle of all the world's religions.

The authors on Mr. Worthington's bookshelf are exactly the ones Kate O'Flaherty read as a schoolgirl: Bulwer (the first author in her commonplace book), Racine, Molière, Scott, Shakespeare. Yet Mr. Worthington is most inspired by the least significant facts: He announces with great seriousness that Saint Monica, the mother of the great Saint Augustine, was a "wine bibber."

When she wrote about the Worthingtons' daughter, a pale and drooping Sacred Heart pupil, Kate Chopin satirized another target she knew intimately. (Although she was no longer a practicing Catholic by the 1890s, Kate still paid her dues to the Children of Mary Sodality.) Her Lucilla believes that "a relaxed tendency of the spinal column" is "a forbidden indulgence"; she wears her dull convent uniform everywhere; and she performs little religious rituals that seem incongruous and bizarre to a Louisiana servant. Ninette, the Louisiana planter's child (probably named for Nini, Kate's ten-year-old niece) has much more common sense.

Kate also evidently intended to make some kind of point or inside joke by using the last name Hosmer for her hero David and his sister Melicent. Hosmer was a common St. Louis name: During Kate's youth, the future sculptor Harriet Hosmer had attended the St. Louis Medical College in the building that became the Gratiot Street Prison, and by the 1890s three of her statues were displayed in St. Louis. In 1885, Frederick L. Hosmer of St. Louis published a volume of religious poetry, *Thoughts of God in Hymns and Poems*, and in 1894 he became pastor at the Church of the Unity, the Unitarian church in St. Louis (but that was four years after *At Fault*). Fanny and David Hosmer are remarried by a Unitarian minister, and Kate Chopin knew many local Unitarians, among them the Eliot family and Anna L. Moss, one of her literary correspondents.

But the most intriguing Hosmer–*At Fault* connection concerns James Kendall Hosmer, a Washington University professor of literature and author of historical books, including *The Colored Guard, History of the Jews,* and *Short History of German Literature*—all books which would have interested Kate Chopin. In 1890, when Chopin wrote *At Fault,* J. K. Hosmer had a six-year-old daughter whose name was Melicent—and Kate Chopin's use of the name Melicent Hosmer in *At Fault* must have meant something to contemporary St. Louisans. But its significance is now lost.

In *At Fault,* Kate Chopin told several interlocking stories, only one of them a man's story: the tale of Joçint—part-black, part-Indian, rebellious, and dangerous. Joçint is an adolescent, like Kate's sons: In 1890, her sons ranged in age from twelve to nineteen. Kate herself was an indulgent mother who did not force her children to go to school, or to get jobs, and she—like Thérèse—had some sympathies with Joçint, who hates the monotonous sameness of his work at Hosmer's sawmill. But Joçint is rude toward his father, brusque to everyone, and eventually deadly. When he sets fire to the mill, another impulsive, rebellious young man, also a motherless son—Grégoire—kills him.

Kate Chopin knew many families who had buried sons: In Cloutierville, Numa and Fanny DeLouche—Loca Sampite's brother and his wife—lost two sons in one day. During the war, virtually every Confederate family, including Kate's own, had buried sons. Still, there was a special grief for sons who killed themselves through their own wildness—like young Tom O'Flaherty, dead of a broken neck after his reckless buggy race. (At the time Kate wrote *At Fault,* Tom had been dead for sixteen years.)

Although she made Joçint in *At Fault* a mixed-blood character, Chopin did not draw on the "tragic mulatto" literary convention of the 1890s: the portrayal of mixed-blood males as always militant, rebellious, and melancholy, because of their warring racial inheritances. Joçint chooses to be violent: Environment interested Kate more than heredity. With Joçint, she described the turmoil and grief that disobedient sons bring to their parents—and as the mother of sons, she pondered how best to raise young men so that they would thrive, instead of destroying themselves and others.

With the character of Grégoire, Kate Chopin created another kind of young man: an earthy yet dandyish fallen aristocrat who loves both guns and fancy high-heeled boots—not unlike the charming Frenchmen she knew in Cloutierville. But *At Fault*'s new kind of Cane River society has no room for the old-fashioned feuding, dueling way of life that Grégoire represents. In Grégoire, Kate depicted a young man with high spirits and strong passions, but no direction or self-discipline—a son to worry every aunt or mother.

Chopin was also interested in young women, for Lélia would be joining St. Louis society in the next decade. In *At Fault,* Melicent Hosmer is a heartless

St. Louis flirt who visits her brother David and has a striking effect on the Cane River community—not unlike the impression Kate Chopin herself made when she first appeared with her citified ways and fashionable gowns. Kate might not have known what village people were saying about her in the early 1880s in Cloutierville—but in recollection a decade later, she saw more than a little humor in the figure she cut.

At first, Melicent has trouble hiring servants: "[T]he negroes were very averse to working for Northern people whose speech, manners, and attitude towards themselves were unfamiliar." Melicent's tastes are also considered extravagant and peculiar. She adorns her rooms with "bizarre decorations that seemed the promptings of a disordered imagination," including yards of "fantastic calico" in impossible designs; palm branches; pinecones; ferns; bright-hued bird wings. And when Melicent dresses in her best finery, a black outfit relieved by a giant bunch of geraniums, she wears a hat with a "great ostrich plume" and hints at displaying her ankles—just as Madame Chopin did in her promenades on horseback down Cloutierville's one street.

For Melicent and Grégoire, Kate put in a favorite Cloutierville story: that Harriet Beecher Stowe had visited the area in the 1840s, and met a slave woman whose story inspired the writing of *Uncle Tom's Cabin*, with its villainous Simon Legree. Melicent and Grégoire visit the lonely, untended grave of "Robert McFarlane," who is "the person that Mrs. W'at's her name wrote about in Uncle Tom's Cabin." Grégoire claims that McFarlane's ghost still roams the area; Melicent, a Unitarian, scoffs at that (and Kate may have intended a dig at both the credulity of Cane River people and the smugness of St. Louis Unitarians).

With Melicent and Grégoire, Kate made another point—that a romance between a St. Louis-bred woman, with her urban ways, and a Cane River country man, with his taste for whiskey and reckless living, could not last. Like Albert Sampite, Grégoire has "undisciplined desires and hot-blooded eagerness"; he also feels himself Melicent's "equal in the aristocracy of blood, and her master in the knowledge and strength of loving." Nevertheless, Melicent is snobbish about the way Grégoire talks: His voice is too low, his words impolite. She believes that Grégoire, a romantic companion for a Louisiana fling, is not the kind of man who will ultimately make her happy.

By 1890, Kate Chopin was forty years old, and no sentimentalist. Had she stayed in Louisiana, she would not have found her avant-garde circle of writers and journalists; she might never have written for publication. Still, *At Fault* suggests that St. Louis left Kate, in some ways, sensually starved.

In *At Fault*, Louisiana is a place of warmth and life, spontaneity and beauty. It is a welcoming, abundant place, in which everything grows and flourishes. In Kate Chopin's own life, Louisiana was associated with love, motherhood, coming of age, and passion—while her later life in St. Louis, an industrial city of the North, was a time for the intellect, for emotion recollected in tranquillity.

Still, it was not the keenly intellectual side of St. Louis—the books, the reviewers, the company of literary friends—that Kate chose to describe in her first published novel. Instead, in *At Fault*, she portrayed the past—what had been, and what might have been.

Kate Chopin had begun *At Fault* in July 1889, during St. Louis's fierce summer heat. She continued writing through the winter, and completed it on April 20, 1890—with a springlike happy ending, a marriage after long hardship and separation. She hired a Miss Keleher to type the manuscript, and offered *At Fault* to *Belford's Monthly* in Chicago, which printed one novel per issue—but *Belford's* said no. Kate also showed the manuscript to her friend Charles Deyo, a journalist, but did not record his opinions.

She kept writing regularly, and learning about literary markets. That April she translated a dramatic French short story: Adrien Vely's "Monsieur Pierre" describes a soldier in love with a seamstress whose husband beats her. By accident, the husband is shot by a sentry, freeing his wife to be with the man she chooses. "Monsieur Pierre" was the first of several translations that Kate sold to the *St. Louis Post-Dispatch*, where it appeared on August 8, 1892. It was also a sign that the departure of an unwanted spouse was still on her mind.

Some two weeks after she finished *At Fault*, Kate began writing another novel, called *Young Dr. Gosse*, which she worked on until November 27, 1890. Throughout most of the 1890s, she tried to publish it, either through magazines or book publishers, and a friend called it her "very strongest work"—but everyone rejected it, and eventually she destroyed the manuscript.

Now at midlife, Kate Chopin was impatient for literary recognition. After *Belford's* rejected *At Fault*, she decided to have it printed at her own expense, by the Nixon-Jones Printing Company in St. Louis. One thousand copies, with pale green covers, were ready on September 27, 1890, and within a week, Kate had sent them out.

According to her notations, she sent 250 copies to Book and News Company, apparently a distributor. Twenty-five copies went to William Barr, twenty-five went to Crawford's, and two to the St. Louis Mercantile Library. Chopin sent single copies to Mrs. Johnston, "ed. *Spectator*," the St. Louis magazine which had published "With the Violin"; to Dr. Kolbenheyer; to John A. Dillon of the *Post-Dispatch*; to the *Harper's* editor William Dean Howells; and to many other periodicals—among them *St. Louis Life*, *St. Louis Star-Sayings*, the *St. Louis Globe-Democrat*, the *New Orleans Times-Democrat*, the *New Orleans Daily Picayune*, the *New Orleans Abeille* (the French-language newspaper), the *Literary World* of Boston, *The Critic* in New York, and *The Nation*. She also gave one copy to her typist, Miss Keleher.

On October 4, her first review appeared in print.

The reviewer in the *St. Louis Spectator* considered *At Fault* an example of refined and well-written fiction. Even the minor characters were believable, and the reader sympathized with them.

A day later, the influential *St. Louis Post-Dispatch* printed a much longer review. John A. Dillon, the *Post-Dispatch's* editor, was a friend of Kate's, or at least a literary adviser: She had given him her story "A Poor Girl" to read the year before, and he had given the story damning praise. Harvard-educated, intellectual, and liberal, Dillon had encouraged Kate's writing, but disliked her subject matter.

The anonymous *Post-Dispatch* reviewer took a generally favorable view of *At Fault*, noting that some of the main characters were St. Louisans. The reviewer liked Kate Chopin's avoiding the didactic approach, and the review praised the humorous characters, the vitality of the plot, the moral questions raised, and the "ARTISTIC SKILL" (printed in capitals) in Chopin's handling of Fanny's death.

But the critic also had objections. "One shudders at hearing Hosmer tell his wife to 'shut up,' and we protest against Melicent's five engagements. If she really was engaged five times it ought not to be mentioned."

A week later, *At Fault* won strong praise from *St. Louis Life*, a weekly edited by Kate Chopin's friend and booster Sue V. Moore. *St. Louis Life* had been founded in December 1889, less than a year before *At Fault* appeared, with plans to be a "light and humorous" weekly, with "society comment" which would be "always bright, fresh and entertaining, without peering into the privacy of the home circle or in any way offending good taste."

Sue V. Moore especially dedicated herself to promoting the St. Louis literary community, and in her October 11, 1890, column "People We Know," she called *At Fault* "a pleasing story, exceptionally well-told, and proves that Mrs. Chopin possesses a talent that should prove a source of pleasure to the public and profit to herself." (Sue V. Moore, the only working newspaperwoman to review *At Fault*, was well aware of the financial side of writing.) Kate Chopin also possessed "an intuitive perception of what is fitting and artistic," and so did her characters, who "are witty, tender, or commonplace, just as she means them to be." Mrs. Moore concluded that *At Fault* was remarkably polished for a first book.

The *St. Louis Republic*, the city's most conservative newspaper, was less pleased. In the column "Literary News," on Saturday, October 18, the *Republic* reviewer called *At Fault* "a clever romance of Louisiana life," about a woman who would like to be married to someone else's husband. "Indeed, "said the reviewer, "the women who love other women's husbands and the men who love other men's wives always do feel that way; as bachelors' children are always admirably reared, they could always make the beloved one happy."

After a listless plot summary, the *Republic* reviewer objected to Kate Chopin's grammar and diction:

> Hosmer's wife, Fanny, is a fatal terror; she "guesses," she drinks to excess of whiskey, she steals from an old darkey's cabin, and uses slang that gives one shivers; but as the fair author herself, in the narrative portion of the volume, speaks of a railway station as a "depot" and a shop as a "store"—mistakes that might do in the mouth of one of the characters, who many of them use "aint" for is not, but mar the value of the book when used in the narrative portion—she may have made Fanny worse than she intended.

The *Republic* reviewer concluded, grudgingly, "Some of the secondary characters are particularly well drawn, and the local color is excellent."

Kate Chopin bristled at the criticism, and the *Republic* printed her reply the following week:

> Will you kindly permit me through the columns of your paper to set *The Republic* book reviewer right in a matter which touches me closely concerning the use and misuse of words? I cannot recall an instance, in or out of fiction, in which an American "country store" has been alluded to as a "shop," unless by some unregenerate Englishman. The use of the word depot or station is optional. Wm. Dean Howells employs the former to indicate a "railway station," so I am hardly ready to believe the value of "At Fault" marred by following so safe a precedent.

Howells, in fact, did use the word *depot* frequently in his divorce novel *A Modern Instance*, in which he also used slang to characterize Bartley Hubbard, the shallow, dissolute husband. The reviewer's objection was to Kate Chopin's realism—an objection she would encounter throughout her literary career from those who saw themselves as the genteel guardians of taste.

When Chopin wrote about divorce in *At Fault*, she clearly was following the precedent of Howells, the genteel *Atlantic* and *Harper's* editor whose *A Modern Instance* was one of very few divorce novels published in the United States. Chopin kept copies of Howells's novels, short stories, and books of criticism in her library; she read his comic works aloud to her friends; and she wrote "good" and "excellent" in the margins next to passages she especially admired. A year after At Fault, she modeled her only extant play, a comedy of manners called An Embarrassing Position, on Howells's work. She also sought Howell's approval, sending him At Fault and being delighted with a note of praise he sent for her children's story "Boulôt and Boulotte," published in Harper's Young People in 1891. (The note no longer exists.)

Yet Kate Chopin was much less conventional than William Dean Howells, who liked his heroines young, virginal, and reined in—but even A Modern Instance had been censored when the 1881 magazine version was put into book form in 1882. Most references to physical contact, including kisses between the main characters, were omitted.

Literary moralists and censors always offended Kate—and they dogged her from the beginning of her career.

More positive reviews of At Fault appeared. In December, another local magazine, Fashion and Fancy, predicted a bright future for the native St. Louisan: "[W]e trust Mrs. Chopin will attain a permanent place in that bright galaxy of Southern and Western writers who hold today the foremost rank of America's authors." Although At Fault at times revealed an "amateur's hand" and suffered from a surplus of secondary characters, Fashion and Fancy found it "a very meritorious one" with "unmistakable indications of strength."

The New Orleans Daily Picayune (October 12) published the first notice outside St. Louis, a minimal three sentences: "The author of this interesting novel is the widow of the late Oscar Chopin, commission merchant in New Orleans, and lived here ten years—from 1870 to 1880. She afterwards resided on a plantation in Natchitoches parish, where the main incidents of the story occur. The life of a handsome Creole widow of 30 is charmingly related in the book."

It was a year before Kate Chopin was reviewed in a national periodical, and The Nation (October 1, 1891) mocked the many plots in At Fault: "It is not quite clear who is cast for the title-rôle in At Fault, since all the characters have valid pretensions to the part." The reviewer suggested candidates:

> There is the lady who drinks and the gentleman who gets a divorce from her, the widow who loves and is beloved by him, but who persuades him to remarry his divorced partner and bring her to the Louisiana plantation, where she (the widow) may have a fostering care of the two and help them do their duty to each other. There is also the young lady of many arrangements, the negro who commits arson, the young gentleman who shoots him, the Colonel who shoots the young gentleman, the St. Louis lady who goes to matinées and runs off with the matineé-going gentleman.

Evidently irritated by a plethora of possibilities, *The Nation* suggested that "It may not be amiss, in deciding who is 'At Fault,' to consider as well the claims of the author, the publisher, and the reader." Still, *The Nation's* review was not thoroughly hostile: Kate Chopin showed an aptitude with dialects, skill in characterization, and "a touch which shows that the array of disagreeables was born rather of literary crudity than of want of refinement."

Still, the major problem for *At Fault* was not Kate Chopin's skills, but the lack of recognition. Except for *The Nation*, the only reviewers were those in places where she had lived. In Natchitoches Parish, the weekly *Enterprise*— edited by Phanor Breazeale's brother—printed the longest review that *At Fault* received, on page one of its December 4, 1890, edition. The review, signed by "Flora," was a plot summary full of misspellings and typographical errors, followed by some moral objections to *At Fault:*

> While we have nothing but praise for the delineation of her characters and for the literary merits of the work—though at times the style is apparently swollen and high-sounding—we find that the love or love-making which existed and was somewhat continuous between Thirese and Hosmer, to be out of place, or in other words improper. Such a feeling between the parties seems to mar the beauty of their lives which rests upon such a pure and high plane. In fact there is a contradiction between their lives when separated and when together. The denouncement is a relief and a satisfactory solution of the situation.

Flora anticipated later reviewers in pigeonholing Kate Chopin as a local-color writer.

> The character of Gregoire is a type of the uninstructed Creole and the language and expressions put in his mouth are true to nature. His canoe-ride with Melicent on Lake du Bois is a delightful description of such pastimes in Louisiana, but the scene at McFarland's grave is rather highly colored and hardly probable in parties so newly acquainted.

> The negro character are exceedingly well reproduced and the authoress traces with a mistress' hand the peculiarities of the African's dialect. Pierson describes in the natural Etheopian style Gregoire's spree in Cloutierville and the light and shade thrown in by Belinda's remarks are perfect specimens of negro mannerism. Marie Louise and Morico form exquisite pictures of the old time darkies and

remind the writer of the race and characteristics of his old nurse and yard-servant of the long ago.

Flora was far more forthright than most St. Louis reviewers about Fanny's problem.

> Another thrilling incident is that of the caving bank with Mrs. Hosmer and the rescue of her lifeless body by the almost super-human efforts of her husband. Here the authoress forgot to drop a tear over Marie Louise's watery grave. Mrs. Hosmer who is the one "At Fault," and ostensibly the heroine of the story, leads the life of a drunken sot, and her manoeuvres and devices in securing her liquor form an ingenious by-play.

Flora praised the characterizations of local and St. Louis people: "This portion of the novel is indited in the reportorial style and is a valuable auxiliary to the story." Also, "The authoress indulges in brief philosophical reflections to which we refer the reader."

"The perusal of the work afforded us much pleasure," Flora concluded, "and we hope that Mrs. Kate Chopin will again favor us with another. Upon the whole, 'tis our humble opinion that while we cannot accord genius to the fair authoress we are willing to admit that she is a lady who possesses talents of no common order."

Not mollified by the conclusion, Kate Chopin—in St. Louis, writing the children's story "A Red Velvet Coat"—retorted immediately. Her December 9 answer was printed in the December 18 issue of the *Natchitoches Enterprise,* under the headline AT FAULT. A CORRECTION.

> While thanking your reviewer for the many agreeable and clever things said of my story "At Fault," kindly permit me to correct a misconception. Fanny is not the heroine. It is charitable to regard her whole existence as a misfortune. Therese Lafirme, the heroine of the book is the one who was at fault—remotely, and immediately. Remotely—in her blind acceptance of an undistinguishing, therefore unintelligent code of righteousness by which to deal out judgments. Immediately—in this, that unknowing of the individual needs of *this* man and *this* woman, she should yet constitute herself not only a mentor, but an instrument in reuniting them.
>
> Their first marriage was an unhappy mistake; their re-union was a crime against the unwritten moral law. Emerson says: "Morals is the science of substances, not of shows. It is the *what* and not the

how. . . . It were an unspeakable calamity if anyone should think
he has the right to impose a private will on others. That is a part
of a striker, an assassin."

Towards the close of the story, Therese acknowledges her error,
and Hosmer reads her a brief lecture upon the "living spirit," the
"dead letter," etc.

I ask to straighten this misconception—of Fanny having been "at
fault," because it is one, which if accepted by the reader is liable
to throw the story entirely out of prospective [sic].

At least one very interested party was in Natchitoches at the time Kate's
correction was published. On page 3 of the *Enterprise*, next to her letter, a list
of hotel arrivals included "Albert Sampeti." By December 1890, Albert Sampite had long been estranged from his wife, Loca, to whom he had been legally
married for twenty-two years. He was forty-six, still handsome and wealthy,
and still a ladies' man.

When Kate's letter appeared in the *Enterprise*, literary readers might have
seen some parallels with William Dean Howells's moral judgments in *A Modern Instance*. But those who knew about Kate Chopin and Albert Sampite
might have recognized that more than a literary quarrel was at stake. Kate's
letter suggested several interpretations.

Was Kate Chopin denying Fanny's (Loca's) importance, trying to deny her
suffering—especially through the callous-sounding statement, "It is charitable
to regard her whole existence as a misfortune"? Was Kate absolving David
(Albert) for his transgressions against the marriage bond? Or was she blaming
Thérèse (herself?) for judging others too harshly?

In *At Fault*, David has greater emotional depth than either of the women:
He blames Fanny, but also pities her. Just before his wife dies, David has
become the kind of man most favored in women's fiction: the sensitive and
empathetic man who can understand a woman's feelings. When she finished
At Fault, half a dozen years after leaving Cloutierville, Kate Chopin evidently
believed that men could make that empathetic leap—and *At Fault* may record
a remembered hope that Albert Sampite could become that sensitive man.

But David Hosmer, unlike Albert Sampite, never beat his wife.

Nine days after Kate Chopin's letter appeared in the Natchitoches newspaper, Loca and Albert Sampite signed a document officially dividing their property. Loca received the house and land where they had lived (the land included
two parcels known as the "Chopin tracts"). She was also awarded farm animals,
equipment, tools, a piano, other furniture and household goods, and a thousand dollars.

*   *   *

At Fault did bring in some money: Kate received a total of fifty-one dollars over the next two years, which she duly recorded in her manuscript account notebook with the brown cover and the mischievous child's squiggles on the pages. (But she did not record how much it had cost her to have *At Fault* printed, and she almost certainly lost money on the novel.)

Still, *At Fault* had gained her review attention. It had made her known, and even praised. But it also exposed her for the first time to literary sniping and nitpicking—and that would bedevil her throughout her career.

Chapter 13

A PROFESSIONAL
WRITER

WITHIN A YEAR OF HER heated retorts to Natchitoches and St. Louis critics, Kate Chopin had written sixteen short stories, a one-act play, and an essay on German music, besides translating three French articles into English for the *St. Louis Post-Dispatch*.

The first, "The Shape of the Head," published January 25, involved the question of heredity versus environment—a subject of continuing fascination to her. According to the article, illustrated with drawings, the shape of one's head was no proof of one's character—for highly esteemed men did not necessarily have larger heads than others, and at least one very talented man's head was shaped exactly like that of a notorious assassin.

In "The Revival of Wrestling," published March 8, Kate translated descriptions of wrestling holds and techniques, subjects far removed from her own experience (although they were of interest to her athletic son Felix). But with "How to Make Manikins" (April 5), she translated something she knew intimately: how to amuse children. The manikins, made with scissors, calling cards, white paper, and black and colored pencils, were cut-paper figures of nuns and little girls, including a four-legged one, but "[i]n so representing the child, the designer has no intention of wounding the popular prejudice which favors little girls with the usual number of legs." There followed instructions on how to "lop off the supplementary legs."

All three translations appeared in the *Post-Dispatch* without Kate Chopin's byline: As a translator, she apparently cared more for pay ($5–$8 each) than for name recognition. She was much more ambitious for her fiction, which appeared under her own name. Of the sixteen stories she wrote in 1891, all but two eventually appeared in print (the two unpublished pieces, "Roger and His Majesty" and "Octave Feuillet" were lost or destroyed). With her children's stories, Chopin began appearing regularly in national magazines, especially in *Youth's Companion*—while with her adult short stories, she gained entry into one of the most prestigious literary magazines of the 1890s, the *Century*.

Kate Chopin did not begin the year cautiously. Her first 1891 story, which she wrote on January 10, was about venereal disease—a subject considered taboo by most American writers. At first, she called her story "The Evil that Men Do"; she also tried "A Common Crime," "Under the Apple Tree," and "A Taint in the Blood" before settling on "Mrs. Mobry's Reason." The story was rejected by most of the major liberal and literary magazines: In her account book, Chopin noted that she had sent it to the *Century, Scribner's, Arena, Belford's, Lippincott's, Atlantic, New York Ledger, Cosmopolitan, Inland Monthly, Harper's, Kate Field's Washington, Two Tales, New England Magazine,* and *Vogue*.

It was, in fact, Kate Chopin's most rejected story.

Syphilis was not unknown in the Continental literature she read. Henrik Ibsen's *Ghosts*, about hereditary syphilis, had been performed in Chicago in English in 1887, and by 1890 it had been published in English translation in Chicago and New York.

Sexually transmitted diseases had also been discussed publicly in her own city, a generation earlier: The "St. Louis Experiment" of 1870 was the first American attempt to combat venereal disease by requiring that prostitutes be medically inspected (male customers were not inspected). The ordinance, passed on July 5, 1870, while Kate and Oscar Chopin were on their European honeymoon, in effect legalized prostitution—but within a few years it was overturned for its "moral vileness," in a campaign led by the Unitarian minister William Greenleaf Eliot.

Kate Chopin knew the Eliot family: A month before writing "Mrs. Mobry's Reason," she had become a charter member of the Wednesday Club, the intellectually elite women's club of St. Louis. One of its guiding spirits was Charlotte Stearns Eliot, William Greenleaf Eliot's intelligent and ambitious daughter-in-law. (In 1904, Charlotte Eliot, also a well-known poet and social reformer, published a biography of her father-in-law, who had died in 1888.) Charlotte, whose son Thomas Stearns (later T. S. Eliot) was then a toddler, very likely encouraged Kate Chopin to write on the "social evil" of venereal disease and its tragic effects on innocent wives.

Kate also knew *The Heavenly Twins*, a novel about syphilis in marriage by the British suffragist Sarah Grand. In her 1894 diary, Kate quoted a friend who "thinks the 'Heavenly Twin' a book calculated to do incalculable good in the world: by helping young girls to a fuller comprehension of truth in the marriage relation! Truth is certainly concealed in a well for most of us." *The Heavenly Twins* had been a sensation in England, where it sold twenty thousand copies the first week; George Bernard Shaw compared Sarah Grand with Ibsen and Wagner as a misunderstood genius.

Evidently the success of *The Heavenly Twins*—"the summer's literary sensation" in St. Louis in 1893—enabled Kate Chopin to sell her story at last. Kate (or her editors) sometimes changed characters' names—and when "Mrs. Mobry's Reason" appeared in the *New Orleans Times-Democrat* on April 23, 1893, its characters and plot bore striking resemblances to *The Heavenly Twins*. Sarah Grand had called her heroine *Edith*; Kate Chopin used the name *Editha*. In both stories, a young woman marries unwisely: Grand's heroine marries the villainous, syphilitic Menteith, whose first name is *Mosley*: Chopin's Editha, although she knows something is wrong, nevertheless marries John *Mobry*— and both are punished. But Chopin's plot did vary from Ibsen's and Grand's: In her version, the fault lies in the mother's bloodline, not in the father's sins.

Kate Chopin gave "Mrs. Mobry's Reason" a European air, with allusions to Wagner: The story's dark fatalism is more European than American. Yet she set the story in the pretty Missouri countryside, with hillsides "crisp and silvered with dew," and a river "that twines like a silver ribbon through the green slopes of Southern Missouri," and runs "like liquid crystal over the shining pebbles beneath." Kate herself loved the country of the Meramec, easily reachable by electric railway: In her 1894 diary, she described a day in the country in Glencoe, where she saw "through the ravine deep down on the other side in a green basin, a patch of the Meramec glistened and sparkled like silver."

She wrote the doomed "Mrs. Mobry's Reason" in January, always a cold, unpleasant month in St. Louis, but she created the sunny, gently satirical story "A Shameful Affair" in June 1891, possibly in the Meramec country. (As her letters show, she was in St. Louis on May 28, but in Sulphur Springs, Missouri, on July 12.)

In "A Shameful Affair," Chopin described a supercilious young intellectual, Mildred, who eschews fashionable summer resorts and prefers a farm near the Meramec River. Endeavoring to pursue "exalted lines of thought," she is nevertheless attracted by a certain sun-bronzed farmhand, although "[f]armhands are not so very nice to look at, and she was nothing of an anthropologist." Once Mildred contrives to be alone with the farmhand, he impulsively kisses her, leaving her in a delicious quandary: Does she dare tell anyone that "her chaste lips had been rifled of their innocence"? She also learns that the farmhand is actually a well-bred "crank" who prefers farm labor to book learning, and his name is Fred—probably Kate Chopin's teasing wink at her fifteen-year-old son Fred, the most outgoing and boisterous of her boys. By the end of the story, both Mildred and Fred have blushed, apologized, and said much more than they intended to.

With her Missouri stories, Chopin attempted to use local color, for stories featuring quaint regional customs and manners were very popular in magazines of the 1890s. The farm wife in "A Shameful Affair" speaks a German-inflected English ("He don't talk no more un ven he vas deef und dumb," she says). In another Missouri story, "The Going and Coming of Liza Jane," Kate reproduced country accents: Characters say, "It's a wonder you wouldn't of took the two horse wagon," and "fix that thur road and throw a bridge acrost Bludgitt creek."

But Kate found that Missouri local color was not easy to sell. "A Harbinger," a six-paragraph story of a summer infatuation, was accepted on the first submission to Mrs. Johnson at *St. Louis Magazine*—but the magazine had a very small circulation. "A Shameful Affair" was rejected by nine publishers before the *New Orleans Times-Democrat* took it on March 20, 1893, and Chopin's urban Missouri comedy of manners, "An Embarrassing Position," was refused by five magazines and three individuals (including the New York producer Augustin Daly), before it was accepted by the *St. Louis Mirror*.

"The Going and Coming of Liza Jane" was rejected by twelve publishers, but its subject was also much more unconventional: Its heroine leaves her country husband because novel-reading has made her yearn for "higher life" (jewels, promenades, carriages). (Liza Jane also anticipates *The Awakening*: She wants to "taste the joys of ixistence," just as Edna wants "the taste of life's delirium.") Eventually Liza Jane, after some "sin or suffering," returns to her husband for Christmas—and so Kate managed to syndicate the story with the American Press Association for Christmas 1892, under the title "The Christ Light."

Kate had submitted "The Going and Coming of Liza Jane" to a *Short Stories* magazine competition, but it did not win. Throughout 1891, she entered other contests in an attempt to make her mark quickly: "An Embarrassing Position" was her entry for the *New York Herald*'s drama competition and "The Maid of St. Phillippe" for *Youth's Companion*'s folklore contest—but again she did not win.

Still, "The Maid of St. Phillippe" was more easily accepted: Only *Scribner's*, the *St. Louis Post-Dispatch*, and the *Century* rejected it before *Short Stories* took it on May 1892, for publication that November. It was only the second Chopin story about a young woman who rejects marriage (the first was "Wiser than a God")—and it was Kate's first, and only, use of the stories her great-grandmother had told her from St. Louis history. Although historical fiction was very popular, she never attempted it again—and five years later, with some comical exaggeration, she explained why.

At one point, she wrote, she had decided to create a tale "that should convince my limited circle of readers that I could rise above the commonplace.

> As to the choice of "time," the present century offered too prosaic a setting for a tale intended to stir the heart and the imagination. I selected the last century. It is true I know little of the last century, and have a feeble imagination. I read volumes bearing upon the history of the times and people that I proposed to manipulate, and pored over folios depicting costumes and household utensils then in use, determined to avoid inaccuracy. For the first time in my life I took notes,—copious notes,—and carried them bulging in my jacket pockets, until I felt as if I were wearing Zola's coat. I have never seen a craftsman at work upon a fine piece of mosaic, but I fancy that he must handle the delicate bits much as I handled the words in that story, picking, selecting, grouping, with an eye to color and to artistic effect,—never satisfied. The story completed, I was very, very weary; but I had the satisfaction of feeling that for once in my life I had worked hard, I had achieved something great, I had taken pains. But the story failed to arouse enthusiasm among the editors. It is at present lying in my desk. Even my best friend declined to listen to it, when I offered to read it to her.

Kate concluded that "a writer should be content to use his own faculty" to reach a sympathetic audience. A writer who did so, "attains, in my opinion, somewhat to the dignity of a philosopher."

During 1891, Kate Chopin was trying to find a sympathetic audience, and she alternated between setting stories in rural Missouri or Louisiana—but Louisiana, with its unique cultural mélange, proved much more popular with editors. Her Louisiana children's stories were sometimes accepted on the first submission; few took more than three attempts. Four of her 1891 stories appeared in *Youth's Companion* ("For Marse Chouchoute," "A Wizard from Gettysburg," "A Rude Awakening," and "Beyond the Bayou"); two in *Harper's Young People* ("A Very Fine Fiddle" and "Boulôt and Boulotte"); and one each in *Two Tales* ("Love on the Bon-Dieu") and the *New Orleans Times-Democrat* ("After the Winter"). Her adult stories set in Louisiana also gained her national publication, in *Vogue* and the *Century*.

For Louisiana, Kate drew on her memories and intuitions. She used Cloutierville as the setting for "For Marse Chouchoute," the story of a black boy's loyalty to a white boy, and the story was reprinted in the *Natchitoches Enterprise* for September 8, 1892, taking up almost the whole front page. In "A Wizard from Gettysburg," she described a shell-shocked Civil War veteran who finally finds his way home to Louisiana, decades after the conflict; in "A Very Fine Fiddle" and "Boulôt and Boulotte," she made gentle fun of the misunderstandings of children. One child sells a priceless violin by mistake; two others carry, rather than wear, their expensive new shoes. In her Louisiana stories, Kate used the gossip she had heard in her Cloutierville years—and villagers assumed, often rightly, that she was drawing on real people for inspiration. She wrote about Saturday afternoon trading and shopping, old women with their herb remedies, the making of delicious *croquignoles*, and the tales of witches.

But in her first year as a professional writer, Kate Chopin was already leaning toward more controversial subjects—such as the prejudices and insensitivities of a priest ("Love on the Bon-Dieu"); the never-ending trauma of war ("Beyond the Bayou"); and the seduction of innocent country women into prostitution ("Dr. Chevalier's Lie").

Halfway through the year 1891, on June 20, Loca Sampite's separation from her husband, Albert, took legal effect. She had charged him with desertion: According to legal documents, he had been sent three summonses in consecutive months, directing him to "return to the matrimonial domicile," but he had refused to do so. The Sampites' community of assets had been legally divided, and Loca was granted "the care and control of her children."

Some three weeks later, Kate Chopin, in far-off Missouri, wrote "A Rude Awakening," in which seventeen-year-old Lolotte is tormented by the laziness and irresponsibility of her father, Sylveste—whose unusual name suggests a link with Sylvère DeLouche, notorious in Cloutierville for his heavy drinking. He was also the estranged husband of Maria Normand DeLouche, the woman who was now the focus of Albert Sampite's attentions.

According to some Cloutiervillians, Albert Sampite had broken up the DeLouches' marriage and set up Maria Normand in a separate house—for which he gave her a particularly pretty hurricane lamp with amethyst-tinted glass. Evidently he was not sentimental about possessions: It was the lamp Kate Chopin had given him when she left Cloutierville.

And so, when Loca Sampite charged Albert with desertion, she was recognizing an accomplished fact: Maria Normand DeLouche's home, just across the horse pasture from the house where he had taken up residence, had become his real home.

Kate Chopin knew, of course, about goings-on in Cloutierville—but her life was now in St. Louis. The day before she wrote "A Rude Awakening," with its sly allusion to Sylvère DeLouche, she took a further step toward realizing one of her greatest literary ambitions.

She was staying at Sulphur Springs, Missouri, in July when she sent the final version of "A No-Account Creole" to editor Richard Watson Gilder of the *Century* magazine. She had been revising the story, originally called "Euphrasie" or "A Maid and Her Two Lovers," for some three years. *Belford's* had rejected one revised version ("Letter: too long—if I cut it—to 5 or 6,000 may prove acceptable," Kate recorded in her account book.) *Harper's, Home Magazine, Chaperone,* Mrs. J. A. Logan (?—Kate's handwriting is unclear), *Scribner's,* and *Cosmopolitan* all rejected it, two of them also calling it "too long." But on July 5, 1891, the *Century* returned it for revision "with flattering letter," Kate recorded in her notebook.

The *Century* was one of the most prestigious and influential literary magazines in the nation. Editor Gilder published George W. Cable and Mark Twain, William Dean Howells and Grace King—although, like other editors, he rejected Stephen Crane's *Maggie: A Girl of the Streets* as too sordid. Gilder wanted realism softened by idealism, and Kate Chopin wanted her writing to appear in his magazine.

Evidently Gilder's advice showed Kate Chopin how to make her story conform to the genteel tradition—and her answer was both fawning and defensive. "The weakness which you found in 'A No-Account Creole' is the one which I felt," she wrote to him on July 12, 1891. "I thank you more than I can say, for your letter. My first and strongest feeling upon reading it, was a desire to clasp your hand." Her main concern was the character of Euphrasie: "I hope I have succeeded in making the girl's character clearer. I have tried to convey the impression of sweetness and strength, keen sense of right, and physical charm beside."

She had also eliminated passages "that seemed to me crude; but I made no attempt to condense the story. I knew that I could not without evolving something totally different in the effort. The thing drags lazily I know—I hope not awkwardly, and I believe contains nothing irrelevant. I trust a good deal to the close for rousing the interest of the reader if it may have flagged by the way." (In the story's closing, Euphrasie's fiancé releases her from her promise, thus handing her to the man she really wants. Euphrasie owes her happiness to men's notions of honor.)

Kate concluded to Gilder, "I shall confess that your letter has given me strong hope that you may find the story worthy of publication."

Gilder did, and wrote a memo on August 3 to his assistant: "Please write to Mrs. Chopin (at Sulphur Springs, Mo.) & tell her Mr. Gilder thanks her for the alterations & accepts the story with very sincere pleasure—& that the publishers will send her a check before long." On August 3, 1891, Kate received one hundred dollars for "A No-Account Creole," by far the largest payment for anything she had written up to that point.

During 1891, she collected four royalty checks for At Fault, adding up to $48.60; her next-largest check was $40 from Youth's Companion for the story "A Rude Awakening." For the children's stories "A Very Fine Fiddle" and "Boulôt and Boulotte," she received five dollars each from Harper's Young People.

In December, she made a short trip to the Cane River country, as reported in the "Personal" column in the Natchitoches Enterprise for December 10, 1891:

> Mrs. Joseph Henry and sister Mrs. Oscar Chopin, of St. Louis, spent several days in our city the past week as guests of their brother and sister, Mr. and Mrs. Phanor Breazeale. Mr. Oscar Chopin, Jr. accompanied his mother. Mrs. Chopin is the authoress of that charming story At Fault, the plot and scenes of which were laid in this parish, and several other interesting stories. She has lately written another novel which will make its appearance in one of the leading American Magazines. Mrs. Chopin returned to St. Louis on last Tuesday. Mr. Oscar will remain in these parts for several months, dividing his time between Derry and this city.

(The new novel, evidently Young Dr. Gosse, was never published.)

Kate still owned the large white house in Cloutierville and rented it to a family named Colvin—but whether she visited Cloutierville on this trip is not recorded. Nor can it be known whom she saw—or did not see.

Once Kate returned to St. Louis, she was inspired to write nine Louisiana stories in eight weeks—and in some of them, she began to violate genteel canons of taste.

Her last story of 1891, "After the Winter," was about a blacksmith's daughter in the Cane River country—possibly inspired by Emma Perrier, her young Cloutierville neighbor (although by 1891, Emma Perrier was twenty-four). "After the Winter" describes a misanthrope whose child has died and whose unfaithful wife left him while he was fighting with the Louisiana Tigers during the war. He has cursed everyone, God included, but flowers, the spring, and the power of music all cure him—and the story was immediately accepted by Youth's Companion for Easter.

But it was never published there: Possibly one paragraph led the editors to conclude that the story was not suitable for children. The first unfaithful wife in a Kate Chopin story appears in "After the Winter," and Kate suggested that she was not an isolated case: "Then, there are women—there are wives with thoughts that roam and grow wanton with roaming; women whose pulses are stirred by strange voices and eyes that woo; women who forget the claims of yesterday, the hopes of to-morrow, in the impetuous clutch of to-day." (The story did finally appear in the *New Orleans Times Democrat* in 1896—at Easter.)

Kate Chopin's December trip to the Cane River country evidently cemented her decision that Louisiana would be her special setting and inspiration. By the early 1890s, too, she had discovered the particular writer who most inspired her. Guy de Maupassant, the French amoralist, replaced William Dean Howells as her literary model.

"About eight years ago there fell accidentally into my hands a volume of Maupassant's tales," Chopin wrote in September 1896, after the *Atlantic* asked her for an essay about herself.

> I had been in the woods, in the fields, groping around; looking for something big, satisfying, convincing, and finding nothing but— myself; a something neither big nor satisfying but wholly convin- cing. It was at this period of my emerging from the vast solitude in which I had been making my own acquaintance, that I stumbled upon Maupassant.

Her St. Louis literary circle consisted of people who read Guy de Maupas- sant, and other French and Continental writers, but his work was something special to Kate Chopin, for, she wrote:

> I read his stories and marvelled at them. Here was life, not fiction; for where were the plots, the old fashioned mechanism and stage trapping that in a vague, unthinking way I had fancied were essen- tial to the art of story making. Here was a man who had escaped from tradition and authority, who had entered into himself and looked out upon life through his own being and with his own eyes; and who, in a direct and simple way, told us what he saw. When a man does this, he gives us the best that he can; something valu- able for it is genuine and spontaneous.

"You probably like to think that he reaches you exclusively," she wrote, but "[s]omeway I like to cherish the delusion that he has spoken to no one else so directly, so intimately as he does to me."

In "The Maid of St. Phillippe," she had used the "old fashioned mechanism and stage trapping"; with "A Shameful Affair," she still relied on William Dean

Howells's genteel approach to romantic comedy. But with such stories as "Mrs. Mobry's Reason" and "After the Winter," Kate was venturing into a deeper, Continental kind of realism. Through Maupassant, she had found a way to write the kinds of stories that she brooded over—adult stories of forbidden desire.

Kate Chopin was not a disciplined writer who sat down every day, pen in hand, for a given number of hours. Nor was she a painstaking editor of her own work: Her surviving manuscripts show that she rarely revised or retouched what had come to her in the first glow of inspiration. Rather, according to her son Felix, a short story would "burst from her: I have seen her go weeks and weeks without an idea, then suddenly grab her pencil and old lapboard (which was her work bench), and in a couple of hours her story was complete and off to the publisher."

Harrison Clark of the *St. Louis Republic* gave a similar report: "Mrs. Chopin writes fluently, rapidly, and with practically no revision. She declares it is either 'easy to write, or utterly impossible,' and therefore she has no fixed plan except a general one of working in the morning."

Even Kate herself claimed, with her characteristic pose of ironic modesty, that "I have not the writing habit." She did her writing most often in the morning, she said, "[o]n a lapboard with a block of paper, a stub pen and a bottle of ink bought at the corner grocery, which keeps the best in town."

But it was the quickness of her mind and pen that most impressed her friends. The poet William Schuyler wrote about her nimble method of creation: "When the theme of a story occurs to her, she writes it out immediately, often at one sitting, then, after a little, copies it out carefully, seldom making corrections. She never retouches after that."

In early 1892, in the afterglow of her December visit to the Cane River country, Kate had many such sittings. As she wrote later:

> Story-writing—at least with me—is the spontaneous expression of impressions gathered goodness knows where. . . .

> There are stories that seem to write themselves, and others which positively refuse to be written—which no amount of coaxing can bring to anything. . . . I am completely at the mercy of unconscious selection. To such an extent is this true, that what is called the polishing up process has always proved disastrous to my work, and I avoid it, preferring the integrity of crudities to artificialities.

In January of 1892 alone, Kate Chopin wrote four stories, three of them in two days ("The Bênitous' Slave," "A Turkey Hunt," and "Old Aunt Peggy").

She sent the three off to the publisher immediately, on January 8, and *Harper's Young People* accepted them all on January 28. Kate was paid seven dollars each for the first two, and three dollars for "Old Aunt Peggy," the shortest.

The first two, soon published, fit common formulas: "The Bênitous' Slave" describes an old black man, in Natchitoches, who still wants to serve the white family he served before the war; "A Turkey Hunt" concerns an odd-looking black child whose sphinxlike placidity leads others to consider her a lazy liar. But "Old Aunt Peggy" is different: She is an ancient and sly ex-slave, who likes to claim that she is about to die in order to wheedle goodies from her former master. The *Harper's Young People* editors evidently changed their minds after they accepted "Old Aunt Peggy": They may have decided that a tale of lying was not suitable for young readers, and they did not publish the story.

But Chopin's next short story, "The Lilies," was squarely in the junior version of the genteel tradition. Gentility and virtue are victorious: An innocent child redeems the adults around her by complaining fastidiously about an old misanthrope's cooking and housekeeping and encouraging her poor but honest mother to meet him. *Wide Awake* accepted the story for Easter.

From February through May of 1892, Kate continued to write local-color sketches and children's stories: When *Vogue* bought "Ripe Figs," her very short sketch of women in the bayou country, that gained her more national attention. But four of her children's stories did not find publishers, including "A Little Free-Mulatto," a happily-ever-after tale of color caste in the Cane River country, and "Croque-Mitaine," a gentle story poking fun at credulous children who fear a masked man on Halloween. Two other stories evidently disappointed Kate enough that she destroyed the manuscripts: of "Mittens" (seven hundred words) and "Bambo Pellier" (thirteen thousand words) only the titles, lengths, and submission records remain in her account book. She submitted "Bambo Pellier" for a *Youth's Companion* serial contest that she did not win.

After "Bambo Pellier," Kate Chopin—obviously chafing against the virtuous formula of children's stories—switched to writing adult stories in which she could portray the conflicts that most interested her: the problems of romance, independence, passion, and divided loyalties. Although Chopin never thoroughly abandoned writing for children, she also began playing even more with the formulas for children's genteel literature, stretching them to include her own inside jokes and pokes at adult pomposities.

By the end of 1892, writing when inspiration struck her—and not writing at all between April and July—Kate had produced fifteen short stories and one unpublished poem ("A Fancy").

She had also decided to be a loner, not a clubwoman.

On December 1, 1890, Kate had been unanimously accepted into the select Wednesday Club of St. Louis, as one of its first hundred members.

Other charter members included Charlotte Eliot, Mrs. William Schuyler, the author-translator Thekla Bernays, and many women who had belonged to the Woman-Suffrage Association of Missouri. According to its incorporation papers, the Wednesday Club's purpose was "to create and maintain an organized center of thought and action among the women of St. Louis, and to aid in the promotion of their mutual interests, in the advancement of science, education, philanthropy, literature and art, and to provide a place of meeting for the comfort and convenience of its members." By May of 1891, at the end of its first year, the club decided to join the General Federation of Women's Clubs and make its headquarters in the Studio Building at the corner of Jefferson and Washington Avenues.

For a while, Kate Chopin seemed to think that the Wednesday Club was worthwhile for her own work (or for what she called her "commercial instinct")—but that state of mind lasted less than two years. Although she enjoyed her euchre (card-playing) club, she found study clubs and clubwomen more an irritant than a pleasure, and Mrs. Charles Stone (Margaret M. B. Stone) particularly fell under her disapproval.

In the 1890s, Mrs. Stone directed the Modern Novel Club, to promote "appreciation of the modern realistic problem novel." She had also written *The Problem of Domestic Service*, an 1892 pamphlet in which she advised bourgeois women about the "management of girls": Ladies were advised to find girls of a genteel background and train them well "while they were yet young enough to be controlled." Housekeeping, she wrote, could be enjoyable, "especially for people not troubled with artistic and literary longings." But Kate Chopin, who wrote about Mrs. Stone in her diary for June 2, 1894, saw her as a self-pitying dilettante.

> Mrs. Stone looks like a woman who accepts life as a tragedy and has braced herself to meet it with a smile on her lips. The spirit of the reformer burns within her, and gives to her eyes the smouldering, steady glow of a Savonarolas. The condition of the working classes pierces her soul; the condition of women wrings her heart. "Work" is her watch word. She wants to work to make life purer, sweeter, better worth living. She has written a novel and some short stories which I have never read. Her experience with publishers has not been happy, but she does not mind. She does not live for herself but for others and she is just as willing to reach the "world" through her personal work as through the written word. Intentions pile up before her like a mountain, and the sum of her energies is Zero! It is well that such a spirit does not ever realize the futility of effort. A little grain of wisdom gained from the gospel of selfishness—what an invaluable lesson—lost upon ears that will not hear.

The Wednesday Club required work from its members: At the May 1891 meeting, Kate was assigned to write an essay on "Typical Forms of German Music," to be assisted by Mrs. Oscar Herf and Mrs. Frank B. Nichols. When Kate presented her essay at the December 9 meeting, according to the Wednesday Club records, "Mrs. Herf gave some additional points of interest concerning the great German composers under consideration." Mrs. Herf also sang selections from Bach, Handel, Mozart, Haydn, and Beethoven, after which "some discussion followed in which Mrs. Green, Mrs. Chopin and others joined and the subject was closed by Mrs. Taussig with an analysis of the Symphony and the symphonic poem."

By the next meeting in January 1892, Wednesday Club members had divided themselves into six sections—Art, Current Topics, Education, History and Literature, Science, and Social Economics—each with officers, programs, and essayists. The Wednesday Club joined the Citizens' Smoke Abatement Association to work on clean air, and by the end of the club year, the membership limit was raised to 175 members—but by then Kate Chopin had resigned.

She may have preferred not to join a section; she may have disliked the emphasis on structure, organization, and committees (she often wrote of wanting to follow her fancy rather than rules). As the daughter of a slave-owning family who had supported the "wrong side" in the Civil War, Kate may have wanted to flee from political agitation. (Charlotte Eliot's father-in-law had been one of St. Louis's most outspoken abolitionists.)

Kate may also have disliked the club's emphasis on uplift. Most of the Wednesday Club women were literary appreciators rather than creators; many were women whose children were grown and away from home, and who had few outlets for their energies. In an early draft of her essay called "Confidences" six years later, Kate criticized a "Madame Précieuse," who had insisted that Kate "cultivate the religious impulse." Kate omitted Madame from the published article, which appeared in the *Atlantic*, but she still maintained her distaste for high-flown discussions of ideas. A preaching voice, she claimed, had told her:

> "Go forth and gather wisdom in the intellectual atmosphere of clubs,—in those centres of thought where questions are debated and knowledge is disseminated." Once more giving heed, I hurried to enroll myself among the thinkers, and dispensers of knowledge, and propounders of questions. And very much out of place did I feel in these intellectual gatherings. I escaped by some pretext, and regained my corner, where no "questions" and no fine language can reach me.

Kate also disliked "society," as she noted in her 1894 diary after reading her stories for a group of ladies: "But how immensely uninteresting some 'society' people are! That class which we know as Philistines. Their refined voices, and refined speech which says nothing—or worse, says something which offends me. Why am I so sensitive to manner."

A month later, when a man at an evening party praised some performers for showing that "acting upon the stage can be done by ladies and gentlemen," Kate wrote in her diary, "It took quite an effort to withhold my wrath at such statement. God A'mighty! Aren't there enough ladies & gentlemen sapping the vitality from our every day existence! are we going to have them casting their blight upon art."

For Kate Chopin, who had known a more sensual existence in the warm, outdoor world of Louisiana, refined and indirect speech would have seemed stilted, strained, bloodless, even comical. In the Cane River world, she had known an earthy life, with the smell of cape jessamine at night, and the sight of white cotton bursting from the bolls, and the changing colors and scents of each planting season. And the man she knew best in Louisiana, after Oscar, the planter Albert Sampite, was no gentleman, no prissy parser of parlor sentences.

Kate Chopin's withdrawal from the Wednesday Club was noted in the minutes for April 4, 1892: "Mrs. Chopin resigned from the club." Undoubtedly Kate had reasons to leave when she did, for she had just written "Miss McEnders," a story satirizing St. Louis social reformers like the members of the Wednesday Club. Five days after her withdrawal, she wrote another story ("Loka") mocking the Christian endeavors of clubwomen, this time Louisiana ladies who fail to civilize the "savage" Loka.

Kate continued to attend social gatherings with people whose ideas she did not respect, because of her "commercial instinct" as a writer—but she reserved for herself the quiet and solitude that a writer needs. By leaving the Wednesday Club, she gave herself more time to retreat to her own "corner."

Chapter 14

LOUISIANA INSPIRATION, ST. LOUIS AMBITION

IN 1892 AND 1893, KATE Chopin looked both backward and forward—drawing on her Louisiana past for stories while taking dramatic steps to promote her new literary career.

Sometimes her inspirations were obvious. In mid-June 1892, for instance, a devastating flood in Natchitoches Parish destroyed most of Albert Sampite's crops. Barely a month later, Kate Chopin created the character of Alcée Laballière—a wealthy and handsome planter whose entire crop is destroyed by a cyclone.

In his first appearance, in "At the 'Cadian Ball," Alcée is hardworking: "It was an every-day affair for him to come in from the field well-nigh exhausted, and wet to the waist." He is earthy, impulsive, sensual—and his mother's graceful goddaughter Clarisse drives him mad with her off-and-on airs. Still, "he must have been crazy the day he came in from the rice-field, and, toil-stained as he was, clasped Clarisse by the arms and panted a volley of hot, blistering love-words into her face. No man had ever spoken love to her like that."

Clarisse rejects him, disdainfully—and when, a day or two later, the cyclone ruins all that he has worked for, Alcée says nothing at all, meeting Clarisse's sympathetic words with "mute indifference." For solace, Alcée drinks more than a little whiskey and then rides off to the 'Cadian (Cajun) ball, where he entrances the women with his "handsome eyes" and "feverish glance."

"At the 'Cadian Ball" proves to be about a four-way dance. Bobinôt, tongue-tied, "dull-looking and clumsy," yearns for Calixta, the sensual "Spanish vixen"; she wants Alcée, with whom she spent a mysterious, scandalous time in Assumption Parish, the year before. When Alcée is near her, "Calixta's senses were reeling; and they well-nigh left her when she felt Alcée's lips brush her ear like the touch of a rose." But then the dainty, prissy Clarisse makes up her mind to chase Alcée—and she takes him away from the ball. The sullen, abandoned Calixta agrees to marry Bobinôt, but refuses to kiss him.

For Kate Chopin, "At the 'Cadian Ball," was a "what if" story: What if someone else, not Loca, had been there when Albert Sampite was choosing a bride? *Clarisse* is not unlike *Catherine*, and the genteel Clarisse does defeat her more earthy rival: For Alcée at the end, "[t]he one, only, great reality in the world was Clarisse standing before him, telling him that she loved him." The character Alcée resembles Albert Sampite in wealth as well as hard work: Albert was said to own so much land that one could ride all day and never come to the end of it. And in the character of Alcée, Kate also recorded the hard-drinking and brutal, passionate behavior that she remembered.

At least one other character would also have been recognizable in Cloutier-ville. Of "that little Spanish vixen Calixta," Kate wrote, "Calixta's slender foot had never touched Cuban soil; but her mother's had, and the Spanish was in her blood all the same." Calixta does not look traditionally Spanish: Her kinky hair is "flaxen" and she has blue eyes ("the drowsiest, most tantalizing that ever looked into a man's"). But Kate's Cane River country neighbors knew just such a Spanish vixen, a rebellious spirit, raised in Cuba, who was both blond and blue-eyed: Maria Normand DeLouche, the woman who had replaced Kate Chopin in Albert Sampite's affections.

Maria Normand was born in Louisiana, but her father, Jules Normand, a photographer, entrepreneur, and inveterate traveler, had taken the family to Cuba for most of her youth. She attended convent school in Matanzas, and when the Normands were leaving to return to Louisiana, she had made a desperate leap over the side of the ship—but was brought back, against her will.

In Cuba, she had had an admirer, Gaspar Hernandez, who gave her a copy of *Faust* and asked her father's permission to marry her—but Jules Normand did not tell his daughter. Some years later, after he had been in New York, Gaspar Hernandez wrote to Maria Normand, wanting to marry her on his way back to Cuba—but she refused: She was engaged to someone else. (Still, she kept his photograph, with its Spanish inscription to *"mi querida Maria"* and a pledge that he would always love her.)

Photographs of Maria Normand show her as a lush beauty, with Calixta's "broad smiling mouth and tiptilted nose" and "full figure": Even as a girl, Maria had been noted for her voluptuous figure. Maria Normand wore Spanish mantillas and sometimes posed with flowers in her naturally curly golden hair, which she set in ringlets by wrapping it around a malacca cane. "Beauty is a fault in your house," a friend once told Jules Normand—and her beauty was not altogether a gift for Maria Normand.

Perhaps on impulse, or out of desperation, she married, at twenty-eight, a man like Bobinôt of "At the 'Cadian Ball": her next-door neighbor Sylvère DeLouche—whose sister Loca was already married to Albert Sampite. Maria's mother had violently opposed the marriage, and it soon foundered, despite the births of a daughter and son. Sylvère was known as a "sodden drunk" and a "wastrel" who refused to work, preferring to order whole casks of whiskey from New Orleans and drink them all himself. Sometimes he would simply leave home. Later in life, Maria often said wistfully that she wished she had never disobeyed her mother.

But Albert Sampite was there to console his sister-in-law. Maria Normand— as she was always called—and Sylvère DeLouche lived apart for most of their lives. And she lived just across a horse lot from Albert Sampite, whose company she much preferred to that of her husband.

Loca remained in the original Sampite home: She carefully kept her legal rights separate from her husband, and in 1892 her mother, Mrs. Scruggs, gave land to her children, and clearly not to Albert Sampite.

Albert lived alone in an adobe house covered with moss and vines, where children enjoyed pulling spiders and snails out of the moss. Sometimes their son Alphonse would go hunting with his father, as Albert wrote to Loca in April of 1892: "Why don't Alphonse write. I haven't hunted any since he was here, he can make war to snails of nothing else." Albert also complained that Loca was always asking for money: Although they lived within walking distance, they communicated by letter, and she also sued him in December 1893, possibly for support money.

When she did have to see Albert in person, Loca Sampite would take with her a big black bullwhip for self-protection.

Nevertheless, Albert Sampite had much in common with the dashing Alcée Laballière in "At the 'Cadian Ball," and Maria Normand's husband, Sylvère DeLouche, was not unlike the clumsy Bobinôt. In a portrait taken in the 1890s, Albert Sampite looks proud, self-confident, well-dressed, with a pointed, well-trimmed beard. But Sylvère DeLouche, a large-nosed man with nervous eyes, a mustache, and a small beard, had one portrait taken in a stiff Napoleonic pose, hand inside his coat—and another taken with his horse, Charlie, who fills most of the picture. Charlie was evidently his closest companion: When Sylvère could no longer manage matters, Charlie knew the way home and could open the gate for his rider.

The story "Loka," Kate Chopin's most critical portrait of Cloutierville women, was not published in *Youth's Companion* until December of 1892, and it appeared to be a Christmas conversion story: The savage Loka, patronized by Christian clubwomen, is transformed by her love for a baby. (The reactions of Cloutierville people, especially Loca Sampite, were not recorded.)

Throughout 1892 and 1893, Kate corresponded with Cane River country relatives, and the changes in their lives shaped and inspired her writings. On August 27, 1892, her sister-in-law, Cora Henry Chopin, the wife of Oscar's brother Lamy, died at the age of thirty-five; their daughter Eugénie ("Nini") was twelve. Kate had been writing Louisiana stories all summer, and on that day she began one of her most elegaic tales of the past: "Ma'ame Pélagie," the story of three generations of Cane River women.

The central figure lives in the past: Ma'ame Pélagie, now queenly and white-haired, yearns for the way her family lived in their stately plantation home on the Côte Joyeuse before the war. She recalls the grand balls, and the buttons of her fiancé's uniform digging into her bosom in their last embrace; she re-members the servants fleeing, and the mansion in flames. Now she lives with her much younger sister in a cabin on the grounds—hoarding every picayune, dreaming of rebuilding the mansion. Finally, for the sake of her young niece, who withers and sickens amid dead dreams, Ma'ame Pélagie surrenders. She will build a new house instead—although "her soul had stayed in the shadow of the ruin."

When Kate Chopin lived in Cloutierville, she could walk to what was left of Magnolia, the prominent Hertzog family's stately manor house. Famous before the war for its stables and prizewinning racehorses, it was still sur-rounded by live-oaks and magnolias. From where the gallery used to be, Kate could gaze over the lush green fields and listen to the crickets and birds surviv-ing in the burned-out ruins. The shell of the Hertzogs' ruined Magnolia man-sion, like so much that she saw, had lingered in Kate's mind.

By the time "Ma'ame Pélagie" was published, in the New Orleans Times-Democrat on December 24, 1893, Lamy Chopin had remarried. The new Mrs. Chopin, twenty-one years younger than her husband, was the former Fannie Hertzog—who had grown up on Magnolia plantation land but in the overseer's house, after the manor house was burned. All her life, Fannie Hert-zog, herself a poet, had heard stories like "Ma'ame Pélagie," about the ram-paging Yankees who burned everything before them, turning the road all the way to Natchitoches into a solid flame.

When Kate Chopin wrote "Ma'ame Pélagie," the house was still a ruin: According to the historian J. Fair Hardin, its traces "stood for years like ghostly sentinels, guarding as it were, the historic memories of bygone days." But six years after "Ma'ame Pélagie," the Hertzog family rebuilt Magnolia, on the original square brick foundation, still amid the live-oaks and flowers that had given the house its name. Later visitors could see the site of "Ma'ame Pélagie" as it had been in all its glory.

Reflecting again on her past in late 1892, Kate Chopin wrote one more somber story about a Cane River woman. On Thanksgiving Day, November 24, she wrote the tale of a foundling, the child Désirée who appears on the doorstep of the Valmondé mansion. The Valmondés raise her as their own, until a wealthy, passionate planter falls in love with her "as if struck by a pistol shot"; they marry, happily, until she gives birth to a child who is not entirely white. The husband sends Désirée away, and her mother implores her to come home—but Désirée turns toward the bayou with her child and is never seen again. Then, in the startling ending, the husband learns that his own mother, who died when he was young, was the one who belonged to "the race that is cursed with the brand of slavery."

In "Désirée's Baby," Kate Chopin gave Désirée's husband, one of the most evil men in her fiction, the name Armand—a combination of Albert and Normand. Like Albert Sampite, the fictional Armand is unfaithful, brutal, brooding—and Satanic in appearance. Like Albert, too, Armand casts off his wife when she ceases to please him. But in real life, the deserted Loca Sampite was no romantic who lived only for her husband's love. Instead of turning toward the bayou, Loca Sampite had gone back to her mother, with her children, and she had survived.

For many Americans, 1893 was a devastating year. The Wall Street financial panic spread over the nation, forcing bankruptcies, throwing thousands out of work. In the South, cotton growers were ruined; in St. Louis, infants born into poor families starved and died in the sweltering tenements.

Kate Chopin, whose income came mostly from rental properties, was largely insulated from financial disaster. Her large white house in Cloutierville was rented out to Dr. S. O. Colvin, his wife, and two daughters, and she still owned some Cane River country land. In St. Louis, she still collected rent on the Seventh Street plot, now in the heart of the business district, that her father had bought more than forty years earlier.

Kate Chopin would never make a living from her writing, although she was writing quickly and earning as much as fifty dollars per story (the price the *Century* paid for "Azélie"). In 1893, Chopin earned a total of $189 from the sale of eleven stories, and she also wrote ten stories, nine of which were eventually published. (The exception was "An Idle Fellow," a first-person meditation rejected by seven magazines before Chopin put it aside in October of 1894.) In April 1893 alone, four Kate Chopin stories appeared in print: "The Lilies" (*Wide Awake*), "In and Out of Old Natchitoches" (*Two Tales*), and "A

Shameful Affair" and "Mrs. Mobry's Reason" (both in the *New Orleans Times-Democrat*).

Kate was still pushing at genteel strictures: In "In and Out of Old Natchitoches," a Cane River country schoolteacher is attracted to a sauntering New Orleans gambler who has a habit of trifling with women. In the story's most sexually charged scene, he "held the rose by its long, hardy stem, and swept it lightly and caressingly across her forehead, along her cheek, and over her pretty mouth and chin, as a lover might have done with his lips. He noticed how the red rose left a crimson stain behind it." The maidenly Suzanne is well aware of the sexual overtones: "She had been standing, but now she sank upon the bench that was there, and buried her face in her palms. A slight convulsive movement of the muscles indicated a suppressed sob."

Kate Chopin did not attempt to sell that story to the *Century* magazine, whose straitlaced editor, Richard Watson Gilder, barred any hint of sexuality. She received fifty dollars for the story from *Two Tales*, a Boston journal that was too avant garde for its audience, and lasted just two years (1892–93).

Kate was creating her own literary world in the Cane River country, with interlocking families: the Santiens, the Laballières, the Lafirmes. Possibly for commercial reasons, she also set several of her 1893 stories in New Orleans: "A Matter of Prejudice" (*Youth's Companion*) describes a Frenchwoman who has never in her life crossed Canal Street and disdains anything American; "In and Out of Old Natchitoches" shows the Cane River country teacher's flight to New Orleans; "A Lady of Bayou St. John" (*Vogue*) and "La Belle Zoraïde" (*Vogue*) take place in New Orleans during or before the Civil War, with wrenching portrayals of death and love, slavery and mastery. And in "At Chênière Caminada" (*New Orleans Times-Democrat*) Kate Chopin wrote her first Grand Isle story, a foreshadowing of *The Awakening*.

But by 1893, Kate was ambitious for literary success beyond the easy acceptance she was finding in *Youth's Companion* and *Vogue*. Although some regional short-story authors were nationally known and esteemed, it was difficult for writers outside the Northeast to receive literary attention—and so Kate decided on a self-promoting journey, as she wrote editor Marion A. Baker of the *New Orleans Times-Democrat* in May of 1893:

> I leave tonight for a two weeks absence in New York and Boston, and shall combine the business of seeking a publisher with the pleasure of—well, not seeking a publisher. I want to say, that any suggestion, recommendation, helpful hint, you might be kind enough to offer in the matter would be gratefully accepted and appreciated.

With her novel *Young Dr. Gosse* and her "Collection of Creole Stories," Kate left St. Louis on May 4, 1893, the day that the financial panic hit New

York. Newspapers were full of trust closings and bank failures—and during the week, *The New York Times* reported that Lizzie Borden had finally been arraigned in New-Bedford, Massachusetts, charged with murdering her father and stepmother.

Kate offered her "Collection of Creole Stories" to the Century Company; she also tried Appleton's, which published books and magazines, for *Young Dr. Gosse* and the story collection. She wrote to *Century* editor Gilder on May 10 with scrupulous care:

My dear Mr Gilder

I have left the MS of a novel—which I forgot to mention the other day—with the Messrs. Appleton. In using your kind note of intro- duction, however, I explained that it had no connection with the novel, of which you knew nothing, but had been written in refer- ence to a collection of short tales that you had subsequently con- sented to have read by the Century company.

I hope my action will not seem objectionable to you, or that you will not consider it, in any sense, a misuse of your cordial assis- tance.

Thanking you heartily for the same,

I am very faithfully yours
Kate Chopin

No information survives about Kate Chopin's meeting with Richard Watson Gilder, a meeting that would have taken place at the *Century*'s magnificent office on Union Square, with its polished floors, Turkish carpets, and stained-glass doors. Chopin might even have been invited to one of the "at home" evenings that Helena and Richard Watson Gilder held on Friday nights for visiting writers.

No records survive from the Boston part of Kate's trip. (A year later, after her second book was published, Rankin reports that "friends and the publisher advised her to go to Boston where the atmosphere was supposed to be literary. She went, and after three days fled home to St. Louis"—but nothing more can be discovered about such a trip.)

Possibly there had been more attractions for her in New York—including a romance.

❖ ❖ ❖

Kate Chopin had many male admirers. Her first biographer, Daniel Rankin, wrote that he had talked with men who had loved her, and "[a]ll declare they felt themselves in the presence of a rare woman who attracted them by an alluring quality which they found incapable of analysis. All speak of her charm, which made her attractiveness a contribution to the joys of life. All recall as vivid memories occasions with her when, as they watched the firelight shadows flicker on the wall of her study and pass like a caress over her face, they thought of her not as a widow with a household of children, but as a woman of mysterious fascination. . . . She knew she possessed a quality of sex that is inexplicable, and she realized its power."

But Rankin, interviewing people in 1930, a quarter-century after Kate Chopin's death, could not have spoken to many men of her generation. Her friend Dr. Kolbenheyer, who first encouraged her to write for publication, had died in 1921; the first editor to publish her, John A. Dillon, died in 1902; and the *St. Louis Mirror* editor, her friend William Marion Reedy, died in 1920. Albert Sampite, in Louisiana, had been dead for seventeen years. Even Kate's brother-in-law, Lamy Chopin, had been dead for twenty years, although his widow, Fannie, was one of Rankin's informants. Very few of Kate Chopin's contemporaries remained, and Rankin was recording what other, younger informants told him about her admirers—fragmentary recollections to which he added his own musings.

Still, there was gossip. Kate Chopin's niece Julia Breazeale, born in Natchitoches in 1895, heard that one of Kate's suitors had been the *St. Louis Post-Dispatch*'s editor in chief; Kate's granddaughter Marjorie Chopin, born in St. Louis three years after Kate's death, heard that Kate had been romantically involved with a New York literary man who was married to an invalid wife. That affair was said to be one reason that Kate Chopin stopped attending the Catholic church.

Both pieces of information point to the same man: John Alvarez Dillon, who lived in New York at the time of Kate's visit in 1893, and also during the winter of 1898–99, when she returned to New York.

Dillon was a St. Louisan, born in 1843 to a mother from an old French family and an Irish immigrant father. He was educated at the Christian Brothers College, virtually next door to the O'Flahertys' home, and he spent the Civil War years at Harvard: He was twenty when the Union government instituted a draft, but evidently his parents bought him an exemption. In 1865, he married Blanche Valle of St. Louis, whose mother was a Chouteau (St. Louis's equivalent of the Astors), and their honeymoon lasted for two years of "aristocratic leisure" in Italy.

By 1876, there were seven Dillon children, and Dillon had become one of the *St. Louis Globe-Democrat*'s best editorial writers, but he was always a little out of place. According to one historian, Dillon had "an easy but unostentatious familiarity with history, the classics, and literature, and a refined, somewhat rueful sense of humor. In time Dillon became schooled in the rough and tumble of journalism, but he was sensitive, easily discouraged, and sometimes apologetic—an oddity in a day of personal journalism when editors habitually composed libelous attacks upon their enemies." He was much like the mature Kate Chopin: intellectual, well-read, with a keen sense of humor.

Then, in 1879, John A. Dillon—dignified, sober-looking, with dark hair, blue eyes, and a neat mustache—opened a thoroughly incongruous partnership that lasted for the rest of his life. When he merged his year-old *St. Louis Evening Post* with the *St. Louis Dispatch*—just purchased by the gawky, scraggly-whiskered, frenetic Hungarian immigrant Joseph Pulitzer—the two men created the *Post-Dispatch*, a great crusading newspaper that exposed corruption and graft while reveling in local gossip. From the beginning, too, there was a link to Kate Chopin: Pulitzer's corporate vice president was Dr. Frederick Kolbenheyer, with whom he had hobnobbed at Fritz Roeslein's German bookstore in the early 1870s.

When Kate Chopin returned to St. Louis in 1884, John A. Dillon was editor in chief of the *Post-Dispatch*. He wrote editorials supporting women's equality, and the five Dillon daughters were among the first young women from St. Louis families to be educated beyond finishing school: All went to the Harvard Annex (later Radcliffe College).

Very early in her career, Kate Chopin sought John A. Dillon's literary advice. In May 1889, she had sent a short story, "A Poor Girl," to *Home Magazine*, where it was rejected on December 1. "Objection to incident not desirable to be handled," Kate noted in her account book, although the magazine also found the story "well written full of interest" and "would reconsider if changed." Although she rarely asked anyone for advice, she gave the story to Dillon to read, probably because his *Post-Dispatch* had published "A Point at Issue!," her first short story in print. (She did not note Dillon's advice in her account book.)

By June of 1891, John A. Dillon had moved to New York, summoned there by Joseph Pulitzer to edit the *New York World*, but Kate Chopin evidently still considered him an important literary connection: Later, when she published her first short-story collection, she made a point of sending him a copy. "Mr. Dillon has sent me a very frank and enthusiastic letter from New York after reading 'Bayou Folk,' " she wrote in her diary for May 28, 1894. "He sent me a feeble note some weeks ago, a note of faint and damning praise, where he pretended to have read it. It must have been hard for him to set aside the prejudice which I know he has had against my work, and for that reason so much more do I appreciate his frank letter."

Dillon's is the only reader's reaction that Kate Chopin recorded in her diary for that year. She valued his opinion in a special way—but the exact nature of their relationship cannot be known.

In late spring 1893, Kate Chopin had returned home from New York with new vigor, but without great results. Later in May, both the *Century* and Appleton's rejected her "Collection of Creole Stories." C. L. Webster, another New York publisher, refused it on June 29, but with some encouragement: "request to consider again next Winter if not placed by that time," Kate noted in her account book. Appleton's rejected *Young Dr. Gosse* in June, and the Arena Publishing Company rejected it in July, while—apparently undaunted— Kate sent her collection of Creole short stories to Houghton, Mifflin in Boston on July 1.

Always, she kept writing. On May 24 and 25, she produced "Madame Célestin's Divorce," the story of a Natchitoches woman who, wanting to divorce her husband, meets with the bishop. Her description of the meeting is—next to *At Fault*—Kate Chopin's strongest indictment of the Catholic view of marriage. (The fact that she wrote it just two weeks after her trip to New York suggests that she may have had John A. Dillon—or someone—in mind.)

The bishop, Madame Célestin says, eloquently described the temptations of divorce: "How it is the duty of a Catholic to stan' everything till the las' extreme. An' that life of retirement an' self-denial I would have to lead—he tole me all that." But "[t]he bishop don't know w'at it is to be married to a man like Célestin, an' have to endu' that conduc' like I have to endu' it. The Pope himse'f can't make me stan' that any longer, if you say I got the right in the law to sen' Célestin sailing." The local lawyer imagines marrying Madame, although they would have to leave Natchitoches—but in the end Célestin returns, promising to "turn ova a new leaf."

The story supports marriage in the end, but grudgingly—and the genteel *Century* rejected it by return mail.

In June of 1893, Kate abruptly turned to poetry, and sent *Vogue* six love lyrics: "The Song Everlasting," "You and I," "It Matters All," "If the Woods Could Talk," "A Sentimental Serenade," and "A Message." Two of them ("If the Woods Could Talk" and "You and I") were about past loves and secrets, and "You and I" asks the pointed question: "Was it love did we feel? was it life did we live?" *Vogue* rejected all six poems.

On the same day that she sent the poems, Kate also wrote the sketch "An Idle Fellow," in which the narrator berates herself for being too bookish, and learning too little from nature. She would do better, she tells herself, to follow the example of her friend Paul, who has deep intuitions: In people's eyes, "he reads the story of their souls." "An Idle Fellow," more unpolished than most of Chopin's short stories, never found a publisher.

During the summer of 1893, Kate also had guests: Lamy and Fannie Hertzog Chopin visited her on their honeymoon trip to the Columbian Exposition in Chicago, where Lamy exhibited a cabin from his plantation, advertised as the original "Uncle Tom's Cabin." Daniel B. Corley, a Texas huckster, had talked Lamy into the venture—a financial loss—and after the fair both the cabin and Corley disappeared. (The escapade also precipitated a long-lasting feud between Lamy and his brother-in-law Phanor Breazeale, who denounced the cabin as a hoax.)

Women were well represented at the fair, only a short train ride from St. Louis. In the Woman's Building, there were displays of women's achievements, including "Modern Woman," the Impressionist Mary Cassatt's celebrated mural, with its madonnalike female figures (possibly an inspiration for the figure of Madame Ratignolle in *The Awakening*). There was also controversy: At the Congress of Representative Women, black women protested their exclusion. The Chicago educator and reformer Fannie Barrier Williams pointed out that the untold stories of black women included "much that is sorrowful, much that is wonderfully heroic, and much that is romantic in a peculiar way in their history." Williams also spoke bluntly about the exploitation of slave women: Treated like animals, they were "not allowed to be modest, not allowed to follow the instincts of moral rectitude." They "could cry for protection to no living man"—nor could they rely on white women for help.

The fair seems to have fed Kate Chopin's imagination. In late August, she used the shimmering colors and sunny pastels of Impressionist painters like Mary Cassatt in "A Lady of Bayou St. John": The young Madame Delisle resembles a painting, with "the brilliancy of her golden hair, the sweet langour of her blue eyes, the graceful contours of her figure, and the peach-like bloom of her flesh." The Frenchman who woos her is also out of an Impressionist painting, dressed for a boating party: "clad always in cool, white duck, with a flower in his buttonhole."

But on the day that *Vogue* published "A Lady of Bayou St. John" (September 21, 1893), Kate Chopin wrote the story's darker counterpart. "La Belle Zoraïde," the tale told by Madame Delisle's slave Manna-Loulou, is the story that the black women told at the Chicago fair: the story of a woman of color whose body is not her own. Although Zoraïde's owner has engaged her to marry "a little mulatto" she detests, the light-skinned Zoraïde chooses to love "le beau Mézor," ebony black, who dances the Bamboula in Congo Square. She becomes pregnant by him, and hers is the first childbirth scene that Kate Chopin wrote for publication: "But there is no agony that a mother will not forget when she holds her first-born to her heart, and presses her lips upon the baby flesh that is her own, yet far more precious than her own." Then Zoraïde's cruel mistress says that the baby has died—whereupon Zoraïde goes mad with grief and spends the rest of her life clutching a bundle of rags, crying, "Li mouri" ("She is dead").

In "La Belle Zoraïde," Kate Chopin—the daughter of slave owners—looked on the thoughtless white world through the eyes of a woman of color, at a time when her Louisiana contemporaries Grace King and Ruth McEnery Stuart were still writing about happy slaves and tragic octoroons. Kate Chopin's Zoraïde, like the black women in Chicago—and like Chopin herself—insists on her own free will and her own destiny.

Also in the summer of 1893, the Old City House in St. Louis, the Sacred Heart Academy where Kate had gone to school, was dismantled. The nuns were leaving the congested city for a new country setting—and so another part of Katie O'Flaherty's past, the place where she had read books and told stories and played the piano, was gone. The last mass was said there on August 3.

That fall, on October 1, a hurricane destroyed the Grand Isle that Kate had known, and she wrote the story "At Chênière Caminada" from her memories.

But she did not need to dwell in the past. On August 11, Houghton, Mifflin had written that they wanted to publish her "Collection of Creole Stories"—and so, as 1893 ended, Kate Chopin was looking forward to her first nationally published book.

Chapter 15

BAYOU FOLK

THE FIRST NOTICE OF KATE Chopin's *Bayou Folk* appeared in *Publishers Weekly* on March 17, 1894, in a Houghton, Mifflin advertisement on page 450, for books to be published March 24.

> Under this title Mrs. Chopin includes several tales drawn from life among the Creoles and Acadians of Louisiana. They are faithful, spirited representations of unfamiliar characters and customs, but picturesque and altogether worthy of description and literary pres- ervation. The dialect of these semi-aliens is given, but not at such length as to be tedious; and it distinctly aids in imparting to the stories a genuine "local color." These stories are quite unlike most American tales, and cannot fail to attract much attention.

The first printing was a respectable 1,250 copies, selling at $1.25 each, and the volume was quite attractive, according to a lead review in *The Cottage Hearth*, a Boston home journal: "The book is simply, though beautifully bound in dark green and gold, and will be an addition to any library."

Of the twenty-three stories in *Bayou Folk*, all but four had been published before. Two of the new ones were sketches of Louisiana characters ("Old Aunt Peggy" and "A Gentleman of Bayou Têche"), and two were criticisms of mar- riage. In one, a wife leaves her violent husband ("In Sabine"); in the other, she thinks about divorce ("Madame Célestin's Divorce").

At Houghton, Mifflin's request, the first three *Bayou Folk* stories brought the "Santien boys" together. In "A No-Account Creole," the farmer Placide Santien gives up the young woman he loves; in "In and Out of Old Natchitoches," the gambler Hector Santien claims not to care about the schoolteacher Suzanne; and in "In Sabine," Grégoire Santien helps a beaten wife to escape, then rides off alone to Texas.

All three stories center on hotheaded young men, but the women characters grow progressively stronger. In "A No-Account Creole," the heroine expects to marry a man she does not love; in "In and Out of Old Natchitoches," she flirts with a gambler but returns to another man, who (she knows) has a bad temper and drinks too much. But in "In Sabine," the heroine leaves her brutal husband and goes off alone, to take her own risks. Kate wrote the Santien stories between 1888 and 1893—years in which she was also growing more vocal and more independent.

The rest of the *Bayou Folk* stories were arranged for variety: "Désirée's Baby" appears after half a dozen children's stories, while other adult stories, such as "Madame Célestin's Divorce," are intermixed with short sketches like "A Turkey Hunt." But the final five stories—"Ma'ame Pélagie," "At the 'Cadian Ball," "La Belle Zoraïde," "A Gentleman of Bayou Têche," and "A Lady of Bayou St. John"—are about adults and wrenching moments of decision. All but the "Gentleman" describe women who defy old patterns: They choose their own homes, their own lovers, and their own fates. The final stories point toward a different Kate Chopin, who would not be contented with charming local-color sketches.

In *Bayou Folk*, Chopin drew on her Cloutierville years for the varied dialects, ranging from standard French (which she rendered as standard English) to the patois spoken by poorer whites and blacks. She used real-life places as settings, notably Cloutierville and Shallow Lake House, the site of "For Marse Chouchoute." Some real-life characters were recognizable: Chartrand for the storekeeper Charles Bertrand in "Love on the Bon-Dieu"; Coton Maïs, the name of an Isle Brevelle family, for the ferryman in "Désirée's Baby." Dicey, the servant in "A Gentleman of Bayou Têche," had a real-life counterpart famous for her intuitions.

Kate Chopin did write about romance—often about men who fell passionately in love with women who were much more practical ("Azélie," "Love on the Bon-Dieu," "A Visit to Avoyelles"). But Chopin mostly imagined a world beyond marriage: Seven of her stories show fathers without wives, and two more have absent husbands who never appear. Only Baptiste in "Loka" and Jules in "A Visit to Avoyelles" are loved and lovable husbands, but Jules's wife (like Kate Chopin) is worn out from bearing four children in seven years. The other two *Bayou Folk* husbands—Armand in "Désirée's Baby" and Bud Aiken in "In Sabine"—are cruel and violent men who drive their wives away. They most resemble the other side of Albert Sampite.

The first review of *Bayou Folk* appeared in *The New York Times* on Sunday, April 1, 1894, under the headline "Living Tales from Acadian Life." It was anonymous, as were most American book reviews in the 1890s, and it filled nearly an entire column, with five long paragraphs. It was one of the longest notices *Bayou Folk* received—and one of the oddest.

The *Times* reviewer, obviously intrigued by *Bayou Folk*'s setting, devoted all but two sentences to pronouncements about Louisiana life and culture—many of them wrong. "The Acadian land of Louisiana, of which Kate Chopin writes, is flat," the *Times* review began, "and has the color of Peruvian gold. The Mississippi is like the Nile—lavish and deadly. The bayous are grayish, under large, dark trees in forests inextricably entangled. Trees, plants, flowers, and people grow riotously. There is extravagance of life, but if the people had an architecture it would be, as was the ancient Egyptian art, emblematic of immobility. The river is their Medusa."

The reviewer's Mississippi River was not Kate Chopin's: Of *Bayou Folk*'s twenty-three stories, all but four take place in the Cane River country, a hundred miles from the Mississippi River. In the remaining four ("A No-Account Creole," "In and Out of Old Natchitoches," "A Lady of Bayou St. John," and "La Belle Zoraïde"), the river is mentioned only in passing: no floods, no turnings to stone. Moreover, the *Times* reviewer, like most northerners, imagined that Louisiana bayous were overgrown swamps, rather than streams (Bayou St. John in New Orleans was a large, clear stream used for boating).

The *Times* reviewer made a point of explaining the origin of the Acadians, who "went to Louisiana when England won her war with France in America. Chateaubriand, Cooper, and Longfellow obtained for them recruits of good quality, but they were not men of affairs. The Catholic Church never abandoned them. They are still Frenchmen of the seventeenth century" who speak "an ancient French that priests and teachers vainly correct." Although some were educated, "the Creoles of New-Orleans call the Acadians ''Cajans,' disdainfully."

The *Times* reviewer was the first of many to misspell *Cajuns*, which Kate Chopin had spelled correctly in "A Gentleman of Bayou Têche." The reviewer also confused the Acadians (French-speaking refugees from Canada) with Creoles (Louisiana residents of pure French or Spanish ancestry)—although the reviewer did appreciate the unusual French names of Kate Chopin's characters, their melding of French and English, and their distinctive speech, in which they "slightly chant their phrases in agreeable Southern voices."

But the reviewer, overall, seemed to view the bayou folk of Louisiana as an exotic, not-quite-American species, "oscillating from the extreme of joy to the extreme of sorrow," and typically placing "a hut near a plantation palace built with a peristyle like a Greek temple." They were "barbarians softened by Catholicism," with a "pagan primitiveness."

Then, in the final two sentences, the *Times* reviewer gave an opinion, the first national critical judgment of Kate Chopin as a short-story writer: "A writer needs only the art to let these stories tell themselves. It is not an art easily acquired, but Kate Chopin has practiced it with force and charm in the several stories of her agreeable book."

Charming was a recurring word in later reviews of *Bayou Folk*: The *Portland Transcript*, for one, said, "These Creole and Acadian tales are so fine that no words save 'charming' and 'fascinating' will serve to describe them." According to *The Argonaut* of San Francisco, every story in *Bayou Folk* was "full of quaint charm"; —the *Boston Beacon* called the *Bayou Folk* stories "very charming in their delicacy of portraiture and felicity of coloring," with "the simplicity and grace of perfect truth." The *Hartford Daily Courant* praised the stories' "quaint dialogue and romance among unsophisticate [sic] forms of life" and called them "very charming in themselves," and eventually "of value as historic documents."

But at least one other reviewer felt the need to parade her own perceptions of Louisiana, rather than discuss what Kate Chopin had written. In *The Critic*, a New York monthly, Jeanette Gilder devoted a long paragraph to describing sluggish bayous, "the abodes of humidity, shadiness, shy sylvan life, the terrifying alligator, the cane-brake, the melodious mosquito . . . Along these Acherontian streams used to wander the Chacta Indians, and villages of them may still be seen here and there, while the silent *pirogue* or the 'Cadjen *bâteau* steals over the sombre waters and occasionally scares up a dazzling heron, a whirring *poule d'eau* or a flashing 'parrokeet.' "

The *Critic* reviewer did recognize that most of *Bayou Folk*'s stories take place in "Middle-Upper Louisiana," rather than in the Acadian country and New Orleans, but the reviewer seemed determined to downplay what "Miss (?) Chopin" had achieved: *Bayou Folk* was an "unpretentious, unheralded little book," with some sketches "like rude cartoons whose very rudeness brings out a more vivid effect." Still, Louisiana, the reviewer declared, "has another remarkable observer in this 'unannounced' lady" with her "photographic realism, shrewdness of observation and a fine eye for picturesque situations: which is only saying that Miss Chopin is herself, and nobody else."

The *Atlantic* also called Kate Chopin a unique talent and an "artist, and the entire ease with which she uses her material is born not less of an instinct for story-telling than of familiarity with the stuff out of which she weaves her stories. . . . Now and then she strikes a passionate note, and the naturalness and ease with which she does it impress one as characteristic of power awaiting opportunity." Kate Chopin, *The Atlantic* concluded, was "a genuine and delightful addition to the ranks of our story-tellers."

Other reviewers gave *Bayou Folk* similar praise, usually in one-paragraph reviews. *Public Opinion* liked *Bayou Folk*'s "Romance, pathos, humor, nobility and meanness, weakness and strength," all mingled so that "the close of the story leaves an agreeable impression—things come out right." The New Orleans *Daily Picayune* called *Bayou Folk* a "charming book" whose author "knows the country well and describes it charmingly, but the great charm of the book, besides its fluent, easy style, is the tender appreciation of the people of whom it treats. . . . [It] will make the author popular throughout the state."

But the *New Orleans Times-Democrat*, which sometimes published Chopin stories, questioned whether her "fresh and charming" stories were accurate. She "has the dialect down fine," the reviewer wrote, but of the sketches: "It may be that they are not all absolutely true to the letter of life, but they are true to its spirit, and some of them might well have been actual happenings."

Two reviewers did recognize Kate Chopin's major literary influence. According to *Review of Reviews*, *Bayou Folk* was "decidedly one of the best volumes of short stories which has appeared for some time," with stories that "might remind some readers of certain of finished bits of Maupassant and other French 'short story' masters." The *Pittsburg Bulletin* added that Kate Chopin's "observations of people and places seem to have been made after Flaubert's advice to his great pupil, De Maupassant, and her dramatic effects are worthy of that artist."

But only two national reviewers considered matters of literary technique. According to *The Nation*, Kate Chopin's "pen is an artist's in choice of subject, in touch, and in forbearance. There is never a word nor an idea too much, and in the score of sketches in which the same names often recur, there is no repetition, nevertheless, of herself or of others." According to *The Literary World*, "Some of these stories, by Kate Chopin, are little more than *croquis*—just a brief incident of [sic] idea sketched in with a few rapid strokes and left to the imagination of the reader to be *materialized*, if we may so speak. Others are longer and more finished, but all are full of that subtle, alien quality which holds the Creole apart from the Anglo-Saxon—a quality we do not quite understand and can never reproduce, but which is full of fascination to us from the very fact that it is so unlike ourselves."

In St. Louis, Kate Chopin got a great deal of attention. "Mrs. Kate Chopin's book 'Bayou Folk' is the best literary work that has come of the Southland in a long time. It is best because it is truest," William Marion Reedy wrote in the *Mirror*. He despised the "floridity of style" in many Southern writers, and called Kate Chopin "cleverer than Cable" and "a much stronger delineator" than

Mary Noailles Murfree. Reedy admired Chopin's "dramatic instinct," her humor ("of the quiet kind that produces an effect half way between a chuckle and a laugh"), and her restraint with dialect, which did not produce "that cheapest and most tawdry effect that has been called 'local color.'" Reedy commended the book to St. Louisans, most of whom did not know "that the talented authoress thereof resides in this city."

The *St. Louis Republic*'s one-paragraph review, unsigned by its author, W. R. Kelsoe, called *Bayou Folk* "an interesting little volume of Louisiana folk tales" whose author is "Mrs. Kate Chopin of this city. The descriptions are true to life, and the stories are well told. Life among the Creoles and Acadians of Louisiana is depicted in a manner which shows the author to have lived among them and to have thoroughly understood them."

The *St. Louis Post-Dispatch* also praised *Bayou Folk*, in five enthusiastic paragraphs. There was an "added charm," the reviewer wrote, in rereading the stories as a "connected narrative" with "real and human" characters living where "simplicity is still the rule and nature is not obscured by the veneer of civilization." The reviewer liked the humor and lack of sentimentality, and particularly praised "A Lady of Bayou St. John" as "a psychological study of the recesses of a woman's heart."

The reviewer, undoubtedly someone Kate Chopin knew from local literary gatherings, also knew that the stories were not entirely fiction: "She seems to have gone straight to the hearts of the Natchitoches folk. She has heard their little confidences of joy and grief." *Bayou Folk* showed a "delicacy of touch" and a "sureness of handling" with "a perfect confidence and an earnest of power only half-displayed," and "an almost austere adherence to art," with "moderation and economy of expression." For local readers, "That Mrs. Chopin is a Southern woman and St. Louisan is another source of gratification while reading this book."

Kate Chopin knew many newspaper people, but the reviews of *Bayou Folk* surprised her. She had expected serious discussion of her writing, but critics sometimes even misunderstood her plots: the *Post-Dispatch*, for instance, called "In Sabine"—the story of a brutal husband who abuses his wife—"full of humor."

"In looking over more than a hundred press notices of 'Bayou Folk' which have already been sent to me," Kate wrote in her diary on June 7, "I am surprised at the very small number which show anything like a worthy critical faculty." The worthwhile ones "might be counted upon the fingers of one hand. I had no idea the genuine book critic was so rare a bird. And yet I receive congratulations from my publishers upon the character of the press notices."

She grumbled in her diary over the critical reception of another writer, Mary

E. Wilkins, whose novel *Pembroke* "is the most profound, the most powerful piece of fiction of its kind that has ever come from the American press. And I find such papers as the N. Y. Herald—the N. O. Times Democrat devoting half a column to senseless abuse of the disagreeable characters which figure in the book. No feeling for the spirit of the work, the subtle genius which created it."

As early as 1894, Kate Chopin knew that reviewers preferred books they could praise for being charming, wholesome, and agreeable. Five years later, when she published *The Awakening*, she would be accused of the same sins that Mary E. Wilkins had committed in *Pembroke*, her novel about a stern New England will. Chopin, like Wilkins, would be accused of writing something unhealthy, unwholesome, and simply "disagreeable."

In late June 1894, buoyed by the acclaim for *Bayou Folk*, Kate Chopin attended her first literary conference, the annual meeting of the Western Association of Writers. Founded in 1886 by would-be authors, the association met at Spring Fountain Park in Warsaw, Indiana, not far from Winona Lake, a 160-acre resort with artificial lakes and islands, flowers, hotels with spacious verandas, a small steamboat and "the great battle panarama The Siege of Chattanooga." There were also shady wooded paths along the lake, where James Whitcomb Riley sometimes held forth.

The "Hoosier Poet" was one of two well-known writers in the group; the other was the historical novelist Mary Hartwell Catherwood. Paul Laurence Dunbar, just launching his career, read a poem called "Character Sketch" at the meeting Kate Chopin attended. But mostly the group consisted of bookworms and would-be poets, and there were nay-sayers: One newspaperman called the Western Association the "Literary Gravel Pit Association"; another termed it "The Writers Singing Bee"; and the *Indianapolis Journal* implied that the annual convention was just an excuse for unpublished poets to "get together and pelt each other with verses."

The Association conference lasted from Tuesday through Friday, June 26–29, but Kate was a late arrival from Anderson, Indiana: "It was a great pleasure for me to walk through the beautiful streets of Anderson at 5 o'clock last Tuesday morning," she wrote in her diary. "The yards were green with foliage and crisp with the early due. We stopped for breakfast at an inviting looking boarding house, whose landlady waited herself, upon table—paint, cosmetics and all at that early hour! Northern Indiana at this season of the year is really a garden spot."

Chopin probably attended the conference with her friend Harriet Adams Sawyer of St. Louis, an association vice president, music lover, and "harmless poet." Mrs. Sawyer, an admirer of *The Heavenly Twins* for "helping young girls to a fuller comprehension of truth in the marriage relation," had a musically gifted daughter who was, according to Kate, "more rusé than her mother."

The Tuesday morning conference session began with a humorous poem, followed by four days of literary discussion, poems, and the reading of papers on such subjects as "Sanitization, Mentally and Physically," "The Schoolmaster in Literature," "The Newest Light on the Oldest Art," and "The Novel— Its Uses and Abuses."

Kate Chopin did not appear on the program—but she evidently watched, listened, and disapproved, as she wrote in a blunt diary entry as soon as she returned home, on June 30: "Provincialism in the best sense of the word stamps the character of this association of writers, who gather chiefly from the State of Indiana and meet annually at Spring Fountain Park. It is an ideally beautiful spot, a veritable garden of Eden in which the disturbing fruit of the tree of knowledge still hangs unplucked."

Chopin described the writers in very unflattering terms: Although Riley, Catherwood, and Lew Wallace (author of *Ben Hur*) had made an impact on "the world beyond," she wrote, most of the association's members were "singers" whose worship of nature and country life was "the chief burden of their often too sentimental songs." They held a wholesome faith in God, the church, the land, and social institutions, and disliked anything that might ruffle them: "Among these people are to be found an earnestness in the acquirement and dissemination of book-learning, a clinging to past and conventional standards, an almost Creolean sensitiveness to criticism and a singular ignorance of, or disregard for, the value of the highest art forms."

They were out of touch with real life, she felt: "The cry of the dying century has not reached this body of workers, or else it has not been comprehended." They had missed much: "There is a very, very big world lying not wholly in northern Indiana, nor does it lie at the antipodes, either. It is human existence in its subtle, complex, true meaning, stripped of the veil with which ethical and conventional standards have draped it."

Still, if the Western Writers' "earnestness of purpose and poetic insights shall have developed into students of true life and true art, who knows but they may produce a genius such as America has not yet known."

Chopin sent her piece on "The Western Association of Writers" to *The Critic*, which had published its favorable review of *Bayou Folk* on May 5 and liked articles that were "cultivated, varied, and gossipy." As Kate jotted hastily in her diary, "Critic accepted my paragraph upon 'The Western Association of Writers' to be published this week, and offer me a years subscription to the paper— not bad when I expected nothing for it, and hardly thought it would be used."

The Critic published the essay on July 7, and Kate Chopin's criticisms were soon reprinted in the *Indianapolis Journal* (July 16), on the front page of the

Brookville (Indiana) *American* (July 19), and in other newspapers. Middle Western readers saw what Kate Chopin of St. Louis really thought: that the Western Association of Writers was a bunch of literary bumpkins.

A few days later, Kate was attacked in print for the first time.

The essay, unsigned, appeared in the *Minneapolis Journal* on July 21. It was reprinted, verbatim, in the *Cincinnati Commercial Gazette* a week later, and almost certainly by other newspapers around the Middle West. The article began by misspelling Kate's last name: "Kate Chapin, in the Critic, writes unkindly and bitterly of the Western Association of Writers, because it is provincial enough to stick to Indiana and meet every year at Spring Fountain Park."

Chopin's critic was insultingly familiar: "Kate says these literary people have 'a singular ignorance of, or disregard for the value of the highest art forms,' and are not students of 'true life and true art.' That may all be, but Whitcomb Riley belongs to that association, and he is a literary artist of a very extraordinarily talented kind. It depends upon what Kate calls 'highest art forms.' "

To Kate Chopin's critic, "It would seem that Riley struck a very high form of art when he showed he was able to give to the world such poems of the common people of his section that they saw the likeness and went after his verses as they go for the sugar trees in the spring. It is a case of high art like that of the Greek painter who painted fruit so true to nature that the birds flew down and picked at his canvas." As for the Association, Kate's detractor concluded, "The Western Association of Writers, however, has members outside of Indiana. There is much Indiana talent in it, and Indianians are a little clannish; but the association is intended to have a wide, interstate scope, and it will probably have it in time."

Kate Chopin never answered her critic in print, but in her private writings she expressed a deep melancholy. By late July, she was staying at the Cedars, a former plantation and resort village in Sulphur Springs, Missouri, twenty-three miles southwest of St. Louis, on the Mississippi River. On vacation, she liked to stay up late: In Indiana she had delighted in her 5:00 A.M. walk, and at the Cedars she wrote a meditation at 11:00 P.M. on July 24, three days after the criticism of "Kate Chapin" appeared in the Minneapolis *Journal*.

She began in a mood of despair: "I am losing my interest in human beings; in the significance of their lives and their actions. Some one has said it is better to study one man than ten books. I want neither books nor men; they make me suffer. Can one of them talk to me like the night—the Summer night? Like the stars or the caressing wind?"

But then she began to take a healing, almost erotic pleasure in her surroundings: "The night came slowly, softly, as I lay out there under the maple tree.

It came creeping, creeping stealthily out of the valley, thinking I did not notice. . . . The night is solemn and it means mystery. . . . My whole being
was abandoned to the soothing and penetrating charm of the night. . . . The
wind rippled the maple leaves like little warm love thrills."

But then, her spell was broken: "A man came to-day with his 'Bible Class.'
He is detestable with his red cheeks and bold eyes and coarse manner and
speech. What does he know of Christ? Shall I ask a young fool who was born
yesterday and will die tomorrow to tell me things of Christ? I would rather ask
the stars: they have seen him."

The religious note at the end was not characteristic of Kate Chopin, and a
few months later, she would be reviewing one of the Catholic Church's pro-
hibited novels for *St. Louis Life*. If she worshiped anything, found solace in
anything, it was in nature, and in the night—and in herself.

On the following day, Kate wrote the story of "Dorothea" in her diary, about
a three-year-old whose mother had died in childbirth during the winter. At a
summer resort, Dorothea adopts another guest as her "mama," but when the
guest leaves, Kate wonders, "What will poor little Dorothea do now." The
story, more literary than many of Kate's diary entries, may have been fiction,
but she never attempted to publish it. It lacked the happy resolution that *Youth's
Companion* and other children's magazines insisted on—and as a mother, Kate
may have felt that it was too sad.

The next day, Kate wrote an entirely different story, "Juanita," about "a
character who does not reflect credit upon her family or her native town of
Rock Springs." A very large young woman (five feet ten, over two hundred
pounds), Juanita has a "fresh and sensuous beauty" that men find irresistible.
She takes up with a poor, shabby, one-legged man, who is also the father of
her child (they claim there was a secret marriage). Juanita is last seen going
with her husband into the woods, "where they may love each other away from
all prying eyes save those of the birds and the squirrels. But what do the squirrels care! For my part I never expected Juanita to be more respectable than a
squirrel; and I don't see how any one else could have expected it."

"Juanita," with its jaunty ending, was Chopin's first story set in Missouri in
three years, and it was inspired by the true experiences of a postmaster's daughter, Annie Venn of Sulphur Springs, whose mother disapproved of everything
except the baby.

For Kate, "Juanita" may have been just a literary exercise. Usually she sent
stories out the day she finished them, but she waited ten months before she
sent her nighttime meditation, "The Night Came Slowly," and "Juanita," together, to *Moods*, a Philadelphia magazine that accepted them immediately
and published them under the title "A Scrap and a Sketch" in July 1895.

In other stories she wrote in 1894, Kate Chopin was also creating stronger, less conventional female characters. In her first story of the year, "A Respectable Woman," she described a woman who was attracted to her husband's best friend—and who might pursue the attraction. In April, Kate wrote "The Story of an Hour," about a woman who revels in the report that her husband is dead; in November, she wrote "Her Letters," about a woman who takes a passionate secret with her to her grave.

Kate also kept a diary, a brown-covered school composition notebook she called "Impressions. 1894." It is the only surviving diary from her adult years, and it gives, in her own words, the sole picture of her mental and professional life in the 1890s, the decade of her literary success.

Kate Chopin opened "Impressions" with an odd encounter. "It was at first an amusing figure which very soon became interesting and pathetic—the old gentleman whom I found sitting at Mrs. Moore's elbow today when I went into her office," Kate wrote in her diary for May 4. The man was reading, aloud, his poem "on the subject of the commonweal army"—one of those "endless refrains written on foolscap—pages and pages of it."

While Kate sat, watching, Sue V. Moore—editor of *St. Louis Life*—proved to be "a kinder and gentler woman than I thought for she listened quite patiently," and told the man that the *Arena* magazine might be interested in his writing ("That was hardly kind," Kate thought). As he left, the man bowed apologetically to Kate, and "looking into his gentle old gray bearded face I was forced to forgive him."

Then Kate found out why the editor had been so tactful: "The old fellow it appears is an anarchist!" That gave the whole scene a comic cast: "Fancy an anarchist armed with no more serious a bomb than a poem which he carries into the offices of publishers there to accomplish its deadly work. I believe it is not today or tomorrow that this insidious explosive will get in its work on the public—not while there remains the live body of a publisher to stand between."

Kate used the diary for a few more "Impressions," thumbnail sketches: A woman at a photographer's office, Kate recorded, was at fist "repellant, with her short fat figure and short brown curly hair. But there is a straightforwardness, a dignity and gentle refinement about her manner that surprises and attracts. She draws me, somehow." (Chopin never mentioned the woman again, although Lacodie's wife in "A Sentimental Soul" resembles her somewhat; for a writer, everything is material.) Eventually Kate used her "Impressions" notebook for writings she would send out for publication: two essays, three translations from Guy de Maupassant, eight poems, and four short stories. Virtually all were eventually published, and little changed from her original notebook copies (which may not have been first drafts).

Also in her diary, Kate Chopin described parties at which anarchism was discussed (with the panic of 1893, radical ideas were in the air). She often mentioned her card playing, calling herself a "euchre fiend," and she recorded her bewilderment and annoyance with society people, inept reviewers, and would-be authors—for by mid-1894, in St. Louis, she had become a celebrity.

"I fear it was the commercial instinct which decided me. I want the book to succeed," Kate explained to her diary on May 4, six weeks after the publication of *Bayou Folk*. She had missed her euchre club again, because "Mrs. Whitmore insisted upon having me go out to her house to meet Mrs. Ames and her daughter Mrs. Turner, who were anxious to know me and hear me read my stories." In April, the *St. Louis Mirror* reported, "The members of the Duodecimo Club had the pleasure of listening to Miss Chopin reading from her book at their meeting Monday afternoon at the residence of Mrs. J. S. James, 4130 West Bell place. She is very well spoken of as a reader."

The *Mirror's* William Marion Reedy liked to mock those society people who did not appreciate Kate Chopin. On April 15, in the same issue with his praise of *Bayou Folk*, he included a satirical exchange:

> . . . a member of the Writers Club, that most remarkable organization the shining lights of which are Mr. James Falsetto Cox and Mrs. J. Belisarius Legg, called upon a friend of mine a short time ago and asked him to do something in the literary line for one of their meetings.
> "Why don't you," said he, "have Mrs. Chopin deliver an address to you."
> "Who?" said this particular grass widow of the Writers' Club.
> "Why, Mrs. Chopin."
> "Mrs. Showpan! Don't know her. She isn't a writer."
> My friend then told the Writer of Mrs. Chopin's fame, but the Writer did not deem her worth inviting to the riot of reason and flood of soul at the meeting of the Writers' Club. The idea of regarding a mere producer of tender and witty stories as a Writer to be compared to the galaxy of ladies who write the society "articles"—a line, line-and-a-half or two-line announcements of arrivals and departures—is preposterous.

But truly literary people knew all about Kate Chopin: Sue V. Moore had assiduously been promoting her friend in the pages of *St. Louis Life*. On January 6, in its "Society" column, the magazine had noted: "Mrs. Kate Chopin, of Morgan Street, has a charming story in the January *Century*, called 'A No-Account Creole.' It is one of the best that this gifted writer has published. Mrs. Chopin has made a great reputation in the East as a writer of dialect stories.

Many think she handles the soft French Creole dialect better even than Cable, who was the first to open that rich vein in our varied American literature. Mrs. Chopin is writing a story for the *Atlantic* by request of the editor."

The prestigious *Atlantic* had indeed solicited a story from Kate Chopin, but rejected "At Chênière Caminada." Still, H. E. Scudder sent a very encouraging letter:

> It can perhaps be of little moment to you, but when I publish for the first time a story by a writer I like—especially when the writer has already won recognition—to have it distinctly an acquisition, and I am bound to say that though this story has in it the tone of your work, it is by no means one I should select with which to introduce you to the readers of the Atlantic. Indeed, had it been offered with your other stories for the book I am inclined to think I might have pleaded with you to omit it. This is not to say that the story is ill told, but that the motif has been used so much; there is really not much to distinguish it from other of its kind save the difference which comes from costume so to speak.

> Pardon me if I am too blunt in this decision, but I wanted you to know how honestly I wish a story from you, and how greatly I regret that this is not the one I want!

The Atlantic rejected two more Chopin stories, "In Sabine" and "A Gentleman of Bayou Têche"—but finally, in March, the magazine accepted "Tante Cat'rinette." Chopin received forty dollars, not her highest payment to date, but *The Atlantic* had a particular cachet among literary people, especially in New York and Boston.

In fact, Kate's was a singular achievement. Agnes Repplier, the Philadelphia novelist and essayist, used to tell aspiring authors that she had been publishing for almost fifteen years before she got into *The Atlantic*, which she called "the taste of the brightest corner of the American literary world." Kate Chopin had accomplished that feat in only five years. (Chopin eventually sent *The Atlantic* a total of thirteen stories—one of them twice—from which they accepted just two more, "Athénaïse" and "Nég Créol.")

"Tante Cat'rinette" made Kate Chopin's *Atlantic* debut in September 1894. Although editor Scudder thought it a fit demonstration of her talents, it was little more than a rethinking of her earlier "Beyond the Bayou." Both depict devoted slaves who, after the war, take enormous risks to save a cherished child in their former owner's family. Tante Cat'rinette even follows directions (she thinks) from her former master, who died years earlier. The *Atlantic* editors, based in Boston, evidently preferred short stories that did not disturb comfortable ideas about race and class.

Even Kate Chopin, on the day that she read the proofs for "Tante Cat'rinette," felt a need for something fuller and racier. "Received Copy of 'Tante Cat'rinette' from Atlantic for correction," she wrote in her diary for July 6. "Suppose it will appear in September. Read a few delicious comedies of Aristophanes last night."

Although she was ambitious for literary recognition, Kate Chopin recognized that the *Atlantic* would not be interested in the kind of amoral French stories she was reading and studying. The next item in her diary, five days later, is a translation of Guy de Maupassant's *"Un cas de divorce"*—in which a woman seeks a divorce because of her husband's "strange sexual perversion," an erotic obsession with flowers. Chopin translated *semence* (semen or seed) as "life," possibly to make her translation more acceptable, but the story was still far too graphic for American editors, with such lines as "I have hot houses to which no one penetrates but myself. . . . [The orchids] spread their flanks, odorant, and transparent, open for love and more tempting than all women's flesh."

Chopin's translation of "A Divorce Case" never found a publisher.

Meanwhile amateur authors were pursuing Kate: Her neighbor Mrs. Hull "solicited an interview to talk over a desire which she has to get into print," Kate noted in her diary. Lizzie Chambers Hull, nearly fifty, was "a delightful little woman; so small—hardly bigger than a child of ten, with a homely irregular face and a forehead of unusual height, debth [sic] and bumpiness." The mother of four and the wife of a coal merchant, Mrs. Hull belonged to the Wednesday Club and "knows she can write as good stories as she reads in the magazines (such belief in her own ability is a bad omen)."

Although Mrs. Hull was an entertaining observer of people, Kate doubted her ability to "give these impressions literary form." Still, "I never pick up such a MS but with the hope that I am about to fall upon a hidden talent." But the first thousand words—which Kate read before visitors arrived—were "all employed to tell how a black girl came in possession of her name. It should have been told in five lines." Eight days later, Kate finished reading Mrs. Hull's story, on "a theme which Cable has used effectively. A girl with negro blood who is loved by a white man. Possessing a noble character she effaces herself and he knows her no more—she dies of consumption."

Mrs. Hull did at least write good English, Kate noted, and knew her subject, and "I have no objection to a commonplace theme if it be handled artistically or with originality." But Mrs. Hull lacked the needed spark: "I fear she will not be able to give the literary form which goes to the making of an acceptable story. No freshness, spontaneity or originality of perception. The whole tendency is in the conventional groove."

Lizzie Hull needed to do what Kate Chopin had done: "study critically some of the best of our short stories. I know of no one better than Miss Jewett to study for technique and nicety of construction. I don't mention Mary E. Wilkins for she is a great genius and genius is not to be studied. We are unfortunately being afflicted with imitations of Miss Wilkins *ad nauseum*." (Evidently Kate considered the New Englander Sarah Orne Jewett suitable reading for her neighbor; she did not even mention Guy de Maupassant.)

There were also bad models about: "I cannot yet discover any serious significance in the present craze for the hysterical morbid and false pictures of life which certain English women have brought into vogue. They appeal to a certain order of mind just as Miss Breddon appeals to another and E. P. Roe to a third." (E. P. Roe was an American clergyman turned novelist; Mary Elizabeth Braddon was an English writer of sensational novels—and Kate Chopin, not above trading on other writers' popularity, gave one of her short stories the same title as a Braddon novel, *Dead Men's Shoes*.)

Meanwhile, there were nonliterary irritants in Kate's life—such as parrots: "detestable birds with their blinking stupid eyes and heavy clumsy motions. I never could become attached to one," she wrote in her diary in May. Moreover: "It made me positively ill today when I had gone to pass a few hours with Blanche, to be forced to divide her society and attention with her own parrot and a neighbor's which she had borrowed. Fancy any sane human being doubling up an affliction in that way."

But Blanche, probably her Charleville cousin Blanche Bordley, also rewarded Kate with "delicious homegrown strawberries (the first) for luncheon. Their flavor somehow recalled James Lane Allen's exquisite story 'A Kentucky Cardinal,' begun in the May Harpers. What a refreshing idealistic bit it is, coming to us with the budding leaves and the bird-notes that fill the air." (Allen, a Kentuckian living in New York, was a year older than Kate Chopin, and also wrote nostalgically about nature and country life. As late as 1900— after both had endured charges of immorality and coarseness in their writing— Kate would call him "the incomparable James Lane Allen.")

But long before that, Kate had resigned herself to Blanche's fondness for birds, and even gave her three in December 1895, with a verse:

> I might have sent you flowers
> Or of bonbons sent you showers!
> But knowing where your love lies

> Why send what you would dispise?
> So to fill your soul with glee,
> Why, I send you puffins three.

Two days after visiting Blanche and her parrot, Kate began writing "Lilacs," about the widowed Adrienne Farival who retreats to the Sacred Heart convent every spring—never telling the sisters who love her that for the rest of the year, she is a decadent woman of the world, an actress who takes lovers. (In Paris, Adrienne even has a clumsy green parrot, who blinks "stupidly" when coaxed to speak.) But one spring, when Adrienne smells the lilacs and rushes from Paris to the convent, she is barred from entering. A lay sister hands her a letter, returns her presents, and—in the last image of the story—sweeps away the lilac blooms Adrienne had left behind on the convent portico.

"Lilacs" had its counterpart in Kate Chopin's life: She had chosen the worldly life, while Kitty Garesché had joined the Sacred Heart nuns, five months before Kate's wedding. Kate was living in New Orleans when Kitty made her profession, and in July 1885 Kitty's mother had died, just a month after Eliza O'Flaherty. In 1888, Kitty, who had been teaching at the Sacred Heart school in Chicago, returned to St. Louis to be mistress of studies at Maryville, a new Sacred Heart school. By then, Kate was on the verge of a literary career: The poem "If It Might Be" appeared in print on January 10, 1889.

But when Kate visited a St. Louis convent five years later, it was to see another school friend. It was May 20, four days after she had written "Lilacs," and Kate was still musing about cloistered and worldly women: "Those nuns," she wrote in her diary, "seem to retain or gain a certain beauty with their advancing years which we women in the world are strangers to. The unchanging form of their garments through years and years seems to impart a distinct character to their bodily movements."

And so, Kate wrote, "Liza's face held a peculiar fascination for me as I sat looking into it enframed in its white rushing," and "in less than twenty minutes those twenty years had vanished and she was the Liza of our school days." Kate's description of Liza was worldly: "The same narrow, happy eyes with their swollen upper lids; the same delicious upward curves to the corners of her pretty mouth. No little vexatious wrinkles anywhere. Only a few good strong lines giving a touch of character that the younger Liza lacked perhaps. The conditions under which these women live are such as keep them young and fresh in heart and in visage."

The Sacred Heart nuns, she knew, did mingle the romantic with the religious, the sensual with the sacred: "One day—usually one hey-day of youth they kneel before the altar of a God whom they have learned to worship, and they give themselves wholly—body and spirit into his keeping. They have only to remain faithful through the years, these modern Psyches, to the lover who lavishes all his precious gifts upon them in the darkness—the most precious of which is perpetual youth."

Kate also wondered "what Liza thought as she looked into my face. I know she was remembering my pink cheeks of more than twenty years ago and my brown hair and innocent young face. I do not know whether she could see that I had loved—lovers who were not divine—and hated and suffered and been glad. She could see, no doubt the stamp which a thousand things had left upon my face, but she could not read it. She, with her lover in the dark. He has not anointed her eyes for perfect vision. She does not need it—in the dark."

As Kate left the convent, the friend who accompanied her said of Liza, "Would you not give anything to have her vocation and happy life!"

Kate gazed around at the grass and the trees, and saw an old man leaning on a cane, "walking down the path holding a small child by the hand and a little dog was trotting beside him. 'I would rather be that dog' I answered her. I know she was disgusted and took it for irreverence and I did not take the trouble to explain that this was a little picture of life and that what we had left was a phantasmagoria."

Kate wanted reality, she wrote in her diary eleven days later, the kind of reality an earthly lover could provide: "There are a few good things in life— not many, but a few. A soft, firm, magnetic sympathetic hand clasp is one. A walk through the quiet streets at midnight is another. And then, there are so many ways of saying good night!"

Sometimes Kate grew moody: "Am I becoming more sensitive and suscepti- ble. Things which bore me and which I formerly made an effort to endure, are insupportable to me," she wrote on June 7. Meanwhile, "[m]y love and reverence for pure unadulterated nature is growing daily."

Sometimes, during the time when the *Bayou Folk* reviews were flooding in, she most appreciated the opportunity not to be literary.

"God! what a delight it was—the pure sensuous beauty of it, penetrating and moving as love!" Kate wrote about a May 28 excursion, with twenty other women, to the hills of Glencoe, outside St. Louis. She noted the "intensely blue" sky, the silvery Meramec River, and the log cabins ("ruder and more primitive than the negro cabins of Louisiana"). She described rural characters, including a skeleton-thin man who turned his back on the visitors, while a "half-dozen barefooted, fat children stared, however, and so did the dog." A black woman "laughed and bowed pleasantly to us," while a rough-looking fellow, bending over a plow, reminded her of "one of Hamlin Garland's impersonations."

Kate mentioned that to a woman next to her, who "didn't seem to know what I meant and I was glad of it. I hadnt come to the Glencoe hills to talk literature! She is the little woman who calls me Mrs. Chovin and hasnt the slightest idea that I write. Its delicious."

Chapter 16

LITERARY CELEBRITY

"HOW CURIOUSLY THE PAST effaces itself for me!" Kate Chopin wrote in her diary on May 22, 1894, her son Jean's twenty-third birthday. "I sometimes regret that it is so; for there must be a certain pleasure in retrospection."

Still, "I cannot live through yesterday or tomorrow. It is why the dead in their character of dead and association with the grave have no hold upon me. I cannot connect my mother or husband or any of those I have lost with those mounds of earth out at Calvary cemetery. I cannot visit graves and stand contemplating them as some people do, and seem to love to do."

Nevertheless: "If it were possible for my husband and my mother to come back to earth, I feel that I would unhesitatingly give up every thing that has come into my life since they left it and join my existence again with theirs. To do that, I would have to forget the past ten years of my growth—my real growth. But I would take back a little wisdom with me; it would be the spirit of a perfect acquiescence."

In the ten years since her mother's death, Kate Chopin's life had thoroughly changed. She had moved away from her relatives and joined a literary circle; she had become a nationally famous author. With her mother still alive, Kate might not have written "The Story of an Hour," about a woman happy to be widowed by a railroad crash. With Oscar still alive, Kate might not have written about that woman's "monstrous joy" at the loss of her husband. Had both been living, Kate might not have been a writer at all. Grief had spawned her career; ambition and acclaim intensified it.

❅   ❅   ❅

In the 1890s, many authors were celebrities. They went on tour and visited exotic locales; their adventures were reported in Sunday magazines. But to the book-buying public, Kate Chopin was virtually unknown, and the success of *Bayou Folk* made her into a subject of curiosity. Abruptly published by a famous house—Houghton, Mifflin—she appeared to have no antecedents.

She had been published frequently in *Youth's Companion* and *Harper's Young People*, but those circulated mostly to households with children; she had appeared in *Vogue*, but its circulation outside New York fashionable circles was small. Other literary magazines, such as *Moods* and *Two Tales*, were short-lived and poorly distributed. The *Century* magazine had published just one of her stories.

The *Providence Sunday Journal*, for one, had wondered about the author. A *Bayou Folk* review began with the comment, "A new name is signed to the sketches of 'Cajun life that make up this volume, but if they are the work of an unpracticed hand they are marvellous in the finished artlessness of their art." Others wondered if "Kate Chopin" was even a real name.

Sue V. Moore, editor of *St. Louis Life*, was the first to answer readers' questions. "Very few authors have made such a success with their first book as has fallen to the share of Mrs. Chopin, and St. Louis has now the honor of being the birth-place and home of one of the foremost writers of American fiction," Moore wrote in a June 9, 1894, article. It was another opportunity to boost her friend's literary career, for *Bayou Folk* reviewers had recently placed Kate Chopin in distinguished literary company, "beside Miss Wilkins, Grace King, George W. Cable and other American authors of acknowledged fame."

The reviews, quoted in Moore's article, praised Kate Chopin's use of dialect and her descriptions of Louisiana life, and Moore added that "Mrs. Chopin herself is a Creole and has lived much of her life in New Orleans and on her Natchitoches plantation"—although she had begun life as "one of the belles of St. Louis."

Knowing that audiences were eager for personal tidbits, Sue V. Moore wrote that Kate Chopin was "the exact opposite of the typical bluestocking," without "literary affectations," "fads," or "serious purpose in life." She did not consciously observe people to use them in stories, but she was an omnivorous reader, preferring Guy de Maupassant over all other French writers. Walt Whitman was "one of her favorites in English, and she always has a copy of his prose writings, as well as his 'Leaves of Grass,' at hand."

As for Kate Chopin herself: "In appearance she is a very pretty woman, of medium height, plump, with a mass of beautiful gray hair almost white, regular features, and brown eyes that sparkle with humor. Her five tall sons and pretty young daughter, who have all inherited from some ancestor a height and slenderness that the mother does not possess, make a most attractive family group, the beauty of which is greatly enhanced by the thorough *entente cordiale* that exists among them. They all take the greatest interest in their mother's work."

Sue V. Moore's "Kate Chopin," with an autographed sketch of Kate wearing a fluffy hat and looking sternly at her audience, found favor with readers and editors. Most of it was reprinted in *Current Literature* two months later, in a section on "General Gossip of Authors and Writers," and a year later in *Book News*.

Meanwhile Chopin's friend William Schuyler had also written a profile, which Kate mentioned in her diary for May 28, 1894: "Mr S. has agreed to write a personal sketch of me which 'The Writer' has asked for. He has done it admirably. I don't know who could have done it better; could have better told in so short a space the story of my growth into a writer of stories."

By 1894, William Schuyler was thirty-nine and part of Kate's circle, although his wife was a puzzle: "Mr. and Mrs. Schuyler were here one evening," Kate also wrote in her diary for May 28. "I never saw her so attractive, sparkling, scintillant like a charged battery. But I do not *know* her, or even think I know her." (It was also not uncommon for wives of her male friends to be standoffish around Kate Chopin.)

Schuyler, the hawk-nosed, beetle-browed son of an Episcopalian minister, was a novelist and musician who had made one of the first serious studies of the spirituals sung by southern blacks. He also admired Brahms and Wagner long before other Americans did. Later, he became the future author Fannie Hurst's teacher at Central High School, and he composed musical settings for literary works, including Stephen Crane's "Black Riders" and Kate Chopin's "In Spring," "You and I," and "The Song Everlasting." Kate, in turn, composed at least one affectionate Christmas verse for the Schuylers, an 1895 poem, "To Hider Schuyler."

Will Schuyler's 1894 article on Kate Chopin agreed with Sue V. Moore's on most points. Both recounted Kate's ancestry; both described her writing methods (requiring very little revision); both praised her characterization. But Schuyler pointed out that Kate Chopin "is not the 'young person' that many of her reviewers are bent on thinking her to be. This wrong impression of theirs regarding her, while it is in some respects flattering, is one which Mrs. Chopin seems anxious to correct."

Kate Chopin was French and Irish, Schuyler wrote, deriving her "delicate and sensuous touch and the love of art for art's sake" from her Celtic and French blood. She grew up in a slave-owning household; she was a "teller of marvellous stories" who also loved to read. After school she had become "one of the acknowledged belles of St. Louis, a favorite not only for her beauty, but also for her amiability of character and her cleverness." She became a wife, mother, and widow, and returned to St. Louis.

Schuyler believed that Kate Chopin's writing career had been unfortunately slowed down: "perhaps, had Mrs. Chopin's environment been different, her genius might have developed twenty years sooner than it did." Her first efforts, "crude and unformed," were rejected, but she reacted very professionally: "She did not, as an unappreciated genius, abuse the editors, but began to study to better her style." She also kept to high standards: "She is particularly favored in not being obliged to depend upon her writing for her livelihood. There is, consequently, no trace of hack writing in any of her work."

As for Chopin's reading, Schuyler reported that she enjoyed Molière, Alphonse Daudet, and especially Maupassant, but disliked Émile Zola, who, "while colossal in his bigness, takes life too clumsily and seriously, which is the fault she also finds with Ibsen." She also disliked most contemporary English women writers, calling them "a lot of clever women gone wrong" who needed "a well-directed course of scientific study" to "make clearer their vision": They were too far removed from nature. Chopin had "great respect for Mrs. Humphry Ward's achievements; but Mrs. Ward is *au fond*, a reformer, and such tendency in a novelist she considers a crime against good taste."

(There may also have been some professional rivalry in Kate Chopin's assessment of Mrs. Humphry Ward. Although they were exactly the same age, Mrs. Ward had been publishing novels in England since 1882, eight years before *At Fault*. When their books were reviewed together, in the *Providence Sunday Journal* in April 1894, *Bayou Folk* got one paragraph—but Mrs. Ward's *Marcella* received two whole columns.)

Kate Chopin did admire American writers, Schuyler said, and felt that they might even surpass the French, "were it not that the limitations imposed upon their art by their environment hamper a full and spontaneous expression."

Schuyler did not neglect Kate's Louisiana ties: "from time to time" she returned to Natchitoches for business and to "refresh her recollections of that land of creoles and 'Cadians. The people of Natchitoches always receive her enthusiastically, since they thoroughly endorse her artistic presentation of their locality and its population; for Mrs. Chopin is not, like most prophets, without honor in her own country." (If Schuyler knew that Cloutiervillians were highly critical of Kate Chopin, he did not say so. Many people had recognized themselves, or thought they did, in *Bayou Folk*, and they were not pleased.)

Will Schuyler made Kate Chopin very pleasing in every respect: "Personally, Mrs. Chopin is a most interesting and attractive woman. She has a charming face, with regular features and very expressive brown eyes, which show to great advantage beneath the beautiful hair, prematurely gray, which she arranges in a very becoming fashion. Her manner is exceedingly quiet, and one realizes only afterward how many good and witty things she has said in the course of the conversation."

Outside St. Louis, Kate was also becoming a celebrity. She was selected as one of the "representative Southern Writers" in *Southern Magazine*, and in October she sent clippings and a letter to the author, a Parkersburg, West Virginia, poet named Waitman Barbe.

"I have no fixed literary plans," she told Barbe, "except that I shall go on writing stories as they come to me. It is either very easy for me to write a story, or utterly impossible; that is, the story must 'write itself' without any perceptible effort on my part, or it remains unwritten."

The *Bayou Folk* stories, she said, took no more than two or three sittings, a few hours each, except for the first one ("A No-Account Creole," which she had been revising off and on for several years). Soon she would be publishing in the *Century* a "story of more than 3000 words" which was "written in a few hours, and will be printed practically without an alteration or correction of the first draught." (That story was "Azélie.") Although she never discussed a story or sketch with anyone before she wrote it, she did not need "to be secluded in order to write. I work in the family living room often in the midst of much clatter."

She had definite career plans, she told Barbe: "I have ready another collection of Creole tales which I hope to have published in book form after they have made their slow way through the magazines." But her "first efforts in literature took the form of two novels of fifty and sixty thousand words. They were written in 1890. The novel does not seem to me now be my natural form of expression. However should the theme of a novel present itself I should of course try to use it. I do not consider one form of more value than the other."

Kate was still seeking a publisher for her second novel, *Young Dr. Gosse*. In 1891, the *Arena Magazine* had offered to publish it at her expense, but she declined; Will Schuyler, in his article, had called it her "very strongest work." In September 1894, just as Schuyler's article appeared in *The Writer*, Kate sent the manuscript to the newly established publishers Stone & Kimball in Chicago. *Young Dr. Gosse and Théo*, she told them, was a forty-five-thousand word story, with a prologue that "introduces the reader to a Parisian scene; the story proper opens ten years later and is acted in America." (Nothing else is known about the novel's plot.)

After Stone & Kimball's rejection, Kate tried to interest the New York editor Joseph Marshall Stoddart in *Young Dr. Gosse*, but conceded that "I have undergone two or three changes of mind regarding the book. It was written in '91—before I had found my way to the short story. I have been told, and believe, that it is interesting. As a piece of literature it does not satisfy me, and certain of its features I would treat differently to day." She tried the Transatlantic Publishing Company, and sometime after its rejection (the tenth), she gave up on *Young Dr. Gosse* and destroyed the manuscript.

Kate Chopin kept building her career as a writer. During 1894, she wrote thirteen stories, four essays, and two Maupassant translations; she published one poem, eight stories, and all four essays. In early 1895, she syndicated "In Sabine" and "In and Out of Old Natchitoches" with the American Press Association.

She also advanced into new markets. At the *Catholic Home Journal*'s request, she sent a story ("A Dresden Lady in Dixie"), and was paid an unusually high fee for a small magazine (sixty dollars). It was also an odd story for a Catholic journal: An old man confesses to stealing a china figurine, but claims that the Devil made him do it ("Satan keep on shovin' my han' ").

Kate reached another audience with "Cavanelle," published in *The American Jewess*. There she accepted a much lower payment (only ten dollars)—probably out of friendship with the editor, Rosa Sonneschein, who had left St. Louis after a scandal.

Sonneschein had come to St. Louis from Hungary after the Civil War, as the wife of a Reform rabbi (Solomon Hirsch Sonneschein of Shaare Emeth). An energetic woman, Rosa Sonneschein had organized the Pioneers, the first literary society for Jewish women, and one of the oldest women's literary clubs in the United States. (It was a model for the Wednesday Club.) As a young St. Louis matron, Rosa Sonneschein had been "a dashing figure," according to those who knew her: She brought new clothes from Europe every year, and always had a coterie of young male admirers. She smoked small cigars and told stories well, and was (according to her grandson) "an entertaining if sometimes acid commentator on people and events, parochial or global." She was also no mother-woman: Babies bored her.

Kate Chopin probably met Rosa Sonneschein sometime in the early 1890s. The St. Louis literary colony was a small one, and interesting women were sought after for clubs and readings. Kate, always a cigarette smoker, liked women who smoked; she and Rosa shared an interest in writing, but Rosa was much more dramatic. When their photographs were taken, Kate Chopin wore conventional evening gowns, but Rosa Sonneschein dressed up in exotic costumes with veils and laces (as if playing Rebecca in *Ivanhoe*).

Then, a year after Kate Chopin published her divorce novel, *At Fault*, Rosa Sonneschein left her husband. She was a Zionist, and he was anti-Zionist, and he had been dismissed from Shaare Emeth under murky circumstances. He also drank, beat his wife, and chased other women. (He claimed that Rosa had been having an affair with the president of the congregation—and that she had refused to sleep with her own husband.) Their divorce was scandalous, Rosa received no alimony, and she moved to Chicago, probably to escape the no-toriety. She needed money—and so she launched a magazine.

The American Jewess, first published in April 1895, was a handsome maga-zine, with woodcuts and engravings, as well as poems, short stories, book re-views, and articles on fashion, the arts, child care, and fads, including a taste for tobacco-chewing among New York belles. It was a women's rights maga-zine, with a column called "The Woman Who Talks," for "the ventilation of all subjects pertaining to woman." If she were "ultra-advanced," the editor wrote, she might have called herself "the woman who sees, feels, hears, smells, smokes"—but she decided not to.

Kate Chopin was the only non-Jewish contributor to the first issue, and her story was not about Jews, nor even particularly about women. "Cavanelle," set in New Orleans, depicts an "innocent, delightful humbug" of a shopkeeper who thinks that his sister's quavering singing voice is the quintessence of mu-sical perfection. When she dies, Cavanelle finds another penniless relative to care for and hover over—and the narrator concludes that Cavanelle himself is an angel.

"Cavanelle" had not been an easy story for Kate Chopin to write or publish. It had taken her a full week to finish it (July 31–August 6, 1894), and six national periodicals had rejected it before she sent it to *The American Jewess*. There it was edited much more heavily than most of her stories: Some sixty-five changes were made, mostly in wording and sentence construction. Chopin often said that she disliked revising, preferring the spontaneity and integrity of her own "crudities"—but Rosa Sonneschein had more exacting standards, in part because her reading audience's first languages were German or Yiddish.

Apparently Kate Chopin submitted to the heavy editing—and the low pay-ment—because of her relationship with Rosa. She did the same for Sue V. Moore and *St. Louis Life,* and for William Marion Reedy and the *St. Louis Mirror* (but Reedy's weekly did have national circulation).

For Rosa Sonneschein, a story by the well-known writer Kate Chopin was a coup. On her first editorial page, Sonneschein praised her star author: "MRS. KATE CHOPIN whose gifted pen contributes to our initial number a delightful sketch of Creole life, is one of the most interesting and unique writers of the *fin de siecle.* Since the appearance of her book 'Bayou Folk,' a collection of most charming tales, Kate Chopin has become an acknowledged literary power." Sonneschein, having herself escaped from a violent husband, especially praised "Désirée's Baby" as the "most remarkable" of the *Bayou Folk* stories, one which "set the critics wild with enthusiasm."

"Cavanelle" was illustrated with a languorous photograph of Kate Chopin, seated in a high-backed chair and swathed in dark draperies. Her eyes look deep-set and wistful, and her hand holds, limply, one long-stemmed rose. The pose is more theatrical than Kate Chopin's usual photographs—probably the influence of Rosa Sonneschein's own dramatic flair.

"Cavanelle" did draw readers to *The American Jewess*—and increased Kate Chopin's fame as well as Rosa Sonneschein's. The *Chicago Daily News* pointed out that the first issue had "one of Kate Chopin's bright southern sketches," and the *St. Louis Star Savings* noted that "Cavanelle" was "from the artistic pen of this gifted story writer." *The Independent* (New York) listed as the new magazine's contributors "Kate Chopin, Elizabeth C. Cardoza, Rebekah Kohut and other well-known writers," and the *Chicago Israelite* concluded, "The short story by Kate Chopin is a gem, and indicates that the rising star has struck out an orbit of her own."

In the fall of 1894, Sue V. Moore of *St. Louis Life* gave Kate Chopin her first forum—perhaps because Kate had complained about the reviews of *Bayou Folk*.

Kate reviewed three books—none of which she liked wholeheartedly, and one of which she despised. She may have chosen them herself, from her own reading: *Crumbling Idols*, a collection of essays by Hamlin Garland; a magazine's edition of the letters of Edwin Booth, the famous actor; and *Lourdes*, a new novel by Émile Zola, which Chopin had read in French.

Kate knew Hamlin Garland as a fiction writer, whose 1891 short-story collection, *Main-Travelled Roads*, had been well received. Garland's literary region was the upper Middle West, and his description of a poor woman's yearning for the trappings of rich people's lives ("A Day's Pleasure") anticipates Kate Chopin's urban story, "A Pair of Silk Stockings"—but Garland had less empathy than Kate Chopin for women who yearned for more than domestic life.

Chopin had studied Garland's work, just as she studied Mary E. Wilkins and Sarah Orne Jewett. Sometimes she echoed his language: In Garland's "A Branch Road," one male character's rage shows "the instinct of possession, the organic feeling of proprietorship of a woman." Kate Chopin, in the story "Her Letters," shortened that Darwinian phrase to "the man-instinct of possession." With Garland, as with other writers like Mary E. Wilkins, Kate Chopin seemed to be holding a dialogue: responding to their writing, refining what they said and how they said it. (By the late 1890s, other writers would be answering Kate Chopin's work: Mollie E. Moore Davis, in "A Bamboula," responds to "La Belle Zoraïde.")

Chopin was not impressed with Garland's *Crumbling Idols*, twelve essays on literature and art. Garland argued, in Whitmanesque pronouncements, that the "West" (Wisconsin, "Dakota," and the upper Midwest as well as California) would be the next literary center of the United States. But Kate Chopin was reviewing Garland's book just three months after her tiff with the Western

Association of Writers, and she cringed at Middle Western protestations of universality.

Garland's ideas were true, if not new, she wrote, and no one would dispute his claims that "the youthful artist should free himself from the hold of conventionalism; that he should go direct to those puissant sources, Life and Nature, for inspiration and turn his back upon models furnished by man; in a word, that he should be creative and not imitative." But Garland overdid his argument, Kate Chopin felt: He "undervalues the importance of the past in art and exaggerates the significance of the present." She was not persuaded by an angry young man, ten years her junior, who wanted to tear down the past.

> Human impulses do not change and can not so long as men and women continue to stand in the relation to one another which they have occupied since our knowledge of their existence began. It is why Aeschylus is true, and Shakespeare is true to-day, and why Ibsen will not be true in some remote to-morrow, however forcible and representative he may be for the hour, because he takes for his themes social problems which by their very nature are mutable. And, notwithstanding Mr. Garland's opinion to the contrary, social problems, social environments, local color and the rest of it are not *of themselves* motives to insure the survival of a writer who employs them.

She also disliked Garland's "exaggerated and uncalled for" claim that the East was dead as a literary center. "The fact remains that Chicago is not yet a literary center, nor is St. Louis (!), nor San Francisco, nor any of those towns in whose behalf he drops into prophecy." She thought Garland was "too young to assume the role of prophet becomingly; and he somehow gives the impression of a man who has not yet 'lived.' "

She also twitted him for his views on "love-life," which he argued should not be depicted in literature—for the word "love," he claimed, was "used charily" among the middle classes. Garland, Kate wrote slyly, "would even lightly dismiss from the artist's consideration such primitive passions as love, hate, etc. He declares that in real life people do not talk love. How does he know? I feel very sorry for Mr. Garland."

Kate also had criticisms of the other two books she reviewed for *St. Louis Life*. "The Real Edwin Booth," a selection from the actor's letters, had appeared in the October 1894 *Century* magazine, and Chopin felt that the late actor's privacy had been violated. If he had been able to see the publication of his letters, "never intended for the public eye," she wrote, "it is easy to fancy him quoting from one of them, 'I shrink from the indelicacy.' " The letters were mostly conventional, and did not, she felt, show the real Edwin Booth, sensitive and reserved. She seemed to be describing herself as well as Booth: "The *real* Edwin Booth gave himself to the public through his art. Those of us who most felt its magnetic power are the ones who knew him best, and as he would have wished to be known."

Kate did not wish to know Émile Zola, whose clumsiness and crudity she found detestable in her review "Émile Zola's *Lourdes.*" She considered the book "a mistake, not in its conception, but in its treatment." It was exhaustive; it had no real plot, and "more than two-thirds of the time" it was "swamped beneath a mass of prosaic data, offensive and nauseous description and rampant sentimentality."

What offended her most, though, was its creaky obviousness (the old stage machinery she had learned to discard through studying Guy de Maupassant). Of Zola, she wrote, "Not for an instant, from first to last, do we lose sight of the author and his note-book and of the disagreeable fact that his design is to instruct us." The instruction, she noted, often took place under ludicrously awkward circumstances. Whenever a character went for a walk, he was sure to be accosted by someone who insisted on filling his ears with pages of documentary information about Lourdes—which Zola, Kate wrote ironically, "thus subtly conveys to us." The hero, for example, "goes to the barber's to be shaved, but we know better by this time." The real purpose was to have the barber rail about clerical abuses at Lourdes, so that Zola could make his opinions known.

Still, Chopin admired some things. The "remarkable cure" of the character Marie Guersaint illustrated a "fine psychological point": "the possibility of the combined will-power of a mass of humanity forcing nature to subserve its ends." She also liked Zola's treatment of Catholicism, even "the most trifling mannerisms of its votaries," which "he handles delicately and captivatingly."

Meanwhile she herself was paying no attention to the church's opinion of books: " 'Lourdes' has been roundly denounced by Catholics," she wrote, "and, I think, the ban of the Church set upon it. I cannot see why. It is a book which I think a good Catholic would greatly enjoy reading, the only and easy condition being to set aside Mons. Zola's point of view and color his facts with one's own."

Kate Chopin's essay on "Émile Zola's 'Lourdes' " was published in *St. Louis Life* on November 17, 1894, and the following day she began to write her own story satirizing unimaginative interpreters of church teachings.

"A Sentimental Soul" depicts a shabby New Orleans shopkeeper who anticipates Mademoiselle Reisz of *The Awakening* with her "rusty black lace" and her "painfully and suspiciously black" hair. Kate gave her Mamzelle Fleurette a passionate infatuation with Lacodie—who, like Émile Zola, has fiercely expressed "radical opinions upon the rights and wrongs of humanity at large and his fellow-workingmen in particular." Although her love is unspoken, Mamzelle finds that flowers smell sweeter and birds' songs seem more melodious—but when she tells her usually bored priest that she loves another woman's husband, he is startled and indignant.

When the atheist Lacodie falls ill with a fever (much like the one that took Oscar Chopin), he refuses to see a priest, and dies. Mamzelle Fleurette grieves silently, until his widow marries again. Then Mamzelle pastes Lacodie's picture on her homemade altar, with her crucifix and her picture of the empress Eugénie, and revels in her role as his only true widow. Now, she is contented—and says nothing at all to her priest.

Mamzelle Fleurette's decision to "take her conscience into her own keeping" enables her to create her own shrine, her own private Lourdes. Kate Chopin, too, had long ago decided that she would be her own priest, her own conscience, and her own judge.

Kate was, for a while, reluctant to abandon the local-color stories that had brought her success—and she tried new twists. Instead of black characters sacrificing themselves for whites (as in "For Marse Chouchoute," "Beyond the Bayou," and others), she wrote reversals: White characters make the sacrifices. In "Ozème's Holiday," the white Ozème gives up his carefully planned vacation to pick cotton for a needy black family; in "Odalie Misses Mass," thirteen-year-old Odalie gives up showing off her new finery at church because there is no one to sit with her "old friend and protegée, Aunt Pinky."

The *Century* took "Ozème's Holiday" but rejected the more unconventional "Odalie Misses Mass." Even among writers who glorified Old South devotion between the races, few described friendships across the generations—and even fewer depicted friendships in which the black person never groveled, and the white person never condescended. Odalie and Pinky are equals and friends, one of the first such pairs in Kate Chopin's fiction.

As she turned away from charming local-color stories, Kate also pondered moral questions in her fiction. As she knew well, what was considered "moral" for a woman was often reduced simply to physical "chastity"—a problem in the story "Her Letters."

Chopin had at least one inspiration from real life: Carrie and George Blackman, organizers of the St. Louis Artist's Guild, were well known for their Sunday night soirees for local artists and writers, among them Kate Chopin, Will Schuyler, Thekla Bernays, and George Johns of the *Post-Dispatch*. The Blackmans, parents of four children, were Kate Chopin's age, and Carrie Blackman—known as the "Egeria of the St. Louis salons"—disturbed Kate in some way she could not quite define.

In her diary for June 2, 1894, Kate described "Mrs Blackman—a woman with the artistic temperament—woefully unballanced I am afraid. Her face is very beautiful and attractive—particularly her large dark eyes. I can understand how her husband gives offense to other women by losing himself in contemplation of his wife when in company. There seems however always an *arrière pensé* with her, which acts as a barrier between us." Something about Carrie Blackman also bothered Kate the following autumn, 1895, when Kate sent a poem:

"To Carrie B."

Your greeting filled me with distress.
I've pondered long and sore to guess
What 'twould express.

Ah, Lady fair! can you not see:
From gentlemen of high degree
I always flee!

(The occasion for the poem cannot be known—but it suggests that Kate had again been accused of flirting or trifling with men.)

The enigmatic Carrie Blackman was a painter, one of whose most admired portraits, colored with rich golden tints, showed a young woman reading a letter. Kate Chopin began "Her Letters" with a woman reading letters—and Chopin imagined that the woman had a deep, troubling secret (an *arrière pensée*) that she hid from everyone, including her husband.

The woman, nameless, knows that she is dying, and she is rereading "precious and imprudent" letters from a lost lover. To her devoted husband, she leaves a message with the packet of letters: "With perfect faith in his loyalty and his love, I ask him to destroy it unopened." But after her death, the letters he destroyed prey upon her husband's mind: "What secret save one could a woman choose to have die with her?" Tortured by doubts, he cannot continue living.

Kate also asked moral questions in her best-known story from 1894, "The Story of an Hour," a criticism of the ideal of self-sacrifice that still haunted women at the end of the century. In it, a wife who learns that her husband has been killed in a railroad accident rejoices in her freedom—until he returns after all, and her weak heart cannot take the shock.

The story was one of Kate's shortest, only one thousand words, but one of her most radical. Mrs. Mallard was a good wife, and Mr. Mallard a good husband, and "The Story of an Hour" was an attack on marriage, on one person's dominance over another in "that blind persistence with which men and women believe they have a right to impose a private will upon a fellow-creature. A kind intention or a cruel intention made the act seem no less a crime." The demand for self-sacrifice was the crime.

Vogue published "Her Letters," but at first shied away from "The Story of an Hour." But when Kate submitted it a second time (after rejections from the *Century, Short Stories,* and the avant-garde *Chap-Book*), *Vogue's* editors had changed their mind—possibly because of *Bayou Folk's* excellent reviews. "The Story of an Hour" appeared in the December 1894 *Vogue,* and was reprinted in *St. Louis Life* on January 5, 1895. (Its original title was "The Dream of an Hour"; "The Story of an Hour" is a modern renaming.)

By the end of 1894, Kate Chopin was already coming into conflict with traditional views of what should be written, particularly about independent women. But she did not seem inclined to stop, and her friends abetted her.

Chapter 17

A St. Louis
Salon

KATE CHOPIN CAME "CLOSER to maintaining a salon than any woman that has ever lived in St. Louis," according to her friend Vernon (Bunnie) Knapp, the Chopins' honeymoon companion in Germany. Kate Chopin was "the most brilliant, distinguished, and interesting woman that has ever graced St. Louis," Knapp wrote. At her modest home on Morgan Street, "her friends and the friends of her children could at all times go and find entertainment, instruction and pleasure."

Hers was not the sole salon in St. Louis: Mrs. Otto Forster often gave receptions for visiting ambassadors, princes, and potentates (and sycophants, according to the populist editor William Marion Reedy). Kate Chopin knew Mrs. Forster, *née* Phil Espenschied: They were invited to the same debutante parties, along with Kate's sons Jean, Fred, and Felix. (Her other sons were less sociable: George was a medical student, and Oscar, an artist who illustrated private copies of *Bayou Folk* with water colors, spent much of his time in Louisiana.)

Carrie and George Blackman also held their Sunday night at-home gatherings, where the St. Louis intelligentsia could meet and mingle informally. But the Blackmans' soirees were attended more by a younger crowd: Orrick Johns, son of Kate Chopin's friend, the *Post-Dispatch* editor George Johns, later remembered her as "the beautiful and exquisite writer of the 'Cadians." Others of her own generation remembered her more distinctly.

They deferred to her opinions. When the newspaperman William Vincent Byars published a volume of poetry, George Johns wrote to him, "Your little book has made a hit among the congregations of stubborn cranks who meet on our hill—I read some of it to Kate Chopin one night this week and she was charmed with the music of the verse and kept the book to try the contents."

The Johnses, the Schuylers, and Kate Chopin shared an informal social life. They organized musicales (Kate played the piano); they visited one another for evening receptions and calling days; and they met for Sunday evening suppers—"al fresco in the summertime," Kate's son Felix recalled.

Byars could not easily join the "stubborn cranks": He and his wife had a dozen children, and lived in suburban Kirkwood. Still, he was the kind of eccentric that Chopin's circle attracted: a gaunt man, laden with books, pipes, and a cane or umbrella, and always shabbily dressed, since he could not bear to throw out old clothes. Because he had impossible handwriting, Byars became the first newspaperman in St. Louis to use a typewriter, and it made him prolific: Between 1890 and 1897, he published seven books of verse. He had a passion for languages, especially Sanskrit, which he would declaim at social gatherings—with "a curious kind of delighted whinny at the end of a speech," testifying to his "sheer excitement of thought."

When he could come, Byars fit in well at Kate's Morgan Street house, "just a nice American home, in which she reared a large family on a modest income," according to Knapp. The neighborhood was not elegant or exclusive, although in 1897 some Morgan Street residents campaigned against having the Hepzibah Home for "the reformation of fallen women" in their neighborhood. (*Mirror* editor William Marion Reedy mocked their lack of charity, wondering if they feared the wailings of fatherless infants with a "birthright of shame," or whether they simply did not want to be reminded of "sin.")

Chopin enjoyed living in an unpretentious neighborhood: "I like to look out of the window," she wrote in 1897, because "there is a good deal of unadulterated human nature that passes along during the length of a day. Of course I do not live in Westmoreland Place"—one of St. Louis's exclusive gated areas where the group Reedy called "swells" lived behind barriers. Kate's neighbors included a coal merchant, two physicians, and a dentist, but mostly 3317 Morgan sat amid boardinghouses, occupied by an ever-changing population of mostly young men.

Kate Chopin's regular reception day was Thursday, the traditional day for "ladies in the West End." Fashions in calling cards changed regularly, and the style of one's card, an etiquette authority wrote in 1898, "speaks volumes for the owner's familiarity with approved customs in polite and refined society." Visiting cards were always white and engraved, but Roman replaced script lettering in 1898, and cards were smaller and heavier than before. Rules were strict: A first daughter would be "Miss Smith," but successive daughters were to insert their first names between "Miss" and "Smith." Lélia's name was correctly written as "Miss Chopin"; Kate Chopin, as a widow, was correctly known as Mrs. Kate Chopin, never as Mrs. Oscar Chopin.

Kate disliked the social calling ritual, and *St. Louis Life* once printed a blind item believed to refer to her:

> A clever woman writer recommends a sort of social clearing house where women can pay off all their calls in one afternoon, and thus get rid of the greatest incubus a fashionable woman has to carry. The calling habit is the greatest drain on a woman's time that she has to contend with. It deprives her of half her pleasure in life— for when she is making her calls she wishes she might have it over, and when she is not making them the thought of a neglected duty takes all the pleasure out of what she may be doing. The social clearing house would be a building where all the women of a certain set might assemble at an appointed time and exchange visiting cards and greetings, thus getting the whole business over in a few hours, while under present regulations it occupies days and weeks.

In St. Louis, calling was not restricted to daytime hours (as it was in New Orleans), nor were calls made solely by ladies. Kate's salon took place in the evening, and both sexes attended.

"Kate Chopin loved cards, coffee, and a cigarette," one informant told Rankin. (Ladies were generally expected to serve tea, chocolate or coffee and wafers to callers, and sometimes light wine and cake.) In her living room, Kate had a grate fire and "a sort of day bed made by carpenters, wider than modern daybeds, and with deep cushions," her son recalled. Her friends shared her love of comfort and self-expression: William Vincent Byars, for instance, believed in the consolation of a good groan—and could groan, "Ah me!" in several different languages.

Many of her friends enjoyed performing: Will Schuyler could play the piano, sing German and Italian folk songs, chat enthusiastically about the latest books, and praise and denounce current Italian painters—all in one short visit. But at her salon, in her living room, Kate Chopin was, according to her son Felix, "pretty much the center of the party." Her prematurely gray hair "was becoming. Later, she became stout, but even then was a handsome woman"—around whom people flocked.

"All the literati" came to her salon, according to her son George; Vernon Knapp said that she attracted all the "visiting literary and artistic lights." She possessed, Knapp wrote, "every grace and talent essential to the maintenance of a brilliant social circle; brilliant in the sense of mentality and wit." Kate Chopin's storytelling attracted friends and visitors, and one friend later said that in Kate's writing, "I can hear you speaking, describing incidents in your own cute, inimitable way."

Kate was known for her understanding, and ability to draw people out. But sometimes she failed: "Ferriss came," she wrote in her 1894 diary. "I do not quite understand him. Have not got near enough." She preferred his wife: "Mrs. Ferriss a frank, wholesome woman, amiable & natural; no doubt a good friend and excellent mother and wife; with nothing of the *precieuse* offensiveness of manner to which I have become more sensitive than ever."

Visitors to Kate's salon sometimes grew polemical, and Charles L. Deyo, exchange editor for the *Post-Dispatch*, was among the most opinionated. Kate had trusted Deyo's literary judgment early in her career, when she showed him her manuscript of *At Fault*—but four years later, she thought him very much lacking. In 1894, she wrote in her diary that Deyo had spoken the previous evening "of the ecstatic pleasure which he finds in reading Plato. He seems to have reached the sage by stages: through Browning then Pater. He feels that there is nothing for him beyond that poetic height. And when Plato begins to pall—as he will in a few years, he wonders what life will have to offer him and shudders already in anticipation of the nothingness."

Chopin did not sympathize with Deyo's willed ennui: "This is to me a rather curious condition of mind. It betokens a total lack of inward resource, and makes me doubt the value of the purely intellectual outlook. Here is a man who can only be reached through books. Nature does not speak to him, notwithstanding his firm belief that he is in sympathetic touch with the true—the artistic. He reaches his perceptions through others' minds. It is something, of course that the channel which he follows is a lofty one; but the question remains, has such perception the value of spontaneous insight, however circumscribed."

Deyo did like to philosophize. After another gathering, Kate recorded that "Deyo talked anarchy to me last night." Anarchy and anarchism were in the air in 1894: Between Deyo's speeches about Plato (June 6) and anarchy (July 4), Kate had attended the Western Association of Writers meeting—but even in small-town Indiana, the Pullman strike in Chicago had dominated the front pages.

"There is good reason for his wrath against the 'plutocrats,' the robbers of the public," Kate Chopin wrote in her diary about Deyo, "—but there seems too much personal feeling in his invectives. His *real* grievance is ill health though he doesn't know it—He believes in equal opportunities being afforded to all men, and feels that he has been hampered in the race by the necessity to gain a living. I didn't remind him that his opportunities to follow the direction of his talents have been unusually favorable. He has had a pen in his hand for the past five years or more—what has he done with it?"

Deyo evidently had no impact. Although he was on the *Post-Dispatch* staff through the 1890s, he is not mentioned in newspaper histories or memoirs. Nor was he politically effective as a founding member of the St. Louis Single Tax League, created to promote the philosophy of Henry George, author of *Progress and Poverty*. Georgists believed that all wealth flowed from the ownership of land, and that only land should be taxed.

Kate Chopin had little interest in political theories, and her only reference to Georgism appears in "Miss McEnders," her own satire on plutocrats. Georgie McEnders, a rich and patronizing young lady who rushes from one reform club to another, has on her schedule "Eight o'clock—hear Henry George's lecture on Single Tax." In Chopin's eyes, Miss McEnders's busy days were much like Charles Deyo's anarchical speeches: noise without accomplishment.

There was another man in Kate Chopin's circle who could be trusted to support anarchical ideas. Her grandchildren heard that he was "bordering on a bomb thrower," and throughout his life he never lost his indignation at injustices, of the kind Kate recorded in her diary for May 4, 1894: "The Doctor told interesting stories about the ignorance, filth, beastiality of country life in Poland."

"The Doctor" was Frederick Kolbenheyer, the physician for most of St. Louis's newspapermen. Kate's children knew him as "a man of great learning, who would speak for hours on the life and career of Napoleon." He was also "a fascinating talker, both by virtue of his deep and versatile knowledge, and his personal charm." He had deep dark eyes and a prominent and forceful nose; he was mostly bald, with a luxurious dark beard that dominated his face (and sometimes frightened small children).

Kolbenheyer frequently expressed his political opinions in articles in St. Louis's German-language newspapers, and he also published in *The American Jewess*, where editor Rosa Sonneschein reported that he was born in 1843, "a scion of an old Hungarian patrician family." He was "the nephew of General Goergoy, of revolutionary fame," he attended college in Teschen, and then studied philosophy and medicine in Vienna, "where he remained a practicing physician until the spring of 1871. Then he came to America and made St. Louis his home."

Sonneschein's bland summary evaded some truths. Although Kolbenheyer—born in Bielitz, a town in Austrian Poland—was the son of a large landed proprietor, he had emphatically rejected his father's way of life. In Vienna, where he studied with the noted Dr. Nothnagel, Kolbenheyer had become a dangerous radical and a member of the Liberty party. When his antimonarchist sentiments became known to the Hapsburg regime, it was strongly suggested that he leave the country.

The doctor's first St. Louis address was 710 South Fourth Street, not far from Fritz Roeslein's German bookstore at 22 Fourth Street. Joseph Pulitzer, then a recent Jewish immigrant from Hungary, was a frequent bookstore visitor, as were Carl Schurz and Emil Preetorius, editors of the *Westliche Post*, the city's major German-language newspaper. Soon, Rosa Sonneschein reported, Kolbenheyer had "become one of the leading physicians of the Western metropolis, and to-day he is one of the most popular of men, as he has evidenced his broad intellect and sincere love for humanity on innumerable occasions." He knew the works of Kant, Schopenhauer, and Hegel far better than anyone else in his circle, and he belonged to the prestigious Germania Club, dedicated to recreation and "scientific culture."

By the 1890s, the Kolbenheyers had moved several times, finally settling at 2006 Lafayette Avenue, still on the poorer South Side. The doctor and his wife and daughter lived simply, with just one household servant. His neighborhood and profession kept him in contact with Eastern European immigrants of all nationalities, and according to Rosa Sonneschein, he had "proven himself to be a staunch friend of the Jews." His "intimate contact" had "qualified him to study and judge the Jewish heart, which he understands thoroughly, because he is entirely free from prejudice. He regards Judaism purely from a historical and scientific standpoint, and, occupying this position, it is not difficult for him to judge of it justly."

As for his writing, Sonneschein wrote, "Dr. Kolbenheyer looks upon his literary work only as a pleasant pastime during the few leisure hours his large practice permits him to enjoy. What he writes is rarely intended for the public, and that which has been published was secured from him only by the personal persuasion of his friends." One of those friends was undoubtedly Kate Chopin, who had already been published in *The American Jewess* and who owed much to Frederick Kolbenheyer: Not only had he been her obstetrician, but he had also been the first to encourage her to write for publication.

"Jewish Blood" by "Dr. Friedrich Kolbenheyer" appeared in *The American Jewess* in installments from April to September 1896. (It may be Kolbenheyer's only published story in English.) The main characters are two Jewish brothers in the western United States: Aaron, an unsightly hunchback with a twisted personality, and Jacob, handsome and thoroughly winning. Both love Clara, a beautiful Catholic orphan raised by their family—and she loves Jacob. But his father forbids the marriage: To him, intermarriage for Jews is "the most suicidal of all our faults and follies." After Jacob renounces Clara, she runs away, leaving a self-sacrificing note (not unlike Robert's "Good-by—because I love you," in *The Awakening*). By the time they meet again, much later, Clara is fatally ill. She and Jacob marry, but it is "only a sacred union of the soul. In such circumstances there could be no question of a fusion of blood."

As editor, Rosa Sonneschein praised Kolbenheyer's "masterly character delineation," in portraying "the justness of the sentiment existing in the heart of Jews against intermarriage"—but it was not the kind of story that Kate Chopin would have written. Her crippled characters (such as "Nég Créol") are dignified rather than warped, and her plots do not turn on coincidences and eavesdroppings (the "old fashioned mechanism and stage trapping" that she abandoned when she discovered Guy de Maupassant). Nor did she use archaic dialect: One of Kolbenheyer's characters says, "Be still, rebellious heart, 'tis no business of thine." Kate Chopin, as a writer, was a realist; Frederick Kolbenheyer was a romantic—and when they wrote to one another, as they frequently did, that was undoubtedly one of the subjects for argument and controversy.

Kate was very fond of the doctor, and wrote in her 1894 diary, "My friend whose birthday I remembered with a little gift, a sip of champagne & 'wish you luck' looked positively a little sadder on the 31 of May, remembering that he was making his 51st notch. 'Ah, if it were only forty one' he sighed." Kate professed to be unworried about growing older: "What sentimentality over a birthday, oh dear! Let me alone with birthdays—so meaningless. I have known rusé old ladies of 16 and giddy young girls of 35 . . . Days are what count—not years. . . . I wonder if I shall ever care if it is 43 or 53 or 63. I believe not."

But Frederick Kolbenheyer cared passionately about most things. He had "an emphatic and outspoken manner, and a temper that was choleric when roused by opposition." A "constant visitor" at the Chopin home, according to Rankin, he was "a decided agnostic; genial, witty, determined, a man of tremendous mental capacity, whose cultured insinuating conversations carried conviction to Kate Chopin, to the extent at least that she no longer remained a Catholic in any real or practical way." Kolbenheyer was, Rankin wrote, "a cordially accepted intimate friend, almost an ardent admirer of Kate Chopin."

Whether Rankin was implying that they were lovers cannot be known. Perhaps Frederick Kolbenheyer was Kate Chopin's trusted confidant, like Dr. Chevalier in "Dr. Chevalier's Lie" and Dr. Mandelet in *The Awakening*—open-minded men who have seen all kinds of human failings and are rarely surprised. Chopin called him "the Doctor" in her diary, and "Dr. Kolbenheyer" in her manuscript account book, but that kind of formality was common: Even wives frequently called their husbands "Mr.   ." Kolbenheyer was married to "the Viennese sweetheart of his youth"—but beyond her age (five years younger than his), her first name, and her naturalized American citizenship, nothing is known about Agnes Kolbenheyer. Possibly theirs was an arranged marriage, since he was from a wealthy family.

Kate Chopin was admired by many men, and her son Felix thought that Dr. Kolbenheyer was one of them: "Kolby had eyes for Mom," he used to say with a laugh. But whether Kate also had eyes for Kolby is unknown. Both of them took that secret with them to the grave.

Kate Chopin was an intriguing figure to the younger generation in St. Louis. She was "the most individual feminine talent America has produced," her friend's son Orrick Johns wrote in Reedy's *Mirror*, seven years after Kate's death. "The younger generation has a rare experience before it if it can discover and assimilate Mrs. Chopin's art. . . . To one who has read her as a boy and come back to her again with powers of appreciation more subtly developed, she breathes the magic of a whole chapter in his life."

Johns reveled in the sensual, adult, amoral atmosphere of her stories: "She had the courage to acknowledge the existence of the flesh. Which one of us does not know the existence of it! . . . . Like every ordained artist, she did not write for 'the young person.' " Johns praised Chopin's portrayal of well-matched wives and husbands, acknowledging that "even the best of marriages have their complexities." But young Johns, in his own memoirs, did not speculate in print about the "complexities" of his parents' marriage—and the role that Kate Chopin might have played in them.

His parents were a few years younger than Kate: In the late 1870s, George Johns had courted Minne McDearmon at school, leaving tobacco, cigarette papers, and "pash notes" in a tree for her. She accepted the bribes, and married him in 1884, the year Kate returned to St. Louis from Louisiana. In her young married days, her son Orrick wrote later, Minne had been very daring: She had smoked cigarettes with "Kate Chopin and Florence Hayward, our town's advanced literary ladies at that time." Florence Hayward was a globe-trotting journalist and opera lover, with an exuberant sense of humor and a no-nonsense manner. Kate Chopin was already dashing and unforgettable.

By background, George Sibley Johns had some things in common with Kate Chopin. Although he was a rural Missourian, he had also grown up with a mammy in a Confederate, slave-owning family. But by the time he was five, in 1862, the blacks were all gone and a new era had begun. Although the Civil War seemed to him, in St. Charles, Missouri, mostly "a few street fights and the talk of the old folks," the Johnses' preacher had been arrested and sent to the Gratiot Street Prison, next door to the O'Flahertys. At Princeton, Johns began a lifelong friendship with Woodrow Wilson; by the early 1880s, Johns was in St. Louis, chasing scoops on foot. In 1883, he joined the *Post-Dispatch*, where—except for two brief spats—he stayed for forty-four years. For a while, he was a drama and music critic, but switched to writing editorials, because he wanted to make a mark on the world.

In St. Louis, George and Minne Johns had at first joined a fast crowd, the kind her straitlaced father disapproved of: "book-reading, cigarette-smoking, music-making, picture-painting, story-writing"—people like Kate Chopin, Florence Hayward, and William Vincent Byars. With these people, according to his son, George Johns began "enlarging his intellectual experience, revivifying his democratic values, breaking down the puritan sexual taboos by copious draughts of Whitman, Swinburne, French fiction, Hugo, and, when translations began to arrive, Tolstoy."

This crowd overlapped with the *Post-Dispatch* crowd—Frederick Kolbenheyer, Charles Deyo, John A. Dillon—and the *Post-Dispatch* consistently gave Kate Chopin her longest and most enthusiastic reviews. Although she was not a great believer in reform, her *Post-Dispatch* friends, especially George Johns, were fighting newspapermen in the Pulitzer tradition. As a savage young editor, Johns once called a rival editor "the head physician of a hospital for jackasses," and when the editor called Johns a son of a bitch, Johns punched him hard enough to land him in the hospital.

By the 1890s, when Kate Chopin was one of the best-known members of their social circle, Minne Johns had become more conservative and decorous. When her sons grew up, she disapproved of their girlfriends' cigarettes, and Kate Chopin was a bad example. It was rumored that she sometimes greeted guests while in her bathtub, smoking a big black cigar; it was a fact that she smoked Cuban cigarettes and knew about even more exotic varieties.

Kate's 1897 story "An Egyptian Cigarette" begins with a gift of handmade, yellow-wrapped cigarettes bought from "a species of fakir" in Cairo. The female narrator slips into the "smoking-den" to recline and try them out, since "[s]ome of the women here detest the odor of cigarettes" (that may have been a dig at Minne Johns). Soon the Egyptian cigarette's gray-green smoke fills the smoking room, with its "exclusively Oriental" furniture, and the visions begin: desert sand, hot sun, stars, oracles, lilies and garlands and pagan gods, waters, birds, and death. Then, abruptly, the narrator awakens from the spell, in which she has "tasted the depths of human despair." She wonders what other visions might come from the "mystic fumes," but she crumples the cigarettes and throws them away.

That kind of exotic *fin-de-siècle* story was rare for the Middle West (although St. Louis did have Chinese opium dens, occasionally exposed in sensational newspaper articles). Hallucinogenic cigarettes and sensual Oriental luxury were associated with decadent Europeans, such as Algernon Swinburne, Oscar Wilde, and Aubrey Beardsley—not with middlewestern wives and mothers. Kate Chopin, who published the story in *Vogue,* was a very different sort of woman from the midwestern Minne Johns—and reports of Kate's friendship with the Johns family mention George Johns, but not his wife.

George Johns, himself a dapper man, evidently saw Kate Chopin's salon as a potential civilizing influence for his friends, including O. K. Bovard, a *Post-Dispatch* reporter who had earlier been fired from the *Globe Democrat* for smoking a cigar in the bookkeeping room. Bovard, though impeccably dressed, was utterly lacking in manners and polish. Probably it was to school him in social graces that Johns brought him to Kate Chopin's "Thursdays," where the talk was always wise and witty, with a French flavor. Bovard became a regular visitor at Kate Chopin's salon—but Minne Johns did not.

George Johns never became wealthy, and for many years he and Minne raised their five sons on little more than fifty dollars a week: Kate Chopin was earning more than that for one short story. Minne McDearmon, unlike Kate O'Flaherty, had given up a promising career for marriage: She possessed a lovely soprano voice and had trained with several teachers, but told her son that she was too shy to perform (much like the frail Mathilde in Kate Chopin's story "Cavanelle"). Minne Johns, like Kate Chopin in her twenties, had been engulfed by motherhood, including three babies in the first four years of marriage, but there was also a family tragedy. The second son, Orrick, was only seven in 1894 when, after a trolley accident, his left leg had to be amputated on the Johnses' kitchen table.

Minne Johns was a frustrated artist—while Kate Chopin, by the mid-1890s, was a fulfilled artist who had also escaped the restrictions of motherhood and conventionality. Kate was free to attend parties and concerts and readings, and listen with delight to the intellectual arguments and posturings of members of her "salon"—but Minne Johns's life revolved around household responsibilities.

Minne and George also had "no intellectual interests in common," according to Johns's brother: Minne did not care about books or ideas, and had little curiosity about George's newspaper life. "Yet I have never seen two people more absolutely loyal and devoted to each other," Johns's brother added. Minne Johns could seem very conservative: She once startled a dinner party by remarking loudly to a neighbor, "I think sex is *terrible*, don't you?" and once claimed to her son (perhaps jokingly) that she had never seen her own nude body, and neither had any man.

Kate Chopin did not consider sex or nudity terrible, and when Orrick Johns described her portrayals of marriage, his language was careful and contradictory, as if defending both his parents and his father's dashing friend: "If her own culture had been possible to Mrs. Chopin's critics they would have felt the charm of her conception of the perfect marriage. Again and again she has drawn it as an existing thing. They would have found in her the priestess of the monogamous relation, when it is true and when it is simple. An eternal bloom of sympathy, even of romance, clings to the lives of her well-mated husbands and wives. Yet she was modern." Kate Chopin knew that "marriage is not a condition but a progress. And she was the faithful guardian of the genuine rights of women."

Orrick Johns ignored the fact that only one marriage in Kate Chopin's fiction is presented as entirely happy: that of the Ratignolles in *The Awakening*, a marriage Edna Pontellier considers stifling. Yet Madame Ratignolle is not unlike Minne Johns: devoted to her family in everything, including her music; uninterested in the world of ideas or dangerous thoughts. *The Awakening*'s Mademoiselle Reisz, dedicated to her career and her eccentricities, has more than a little similarity to the independent journalist Florence Hayward. And Edna, of course, possesses Kate's own desire to experience everything.

Kate Chopin was a glamorous figure who made most other women seem drab, and her young niece Julia Breazeale in Louisiana often heard that the editor in chief of the *St. Louis Post-Dispatch* was a pursuer or admirer of "Aunt Katie." After John A. Dillon's departure for New York, the chief executive was George Johns.

Kate Chopin was sometimes flirtatious, and one of the poems she sent to the *Chap-Book* in 1895 suggests that she had been misinterpreted by a man—who could have been George Johns, or John A. Dillon, or Albert Sampite, or Frederick Kolbenheyer.

> Then Wouldst Thou Know
> (also called "If Some Day")
>
> If some day I, with casual, wanton glance
> Should for a moment's space thine eyes ensnare;
> Or more, if I should dare
> To rest my finger tips upon thy sleeve,
> Or, grown more bold, upon thy swarthy cheek;
> If further I should seek
> With honey-trick of tone thy name to call,
> Breathing it soft, in meaning whisper low,
> Then wouldst thou know? . . .

Whether Kate Chopin's daring—in thought or in deed—involved more intimacy with George Johns cannot be known, although there is room for speculation.

Once, at Joseph Pulitzer's estate, he and George Johns and others were discussing an editor who had been fired after an affair with one of the staff women. Pulitzer was astonished that the culprit was that particular editor: "I wouldn't have expected it of him, a little fellow like that"—but "if it had been Johns, I would not be surprised. Yes, Johns might do a thing like that." Then Pulitzer added, to Johns: "You mustn't think I intend any reflection on you. You know I am blind, an invalid, and say things. But I insist, I would not have been astonished if this Don Juan had been you."

Many years after that, in 1937, George Johns confided to his son, "At seventy I begin to regret some of the sins I could have committed but didn't." But if those uncommitted sins involved Kate Chopin, George Johns did not confide his longings to print, and so they remain a mystery.

There were few mysteries about another Chopin friend and visitor—William Marion Reedy, the raffish editor and proprietor of the *St. Louis Mirror*. Reedy's weekly paper, which lasted until his death in 1920, covered world events, St. Louis news, economic trends, books, theatrical performances, and society gossip. He was one of the first American editors to publish Oscar Wilde, Fannie Hurst, Theodore Dreiser, Amy Lowell, James Joyce, and many others, and his paper reflected his taste and opinions. Writing under his own name and half a dozen pseudonyms, among them "Uncle Fuller" and "Touchstone," Reedy rarely refrained from praise or vituperation.

Born in December of 1862, too late to remember the war or slavery, "Billy" Reedy had not known the comfortable kind of life Kate Chopin, George Johns, and John A. Dillon remembered. Reedy grew up poor in Kerry Patch, the north-side Irish ghetto—but, drilled by his mother, he learned Latin and worked his way through the Christian Brothers College. As an adult, Reedy was handsome, with penetrating dark eyes and unusually white, soft hands for a man—both characteristics that Chopin gave her newspaperman character, Gouvernail, in the story "Athénaïse." But people were more apt to notice Reedy's girth: As he grew older, he grew more and more rotund.

Billy Reedy's tales of his boyhood evidently inspired Kate Chopin's longest short story, "A Vocation and a Voice" (1896), about a poor and nameless fifteen-year-old boy who lives in "The Patch" and hungers for something richer. Like Reedy, the boy loves church Latin and serving at mass—but is torn between flesh and spirit. One day, near "Woodland Park" (St. Louis's Forest Park), the boy joins up with two vagabonds: Suzima, the fortune-telling "Egyptian Maid, the Wonder of the Orient," and her truculent, often drunken companion Gutro ("The Beast"). The boy is entranced by Suzima's lovely singing voice, and one day, unawares, he comes upon her, naked, bathing in a pond: "Her image, against the background of tender green, ate into his brain and into his flesh with the fixedness and intensity of white-hot iron."

A little later, Suzima introduces the boy to sex: "Turning, she folded her arms about him and drew him close to her. She held him fast with her arms and with her lips." Following genteel custom, Kate paused, letting white space indicate a sexual encounter, and began a new chapter: "A few days had wrought great changes with the boy . . . He seemed to have been brought in touch with the universe of men and all things that live." To him, Suzima is "the embodiment of desire and the fulfillment of life." But after a drunken quarrel with Gutro, the boy runs away to a monastery to hide from the world—until one day, when he is building a wall, he hears Suzima's singing. He leaps over the wall, to follow her.

Like the boy, Billy Reedy wallowed in a sea of temptation, liquor, and lust, but he also had Suzima's generous spirit. He was extravagant with money, and rarely choosy about his companions, who were often the politicians, prostitutes and gamblers whom he met in downtown bars and "sporting houses." But in November of 1893, Billy Reedy succumbed to his weaknesses and created a scandal: During a prolonged binge, he married Addie Baldwin, one of St. Louis's best-known madams. She paid for his taking the Keeley Cure for alcoholism, but finally divorced him in 1896 for desertion.

Then Billy Reedy began receiving notes from Lalitte Bauduy, a young lady from an impeccable society background (she was distantly related to Kitty Garesché). Lalitte Bauduy wrote that she wanted to meet Reedy, to discuss the Single Tax with him—but he discarded her notes, thinking they were a hoax. They were not, and she pursued him—and he pursued her. He also applied to have his marriage annulled, but an ecclesiastical court said no. A day later, in March of 1897, Billy Reedy and Lalitte Bauduy eloped. Her father, a St. Louis surgeon who had experimented with hydrochlorate of cocaine on alcoholics, violently denounced the marriage, and the Catholic Church excommunicated Reedy—who denounced St. Louis's Archbishop Kain as a "Tittlebat Titmouse Torquemada."

And so Reedy, like Kate Chopin, became a lifelong opponent of stringent divorce laws—and through the 1890s, they appreciated each other's work. Early in Chopin's career, Reedy had reprinted "Désirée's Baby" with a laudatory introduction (but no payment: He was always on the brink of bankruptcy). For Christmas in 1895, she sent him a box of his favorite food, cigars, with a poem:

To "Billy" with a Box of Cigars

These may be, without question,
Rather bad for your digestion.
But the Powers have not sent me
To preach sermons; they've but lent me

A keen desire to please you
Now and always without end,
And a little wish to tease you
With the fondness of a friend.

By then, Chopin was known as the "leader of a literary set in St. Louis society," and she was part of an intellectual elite, Reedy testified in the June 3, 1897, issue of the *Mirror*. "Two Belles," he claimed, had sent him a letter listing St. Louis women's claims to distinction. Reedy—who quite probably wrote the letter himself—listed the most popular young women, "the more handsome spinsters," the young matrons distinguished for beauty and popularity, the most notable "dames, or it might be dowagers," and the "best ten wheelwomen," or bicycle riders. The lists included many of Kate's friends: her euchre partner Mrs. Julius S. Walsh; her visiting companion Mrs. David R. Francis; her friend's daughter Bertha Sawyer; and numerous Gareschés and Bauduys.

Then, finally, Reedy's "Two Belles" listed "the intellectual women of St. Louis"—twenty of "such indubitable cleverness that we think there will be no complaint of any individual therein against her associates. These are our Minervas." The list included the essayist-translator Thekla Bernays, the novelist-reformer Margaret M. B. Stone, the *Mirror* reviewer Frances Porcher, several Hegelian philosophers—and, at the top of the second column, Reedy listed among the Minervas "Mrs. Kate Chopin."

Reedy took every occasion to praise Kate Chopin's writing. When *Town Topics*, in New York, listed the authors it thought should be named to an American Academy of Letters (if there were one), Reedy pointed out the magazine's exclusions in his January 8, 1898, issue: "There are no women in the *Town Topics* list and yet we can run over the best work that comes to mind and note that a great deal of it has been achieved by women. If we were to take out of contemporary American literature, Mary E. Wilkins, Kate Chopin, Margaret Deland, Molly Elliott Sewall, Alice French (Octave Thanet), Alice Brown, Louise Imogen Guiney, Agnes Repplier, Gertrude Atherton, Elizabeth Stuart Phelps Ward, Mrs. Catherwood, there would be left a vacancy of considerable size."

Unlike many of his contemporaries, Reedy never overlooked women writers: In the next generation, Fannie Hurst, Zoë Akins, and Sara Teasdale would all benefit from his encouragement. But except for Akins—with whom he may have had a romantic fling—Reedy was not close friends with those writers. With Kate Chopin, he was close friends, and sometimes allies.

On at least one occasion in 1897, Kate Chopin and Billy Reedy took on the same satirical subject: *A Society Woman on Two Continents*, a vanity-press memoir published by Kate's former Sacred Heart classmate Sallie Britton. Sallie now called herself "Sarah Maria Aloisa Spottiswood Mackin," and Kate Chopin, who never called herself anything other than Kate Chopin, did not comment on the grandiose variety of names her old classmate used—nor did Kate say anything directly about the self-promoting quality of the book.

But she said a great deal indirectly. Hearing that Sallie had written her memoirs, Kate wrote, "I was seized with an insane desire to do likewise." When they were girlhood neighbors, Kate recalled, Sallie would often invite her to stay overnight, but Kate's mother never allowed it, "because Sallie was not a Catholic! And to-day, here she is, not only a Catholic, but actually receiving a golden rose from the Pope! While I—Well, I doubt if the Holy Father has ever heard of me, or if he would give me a golden rose if he had."

As for Kate's own "insane desire" to write her memoirs: "I found that my memory was of that order which retains only the most useless rubbish." As if talking to a friend, she rejected writing about her wartime adventures (tearing down the Yankee flag, helping prisoners to escape), and instead slyly suggested something very like Sallie Mackin's name-dropping book: "I want to tell of interesting and entertaining things; whether I received much attention, and whether I was a great belle or not; that sort of thing. Do you remember if I ever met any people of distinction?"

She dropped the subject without ever answering that question—but she evidently also discussed A Society Woman on Two Continents with Billy Reedy, who reviewed it with the Mirror under the pen name "Arbaces McFudd." What Kate Chopin did gracefully, Reedy did with all his roaring Latinate verbiage. To Reedy, Sallie Mackin was "a 'sassiety' woman in the fullest meaning of the slangology of the phrase," and only her modesty "induces her to refrain from spreading herself all over this terraqueous sphere." Reedy did not hesitate to name her a snob: Her Home Circle balls he called "hot rags." He suggested that she not neglect the annual festivities of the "Ninth Ward Chowder Coterie"; and he supposed that someone with "so much name" really ought to have a great deal more to say.

Kate Chopin herself was somewhat tongue-tied in her only known meeting with a national literary celebrity.

When the best-selling author Ruth McEnery Stuart visited St. Louis, she did not go to Kate Chopin's salon. Instead Kate traveled to the home of Mrs. E. C. Sterling "on the morning of the big snow," (February 3, 1897), according to Kate's report in the St. Louis Criterion. Stuart was on tour, the Wednesday Club entertained her, and she gave a public reading at Memorial Hall, sponsored by the Isabel Crow Kindergarten Association.

Kate Chopin had long admired Ruth McEnery Stuart, she wrote. Stuart's

"Carlotta's Intended" was, Chopin said, "a tale of such marked excellence that it left an impression upon my mind which has never been disturbed." The characters and New Orleans dialects struck her as "singularly true to nature," and in other Stuart short stories, "I have never failed to find the same wholesome, human note sounding through and through them. . . . Her humor is rich and plentiful, with nothing finical or feminine about it. Few of our women writers have equalled her in this respect. Even Page and Harris among the men have not surpassed her in the portrayal of that child-like exuberance which is so pronounced a feature of negro character, and which has furnished so much that is deliciously humorous and pathetic to our recent literature." (Kate Chopin's description of black people—jarring to current sensibilities—would have been considered liberal in her day: Thomas Nelson Page and Joel Chandler Harris were far more committed to the "happy darky" stereotype. By the time she met Ruth McEnery Stuart, Kate Chopin had virtually given up writing dialect stories and using blacks as major characters.)

Ruth McEnery Stuart, a native New Orleanian two years younger than Kate Chopin, had begun her writing career out of desperation: Her planter husband had died suddenly, leaving her penniless, with a small son. By the early 1890s, not long after she began publishing in national magazines, Stuart had gone to live in New York. There she "remained a southern lady in a northern city, a charming and fashionable hostess for literary gatherings," according to one biographer. She was "a slender, dark-eyed, middle-aged widow" for the rest of her life (she lied about her age), and for a short time, an editor at *Harper's Bazar*. She was also one of very few women to be successful stage performers: Her dialect stories particularly lent themselves to public readings.

Like Kate Chopin, Stuart wrote about rural Louisiana, but most of her tidy, well-shaped stories end neatly with marriage or death. Stuart did not deviate from genteel rules: In "A Golden Wedding," a couple separated for fifty years must go through another wedding ceremony before spending the night under the same roof. In the 1890s, Stuart did not experiment with deeper passions or slice-of-life short stories. As a professional writer who earned a living from her work, she could not afford to.

She and Kate Chopin evidently read each other's stories: Stuart's "The Unlived Life of Mary Ellen," about a young woman who loses her mind and carries about a large doll for the rest of her life, is reminiscent of Chopin's "La Belle Zoraïde." And Chopin's "Nég Créol," the story of a former slave who supports his former owner, is a much more dignified version of Stuart's "Caesar." But Kate Chopin had the luxury of writing what she chose; Ruth McEnery Stuart had to follow popular taste.

The two writers had a pleasant and warm meeting, on a silent, snowy, beautiful day. Kate had been preoccupied, she wrote, with "the disturbing anticipation of meeting an unfamiliar personality—a celebrity, moreover. I had met a few celebrities, and they had never failed to depress me." But Chopin suspected that Stuart, like herself, was appreciated everywhere but in Louisiana, and she imitated Stuart's dialect writing to make that point (Chopin's own dialect writing was much easier to read).

> I am quite sure that when Mrs. Stuart occasionally wanders back to *Les Avoyelles* there comes sauntering up to her some black wench or other, who accosts her with:
>
> "G'long Mis' Ruth! you knows des well as me, we all colo'ed people we don' talk dat away lack you makes us talk in yo' books!" And I am greatly mistaken in this guess work if some old chap from Bayou de Glaize hasn't said more than once, "Hit seems Ruth MicHenry's took to writin' books. But land! they ain't like no books I ever seen! Thes about common eve'y day talk an' people!" In short, Mrs. Stuart is a prophet outside of *Les Avoyelles*.

Chopin wanted to talk with Stuart about her characters—but instead made small talk: "I have met Mrs. Stuart, and did not speak of her stories."

Kate Chopin found Ruth McEnery Stuart to be delightful, with a soothing voice, a "natural and sympathetic manner," with no sharp edges or "unsheathed prejudices." Kate wanted to sit beside her for hours ("I know she would not have bored me the whole day long"). Unlike Kate's own loquacious circle, "I know she does not inflict the penalty of speech upon sympathetic companionship." Instead, Ruth McEnery Stuart left Kate Chopin with "the memory of a captivating presence, which lingered with me the whole day like the echo of some delicious strain of music that one cannot and would not banish."

Chopin also gave Stuart a copy of *Bayou Folk*, personally inscribed "To Ruth McEnery Stuart" with a message: "The snow lay everywhere, thick and soft; the tree-branches were bent like bows beneath its weight. A white silence muffled the earth and its chill reached my very soul.

"But I heard the voice of a woman; it was like warm music; and her presence was like the sun's glow through a red pane.

"The snow lay everywhere; but its silence and its chill no longer touched me. For the voice of the woman lingered in my ears like a melting song, and her presence, like the warm red glow of the sun still infolded me."

Ruth McEnery Stuart had much to attract Kate Chopin: the musical voice, the serenity of manner, the literary fame. Chopin, who always kept a slight reserve in company, envied one who could be "a perfect womanly woman," putting all others at ease. Ruth McEnery Stuart, a native southerner, perhaps had the warm charm and social graces that Kate Chopin never quite mastered in her years in Louisiana. But while Stuart would continue to write, indefinitely, the same kind of story, with "whole-souled darkies" and happy endings, Kate Chopin had covered that ground—and wanted to move on.

Of the women in Kate Chopin's salon and circle, none left memoirs mentioning her: There are no Chopin comments or reminiscences in the papers of Thekla Bernays, Charlotte Stearns Eliot, or Florence Hayward. When Chopin's children gave Daniel Rankin a list of her friends to consult, the only woman included was her childhood friend Kitty Garesché.

The Chopin children may have been protecting her memory (or her friends), and the women who knew Kate may not have been in a position to record their memories. Bernays was a translator and essayist; Eliot was a poet and biographer; Hayward was a humorist and travel writer—and Chopin's other society friends were mostly euchre players, not authors.

Yet the silence may also mean that Kate Chopin was far more popular with men than with women. She was critical of women reformers and women of society pretensions; she may, herself, have been considered something of a snob.

Or she may simply have been too racy, too dashing, too avant garde, too handsome, and too threatening for the wives of her male friends. The silence about her may be a silence of jealousy, or apprehension.

Chapter 18

INTIMATE AND
UNTIDY STORIES

KATE CHOPIN, AND THE other members of her salon, persisted in reading authors who were considered improper.

Although she read carefully the writings of her American competitors—Ruth McEnery Stuart, Mary E. Wilkins, Sarah Orne Jewett—Chopin's model remained Guy de Maupassant. Her style, like his, was crisp and clean; her storytelling, like his, was a matter of letting stories unfold—not hammering home morals. But as an American, Kate Chopin was restricted. American magazines, as Billy Reedy constantly complained, were edited for "the young person"—not for adult readers. Nevertheless, after *Bayou Folk*, Chopin began writing more sensual stories—testing the limits as to what could be published in the United States.

She continued studying Maupassant, who had died of syphilis in a French insane asylum in July of 1893. (He was forty-two, six months younger than she was.) She had long known his stories in French, and some of her most haunting tales resemble the Maupassant stories she began translating a year after his death. Chopin's "Her Letters" resembles Maupassant's "It?" ("*Lui?*") and "Night" ("*La Nuit*"): All are portraits of men obsessed with aloneness, darkness, and night imaginings. Chopin's melancholy night meditation, "The Night Came Slowly," has much in common with Maupassant's "Solitude," in which a man mourns his "isolation of self." And Maupassant's "Suicide" anticipates *The Awakening* in its description of "a solitary existence left without illusions"—an existence described in a letter found next to a loaded, used revolver.

Madame Victoire Verdon Charleville, Kate O'Flaherty's great-grandmother and first teacher *(Courtesy Elizabeth Shown Mills and Gary B. Mills)*

Below, Thomas O'Flaherty and Eliza Faris O'Flaherty, Kate's parents
(Missouri Historical Society)

George O'Flaherty, Kate's beloved half brother, with his stepmother, Eliza Faris O'Flaherty
(Missouri Historical Society)

First baby picture, probably by a traveling
artist who used the same body portrait for
every girl child—but the head is Kate's
(The Bayou Folk Museum)

Below, Kate O'Flaherty
as a five-year-old
ruffian, c. 1855

Right, Kitty Garesché: Kate's closest
school chum, later a Sacred Heart nun
(Courtesy Dorothy Garesché Holland)

1869: "Her very abundant dark hair drooped in a wave, lower on one side than on the other, which gave her a very arch, sprightly expression," according to Kitty.
(Missouri Historical Society)

Oscar Chopin in 1870, at the time of his marriage. *Below*, Kate Chopin with her first four sons: Fred, George, Jean, Oscar. The only portrait in which she wears a cross. *(Missouri Historical Society)*

Kate favored extravagant riding costumes, including hats with plumes and flamboyant lavender colors. Neighbors often disapproved. Picture taken in St. Louis, 1876. *(Missouri Historical Society)*

Below, the Chopins' home in Cloutierville, Louisiana, now the Kate Chopin Home/Bayou Folk Museum *(Bayou Folk Museum. Photograph by John C. Guillet)*

Albert Sampite: "Alcée" in Kate Chopin's stories *(Courtesy Leona Sampite)*

Maria Normand DeLouche. A late portrait: She was known for her wistful expression and curly hair. *(Courtesy Mary DeLouche)*

Below left, John Alvarez Dillon: newspaper editor and one of Chopin's first readers. *Below center,* Dr. Frederick Kolbenheyer: author, anarchist, physician. *Below right,* Rosa Sonneschein: editor, *The American Jewess* *(American Jewish Archives)*

Kate Chopin in 1893: Her admirers compared her to a French marquise. *(Missouri Historical Society)*

Below, Kate's last home, now 4232 McPherson Avenue, St. Louis *(Courtesy Lewis Schucart)*

1899: an ethereal, fin-de-siècle pose
(Missouri Historical Society)

MRS CHOPIN'S WORK ROO
FROM A WATER COLOR SKET
BY HER SON, OSCAR CHOP

Above, Kate Chopin's study, 1899: from a watercolor by her son Oscar

Kate Chopin, 1900, in a sketch by Oscar: the only picture of Chopin with eyeglasses

Over the course of four years—between July 11, 1894, and April 21, 1898—Chopin translated eight Maupassant tales. All were on subjects that particularly engaged her in the years after *Bayou Folk:* sex, solitude, madness, disillusionment, suicide. She may have read the translations at her "Thursdays," where Continental literature was discussed—but she managed to sell only the most conservative ones to local publications. "It?" and "Solitude" appeared in Sue V. Moore's *St. Louis Life* (1895), and "Suicide" appeared in the *St. Louis Republic* (1898).

Two of the rejected stories are far more intimate and strange. "A Divorce Case" describes one man's passionately sexual obsession with flowers, while "Mad?" depicts another's "wildly insane" jealousy over a woman, in language far too graphic for American magazines: "She possessed me, overpowered and bound me up soul and body. I was, I am her thing, her toy. I belong to her smile, to her lips, to the curves of her body and the contours of her face. . . . From between her trembling lips would escape the tip of her tongue, rosy and moist which quivered like that of a reptile."

When the woman in "Mad?" gallops away each morning at daybreak, the madman imagines her "saddle, pressed against her thigh" (even that would have been unacceptable to most American editors). He sees her kiss her horse, without wiping her lips, and he smells "the perfume of heated body—as after the warmth of the bed." When the man finally sets a trap for the woman and her unknown lover, he captures her and her horse—and shoots them both.

Kate asked J. M. Stoddart, a magazine editor, if he had "any market for disposing of translations of de Maupassant." She also offered her translations of Maupassant's six "Mad Stories" to Houghton, Mifflin, her *Bayou Folk* publishers, but without success: They said they did not publish translations from current literature.

Nevertheless, Chopin continued translating Guy de Maupassant, and turned to country stories: "For Sale" has more to do with nature than with the decadent, intoxicating interiors of the "Mad Stories," but it also ends in disappointment and melancholy. "Father Amable," another rural story, includes the claim that organized religion is "directed toward loosening men's purse strings; toward emptying their pockets to fill the coffers of heaven." After Chopin translated that thought, she ceased making a clean copy of her "Father Amable." What remains is a scrawled, mostly illegible draft.

Possibly Chopin decided that "Father Amable" would be too difficult to publish: In the early 1900s, a church official managed to get two anticlerical books withdrawn from the St. Louis Public Library shelves. Moreover, most American public libraries did not even stock the works of Zola, Flaubert, and Maupassant.

Still, when Chopin translated Maupassant, she absorbed much more than his style: She also responded to his worldly sophistication and his ingrained cynicism about youthful romantic dreams. Maupassant's characters live at night, in solitude and disillusionment: Like Edna Pontellier in *The Awakening*, they spend much of their lives asleep, or brooding over what should have been. Maupassant's view was far darker and more melancholy than the stories of *Bayou Folk*—and Kate Chopin's own short stories after 1894 also turned away from sunny Louisiana scenes with neatly crafted endings. She moved toward more intimate, untidy explorations of human passions.

Kate Chopin wrote twenty-five short stories between 1895 and 1897, and found publishers for eighteen. *The Atlantic* was the most prestigious magazine accepting her work: While she had not given up on the *Century*, it had evidently given up on her, and she received a continual stream of rejections. But *The Atlantic* did accept "Nég Créol," her unsentimental reworking of a devoted slave story, and it also took "Athénaïse," her two-part story about marriage and motherhood and what wives and husbands owe each other.

Athénaïse was, of course, the name of Kate Chopin's grandmother—who, at the time the story was published in August–September 1896, had just four months left to live (she died on January 27, 1897). At eighty-seven, Athénaïse Charleville Faris may have been in no condition to read or understand her granddaughter's short story—but the fact that it took Kate eighteen days to write "Athénaïse" suggests some self-doubts. She had had the story in mind for several years, for "In and Out of Old Natchitoches" (1893) includes an allusion to the marriage of Athénaïse Miché—but Chopin's decision to use the unusual name *Athénaïse* points to her thinking about her grandmother, whose marriage had ended with her husband's desertion half a century earlier.

The marriage in "Athénaïse" is unhappy: Athénaïse was immature when she married Cazeau, a much older widower, and both had unrealistic expectations. She runs away, and he brings her back, once—but realizes he is treating her as his father treated his runaway slave. When she runs away again, to New Orleans, she becomes friendly with Gouvernail, a bachelor newspaperman (like George Johns, he writes editorials attacking corrupt legislation). Gouvernail also belongs to an "intellectual coterie" with very advanced ideas: "[A] man or woman lost nothing of his respect by being married." Yet Gouvernail falls in love with Athénaïse, though he suspects she has no literary tastes and "would have rejected The Duchess as readily as Mrs. Humphry Ward." But after Athénaïse has been in New Orleans for four weeks, she feels unwell—whereupon the boardinghouse proprietor explains the facts of life. Enraptured at the thought of motherhood, Athénaïse returns to her husband, and for the first time responds to his passionate kisses.

The *Century* and the *Chap-Book* rejected "Athénaïse," and then, on July

12, 1895, Horace Scudder of *The Atlantic* wrote to Kate Chopin: "I have been delayed in reading *Athénaïse* and am sorry to have postponed so much pleasure. I am delighted with the story, and so I am sure will the readers of *The Atlantic* be."

The Atlantic gave "Athénaïse" a subtitle, "A Story of Temperament," as if to suggest that the story's problem was just a matter of individual peculiarities. But "Athénaïse" is a criticism of the institution of marriage itself: Cazeau, more than once, ponders the fact that his marriage is a mistake, but it is "a thing not by any possibility to be undone." "Athénaïse" includes a discussion of grounds for legal separation—mistreatment, drunkenness, and abuse—but Athénaïse's own objection is not enough: "the sweeping ground of a constitutional disinclination for marriage."

As for Gouvernail, who had already appeared in "A Respectable Woman" and reappears in *The Awakening*, Kate Chopin made him the spokesman for the ideas of her own intellectual coterie in St. Louis. Unlike Robert in *The Awakening*, who cannot imagine that a woman can belong to herself and not to her husband, Gouvernail of "Athénaïse" believes in a freer kind of love: "When the time came that she wanted him,—as he hoped and believed it would come,—he felt he would have a right to her."

But if Kate Chopin had written that kind of story, in which a married woman freely pursues a single man, she could not have published it in an American magazine.

She had little trouble placing holiday stories and local-color sketches—although sometimes she made fun of conventional story types. For Easter 1897, she wrote a standard holiday story, "An Easter Day Conversion" (also called "A Morning Walk"), in which a hard-hearted scientist is converted to belief in "the poet's vision." But by the following Christmas, she was ready to parody the child-as-redeemer stories that were so popular with American magazine editors. Her "A Family Affair" is an anticonversion story: A miserly old woman refuses to change her stingy ways—and so her young niece absconds with half her household treasures.

"A Family Affair" was Chopin's declaration of independence from the kind of story that filled magazines like *Youth's Companion*. Instead of publishing it individually, she syndicated it with the American Press Association, and received her second-highest payment for a short story, seventy dollars.

She may also have had a personal motive for writing "A Family Affair": Her grandmother Athénaïse had died without a will, while living with her daughter Josephine Faris Wilson. Possibly there had been a family squabble over Athénaïse's goods, since three other children survived her: Kate's aunts Amanda McAllister and Zuma Tatum, and her uncle Charles Faris. But if Kate's relatives took "A Family Affair" as a personal affront, they left no records. Kate does not seem to have spent much time with them, and only Charles Faris's wife, Clémence, appears in the guest lists with Kate at St. Louis social gatherings. By the mid-1890s, her relatives may have been too conservative for Kate's tastes.

Kate Chopin despised most rules. There should be an Eleventh Commandment, "Thou shalt not preach," she wrote in October 1896 for an *Atlantic* essay (published in January 1899). "Thou shalt not instruct thy neighbor as to what he should do," she continued. "But the Preacher is always with us. Said one to me: 'Thou shalt parcel off thy day into mathematical sections. So many hours shalt thou abandon thyself to thought, so many to writing; a certain number shalt thou devote to household duties, to social enjoyment, to ministering to thy afflicted fellow creatures.' "

As usual, Chopin expressed anger through a bemused irony. "I listened to the voice of the Preacher, and the result was stagnation all along the line of 'hours' and unspeakable bitterness of spirit. In brutal revolt I turned to and played solitaire during my 'thinking hour,' and whist when I should have been ministering to the afflicted."

She did indeed prefer card playing over almost anything. As the *St. Louis Republic* reported in late 1897, the local author Kate Chopin "finds the greatest enjoyment in cards, and is always ready for a game." Her favorite was duplicate whist, which she usually played with her sons and "their young men friends, among whom are some very good players." Moreover, Kate Chopin "is fond of solitaire, too, and it is a sort of standing joke among her intimate friends to say that if they leave Mrs. Chopin alone for five minutes they'll find her with the cards spread out before her, on their return, deep in the fascinations of one of the many combinations of solitaire."

Kate rebelled, she wrote in the *Atlantic*, against all fixed schedules: She "scribbled" during her "social enjoyment" period; she carved the "household duties" time into fragments, "with which I besprinkled the entire day as from a pepper-box." For a little while she followed the voices that bade her, "Go forth and gather wisdom in the intellectual atmosphere of clubs"; she also tried, and failed, to write the heavy historical fiction the times demanded. (In the late 1890s, the best-selling books were historical novels, among them Charles Major's *When Knighthood Was in Flower* and St. Louis author Winston Churchill's *Richard Carvel*. The most popular book in the St. Louis Public Library was Alexandre Dumas's *The Count of Monte Cristo*.)

Kate Chopin wrote with self-deprecating irony, except on a subject of deep interest to her as a mother and a writer: what young people should read. There was "far too much gratuitous advice bandied about," she said—and the thought that someone would censor another person's reading was abhorrent to her, she wrote in the *St. Louis Criterion* in 1897. She admitted, "There are many phases and features of life which cannot, or rather should not be expounded, demonstrated, presented to the youthful imagination as cold facts, for it is safe to assert they are not going to be accepted as such." But rather than being preached to, youth should have "its privilege to gather wisdom as the bee gathers honey."

Even within Kate's circle, however, there was disagreement about that. The Byarses, for instance, kept a locked case for books possibly "detrimental" to youngsters' morals, among them writings by Balzac and Fielding. But Kate Chopin made condemned books readily available to her children and to visitors, even though the appearance of one such book—Thomas Hardy's *Jude the Obscure*—"communicated a severe shock to the susceptibilities of a woman who was calling upon me."

"Oh! how can you!" the woman exclaimed, "with so many young people about!"

All the more reason to have the book, Chopin thought. Before it was condemned, there had not been any particular interest in reading Hardy's novel. But then "for some inscrutable reason" it was "withdrawn, I am told, from circulation at our libraries," she reported—and so everyone wanted to borrow the book, a ponderous object with the "outward appearance of a Congressional Record." She suspected that most people never finished it, for it was heavy and "unpardonably dull."

Jude the Obscure was not the kind of fiction Kate Chopin enjoyed reading. "From beginning to end there is not a gleam of humor in the book. From beginning to end there is not a line, a thought, a suggestion which could be called seductive. Its brutality is an obvious and unhappy imitation of the great French realist [Emile Zola]." Moreover, the hero of this preachy and gloomy book, Chopin wrote, "arouses so little sympathy that at the close one does not care whether he lives or dies; he might be put upon the rack and submitted to unspeakable torture, and I am sure nobody would object; for no one minds much about the spilling of sawdust or the wrenching of rubber joints!"

To Chopin, *Jude the Obscure* was not sensational. Instead of feeling fear and horror, "You will just keep on munching a cream chocolate, or wondering if the postman has gone by or if there is coal on the furnace." In sum: "The book is detestably bad; it is unpardonably dull; and immoral, chiefly because it is not true"—and it should have been left to "work out its own damnation." (That was a characteristic belief of Kate Chopin's. Two years later, she would use the same phrase about Edna in *The Awakening*, claiming that "I never dreamed of Mrs. Pontellier making such a mess of things and working out her own damnation as she did.")

Nevertheless, Chopin had written about *Jude the Obscure* out of "sympathy for the young person," who might be "led to believe that the work is dangerous and alluring" because the libraries would not give it out. That could leave a youngster "quite convinced that it is pernicious and altogether delightful," and she might be misled into spending a week's allowance to buy the book, to receive only "disappointment and disillusion." The "investigating spirit" in young people should be encouraged, Chopin said, but they should also be warned that books kept from them were usually not worth reading. Either they were dull, not written for youth—or they had no truth in them.

Censorship was another obvious topic for Kate Chopin's salon: Billy Reedy, who admired *Jude the Obscure*, was a vituperative critic of all book bannings. Reedy defended Émile Zola's discussing bodily functions; he praised Oscar Wilde's wit after Wilde was condemned for homosexuality. When postmaster Anthony Comstock suppressed Gabriele D'Annunzio's *The Triumph of Death* in March 1897, Reedy thundered, "When will fatheads learn that genius cannot be suppressed?" And when the Philadelphia School Board banned Victor Hugo's *Les Misérables* as unfit for girls, Reedy roared that they must be "poisoned by the miasma from a filthy heart." When he was himself criticized for publishing an excerpt from Marcel Prévost's *Letters of Women* showing "wifely infidelity," Reedy declared, "If people are looking for filth they will find it."

Almost thirteen months to the day before *The Awakening* was published, Reedy concluded, "There is no great literature that isn't vulgar, in that the forces in it are elemental."

Such beliefs put Kate Chopin (and Billy Reedy) on a collision course with the "conservative element," including most magazine editors in the United States. Although Chopin had once admired William Dean Howells's writings, by the mid-1890s he represented what she was struggling against. As a *Harper's* and *Atlantic* editor, he decided what Americans could read—and he preferred, he said, "the more smiling aspects of life, which are the more American" over the tragic subjects treated by such European writers as Guy de Maupassant. In particular, Howells argued that American authors should avoid "certain facts of life which are not usually talked of before young people, and especially young ladies."

Moreover, serious American writers, Howells declared, "have no desire to deal with nakedness, as painters and sculptors freely do in the worship of beauty." No serious American novelist, he said, would write anything like *Anna Karenina* or *Madame Bovary*, novels about "guilty love." (Howells could not bring himself to use the word *adultery*.)

And even if a writer did treat "guilty love" as Tolstoy or Flaubert had, Howells asked, "what editor of what American magazine would print such a story?"

Yet almost from the beginning of her career, Kate Chopin had skirted so closely to the depiction of "guilty love" that only the most literal-minded could have missed it. As early as *At Fault* in 1890, Chopin was describing a man married to one woman but loving another. Between 1891 and 1895, at least eight Kate Chopin stories included desires and flirtations outside marriage: "The Going and Coming of Liza-Jane"; "Madame Célestin's Divorce"; "A Lady of Bayou St. John"; "The Kiss"; "A Visit to Avoyelles"; "In Sabine"; "A Sentimental Soul"; and "Her Letters."

Nor did Chopin neglect the story possibilities of illicit passion without marriage. In "Lilacs," she intimates that the actress Adrienne Farival has lovers in Paris; in "Juanita," the heroine runs off with a one-legged man who may not be her husband; in "La Belle Zoraïde," the title character becomes pregnant by her lover. And in "At the 'Cadian Ball," the passionate planter Alcée mentions his scandalous weekend with Calixta (the "Spanish vixen").

As early as January 1894, even before *Bayou Folk* was published, Kate Chopin had thrown off Howells's strictures: She ended "A Respectable Woman" with a hint—almost a promise—that "guilty love" would take place. The loving but tempted wife tells her husband that next year when his friend Gouvernail visits them, she intends to be "very nice to him."

"A Respectable Woman" was published in *Vogue*, a magazine read by fashionable society people, and most of Kate Chopin's stories hinting at guilty love were published in that magazine. While *The Atlantic, Harper's, Scribner's*, and the *Century* consistently rejected her most unconventional tales, *Vogue* became her vehicle for escaping the "charming" label attached to her work by *Bayou Folk*.

While few well-known American writers appeared in *Vogue* (and no other local colorists), Kate Chopin found in its pages her own showcase, and she used it to experiment with a more radical realism and a less traditional—and less happy—view of the world.

Vogue had already commented on her talent as well as her beauty. In a photograph collage of *Vogue* writers ("Those Who Have Worked With Us") in the December 6, 1894, issue, Kate Chopin's picture appears at the pinnacle, above all other columnists and regular contributors. The picture shows her wearing a small headdress, with her shoulders draped in a flowing day dress. She looks contemplative, and thinner and sadder than in her best-known picture from 1893, the elegant one in which she gazes serenely at her audience with the air of a slightly smiling marquise.

In the December issue, Chopin was the first author mentioned in *Vogue*'s explanatory text (which misspelled the names of several of her stories): "MRS. KATE CHOPIN.—A beautiful woman, whose portrait fails to convey a tithe of the charm of her expressively lovely face, has been an honored contributor to Vogue almost from its first number. Calin, Desiré's Baby, a Lady of Bayou St. John, Dr. Chevalier's Life, A Respectable Woman, and La Belle Zoraide are among the powerful stories from her pen first presented in these columns." Reviewers of *Bayou Folk*, *Vogue* noted, were "nearly unanimous in singling out Desiré's Baby, one of the Vogue series, as the most original and the strongest story of the collection which, as a whole, they enthusiastically praised. Mrs. Chopin is daring in her choice of themes, but exquisitely refined in the treatment of them, and her literary style is a model of terse and finished diction."

Vogue's editor in chief, whom Kate possibly met on her May 1893 trip to New York, was Josephine Redding—who seems to anticipate Mademoiselle Reisz of *The Awakening*. Mrs. Redding was, according to a colleague, "a violent little woman, square and dark, who, in an era when everyone wore corsets, didn't"—but she always wore a hat, even at home in bed. She was not a woman who conformed to others' expectations.

In the mid- to late 1890s, *Vogue* paid Kate Chopin better and better rates, and published six of her most experimental and ironic stories, including the hallucinogenic "An Egyptian Cigarette." *Vogue* had also deliberately set itself against the censorious. In a November 1894 issue, for instance, the magazine had editorialized, "The Anglo-Saxon novelist, it appears, is again imploring the world to free him from the fetters imposed on him by the Young Person . . . . The pink and white—débutante afternoon tea—atmosphere in which convention says we must present love, means intellectual asphyxiation for us."

Kate Chopin's later *Vogue* stories had none of Howells's "smiling aspects of life." In "Two Summers and Two Souls," she described the end of a summer romance between a young country woman and a handsome, impetuous city fellow, for whom their five weeks seemed "a flash, an eternity, a rapturous breath, an existence—a re-creation of light and life, and soul and senses." Chopin described the man's intensity in language similar to Maupassant's in the "Mad Stories": "He talked like a mad man then, and troubled and bewildered her with his incoherence. He begged for love as a mendicant might beg for alms, without reserve and without shame, and the passion within him gave an unnatural ring to his voice and a new, strange look to his eyes that chilled her unawakened senses and sent her shivering within herself."

Chopin's *Vogue* stories were often about separation and loneliness. In "Suzette," an unlucky, hard-drinking young man has fallen into the Red River and drowned—but Suzette, who once loved him, ignores the news: His love had become a "weariness." In "The Recovery," a woman who has been blind for fifteen years gets back her sight—but is appalled at how she has aged: "The blessed light had given her back the world, life, love; but it had robbed her of her illusions; it had stolen away her youth."

In the *Vogue* stories, following Maupassant rather than Howells, Chopin was taking a much somberer view of life. Youth was prey to illusions, she suggested, and love did not last if health and beauty were gone. In "The Unexpected," two sweethearts are parted when the man contracts tuberculosis—and when the fond Dorothea finally visits Randall, she is appalled by his waxy skin, sunken eyes, and wasted body. She vows that she will never marry him: "not for all his thousands! Never, never! not for millions."

That story would have had a particular appeal to *Vogue*'s young lady readers, some faced with marrying for millions instead of sentiment: In the 1890s, it was fashionable for American heiresses to marry European royalty. But *Vogue* even published Chopin stories critical of its own audience.

Chopin's "The Blind Man," for instance, describes a shabbily dressed, "stupid" blind man who is tormented and abused by wealthy people. When he finally reaches a street where electric cars are "thundering up and down," shaking the ground, "something horrible" takes place. Women faint, men grow sick, the motorman turns gray, and crowds rush to see "the dead and mangled figure"—of one of the wealthiest, most influential men in town. He was, Chopin wrote with obvious intent, a man noted for prudence and "foresight." Meanwhile, the blind man, not knowing what the commotion is about, crosses the street and stumbles on in the sun.

The title of Chopin's last *Vogue* story of the 1890s, "A Pair of Silk Stockings," suggests a tale for the rich—but it is really a message to *Vogue* readers about how the other half lives. Its central character, a struggling mother who once had "certain better days," must now scrimp to buy necessities for her children. But when Mrs. Sommers suddenly finds herself with fifteen dollars, she yields to temptation and spends all the money on herself: silk stockings, new boots, kid gloves, a tasty lunch, and a matinee. On the streetcar home, she feels "a poignant wish, a powerful longing that the cable car would never stop anywhere, but go on and on with her forever."

Mrs. Sommers was the kind of woman that *Vogue* readers might pass by on the street without noticing—but by the late 1890s, living frugally in St. Louis, Kate Chopin had seen the effects of poverty and urban strife on women. *Vogue*, unlike other magazines, did not expect her to write for "the young person" about domesticity and womanly self-sacrifice. *Vogue* allowed her to describe what she had seen, honestly and fearlessly.

Vogue moved with her; other magazines refused.

After 1895, there were stories that Kate Chopin had trouble placing.

Some of them had no apparent offense. Seven magazines rejected "A Mental Suggestion," a romantic comedy about posthypnotic suggestion—the kind of extrasensory perception that Chopin believed in, because of a "curious psychic experience" her son Felix remembered years later. She had gone to see a play with a friend at the Olympic Theatre, but in the middle of the performance, Chopin suddenly said, "I must go home at once—something has happened to Lélia." She found her daughter sleeping peacefully, but while Kate was in the theater, a grate fire had indeed set Lélia's clothes aflame. (The quick-witted Lélia had wrapped herself in a rug to put the fire out.)

Despite the magazines' lack of interest in "A Mental Suggestion," the subject of "mental energy and its compelling force or quality" was very popular, as Kate Chopin pointed out in a *St. Louis Criterion* essay. While millions of people's thoughts were concentrated on "the great fist fight" between the heavy-weights Robert Fitzsimmons and James J. Corbett, "I could not help wonder-ing whether this accumulated mental force, projected at a given time upon a common object, could fail to affect in some way the men against whom it was directed. I have had this notion before, in regard to events which have claimed the simultaneous attention of a whole nation." There had been, for instance, the public reaction to the assassination of President Garfield: "It seems to me, for instance, that the united impulse of horror which went out from millions of souls must in some subtle way have reached Guiteau's inner consciousness, after his crime, and made itself felt. But this is something for the psychologists; I had better stop, or I shall have them laughing at me."

Serious topics did not always sell stories, either. When Kate Chopin at-tempted a war story, romantic war tales were popular in magazines, and Ste-phen Crane had also won acclaim in the literary world with *The Red Badge of Courage* (1895), a realistic story of Civil War army life (some librarians and reviewers had objected to his "profanity"). Kate Chopin's only war story, "The Locket" (1897), was also about a young and frightened soldier—but her soldier was a Confederate and a "Frenchy," like Albert Sampite and her Charleville relatives.

As in *The Red Badge of Courage*, there was no heroism in Kate Chopin's account of war—only loneliness, despair, and death—but she could not sell "The Locket." Between March 1897 and December 1898, it was rejected by nine periodicals, and by 1898 it was also out of step with its times, for the Spanish-American War had begun, amid waves of patriotic fervor. Kate Cho-pin was not only expressing an unpopular sentiment, showing war as grief rather than glory, but she was also intruding on masculine territory—and a woman who did so was rarely welcome.

Two other Chopin stories from this period were accepted but never printed. *Youth's Companion* paid fifty dollars for "Madame Martel's Christmas Eve," a kind of Christmas conversion story about a grieving widow who substitutes love for her "big, manly son" for sad memories of her cherished husband—but *Companion* (as Kate designated it in her account notebook) never published the story. Nor did *Companion* publish the Cane River country story of a young people's quarrel, "Ti Frère," for which the magazine paid sixty-five dollars in 1897. On second reading, "Madame Martel's Christmas Eve" may have seemed too somber, while "Ti Frère" may have struck the editors as too graphic a discussion of vice, gambling, and whiskey.

By the mid- to late 1890s, Kate Chopin's stories no longer fit most magazines' expectations. She was much less interested in the marriage plot, and much more attracted to slice-of-life portrayals of people forced to live with disillusionment. But at times she attempted to conform: The *Century* had almost taken "In the Vicinity of Marksville" (later called "A Night in Acadic"), but Chopin could not weaken the main character enough to suit editor Richard Watson Gilder.

She did try. In the story, the bold Zaïda is pursued by a very proper, industrious young man named Telèsphore. Zaïda, no delicate damsel, steps out "freely and casily" with "the air of a young person accustomed to decide for herself and for those about her." (Zaïda's name echoes the romantic *Zaidee* that Kate O'Flaherty and Kitty Garesché read before the war, and one character even uses "Zaïdé" as a nickname). At a Cane River country dance, Zaïda arrives dashingly late and dances with Telèsphore—who, later that evening, stumbles into her plan to meet and marry the drunken, lazy André Pascal. Telèsphore and Pascal square off in a clumsy fist fight that Telèsphore wins, and he takes home the drooping Zaïda.

In the first version of the story, Chopin had not shown Zaïda as tired and dulled after watching the fight: The original Zaïda, her will as strong as ever, had demanded that Telèsphore marry her on the spot. But the *Century*'s Gilder criticized the story, and Kate Chopin wrote to him on January 5, 1897, that she had made "certain alterations which you thought the story required to give it artistic or ethical value . . . . The change in the story will be found to begin on page 53. The marriage is omitted, and the girl's character softened and tempered by her rude experience."

But the story still was not acceptable to Gilder: Possibly André's drunkenness displeased him, or Zaïda's boldness. The story was also antiromantic: Zaïda is not so beautiful as Telèsphore thinks she is—nor are the men as skillful fighters as they ought to be. Kate Chopin came close to parodying sentimental romances and dime novels, and Gilder had never been attracted by satire.

By 1897, Kate Chopin had virtually abandoned the kind of local-color writing that had brought her national acclaim. Although she still owned her house in the Cane River country and kept close family ties with the Breazeales and the Henrys and the Lamy Chopins, her creative and imaginative life was centered in St. Louis. There, she was powerful and popular and very much in vogue—with some people.

Chapter 19

MAKING
ENEMIES

⟝⟞ "THE COURTEOUS EDITOR OF
The Criterion, obeying some misguided impulse, has kindly placed at my disposal a couple of columns of this entertaining journal, in which to exploit my opinions upon books and writers, and matters and things pertaining thereto," Kate Chopin wrote in *The St. Louis Criterion*, in an essay published on February 27, 1897.

The Criterion was the new incarnation of *St. Louis Life*: Kate's friend Sue V. Moore had been replaced by Grace L. Davidson, a retired schoolteacher described as a "stately and somewhat mysterious lady well on in years," who had bought the magazine in 1896. For her editor, Davidson appointed Henri Dumay, a peripatetic Frenchman variously described as a literature professor at Washington University, "a French-born literary adventurer," or a "slightly sinister young Frenchman." (Billy Reedy considered him "pettily piquant and colossally egotistic"—and ultimately Dumay was fired for, among other things, "rhapsodizing the little sanitary stops of a French dancer's dog.")

Kate Chopin knew Dumay, who had translated her "Story of an Hour" into French—and had revised it in the process. Dumay had added two paragraphs at the beginning, shifting the focus from the wife to her husband's friend. Chopin's "railroad disaster" in Dumay's hands became more graphic: Two trains at top speed had crashed into one another, with broken cars and "horrible agonies." Dumay made the wife's friends more talkative; he changed the husband's name from Brently to Roger; and he gave the newly emancipated wife religious language. Dumay's character says, *"Libre, Mon Dieu, libre!"* ("Free, my God, free") rather than simply "Free, free, free." (Whether Dumay ever published his translation is unknown, but he did give a copy to Kate Chopin.)

Under Dumay and Grace L. Davidson, *The Criterion* grew intellectually fancy, according to the populist Billy Reedy: "The articles took on a tone of exalted aestheticism. . . . The comment upon the affairs of the day was written in the clouds." Still, *The Criterion* recognized the value of contributions from St. Louis's best-known writer—for by the late 1890s, Kate Chopin's only local rival for national fame was Reedy himself.

But *The Criterion* had made an error, Chopin wrote wryly: "When a person is politely offered *carte blanche* to discourse upon 'matters and things,' that person is going to talk about herself and her own small doings, unless she is old enough to know better. One must be very old indeed to be old enough to know better." (Less than a year later, Chopin wrote of Robert in *The Awakening* that he "talked a good deal about himself. He was very young, and did not know any better.")

Moreover, according to Kate Chopin, *The Criterion's* "second mistake was in supposing that I had any opinions. Very long ago I could do nothing with them; nobody wanted them; they were not self-supporting, and perished of inanition." Nevertheless: "Since then I have sometimes thought of cultivating a few—a batch of sound, marketable opinions, in anticipation of just such an emergency, but I neglected to do so."

Chopin presented herself as bumbling rather than opinionated—but she had strong ambitions and strong opinions. In the six *Criterion* essays, published between February 13 and March 27, 1897, under the heading "As You Like It," Chopin said what she thought about censorship, *Jude the Obscure*, and her former classmate's memoir *A Society Woman on Two Continents*; she reminisced about her visit with Ruth McEnery Stuart. She made all the essays rambling, comfortable, and engaging—although she was also making fun of much of the conventional wisdom of her day.

In her opening essay, she talked about a "young friend" assigned to write a pompous oration, a thought that made her cringe and laugh (the young visitor, ambitious to be a lawyer, may have been inspired by her son Felix). Whatever you do, Chopin told her friend, "let it be original. Give your own impressions, for goodness sake! However lame or poor, they ought to be of more value than any second-hand material you may chance to gather." But her visitor pointed out that schoolteachers did not want originality—and so he had in mind a grandiose discourse on "Standing Armies." The result was a great roll of sentences, though laudably short, "[b]ut there was no truth in it from beginning to end, and I told him so."

His efforts drew her to think about illusions, the subject of most of her stories after 1895, including *The Awakening*. "We never know what illusions are till we have lost them. They belong to youth, and they are poetry and philosophy, and vagabondage, and everything delightful. And they last till men and the world, life and the institutions, come along with—but gracious! I forgot whom I was talking to. Run on and get your skates. I hear there's great sport out at Forest Park."

Kate Chopin disliked predictability in politics or people, and wrote in *The Criterion* about her enjoyment of literary gossip: "We are told that Macaulay was in the habit of swallowing a book almost at a gulp; just as the ogres used to swallow little children, clothes and all. One longs for a like super-human capacity"—in order to ingest all the "bewildering and tempting variety of wares which the book-stands are offering us to-day."

Chopin seemed to be alluding in particular to the *Century* when she wrote about periodicals that might entertain, amuse, and instruct, but "they are not going to shock us. They hold no surprises in reserve; we should very likely resent the innovation if they were to take upon themselves any such new departure." She was intrigued by "the newer booklets, chiplets, clap-traplets, that we must turn [to] for sensations"—an obvious reference to the *Chap-Book*, the innovative Chicago magazine to which she kept submitting her work without success. The new magazines, she wrote, were invigorating, like a breath from "the new land where 'the modern' holds sway"—France.

Then she shifted abruptly, again, to a seven-paragraph review of *Sister Jane*, a new novel by Joel Chandler Harris, with none of the "modern" traits she admired. The plot was "lamentable," predictably melodramatic, and its author "has not the constructive faculty that goes to the making of even the mediocre novel; while he lacks the 'vision' which gives us the great novel."

Kate Chopin was also concerned, literally, with vision. She had written two stories about blindness ("The Recovery" and "The Blind Man") in the previous year, and she may have been suffering from vision problems related to diabetes—a common problem in women who have had multiple pregnancies. Her "defenseless right eye," she wrote in *The Criterion*, had sent her to the doctor, and she wrote about him with nonchalance, humor, and very little respect. (Her fictitious physicians—Chevalier, Mandelet in *The Awakening*, John-Luis in "Mamouche"—are benevolent authorities, but Kate Chopin in her essays opposed all authorities.)

Her eye doctor, she wrote, had ordered her to look this way and that, and up and down, while "a glance of ten million candle-power" was turned upon her eye, so that "[t]he very wastes and caverns of my inner thought must have been resolved by the searching probe." The verdict was simple: "Only a little inflammation." She should not read, write, or sew, her doctor prescribed. (As Charlotte Perkins Stetson—later Gilman—had shown in her chilling 1892 story

"The Yellow Wallpaper," that kind of advice was frequently given to women—
who could scarcely ever follow it.)

Kate Chopin, for one, wanted to know more.

"And may I clean out closets; go see people; play whist; and think
upon my sins and the means of escaping the penalty thereof?"

"Next, please!"

The snub direct from a professional gentleman in the discharge of
his duty!

She did follow her doctor's advice, she said: Newspapers stayed unread, and
letters unanswered, "and the boys are sewing on their own buttons." One friend
sent her a homemade green eye-shade; another brought "a homeopathic specific of such subtle quality and insidious efficacy that there seems to me to be
no excuse for blindness upon the face of the earth unless she has been misin-
formed."

But there was one pleasure in all this: Someone read aloud to her from *Tales
of Two Countries*, a collection of short stories by the Norwegian author Alexander Kielland. Chopin implied that she had first encountered Kielland's writing in 1897, but his *Tales* had been published in the United States in 1891,
and some of her 1892 stories resemble his: Her "Caline," like his "Parsonage,"
describes a society young man who flirts with a young country woman and
forgets her, while she keeps him in her dreams. Similarly, Chopin's "Miss
McEnders" resembles Kielland's "Good Conscience," a scathing portrait of a
would-be lady bountiful, who rejects a poor family when their unmarried daughter
becomes pregnant.

Kielland had the kind of vision Chopin admired, and she, as usual, gave her
readers advice while pretending not to: "But, speaking of Kielland, I am not
going to advise anyone to read his stories; I would not be guilty of advising
anyone to do anything. I only want to say that they possess a subtle quality that
suited the ear, the understanding, the mood with which I listened to them."
Kielland, like Guy de Maupassant and Alphonse Daudet, was a realist. His
Norwegian country characters, like Kate Chopin's, did not suffer from extreme
deprivation and poverty; his women characters were not confined to domestic
roles; and his plots were not creaky, old-fashioned, and mechanical.

Chopin, however, had no particular interest in Kielland's plots: By that time,
her own stories were being rejected as plotless. She was far more interested, as
Kielland was, in characters and situations. His first story, "Pharaoh," she wrote,
had "a fine psychological touch": A countess, conveyed to a ball, jostled by the

crowd, remembers that she "was not always a countess"—and she feels a "sympathy of blood" with the common people.

Two other Kielland stories particularly impressed Kate Chopin. "At the Fair" appealed to her because of its pathos: A poor little mountebank is shown crying behind the tent, and "[h]e has a yellow and a red leg, and he stands on his yellow leg 'like a stork,' with the red one doubled up under him. '*Maman m'a pris mon sou,*' he wails between sobs. His mother has taken his sou!"

The boy's legs—actually red and green, in his costume—were not all that Kate Chopin saw in the story. A condor, trapped, watches the poor carnival performers and the surging crowds, and dreams of the Andes—just as "the white eagle," in one of Chopin's last stories, "gazes across the vast plain with an expression which in a human being would pass for wisdom."

The other Kielland story Chopin admired, "Two Friends," involved a subject she would not have used: two men in business. Charles is ugly, but a business genius; Alphonse is charming, but has no business sense. After Charles, seething with jealousy, breaks off their partnership, Alphonse forges Charles's name—and then takes a fatal dose of poison.

"The story of 'Two Friends,' " Kate Chopin wrote, "is one of the most subtle delineations of character which I ever read. It is not told as I like stories to be told; but that, perhaps, is because it is Norwegian. I stayed quite still after hearing it, quite still for a long time, pretending to be asleep, thinking of it, wondering at it."

Kate Chopin was far more introspective and reserved than her friend Billy Reedy of the *St. Louis Mirror.* Midway in her series of essays in *The Criterion,* she published two society stories in the same magazine under the pen name "La Tour." Reedy kept silent about the inspiration for the first—but leaped gleefully into print about the second because it concerned a rich person and a rival newspaper. Billy Reedy could not resist spilling what he knew.

Kate did not really conceal her authorship of "The Falling in Love of Fedora," published February 20 in *The Criterion.* She included it in her planned story collection, *A Vocation and a Voice,* and she had submitted to *The Atlantic* (where it was rejected with the comment that it had no plot).

Fedora is not a charming character. At thirty, she is unmarried, with "her own persistent affectation and idiotic assumption of superior years and wisdom." Her sisters' and brothers' summer guests do not interest her, nor does she attract them: "[A]s Fedora was tall and slim, and carried her head loftily, and wore eye-glasses and a severe expression, some of them—the silliest—felt as if she were a hundred years old. Young Malthers thought she was about forty." One day, looking up at the young Malthers, whom she knew as a child, Fedora recognizes that he has become a man. She begins to seek him out, sensing in herself an "inward revolt, astonishment, rapture, self-contumely; a swift, fierce encounter betwixt thought and feeling." When Young Malthers' sister arrives, Fedora insists on meeting her at the station—and before leaving home, Fedora fervently touches Malthers's hat and buries her face in his coat.

To this point, "The Falling in Love of Fedora" resembles "A Shameful Affair," Chopin's 1891 story of a lofty young female intellectual distracted by the presence of a sun-browned farmhand. "Fedora" also resembles an undated Chopin manuscript called "The Impossible Miss Meadows," about a shabby female visitor to a Wisconsin summer resort who is very much resented by the good-looking and popular young people of the family. The mother tries to cheer up Miss Meadows, but the boys groan and slink away—whereupon the story ends, incomplete. "The Impossible Miss Meadows," not listed in Kate Chopin's account book, may have been a draft for "The Falling in Love of Fedora."

But Chopin gave "Fedora" a twist—and one that made it hard to publish.

When Fedora meets Malthers's sister, who resembles her brother, Fedora greets the sister in "her usual elderly fashion." Fedora gathers the reins, puts her arm around Miss Malthers's shoulders, and "[w]hen the girl looked up into her face, with murmured thanks, Fedora bent down and pressed a long, penetrating kiss upon her mouth."

As for the reaction: "Malthers' sister appeared astonished, and not too well pleased. Fedora, with seemingly unruffled composure, gathered the reins, and for the rest of the way stared steadily ahead of her between the horses' ears."

Kate Chopin left no clues as to why she wrote the story, or what that gesture was intended to mean, or why she published the piece under a pen name. Perhaps it was a true, or almost-true, story from St. Louis society. Possibly something like Fedora's penetrating kiss had been bestowed upon Lélia Chopin by an admirer of her brother Jean, a society favorite. One society columnist described the "slender beauty of Jean Chopin, who is a splendid dancer, if he is tall"—and at a society wedding, Jean was seen "gazing entrancedly down into the eyes of a pretty girl at his side. Isn't Jean Chopin the very tallest thing except the Eiffel Tower that you ever saw?" Two young society women were also giggling about Jean and his companion: "O, I reckon she has been taking the High Jean treatment."

The character of Fedora does bear some resemblance to the St. Louis journalist Florence Hayward, who was tall, slim, and bespectacled—and whose name could be an anagram for "Fedora." By her own account, Florence Hayward did have a curmudgeonly side, and she also had a younger sister with an active social life among a set of young people—but whether Kate Chopin had Florence Hayward, or anyone, in mind when she wrote "The Falling in Love of Fedora" cannot be known.

"The Falling in Love of Fedora," whatever its meaning, did find a publisher, in a little more than a year. But "Miss McEnders," the second story published under the name "La Tour," took five years.

Chopin had written it on March 7, 1892, while the St. Louis daily newspapers were fighting a circulation battle. She naturally sided with her friends at the *Post-Dispatch* over the *Republic* and the *Globe-Democrat*, and her story may have been intended as a weapon against the *Globe-Democrat*. Less than a month after writing "Miss McEnders," Chopin had resigned from the Wednesday Club—and the timing suggests that a particular incident may have triggered her story and her resignation.

Chopin's "Miss McEnders" is a cuttingly described character. At the start of her story, the wealthy Georgie McEnders is "a charming young woman of twenty-five" with "a burning desire to do good—to elevate the human race, and start the world over again on a comfortable footing for everybody." She belongs to "a committee of ladies to investigate [the] moral condition of St. Louis factory-girls," and her schedule includes women's club meetings, social calls, dinner, and a lecture on the Single Tax. Although she believes that she works unselfishly for others, Georgie is always aware of the impression she is making: Before reading a paper on "The Dignity of Labor" for the Woman's Reform Club, she finishes "an elaborately simple toilet of gray and black."

Then Georgie discovers that her dressmaker, Mademoiselle Salambre, has a small child but no husband. Georgie fires Mademoiselle, who retorts with a challenge. Let the self-satisfied "Mees McEndairs" ask anyone on the street how her father really made his money and what kind of a man her fiancé really is.

Georgie quizzes passersby about her father. An old gentleman says she should not ask "indiscreet questions." A plumber reports that Mr. McEnders made his fortune in "the Whisky Ring." But a newsboy gives the bluntest explanation for where Mr. McEnders got his money: "He stole it; dats w'ere he got it." As for her fiancé, Georgie does not even ask: Chopin may have intended readers to think he was the father of Mademoiselle Salambre's child. At the end of "Miss McEnders," Georgie finds a box of white spring blossoms from her fiancé, and flings them into the dark ashes of the fireplace.

"Miss McEnders" was not easy to sell to magazines: Possibly its attack on ladies of the capitalist class made editors uneasy. First it was rejected by *Two Tales* and the *Arena*, and then Chopin sent it to the *New England Magazine* because of "the liberal views expressed by Mr Walter Blackburn Harte in his 'Corner at Dodsbys.'" But the magazine kept her story for an entire year before rejecting it. Chopin did not send "Miss McEnders" to the *Century*, where Mademoiselle Salambre's unmarried motherhood would have been unacceptable—and after the *New Orleans Times-Democrat* and *Vogue* also refused it, she stopped sending the story out.

Then, four years after *Vogue*'s rejection, "Miss McEnders" by "La Tour" suddenly appeared in the *St. Louis Criterion* on March 6, 1897—almost five years to the day after Chopin had written the story.

A week later, Billy Reedy gave his *Mirror* readers the inside scoop.

The Criterion, Reedy wrote, was now "printed on fine paper and beautifully illustrated, and edited by an intimate advisor of God, one M. Henri Dumay." Although it had "blossomed forth in a shape and style that argued the discovery of 'an angel,' " Reedy wrote, "I doubt if funds will be forthcoming henceforth." Last week's *Criterion* had published a "bit of fiction" that could have the effect of "cutting off the wherewith."

The story had shown how a certain Miss McEnders had "determined to spend her life in charity. She went about doing good and incidentally lecturing people on their morals," Reedy reported. Georgie McEnders also discovered that her father's money "was stolen from the Government by the Whisky Ring, of which the charitable heroine's father had been a member."

To St. Louisans, the name of the man who profited most from the Whisky Ring scandal in the 1870s was well known: William McKee, editor of the *Globe-Democrat*. Convicted in 1876 of collecting a thousand dollars a week by siphoning off taxes from illicitly brewed whisky, McKee had been sentenced to two years in prison and fined ten thousand dollars. But he served only six months, spending most of his nights at home with his family. (He died in 1879, while Kate Chopin was living in Louisiana.) McKee clearly bore some resemblance to Georgie McEnders's father in the story by "La Tour": William McKee, like Horace McEnders, did have "closely-cropped sidewhiskers," "thin, firm lips," and "a good-humored shrewdness" in the eyes.

Reedy did not hesitate to point out other real-life parallels to the *Criterion*'s "Miss McEnders."

> It must have been a most interesting story to the "angel" of the paper, because the said "angel" is none other than Miss Ellen McKee, daughter of William McKee, and the chief stockholder in the "Globe-Democrat." The unfortunate history of the entanglement of Miss McKee's father with the Whisky Ring is a local tradition. Miss McKee is devoted to charities of all kinds, including the maintenance of fashionable weeklies, and there can be no doubt that "The Criterion" 's story was a satire upon the person whose money gives it life. The publication of the tale is a splendid example of biting the hand that feeds, for it is impossible that anyone who read the story should have been ignorant of the purpose of the recital. It is said

that "The Criterion" 's patroness has been terribly wounded by the
fiction feature of last week, and that she has been unable thus far
to bring herself to believe the "explanation" that the story was not
intended to mock her philanthropic tastes and revile her father's
memory.

Kate Chopin could not have anticipated that *The Criterion*, supported by the
Whisky Ring king's daughter, would publish her five-year-old story. But Chopin had been a consistent critic of patronizing philanthropists: Two weeks earlier, in *The Criterion*, Kate had made—under her own name—a sly remark
about a friend who was to deliver an address before "an Intellectual Society for
the Prevention of Cruelty to Adults." Chopin also had a longstanding personal
reason to dislike the McKee family: Before the Civil War, William McKee, a
New York Irishman, had founded a fiercely antislavery newspaper in St. Louis.
He was prominent in the parades and speechmaking for the opening of the
Eads Bridge, for which Kate came back to St. Louis in 1874—and so his presence was both inescapable and galling.

Kate Chopin evidently did have Ellen McKee in mind when she wrote "Miss
McEnders." The name "McEnders" is an intentional clue—easily abbreviated
as "McE" or "McKee." Further, no one else's father had made so much money
in the Whisky Ring and spawned a daughter so renowned for her charity. Ellen
McKee, sixty-one years old the year "Miss McEnders" was published, had long
been noted for her gifts and donations. When she died in 1905, she left an
estate worth over a million dollars, much of it for charities.

Nor was any other St. Louis woman so well known for her refusal to flaunt
her own wealth. William McKee had been famous for simple habits, such as
walking to work and spending evenings at home—and Mrs. McKee and Ellen,
their only child, were said to own no more than two hundred dollars' worth of
jewelry. Chopin's Georgie McEnders shares an appreciation for the simple life—
or at least the appearance of it. In the first paragraph of "Miss McEnders,"
Georgie dresses for a Woman's Reform Club meeting by divesting herself of
rings, bangles, and brooches—"everything to suggest that she stood in friendly
relations with fortune," because "if she was blessed with an abundance of wealth,
she possessed a no less amount of good taste."

Whether anyone else knew that Kate Chopin had written the attack on Ellen
McKee cannot be known. Even Billy Reedy, perhaps out of friendship or chivalry, had not revealed the identity of the author "La Tour."

After "Miss McEnders," Kate Chopin gave up satirizing St. Louisans, but
Billy Reedy kept alive his vendetta against the McKee circle: Ellen McKee's
vulnerable point, he wrote six months after "Miss McEnders," was her belief
in ghosts. *Criterion* owner Grace L. Davidson reportedly "had access to the

spirits," who would suggest "things that Miss McKee should do." And so, "at spook behest," Ellen McKee bankrolled *The Criterion* to move to New York— where, Reedy said, it became even more noted for "priggish dullness" than it had been in St. Louis.

But Kate Chopin preferred not to harp on old feuds. After "Miss McEnders," her only story inspired by a specific St. Louis character was "A Vocation and a Voice," based on Reedy's boyhood. Nevertheless, she was developing a cadre of enemies in St. Louis. Some would damn her new short-story collection with faint praise—while others would wait for *The Awakening*.

Chapter 20

A NIGHT IN ACADIE: "IS LOVE DIVINE?"

IN NOVEMBER 1897, THREE-and-a-half years after *Bayou Folk*, Kate Chopin's second short-story collection was published.

Living in the Middle West had been a handicap. Her contemporaries—Ruth McEnery Stuart, James Lane Allen, Theodore Dreiser—had all been able to move to New York, where they regularly met publishers and editors. But Kate Chopin remained in the "provinces." For her second collection, she did not even approach the New York publishers who had declined her first one.

Chopin did keep on good terms with Boston publishers, although she was not always tactful or straightforward. When *The Atlantic*'s Walter Hines Page invited her to contribute to the *Men and Letters* series in the fall of 1896, Kate's essay described her discovery of Guy de Maupassant and her dislike for preachy writers, but she began ironically, "There is somewhere registered in my consciousness a vow that I would never be confidential except for the purpose of misleading." And so, for the essay, she created a persona: "I disguised myself as a gentleman smoking cigars with my feet on the table. Opposite me was another gentleman (who furnished the cigars) entrapping me into disclosures by well turned questions, after the manner of the middle men at the 'Minstrels.' "

Editor Page was dissatisfied with her dialogue: "I say all this with some diffidence because I appreciate the reason why you shrank from a direct 'confession,' " he wrote to Kate Chopin on October 9, "but after all, isn't direct statement the only satisfactory way (to your readers) to get at it?"

Kate tried again, still using her male persona, but in her next draft she also made fun of Page: "A person of sounder judgment than myself convinced me that the device was more clumsy than clever, and likely to bewilder rather than to deceive. He appreciated what he supposed to be the underlying notion of my diffidence and intimated that he really understood I might be ashamed of myself. In this he is mistaken. Like the colored gentleman in the Passemala I am sometimes 'afraid o' myse'f' but never ashamed."

Chopin also created a "Madame Précieuse," to whom she ascribed her own increasing dislike for religious pieties (which were not usually criticized in *The Atlantic*. Kate was pushing at boundaries again). Madame, Kate wrote, "often tells me that I have no soul (some people will tell you anything) and that my work consequently lacks that dignity as well as charm—which the spiritual impulse infuses into fiction. 'You have eyes, ears, nose, fingers and—senses—nothing else; you are a brute, you have no soul,' and—being rather fond of me—she weeps about it—in her lace handkerchief."

As many Sacred Heart graduates did, Chopin herself made gentle fun of the whole subject:

> In vain have I represented to her that at an early and credulous age
> I was told that the soul was a round, white, luminous substance
> or—copying some misunderstood portion of my anatomy—beauti-
> ful and luminous in a state of grace, but spotted black and hideous
> by sin—every fresh offense adding a new disfigurement, and that I
> have never been able wholly to disassociate the idea of soul from
> that first material impression. But she accepts no apology. She says
> that any kind of a soul—no matter how material—is better than
> none at all. She sometimes makes me feel that I am stubbornly and
> persistently rejecting some beautiful and precious adornment that
> has been offered to me as a velvet cushion.

Page accepted Chopin's revision by return mail on October 23, 1896, but her essay, "In the Confidence of a Story-Writer," did not appear in *The Atlantic* until January 1899—and then it appeared anonymously, and considerably shortened. Both Guy de Maupassant and "Madame Précieuse" (with Kate's discussion of souls) were gone—and the essay was a much more general criticism of didactic writers and advice givers. It could have been written by anyone, except that the ending described the Chopin salon: "Every writer, I fancy, has his group of readers who understand, who are in sympathy with his thoughts or impressions or whatever he gives them." Although she did not live in New York, Kate Chopin did have kindred spirits.

Meanwhile, *Bayou Folk*'s original printing of 1,250 copies had sold out, and

500 more copies were printed in 1895. Chopin continued to receive small royalty checks through 1902, adding up to a total of $35.97—and as early as 1895, she had been asking Houghton, Mifflin (editorially linked with *The Atlantic*) about publishing a second collection.

Finally, on January 20, 1897, the company's H. E. Scudder answered her. First he rejected a story she had sent to *The Atlantic* (probably "The Falling in Love of Fedora"): "You always make your scenes vivid to me, but sometimes they are of consequence,—a real story is involved—and sometimes there seems to be, as in this case, scarcely any story at all." As for a second short-story collection:

> I had enquiries made as to the success of *Bayou Folk*, and the result was not very encouraging. Yet the firm is always loth to seem inhospitable to one whom they have once included in the lists. Let me, in turn, ask you a question. You have now and then sent me a story long enough to run through two or three numbers in the magazine. Have you never felt moved to write a downright novel? The chance of success in such a case is much greater than with collections of short stories.

Five months later, Kate began writing a "downright novel," which became *The Awakening*—but for her second short-story collection, she turned to Stone & Kimball, the new Chicago firm that had published Hamlin Garland's *Crumbling Idols* and the avant-garde *Chap-Book*, to which Kate had been eagerly submitting poems and short stories: "I would greatly like to see one of them—some of them—something—anything—over my name in the Chap-Book," she wrote to Stone & Kimball on January 2, 1896.

Stone & Kimball, founded by Harvard undergraduates Herbert S. Stone and Hannibal Ingalls Kimball, was noted for beautiful books and very modern authors. Among the *Chap-Book*'s contributors and subjects were Aubrey Beardsley, Octave Thanet, Stephen Crane, Stéphane Mallarmé, Hamlin Garland, George Bernard Shaw, Louise Imogen Guiney, and Louise Chandler Moulton. The *Chap-Book*, like Reedy's *Mirror*, denounced censorship—and when Oscar Wilde's books were withdrawn from the British Museum after his trial for homosexuality, the *Chap-Book* called the removal "an act of bigoted and blind fury."

Still, Stone & Kimball were not interested in publishing Kate Chopin. They declined *Young Dr. Gosse and Théo*, and two Chopin poems and nine short stories, three of which eventually appeared in *Vogue* ("The Story of an Hour," "Lilacs," and "An Egyptian Cigarette.")

For her collection, Chopin then tried Way & Williams, Stone & Kimball's friendly Chicago rivals. W. Irving Way and Chauncey L. Williams, whose partnerhip had just begun in 1895, wanted to create a "Literary West" by publishing books that stretched the boundaries of what was permitted. They were also shrewd promoters, as they showed with Kate Chopin's untitled collection: Her first story, the tale of the bold Zaïda and her two suitors, originally bore an uninteresting name, "In the Vicinity of Marksville." That was changed to "A Night in Acadie," which became the title of the collection—and it was both a pun and a clever commercial ploy.

The title A Night in Acadie not only used the name of French Louisiana (Acadia), but also suggested "Arcady" or "Arcadia," a place of rural peace and simplicity. The popular Louisiana writer "Catharine Cole" (Martha Field) included "A Little Good-bye to Arcady," a New Orleans local-color story, in her collection Catharine Cole's Book—also published by Way & Williams in 1897. (Catharine Cole, on the editorial staff of the New Orleans Times-Democrat, certainly knew Kate Chopin's work: Chopin had published half a dozen stories in her newspaper.)

But A Night in Acadie's title also drew on the commercial and scandalous success of another book: Summer in Arcady by James Lane Allen, the Kentucky gentleman whose story A Kentucky Cardinal Kate Chopin had admired so much. Chopin probably never met Allen, although she visited New York at least twice while he lived there (in 1893 and 1898): Allen was a reclusive bachelor whose friends said he "appears to have practiced repression in his life." Nevertheless, by 1895, he, too, was pushing at the censors—and Chopin would have read his novel Butterflies, serialized in Cosmopolitan between December 1895 and March 1896.

It was called "the 'Romeo and Juliet' of Kentucky and Southern life," and Allen's story described a young woman and man drawn together by inescapable sexual longings during a hot, germinating Kentucky summer. Still, Allen pulled away from describing an actual sexual encounter. His would-be lovers are interrupted by the attack of a great black bull—and their consummation takes place only after the book ends, and after they have been properly married.

Butterflies, somewhat toned down and retitled Summer in Arcady, was published by Macmillan in book form in 1896. (Phrases like "helpless surrender" were omitted, although "laughing round-breasted girls" remained.) Yet Allen's novel remained insistent, amoral, with the kind of brooding refrain that Kate Chopin would use in The Awakening: "Nature is lashing everything—grass, fruit, insects, cattle, human creatures—more fiercely onward to the fulfilment of her ends . . . far out on the deeps of life Nature, like a great burying wave, was rolling shoreward."

Although Allen had carefully observed the ultimate taboos—his characters do not make love outside marriage, and their consummation is not shown—

reviewers still attacked *Summer in Arcady*. L. W. Payne, Jr., in *The Sewanee Review*, voiced typical objections: "Again we ask, why could not Mr. Allen have given us a purer story of love, and made of his beautiful Arcady of Kentucky the idyllic home of these happily mated children of nature? . . . We are ready to agree that the story has been enacted over and over again in our very midst, still the wonder is that any author should be willing to put his time and talents upon such carnal evidences of our human weaknesses when the world is so full of better themes." Even *Vogue* suggested that although *Summer in Arcady* had broken new ground for American writers in its depiction of sensuality, "the product of moral forces working over good intentions is in this case revolting . . . it is simply better to describe the book as unclean."

But whatever condemnation *Summer in Arcady* received did not damage James Lane Allen's writing career. His *The Choir Invisible* was the best-selling novel in the United States in 1897, the year that Way & Williams brought out Kate Chopin's new collection of Louisiana short stories, with its title transparently designed to echo Allen's novel.

In A *Night in Acadie*, few of Kate Chopin's twenty-one stories are actually about Acadians ("Cajuns"), but all take place in Louisiana, and most in the Cane River country. After "A Night in Acadie," the book contained "Athénaïse," "After the Winter," "Polydore," "Regret," "A Matter of Prejudice," "Caline," "A Dresden Lady in Dixie," "Nég Créol," "The Lilies," "Azélie," "Mamouche," "A Sentimental Soul," "Dead Men's Shoes," "At Chênière Caminada," "Odalie Misses Mass," "Cavanelle," "Tante Cat'rinette," "A Respectable Woman," "Ripe Figs," and "Ozème's Holiday."

Some of the stories were about courtship, like those in *Bayou Folk*; some described devoted servants. Some were about men who gained self-knowledge: Polydore learns that he must not fake an illness to avoid work; Mamouche gives up mischievous pranks; Gilma in "Dead Men's Shoes" declines his inheritance; Tonie in "At Chênière Caminada" prefers his dreams of a dead young woman to the possibility of losing her while she is alive.

But more of the stories in A *Night in Acadie* described women's awakenings. Athénaïse is transformed by the discovery of her pregnancy; Caline's life is changed by the visit of a young society man who draws her picture; Mamzelle Aurélie in "Regret" begins to question her own self-sufficiency; Madame Carambeau in "A Matter of Prejudice" surrenders her hatred of everything not French. Chopin's women characters also have forbidden thoughts: Mamzelle Fleurette in "A Sentimental Soul" enjoys being the true widow of a man she scarcely knew (but worshiped) while he was alive, and Mrs. Baroda in "A Respectable Woman" is powerfully attracted to her husband's best friend.

The stories in A Night in Acadie were more subtle and intimate than those in Bayou Folk—and reviewers did not find them so immediately pleasing.

A Night in Acadie received fewer reviews than Bayou Folk, in part because Way & Williams did not have Houghton, Mifflin's distribution and promotion network. The Independent gave the book one paragraph: "The romance and the reality of rural Louisiana has never been better sketched than by this author. These Acadian stories are exquisitely told. They are like aquarelles. The opening tale, from which the book gets its title, is a delicious piece of creole bucolic life, full of tenderness and truth. 'Azélie' is another charming bit, with just the shadowy, irresponsible sentiment of the cane country in it. 'Ozème's Holiday' touches a fine human chord; indeed, all of these stories are good, with a flavor and a fragrance purely creole."

The New Orleans Daily Picayune was also favorably impressed: "In originality and interest, as well as in the quality and variety of material, these stories show no falling off from the standard set in Mrs. Chopin's previous book. In this, as elsewhere, she deals with the Creoles of southern Louisiana, traversing much the same field as that so successfully worked by Mr. Cable. Mrs. Chopin, however, has a keener insight into the character of the Creole than Mr. Cable, because she loves, as well as understands, them. She has much of Mr. Cable's literary ability, and more than his sympathy for the rude courage and self-abnegation of the Creole fisherfolk."

The Nation's one-paragraph review defined Kate Chopin as a major regionalist: "Kate Chopin tells a story like a poet, and reproduces the spirit of a landscape like a painter. Her stories are to the bayous of Louisiana what Mary Wilkins's are to New England, with a difference, to be sure, as the Cape jessamine is different from the cinnamon rose, but like in seizing the heart of her people and showing the traits that come from their surroundings; like, too, in giving without a wasted word the history of main crises in their lives. That Cape jessamine is sometimes a thought too heavy is perhaps inevitable in the heated South. But enough there is of artistic in the best sense to hold the reader from cover to cover, transported for the time to a region of fierce passions, medieval chivalry, combined with rags and bad grammar, a soft, sliding Creole accent, and the tragedies and comedies that loom with special meaning in a sparsely settled country."

But The Critic, edited in New York by Richard Watson Gilder's sister Jeanette, sounded a faint note of alarm about A Night in Acadie. Although The Critic admired Chopin's "simple, childlike southern people" overall and the "delicacy and understanding of both man and woman" in the story "Athénaïse," the reviewer also felt that the story was "marred by one or two slight and unnecessary coarsenesses."

The Critic did not specify those "coarsenesses"—which may have been Athénaïse's shuddering at her husband's earthy ways (his boots, his dirty feet), or her attraction to another man, the courtly Gouvernail. Or *The Critic* may have disliked Athénaïse's response to her husband's kiss, after her discovery of her pregnancy: "He felt her lips for the first time respond to the passion of his own." *The Critic*, like most reviewers who criticized "coarseness," left readers to find the coarseness on their own, and focused on the stories that were clean and more pleasing by its standards: "Regret," "A Dresden Lady in Dixie," "Nég Créol" and "Odalie Misses Mass." "All the stories are worth reading," *The Critic* said, and "[t]he author is sympathetic and tender, and shows a knowledge of the human heart, young as well as old, as 'Polydore' and 'Mamouche' prove."

Yet *The Critic* also had a literary objection, the same one that editor H. E. Scudder had made against "The Falling in Love of Fedora": Kate Chopin was no longer telling stories in the traditional way. Bored with the predictable crisis and resolution of most short stories, she was writing more rambling stories— describing the texture of everyday life, finding a lyricism in dailyness (Sarah Orne Jewett was doing the same in her New England stories). *The Critic* did not care for Chopin's experiments, and complained, "She is never very exciting or dramatic; there is even a slight feeling after reading about six of the stories, that one has read something very like the seventh before; but to anyone who wants to be quietly and soothingly interested for an hour, they are to be recommended."

In St. Louis, however, *A Night in Acadie* was important news, highlighted in all the newspapers and literary journals. Billy Reedy, the first to review the collection, wrote that Kate Chopin was "a home author, who has achieved merited distinction in the realm of the short story." She "is one of very few women who have been successful in that line of literary execution which called forth the highest genius of Poe and De Maupassant. Mrs. Chopin is much impressed with the latter genius and he colors her style more, perhaps, than any other influence in letters. She is not an imitator. She has the great word-etcher's spirit." *A Night in Acadie*, Reedy said, "is a volume of delight to the reader, whether he or she be acquainted or not with Mrs. Chopin's style and stories."

Reedy praised Kate Chopin's style: "[D]elicious is the word that sums it up and she has a rare power of making an intensely interesting story out of a few simple happenings." He particularly liked "Athénaïse," and recorded his impression of the story's meaning (probably colored by discussions with Kate herself): "It is not the man she hates, although she makes the mistake that many wives do of thinking it is, but it is the institution, and so she runs away, as many other wives under the first impulse of rebellion would like to do. In her case she is led back by a stronger power than convention or force; a little life, of which she was ignorant when she wilfully shook off the galling fetters, will some day be her own—and his. So a great passion of love, lain dormant, starts up, wide-eyed and strong, and she goes back to the father of her child a wife in very deed and truth."

Reedy, typically, most admired Kate Chopin's efforts to write about adult passions: "[T]he touches of life are pictures of the same old human nature that is old as mankind and as puzzling and new to-day as when the first murderous instinct awoke to life in the heart of Cain or the first grand passion of love entered Eden and sent a man and woman from thence to be the one compensation left for all that temptation had lost them."

Two days later, Kate Chopin's friends at the *Post-Dispatch* printed their first notice of A *Night in Acadie:* "Mrs. Chopin is a St. Louis lady and St. Louis can justly be proud of her. Her style is finished and her insight of the life she describes thorough. Each of the twenty-one stories in this collection has its own charm. The whole form a string of literary jewels that are unique and pleasing."

The *Republic* was also quick to reprint and review portions of the book: One day after the *Post-Dispatch*'s notice, the *Republic* included in its Sunday magazine section condensations of "A Night in Acadie" (illustrated with a large woodcut) and "Azélie." But the *Republic* review mingled praise and puzzlement: "The author knows her characters well. She invests the folk who walk through her pages with such an appearance of reality that one imagines one is recalling an old and well-known tale. Perhaps the matter-of-fact reader may be a little disappointed on account of the vagueness of the endings of many stories, but the spirit which the author conjures up enables one to read on to the close of the episode."

The *Republic* reviewer—possibly assistant editor Mary Louise Dalton—also suggested a way for Kate Chopin to fix one of her inconclusive stories. At the end of "A Night in Acadie," Zaïda and Telèsphore are driving away from the house where he has knocked down the man she had planned to marry. Telèsphore, always precise, finds his watch is broken—and, the story concludes, "almost for the first time in his life Telèsphore didn't care what time it was." According to the *Republic* reviewer, "That is all of that story. It might have been a little more satisfactory to the reader if old Gibson [a justice of the peace] had come home in time to marry Telesphore and Zaida, and then they might have gone home man and wife, but the author would not spoil her 'Night in Acadie' in such a way."

(In fact, Kate Chopin had originally ended her story that way, with Zaïda's demanding that Telèsphore marry her on the spot—but Chopin had changed the ending because Richard Watson Gilder of the *Century* disliked it.)

The *St. Louis Globe-Democrat* also reported on A *Night in Acadie*—but in a way that any professional writer would recognize as disparaging.

Chopin was never friendly with *Globe-Democrat* people, except for the globe-trotting journalist Florence Hayward. Eight months before *A Night in Acadie*, "Miss McEnders," the attack on *Globe-Democrat* owner Ellen McKee and her late father, had been published—and although the story appeared under the name "La Tour," Chopin's authorship was no doubt whispered around St. Louis. When *A Night in Acadie* appeared, the *Globe-Democrat* could not ignore it—but its notice was grudging and inaccurate.

Unlike the other papers, the *Globe-Democrat* gave no indication that Kate Chopin was a St. Louis author. Its review began with a description that applied more aptly to *Bayou Folk:* "Visions of the bright Southland, with its magnolias and jessamines, its mocking-birds warbling through the night, its air fragrant with the odors of a thousand flowers, are conjured up by Kate Chopin's new book, 'A Night in Acadie' (Way & Williams)." The reviewer explained the history of the Acadians: Expelled by the British from Nova Scotia, they found their way to Louisiana. (Those Acadians were not, of course, Chopin's main subject.) The *Globe-Democrat* reviewer digressed about French peasants, Vikings, and troubadours, and then opined, "Personal character may inhere in a race as well as in a family, and is often displayed to better advantage. Kate Chopin has in her tales reproduced some of the most striking features of French Creole character and with touches of genuine genius. Here and there are trivial exaggerations in character painting and in dialect, but probably only such as are required by the art of the novelist."

Finally, in its faintly praising last paragraph, the *Globe-Democrat* reviewer did mention a few of Kate Chopin's characters, but mostly children—as if her adult characters were not worthy of notice. And about Chopin's story "Mamouche," the *Globe-Democrat* published the kind of error that results from carelessness or spite: The title character's race (white) is specified on the first page, but the *Globe-Democrat* identified him as a "mischievous little darky given to all sorts of pranks and tricks." The *Globe-Democrat*, silent about Chopin's stories of awakened women, made her into another Ruth McEnery Stuart, portraying "happy darkeys" and wholesome children.

But the *Post-Dispatch*, two weeks later, leaped to Kate's defense, with two full columns of intelligent praise, possibly by Kate's friend Charles L. Deyo. "A great truth that is fast slipping away from us is the absolute independence of art—art nourished by imagination and revealing beauty," the *Post-Dispatch* began, quoting the essayist Agnes Repplier. There are still, the *Post-Dispatch* said, writers who "keep fast their hold upon this beautiful escaping art—who have no problems to unfold, no theories to expound, no fatal habit of imparting opinions—and among them must be ranked Kate Chopin."

The *Post-Dispatch* review amounted to a forum for Kate Chopin's ideas—that an author must show, and not tell; must portray, but not preach. Probably drawing on conversations at the Chopin salon, the reviewer compared her writing to other arts: "[O]ne is more and more moved to an enthusiasm of intellectual gratification over the assured touch, the perfect balance of values—to speak in painter language—the flashes of insight and the keen artistic sense that holds back the word too much." The writer found in Kate Chopin's "delightful short stories," a "simplicity and directness of treatment combined with an invariable verity of motive" that "is borne in upon the consciousness of the reader from the very beginning of the story and produces a feeling of confidence similar to that felt at the beginning of a difficult aria by a singer of tried and assured powers. One feels that one is in the hands of an artist and that all is well."

Chopin, the reviewer said, "has gifts as a writer that go deeper than mere patois and local description and to which any background would be but an incidental. Psychological truth can be found in everything she writes. She knows the characteristics of the black race through and through and strikes an elemental note now and then to prove it. I know of nothing that Joel Chandler Harris has written that so graphically expresses the pure Congo African and the animate world of nature, as some of the passages from Mrs. Chopin's story 'Tante Cat'rinette.' "

Similarly, "Nég Créol" showed "one of Mrs. Chopin's most characteristic literary touches—that of surprising the reader with a climax that is a veritable spiritual illumination. I know of no one, not even the writer whom she most suggests, Maupassant, who is so clever at this. It seems a pity to have to point it out—it is so subtly put."

While praising "Tante Cat'rinette" and "Ozème's Holiday" for their characters' sincerity and unselfishness, the reviewer noted that they were "so unlike the smug complaisance of the Pharisee, or the sickly sentimentality of the organized charity worker, that one's faith in the better side of human nature is strengthened and renewed after each reading." (The criticism of charity workers would have been read as yet another jab at the philanthropist Ellen McKee of the *Globe-Democrat*.)

The *Post-Dispatch* reviewer also answered those who ignored Chopin's adult stories (the *Globe-Democrat*) or found "coarseness" in them (*The Critic*). The reviewer praised "Athénaïse," the story resolved by pregnancy, for its "wonderful insight into the heart of woman. . . . the fact that Mrs. Chopin has not hesitated to use one of nature's hidden secrets for its motive, proves alike the freedom of her spirit and her sureness of herself."

The reviewer did know Kate Chopin, he admitted, and hinted at some things unsaid: "Deliciously wholesome is her humor, and in considering both the woman and the writer, I am reminded of that famous definition of the heroine in George Meredith's 'Egoist,' where he speaks of her as a 'rogue in porcelain.' Our 'rogue in porcelain'—physically reminding one of Dresden—flashes many a witty thing, but none more roguishly than this, right into the face of Philistia. 'But for all his "advanced" opinions Gouvernail was a liberal-minded fellow; a man or woman lost nothing of his respect by being married.' Now what may she mean by that? inquires your matter-of-fact person—but the 'rogue' will never tell you."

Kate Chopin had always had secrets—as all her friends knew—and at the time the *Post-Dispatch* reviewed A *Night in Acadie*, she was already writing her most telling condemnation of marriage, *The Awakening*. When the *Post-Dispatch* reviewer described Chopin's career, he was writing one of the last favorable reviews she would receive in a St. Louis newspaper—and anticipating what would be most criticized in her next book:

> To sum up in brief the qualities of Mrs. Chopin, the writer: She is an instructive psychologist and absolute mistress of art form. Her art is sincere, delicate and full of the human quality, without which, art cannot be, for, according to Swedenborg, art is love. She is modern, universal and untrammeled by convention. She will do greater things than she has done, just as her second book, "A Night in Acadie," is greater than her first "Bayou Folk." In the latter the grace and delicacy of her art is paramount; in the former an intellectual and spiritual quality is added that keeps one brooding long after the spell of charm has passed.

One other local journal commented on A *Night in Acadie*, and the reviewer was a man Kate Chopin had known all her life: Alexander DeMenil, editor of *The Hesperian*. They had grown up in the same French social circles: DeMenil's mother was a Chouteau, and he had been educated at the Christian Brothers school and Washington University. He was a very handsome man, just a year older than Kate, and as a lawyer and city council member, he was known for his love of debate and his extravagant gestures.

DeMenil saw himself as an esthete. He wrote for newspapers and literary magazines and edited the *St. Louis Illustrated Magazine* in the 1880s: Among his contributors were the poet R. E. Lee Gibson, who later wrote a sonnet praising Kate Chopin, and the fiction writer Fanny S. Roper, who—as Frances Porcher—would write a damning review of *The Awakening*. DeMenil called his *Hesperian*, first published in 1894, a "high tone magazine," appealing to the "educated and thinking classes," while Billy Reedy was reminded of "the old thundering quarterlies of Britain which enshrine such a great and glorious body of English eloquence." Still, Reedy conceded, *The Hesperian* "serves a good purpose in introducing the readers to intelligent and appreciative estimates of the standard writers, and putting them in the right way to become lovers of the best thought and writing."

DeMenil liked A Night in Acadie, but from a lofty perch. Kate Chopin, he wrote, "pictures vividly a race and a life which are as innocent of the refinements and knowledge of higher civilization as it is possible for an exclusive, strongly opinionated, and self-isolated people clinging to the forms and traditions of a past civilization, and surrounded by American push, energy, and ambition, to be. But there is a humanity and a self-forgetting love, a rude courage and an inward sense of honor about them, as genuine as can be found in any other race in our country, and many of them are all the more pathetic for the uncouthness of their language, and some for the density of their ignorance."

DeMenil admired Kate Chopin's "vein of quiet humor" in "the development of certain peculiarities in the characters of her creations"; he also found her stories "extremely interesting as studies of life." Moreover: "Her touch is far more deft than Mr. Cable's; her insight is more femininely subtle (if we may use the word); pain, sorrow, affliction, humbled pride, rude heroism—enter more completely into her sympathies. She feels and suffers herself more intensely with her characters."

Yet in DeMenil's elite view, Kate Chopin could not possibly have seen the Cane River country people as her social equals: "[S]he is herself to the manor born—springing from an old and honored French family of St. Louis, reared and educated among, and with, the old Creole stock of the town—a race, let it be said for the first time, only a few removes higher than the Louisiana race, and possessing many of the same characteristics—and latterly, during some fifteen or eighteen years, a resident among the very element she so faithfully portrays, she has thought, felt, hoped, and lived intimately (as a superior) with the very people she gives life to in her books." In sum, Kate Chopin was her characters' "sympathetic historian, and not their caviling reporter. The critics have not yet understood the full excellence of her work."

Kate Chopin also felt that she was not fully appreciated, and in early 1898, she wrote to Richard Watson Gilder for advice about literary agents. "I am afraid I do not know of any good agency here except Pond's," Gilder wrote back from New York on March 8, 1898. "Why not Pond's? How about the Redpath Agency of Boston, Chicago, etc.? Has it a branch in St. Louis? I believe Mr. Kennan is now with the Redpaths."

As soon as she received Gilder's letter, Chopin traveled to Chicago, where the Redpath Agency was one of the oldest American literary agencies, first founded to provide lecturers on the lyceum circuit. The Redpath Agency could have started Kate Chopin on a series of platform performances, like those of

Ruth McEnery Stuart: In St. Louis, Chopin had been giving readings of her own dialect stories since 1894, and in February 1898, she was paid twenty-five dollars for a reading at the St. Georges Guild. But perhaps because Chopin was more reserved than Stuart, nothing came of her efforts to find an agent.

In Chicago, Chopin may also have visited Way & Williams, the publishers of A *Night in Acadie*. On January 21, 1898, they had accepted her new novel, called A *Solitary Soul* in her notebook (and published as *The Awakening*).

Chicago, like its rival St. Louis, supported a thriving community of writers: In the 1890s, Chicagoans produced some seventy literary periodicals. Studios, especially the informal Little Room, served as salons for artists, authors, and society people who shared tea and intellectual conversations. (Thorstein Veblen drew on this world for his *Theory of the Leisure Class*, published in 1899.) In St. Louis, visiting writers were brought to Kate Chopin's salon; in Chicago, Kate herself was honored by at least one member of the local literary colony.

Lydia Arms Avery Coonley Ward was a contributor to Chicago periodicals and the author of *Under the Pines and Other Verses*, published by Way & Williams in 1895. Ward evidently hosted a social gathering in honor of Kate Chopin, who wrote to her on March 21, "I feel as though I could not delay in expressing to you my thanks for your kind attention during my brief visit in Chicago, and also my regret at being unable to see you again and bid you good-by. I shall cherish the hope of meeting you again. Wishing to be affectionately remembered to your mother and the dear son, I am ever sincerely yours Kate Chopin."

Chopin had also been seeking a publisher for her third story collection, A *Vocation and a Voice*, which contained her most advanced stories—among them "An Egyptian Cigarette," "Juanita," "The Story of an Hour," and "The Nun and the Wanton" ("Two Portraits"). She needed an untraditional publisher, one who would not demand still another collection of charming, neatly rounded Louisiana stories. She had begun trying to sell the collection as early as 1896, and it was rejected by the Atlantic, the Bodley Head (publishers of Aubrey Beardsley), and F. Tennyson Neely, another young Chicago publisher, whose authors included James Whitcomb Riley and Jules Verne.

In April 1898, possibly as a result of her Chicago trip and assurances that her new novel would be well promoted and distributed, Chopin sent A *Vocation and a Voice* to Way & Williams, and it was accepted that month. She had, at last, a regular publisher.

Meanwhile, Kate Chopin was a socially sought-after person in St. Louis— although she had the habit of disappearing from parties or neglecting social obligations, and then sending apologetic notes. Not long after A *Night in Acadie* was published, she missed a lecture at Washington University, and had to send a note; to Mrs. Dexter Tiffany, whose son was a friend of her children's, Chopin wrote similarly, "You are *too* amiable; I must thank you in person for your kindness in overlooking my lapse." She did attend the exhibition of water colors by Cornelia Maury, a St. Louis painter, and wrote Maury that "I hope to look into your Studio some afternoon before long, if you will let me."

By the winter of 1897–98, Kate Chopin was one of St. Louis's most prominent persons. John Devoy's *History of the City of St. Louis and Vicinity*, published in 1898, devoted half a page to Kate Chopin: Few men, and only one other woman, were given more space. (The woman was Mrs. Margaret A. E. McLure, the eighty-six-year-old founder and president of the Daughters of the Confederacy of St. Louis.)

A Night in Acadie, Devoy reported, had "met with universal approval," and Kate Chopin's Louisiana stories were noted for tenderness, humor, and true-to-life dialect. Chopin herself also met with Devoy's approval, in a slightly patronizing way for a woman just turned forty-eight: "Mrs. Chopin is a well-preserved woman of commanding appearance and charming personality. Her conversation is always polished and impressive. She is perfectly familiar with all the topics of the day, and on them she speaks fluently and intelligently. Mrs. Chopin resides with her family at 3317 Morgan Street, where she entertains her many friends."

But Kate Chopin did not confine her friendships to her salon: She and her family were also members of St. Louis' "400" (the city's exclusive clique), and their doings were reported in society columns. On February 6, 1896, for instance, Chopin attended the Chadbourne reception for several hundred ladies, and was one of eight women "dispensing the cafe frappe," according to the *Mirror*. Her daughter Lélia's attendance at Minnie Maddern Fiske's performance at the Fourteenth Street Theater in December of 1897 was reported, and a year earlier, the *Mirror* had called Lélia, now sixteen, "a strickingly [sic] handsome girl, with dark eyes and hair," who wore a "white Paris muslin gown" to a dance for her young neighbor and friend, Augusta Chase.

Kate Chopin was frequently entertained by other people in the winter of 1897–98, while she was finishing *The Awakening*. On December 1, 1897, she was present for the debut reception of Louise Espenschied, in the Espenschieds' elaborately decorated home on Washington Avenue. Chopin's relatives also kept her socially active: On January 24, 1898, she attended "an elegant afternoon tea" given for several hundred society women by her cousin Blanche Bordley, at 4472 Forest Park Boulevard. Blanche's sister, Virginia Lynch Donovan, who assisted her "in a half mourning toilette," was the godmother to Kate Chopin's son George. Lélia Chopin attended the Bordley tea with her mother, the newspapers reported, and served chocolate with several other young ladies.

The Chopin sons were also busy in society. George, called the handsomest of the Chopin sons, had graduated from Washington University and was a student at the Missouri Medical College. With his brother Jean, he attended a ball hosted by Dr. and Mrs. Otto Forster and their daughter in honor of guests from Texas, New York, and Kansas City. Jean, a social favorite for his dancing ability, also attended a "Dutch supper" hosted by Mrs. John O'Fallon Delaney, at which the guests made Welsh rarebit and danced.

Sometimes social and artistic circles overlapped. For a reception on February 11, 1898, Mrs. Huntington Smith of 2621 Locust Street "endeavored to gather together women who would be congenial, both socially and professionally" to meet her Indiana childhood friend, Miss Susan Ball, the *Post-Dispatch* reported. "As a consequence, some of the brightest and most intellectual women in St. Louis society were present," including Kate Chopin. Miss Ball was "a litterateur of no small merit," descended from "a family of scholars" and herself the editor of the *Women's World*, and at the reception a singer from Chicago performed, along with a clarinet soloist. The guests "numbered only 80, as the affair was impromptu and very informal."

Four days later, Kate Chopin appeared at the Chart Club of St. Louis, as reported in the *Post-Dispatch:* "After a discussion by the leader of the club, Mrs. M. I. Johnston, and several other bright women on various topics of public interest, Mrs. Kate Chopin read, in her charming and characteristic manner, 'A Night in Acadie' and 'Polydore,' two short sketches from her own pen. In speaking of Mrs. Chopin to the members of this division of the Chart Club, Mrs. Johnston said:

" 'We are proud of the fact that a sister St. Louisan has made such valuable contributions to literature. The portrayal of character, habits and manner in the Gulf States, with their phases of French and Spanish creole, negro and Indian, is a marked feature of nineteenth century literature. Writers on these subjects have drawn on a deep mine of poetry and romance, and will give the next generation correct ideas of an institution and regime that has passed away. In the front ranks of the dialect writers stands Mrs. Kate Chopin.' "

In January 1898, Kate Chopin finished writing *The Awakening*—which she had begun in June 1897—and although she claimed that she never discussed her writing with anyone, both the *Mirror* and the *Post-Dispatch* published items that seemed to stem from discussions of her new novel.

On January 13, Billy Reedy devoted the *Mirror's* front page to a discussion of "Wives and Husbands": "Woman's latest discovery is that the husband is a drag," Reedy wrote. "The woman generally is becoming more individualized in matrimony. Woman has evolved from a doll into a human being"—something he heartily approved of. "A certain amount of independence for a woman is a very good thing. Old ladies will tell any one that it is good for the marital institution for women not to be too pliant and submissive to their husbands, just as they maintain that it is mistaken policy to try to prolong the honeymoon indefinitely, instead of getting away from each other occasionally."

Reedy did not approve of clinging women (like Chopin's Madame Ratignolle): "Women who submit to complete obliteration in matrimony will find, in time, that they will not need to obliterate themselves, for they will be ignored." Reedy also described Edna Pontellier's central conflict when he wrote, "Woman's truest duties are those of wife and mother, but those duties do not demand that she shall sacrifice her individuality."

The proper role of women—especially upper-class women—was one of the *Post-Dispatch*'s great concerns during the social season of 1897–98, and the newspaper launched a series of interviews on problems facing St. Louis society women.

One week the contributors, including Kate Chopin's euchre-playing friend Mrs. Julius Walsh, answered the question "What Is the Unforgivable Sin in Society?" One contributor, Mrs. Charless Cabanne, said that the unforgivable social sin was "[l]ack of wealth," although it need not be that way: "The 'tacky' people one meets at a large social function are often more entitled to social position, by reason of culture and refinement, than those who have greater wealth and present a finer appearance." Kate Chopin, known for her intellect but without enormous wealth, was most often invited to such large social functions—and she may have been one of the "tacky" people referred to.

Mrs. Leroy Valliant said that the unforgivable sin in society is "the bad behavior that springs from an impure character. That will cause a woman's downfall sooner than anything else." Mrs. G. F. Paddock felt that "[b]rains is of more importance in society than money," and "there are many people who are invited everywhere and who go everywhere, and who have nothing to recommend them except their charms of mind or person, or both." These people Mrs. Paddock called "the true ornaments of society." But Mrs. Walsh, of the four respondents the one best known to Kate Chopin, answered that in society the rule was "Wealth first, brains afterward."

Kate Chopin was just finishing *The Awakening* when the *Post-Dispatch* called on her to answer the question "Is Love Divine?"

Two other St. Louis society women answered with her, in a column published on January 16, 1898. Mrs. Shreve Carter said that "all true women must cherish the belief, deep down in their hearts, that there exists, or will exist, some time and somewhere, their kindred soul, their dual spirit." Mrs. Tudor Brooks, Chopin's Morgan Street neighbor and president of the Golden Chain Humane Society, felt that love must be divine. People are not machines, she said, and asked, "Is there nothing in us, nothing inborn, inexplicable, which finds satisfaction nowhere save in human sympathy and love? Certainly it would be difficult and distressing to believe that love, the motive power of the universe, existed as a material something to be idly picked up or wantonly destroyed by creatures incapable of knowing or appreciating so great a blessing."

The *Post-Dispatch*'s third respondent was Kate Chopin, who "has written stories of Southern life and as a novelist should know what love is." Kate answered, "It is as difficult to distinguish between the divine love and the natural, animal love, as it is to explain just why we love at all. In a discussion of this character between two women in my new novel I have made my heroine say: 'Why do I love this man? Is it because his hair is brown, growing high on his temples; because his eyes droop a bit at the corners, or because his nose is just so much out of drawing?' "

(In *The Awakening*, Chapter XXVI, the words are somewhat different. Mademoiselle Reisz, speaking of Robert, asks Edna, "Why do you love him when you ought not to?" and Edna replies: "Why? Because his hair is brown and grows away from his temples; because he opens and shuts his eyes, and his nose is a little out of drawing." Kate Chopin always claimed that she did very little revision—but her *Post-Dispatch* answer shows that she did make changes.)

Fifteen months before her novel appeared, Chopin had more to say: "One really never knows the exact, definite thing which excites love for any one person, and one can never truly know whether this love is the result of circumstances or whether it is predestination." Her answer hinted at Edna's animal attraction for Arobin (not unlike her own passion for Albert Sampite, fifteen years earlier). She also suggested that choice played a very small role in love. "I am inclined to think that love springs from animal instinct, and therefore is, in a measure, divine. One can never resolve to love this man, this woman or child, and then carry out the resolution unless one feels irresistibly drawn by an indefinable current of magnetism."

Typically, Chopin was diplomatic and unrevealing in her conclusion: "This subject allows an immense field for discussion and profound thought, and one could scarcely voice a definite opinion in a ten minutes talk. But I am sure we all feel that love—true, pure love, is an uncontrollable emotion that allows of no analyzation and no vivisection."

A week later, a *Post-Dispatch* editorial—possibly spawned by salon discussions—reflected on Kate Chopin's novel in still another way. According to the editorial, headlined THE KILLING PACE, "Within a month four young women of high social position have committed suicide under circumstances which seemed to indicate sympathetic motives." The writer, probably George Johns, described the cases: "The suicide of Miss Leila Herbert, the daughter of ex-Secretary

Herbert, was followed by that of an intimate friend, Miss Anna Virginia Wells. A few days after, Miss Mary Waite, daughter of the ex-Governor of Colorado, took poison. Then Lucile Blackburn Lane was shot under peculiar circumstances and Harriet Keith Owens, a friend of Miss Lane in Kentucky, immediately after reading of the shooting, put a bullet through her brain."

There were no economic explanations, the writer said: All the victims were "petted daughters of society," not pinched by poverty or overwork. And so he mused, "Aside from the possibility of morbid emotional excitement to which all human beings are liable, there was no strain upon them, except the strain of social activity and rivalry. Does the conjunction of suicidal attempts indicate a tendency in that direction among the women of society? Has high society struck the pace that kills?"

The subject continued to be controversial, for two weeks later, in a roundup society-page interview, the *Post-Dispatch* posed the same question, "Has High Society Struck the Pace That Kills?"—and Kate Chopin was one of the answerers.

The other respondents included Mrs. Maria I. Johnston, a lecturer for the Chart Club, "composed of ladies of fashion," for whom Chopin would read "A Night in Acadie" and "Polydore" two weeks later. Mrs. Johnston said that society's conditions did not drive women to suicide, for society women had fewer strains in their lives than poorer women. She attributed the suicides to "diseases or heredity," rather than environment, and added, "For ages women have taken their lives to escape dishonor. In the present state of society, when women are so carefully guarded, this cause is infrequent."

The *Post-Dispatch*'s second respondent, Mrs. John Green, "litterateur, expert whist player and prominent society woman," had been one of the earliest members of the Wednesday Club. Mrs. Green called society "a benefit to women who have no definite occupation. . . . It keeps their minds active and saves them from ennui. It has been the salvation of many a woman." She also claimed that the suicide rate among society women was decreasing, and that young women who did commit suicide tended to be "sensitive" and "morbid" (words later applied to Edna Pontellier by hostile critics).

The third respondent, Mrs. Martha Davis Griffith, was designated as "[l]ecturer, authoress and leader of the Literary Symposium, an organization of society women." Mrs. Griffith said that society created strains for nervous and excitable people, including women with "a hysterical tendency. . . . Strong willpower can overcome a woman's inclination to be flighty, whatever her station in life, but women who are so inclined would do well to keep out of society, as nearly as they can consistently with their station in life."

Of the four respondents, only Kate Chopin adopted a somewhat antagonistic attitude toward the question, and avoided blaming the victim. Mrs. Kate Chopin, identified as "[l]eader of a literary set in St. Louis society and author of many stories of Creole life," said about high society, "Leadership in society is a business. It is a good thing for women who have no other occupation to engage in it and endeavor to keep up with the social whirl. There is nothing about it that I can see that would tend to produce an unhealthy condition of mind.

"On the contrary, it prevents women from becoming morbid, as they might, had they nothing to occupy their attention when at leisure."

She also sensed, beneath the question, an unspoken double standard that irritated her. "Business men commit suicide every day, yet we do not say that suicide is epidemic in the business world. Why should we say the feeling is rife among society women, because half a dozen unfortunates, widely separated, take their own lives?

"The tendency to self-destruction is no more pronounced among society women than it ever was, according to my observation.

"The desire seems to come in waves, without warning, and soon passes away. The mere reading of a peculiar case of suicide may cause a highly nervous woman to take her own life in a similar manner, through morbid sympathy.

"But do not men do the same thing every day? Why all this talk about women?"

The *Post-Dispatch* interviews appeared on February 6, 1898—and a week later, everyone was indeed talking about men. On February 15, in far-off Cuba, the United States Navy's battleship the *Maine* was blown up, presumably by the Spanish overlords who controlled Cuba. The newspapers and the jingoists—then a proud term—cried out for war.

Many of Kate Chopin's acquaintances had links with Cuba. In St. Louis, the Gareschés and Bauduys had Cuban ancestors; in Louisiana, Maria Normand, Albert Sampite's intimate companion, had grown up in Cuba and was famous for her exotic Cuban ways. One of Kate Chopin's own ancestors, her great-grandmother's sister Pélagie, had married a Spaniard, traveled with him to Havana, and was never heard from again—probably one of the stories Madame Charleville had told young Katie O'Flaherty.

The newspapers were full of Cuba, the last Spanish possession in the New World. Cuban rebels had been fighting for freedom since 1868, and Cuba, a tropical isle only ninety miles from Florida, had a voluptuous aura for Americans (Florida itself was mostly swampland and Indian huts). When the Spanish brutally subdued the Cuban rebellion, American congressmen and newspapers screamed for United States intervention—and John A. Dillon and Joseph Pulitzer's *New York World*, along with William Randolph Hearst's *New York Journal*, led the pack. Both papers printed atrocity stories from Cuba; both concocted lurid scenarios when they lacked facts. But Dillon's *World* was not so sensational as the Hearst paper, which after the February explosion in Havana ranted continually, "Remember the *Maine* and to hell with Spain!"

Events moved quickly. On April 20, Congress declared war; on April 22, President McKinley ordered a blockade of Cuba; on April 23, he called for 125,000 volunteers. Flags sprouted on porches and streets all over the United States; new factories and military recruiting booths sprang up everywhere. Young men who volunteered collected free drinks—and enthusiastic kisses from young women.

Billy Reedy at first joked that war over Cuba was just a plot to cut off his cigar supply. Kate Chopin, who smoked Cuban cigarettes, may have felt the same way—but she also had soldier-age sons. In St. Louis, Reedy was virtually the only public foe of the "zanies" who "howled for war"—but the war crisis also gained him ten thousand new subscribers, pushing his circulation ahead of *The Atlantic*, *The Nation*, and most other established journals of opinion. Reedy, who called the warmongering newspapers "treasonable, contemptible and ridiculous," wrote that the Spanish-American War made the United States into an imperialist power, and "[i]mperialism is a word of ugly memories and the thing itself is about equally compact of glory and of foulness."

Nevertheless, a mob of would-be soldiers surged into Jefferson Barracks in St. Louis, clamoring to enlist. For young men like Kate Chopin's sons, the Civil War was now the glorious cause, its horrors forgotten. Felix, her youngest boy, ached to join the new military venture: At Central High School (class of 1898), he was a star athlete, winning gold medals in hurdles and pole vaulting at the school field day, managing and quarterbacking the football team. But Felix was very thin and frail-looking and weighed only 140 pounds—and when the army rejected him, he was devastated.

But Fred Chopin, who had turned twenty-two in January of 1898, joined Light Battery A, and prepared for glory—while his mother remembered her half-brother George's death in the army, in his twenty-third year.

Fred and the other eager recruits camped out on the parade ground at Jefferson Barracks—the site of Camp Jackson, the opening battle of the Civil War. The soldiers of Battery A, an aristocratic artillery unit formed by an ex-Confederate major to quell the railroad riots of 1877, trained for just three weeks. In the morning, they drilled, and in the afternoon entertained guests, mostly young women bringing cakes and other treats. "The popular boys now in society," the *Republic* reported, "are Chopin, Carr, Boogher, Humphrey, Niemeyer, et. al, and their circle of worshiping maidens is increasing every day."

With three other soldiers, "Freddy" Chopin posted messages for visitors, such as "We are always glad to see you—with a cake box," and "If you are our sweethearts, you know what to do, but be careful. Corporal Saunders, in charge of this section, is a bachelor." But another message would not have amused his mother: "We are fond of war pictures. Those that represent us as facing bursting shells and walking over the mangled remains of our comrades and dead horses, and that have vultures in the air, are especially fascinating to a young soldier in camp."

On May 16, Fred Chopin and the men of Battery A left for Chickamauga National Park in Georgia for further training. An enormous crowd saw them off, and the *Republic* described their mothers weeping at Union Station. At Chickamauga, Fred was known as "the sweet singer of the battery and the best darkey story teller," but "[t]here is no truth to the rumor, said to be circulating at home, that Fred Chopin has applied for permission to put a piano in his tent. He has a harmonica and a jews-harp." By July 7, however, "[a] piano came on the *Post-Dispatch* car for Fred Chopin, and he has set it up in the canteen, as his section objected. This gives the canteen the general tone of a free-and-easy, but the boys are very orderly." A week later, during a visit to a Chattanooga hotel, Fred and "some of the boys" found a piano in the parlor— whereupon Fred began playing some of "his great grandfather's pieces," and after the other boys began singing, a crowd of three hundred gathered to applaud and sing.

Meanwhile, at home, Kate Chopin and the other mothers of soldiers were organizing a benefit for Battery A, a combined lawn party of the United Daughters of the Confederacy and the Daughters of the American Revolution on June 21. It was "the event of the summer," with the Fair Grounds lighted by Japanese lanterns, young ladies dressed to represent each military company, and military bands, choruses of "song birds," and "darky jubilee singers."

The "patronesses" of the event included all of Kate Chopin's society acquaintances: Mrs. Julius Walsh, Mrs. Otto Forster, Mrs. Dexter Tiffany, Mrs. Alexander DeMenil. It was a brilliant occasion—but for women who remembered the earlier war and the bright young men who had marched off and never returned, it was not all a scene of joy.

Then, almost immediately, the war their sons had enlisted for was over. The first American invaders arrived in Cuba on June 20; on July 1–2 they charged up San Juan Hill—and on July 17 the Spanish general José Toral surrendered, ending the Cuban war. But Congress, the president, and William Randolph Hearst were not satisfied. They demanded a wider war.

And so, on July 27, Battery A sailed for Puerto Rico. On September 8, they were just about to open fire for the first time when the president's proclamation reached them: The war was over. (The artillerymen were bitterly disappointed.) They were back in St. Louis by September 17, cheered by an immense crowd in Union Station, and honored at a magnificent banquet that they could scarcely eat—"but they wept at the sight of real food," according to one historian. They were mustered out by November 30—except for the four men who had died in the war, mostly of diseases.

That summer, Kate Chopin wrote very little. From the time she began writing seriously in the early 1890s, Chopin had written about a dozen stories a year—but after finishing *The Awakening*, she was mostly silent. (She also never indicated when—or why—the title of her novel was changed from "A Solitary Soul" to *The Awakening*.)

In January and February, she had produced the two responses in the *Post-Dispatch*, on "Is Love Divine?" and "Has High Society Struck the Pace that Kills?" After the sinking of the *Maine*, she wrote one Cane River country children's tale, "A Horse Story," in which the young Acadian Herminia rides a "dejected looking sorrel pony," Ti Démon. Also in March, while Americans waited for their country to declare war on Spain, Chopin wrote "Elizabeth Stock's One Story," one of her most bitter and hopeless stories, beginning with the death in St. Louis of the main character—a poor and lonely postmistress from a small Missouri town.

"Elizabeth Stock's One Story" was a somber version of Bret Harte's popular "Postmistress of Laurel Run," a comical romance about a pretty widow who diligently delivers the mail. The public still acclaimed Bret Harte—but Kate Chopin seemed to be losing her willingness, or her ability, to write for the popular taste.

She could not find a magazine that would publish "A Horse Story" or "Elizabeth Stock's One Story"—probably because both stories end in death rather than the upbeat optimism American magazines preferred. The *Century, Youth's Companion, The Atlantic, Cosmopolitan, Saturday Evening Post, Harper's,* and *Scribner's* all said no. After the last rejections in February 1899, Chopin stopped sending out the stories—perhaps believing that after *The Awakening* appeared in April, magazines would be more interested in her new, somber work. She also kept "Elizabeth Stock's One Story" with the stories she planned to publish in her third collection, *A Vocation and a Voice*.

She did other, scattered bits of writing in 1898. In April, while Congress was declaring war, Chopin translated Guy de Maupassant's "Father Amable," but was evidently distracted, and never completed a clear copy to send to a publisher. In the latter half of the year, she wrote a few verses about gift-giving and going a-Maying, and produced one very lush poem about night and wine, called "Lines Suggested by Omar." The last stanza did resemble the *Rubaiyat*:

> Ah! drink, my soul, the splendor of the day;
> Quaff from the golden goblet oft and deep.

Darkness will come again; too long 'twill stay—
The everlasting night of dreamless sleep.

In late August, Chopin traveled to White Oaks, Wisconsin, and wrote about the countryside: "Of all the places on earth I know/I'd rather stay where the white oaks grow. . . ." Later, autographing a copy of *Bayou Folk* for a Louisiana friend, she obligingly wrote the same poem, but changed "white oaks" to "live-oaks," to suit the Louisiana landscape. She sent some of her poems to magazines, but no one wanted them.

For Kate Chopin, much of 1898 was a year of waiting—and a year of worrying about war. But in July of 1898, two days after the fight in Cuba had ended, when she thought her warrior son would be coming home, Kate Chopin wrote her greatest story of sexual pleasure, a startling fantasy of sensuality called "The Storm."

Chapter 21

"THE STORM" AND THE AWAKENING

KATE CHOPIN HAD VISITED Natchitoches Parish in June of 1897, the same month that she began writing *The Awakening*. According to the *Natchitoches Enterprise* on June 24, she planned a long stay: "Mrs. Kate Chopin, whose dialect stories of Creole life have won her an enviable record in the literary world and whose charming personality makes her a longed for and appreciated visitor wherever she goes has arrived with her daughter, Miss Lelia, from their home in St. Louis and will spend the summer with Mr. and Mrs. Joseph Henry at Derry."

The Henrys, Oscar's sister Eugénie and her husband, had a large and gracious home (where "old Joe Henry," seventy years old, would die a year and a half later). From there, Kate and Lélia could visit Marie and Phanor Breazeale and Lamy and Fannie Hertzog Chopin, as well as the restoration of Magnolia plantation, the inspiration for "Ma'ame Pélagie."

In Cloutierville, Father Beaulieu was still the presiding priest, although he performed his last wedding ceremony that August, with a painful "carbuncle" on his shoulder or back. Evidently it was cancer, for he died not long afterward.

There were still relatives in Cloutierville, including many Benoists and Charlevilles; there were still the same neighbors, including Scruggses and Perriers. Kate visited the Flanners, cousins by marriage, and much later Florian Flanner remembered receiving an autographed copy of A *Night in Acadie* from Kate with "a lovely little note."

There was always new gossip to exchange—and in Cloutierville, there were still the Sampites. Albert Sampite was by now a grandfather, and always a restless traveler, seeking better cotton prices and amusement in New Orleans and Natchitoches and Alexandria. Albert and Loca Sampite had lived apart since their legal separation in 1891, and she was still said to carry a black bullwhip when she went to see him.

The Cane River world had not changed during Kate Chopin's thirteen years in St. Louis. The round of the seasons was still slow and warm, and in the summer there were gentle rain showers nearly every day, while the cotton plants grew tall and green. June and July were lingering, lazy times, while the Sampite cotton ripened in the simmering sun, and the scents from the piney woods, the sassafras, the camomile, and the roses filled the air. In Cloutierville, Maria Normand's garden included cape jessamine, the night-blooming gardenia with its uniquely voluptuous scent. The nights, filled with the dronings and hummings of insects and the croaks of frogs, were much darker than they ever were in cities—and the night was still a time of silence and mystery and sin.

Kate Chopin had planned to spend the summer in Louisiana, but left after less than two weeks. A week after its first report, the *Natchitoches Enterprise* noted that "Mrs. Kate Chopin spent Tuesday in Natchitoches returning to Derry Wednesday morning from whence she will leave for her home in St. Louis in a day or two."

She could scarcely have missed seeing the Sampites when she visited Cloutierville—and possibly it was Albert, or Albert's well-known romance with Maria Normand, that sent her home so quickly.

A little more than a year later, after she had finished *The Awakening*, Kate Chopin wrote "The Storm," a story about the consummation of some lingering desires.

In 1892, when she wrote "At the 'Cadian Ball," Kate Chopin had been a literary beginner, reluctant to write the kind of story that could never be published. But by the summer of 1898, she had no such inhibitions.

She wrote "The Storm" in one sitting on July 19, 1898, just after peace was declared in Cuba. Possibly her son's going off to war had reminded her of another young warrior, Albert Sampite, who had trudged home barefoot and bleeding from the siege of Vicksburg. But Albert Sampite was no longer that young warrior—nor was Kate Chopin the dashing young woman who had scandalized Cloutierville. By 1898, they were both middle-aged: Kate was forty-eight, and Albert was fifty-four.

In "At the 'Cadian Ball," Chopin had created a romantic triangle, with the French planter Alcée Laballière, his dainty cousin Clarisse, and the "Spanish vixen" Calixta—who had the blue eyes, curly blond hair, and Cuban ways of Maria Normand. (Loca Sampite, an intelligent woman who suffered because she lacked Maria's glamour, had nothing in common with the character Clarissc.) At the ball itself, Alcée had flirted with Calixta and reminisced about their time together in Assumption Parish—a time everyone gossiped about. But when Clarisse came to fetch Alcée, he followed her. Calixta made do with Bobinôt, an awkward fellow who adored her, and the ball was over.

But the relationships Kate Chopin had drawn in "At the 'Cadian Ball" were not over in her mind, or in fact. The beautiful Maria, who cheered each Cuban victory, was still legally married to the hapless, heavy-drinking Sylvère DeLouche, Loca Sampite's brother. Children called her, properly, "Madame Sylvère," but Cane River country adults called her by her maiden name: Maria Normand.

By the summer of 1898, Maria was forty-five, still known for her beauty and her wistful expression. She lived with her twelve-year-old daughter and thirteen-year-old son across the horse lot from Albert Sampite, still a handsome man with an irresistible French charm, when he wanted to use it. People said that Albert was paying her bills.

For "The Storm," Kate Chopin imagined her " 'Cadian Ball" characters five years later, and married: Alcée to the graceful Clarisse, and Calixta to the clumsy Bobinôt. The story begins with Bobinôt, an indulgent father something like Oscar Chopin, and his four-year-old son Bibi, stranded by a storm at the village store. While they wait out the weather, Bobinôt and Bibi buy Calixta a favorite treat, a can of shrimps.

Calixta, at home, is "sewing furiously on a sewing machine"—a much-prized invention when Kate Chopin lived in Cloutierville. Mrs. Scruggs, Loca Sampite's mother, had been the first in the area to own a sewing machine. But in the Cane River country in the 1890s, the woman most famous for her sewing—the fine stitching she had learned in convent school in Matanzas—was Maria Normand. When Albert Sampite gave her some of his most valuable land, she said it was in exchange for the sewing she did for him. Sewing had always been important to her: When the Normands left Cuba after the Civil War, Maria was almost sixteen, and her admirer, Gaspar Hernandez, gave her an elegant mirrored sewing box with a blue satin lining. She cherished it all her life, using it to store her money and her most valuable papers.

Sewing furiously in the heavy heat of the approaching storm and darkness, Calixta in "The Storm" suddenly realizes she must close the windows and doors—whereupon Alcée Laballière rides in at the gate. He wants to wait on the gallery until the storm is over, but Calixta invites him inside, their voices startling her "as if from a trance."

Kate Chopin did not describe Alcée: She remembered him well enough. But Calixta she identified unmistakably with Maria Normand: "A little fuller of figure than five years before when she married; but she had lost nothing of her vivacity. Her blue eyes still retained their melting quality; and her yellow hair, dishevelled by the wind and rain, kinked more stubbornly than ever about her ears and temples."

The rain beats down, while Calixta and Alcée sit in the one room that serves as "the dining room—the sitting room—the general utility room." The door is open, and the adjoining room "with its white, monumental bed, its closed shutters, looked dim and mysterious."

A crack of thunder, and a bolt of lightning much too close, terrify Calixta— and Alcée's arms are around her, arousing "all the old-time infatuation and desire for her flesh." He pushes back her warm, steaming hair; her lips are "as red and moist as pomegranate seed"; her white neck "and a glimpse of her full, firm bosom disturbed him powerfully." In her eyes, he sees "a drowsy gleam that unconsciously betrayed a sensuous desire."

> "Do you remember—in Assumption, Calixta?" he asked in a low voice broken by passion. Oh! she remembered; for in Assumption he had kissed her and kissed and kissed her; until his senses would well nigh fail, and to save her he would resort to a desperate flight. If she was not an immaculate dove in those days, she was still inviolate; a passionate creature whose very defenselessness had made her defense, against which his honor forbade him to prevail. Now— well, now—her lips seemed in a manner free to be tasted, as well as her round, white throat and her whiter breasts.

Kate made the passion a matter of mutual power and desire: "They did not hear the crashing torrents, and the roar of the elements made her laugh as she lay in his arms. She was a revelation in that dim, mysterious chamber; as white as the couch she lay upon. Her firm, elastic flesh that was knowing for the first time its birthright, was like a creamy lily that the sun invites to contribute its breath and perfume to the undying life of the world."

Kate's two lovers come together without deception or guilt:

> The generous abundance of her passion, without guile or trickery, was like a white flame which penetrated and found response in depths of his own sensuous nature that had never yet been reached.

> When he touched her breasts, they gave themselves up in quivering ecstasy, inviting his lips. Her mouth was a fountain of delight.

(Chopin was violating more than one taboo: Although James Lane Allen in *Summer in Arcady* and Thomas Hardy in *Jude the Obscure* had described their heroines' breasts, women writers did not do that in 1898. As late as 1920, Willa

Cather's references to a woman's thigh and breast were omitted from a story published in the *Smart Set* magazine.)

And then Kate Chopin moved beyond Allen's delicate description of desire as the "borderland of mystery and reality." Alcée touches Calixta's breasts, and her mouth, "[a]nd when he possessed her, they seemed to swoon together at the very borderland of life's mystery." Afterward, "[h]e stayed cushioned upon her, breathless, dazed, enervated, with his heart beating like a hammer upon her. With one hand she clasped his head, her lips lightly touching his forehead. The other hand stroked with a soothing rhythm his muscular shoulders."

Outside, the storm dies down. The thunder grows distant, the rain beats down slowly, inviting them to sleep—but they dare not. Then the sun comes out, "turning the glistening green world into a palace of gems." Calixta watches Alcée ride away. He smiles, and she laughs aloud.

Meanwhile her husband and son are trudging home after the rain, Bobinôt fussing over the mud on Bibi's clothing and fearing Calixta's wrath. But instead she greets them both with chattery enthusiasm and effusive kisses—especially when Bobinôt gives her the can of shrimps. At dinner, they laugh so loud "that anyone might have heard them as far away as Laballière's."

Alcée, meanwhile, writes a loving letter to his wife Clarisse, at Biloxi with the babies, and encourages them to stay a month longer if they like. Clarisse, in turn, is charmed by the letter and the freedom of Biloxi, "the first free breath since her marriage," for "[d]evoted as she was to her husband, their intimate conjugal life was something which she was more than willing to forego for a while."

And so, Kate Chopin concluded, "[T]he storm passed and every one was happy."

Kate had changed in the six years between writing "At the 'Cadian Ball" and "The Storm"—and so had the character of Alcée. In the first story, Alcée is hot-tempered, morose, a heavy drinker, much like the Albert Sampite Kate Chopin had known. But in "The Storm," Alcée is a charming, well-behaved gentleman who helps Calixta take the laundry off the clothesline before they take passionate advantage of the moment. He has matured—and Calixta has come to know her own desires.

When Chopin wrote *The Awakening*, and then "The Storm," she was considerably older than Edna or Calixta. She was living among freethinking intellectuals who made fun of bourgeois proprieties—and she had grown much bolder. The action in "At the 'Cadian Ball" takes place mostly at night, at back doors, with sly and hidden hints; "The Storm" proceeds boldly during the day, in the married woman's own home. By the summer of 1898, when she wrote "The Storm," Kate Chopin had been living in St. Louis for fourteen years, the years of her real growth. She had come to feel that there was no shame in sexual desire—only in hypocrisy.

In Cloutierville, anyone who read Kate Chopin's "The Storm" would have recognized Maria Normand in the character of Calixta, and Albert Sampite in the character of Alcée. But Kate Chopin had no intention of letting anyone in Cloutierville ever read "The Storm": She never made any attempt to publish the story.

In November 1898, Kate Chopin suddenly gained a new publisher, as the Chicago firms reshuffled themselves. She had been under contract to Way & Williams, who dissolved their three-year-old business in 1898; a year earlier, their rivals Stone & Kimball had dismantled their own company. When Herbert S. Stone & Company took over the books and assets of both publishers, Stone acquired *The Awakening* (which he officially accepted in January 1899) and Chopin's forthcoming story collection, *A Vocation and a Voice*.

When Kate traveled to Louisiana that December, she told her friends and relatives that a new novel was in the works.

According to the *Natchitoches Enterprise* of December 15, 1898, "Mrs. Kate Chopin (the noted writer) of St. Louis is the guest of her sister-in-law, Mrs. Phanor Breazeale. All of her old friends and admirers are glad to welcome her and many new ones were delighted to form the acquaintance of this gifted woman whose personality is as charming and unique as her genius."

The *New Orleans Times-Democrat* for December 18 also noted Kate Chopin's visit: "Last Friday's train brought to Natchitoches one who, although she is not a native, has spent some years of her life in the parish, and has many relatives and friends who welcome her with open arms. This refers to that beautiful and talented woman, Mrs. Kate Chopin of St. Louis, who has made a brilliant success in the literary world. Her last novel has not yet been published, but judging from her former works there is indeed a treat in store for all lovers of fiction."

She was celebrated: "While here Mrs. Chopin is the guest of Mr. and Mrs. Phanor Breazeale, and has been the recipient of many social honors. Mrs. Camilla Breazeale entertained at a musicale on last Sunday afternoon in honor of Mrs. Chopin, Mrs. T. P. Chaplin entertained at a whist party Tuesday night, and Mrs. M. L. Walmsley at a musicale Wednesday night."

Mrs. Camilla Lachs Breazeale was also responsible for Kate Chopin's newspaper coverage: As editor of the *Natchitoches Enterprise*, she was one of the most powerful women in town. She was the widow of Hopkins Payne Breazeale, the older brother of Phanor Breazeale, and she was a large, attractive woman, strong-minded and unconventional, known for her cleverness and her old-fashioned clothes.

Like Kate Chopin, Camilla Lachs Breazeale had been a Sacred Heart schoolgirl, but she was Jewish, and raised her daughters as Jews, with romantic names: Carmen and Cecil and Wynonah. (In her own story of a female eccentric, "The Falling in Love of Fedora," Chopin had given the protagonist's sister the name Camilla.) When her husband died suddenly, leaving her with four children under the age of seven, Camilla Breazeale appointed herself editor-proprietor of his newspaper, the *Natchitoches Enterprise*, and ran it for half a century. She was also district chair for the Woman Suffrage party of Louisiana, which by 1898 had got Louisiana women a limited voting right.

Camilla's daughter Carmen, nine years old in 1898, was one of the active, inquisitive children who flocked around Kate Chopin—and on one special occasion, she and her sisters were deputed to serve at a tea that Marie (Mrs. Phanor) Breazeale gave for her famous sister-in-law from St. Louis.

Carmen Breazeale's grandmother, who lived in the same household, checked the three young girls' bows and sashes before they went down the back stairs, and then (according to Carmen's recollections nearly eighty years later): "Grandmother ushered us into the room where Kate Chopin was sitting on the old antique love seat, and when my grandmother looked up, there was Kate Chopin with her hair cut short, her legs crossed, and smoking a cigarette! My grandmother just ushered us very quickly right out of the room, wouldn't even let us stop to see what it was all about.

"My mother followed us, but my grandmother said to her, 'I am not going to let the children be contaminated!'

"Mother told her, 'Miss Emily, I am sorry to have to go against your wishes this time. The girls will serve.' "

Carmen and the other girls were filled with "awe and wonderment" at the sight of Kate Chopin—whose skirt was either short or riding up, for her legs were showing and her foot was swinging jauntily in the air. Her hair was dark and bobbed, ear-length, Carmen remembered decades later, although her cousin July Breazeale remembered "Aunt Katie" with pretty white hair and bright red cheeks. Possibly Kate Chopin wore a wig for the occasion—but whatever she wore, it did not please the Breazeales' grandmother: "If *that* is an example of your literary friends, I won't meet them," she declared—and she never did.

Carmen Breazeale learned early that Kate Chopin was considered "a little too wild for a properly brought up young girl to model herself after"—although her even-younger cousin July Breazeale was allowed to think of her aunt Kate as a "beautiful, charming, exciting" visitor.

"July" (Julie) Breazeale was the third of Marie Chopin and Phanor Breazeale's four daughters (the others were Marie, Gladys, and Katherine), and they lived in a big Natchitoches house in which there were always parties. Marie Chopin Breazeale was known as a "gracious, dignified hostess," and during

Kate's December 1898 visit Marie entertained the Round Table Club for "a most interesting game of progressive euchre," according to the newspaper. The first prize was a handsome cake plate; the consolation prize was "a lovely little 'nigger' doll baby"; and the "dainty refreshments" consisted of chicken salad, sandwiches, chocolate, and whipped cream.

Marie Breazeale and her sister-in-law Kate delighted in each other's company and gossiped in French, Marie's first language. Marie's husband, Phanor, had become a well-known local politician, elected district attorney and a leader in the Louisiana Constitutional Convention. The penniless young man Marie Chopin's family had so disapproved of had become a substantial citizen.

Little July Breazeale did see her father smoke cigarettes with Aunt Katie— but July was too young to be shocked. Kate and Phanor would swap stories and play whist on Sundays—although on one occasion when a minister came to call, Kate hid her cards on her lap until he departed. Like Kate's St. Louis friends, Phanor Breazeale was a great reader and an agnostic, and he disparaged marriage as a social institution and thought no one should get married. He also liked to spin yarns about his own adventures during Reconstruction, but his tales were more than just entertainment to Kate Chopin.

According to Daniel Rankin, the plot of *The Awakening*—the tale of a French Quarter woman with desires that marriage cannot fulfill—is based on a true story that Kate Chopin heard from Phanor Breazeale (probably in French, since the Breazeale children spoke only English). Breazeale reportedly claimed that the woman was well known among New Orleans Creoles, and so was the ending of her story. But half a century after her father's death, his daughter July Breazeale Waters suggested that if he did give Kate Chopin the idea for *The Awakening*, it might not have been true in the first place: He was also a storyteller.

Kate Chopin may also have understood the story very differently from the way Phanor Breazeale told it. Two months after her December 1898 Natchitoches visit, and just after she read the proofs for *The Awakening*, Chopin wrote a poem—that can be read as a defense of Edna Pontellier against a man who has made light of her story.

The Haunted Chamber

Of course 'twas an excellent story to tell
Of a fair, frail, passionate woman who fell.
It may have been false, it may have been true.
That was nothing to me—it was less to you.
But with bottle between us, and clouds of smoke
From your last cigar, 'twas more of a joke

Than a matter of sin or a matter of shame
That a woman had fallen, and nothing to blame,
So far as you or I could discover,
But her beauty, her blood and an ardent lover.
But when you were gone and the lights were low
And the breeze came in with the moon's pale glow,
The far, faint voice of a woman, I heard,
'Twas but a wail, and it spoke no word.
It rose from the depths of some infinite gloom
And its tremulous anguish filled the room.
Yet the woman was dead and could not deny,
But women forever will whine and cry.
So now I must listen the whole night through
To the torment with which I had nothing to do—
But women forever will whine and cry
And men forever must listen—and sigh—

Kate Chopin's 1898 visit was not solely social. On Saturday, December 17, she sold her Cloutierville home—the big white house where Lélia had been born, and where Kate had lived with Oscar and all the children. She had been renting out the house since 1884, and may have needed money for Lélia's debut: The buyer, a sixty-four-year-old German-born merchant named Pierre Rosenthal, paid twenty-five hundred dollars for the home. But the sale was also a break with the past: Kate could no longer return to Cloutierville to live.

She may have planned a longer visit. The Cane River country in December had its beauty, with the quiet river, brown fields, blue smoke rising from chimneys, and blue mists hanging in the trees just before dark. Sometimes, as in her story "The Return of Alcibiade," there might be a "thin wafer of ice" covering pools of water in the road. Or, as in "After the Winter," on the rawest of December days there might be a "fine, cold, mist falling."

But within a week she had departed again. On December 22, the *Enterprise* reported that "Mrs. Kate Chopin left for New Orleans on Friday night where after a short visit she will return to her home in St. Louis. While in Natchitoches she was the recipient of much social attention."

Kate was also highly esteemed in New Orleans, where she had received one of the sincerest forms of flattery: One of her short stories had been plagiarized. Her "Boulôt and Boulotte" appeared almost word for word in *The Creole Monthly* (I:4, June 1896) under the name "Moune and Mounette," by "Lola Alvez," with no credit to Kate Chopin.

By the late 1890s, New Orleans also had its literary salon, presided over by Mollie E. Moore Davis—whose "A Bamboula" (1896) resembles Kate Chopin's "La Belle Zoraïde." Davis also published in *Youth's Companion* and *The*

Atlantic, and she was a popular novelist whose works outsold Kate Chopin's. At her home at 406 Royal Street in the French Quarter, Davis held "Fridays" at which her callers included "Belles, beaux, papas, mamas, poets, painters, musicians, journalists, statesmen, scientists, churchmen, men and women of letters, foreign and home-bred officers, military and naval."

Her literary guests included such New Orleanians as "Pearl Rivers" (Eliza Nicholson, editor of the *Daily Picayune*) and "Catharine Cole" of the *Times-Democrat,* along with many out-of-town visitors—among them Richard Watson Gilder, George W. Cable, Ruth McEnery Stuart ("brightest of story-tellers"), and Kate Chopin. As at Chopin's salon, guests often gave readings from their works, and Davis—like Kate Chopin's friends—enjoyed ghost stories.

Then, according to the *New Orleans Times-Democrat:* "Mrs. Kate Chopin, after a short stay of one week, has returned to her home in St. Louis, where she will remain during the Christmas holidays, then will spend the rest of the winter in New York." But if Kate went to New York as planned, she spent little time there. On January 10, 1899, she was at home, sending her manuscript on "Typical German Composers" to *The Atlantic* (it was rejected). She wrote and rewrote a group of poems, and in late January and early February produced the chilling short story "The Godmother" and her last local-color story before *The Awakening,* "A Little Country Girl."

Still, Kate Chopin's travels in 1897 and 1898 suggest that she was seeking something—or someone.

During June 1897, when she began *The Awakening,* her friend John A. Dillon—still, as always, married to Blanche Valle—had made a visit to St. Louis from New York. Then, in December 1898, four months before *The Awakening* would appear, Kate planned her trip to New York, where Dillon had lived since 1891.

She had sought Dillon's approval in the past. He had liked *Bayou Folk,* but not *At Fault* (and there is no record of his reaction to *A Night in Acadie*). But if Kate had told him that she had written about a woman who finds marriage too confining, most likely the genteel Dillon would not have approved.

Kate Chopin carefully recorded her short stories in her account notebook, but was careless about her poems: They appear in variant forms, without clear dates. She may have thought less of them—or may have wanted to keep anyone from linking them with specific events or people. In at least one case, she tried to mislead would-be gossipers: On the back of the poem "An Hour," which asks for more time to live and love, Kate wrote, "This is not dedicated to you or to anybody."

Before February 1899, she had a burst of inspiration, and wrote a dozen poems about nature, love, secrets, and sensuality. The *Century* accepted "I

Opened All the Portals Wide," the third (and last) Kate Chopin poem ever to be published, but the others remained in manuscript, refused by all the magazines she tried.

While she waited for *The Awakening* to appear, Kate Chopin wrote two stories about folly.

February 1899 was one of the coldest months in St. Louis history. A few days before Kate's forty-ninth birthday, February 8, a blizzard was predicted; on February 9, the thermometer registered 16 degrees below zero, the coldest February temperature ever recorded. Possibly thinking a sad tale was best for winter, Kate wrote "The Godmother" between January and February 6, 1899, and then "A Little Country Girl" five days later, when the weather had warmed slightly.

"The Godmother" is Tante Elodie, who dotes on her godson Gabriel, who is in turn smitten with a young woman at "the Normal" (the teachers' college in Natchitoches). Gabriel drinks too much and behaves rudely—and one night, while Tante Elodie is saying her nightly prayers, Gabriel comes to announce that he has killed a man down at an old cabin. Tante Elodie cleans Gabriel's clothes; she provides an alibi and coaches him; she even treks to the cabin herself and takes the murder weapon, a knife, from the body of the dead man. No one ever suspects Gabriel—but he has lost all interest in everything he pursued before the murder: reading law, the young woman at "the Normal." He goes away and is killed in a fall from his horse, leaving Tante Elodie alone in her corner.

For the character of Gabriel, Kate drew on many young men she had known: her brother Tom, reckless with horses; her son Fred, discontented with a life of inaction after the war; her other sons, paying attention to one young woman and then another. Tante Elodie had much in common with Kate Chopin: Both "attracted youth in some incomprehensible way," but needed to be alone, to think; both loved cards, especially solitaire; and both believed that all morals and ethics are relative.

"A Little Country Girl," a much lighter story, was also about morals and ethics—about a girl who makes "diabolical wishes" for the circus, then blames herself for unleashing a horrific thunderstorm. In the end, a jolly priest tells her that she is no "Magician" or "Sorceress": She is a lonely, imaginative child.

Youth's Companion accepted "A Little Country Girl," but never published it. "The Godmother" was published in Reedy's *Mirror* on December 12, 1901, just after the sudden death of Billy Reedy's young wife, Lalitte Bauduy, from an obscure bacterial infection. Reedy's farewell poem to his wife appeared in the same issue with Kate Chopin's story of blood, desertion, and death.

Meanwhile, in the months before *The Awakening* appeared, Kate Chopin was being pursued by literary admirers, among them the poets R. E. Lee Gibson and Madison Cawein. Gibson, head clerk at the St. Louis Insane Asylum, had published several pamphlets of his poetry; Cawein, a Kentucky poet, was better known, with poems in *Youth's Companion, The Atlantic, Harper's, Lippincott's,* and many other magazines. Both were ambitious for literary recognition, both admired Kate Chopin's work—and both wanted her to admire theirs.

On February 26, Gibson—also a friend of Dr. Kolbenheyer's—wrote to thank Kate for her kind words about Cawein's *Idyllic Monologues,* and said he would be sending her his "three unpretentious little booklets" of poetry. Gibson called *A Night in Acadie* and *Bayou Folk* "almost my favorite volumes of the few, very select and fondly-cherished books that I possess." He lavished praise on Chopin's writing: "[W]hat a sweet, tender story 'Loka' is, in your Bayou Folk,— and how mightily it has pleased me. It seems to me as beautiful and strong and touching as any of Kipling's . . . Very fine, too, are 'Athénaise,' 'Regret,' 'A Night in Acadie,' and one other exquisite bit of etching—a masterpiece in miniature, 'Caline,'—which impressed me powerfully."

Eventually Gibson and Cawein would visit Kate Chopin, after her fortunes had changed—but in the spring of 1899, the early notices about *The Awakening* gave her reason to feel powerful.

The Awakening's first review, by Lucy Monroe in the March 1899 *Book News,* was extremely favorable. Monroe called Chopin's work a "remarkable novel," one

> so keen in its analysis of character, so subtle in its presentation of emotional effects that it seems to reveal life as well as to represent it. In reading it you have the impression of being in the very heart of things, you feel the throb of the machinery, you see and understand the slight transitions of thought, the momentary impulses, the quick sensations of the hardness of life, which govern so much of our action. It is an intimate thing, which in studying the nature of one woman reveals something which brings her in touch with all women—something larger than herself. This it is which justifies the audacity of "The Awakening" and makes it big enough to be true.

In Monroe's view, Kate Chopin was "an artist in the manipulation of a complex character, and faulty as the woman is, she has the magnetism which is essential to the charm of a novel." *The Awakening,* Monroe wrote, "pictures, too, with extraordinary vividness, the kind of silent sympathy which is some-times the expression of the love that goes deep. The men in the book are capital, with the exception, perhaps of Robert, who is a bit wooden; and Edna's husband especially is drawn to the life. In construction, in the management of movements and climaxes, the thing shows a very subtle and a brilliant kind of art." The book, she noted, was published by Herbert S. Stone & Company.

Lucy Monroe's praise was hardly disinterested. She was Stone's "chief reader and literary editor" and very likely responsible for Stone's buying *The Awakening*. Also an art critic, Lucy Monroe was a regular member of the Little Room artists and writers group in Chicago, although she had been traveling in Europe with her sister Harriet when Kate Chopin visited their city.

In her teens, Lucy Monroe had stayed at fashionable resorts like Grand Isle; in London, she and her sister had met Sarah Grand, author of *The Heavenly Twins* and a strong proponent of women's rights in marriage. Lucy Monroe's sister Harriet, like Kate Chopin's Mademoiselle Reisz, used to say that she wanted only a perfect lover, a *"grand esprit,"* and so never married; Harriet and Lucy often discussed disillusionment as a fact of life and a theme in art.

Harriet later founded *Poetry* magazine, after Lucy married an attorney and moved with him to Peking—but at the time Stone bought *The Awakening*, Lucy was an independent New Woman in Chicago whose ideas were very much like Kate Chopin's. Her *Book News* review appeared a month before publication, and would have been very influential with the book trade.

The next announcement was in *The Book Buyer* for April 1899, with a por-trait of Kate Chopin in ruffled hat and boa. Her *Bayou Folk* "had many de-lighted readers," *The Book Buyer* reported, and her new novel, *The Awakening*, "is said to be analytical and fine-spun, and of peculiar interest to women."

The first St. Louis notice, in the *St. Louis Republic* for March 25, 1899, was also encouraging: "The phase of development which Mrs. Kate Chopin describes in 'The Awakening' is rare in fiction, but common enough in life. A woman who has been merely quiescent, who has accepted life as it came to her, without analysis and without question, finally awakens to the fact that she has never lived. Mrs. Chopin tells the whole of her story, with its inevitable consequences of joy and suffering. Quietly as the work is done, it makes her intensely real; it brings her out with extraordinary distinctness and force. It is the work of an artist who can suggest more than one side of her subject with a single line. The environment is Southern, and it is by no means the book of a single character."

That would be one of the last good notices *The Awakening* received.

In *The Awakening*, Kate Chopin reflected on the life of a woman almost the age of her son Jean: Edna Pontellier has her twenty-ninth birthday in *The*

Awakening. When she herself was twenty-nine, Kate Chopin had moved to Cloutierville and given birth to her last child. Then her own bittersweet romance with another man had taught her about passion and pain and disillusionment—and had set her on the path to becoming a published author.

Kate did not write her autobiography in *The Awakening*, but she drew on and reshaped what she had learned in forty-eight years.

Edna Pontellier of *The Awakening* is the mother of two sons and the wife of a man who loves and protects her but scarcely interests her at all. As a child, Edna was reserved, like the youthful Katie O'Flaherty who confided her satirical comments to her diary. The young Edna, whose mother died young, had always stifled her feelings, especially her affections, and expected her life to be an "outward existence which conforms" and "an inward life that questions."

But Edna as a schoolgirl has a more romantic fantasy life: Her friends, all of them self-contained like herself, are intellectual rather than confiding. There is no one to direct Edna's energies away from infatuations—with a cavalry officer who resembles Napoleon, with a young man engaged to a neighboring young lady, and finally with a famous tragedian whose portrait she treasures.

Edna has always lived in dreams, in a world of illusions, and marrying Léonce Pontellier appeals to her as a way to rebel against her stodgy Kentucky Presbyterian family, who violently oppose her marrying a Catholic. For Edna, the New Orleans Creole Léonce Pontellier is safe. He is middle-aged and financially secure; he is devoted to her; and his presence will, she thinks, insulate her from the dangerous consequences of her imagination.

Oscar Chopin was not, of course, anything like Léonce Pontellier: Edna's marrying the stolid, settled Léonce, twelve years her senior, is more like Eliza O'Flaherty's marriage. Kate's mother had married a man more than twice her age for security, not for adventure or romantic dreams. Edna—perhaps like the young Eliza O'Flaherty—gives birth to two children without giving much thought to the meaning of her life. But one summer, in the brooding, seductive atmosphere of Grand Isle, full of the lushness of temptation, Edna awakens from her life of drifting.

Her inspiration comes partly from her first intimate friendship with a woman. Inspired by the beauty and warmth of her Creole friend Madame Adèle Ratignolle, Edna begins to wonder about her own place in the universe. Amid the bright Impressionist colors and streaks of light at Grand Isle, Edna learns to swim, feeling "as if some power of significant import had been given her to control the working of her body and her soul." She is inspired to tears by the magnificent piano playing of the otherwise disagreeable Mademoiselle Reisz, who lectures her on the duty of the artistic soul. And, for the first time since her marriage, Edna is attracted to another man.

Robert Lebrun, son of the owner of the Grand Isle cottages, is charming, and each summer he devotes himself to a different lady, playing at being the gallant lover—but Edna is different. When Robert leaves for Mexico, abruptly, Edna recognizes in herself the same bitter infatuation, the feeling of having lost something precious that was never her own.

When the summer resort season ends, Edna is back in New Orleans and radically discontented. She devotes days to her painting, and makes plans to sell her work; she neglects her household duties, and goes out on the day she is supposed to receive callers. She takes long solitary walks, reveling in her own company. Eventually, when her husband and children are away, she holds a luxurious dinner party, at which the guests wear eccentric costumes and recite Swinburne, and she is "the regal woman, the one who rules, who looks on, who stands alone"—after which she moves into a little house around the corner from her husband's home.

There, she carries on her affair with another man—the notorious man-about-town Alcée Arobin, with whom she shares "the first kiss of her life to which her nature had really responded. It was a flaming torch that kindled desire." Afterward, she feels no shame or remorse, only "a dull pang of regret because it was not the kiss of love which had inflamed her, because it was not love which had held this cup of life to her lips."

Robert returns to New Orleans (after having had a romance with a young woman in Vera Cruz). Edna confesses her love to him, and Robert admits that he loves her in return—but he is shocked at her sexual overtures (she kisses him with "a voluptuous sting"). Robert still views her as her husband's possession. Then Edna is called away to attend Adèle Ratignolle, who is giving birth—and when Edna returns, after a "scene of torture," she finds that Robert has gone. After a sleepless night, in which she faces despair and the fact that "there was no one thing in the world that she desired," Edna goes to Grand Isle and swims out until her strength is gone.

When Kate Chopin quoted from *The Awakening* in the *St. Louis Post-Dispatch* society column, she was answering the newspaper's question: "Is Love Divine?" But in *The Awakening*, she also posed and answered another underlying question: "Is Motherhood Divine?"

Chopin described Edna Pontellier as not a "mother-woman," unlike her friend Madame Ratignolle, the golden madonna who resembles the blond, blue-eyed heroines of Sir Walter Scott novels. But Madame Ratignolle is not the virginal maiden of American literature: Every two years she has another baby, and *The Awakening* takes place over the nine months of her pregnancy.

When Kate Chopin wrote about Adèle Ratignolle's "condition," she was breaking new ground (although no reviewers noticed it): *The Awakening* is virtually the only American novel of its era to describe a pregnant woman. Adèle

Ratignolle is also a bountifully pregnant woman, glorying in her condition, which she continually makes the subject of her conversation. (George Moore's 1894 English novel *Esther Waters* had been refused by English circulating libraries because it included scenes in a lying-in hospital. The first legal American edition was scheduled for publication in the same month as *The Awakening*—and by the same daring publisher, Herbert S. Stone & Company.)

In *The Awakening*, Kate Chopin described—with the discretion required in the 1890s—the stages of pregnancy she knew so well. Adèle Ratignolle claims to have fainting spells; she worries over whether she should eat certain delicious bonbons, lest they be too rich for her. She is always sewing and crocheting tiny garments, with the mother-woman's habit of being constantly busy.

During her New Orleans years, with the summers in St. Louis or Grand Isle, Kate Chopin had observed the social customs that she recorded in *The Awakening*. At Grand Isle, pregnancies and childbirths were a popular topic of conversation, with the freedom of summer resorts and the understood Creole "absence of prudery," which co-exists with an "inborn and unmistakable" chastity in the women. When Adèle Ratignolle tells an old Creole gentleman the "harrowing story of one of her *accouchements*," she shocks Edna, but no one else.

In New Orleans, though, there were limits to a pregnant woman's freedom: Once Adèle is in an advanced stage, and *souffrante*, she cannot be seen in public. That would have been Kate Chopin's experience with her sons Frederick and Felix, and perhaps with Lélia as well: The boys were born in January in New Orleans, and Lélia in December in Cloutierville, and their mother would have been obviously pregnant by the end of the resort season.

Kate Chopin also described, with as much candor as she could, Adèle Ratignolle's last *accouchement*: Adèle's anger at the doctor's delay, her demands for her friend Edna, her cries. Watching her, Edna remembers her own births (so much like Kate Chopin's): the "ecstasy of pain, the heavy odor of chloroform, a stupor which had deadened sensation."

Watching Adèle makes Edna profoundly sad, and her despair only deepens when she realizes that Robert has abandoned her—for it was not only her own motherhood that Kate drew on for the plot of *The Awakening*. Edna has one other source of transcendence: the dream of the perfect romance, with an extraordinary man who can ignore the petty dictates of a bourgeois society.

She thinks Robert is that love, but (as the doctor says toward the end of the novel), "youth is given up to illusions . . . a decoy to secure mothers for the race. And Nature takes no account of moral consequences." Edna has already refused to say no to experiences that awaken her further, including her affair with Alcée Arobin, a man who loves horses, women, and the night.

But, as Kate Chopin showed in *The Awakening*, even the trio of men cannot meet all of Edna's needs: She wants something more, something perpetually out of reach, something she cannot even name in her thoughts before her last swim. Her painting is not enough, and in her last minutes she thinks that Mademoiselle Reisz would laugh at her, for lacking the artist's courageous soul. Edna finally renounces life—as Kate Chopin renounced a large portion of her life, when she decided to leave Cloutierville and return to St. Louis.

When Kate Chopin drew on her own experiences for *The Awakening*, she did not thoroughly disguise them: *The Awakening* records her own dilemmas and her own choices. When she named Edna's lovers, Kate Chopin gave them each a part of Albert Sampite's name: Al-cée (Al. S——é) and Ro-BERT. Alcée is the man who appeals to Edna's body; Robert is, she thinks, the mate of her soul.

Albert Sampite, of course, proved to be neither, and *The Awakening* can be read as a cautionary tale about the promises of men.

There are warnings in the novel: Adèle warns Robert that Edna may take him seriously—as Kate Chopin, a Cloutierville outsider and a widow, may have taken Albert Sampite's attentions more seriously than he intended. Dr. Scruggs, like Dr. Mandelet in *The Awakening*, may have warned her that "youth is given up to illusions"; Eliza O'Flaherty may have beseeched her, as Adèle does, to "remember the children."

When Kate Chopin left Cloutierville for St. Louis, she left her lover to go to her mother—the same choice that Edna makes in *The Awakening*: She leaves Robert to be with the mother-woman Adèle Ratignolle, who is about to give birth. By leaving Cloutierville, Kate Chopin had given birth to herself— had allowed herself to become an independent woman, the center of a circle of men but not dependent on any of them for fulfillment and meaning in her life. Edna Pontellier, disillusioned, had disappeared into the sea; Kate Chopin, with much more practicality and hope, had gone to St. Louis.

In St. Louis, reviewers of *The Awakening* did not even notice that Kate Chopin had violated social taboos in depicting a bountifully pregnant woman as beautiful. They did not comment on her harrowing *accouchement* scene, which by itself would have been considered coarse. Nor did they notice her small indelicacies: Mariequita, the shrimp girl, thinks nothing of a man who ran off with another man's wife; Robert evidently had an affair in Vera Cruz; Robert and his brother Victor both seem to have a more-than-friendly relationship with Mariequita, whose bare feet ooze slime between their toes.

Kate Chopin's critics also ignored her satirical jabs at religion: When Edna goes to mass at Lourdes, she gets sick instead of well, and has to race outside for fresh air. Nor did the reviewers notice that Edna lacks respect for great thinkers: She falls asleep over Emerson.

But Kate Chopin's reviewers could not miss the fact that Edna Pontellier has an affair with another man.

*   *   *

The story of *The Awakening* did have some similarities to a St. Louis scandal taking place while Kate Chopin was writing the novel. In September of 1897, Billy Reedy had reported in the *Mirror* about a romance at a summer resort involving "an elderly married lady of this city." According to Reedy, the un-named lady was, despite her years, "a fine figure of a woman," and "especially is this apparent when she ventures in the sea"—but "she is frivolously inclined and somewhat addicted to sentimentality." That made her an easy mark for "a young Baltimorean with good looks and a taste for poetry" and "romantic professions."

Resort guests were amused at first, and then alarmed when the lady seemed far more devoted than she should have been: She also "insisted that he only could teach her how to swim." When her man went to New York, she tele-graphed him every day; when he returned, she "all but kissed him" and gave him a handsome diamond scarf pin made from her own ring. Soon thereafter, a few letters were sent, and the young man's father appeared at the spa to take his son away. The elderly lady mourned, then quarreled with her husband, and the hotel help said they heard the husband say "something about 'puppy-love letters' and an 'asylum.' "

The lady had not yet returned to St. Louis when Reedy published his report, "but when she comes she will be surprised to find how much news of her season has preceded her."

She and her relatives and friends were no doubt surprised—and distressed—to find what seemed to be her story in *The Awakening*. The *Republic*, which published the first St. Louis review of Kate Chopin's new novel, was also the favored paper of the wealthiest "best people" of St. Louis—and its condemna-tion, and its silences, set the tone for the rest of the St. Louis papers.

On April 22, 1899, Herbert S. Stone & Company officially issued *The Awakening* by Kate Chopin, billed as "author of 'A Night in Acadie,' 'Bayou Folks,' etc." *The Awakening*, which sold for $1.50 a copy, was a slim volume with a light green linen binding decorated with graceful green and wine-dark vines, printed on the sides and spine in red. The book was copyrighted on April 24—almost ten years to the day after Oscar Chopin's body was buried in St. Louis.

Except for the poem "If It Might Be," published in January of 1889, Kate Chopin's entire literary career had taken place in those ten years after Oscar's burial. In that time, Chopin had written three novels, eighty-five short stories, twelve essays, at least twenty-five poems, and one play. She had ceased to see herself primarily as a widow (if she ever did)—and Albert Sampite, rather than

Oscar Chopin, inspired the strongest male characters in her fiction and the hymns to night, parting, separation, and regret in her poetry.

She had also made enemies in St. Louis, and she had not been kind to her own city in her writings: From the superficially silly people in *At Fault* through the supercilious Lady Bountiful in "Miss McEnders," she had presented St. Louisans as philistines mired in trivialities.

Still, she was esteemed in some quarters. On April 13, nine days before *The Awakening*'s publication, Billy Reedy wrote that "St. Louis is not much of a town for literature," but he made a few exceptions: "Of course, the stories of Mrs. Kate Chopin continue to find ready sale all over the United States."

On April 20, two days before *The Awakening* was issued, Kate Chopin attended a euchre party hosted by Mrs. Alexander DeMenil at the St. Nicholas Hotel. The party was "the Mecca for throngs of women in gay spring toilets," the *St. Louis Republic* reported, and the ladies dressed in taffeta, lace, silk, and organdy, with their best jewelry. Some eighty ladies—who included Kate's cousin Blanche Bordley and one titled guest (the Baroness d'Este)—were served a luncheon of entrees, salads, ices, and nesselrode pudding. Afterward, the prizes were distributed—and Kate Chopin won a "fine salad set of solid silver," according to the *Mirror* (the *Republic* said it was gold).

Ten days later, the *Republic* published the first St. Louis review of *The Awakening*.

Chapter 22

"THE STORY OF A LADY MOST FOOLISH"

⟶ THE FIRST ST. LOUIS REVIEW of *The Awakening* appeared on page 11 of the *Republic*'s Sunday magazine for April 30, 1899, with large headlines:

KATE CHOPIN'S NEW BOOK IS THE STORY OF A LADY MOST FOOLISH

The *Republic* review proved to be the longest review *The Awakening* ever received. It provided a running plot summary that filled seven columns and covered nearly half a newspaper page—but the reviewer's summary still left out much of the story.

It began somewhat negatively: "Kate Chopin's new book, 'The Awakening,' is her first long story. Mrs. Chopin is authority for the statement that she prefers the short story to the novel; that is, she prefers to write the short story."

The Awakening, the *Republic* reviewer reported, was the story of "a self-contained woman, a Kentuckian, who married a creole gentleman, and went to live in a creole atmosphere, where nature was acknowledged more frankly than she had ever known. After several years of 'unthinking life,' absorbed in what the author calls 'the externals,' she awoke and learned to love. The tragedy of it all was that she did not love her husband."

Most of the review consisted of quotations from *The Awakening*: about Edna's not being a mother-woman, about her young sons' independent ways, about Madame Ratignolle as the embodiment of beauty and charm, about Edna's past infatuations and romantic dreams, before her sensible marriage.

The reviewer misstated Robert's age (claiming he was thirty-one instead of twenty-six), and then described the novel's main problem, as the reviewer saw it: "Given a woman at a summer resort with nothing to do, more interested in herself and her own emotions than in her husband and children, and a man who had nothing to do except make himself agreeable to the aforesaid woman, and it is like working out an equation in Algebra: 'Let X equal the unknown quantity,' and lo, the problem is solved."

The *Republic* described Edna's falling in love with Robert; his departure and return; her confession that she loved him; and his abandoning her—after which, despondent, she traveled to Grand Isle in despair. The review concluded, "So the woman who did not want anything but her own way drowned herself."

The *Republic's* reviewer left out most of the richness of Edna's life: her passionate susceptibility to music; her quirky friendship with the disagreeable Mademoiselle Reisz; her erratic but skillful sketching and painting. The *Republic* review also omitted Madame Ratignolle's pregnancy and the childbirth scene—and it left out, utterly, any mention of Alcée Arobin.

As described in the *Republic*, *The Awakening* was the story of a foolish wife who could not accept the fact that her life would not be an endless flirtation with Robert—and so she drowned herself. The *Republic* made *The Awakening* into a very different story from the one Kate Chopin told.

That first review was not good—but Chopin was also already receiving letters of praise for her new novel.

On April 28, the poet R. E. Lee Gibson—to whom Kate had sent a copy—wrote her that no story had ever "affected me so profoundly" as *The Awakening*. By the time he reached Chapter XXI—in which Edna visits Mademoiselle Reisz, who plays the piano for her and shows her Robert's letter—Gibson was "so completely engrossed, so absorbed that I could not put the book by until I had finished it." *The Awakening*, he wrote, was "intensely dramatic and awfully sad," and also "exceedingly clever, artistic, satisfying."

Gibson admired *The Awakening's* "quiet humor, the pleasing descriptions; the dramatic situations; the analysis of character and feeling and the consummate skill generally with which the story is constructed." The ending made him feel "bitterly grieved," and "[t]he pathos of it all is overpowering; the impression is painfully sweet and sad. It is heart-breaking."

The Awakening, he said, left him "deeply stirred and strangely fascinated," and "[t]here is no end to my admiration of your undoubted genius." A sentence in Chapter XXI impressed him particularly, as a description of Kate Chopin: "To be an artist includes much, one must possess many gifts—absolute gifts—which have not been acquired by one's own effort." Someone like Kate Chopin, Gibson concluded, "one capable of writing stories like yours is wonderfully gifted above the balance of us, and is worthy of all possible praise and success."

Lewis B. Ely, another friend and a young St. Louis attorney, also wrote to Kate on April 28 about *The Awakening*, calling the book "delicate" and "artistic" and terming it "a *moral* tale rather than an immoral one but I think the moral is a deep one. The book is a sermon against un-natural-ness and Edna's marriage—as I understand it—." He added, "I think there is little in it to offend anybody—"

But Ely was wrong. When Sue V. Moore, former editor of *St. Louis Life*, wrote to Kate in early May, she mentioned that "at Barr's they have sold a good many copies." Mrs. Moore wrote, "Your book is *great!*" and added that she would come to Kate's "Thursday" that week, because "I am so proud to know 'the artist with the courageous soul that dares and defies.' "

But by then the St. Louis reviewers had pounced on *The Awakening*. Over the next month, *The Awakening* was reviewed in Reedy's *Mirror*, the *St. Louis Globe-Democrat*, and twice in the *Post-Dispatch*—and most reviewers took great exception to Kate Chopin's view of a woman's life.

To write the *Mirror's* review of *The Awakening*, which appeared on May 4, Billy Reedy selected a woman who had much in common with Kate Chopin. Frances Porcher was also a short-story writer, a widow, and an avid card player who had attended the sumptuous DeMenil euchre party just before *The Awakening* was published.

Frances Smith Cannon, a tall, dignified woman, was a Virginian by ancestry, but attended Missouri private schools, especially the Pritchett Institute in Glasgow, Missouri. She married a schoolmate, John Hale Roper, who died four years later—whereupon Fannie S. Roper turned to writing society items and short satirical pieces for the *St. Louis Star*. Another *Star* reporter was Billy Reedy—who, once he became editor in chief of the *Mirror*, offered Fannie S. Roper a job.

She was an active contributor of book reviews, short stories, and dramatic criticism for the *Mirror*, while also free-lancing for the *Globe-Democrat*, the *Republic*, and the *Post-Dispatch*, and writing advertising copy for a shoe company. In July 1896, she married Thomas Davis Porcher, head of the book department at the Stix, Baer & Fuller department store; a year later, their son, Francis, was born—but Frances Porcher never stopped writing. Like most nineteenth-century women writers—including Kate Chopin—she claimed to write on an erratic schedule and to prefer domesticity to a career, but in fact she was an ambitious author who valued books, reading, and reviewing.

Porcher, like Kate Chopin and Frederick Kolbenheyer, had been a Gentile contributor to *The American Jewess*. (In her story, "Maurice Latimer, Gentleman," the gentleman is finally run over by a streetcar.) Porcher also admired Guy de Maupassant's stories. Like Maupassant and Chopin, Frances Porcher was interested in ghost stories and suicide: "A Queer Suicide Club," Porcher's short story in the *Mirror* for January 7, 1897, describes an editor who meets the shades of "newspaper suicides," people whose reputations have been destroyed by the "journalistic craze for sensations." (Porcher's story may have been inspired by the suicide of "Little Mac" McCullagh, editor of the *Globe-Democrat*, on New Year's Eve, 1896.)

By 1899, Frances Porcher's career and Kate Chopin's had run along similar lines: Sometimes, as in the December 19, 1895 *Mirror*, they were even published in the same issues. Chopin's contribution was her one play, "An Embarrassing Position"; Fannie S. Roper's work was "Brewster's Present," the story of a middle-aged confirmed bachelor who takes on a protégé, who in turn is ruined by a woman from Brewster's own past.

But Porcher's stories were generally from a male point of view, and rarely sympathetic to women who were other than conventional—women who were cynical, or jealous for good reason, or who wanted to control their own lives. Nor, in her reviews, did Porcher encourage the new writers Billy Reedy favored: She disliked anything unpleasant that strayed from "the ideal." (She despised Henry James's story of divorce, *What Maisie Knew*, as "a nauseating analysis of man and woman nature.")

In 1899, Frances Porcher was much more conservative than Kate Chopin—in her marriages, in her writing, and in her thinking about the subjects Chopin portrayed in *The Awakening*, such as lovers outside marriage, and a mother's obligations to her children. Porcher believed firmly in a writer's responsibility to avoid "morally diseased" characters and "adult sin."

Along with most reviewers, Frances Porcher thought *The Awakening* was Kate Chopin's first novel: "Of an already successful writer's first novel one should not write, perhaps, while the spell of the book is upon one; it is something to be 'dreamed upon,' like a piece of wedding-cake for luck on one's first marriage-proposal, or anything upon which hangs some importance of decision."

Nevertheless, Frances Porcher had raced into print with her review, which continued, "And so, because we admire Kate Chopin's other work immensely and delight in her ever-growing fame and are proud that she is 'one-of-us St. Louisans,' one dislikes to acknowledge a wish that she had not written her novel."

Porcher admired Chopin's "peculiar charm of style" and "beauty of description," but *The Awakening* sickened her: "[I]t is one of the books of which we feel— 'cui bono?' It absorbs and interests, then makes one wonder, for the moment, with a little sick feeling, if all women are like the one, and that isn't a pleasant reflection after you have thoroughly taken in this character study whose 'awakening' gives title to Mrs. Chopin's novel.

"One would fain beg the gods, in pure cowardice, for sleep unending rather than to know what an ugly, cruel, loathsome monster Passion can be when, like a tiger, it slowly stretches its graceful length and yawns and finally awakens."

In Frances Porcher's eyes, Edna's was not even a proper improper passion: It was not love, but something "sensual and devilish." She "played the wanton in her soul." Porcher condemned Edna not for her thoughts, but for her actions: for choosing sensuality over self-sacrifice. The review did not mention Alcée Arobin or Robert Lebrun by name, nor did Porcher say that Edna had two lovers, one representing sexual desire and the other a more honorable yearning: Rather, it implied that Edna had only one "other man." (Porcher also filled her review with such words as *treacherous*, *fickle*, *fiend*, and *demon*.)

The Awakening, Frances Porcher wrote, "is not a pleasant picture of soul-dissection," and in the end, "[i]t is better to lie down in the green waves and sink down in close embraces of old ocean, and so she does."

Still, Frances Porcher acknowledged that Kate Chopin was a fine writer: "There is no fault to find with the telling of the story; there are no blemishes in its art, but it leaves one sick of human nature and so one feels—*cui bono!*"

Two days later, on May 6, the *Post-Dispatch* printed its first notice of *The Awakening*, in just one paragraph: "In 'The Awakening,' Mrs. Kate Chopin has penetrated very far into the secret motives of action. She is not afraid to tell you what she finds there, feeling sure that the truth after all is wholesome. Her heroine is very far from perfect, yet her sins and weaknesses bring her no happiness, and we are led to infer that the established order of things cannot be broken into without heavy payment. There is much beauty, however, in the development of this graceful, fascinating, subtle character, and Mrs. Chopin has described it with extraordinary art. There is no pose in her attitude; it is absolutely simple and sincere."

On May 10, Kate Chopin—so far unruffled by reviews—wrote a poem:

Life

A day with a splash of sunlight,
Some mist and a little rain.
A life with a dash of love-light,
Some dreams and a touch of pain.
To love a little and then to die!
To live a little and never know why!

On the next day, May 11, her relative-by-marriage Camilla Lachs Breazeale printed an announcement in the *Natchitoches Enterprise*: "The title of Mrs. Kate Chopin's new novel is 'The Awakening.' This is the same title given in this country to Tolstoi's latest novel now running in the Cosmopolitan Magazine, but in Europe the last mentioned work is known as 'The Resurrection.' Mrs. Chopin's story, which has just been issued by Herbert S. Stone & Co., deals with life in and around New Orleans."

Two days later, *Publishers Weekly* published a one-paragraph notice, misspelling Edna's name: "A Kentucky girl, brought up among strict Presbyterians, had married a Creole speculator, chiefly because her family had actively opposed the marriage because the man was a Catholic. He took her to New Orleans, and when the story opens she is twenty-eight, the mother of two boys, spending her summer at Grand Isle. In strong contrast is her Creole friend, devoted to husband and children. The descriptions of Creole summer pastimes, the hotel life, the flirtations, chiefly occupy the author. This summer Madame Montpellier awakens to the fact that her indulgent, good-natured husband and her children and home do not satisfy her. Two men stir her emotional nature for a short time. There is a tragical ending."

On that same day, in St. Louis, the most explicit review yet of *The Awakening* appeared—and it was not favorable.

For Kate Chopin, the *St. Louis Globe-Democrat* was the enemy paper. It was the *Post-Dispatch*'s most aggressive rival, and was still owned by Ellen McKee ("Miss McEnders"). Lewis Ely sent Kate Chopin a warning: The *Globe-Democrat*'s review, he wrote to her on May 13, would give her "hysterics."

The anonymous *Globe-Democrat* reviewer began on a positive note: The appearance of a new novel by Kate Chopin, a St. Louis writer, was of local interest. But *The Awakening* was a surprise, "hardly the kind of a book some people would look for from her," a love story of one woman and "several male characters," in which the woman finally swims to her death. "Her very suicide," the *Globe-Democrat* reported, "is in itself a prayer for deliverance from the evils that beset her, all of her own creating."

According to the *Globe-Democrat*, *The Awakening* "is not a healthy book; if it points any particular moral or teaches any lesson, the fact is not apparent." The *Globe-Democrat* was the first to mention Alcée Arobin: Edna is "violently in love" with Robert, but after he leaves for Mexico, "she gets tangled up with another man, a roue whose reputation is very bad; and she does all sorts of imprudent things. . . ." The review did mention "the unique feature of the book" after Robert's return: "Right in the very midst of their mutual declarations of love, she is summoned to the bedside of a woman friend in the throes of childbirth. . . . But she is not forced to choose between duty as a mother and her unholy love, for Robert runs away."

The *Globe-Democrat* praised Kate Chopin's "pretty bits of description of Louisiana Creole life," and said that "two or three minor characters" were "drawn with a deft hand." But the overall verdict was negative: "[I]t can not be said that either of the principal characters claims admiration or sympathy. It is a morbid book, and the thought suggests itself that the author herself would probably like nothing better than to 'tear it to pieces' by criticism if only some other person had written it."

And then, as if he had been waiting in the wings to refute her critics, Kate's friend Charles L. Deyo reviewed *The Awakening* in the *Post-Dispatch*. Deyo summarized the plot, criticizing Léonce Pontellier for treating his wife as "a bit of decorative furniture." He mentioned Edna's dabbling as a painter, her friendship with Mademoiselle Reisz ("who was a witch"), and Robert's departure. Edna was "not good enough for heaven, not wicked enough for hell": In Deyo's words, she was "a derelict in a moral ocean, whose chart she had never studied, and one of the pirates who cruise in that sea made her his prize." Robert, with whom she might have committed "a robust sin," was away, and so Edna's "moment came and with it the man. There is always a man for the moment, sometimes two or three." But "passion without love" was not what Edna wanted, and eventually "she could not forget her womanhood, and to save the remnants of it, she swam out into the sunkissed gulf and did not come back."

Deyo praised the book's "flawless art," and the "delicacy of touch of rare skill in construction, the subtle understanding of motive, the searching vision into the recesses of the heart." And in *The Awakening*, "power appears, power born of confidence. . . . In delicious English, quick with life, never a word too much, simple and pure, the story proceeds with classic severity through a labyrinth of doubt and temptation and dumb despair."

Deyo's discussion took the novel much more seriously than others had—and he was much less hostile toward Edna. *The Awakening* was not a tragedy, Deyo wrote, "for it lacks the high motive of tragedy." Edna Pontellier, "not quite brave enough, declines to a lower plane and does not commit a sin ennobled by love. But it is terribly tragic. Compassion, not pity, is excited, for pity is for those who sin, and Edna Pontellier only offended—weakly, passively, vainly offended."

Deyo refused to use William Dean Howells's traditional standard for judging a book: whether it could be properly read by an innocent young person. No doubt strengthened by discussions at Kate Chopin's "Thursdays," Deyo confronted the issue directly, even sarcastically: "*The Awakening* is not for the young person; not because the young person would be harmed by reading it, but because the young person wouldn't understand it, and everybody knows that the young person's understanding should be scrupulously respected."

Instead, Deyo wrote, *The Awakening* was for "seasoned souls, for those who have lived, who have ripened under the gracious or ungracious sun of experience and learned that realities do not show themselves on the outside of things where they can be seen and heard, weighed, measured and valued like the sugar of commerce, but treasured within the heart, hidden away, never to be known perhaps save when exposed by temptation or called out by occasions of greed, pith and moment."

Kate Chopin's novel was not for timid readers, Deyo said. "No, the book is not for the young person, nor, indeed, for the old person who has no relish for unpleasant truths. For such there is much that is very improper in it, not to say positively unseemly. A fact, no matter how essential, which we have all agreed shall not be acknowledged, is as good as no fact at all. And it is disturbing—even indelicate—to mention it as something which, perhaps, does play an important part in the life behind the mask."

Deyo's conclusion praised *The Awakening* for its adult portrayal of a woman's life: "It is sad and mad and bad, but it is all consummate art. The theme is difficult, but it is handled with a cunning craft. The work is more than unusual. It is unique. The integrity of its art is that of well-knit individuality at one with itself, with nothing superfluous to weaken the impression of a perfect whole."

Those who wished to could read Deyo's as a negative review of *The Awakening*: that the book was "sad and mad and bad," that Kate Chopin should not have revealed "the life behind the mask." But Chopin's friends would have read Deyo's review as praise, for her fearless and honest portrayal of a woman's life.

Deyo's review appeared on May 20, 1899—and then, in an extraordinary move, the *Post-Dispatch* published another review on the next day.

The second review, by "G. B.," began with a philosophical discussion of self-love in three varieties: instinctive, reasonable, emotional. Edna's love for her husband was "reasonable," and in the portrayal of reasonable love, Kate Chopin's *Awakening* was "a work of genius, in that it states a universal principle in particular terms." But Edna's passion for Robert was "involuntary," and "Under repression her passion became perverted into a sensual sanction of Arobin." Then G. B.'s review grew incoherent:

The glaring defect of the book greets one on the title page, which rumor says was furnished by the intelligent publishers.

Life is a succession of awakenings.

From the dawn of consciousness to the eve of senility we are continually arriving.

Edna thought she had solved the riddle, and apprehending wanton-
ness she fled. These publishers thereupon indorsed her error and
called it "The" instead of "An Awakening."

G. B.'s review, oscillating wildly, ended with praise and condemnation:

The science of the human soul and its operations is instinctive in
Kate Chopin. In her creations she commits unutterable crimes against
polite society, but in the essentials of her art she never blunders.

Like most of her work, however, "The Awakening" is too strong
drink for moral babes, and should be labeled "poison."

By the end of May, 1899, only *Book News* and the St. Louis newspapers
had reviewed *The Awakening*. Kate Chopin had reason to hope that national
reviewers might be more sympathetic.

The Critic, for one, wanted a new photograph. Kate sent an unsmiling portrait of herself without a hat (hatlessness was a new St. Louis fad). Her hair
was waved in front and escaping from its pins in back, and she wore a cameo
brooch at the throat of a high-necked gown. Her slightly narrowed eyes were
focused on something in the distance, and her expression was wistful.

She sent the picture to her publisher Herbert S. Stone on June 7, with
Charles Deyo's review of *The Awakening* and a note:

What are the prospects for the book? I enclose a notice which you
may not have seen—from the Post Dispatch. It seems so able and
intelligent—by contrast with some of the drivel I have run across
that I thought I should like to have you read it when you have
the time.

On May 28, she had also written a somewhat satirical answer to her critics,
for *Book News*:

Having a group of people at my disposal, I thought it might be
entertaining (to myself) to throw them together and see what would
happen. I never dreamed of Mrs. Pontellier making such a mess of
things and working out her own damnation as she did. If I had had
the slightest intimation of such a thing I would have excluded her
from the company. But when I found out what she was up to, the
play was half over and it was then too late.

By the time *Book News* published her piece, in July, Kate was definitely on the defensive—but in May, her friends were still writing glowing letters. Lizzie L., a Louisville friend, wrote on May 10 that she had been

> so deeply interested, so absolutely absorbed in "The Awakening" that I could not realize the denoument. It seemed so impossible that Edna should sacrifice her life, although I understand how her nature had become completely metamorphosed under the influence of an infatuation she was powerless to control. Robert was disappointing; he was unworthy the intensity of the feeling he had awakened. His nature lacked the strength & depth of emotion requisite for a grande passion, qualities not usually lacking in the Creole temperament. A little French blood I think is absolutely necessary to make any man interesting.

Lizzie L. felt that "[t]he style of the book is faultless—each character is so graphically portrayed that we forget they are imaginary, & feel depressed when they are no longer with us. I am lonely since I parted from them all. . . ."

> The humor of the book is delicious—like Balzac—but still essentially your own. In many places I can hear you speaking, describing incidents in your own cute, inimitable way. I can see & hear the parrot—the twins are graphic—so is the lady in black—& the lovers—but why particularize, each & everyone is the creation of a genius which all must acknowledge.

In Lizzie L.'s opinion, "the whole book is a grand success, from beginning to end, artistic in every detail & it is such a happiness that the one I love best on earth is capable of such great achievements."

Lizzie L. hoped to see Kate in June in St. Louis and go together "to Cherokee where we can discuss the sorrows of Edna & her dream of love which was never realized"—but in the meantime, Lizzie L. provided a tidbit that she knew Kate would appreciate, as someone with an unceasing curiosity about other people:

> I heard a piece of gossip which I do not like to repeat as it is always dangerous to mention names, but I was told that the party whose name I inclose on a separate piece of paper, was enamored of the well known Lou Triplett & was her only love & chief support. I have always thought of him as an example of everything good and cannot believe the story.

(The name on the separate piece of paper has been lost.)

Six days later, another friend whose signature was "L." and who lived in St. Louis, wrote to "My dear little Katie" about *The Awakening*:

> I am still thinking and talking about *The Book*. There is indeed a variety of opinion concerning it. To me it is a psychological study— the development of a soul—an awakening to the possibilities of life—an emancipation of the whole being from the trammels of conventionalism. But why must it ever & always be in fiction as in fact that those brave enough to make the daring leap are inevitably swallowed in the chasm of defeat. Why not let joy & triumph await those who dare defy the edicts of merciless custom—but all this would be foreign to the school of Realism & you are as realistic as Zola.

L. evidently intended to flatter Kate—and did not know that she detested Zola's writing. L., like Lizzie L., had given *Bayou Folk* to other readers and reported their enthusiastic reactions. L. added that a couple named Paul had read *The Awakening* and called it "the oddest—most uncommon book—different from all other books." Mr. Paul said that

> "Mrs. Chopin stands alone among women writers—there is no one who can touch her. The only writers I would compare her with at all are Turgueneff, Tolstoi & Zola. She is realistic almost to a fault, artistic—daring—O! how I should love to meet that woman. I am expecting still greater things from her—she is an undoubted genius."—His wife says *do please write another book*. No other book seems interesting after yours. I showed them your picture which they pronounced beautiful. I tried to describe you—but no description could ever do you justice.

L., like Lizzie L., saw *The Awakening* as the story of Edna and Robert's failed romance:

> In regard to "The Awakening" it is above & beyond the comprehension of the commonplace. In the delineation of the various feelings of the human heart, dissecting the inner self & laying bare the minutest emotions you are simply marvellous. I did not like Robert—but others like him best—I said he was weak—they said "he was strong" she was weak—I would like to read something on the subject from a competent critic—one capable & appreciative. How I would love to hear from you—Your letters are balm in Gilead flowers in the desert of life.

Within a few weeks after Lizzie L.'s and L.'s letters, reviews of *The Awakening* began appearing in national periodicals and newspapers in other cities.

On June 1, the *Chicago Times-Herald* reported that Kate Chopin's "many admirers" would be

> surprised—perhaps disagreeably—by this latest venture. That the book is strong and that Miss Chopin has a keen knowledge of certain phases of feminine character will not be denied. But it was not necessary for a writer of so great refinement and poetic grace to enter the overworked field of sex fiction.

"This is not a pleasant story," the *Times-Herald* said, but the contrast between Edna and Madame Ratignolle, devoted to her husband and family, "saves it from utter gloom, and gives the reader a glimpse of the real Miss Chopin, who is at her best as a creator of sweet and lovable characters."

On June 3, the *Outlook* (New York) gave a similar report: "*The Awakening* is a decidedly unpleasant study of a temperament." It praised Kate Chopin as a Louisiana local-color writer and said that *The Awakening* was "faithful enough in its presentation of certain phases of human passion and downward drift of character, but the story was not really worth telling, and its disagreeable glimpses of sensuality are repellent."

On June 4, the *Providence Sunday Journal* called Kate Chopin "another clever woman writer" who had greatly disappointed her readers with *The Awakening*: "[T]he purport of the story can hardly be described in language fit for publication. We are fain to believe that Miss Chopin did not herself realise what she was doing when she wrote it," for it "fairly out Zolas Zola." The greatest danger, the Providence paper said, was that "such stories" might

> fall into the hands of youth, leading them to dwell on things that only matured persons can understand, and promoting unholy imaginations and unclean desires. It is nauseating to remember that those who object to the bluntness of our older writers will excuse and justify the gilded dirt of these later days.

On July 18, the *New Orleans Times-Democrat*, which had bravely printed Kate Chopin's short stories on such sensitive subjects as venereal disease, joined the attack on *The Awakening*:

> This unhappy Edna's awakening seems to have been confined entirely to the senses, while reason, judgment, and all the higher faculties and perceptions, whose office it is to weigh and criticise, impulse and govern conduct, fell into slumber deep as that of the

seven sleepers. It gives one a distinct shock to see Edna's crude mental operations. . . . The assumption that such a course as that pursued by Edna has any sort of divine sanction cannot be too strongly protested against. . . . Certainly there is throughout the story an undercurrent of sympathy for Edna, and nowhere a single note of censure of her totally unjustifiable conduct.

Public Opinion was equally censorious, feeling "no sympathy for this unpleasant person" (Edna), but being "well satisfied when Mrs. Pontellier deliberately swims out to her death in the waters of the gulf." *Literature* lamented the fact that "so beautiful a style and so much refinement of taste have been spent by Miss Chopin on an essentially vulgar story . . . the waters of the gulf close appropriately over one who has drifted from all right moorings, and has not the grace to repent."

In late June, Kate did get a few sympathetic readings. The *Boston Beacon* agreed that "*The Awakening,* by Kate Chopin, is emphatically not a book for very young people"—but it called the book a cautionary tale, a criticism of "marriage without real love." The *Beacon* had its own interpretation of Edna's lovers:

> The story is intensified by the appearance of a villain upon the scene who embodies or simulates some of the grace and magnetic qualities which the heroine's nature requires in a man companion and who succeeds in breaking down her reserve so that her judgment is baffled till the real lover in person summons her allegiance. The pure affection of her lover saves the heroine from irrevocable disgrace by a very narrow margin, but it is a powerful stroke on the part of the author to secure a strong artistic effect. In thus dealing with the subject the author emphasizes the immorality of a marriage of convenience.

The *Beacon* was unusual in not condemning Edna's sexual desires:

> There is an evident effort to illustrate without prudery—very much without prudery—that the normal woman is capable without sin of experiencing a full awakening of the entire human nature. One closes the volume, wondering what good, clever old Dr. Mandelet would have said to justify his telling the heroine not to blame herself, whatever came.

The New York Times was even more sympathetic to Edna:

Would it have been better had Mrs. Kate Chopin's heroine slept on forever and never had an awakening? Does that sudden condition of change from sleep to consciousness bring with it happiness? Not always, and particularly poignant is the woman's awakening, as Mrs. Chopin tells it. The author has a clever way of managing a difficult subject, and wisely tempers the emotional elements found in the situation. Such is the cleverness in the handling of the story that you feel pity for the most unfortunate of her sex.

But on the West Coast, where divorce laws had always been less strict than in Boston or New York, the *Los Angeles Times* was harshly critical—calling Edna a "selfish, capricious woman" from "that large section of femininity which may be classified as 'fool women.' " *The Awakening*, the Los Angeles reviewer said,

is like one of Aubrey Beardsley's hideous but haunting pictures with their disfiguring leer of sensuality, but yet carrying a distinguishing strength and grace and individuality. The book shows a searching insight into the motives of the "fool woman" order of being, the woman who learns nothing by experience and has not a large enough circle of vision to see beyond her own immediate desires. In many ways, it is unhealthily introspective and morbid in feeling, as the story of that sort of woman must inevitably be. The evident powers of the author are employed on a subject that is unworthy of them, and when she writes another book it is to be hoped that she will choose a theme more healthful and sweeter of smell.

Meanwhile, Kate's friends continued to write to her about *The Awakening*. Anna L. Moss, a St. Louis clubwoman and book reviewer, wrote on June 25:

My dear friend—

Thanks for the reviews—there is, on the whole, as much discrimination as one could expect from such sources for such a bit of work. I hold one must know and feel much, of art and life, to see how great is the gift which has given us this book: further that only on one who loves such, can the impersonal delicacy of your literary style exert it's full charm.

The reading public, Mrs. Moss felt, was too jaded, too used to writings that bludgeoned the reader with messages—such as Edward Noyes Westcott's *David Harum*, the year's best seller, and Finley Peter Dunne's "Mr. Dooley" stories, about an Irish bartender with satirical opinions on current events. Such a read-ing public, Anna L. Moss wrote,

> can not be expected to bring it's blunt appetite with relish to your
> delicate touches revealing the truth by salient glimpses. The reserve
> which is to my mind the strong and unique feature of your individ-
> ual phase of veritism must fall flat on a public—at least on a major
> fraction of a public—on which materialism has wrought so strongly
> when the cant, the pretence, the smotherings of the human heart
> that disfigure that other great and grand factor in our civilization—
> puritanism—are recalled in connection with your theme—it is not
> surprising that but few of the reviewers are more than funny.

Kate Chopin's work was superior to William Dean Howells's, Anna L. Moss felt: He often used tiresome and vulgar details, but Chopin trusted the reader's imagination.

> You have given us truth with the suggestion and delicacy of the
> true poet, and while yielding no jot in absolute faithfulness have
> left some things to the reader—have paid us the subtle compliment
> of taking for granted that we knew and felt and could see. I am free
> to say that while a great admirer of Tolstoi, Maupassant and our
> own Howells, I find a charm in that personal quality which makes
> your style yours, that is *in it's line* beyond their power for me.

Mrs. Moss praised the unity of *The Awakening* ("one not always reached in realistic fiction"), and Edna's morality: "[H]ow imperious is her demand for freedom and how surely any law but her own brings slavery and death." As for reviewers who criticized Kate Chopin's morality:

> To make moral or immoral use of your gift is our problem, not
> yours. The surety of your sense that preaching is not the province
> of fiction, is delightful. Again the artistic sanity—confidence &
> courage which gives with masculine self forgetness, with true ob-
> jectiveness, with utter lack of mawkish introspection, this revelation
> of a potential woman by a woman, is to my mind of large signifi-
> cance in the line of sex in the artist.

Mrs. Moss also found the ending of *The Awakening* truthful, though sad:

> I wish you believed that the Ednas will somewhere, somewhen,
> somehow grow into a spiritual harmony to which the splendor of

their frailty will contribute beauty—that the freedom and liberty—
into which your heroine went with the exultation of irrepressible
life (and I think the close of the story a fit climax, far preferable to
any inconsistent surface harmony of mutually, destructive psychological states) must contribute to a result grand in the whole, as the
factors she brings are strong and compelling.

Another correspondent disagreed, calling *The Awakening* "the only inartistic
story you have ever written," because of Edna's romance with Alcée Arobin.

The introduction of the Arobin intrigue with Edna was a mistake
as it destroyed the one grand and forgivable passion which becomes
two common loves for mere sexual gratification. At least, so it seems
to me, and it is in this that the story falls in my opinion. Without
the Arobin intrigue the story would have been dramatically stronger
and artistically perfect.

Only part of the letter survives, with no signature, but the confident, joking
tone suggests that the author knew Kate Chopin well.

Have no hesitancy in "damning my eyes" for my presumption, even
if I am mad, for daring to take issue with you and saying saucy
things. If I were not your admirer in matters literary (I'll leave the
personal side out so as to excite no jealousies) I would not dare to
speak so plainly, but I dare hope you will understand.

Personally I love the frank outspoken criticism of the friend even
when it hits the hardest. It brings me back to my work at a new
point of view and with new eyes to see. I am not always convinced
by my friend's argument, but go over my work in its light and am
so far benefitted at any rate.

The correspondent was evidently a writer, too:

Tolstoi was so delighted with my seduction story that he too has
written a serial for the Cosmopolitan, and he too calls it "The
Awakening." You have precedence over him, but isn't it funny you
both should have hit upon the same title.

The hostile reviews continued to pour in. Kate's satiric self-defense finally
appeared in *Book News* in July, the same month that *The Awakening* received
its third known review by a female critic (most reviews were unsigned). The

Pittsburgh Leader's reviewer, who signed herself by her middle name ("Sibert"), was a twenty-three-year-old writer named Willa Cather.

Cather, the first to call *The Awakening* "a Creole *Bovary*," admired Kate Chopin's writing—but detested her subject.

> I shall not attempt to say why Miss Chopin has devoted so exquisite
> and sensitive, well-governed a style to so trite and sordid a theme.
> She writes much better than it is ever given to most people to write,
> and hers is a genuinely literary style; of no great elegance or solidity; but light, flexible, subtle, and capable of producing telling effects directly and simply.

Yet Kate Chopin's story, Cather said, was "new neither in matter nor treatment": the story of a dreamy wife who, at a resort, made the mistake of taking a man's attentions seriously. "The lover of course disappointed her, was a coward and ran away from his responsibilities before they began. He was afraid to begin a chapter with so serious and limited a woman."

Edna, said Willa Cather, belonged to a class of women, "forever clamoring in our ears, that demands more romance out of life than God put into it." Such "women of the Bovary type," Cather wrote, expect

> the passion of love to fill and gratify every need of life, whereas
> nature only intended that it should meet one of many demands.
> They insist upon making it stand for all the emotional pleasures of
> life and art; expecting an individual and self-limited passion to yield
> infinite variety, pleasure, and distraction, to contribute to their lives
> what the arts and the pleasurable exercise of the intellect gives to
> less limited and less intense idealists. . . . They have staked everything on one hand, and they lose. . . .

> Edna Pontellier, fanciful and romantic to the last, chose the sea on
> a summer night and went down with the sound of her first lover's
> spurs in her ears, and the scent of pinks about her. And next time
> I hope that Miss Chopin will devote that flexible iridescent style of
> hers to a better cause.

Chapter 23

PRIVATE PRAISE
AND PUBLIC
CENSURE

DESPITE THE CRITICISM OF
The Awakening during the spring and summer of 1899, not everything was
negative for Kate Chopin as an author. In July, the *Century* printed her poem,
"I Opened All the Portals Wide":

> I opened all the portals wide
> To swallows on the wing.
> It matters not what now betide:
> I've had the taste, the touch, the breath, the scent and song of
> spring.

> Oh, fair sweet spring! abide with me
> In joy the whole time long;
> Bring all thy life, thy light, with thee:
> I fain would keep thy taste, thy touch, thy scent, O spring! thy
> song.

In August, Kate Chopin was featured in "The Lounger," a column in *The
Critic*. Kate was presented as nonchalant and unambitious: The article played
down her dedication to her music, her intellectual circle, and her writing.
Instead, "The Lounger" devoted more than a third of its space to Kate's family
history, and claimed that at the Sacred Heart school, she had been "an indif-
ferent student with a mistaken belief that she possessed musical talent." "The

Lounger" listed *At Fault*, *Bayou Folk*, and *A Night in Acadie*, and then concluded, "Mrs. Chopin is said to avoid the society of literary and 'bookish' people. She does not like to talk about her work. She writes seldom, but with great rapidity and little or no correction." There, *The Critic*'s sketch ended, ominously—without a mention of *The Awakening*, which had already been available for nearly five months.

Later, her children said that Kate Chopin never discussed the negative reception of *The Awakening* with anyone (and Lélia also claimed that her mother "never wrote again" afterward)—but in 1899, Kate's children were busy with their own lives. Jean was the sociable one, while Oscar was a reclusive artist. Fred was pallbearer for a fellow soldier who had died in Puerto Rico; George had his medical studies; Felix attended a dance for the Central High School graduating class, but grieved for his classmate and friend Will "Little Billee" Scullin, a promising law student, who had been in a "deplorable accident" that led to the amputation of both his legs.

Lélia spent the summer of 1899 away from home: She and Kate did not always get along, and there were hints of a social rivalry. Kate, it was said, would pay more attention to doctors and lawyers at parties than to her daughter—and their names rarely appear as guests at the same gatherings. (Later in life, Lélia was noted for imperious manners and dramatic public scenes.)

Lélia was eighteen, tall and attractive, and energetically involved in St. Louis society: She would be making her debut in the fall. In January, she and Felix attended a "domino dance" at the Outten residence on Pine Street, where, according to the society reporter, "The dominos were not removed until 11 o'clock, when the surprises were numerous." In early April, Lélia was part of a "musical and fashionable audience" at the Philharmonic, where she sat with a Mr. Edward Meade; two weeks later she was among the "fashionable folk" at the Apollo Club's final concert, where another guest was Mr. R. Park Von Wedelstaedt, who later that winter would be "rushing" her.

In May, Lélia and her friend Edna Moss (probably the daughter of Anna L. Moss, Kate's correspondent) left for a week's stay at the Sulphur Springs resort; in July, Lélia went to spend the summer at Lake Minnetonka, a Minnesota resort, with the Chopins' neighbors, the Chases. In early August, Lélia—still at the Chases' cottage—won the prize at a thimble bee, and a week later Mrs. Chase gave a "flower german" in honor of Lélia, with Jean Chopin leading the dance. In September, as the summer season was ending, Mrs. Chase gave a "fancy dress party," at which Lélia wore the costume of "a Spanish gitana." When Lélia returned home in mid-September, the *Mirror* reported that in Minnesota she had been "pronounced one of the most beautiful young ladies there and was entertained a great deal."

Meanwhile, Kate remained in St. Louis—and reviews condemning *The Awakening* continued to appear.

On August 1, *The Dial*'s conservative reviewer, William Morton Payne, called *The Awakening* a book "not without charm, but not altogether wholesome in its tendency."

The Nation called Kate Chopin "one more clever author gone wrong": *The Awakening* had the author's "accustomed fine workmanship," with its "hinted effects, the well-expended epithet, the pellucid style," and the skillful description of the "tint and air of Creole New Orleans and the Louisiana seacoast." Still, the morality of *The Awakening* disgusted *The Nation*'s reviewer:

> But we cannot see that literature or the criticism of life is helped by the detailed history of the manifold and contemporary love affairs of a wife and mother. Had she lived by Prof. William James's advice to do one thing a day one does not want to do (in Creole society, two would perhaps be better), flirted less and looked after her children more, or even assisted at more *accouchements*—her *chef d'oeuvre* in self-denial—we need not have been put to the unpleasantness of reading about her and the temptations she trumped up for herself.

By August, most critics seemed to agree that Kate Chopin wrote beautifully, but she had written an improper book. The *Boston Herald* called her style "short, crisp, and breezy," full of charm, but the reviewer shared *The Nation*'s complaints: Edna "wanted to do just what she wanted to," including "love affairs"; she should have flirted less and cared more for others. And so, according to the *Herald*, Chopin's novel was "most unpleasant in its bearings and not exactly profitable reading. . . . The ruptures in love affairs after matrimony are not altogether commendable for fiction, except as stepping stones to better conditions."

The *Herald*'s review appeared on August 12; on August 14 the *Indianapolis Journal* gave *The Awakening* a one-paragraph review, calling the book "not a healthy story, yet it is clever and one feels while reading it that he is moving among real people and events. The ending is abrupt and gives the reader somewhat the impression of being left hanging in midair." Then, on August 24, *The Congregationalist*, originally a religious weekly, published the year's last public verdict on Kate Chopin's novel: "It is a brilliant piece of writing, but unwholesome in its influence. We cannot commend it."

The reviews left Kate Chopin deeply wounded—although she tried to carry on her literary and social life as usual. When Richard B. Shepard, a member of the House of Representatives in Utah, inquired about her books, she sent him a list of all four, and offered to send *At Fault*, since it was not available at booksellers.

Kate also kept up her "Thursdays" and welcomed an appreciative guest: the Kentucky poet Madison Cawein, a friend of the poet R. E. Lee Gibson. In July, Gibson sent Kate a copy of Cawein's latest volume of poems, *Myth and Romance*, with a note of cheer:

> While I am writing to you, may I not quote from a recent letter of Cawein's to me, his most glowing estimate of your fine novel: "The Awakening." He says:

> "I received 'The Awakening,' and thank you most sincerely for the enjoyment of a most beautiful, though a most sad, story. Mrs. Chopin is a writer of the greatest talent. She made me feel everything she speaks of in this fine novel. I could hear the waves of the gulf foaming on the shore; smell the magnolia-scented atmosphere of Louisiana; the sun vibrating on the tropical foliage filled me with languours; and the moon beating softly on the waters of bay and lagoon filled me with unutterable longings. It is a beautiful book as I have said before, and a sorrowful one. But the most lovely things are those, I think, that are founded on pathos, and suggest the mortal human that appeals to us only through its sweet sorrow, that is akin to nothing on earth that we know.

Cawein's letter was dated March 30, before the official publication or the hostile reviews, and he also wrote to Gibson that "if you think it will interest Mrs. Chopin send her what I said about her book which charmed me more than I can tell you; it is intensely human; therein its charm consists. She is a fine writer."

Gibson agreed, and added to Kate that "I have no patience with any one who would fail to recognize the great power and pathos of the splendid story which you have told in 'The Awakening.' "

Cawein, a thirty-four-year-old bachelor, came to St. Louis in August, and Kate Chopin autographed his copy of *The Awakening*: "I shall never lose the delight which Madison Cawein has given me in his poems and his voice."

Also delighted, Cawein wrote to a Louisville friend that Kate Chopin "is a lovely woman of fifty-two, but still fine-looking and capable of exciting the enthusiastic admiration of men much younger than herself. She must have been very beautiful indeed when she was in her twenties and thirties." (Kate was actually forty-nine when Madison Cawein met her.)

Cawein also described the August 17 "Thursday" at Kate Chopin's home:

I met Mrs. Kate Chopin last evening together with a number of charming St. Louis people who seemed to be acquainted with my work, much to my surprise I must say. . . .

We passed a delightful evening of ghost stories and poetry. I thought of how you would have enjoyed it—the ghost stories especially. A Mr. Schuyler told some interesting ones, but I flatter myself that mine—in subject, at least, if not as well-worded as his—were the most thrilling. Mrs. Chopin is a great sceptic, but she seemed to be very much interested; perhaps, if given a chance I might be able to convert her to believing in them.

Kate Chopin did believe in extrasensory perception and spiritual communication between kindred souls (which she had mocked, gently, in the story "A Mental Suggestion")—but she was a cynic compared with Madison Cawein, who claimed to be a pantheist and spiritualist, as well as a believer in ghosts and fairies. (His mother was a medium.)

Madison Cawein never wrote publicly about Kate Chopin, but two years later he published a rare Louisiana local color poem, called "Hoodoo," about a woman who "mutters and stoops by the lone bayou" in a ghostly scene—like the night descriptions in Chopin's unpublished story "Ti Frère." Possibly the evening of telling ghost stories at Kate's Thursday also inspired Cawein's refrain: "*Soon, oh, soon,*" hear her croon,/ "*Woe, oh, woe to the octoroon!*"

Through most of 1899, Kate Chopin's writing career was in limbo. Her short story of a Louisiana misanthrope, "A Family Affair," had been published in the *Saturday Evening Post* for September 9, but after "A Little Country Girl" in February, she delayed eight months before writing another short story. Nor was she sending out stories she had already written: She was waiting for them to appear in *A Vocation and a Voice*, under contract to Herbert S. Stone & Company.

She was also still feeling the sting from the reviews of *The Awakening*: It clearly was not the kind of book that Americans favored. Among the most popular novels for 1899 were Westcott's *David Harum*, Booth Tarkington's *The Gentleman from Indiana*, Charles Major's *When Knighthood Was in Flower*, Mary Johnston's *Prisoners of Hope*, and the St. Louis novelist Winston Churchill's *Richard Carvel*. Most were historical novels; all were considered "healthy," with "kindly sentiment," suitable for a young person to read; and all promoted the traditional values that Kate Chopin, in *The Awakening*, had questioned.

Most society St. Louisans had returned from their summer cottages by October 8, 1899, when Kate Chopin left for the Wisconsin lake country. It was only three weeks after Lélia's return from Minnesota, and her debut was less than two months away.

Kate was in Wisconsin when she received two letters that gave her great pleasure. They had been sent to her c/o Herbert S. Stone, who forwarded them to her "c/o Mr. O. W. Meysenburg, Lake Beulah Station, Wisconsin." (A Mrs. T. A. Meysenburg belonged to St. Louis's Wednesday Club.)

The cover letter was from Lady Janet Scammon Young in London, an admirer of *The Awakening*, who reported that the Dutch poet Maarten Maartens said the novel should be translated into Dutch, Scandinavian, and Russian. But Young was more interested in sharing her own opinions with the writer whose name she assumed was a pseudonym: "Kate Chopin."

"Evidently like all of us you believe *Edna* to have been worth saving—believe her to have been too noble to go to her death as she did," Young wrote—and then she suggested an alternative scenario for *The Awakening*:

> But suppose her husband had been conceived on higher lines? Suppose Dr. Mandelet had said other things to him—had said, for example: "Pontellier, like most men you fancy that because you have possessed your wife hundreds of times she necessarily long ago came to entire womanly self knowledge—that your embraces have as a matter of course aroused whatever of passion she may be endowed with. You are mistaken. She is just becoming conscious of sex—is just finding herself compelled to take account of masculinity *as such*. You cannot *arrest* that process whatever you do; you should not wish to do so. Assist this birth of your wife's deeper womanliness. Be tender, let her know that you see how *Robert*, *Arobin* affect her. Laugh with her over the evident influence of her womanhood over them."

Dr. Mandelet, Young wrote, should advise Léonce Pontellier to trust Edna, to leave her with Robert and with Arobin. If Edna's husband followed that advice, Young had Dr. Mandelet say, "in a year you will have a new wife with whom you will fall in love again; & you will be a new husband, manlier, more virile and impassioned with whom she will fall in love again."

Of course, she hastened to add, Lady Janet Scammon Young found loathesome the French maxim "The lover completes the wife"—but she did believe that "[n]o woman comes to her full womanly empire and charm" unless her "passional nature" has felt "the arousing power of more than one man." But a woman must distinguish between passion and love—and that, Young said, should be the subject of Kate Chopin's next novel.

> *You* can write it. You alone. You are free from decadency. Your
> mind and heart are healthful, free, clean, sympathetic. Give us a
> great hearted manly *man*—give us a great natured woman for his
> wife. Give us the awakening of her whole nature, let her go to the
> *utmost* short of *actual* adultery . . . not for the sake of scenes of
> passion, but that readers may be helped whose self respect is ship-
> wrecked or near it because *they* have gone far and are saying "I
> might as well go all the way."

Lady Janet told a long story of a woman she knew, attracted by other men
but not succumbing—and then apologized: "I have made a long and stupid
story of what *you* would have packed into one of your brief paragraphs—those
paragraphs which are like sunlight and like flowers."

She concluded with a plea to Kate Chopin to "write us a brave book which
will really interpret our sister women to themselves," and offered to help with
"publishers, translators, &c, &c."

Lady Janet also enclosed a letter from Dunrobin Thomson, whom she called
"the great consulting physician of England" and "the soundest critic since Matthew Arnold." Dr. Thomson had written an admiring letter about *The Awakening*, which he called "easily the book of the year." It reminded him, he said,
of *The Open Question* (by Elizabeth Robins, an American-born writer who
campaigned for woman suffrage in England)—"but how vastly superior in power,
ethic and art is this newer book."

The tragic ending of *The Awakening* was unavoidable, Dr. Thomson felt:

> the authoress took the world as it is, as all art must—and 'twas
> inevitable that poor dear *Edna*, being noble, and having Pontellier
> for husband, and Arobin for lover, and average women for friends,
> should die.

And "[t]rust an old doctor," he continued: Edna's "case" was not exceptional. The fault lay with "the accursed stupidity of men," who

> marry a girl, she becomes a mother. They imagine she has sounded
> the heights and depths of womanhood. Poor fools! She is not even
> awakened. She, on her part is a victim of the abominable prudish-
> ness which masquerades as modesty or virtue.

Taught that "passion is disgraceful," the doctor wrote, young women often
become confused about their feelings:

In so far as normally constituted womanhood *must* take account of *something* sexual, it is called "love." It was inevitable, therefore, that *Edna* should call her feeling for *Robert* love. It was as simply & purely passion as her feeling for *Arobin*. "Kate Chopin" would not admit that. Being (I assume) a woman, she too would reserve the word love for *Edna's* feeling for *Robert*.

But husbands should teach their wives to "distinguish between passion and love," Dr. Thomson wrote, so that any natural attraction a wife felt toward other men would not "touch her wife-life, her mother-life, her true self-hood." He had successfully counseled many husbands to do just that, he said.

As for *The Awakening*, the doctor concluded,

> This book has stirred me to the soul. *Edna* is like a personal friend. She is not impure. The art, the local colour, the distinctness of characterisation of even the minor personages are something wonderful.

Kate Chopin, pleased with the Londoners' letters, showed them to her friends, although she might very well have disagreed with them. *The Awakening* is not solely a criticism of Léonce Pontellier's failure to understand his wife—nor is the novel solely about Edna's sexual awakening. Edna's revolt is against the institution of marriage, and the confinement of her dreams, and she ultimately refuses everything: social calls, her husband's bounty, her children's demands for bonbons, her lovers' expectations that she be honorable or amoral, her friends' assumptions about her artistic commitment and her love for her children. In the last scene of the book, she throws off her clothes—her last confinement by the demands of others.

If Kate tried to answer the two Londoners, she might have had an unpleasant surprise: There is no evidence that they existed. Although Maarten Maartens was in London in October 1899, the two Londoners do not appear in any of the registries of physicians or gentry, and they may very well have been invented by Kate's friends to cheer her.

In fact, Florence Hayward—one of the "advanced literary ladies" who sneaked cigarettes with Kate Chopin in the early 1890s—was more often in London than in St. Louis. The author of stories in the *Century* and two books of essays, *Shreds and Patches* and *Two Points of the Compass*, Hayward often wrote back dispatches to the *Globe-Democrat* and the *Republic*. She corresponded with many famous people, among them Mark Twain, and had similar misadventures: She once read in the London newspapers that her sudden death from heart disease was deeply regretted—whereupon she wrote a column assuring friends and creditors that the rumors had been greatly exaggerated.

Hayward, a slim, bespectacled woman with a Confederate background and a brisk style, attended London dinners with writers and suffragists, and she was a self-styled "independent spinster" who often wrote appreciatively about independent women. According to the *Mirror* for November 30, Florence Hayward had "recently returned from abroad"—and could easily have arranged for the London letters to reach Kate Chopin in October. The handwriting is unlike Hayward's—in fact, the "Lady Janet Scammon Young" letter resembles Kate Chopin's handwriting more closely—but that, too, could be arranged.

Even the name "Janet Scammon Young" might have been contrived by someone like Florence Hayward, aware of names in the news. (Hayward and her friends liked to use joking pseudonyms in their correspondence.) In the 1880s, before Hayward became a virtual resident of London, one of the business leaders in Chicago was a man named J. Young Scammon. In 1894, one of the reading authors at the Western Association of Writers meeting was Emma Scammon, and in 1898 the President of the Missouri Federation of Women's Clubs was Laura E. Scammon.

Even if Kate Chopin suspected a ruse, she might have been heartened that someone cared enough to fabricate letters. She was also mentioned favorably in Billy Reedy's October 19 note on "St. Louis Writers": "The people who are always railing at St. Louis would do well to remember that, with all the city's faults, it has contributed some of the greatest American book successes of late years, in the work of Miss Murfree, Mrs. Kate Chopin, Mr. Jesse Lynch Williams and Mr. Winston Churchill, not to mention the continuously popular productions of Henry M. Blossom."

By November 8, Kate was back in St. Louis, where she wrote an apologetic letter to Richard B. Shepard of the Utah House of Representatives:

> My dear Mr Shepard
>
> Since receiving and answering your letters last July I have had a severe spell of illness and am only now looking about and gathering up the scattered threads of a rather monotonous existence. Kindly let me know if you have procured my books or if it is still your desire that I send them to you. . . .

Kate's "severe spell of illness" may have been depression: Her earlier letter to Shepard was dated August 24, a week after the ghost-story party that Madison Cawein attended. That was also the date of the *Congregationalist* review of *The Awakening*, calling her book "unwholesome in its influence." After that last review, Kate would have realized that only a few reviewers (among them Charles Deyo and *The New York Times* critic) had even understood what she was doing in her new novel.

But by November, Kate had recovered her spirits enough to write a short story, "Ti Démon." The title character, an Acadian farmer with a ragged pony, is known for "bovine mildness" and for doting on Marianne, his fiancée—but Ti Démon has a very suave friend, Aristides, who is envied by men and worshiped by "susceptible women." (As Kate no doubt intended, the coarse Ti Démon and the elegant Aristides are much like Bobinôt, the clumsy husband, and Alcée Laballière, the aristocratic planter, in "At the 'Cadian Ball" and "The Storm.")

Aristides corrupts the hapless Ti Démon, taking him to a gambling shack where he drinks too many toddies and forgets that Marianne is waiting for him. When he comes to his senses, hours later, he finds the debonair Aristides with Marianne. The outraged Ti Démon beats Aristides into unconsciousness, and leaves him battered and bleeding in the moonlight—after which Marianne refuses to marry "so murderous a madman."

"Ti Démon" was never published. The *Century* rejected it, and so did *The Atlantic*, admiring its "excellent craftsmanship" but regretting its being "so sombre . . . the sad note seems to us too much accented to let us keep the story for the Atlantic." The magazines, like the reviewers, still wanted the sunny, well-crafted stories of *Bayou Folk*.

Chopin wrote about her feelings in early November, in a piece called "A Reflection" that she never sent out for publication: It, too, would certainly have been too somber for the magazines. "A Reflection" was also a rare, blunt statement about her own emotions from a writer who was usually self-contained.

> Some people are born with a vital and responsive energy. It not only enables them to keep abreast of the times; it qualifies them to furnish in their own personality a good bit of the motive power to the mad pace. They are fortunate beings. They do not need to apprehend the significance of things. They do not grow weary nor miss step, nor do they fall out of rank and sink by the wayside to be left contemplating the moving procession.

In fleeing to Wisconsin, Kate had been escaping "the moving procession" of St. Louis life, including preparations for Lélia's debut—part of the inevitable procession from birth to courtship to marriage to motherhood, all prescribed for a young lady in society. In *The Awakening*, the hectoring Léonce Pontellier tells Edna that "we've got to observe *les convenances* if we ever expect to get on and keep up with the procession"—but on Edna's unhappy days, she sees life as a "grotesque pandemonium" of a procession: "humanity like worms struggling blindly toward inevitable annihilation."

It was that procession that Kate wanted to avoid, she wrote in "A Reflection":

> Ah! that moving procession that has left me by the road-side! Its
> fantastic colors are more brilliant and beautiful than the sun on the
> undulating waters. What matter if souls and bodies are falling be-
> neath the feet of the ever-pressing multitude! It moves with the
> majestic rhythm of the spheres. Its discordant clashes sweep upward
> in one harmonious tone that blends with the music of other worlds—
> to complete God's orchestra.

Being part of the procession was not for Kate Chopin, she knew.

> It is greater than the stars—that moving procession of human en-
> ergy; greater than the palpitating earth and the things growing thereon.
> Oh! I could weep at being left by the wayside; left with the grass
> and the clouds and a few dumb animals. True, I feel at home in
> the society of these symbols of life's immutability. In the procession
> I should feel the crushing feet, the clashing discords, the ruthless
> hands and stifling breath. I could not hear the rhythm of the march.

She concluded with a short note of defiance: "*Salve!* ye dumb hearts. Let us
be still and wait by the roadside."

In late November, however, Kate Chopin made some friendly overtures to
St. Louisans, possibly to smooth the way for Lélia's debut. The *Post-Dispatch*
on November 26 reported that Lélia Chopin had attended two important social
gatherings: a reception for the debutante Viola Robinson, and the year's first
Junior Club Ball, to which "all the prettiest and most popular debutantes of
this year" had been invited. Jean Chopin, always in demand for his dancing
ability, also attended both events.

The same issue of the *Post-Dispatch* included almost an entire page devoted
to "A St. Louis Woman Who Has Won Fame in Literature"—Kate Chopin.
There was a drawing of her first home, labeled "Old Residence on 8th St.
Between Chouteau and Gratiot, Where Mrs. Chopin Was Born"—an immense house with a long flight of stairs, galleries and pilasters—possibly an
artist's embellishment of the truth. Another illustration was more informative:
"Mrs. Chopin's Workroom From a Water Color Sketch By Her Son, Oscar
Chopin" (who spent much of his time painting, drawing and sketching in the
attic and had never been particularly interested in going to school). His watercolor sketch shows a well-appointed room, with well-stocked bookshelves on
either side of the fireplace, an intricate musical clock on the mantel, framed
pictures on the walls above a nude Venus and interesting bric-a-brac on the
shelves. In the armchair, leaning back and looking almost ghostly, is Kate
Chopin (who liked to write in her favorite chair, beside the grate fire).

"Mrs. Kate Chopin's novel 'The Awakening,' " the unsigned article began, "has not had the vogue of Winston Churchill's 'Richard Carvel,' but it has aroused more discussion and probably deeper interest. She is a St. Louisan"— and the *Post-Dispatch* retold her history. She had married Oscar Chopin and lived with him in New Orleans and Natchitoches Parish, where her children were born; she began writing after her husband's death. The article described Kate Chopin as a conscious literary artist:

> As a writer of fiction Mrs. Chopin appeals to the finer taste, sacrificing all else, even pecuniary profit, to her artistic conscience. Her style is clear, frank and terse, never a word too many or too few. In construction her power is especially noticeable because effects are produced without apparent effort. There is nothing of contrivance to be seen. Her art is not a cunning composition, but a living thing.
>
> Mrs. Chopin has been called a southern writer, but she appeals to the universal sense in a way not excelled by any other American author. She is not sectional or provincial, nor even national, which is to say that she is an artist, who is not bound by the idiosyncrasies of place, race, or creed.

In a sidebar, the *Post-Dispatch* summarized Kate Chopin's literary career:

> Mrs. Chopin's first venture in literature was a little story called "Euphrasie," which contained so much promise that she was encouraged to persevere, although the work was never offered for publication. The author's critical instinct was too sure to permit any work to go before the public which could not satisfy the requirements of the best art.

She published *At Fault* in 1890, the *Post-Dispatch* reported (Kate herself often gave 1891, incorrectly, as the date for her first novel). Then *Bayou Folk* "was immediately recognized as the work of a sure-handed artist," and A *Night in Acadie* was "marked by the same finish and classic quality."

> Mrs. Chopin's latest book, "The Awakening," was published a few months ago. The perfection of its art is acknowledged in this country and even more cordially in England, Maarten Maartens recommending its translation into the continental languages of Europe. . . . Another collection of short stories will appear next spring.

Kate Chopin also contributed an article to the *Post-Dispatch's* spread, and she began jauntily.

> On certain brisk, bright days I like to walk from my home, near Thirty-fourth street, down to the shopping district. After a few such experiments I begin to fancy that I have the walking habit. Doubtless I convey the same impression to acquaintances who see me from the car window "hot-footing" it down Olive street or Washington avenue. But in my sub-consciousness, as my friend Mrs. R—— would say, I know that I have not the walking habit.

Instead, Kate wrote, after publishing short stories in magazines, "I forthwith began to suspect I had the writing habit"—yet she denied, as always, her serious ambitions as a writer. She answered the typical questions authors are asked: "Now, where, when, why, what do you write?" In a Morris chair beside the window, on a lapboard, with paper and ink from the corner grocery store, she answered. As for when she wrote, she was tempted to say "any old time,"

> but that would lend a tone of levity to this bit of confidence, whose seriousness I want to keep intact if possible. So I shall say I write in the morning, when not too strongly drawn to struggle with the intricacies of a pattern, and in the afternoon, if the temptation to try a new furniture polish on an old table leg is not too powerful to be denied; sometimes at night, though as I grow older I am more and more inclined to believe that night was made for sleep.

"Why do I write?" Story-writing, according to Kate, was "the spontaneous expression of impressions gathered goodness knows where." But she did not write "everything that comes into my head. . . . I am completely at the mercy of unconscious selection." She was also at the mercy, she wrote, of newspaper editors who might put any kind of question "to a defenseless woman under the guise of flattery"—such as "How many children have you?"

> This form is subtle and greatly to be commended in dealing with women of shy and retiring propensities. A woman's reluctance to speak of her children has not yet been chronicled. I have a good many, but they'd be simply wild if I dragged them into this. I might say something of those who are at a safe distance—the idol of my soul in Kentucky; the light of my eye off in Colorado; the treasure of his mother's heart in Louisiana—but I mistrust the form of their displeasure, with poisoned candy going through the mails.

As for other questions, Kate wrote that she considered "Do you smoke cigarettes?" an "impertinent" inquiry,

> and I think most women will agree with me. Suppose I do smoke cigarettes? Am I going to tell it out in meeting? Suppose I don't smoke cigarettes. Am I going to admit such a reflection upon my artistic integrity, and thereby bring upon myself the contempt of the guild?

Smoking for women remained controversial: Although Kate's son Felix smoked, he disapproved of women who did. (Men were more apt to smoke cigars, as cigarettes were considered less masculine: When Robert in *The Awakening* smokes cigarettes, he explains that he cannot afford cigars.) In 1899, President William McKinley was taking a special cure for smoking, and it had already been rumored that tobacco would damage the lungs. But the main objection to women's smoking was that it was a male prerogative, and so rebellious, independent-minded women often smoked—including half the women writers in London, Florence Hayward reported. Although Kate Chopin was a thoughtful smoker who put her cigarette out if it offended anyone, she preferred not to discuss the subject: "In answering questions in which an editor believes his readers to be interested, the victim cannot take herself too seriously."

In fact, Kate took herself very seriously in the *Post-Dispatch* article, despite the occasional jocular tone:

> How hard it is for one's acquaintances and friends to realize that one's books are to be taken seriously, and that they are subject to the same laws which govern the existence of others' books! I have a son who is growing wroth over the question: "Where can I find your mother's books, or latest book?"
>
> "The very next time any one asks me that question," he exclaimed excitedly, "I am going to tell them to try the stock yards!"
>
> I hope he won't. He might thus offend a possible buyer. Politeness, besides being a virtue, is sometimes an art. I am often met with the same question, and I always try to be polite. "My latest book? Why, you will find it, no doubt, at the bookseller's or the libraries."
>
> "The libraries! Oh, no, they don't keep it." She hadn't thought of the bookseller's. It's real hard to think of everything! Sometimes I feel as if I should like to get a good, remunerative job to do the thinking for some people. This may sound conceited, but it isn't.

If I had space (I have plenty of time; time is my own, but space belongs to the *Post-Dispatch*), I should like to demonstrate satisfactorily that it is not conceited.

Kate's books were indeed available in St. Louis bookstores: *The Awakening* earned $102 in royalties for 1899, while *A Night in Acadie* earned $3.25 and *Bayou Folk* $3.12. The libraries also had her books: The Mercantile Library and the St. Louis Public Library had both purchased multiple copies of *The Awakening*.

But later generations took her comment, "The libraries! Oh, no, they don't keep it" to mean that *The Awakening* had been banned, withdrawn from library shelves—a legend that has persisted for more than half a century, due in part to Daniel Rankin's claim that it was "taken from circulation by order of the librarian of the St. Louis Mercantile Library." But Rankin offered no source and no proof.

Felix Chopin, interviewed fifty years after the fact, believed that *The Awakening* had been withdrawn. In a 1949 discussion with Charles van Ravenswaay, director of the Missouri Historical Society, Felix said that *The Awakening* had

> created a furor which hurt her deeply. In it, a woman permits a man to kiss her on the neck. Many newspapers and libraries treated the book as indecent. The Mercantile Library, among others, took it out of circulation, and Mother resigned her membership as a result. She was broken hearted at the reaction to the book.

Four years later, Felix, then an attorney in charge of the juvenile division of the St. Louis Domestic Relations Court, expanded his charge, saying that the book was "withdrawn from the Mercantile and St. Louis Public Libraries, later being restored to the Central Public Library in a 1906 reprint edition." He also repeated his belief that *The Awakening* shows a man kissing a woman on the neck—something that does not happen in the novel.

The only other contemporary claim that *The Awakening* was banned comes from the testimony of Clarence E. Miller, a nineteen-year-old desk assistant at the Mercantile Library in 1899 and later its head librarian. Sixty-two years later, Miller told Chopin's second biographer, Per Seyersted, that Kate Chopin had come in one day with a woman companion and, according to Seyersted,

> asked politely for her novel. She probably just wanted to prove to her friend that they had banned it, for when Miller told her it was taken from circulation, she simply walked away without anger.

Miller attributed the ban to the "bigoted people on the book-committee." But no one reported the ban at the time, even though Miller himself sometimes wrote for Reedy's *Mirror*.

Kate O'Flaherty had been a member of the Mercantile Library, the city's subscription library, since her eighteenth birthday, in 1868. Her father had been one of the library's first members, joining in 1853, and her brother Tom had been a member in 1866 and 1868.

Officials at both the Mercantile Library and the St. Louis Public Library were critical of fiction-reading. From the 1870s on, both institutions had tried to inspire their readers with "better tastes," despite the public appetite for popular literature. In May 1899, just after *The Awakening* was published, the public library's director, Frederick M. Crunden, told the *Republic* that library readers were now showing "decided signs of a healthy taste for clean literature." They were rejecting "the problem novel, dealing exclusively with sex," and "the novel-with-a-purpose, often written by a hysterical woman with some morbid theory to expound."

But years earlier, public library officials had noticed that the Mercantile's circulation soared when it stocked popular fiction—and so, grudgingly, in 1871, the Public Library had created the Collection of Duplicates, consisting of popular fiction. Borrowers paid five cents a week, so that tax monies would not be used to buy popular fiction. Once the books became less popular, they would be withdrawn or sold.

On April 26, 1899, the St. Louis Public Library bought three copies of *The Awakening* for its Collection of Duplicates; between April 29 and June 28, the Mercantile Library bought four copies. Both libraries obviously thought it an important book, worth keeping in stock—and there is no contemporary evidence that they ever removed *The Awakening* from their shelves.

Eventually books do die. At the Public Library, one copy of *The Awakening* was withdrawn in 1912 and another in 1914, obviously worn out; a third copy was reported missing in 1901, but a replacement copy was bought in 1906. In the Mercantile records, all four copies are marked "condemned" in the library's records—but *condemned* was the standard term for *de-accessioned*, most often meaning that the books were worn out. (More than 75 percent of the books acquired by the library in 1899–1900 are now marked "condemned," including C. M. Sheldon's Christian best-seller *In His Steps* and Charles Major's *When Knighthood Was in Flower*.) Moreover, the "condemned" designation could have been put in the Mercantile records at any point from 1899 to 1959, when the library's procedures changed.

Book bannings were not unknown in St. Louis, and books were sometimes withdrawn from library shelves. In the early 1900s, several anti-Catholic and anti-Irish books were removed from the public library: An Irish judge had objected to the portrayal of Irish peasants as drunken, stupid, and violent (in one of the banned books, Irish characters tore the udders from milk cows). There were also book restrictions, white bookplates decreeing, "This book shall not be loaned to minors," and there were some books kept shelved in the librarian's office.

Whenever books were censored, Billy Reedy would object vociferously: "If people are looking for filth they will find it," he always claimed. Likewise, Orrick Johns, who knew Kate Chopin, loathed censorship and berated those who wanted to suppress Theodore Dreiser's *Sister Carrie*, published a year after *The Awakening*.

But neither Reedy nor Johns reported that *The Awakening* was ever suppressed, removed from libraries, or banned. The St. Louis Public Library's annual reports for 1898–1901 say nothing about banning or removing *The Awakening*.

Kate Chopin was indeed ostracized by some friends (although Rankin's story that she was denied membership in a fine-arts club seems to be a myth). Kate still "had a lot of men friends," according to her niece, although *The Awakening* did create a minor scandal in some circles—and as late as the 1960s in New Orleans, Kate Chopin was talked about as something of a scandalous person.

But in 1899 in St. Louis, the verdict on Kate Chopin was not at all unanimous. If it had been, the respectable ladies of the Wednesday Club, part of St. Louis's social elite, would never have invited her for their Reciprocity Day, at which they put on a program for all the women's clubs of St. Louis. Moreover, they issued their invitation in November—six months after the scathing reviews of *The Awakening* had begun appearing in the St. Louis newspapers.

Clearly the women of the Wednesday Club intended to honor Kate Chopin, no matter what anyone else might say.

The Wednesday Club, which paid Kate fifteen dollars for her reading, had changed since she joined as a charter member in 1890 and resigned in 1892. No longer devoted solely to literary study, it was now a social reform group, with such projects as kindergartens, playgrounds, and bathing facilities for the poor. Its sections now studied education, tenement housing, parliamentary law, equalization of economic opportunity, and philanthropy as well as the arts.

The club's 250 members were "women of brains, of wealth, of influence and undisputed power," according to the *Republic*. One of the ten directors was Mrs. Charles LeRoy Moss, the Anna L. Moss who had sent Kate a glowing letter about *The Awakening*—and as chair of the arts section, she was undoubtedly active in inviting Kate to the Wednesday Club. Kate also knew many other members. The arts section's bibliographer was Mrs. Oscar Herf, who had assisted with Kate's paper on "Typical Forms of German Music" for the Wednesday Club in 1891. Mrs. John O'Fallon Delaney, whose "Dutch suppers" Kate's sons attended, was a member, and so were Charlotte Eliot and Kate's neighbor Mrs. Hull, who had given a paper on Assyria for a November meeting.

On November 29, Kate appeared for an "Afternoon with St. Louis Authors" at the Wednesday Club's cozy rooms in the Y.M.C.A. building. (The rooms' walls were olive-tinted, and covered with "numerous fine etchings and foreign photographs," according to a society reporter.) Each club belonging to the Missouri Federated Women's Clubs was permitted to send ten to twenty delegates, and 397 guests attended the meeting. It was the largest audience Kate Chopin had ever had for a reading.

The program, also called "An Hour with St. Louis Authors," offered a wealth of songs and readings:

> "The Serenade" (from "Three Freshmen")
> "The Artists & Scientists' Use of Words"—Mrs. Robert T. Chase
> "Poems"—Mr. R. E. Lee Gibson
> Songs—words by Mrs. Kate Chopin, music by Mr. William Schuyler
> Verses: "The King of the Fairy Gold" by Miss Ruth Sterling, music by William Schuyler, Miss Ione Huse
> "The Peacock Lea"—Miss Florence Hayward
> "Ti Démon"—Mrs. Kate Chopin
> Mr. Winston Churchill

The Kate Chopin songs were Schuyler's musical settings for the poem Kate had published in the *Century* ("In Spring," also called "I opened all the portals wide"), together with two unpublished poems: "The Song Everlasting" and "You and I." The first two were art songs, praising spring and birds and flowers—but "You and I," which Kate had written before June 1893, was more personal. At the time, much closer to her Louisiana past, she could have been remembering Oscar, or Albert Sampite—but now, to the Wednesday Club, her poem would have seemed just romantic, and nostalgic:

> How many years since we walked, you and I,
> Under the stars and the April sky;
> You were young then, I was not older;
> Then you were shy, nor was I bolder.
> Was it love did we feel? was it life did we live?
> It was springtime indeed, but can springtime give
> The fullness of life and of love? Completest
> When living and loving and roses are sweetest!
> Shall we walk together once more, you and I,
> Under the stars and the summer sky?

The Wednesday Club evidently forgave Kate Chopin—or never blamed her—for the "fullness of life and of love" she depicted in *The Awakening*. The *Post-Dispatch*, similarly, praised Kate's outfit ("black satin with white lace trimmings, jetted front and blue velvet toque") and the tale she chose to read: a "touching little story of creole life."

The following spring, Florence Hayward would organize a group of women to snub and boycott the actress Lillie Langtry for her adulterous life—but she saw no reason to do the same to Kate Chopin, who had written about an adulterous woman. Hayward gladly shared the platform with her friend at the Wednesday Club, and over the following months, Hayward also attended the debutante parties at which Lélia Chopin was introduced to St. Louis society.

"Several entertainments are to be given in honor of Miss Lelia Chopin, who is one of this season's debutantes," the *Mirror* announced, one day after Kate's appearance at the Wednesday Club. Lélia, the *Mirror* noted, was "the only daughter of Mrs. Kate Chopin, who stands now among the first writers of the day."

Lélia's first presentation to society took place a week later, on Wednesday afternoon, December 6, at a tea given by the grandest of Kate's relatives: Mrs. Charles Faris, the former Clémence Benoist. Charles Faris was Kate's uncle; his wife Clémence, five years younger than Kate, was the daughter of the financier Louis A. Benoist and Sarah Wilson Benoist, at whose Oakland estate Kate had met Oscar Chopin some thirty years earlier. (By the 1890s, the Benoists had sold Oakland to the philanthropist Robert Brookings.) Clémence Benoist Faris had one eccentricity: She always wore black in the winter but only white in the summer (a habit Kate used for Madame Lebrun in *The Awakening*). Her sponsorship guaranteed that Lélia would be well received. Clearly Kate Chopin's relatives were untroubled by her novel: There was no family ostracism.

After Christmas, Lélia was constantly busy. According to society columns, she was a guest at teas given by Mrs. John O'Fallon Delaney ("an exceedingly pleasant and fashionable affair") and by Miss Elsie Ford ("a very pretty and fashionable affair"). She danced and played party games at Mrs. Sanford's Cotillion ("a delightful little affair"). She was a "Maid of Honor" at the Flower Pageant and ball hosted by the St. Louis Daughters of the Confederacy, where the reception committee included Charles and Clémence Benoist Faris; she was in the audience for a musicale arranged by Albert Chauvenet Wegman of St. Louis, at his studio in the Conservatorium. (Other guests included Mr. and Mrs. George Johns, Florence Hayward, and Billy Reedy.) In March, Lélia also had a house guest, Edna Tidball.

But the largest and most extravagant event the young debutante attended was the University Club reception in honor of the British actors Ellen Terry and Henry Irving. The two hundred to three hundred women who attended were said to be "distinctly representative of St. Louis's best people," dressed in "the handsomest" clothes seen that season for an afternoon gathering. The guests included Florence Hayward—but not Kate Chopin.

As a young belle herself, three decades earlier, Kate had complained in her diary about the "general spreeing" required of her: "I am diametrically opposed to parties and balls," she had written, "and yet when I broach the subject— they either laugh at me—imagining that I wish to perpetrate a joke; or look very serious, shake their heads and tell me not to encourage such silly notions." With Lélia's debut, Kate may have decided to follow her own "silly notions" at last and skip the spreeing.

Despite the negative reviews of *The Awakening*, Kate Chopin's national reputation as a writer did not appear to be suffering: *Youth's Companion* included "A Little Country Girl" in its preview advertisement for "The Best of Reading for Girls," a list of stories forthcoming in 1900. Earlier Chopin had been listed as one of the *Youth's Companion's* eminent "Story Tellers," along with Hamlin Garland and Octave Thanet—and when she began writing again in 1900, she produced the kind of story that *Youth's Companion* would accept.

On January 23, Kate wrote "Alexandre's Wonderful Experience," about a bedraggled New Orleans orphan who works in an antique store and dreams of riches and success. The plot is a Louisiana local-color version of a Horatio Alger story: Alexandre introduces a poor but genteel lady to a rich doctor, and when they marry, they take Alexandre to live on their plantation—in "a strange, delicious, beautiful dream come true!"

Youth's Companion accepted "Alexandre's Wonderful Experience," and sent Kate fifty dollars.

On February 8, her fiftieth birthday, Kate wrote "The Gentleman from New Orleans," about a quarreling Louisiana couple, Mr. and Mrs. Buddie Bénoîte (whose name would be seen as a reflection on her Cloutierville and St. Louis relatives, the Benoists). Buddie is blustery; his wife, Kate wrote wryly, shows "a certain lack of self assertion which her husband regarded as the perfection of womanliness." When the Bénoîtes go off to a barbecue, their energetic young housekeeper Sophronie flies around cleaning and sewing and opening and closing—until an unknown and very taciturn gentleman arrives. He turns out not to be the expected commercial traveler from New Orleans, but Mrs. Buddie's long-estranged father, and Sophronie is most pleased with her skills at household management.

Youth's Companion accepted "The Gentleman from New Orleans," and sent Kate forty dollars.

On February 9, Kate did attend a social event: an "entertainment" given by Mrs. Joseph Walthew of 4363 Laclede Avenue, in honor of a Mrs. Calhoun. The hostess and guest of honor were both well-dressed, handsome women, according to the newspaper report, and the house was filled with flowers.

Six days later, Kate sent "A December Day in Dixie" to *Youth's Companion*, with an unusually self-deprecating note:

> I can't imagine that you will care for this little sketch, or impression of one snowy day last winter when I arrived in Natchitoches, but I send it anyway, hoping that you might. The impression of that snowy day in the old Southern town and the snow in the forest and upon the cotton fields was fantastic and beautiful and I cannot forget it.

"A December Day in Dixie" had the spirit of *Bayou Folk*: Kate described a saloon keeper, his "piggish little" wife, and the "delicious prattle of Cadian French" when she spoke to their baby, who had recently survived a fall into an unused cistern. "I wondered how he had lived through those two hours of suffering and terror," Kate wrote. "But the little children's world is so unreal, that no doubt it is often difficult for them to distinguish between the life of the imagination and of reality."

She described, lovingly, the dazzling white, soft snow she could see from the Natchitoches train—a beauty utterly lost on her companion, a gentleman who complained about the price of cotton and said the planters might as well "turn half the land into pasture and start raising cattle" (which was exactly what Lamy Chopin had done). The snow was all gone by the next day, when Kate walked across a bridge where "a dear old lady was standing in her dear old doorway waiting for me."

In March, *Youth's Companion* accepted "A December Day in Dixie," and paid Kate ten dollars. But the magazine never published the sketch—nor did it publish "A Little Country Girl," "Alexandre's Wonderful Experience," or "The Gentleman from New Orleans," all accepted between March 1899 and March 1900. *Youth's Companion* had bought stories from Kate Chopin before and not published them—but it was very unusual for a magazine to pay $150 in a year for stories it did not use.

In February 1900, Kate also received some crushing news: Herbert S. Stone & Company decided not to publish her third short-story collection, *A Vocation and a Voice*. The firm was cutting back on its list, and not necessarily making a judgment on Kate Chopin's writing—but she may not have known that.

She did not even try to find another publisher for the collection. Later, she sent out individual stories: "An Egyptian Cigarette" and "The White Eagle" to

Vogue; "The Godmother" and "A Vocation and a Voice" to Reedy's Mirror—and thirteen of the twenty-two stories had already been published, eight of them in Vogue.

(According to Rankin, A Vocation and a Voice was to contain "A Vocation and a Voice," "Elizabeth Stock's One Story," "Two Portraits," "An Idle Fellow," "A Mental Suggestion," "An Egyptian Cigarette," "The White Eagle," "The Dream of an Hour," "Two Summers and Two Souls," "Sketches (The Night Came Slowly, and Juanita)," "The Unexpected," "Her Letters," "The Kiss," "Suzette," "The Falling in Love of Fedora," "The Recovery," "The Blind Man," "A Morning Walk," "Lilacs," "Ti Démon," and "The Godmother.")

Another story collection would have meant national reviews, and prestige, and money that Kate could use: In 1900, she collected a total of $49.77 in royalties from Bayou Folk, A Night in Acadie, and The Awakening.

After The Awakening, Kate Chopin continued writing, slowly—but only one story truly seemed to inspire her: the tale of a girl who escapes the common procession.

Chapter 24

IN DECLINE AND MELANCHOLY

AS 1900 BEGAN, KATE CHO-
pin seemed permanently slowed by the harsh reactions to *The Awakening*. Her
one cheerful story, "Charlie," showed the rompings of high-spirited young
women: Women, especially in the Wednesday Club, had supported her vision
and approved her work. But in 1900, in her writings and her life, Kate was
feeling a great sorrow.

The 1900 census lists Kate Chopin's occupation as "capitalist"—an ironic
designation for one who just scraped along on real estate earnings. The census
also lists her birthdate as February 1849—making her two years older than her
usually listed age, and a year older than her actual one. Her children's birthdates are all listed correctly, and Kate may just have given up a lifelong habit
of fibbing about her age.

According to the census, the Chopin household at 3317 Morgan Street in-
cluded Kate and four of her children: Jean (whose occupation is "Commercial
Trav. El. S."), Oscar ("Artist"), Felix ("Student [Law]"), and Lélia, for whom
no occupation is listed. (According to the city directory, Jean worked as "trav.
Western Electrical Supply Co.") There was also a servant, Annie Porter, a
thirty-year-old black woman whose parents were from Kentucky and Missouri.
Annie Porter had been born in April 1870, just two months before Kate
O'Flaherty married Oscar Chopin.

George and Fred Chopin were living elsewhere. George, now a physician,
was boarding in a house at 8116 North Broadway—but Fred had found life
difficult since he stopped being one of the "spoiled darlings" of Battery A. First

he had gone back to living in his mother's home, while working as a salesman, but he was restless. By 1900, Fred had moved to William L. Thompson's boardinghouse at 510 Washington Avenue, where the other lodgers included three deputy sheriffs. Fred was also switching jobs frequently: The 1900 census calls him an insurance agent, but the city directory lists him as a Geisel Manufacturing Company clerk.

Kate's aunt Amanda McAllister still lived at 1125 St. Ange Avenue, with her son Andrew, a broker, and in 1900 Kate used the name Amanda in one of her last short stories.

An unusual news item may have spurred Kate Chopin to write "Charlie," the story of a tomboy sometimes mistaken for a young man. On November 26, 1899, the day that the *Post-Dispatch* published its full-page tribute to Kate, the newspaper's front page carried a shocking revelation about one Ellis Glenn, a "handsome beau of southern Illinois"—who turned out to be a woman.

A tall and dashing fellow with "curly jet black hair and heavy mustache," Ellis Glenn was the wealthiest and most fashionable young man in his corner of Illinois. He had been engaged to a young woman in Hillsboro, the newspaper reported, but had disappeared three days before the wedding. When he reappeared, he was arrested for forgery, but at the prison refused a bath, "by reason of cramps"—whereupon Glenn's true sex was discovered.

The *Post-Dispatch* claimed that such a case had never been heard of—but women in men's clothes were not unknown. Mary Walker had been a Civil War surgeon; George Sand had been notorious in France for her cigars and men's clothes—and Kate Chopin, early in her writing career, had written of "The Maid of St. Phillippe," the hunter Marianne with her buckskin leggings, gun slung across her shoulder, and long, untrammeled stride. Men's clothes meant mobility and freedom from restriction—and so Kate characterized them in her long story "Charlie," which she wrote in April of 1900.

Like Phanor Breazeale, the father in "Charlie" has many daughters (seven). All are well-behaved except Charlotte ("Charlie"), who wears her dark hair short and close-cropped, and dresses in "a costume of her own devising, something between bloomers and a divided skirt which she called her 'trouserlets.' " (Possibly an outfit like that was the "eccentric clothing" worn by Kate Chopin and her friends. Such clothes were not unusual for schoolgirls, who wore bloomers for basketball.) For her widowed father, Charlie makes an ideal son: riding, shooting, fishing, and bragging—until she wounds a young gentleman during target practice, and is sent to New Orleans to learn to be a lady. (Her sister Amanda, unsympathetic, says, "Charlie's a goose"—and by choosing the name Amanda, Kate may have been making a belated comment on the relationship between her aunt and her mother.)

In New Orleans, Charlie's aunt Clementine plans to teach her all about calling and dining and operas and dress fittings. (The name Clementine—so close to that of Clémence Benoist Faris—may be Kate's comment about her powerful aunt.) Charlie also attends a boarding school, where her teachers pronounce her impossible, but her poems send her classmates into swoons of delight.

Then, suddenly, Charlie is summoned home: Her father has lost his right arm in a terrible accident. She resumes her trouserlets, rides her big black horse again, and takes over the plantation—and although it is implied that she'll eventually marry a neighbor, the story ends with Charlie at her ailing father's bedside, devoting herself to him.

Despite its lively pictures of schoolgirl life, "Charlie" was nevertheless a retreat for Kate Chopin, into material from her Sacred Heart past. Unlike Edna Pontellier, Charlie is still young and malleable, a schoolgirl whose rebellious behavior can be seen as a phase. Kate sent "Charlie" to the most conventional magazine that still accepted her work—*Youth's Companion*—but it was rejected. After the *Century* also said no, she put "Charlie" away, a month after writing it, and never sent it out again.

There was sadness, too, during the month that Kate wrote "Charlie": Her cousin Nina McAllister died. Nina, Aunt Amanda's daughter, had been Kate's younger Sacred Heart schoolmate and the annoying companion on their adolescent trip to New Orleans thirty-one years earlier. Nina was buried April 17 in Calvary Cemetery, and her death left her mother distraught.

A month later, Kate wrote "The White Eagle," the sad story of a little girl who loves to sit under the sheltering wings of a wise-looking cast-iron bird. As an adult, she still takes the bird with her, the last remnant of her lost estate: Eventually he is crowded into a corner of her poor and narrow room. In the delirium at the end of her life, she imagines that the eagle is pecking at her bosom—and after she is buried, the eagle stands like a tombstone on her grave, still gazing "with an expression which in a human being would pass for wisdom."

Only one magazine would be interested in a story so somber (and so reminiscent of Flaubert's "*Un Coeur simple*," the story of a servant who loves her parrot above all other creatures). *Vogue* accepted "The White Eagle" and published it on July 12. It proved to be Kate's last story in *Vogue*.

During the summer of 1900, Kate Chopin seemed to be looking backward, in loneliness and nostalgia. Often, especially in "The Story of an Hour" and *The Awakening*, she had presented solitude as a delectable state for women—but "Alone," a four-stanza poem that she wrote in July, was a lament.

I see the sights that I saw in the Sight
Of Love's dawn-light in its morning's glow;
I dream the dreams that I dreamt in The Dream
When hopes ran high over fears lain low:
I live the life that I lived in The Life
Of our living Love in the Long Ago.

She ended with a sort of hope:

Sweet are the hopes that hope in The Hope
That shows through the Future's Door ajar:
Bright is the light that lightens The Light
That shines from my heart to *you* afar:
Lovely the Life that shall live in The Life
When the Distance no longer my Kisses bar.

The poem seems to be a longing for reunion through death—and just a month later, on August 24, Kitty Garesché's fiftieth birthday, Kate wrote another poem looking both to the past and to death:

To the Friend of My Youth: To Kitty

It is not all of life
To cling together while the years glide past.
It is not all of love
To walk with clasped hands from first to last.
That mystic garland which the spring did twine
Of scented lilac and the new-blown rose,
Faster than chains will hold my soul to thine
Thro' joy, and grief, thro' life—unto its close.

"To the Friend of My Youth: To Kitty" is apparently the last poem that Kate Chopin wrote.

The Chopin children continued in the social round. In December 1900, Lélia, George, and Jean attended a reception for a Parisian visitor, given by Caroline Newman, at whose wedding Lélia would be a bridesmaid several years later. In January 1901, Lélia and Fred attended the new assembly ball—but their mother does not appear in any party lists during the winter. She may have been in Louisiana or New York; she was definitely in seclusion. She may have had financial worries as well: On November 10, she sold some Natchitoches Parish land to her brother-in-law Lamy.

Still, Kate Chopin did gain one new national recognition, as she was included in the first edition of *Who's Who in America*:

> CHOPIN, Kate, author; *b.* (O'Flaherty) St. Louis, Feb. 8, 1851; grad. Sacred Heart Convent, St. Louis, 1868; *m.* 1870, Oscar Chopin, New Orleans, cotton factor (now deceased). Lived in La. 14 years; now in St. Louis. *Author:* At Fault, 1891 A7; Bayou Folk, 1894 H5; A Night in Acadie, 1897 W6; The Awakening, 1899 S1; etc. *Address:* St. Louis.

St. Louis readers were also still interested in Kate Chopin. In December 1900, the *Republic* gave her a literary forum, previewed on December 8 under a very large headline:

WHAT BOOKS SHALL I BUY JUST NOW?

with the promise that the question would be answered in a "graphic and interesting" article about the literary West by "a St. Louis woman who has won a distinct place as a member of this same Western literary guild MRS. KATE CHOPIN. . . ."

The *Republic*, still owned by Kate's lifelong friends the Knapps, gave her the bottom half of the front page of their "book number," a special supplement for December 9, 1900. (Some years later, Florence Hayward claimed that her own piece in the book number, "The Way We Read," had got her fired. It was a criticism of readers who made a "fetich of reading," and of authors who hid their subversive theories in novels. Both writers and readers, Hayward concluded, were "a perverting lot.")

For the *Republic*, Kate Chopin was still among the most important of local authors, and an article by Harrison Clark on "Writers and Books of Note that Have Come Out of St. Louis" featured her prominently, though inaccurately. Clark listed *A Night in Acadie* as Chopin's first, rather than her third, book, and claimed that she had published *At Fault* and *Bayou Folk* between *A Night in Acadie* and *The Awakening*. Clark described Kate Chopin's writing habits as others had:

> Mrs. Chopin writes fluently, rapidly, and with practically no revision. She declares it is either "easy to write, or utterly impossible," and therefore she has no fixed plan except a general one of working in the morning.

For a piece supposed to celebrate St. Louis writers, Harrison Clark was unusually harsh about _The Awakening_:

> This work is pretentious, and is more nearly what is known as a "problem novel" than any other St. Louis book. It has to deal with the heart and the wiles of a woman, and ends tragically. There has been much severe criticism of this book—not so much of the workmanship as of the story; but Mrs. Chopin says she does not mind that.

Still, Kate Chopin minded enough to have the _Republic_ portray her as a very conventional woman: not part of the "perverting lot" of writers Florence Hayward described, and not part of the lofty immoral _fin-de-siècle_ world that ordinary St. Louisans feared. Kate appeared in the _Republic_ book number as a mother, a businesswoman, and a reader who enjoyed uncontroversial books.

The front-page "Portrait of Mrs. Kate Chopin. From a Drawing Made By Her Son, Mr. Oscar C. Chopin, A St. Louis Art Student" was very different from her earlier pictures, in which she wore evening gowns, laces, and ruffles, and often looked ethereal. Oscar Chopin drew his mother as a brisk businesswoman in a business suit with notched lapels, her hair pinned in a neat topknot. She also wears a pince-nez (it is the only picture of her with spectacles). Instead of gazing languidly, Kate Chopin in the 1900 _Republic_ is working: with large, capable-looking hands, she holds up one sheet of paper and reads another.

It was a picture calculated to please conservative people—and that may have been Kate and young Oscar's intent, to portray her as an ordinary, even slightly dowdy, businesswoman, no follower of decadent aesthetic trends. In the _Republic_ portrait, she looks like a very moral, straitlaced person.

Her article is straitlaced, too: "Development of the Literary West," which was "Written for the Sunday Republic by Mrs. Kate Chopin," takes most of three columns and contains few surprises and little humor. (Probably displeased with the article herself, Kate did not keep a clipping among her manuscripts, as she did with her other published works.) She was paid twelve dollars for the article—the last time she was paid for her opinions.

Kate began with a question: "What would Father De Smet with his Indian sketches have thought of Bret Harte and his 'Luck of Roaring Camp'?" Father De Smet, a Jesuit missionary and author of _Western Missions and Missionaries_ (1863) and _New Indian Sketches_ (1865), was one of St. Louis's most beloved early citizens, especially in the old French community. Kate appealed to civic pride by mentioning him first, and by claiming to value him over the controversial Harte.

That was the beginning—that "Luck of Roaring Camp"—so we have all come to acknowledge. It was the first resounding note. It reached across the continent and startled the Academists on the Atlantic Coast, that is to say, in Boston. They opened their eyes and ears at the sound and awoke to the fact that there might some day be a literary West. Something different from the East, of course, and alien, but to be taken seriously, to be observed and considered.

Personally, I like to give precedence to our own well-beloved Father De Smet and his Indian sketches. The little volume with its quaint complimentary offering on the fly-leaf, no doubt, reposes, musty, on many a library shelf in St. Louis, libraries that perhaps ceased to grow when St. Louis began to spread.

The dear old man spoke the English language indifferently well, but he wrote with simplicity and directness. Pinning his faith in God and General Harney, he invaded the great unknown West and conquered it with the abundance of his love. The red man was his most noble friend. Savage tribes became his "dear spiritual children." Hell's Gate Fork and Bitter Root Valley held no terrors for him. The mountains and the great plains were his inheritance. Of all this he tells, and when one has read there is left upon the mind a well-traced picture of the early West, by no means devoid of atmosphere and color.

But the West of to-day is by [sic] no longer the West of Father De Smet and Bret Harte. The red man is vanishing. The buffalo has become a zoological specimen. Trails of the prairie schooner are obliterated. Mining camps are not so very far from the police station, and the bucking broncho is colliding with the automobile.

Chopin was also describing the changes in her lifetime. A year before she was born, her mother's young uncle F. A. Charleville had gone out to California in a covered wagon, with his wife, Gabrielle, to seek his fortune. Kate had grown up riding in horse-drawn carriages and mule cars, and in Cloutierville she had promenaded on her horse in the afternoons, sidesaddle in her best finery. But the automobile was now replacing the romance and danger of travel with efficiency and speed—and a Cloutierville cousin, another F. A. Charleville, would be the first in town to own a car.

Still, Kate Chopin was concerned with literature, not nostalgia—and while she gave the impression of possessing some delicate sensibilities, she also appreciated American regionalist writers:

There is an intensely interesting story developing in the West. Hundreds of men and women, keen with artistic perception, are telling it and telling it well. There is sometimes a two [sic] obvious lack of reserve in their work, often tawdriness, but there is always vigor. Bret Harte has naturally had his followers, but it is pleasing to note that the great majority of Western writers have observed with their own eyes and have chronicled their individual impressions.

What pleasure have we not felt, for instance, in reading the stories—so genuine—of Mary Hallock Foote? Hers is excellent work, with a fine literary quality, damaged somewhat by a too conventional romanticism. But she knows her territory and leaves in the mind of the reader no inclination to question.

Then there is Ambrose Bierce away off in California. He, too, is a product of the West, but he has that peculiar faculty or privilege of genius which ignores subservience. He acknowledges no debt and pays no tribute. His "Soldiers and Civilians" might be called an eccentricity of genius. It is certainly a marvelous flash of the horrors of the possible. Depicting not so much what we are familiar with as what might be, hence, the shudder. His originality defies imitation.

Another Western writer of note is Owen Wister, in whose work there is a suggestion of the spectacular. This effect may be partly due to the profuse illustrations, which usually accompany it. But he gives the impression of a stagy fellow with an eye on his audience in the East. Yet his stories are greatly liked, and this may be a squeamish opinion, not wholly just.

Sincerity, on the other hand, strongly marks the work of Octave Thanet. One almost feels that she and A. B. Frost were created for each other, so graphically does he catch the spirit of her inspirations.

Her heart is essentially with the plain, everyday people. We meet her characters everywhere—crowding the department stores on bargain days, hurrying with bundles through the streets; thronging the lodge meetings and church sociables. She must walk about our Middle Western towns with her mental notebook open, chuckling to herself. But how she gets A. B. Frost to see exactly what she sees is the mystery.

Then Kate named a writer whose work had been criticized for "coarseness." In an apparent effort to please, she claimed to agree with the majority view:

> Along with Bret Harte, the man, it seems to me, who most subtly reflects the western spirit, is Hamlin Garland. At his worst, Hamlin Garland has been guilty of inexcusable crudities in handling men and women. At his best, he has not been surpassed in his field. His best, to my mind, is represented by the long short-story entitled "In The Land of the Straddle-Bug," published several years ago in the Chap Book. Nowhere, except in Tolstoi's "Master and Man," and perhaps Mary Wilkins's "A Solitary," has any recent writer so vividly portrayed an atmospheric condition. The march, the sweep of the season on the Northern prairies, as he depicts it, is like a noble epic. The dreariness, the sinister, gray gatherings of clouds; the bleak rainfall; the still and killing cold and great winding sheets of snow; the flaming splendors of the sun, could only have been told by one whose soul is close to nature. He believes in himself and follows his own light. May he never be tempted to follow false gods.

But Kate Chopin omitted what was most like her own writing in Garland's "The Land of the Straddle-Bug" (the name for three boards nailed together to stake a claim). Garland's story, published in 1894–95, is a tale of cold and hungry settlers on the northern prairies—but it is also a story of adultery. The wife, Blanche, a strong and handsome woman ground down by the tedium of prairie life and her husband's lack of human warmth, falls into an affair with Rivers, a merry-eyed and popular land agent. They spend long hours together, stranded by a sudden fierce thunderstorm—much like Kate Chopin's description, in "The Storm," of stranded former lovers who find one another irresistible.

But Chopin's "The Storm" has far more sensuality than Garland's "The Land of the Straddle-Bug." Garland's Blanche becomes pregnant after only a few hints of intimacy: Garland did not dare write a scene of sexual consummation, as Chopin did in "The Storm." Nor did Garland describe a bountifully pregnant woman, as Chopin did with Madame Ratignolle in *The Awakening*—although both stories take place over a period of nine months and end with thoughts of motherhood, the smell of flowers, and the humming of bees.

When Kate Chopin praised "The Land of the Straddle-Bug" in the *Republic*, she limited herself to discussing Garland as a local colorist—just as critics preferred her as a local-color writer, the author of *Bayou Folk*. She also looked askance at city writers:

Chicago has recently developed, among many writers of talent, a
group of young men whose mental vision seems to be impaired by
the city's skyscrapers, and who are apparently fascinated by the hideous complexities of life which so phenomenal and abnormal a
growth has produced. Their work has its place in the great mosaic
word-picture of the West, but it makes unpleasant reading.

(Chopin would not yet have read Theodore Dreiser's *Sister Carrie:* Billy Reedy
received his copy in late December 1900, and reviewed it enthusiastically in
early January 1901.)

For her local readership, Kate Chopin made a point of praising one St.
Louis writer, the young author of the historical novel *Richard Carvel.*

Here, at home, Winston Churchill has had marvelous success with
his historical romance. He is said to be engaged upon a novel depicting life in St. Louis during the days of Lincoln and Grant. This
is good news. It is not well to let the age slip by unchronicled, and
Winston Churchill, of all young writers, seems best fitted to tell
the story of so important an epoch in the West.

Then, in her last paragraph, Chopin mentioned, with respect, the kinds of
writers she had ridiculed in "The Western Association of Writers," six years
earlier—but her final words could still be read as ironic.

After all, where are we to draw the line? May we not claim Mrs.
Catherwood of the Northwest? James Whitcomb Riley and the whole
State of Indiana that abounds in novelists and minor poets? Will
the South cede to us Madison Cawein, John Fox or the incomparable James Lane Allen? Perhaps we are claiming too much, but
draw the line ever so taut and we still have enough to be proud of
if it were only Mark Twain. The West will surely continue to develop along the lines of a natural and wholesome growth, as yet
unimpaired by intellectual complications.

In "Development of the Literary West" Kate Chopin kept, for the most part,
to a conventional set of literary opinions: praising regionalists, criticizing crudities. But most of the stories she mentioned by name—Wilkins's "A Solitary,"
Garland's "In the Land of the Straddle-Bug," even Harte's "The Luck of Roaring Camp"—were stories of silence, deprivation, hunger, loneliness, and cold.
Most of the protagonists were men, too: In "The Luck of Roaring Camp," the
prostitute Cherokee Sal gives birth and immediately dies. Kate was erasing from

hei public persona most vestiges of interest in women's lives, in comfort, in physical pleasures.

She was making herself into a public puritan.

The new century officially began in 1901, after an evening of fireworks and public celebrations. But Kate Chopin did no writing, or no writing that she kept, for the first nine months of the year—until a friend's admiration briefly inspired her.

On October 10, R. E. Lee Gibson sent Kate a copy of his newly published *Sonnets and Lyrics*, autographed "To Mrs. Kate Chopin, Author, with admiration for her delightful stories, from her friend, R. E. Lee Gibson."

She wrote back on October 13 that his poems showed "a fine, fine spirit and I am proud to know you. What a speaking likeness! Do come when you can and let us talk them over. Mr. Deyo and I have enjoyed reading some of the sonnets together." Kate also praised Gibson to the *Hesperian* editor, Alexander DeMenil, who wrote to Gibson a month later:

> I vastly admire your endurance and determination in keeping on publishing your books in this utilitarian and illiterate town. . . . I saw an old playmate of my happier days yesterday. She speaks very highly of you. I mean Kate Chopin.

Gibson, meanwhile, had paid Kate Chopin a poet's ultimate tribute: His new book included a sonnet about her—although it was not about *The Awakening*:

"Bayou Folk"
To the Author of "Bayou Folk"

> Madam, your work is destined to receive
> Still wider recognition; in these days,
> Among the writers whom we justly praise,
> Few pens such triumphs as your own achieve.
> Witness the stories which you richly weave
> Of Creole life, wherein your art portrays
> Real men and women, and in charming ways,
> Constrains us with them to rejoice or grieve.
> This book of yours which I have read to-night
> Pleases me much: my words but feebly tell
> How I have followed with intense delight
> The fortunes that these bayou folk befell;
> The pen most truly is a thing of might
> In hands like yours that wield its power so well.

By the time Gibson's sonnet appeared, Kate Chopin was no longer writing "of Creole life . . . in charming ways," but Gibson's tribute seems to have lifted her spirits. Three days after she wrote to him, she resumed short-story writing—for the first time since "The White Eagle," nearly a year and a half earlier.

With a burst of energy, as in the early 1890s when inspiration just flowed, Kate produced three children's stories in three days, October 16, 17, and 18: "Millie's First Party," "The Wood-Choppers," and "Toots' Nurses." *Youth's Companion* accepted the first two, but rejected "Toots' Nurses," as did the *Mirror*. Kate received seventy dollars for the two, but only "The Wood-Choppers," a cheerfully sentimental story in the *Bayou Folk* vein, was ever published in *Youth's Companion*.

Evidently she lost interest in both unpublished stories: She had kept copies of such unpublished adult stories as "Elizabeth Stock's One Story" and "The Storm," but the manuscripts of both "Toots' Nurses" and "Millie's First Party" are lost.

In January 1902, Kate Chopin managed to produce one more cheerful tale: "Polly's Opportunity," about a young St. Louis bookkeeper who is waiting for her fiancé to get a new job "when Ferguson opens up in St. Jo." Polly's uncle sends her a hundred dollars, with instructions to spend it all on herself—and that weekend, her fiancé brings good news: Ferguson has at last opened, and they can be married. At the story's end, Polly's boss has sent a brass teakettle as a wedding present, "And he sent it with the humorous injunction: 'Polly, put the kettle on!'"

In March, Billy Reedy published "A Vocation and a Voice" in the *Mirror*: It was the last story sale (forty dollars) recorded in Kate Chopin's account book. *Youth's Companion* published "The Wood-Choppers" in May, and "Polly" in July, and its last line—"Polly, put the kettle on!"—proved to be Chopin's last words to her readers.

Kate Chopin still visited her relatives in Louisiana. Lamy and Fannie Chopin loved to entertain at their plantation house, and Lamy would sometimes charter entire trains to bring their guests from New Orleans, Alexandria, Shreveport, and Natchitoches. On one trip with Lélia to visit Lamy, Fannie, and their small children, Julie and young Lamy, Kate ate a particularly heavy meal, and then insisted on a brisk stroll with Lélia afterward. Both were wearing boots, and inadvertently stepped on and killed several baby chicks who were four-year-old Julie's pets. (Julie never forgave Kate.)

Kate also kept up her Louisiana ties by mail. On February 4, 1902, a few days before her fifty-second birthday, she answered a letter from her sister-in-law Marie Breazeale, whose husband, Phanor, had been elected to Congress. "My dear Marie," Kate wrote,

> I certainly appreciate your letter very much because I know that letter-writing is not one of the things that you enjoy most in life. Indeed it was mighty nice of you to write and I hope you will keep that New Year resolution of letting us hear from you often. I suppose you will be going to join Phanor pretty soon. I don't see how you manage to exist apart from each other unless your affections have somewhat cooled since I was with you.

Kate's letter was newsy and cheerful:

> How I should love to see Phanor in Washington. I know he is just the same old Phanor that he is in Natchitoches. I can't think of anything changing him or moving him from his good humored whimsical self.

In St. Louis, there had been talk since the mid-1890s about putting on a World's Fair to rival the 1893 Columbian Exposition in Chicago, and Kate urged Marie:

> You must have that Womens Federation send you up to our Worlds Fair. *It isn't going to be next year,* notwithstanding the assurances of the officers, not unless they can get some spooks and fairy godmothers to do the work for them.

(Kate had friends on the fair board, including Franklin Ferriss, one of her salon visitors, and Florence Hayward, who was globe-trotting in search of exhibits for the fair.)

In her letter, Kate also sent greetings to the Breazeales' four daughters, the oldest of whom was sixteen: "How are the little ladies? Marie must be nearly a young lady now. Are they all as pretty as ever and is July still in the lead?"

The rest of Kate's letter was devoted to family illnesses. Marie's sister, Eugénie Chopin Henry, was ailing, according to her niece "Nini":

> Nini writes me that Eugenie continues to improve. But I know she must still be far from her old self. I can't bear to think of her condition. What do the doctors say of her prospects of getting entirely well. Let me know what progress she makes. I should love to

> write to her if I thought there was any use. I hope you have told her of our solicitude.
>
> We are all well but the weather is so nasty and cold that I am actually unable to get about or accomplish anything. Aunt Amanda has been very ill off and on and I feel quite uneasy about her. She went through so much sorrow and uneasiness in poor Nina's sickness that she has never gotten over it.

Lélia and the boys "send their love to all," Kate wrote, and she hoped that Marie would be able to "pass by St. Louis" on her way to Washington.

Five weeks later, Eugénie Chopin Henry died. She was fifty-four, only two years older than Kate.

Kate still kept up some St. Louis social life: On May 2, 1902, she was one of the "patronesses" for a lecture sponsored by The French Benevolent Society of St. Louis. The speaker, M. Hugues Le Roux, reportedly had known Flaubert, Daudet, and Maupassant.

In the late spring of 1902, there was something to celebrate: Jean Chopin was getting married. Jean, Kate's eldest, was thirty-one that May, and his fiancée was twenty-eight-year-old Emelie Hughes of Evansville, Indiana. She was a graduate of St. Mary of the Woods College in Indiana, and the daughter of a merchant whose family was "prominent both socially and financially."

Jean Chopin and Emelie Hughes were married by a bishop in the Church of the Assumption in Evansville, on June 4. Many St. Louisans attended because, according to the newspapers: "Mr. Chopin is a resident of St. Louis and comes from one of the oldest French families in that city." After a monthlong honeymoon in Colorado, the Chopins settled at 4429 Berlin Avenue near Newstead, and the 1903 city directory lists Jean's occupation as "dept. mngr. Western Electrical S Co."

Oscar, Felix, and Lélia remained at home with Kate—but she was not writing.

In September 1902, there was a shock: At Joseph Pulitzer's Bar Harbor retreat, John A. Dillon had been thrown from his horse and fractured a rib. He lingered a few weeks and was treated by some of the country's most famous physicians, but double pneumonia and pleurisy set in. He died on October 15, at the age of fifty-nine.

His body was brought back to St. Louis for burial in Calvary Cemetery, and the pallbearers included men Kate Chopin knew: the husbands of Mrs. Julius Walsh and Mrs. John O'Fallon Delaney, and George Johns.

Dillon was another link to Kate Chopin's past—to her early writing days when she eagerly showed him her manuscripts, even though she doubted his sympathy with her work. Although he had been sailing to England with Joseph Pulitzer when *The Awakening* was published, Dillon was said to have praised Kate Chopin's courage: "She had poured herself—thoughts and feelings—into the novel with utmost honesty. She knew so much about life. She was an original genius."

In 1900, Dillon had been working as business manager for the *Chicago Tribune*, not far from St. Louis, and he may have been a more intimate friend. There were those who said, after her death, that Kate Chopin had died of a broken heart because she loved a married man. Dillon's death deepened her depression—and when it was rumored that she had been seen leaving a fashionable church (her first visit to a church in years), perhaps she was having masses said for the repose of John A. Dillon's soul.

That December of 1902, Kate Chopin made a will, leaving her jewelry, wearing apparel, and the lot and stable on Seventh Street between Franklin Avenue and Washington Street to her daughter, Lélia. "All the rest of my property," Kate wrote, "I direct be divided equally, share and share alike, between my sons, or the descendants of such as may be living at the time of my death." She appointed Jean and Felix as executors, and signed the will in the presence of two of her sons' friends, Nobel Willcox and Linn R. Brokaw.

By the following year, she was definitely ailing. She was weak and tired easily (and may have suffered from diabetes or emphysema). She told her children once, "I hope I will die first so that *I* will not lose any one of you."

Then, soon after, Kate moved to 4232 McPherson Avenue, between Boyle and Whittier, across the street from the lawyer Jesse McDonald and his wife, Gertrude, who was John A. Dillon's daughter. Kate was leaving behind the house where she had lived for her entire writing career in St. Louis—and where she had held her "Thursdays" and welcomed her circle of friends and admirers.

Money troubles may have influenced her: In 1903, her brothers-in-law had made four land sales for her in Louisiana. She had owned the Morgan Street house, without a mortgage, but was renting the brown brick home on McPherson. (St. Louis was known for its high rate of home ownership, and switching from owning to renting was unusual.) In 1902, Kate recorded her last earnings from her writing: $3.35 in royalties for *Bayou Folk*, and a total of $105 for three stories: "The Godmother" and "A Vocation and a Voice" in the *Mirror* and "Polly" in *Youth's Companion*. There were no longer any royalties for *The Awakening* or *A Night in Acadie*.

But there was also another reason for Kate to move: 4232 McPherson was virtually around the corner from Jean and Emelie Chopin's home—and the younger Chopins were expecting their first child. Kate Chopin would be a grandmother.

She was renting the McPherson house from another widow, Emily J. Randolph: The house itself was almost new, just finished in March of 1897 as an investment in the Central West End. It was a two-and-a-half story house with a front porch and gable roof, and the second story had dormer windows. The house also had elegant woodwork, a winding stairway, and a comfortable front parlor, as well as a sun room, kitchen, and dining room on the first floor. The second floor had two adjoining front rooms, one suitable for a bedroom and the other for a study—if Kate had still been writing. There was one more bedroom on that floor, probably Lélia's. The third floor, which had three bedrooms, would have been most suitable for Kate's sons—and Oscar, in particular, liked to spend his time drawing in the attic.

Kate occupied the house with four of her children. Felix, now a lawyer with Scullin and Chopin, had offices on 705 Olive Street; Fred, who had returned home, had a job as a superintendent, according to the 1903 city directory; Oscar was still listed as "artist." Lélia, not listed in the directory (single women rarely were), was still socially prominent: In 1903, she was one of the maids of honor in the Veiled Prophet's Court (St. Louis's equivalent of Mardi Gras celebrations).

Oscar, meanwhile, had become an artistic success. By 1904, he was an editorial cartoonist for the *Post-Dispatch* and drew the popular "Weather Bird," who announced the weather on the front page and commented on current events. Oscar usually made the "Weather Bird" male, but on April 4, 1904, when Lélia was about to be a bridesmaid, Weather Bird appeared on the front page of the *Post-Dispatch* in a wedding gown and veil, crying, "I'M SO NERVOUS!!!!" (The day before, Easter Sunday, Weather Bird had appeared in a fancy bonnet with flowers, a fluffy blouse and skirt and high heels, proclaiming, "I'LL BET EVERY GIRL IN CHURCH GETS GREEN WITH ENVY.")

Oscar also drew political cartoons, caricaturing bosses as stubby birds in bowler hats—for whom he provided pointed, and sometimes misspelled, dialogue. He drew President Theodore Roosevelt in toga and sandals, brandishing a mighty sword over a land labeled "PANAMA"; he drew the state legislature as a minstrel show. He enjoyed puns: For the 1904 baseball season, he drew a hand, labeled "GLAD," and drew a sausage machine for producing "ground balls." His dialogue and puns may have been inspired by conversations at home with his mother—and Kate may have aided him with the short poems that sometimes appeared underneath his cartoons.

By 1904, Fred Chopin was listed in the city directory as "clk 3d dist Street

Dept."; Felix remained a lawyer with Scullin & Chopin; and Kate was still listed as "Chopin Kate wid Oscar r 4232 McPherson av."

But by then, another of her sons had returned home. On the morning of July 7, 1903, suddenly, Emelie Hughes Chopin—Jean's young wife—died in childbirth, along with her infant. After the funeral at the New Cathedral Chapel at Maryland and Taylor Avenues, mother and child were buried together in the same grave in Calvary Cemetery, on July 9.

Jean Chopin was shattered.

He moved back to his mother's house, where Kate spent much of her time caring for him. The 1904 city directory lists him as "salesman Wesco Supply Co."—but he had had a nervous breakdown, and never fully recovered from his grief. (He would be the first of Kate Chopin's children to die, succumbing to typhoid just seven years after his mother.)

In early April 1904, Lélia was a bridesmaid for her friend Caroline Newman, who married Rufus Lackland Taylor. Lélia herself was close to an engagement with Frederick Hattersley, whose English-born father had made his fortune in flour. Lélia visited the Breazeales in Natchitoches, where she wore all black and was "so dramatic and interesting," according to her nine-year-old cousin July Breazeale. Lélia also hinted that her family disapproved of her engagement (but the reason was not clear).

On April 30, 1904, the much-acclaimed St. Louis World's Fair was opened— a year late: It had been intended as the centennial celebration for the Louisiana Purchase. Nevertheless, it was known as the Louisiana Purchase Exposition, a celebration of "Universal Progress." The Breazeales in Louisiana made plans to visit "Aunt Katie"; the city was full of excitement.

From McPherson Avenue, Kate Chopin was only six blocks from the eastern edge of Forest Park, where the fair was held—easily reachable by the Lindell Railway. She bought one of the first season tickets, and visited the fair virtually every day, most often alone. It was said that she could not get anyone to go with her—but she may have preferred solitude, as she did for much of her life.

The fair was beautiful and extravagant, the largest ever seen, 1,270 acres that could be traversed by gondola through artificial canals and lakes and la- goons, or by miniature railway, motor car, jinricksha, or "zebu carriage." The most intrepid could ride camels, burros, or elephants.

Kate Chopin was enraptured "when her eye caught the Fair *ensemble* in a certain magical, semi-mystical light," according to family memories. The fair was famous for its spectacular shows of colored lights and crystal-clear water- falls—made possible when St. Louis officials finally appointed experts to clean up the city's water supply. St. Louis's famous muddy tap water, which Kate

Chopin had known all her life, finally became the subject of myth. (Mark Twain used to say that if you let a glass of water stand half an hour, "you can separate the land from the water as easy as Genesis.")

The fair was full of music. Scott Joplin composed "The Cascade Rag" for the fair, whose theme song was "Meet Me in St. Louis, Louis" by Andrew B. Sterling and Kerry Mills; there were also orchestra and band and ragtime concerts. For those eager to soar, there was a giant Ferris wheel, the largest ever built; for animal watchers, there were bears in pits (possibly the first ones Kate had seen since the zoo in Cologne on her honeymoon, where she and Oscar saw "any number of wild beasts that showed their teeth in the most wonderful manner"). The exhibit from the Philippines—a collection of villages, complete with aborigines in loincloths—was a particular favorite of gawkers, but it also provoked violent controversy when rumors swept the city that the Filipinos were killing and eating dogs.

The fair was about the past (including a replica of the Cabildo, from the French Quarter in New Orleans) and about futuristic inventions: the wireless (radio), a Swedish *statisticum* (a kind of computer), X-rays, electric clocks, automatic telephones and answering machines, and automatic picture-takers. Kate Chopin could also view reenactments of the Galveston Flood and the Boer War, witness the Creation, visit the Hereafter, or talk to the Educated Horse—and she could sample the fair's new delicacies. Both iced tea and ice-cream cones were said to be fair firsts, and "fruit icicles" (popsicles) were another treat.

Women were well represented. Helen Keller and her teacher Annie Sullivan appeared as representatives of deaf and blind people, and Jessie Tarbox Beals was the first woman ever to be an official World's Fair photographer. Florence Hayward, the only woman commissioner for the fair, had not only convinced the Vatican to lend precious jewels to be exhibited, but was also active in promoting propriety: For the singing of "America" at the fair's opening ceremonies, she shouted, "Hats off! hats off!" until all the gentlemen complied.

Women had also influenced the fair planning. There was no Women's Building, as there had been at the 1893 Chicago fair, because St. Louis women's clubs, especially the Wednesday Club, wanted women artists' work to compete alongside men's. The St. Louis Fair's board of lady managers had also campaigned against the "indecent dancing" that Little Egypt had performed at the Chicago fair—although "Meet Me in St. Louis" still contained the musical promise to "dance the Hoochee Koochee" (and "be your tootsie wootsie").

Kate Chopin's son Oscar found the fair and fairgoers an endlessly fertile field for cartoons: For the fair's first day, he drew eight faces, headlined SOME TYPES OF AMERICANS CHOPIN THINKS HE MET AT THE FAIR YESTERDAY. They included a top-hatted shocked gentleman, with the caption "TOO MUCH FOR STAID PHIL-ADELPHIA"; a schoolmarmish lady with a lorgnette (COLD, CRITICAL AND FROM BOSTON, OF COURSE); and a mustachioed sharpie in prosperous tweeds (THE NEW YORKER'S EYES WERE OPENED).

Three weeks after the fair's opening, in May, Kate's uncle Charles Faris—the husband of Clémence Benoist Faris, Lélia's sponsor in St. Louis society—died, at the age of sixty-three. He was buried in the Benoist plot in Calvary Cemetery. Kate received a small inheritance from her uncle—but did not live to collect it.

The summer of 1904, like most St. Louis summers, was very humid. One of the earliest complaints of fairgoers had been the lack of free drinking water—finally remedied when several hydrants were opened.

On Saturday August 20, Pennsylvania Day, Kate Chopin had a particularly enjoyable day at the fair. The International Congress of the Deaf opened that day, and there were military drills, band concerts, and a program by Native American school pupils. The highlight was the military display by Pennsylvania companies in full regalia—including helmets, plumes, gold braid, and silver-mounted spurs.

It was also the hottest day since the fair opened, and Kate came home very tired (the result, it was said later, of "unaccustomed exercise and exertion"). At midnight she called to her son Jean, complaining of a severe pain in her head—but by the time he reached her bedside, she was unconscious.

The next day, with her children at her bedside, she recognized her son George, the physician, for a moment, and complained again about the pain in her head. She had evidently had a hemorrhage of the brain, but for a while the doctors thought her condition was improving.

On Sunday night, she lapsed into unconsciousness again—and on Monday, August 22, at noon, with her children nearby, Kate Chopin died.

Kate Chopin's death appeared on the front pages of the *Post-Dispatch* and Reedy's *Mirror*, and on p. 13 of the *Globe-Democrat*.

According to the *Globe-Democrat*, Kate Chopin was "the well-known depictor of Creole life in Louisiana," a St. Louisan who graduated from the Sacred Heart school, and "was extremely popular in society after her graduation, because of her beauty and intellect." (The *Post-Dispatch* said she had become "one of the belles of St. Louis, popular alike because of her beauty and attractive mental attributes.") *At Fault*, the *Globe-Democrat* reported, "had marked the beginning of a distinguished career in works of fiction," while *Bayou Folk* had "created an universal desire to study more of Creole life as the authoress so vividly depicted it, with a vein of quaint humor." The *Globe-Democrat* slighted the rest of Kate Chopin's literary career:

In 1897 "Bayou Folk" was followed by "A Night in Acadie," and two years later her fascinating novel, "The Awakening," was published in Chicago. Since then Mrs. Chopin had published nothing of importance, but it was recently announced that another volume of short stories from her pen was to be issued this year.

Other St. Louis and New Orleans newspapers similarly summarized her writing, praising *Bayou Folk* and *A Night in Acadie* over *The Awakening*:

In 1897 "Bayou Folk" was followed by Mrs. Chopin's second volume of Creole short stories, "A Night in Acadie," which more than confirmed the success already achieved, and in 1899, her novel, "The Awakening," was published in Chicago. This more sustained effort, while esteemed a success, did not overshadow the two preceding volumes, and it is still to the latter that the discriminating reader turns in a study of the best work of their author.

The *Boston Evening Transcript*, in an abbreviated obituary, said that of Kate Chopin's stories,

"Bayou Folk" and "A Night in Arcadie" perhaps brought her greatest credit from the literary world . . . "The Awakening," a novel written by Mrs. Chopin, was published in Chicago in 1899, and, while it met approval, seemingly it did not bring forth the true talent of the author as had "Bayou Folk" and "A Night in Arcadie."

Two more personal remembrances appeared in St. Louis—one from the genteel Alexander DeMenil and the other from the raffish Billy Reedy.

DeMenil published his two-page tribute to Kate Chopin in *The Hesperian*, his elite literary magazine, which had never reviewed *The Awakening*. St. Louis had "lost her foremost female author" with Kate Chopin's death, DeMenil wrote, and praised *Bayou Folk* as a portrait of Kate Chopin's "'own people' (the words she once used to us), for, by inheritance of birth and by marriage, and we may add—by inclination, she was herself, a Creole." DeMenil called her *Bayou Folk* stories "far more *femininely* subtle (if we may use the word)" than George W. Cable's, and gave them high praise—but he mentioned *A Night in Acadie* and *The Awakening* only by name.

Mostly he reminisced about Kate Chopin as a person, and had obviously believed her claims that she was not ambitious or seriously committed to her work:

We remember Katie O'Flaherty when only six or seven years old reading one of Sir Walter Scott's novels! A year or two later she borrowed from a neighbor the poetical works of James Hogg, the Ettrick Shepherd. All her life she was an omnivorous reader. . . . She was not a "blue stocking"—she had none of the manners, airs, affectations and eccentricities of the *poseurs bleu*. She had no fads, no serious purposes in her literary work, no lesson to teach, no moral to point. She took no notes; she declared to us on several occasions that she never studied or even closely observed people, places, or things, or conditions, or circumstances with a view of using them as literary material. She was simply a bright, unaffected, warm-hearted, unpresuming and *womanly* woman.

In his epitaph, Billy Reedy also did not discuss *The Awakening*—but his was the only tribute to acknowledge Kate Chopin's singular intelligence and talent. Unlike DeMenil, Reedy had known Kate Chopin only as an adult, as the center of the Thursday salons, and as a fellow satirist (and gentler debunker) of local pretensions. He was the only obituary writer to call her a "genius."

ST. LOUIS lost a woman of rare intellect and noble character when death removed, last Monday, Mrs. Kate Chopin. A host of friends today honor her memory and cherish the boon of her acquaintance. She was a remarkably talented woman, who knew how to be a genius without sacrificing the comradeship of her children. As a mother, wife and friend she shone resplendent and her contributions to fiction, though few, showed that she possessed true literary genius. She was remarkably clever as a depictor of Creole life and character in the Sunny South. "At Fault," "Bayou Folk," "A Night in Acadie," and "The Awakening" are literary treasures which she has left and which have afforded many a pleasant hour.

The requiem mass for Kate Chopin was celebrated at nine o'clock on the morning of Wednesday, August 24, 1904, by Father Francis Gilfillan, assistant rector of the new Cathedral of St. Louis the King.

The active pallbearers, described as "young friends of Mrs. Chopin and former schoolmates of her sons," were Fred Hattersley, Lélia Chopin's fiancé; Willis Hinckley, later Oscar Chopin's brother-in-law; George Wilson; Lewis B. Ely; Linn Brokaw; and Hallock N. Gillette. The honorary pallbearers were Daniel C. Bordley, husband of Kate's cousin Blanche; George Blackman of the St. Louis Artists' Guild; Judge Franklin Ferriss, a regular member of her "Thursdays"; Eugene Benoist; Hinman H. Clark, Jr.; J. De Pombiray; Judge Shepard Barclay; John F. Carten; and her dear friend from the *Post-Dispatch*, Charles L. Deyo.

(Some of her closest male friends were notably absent from the list. As a militant atheist, Frederick Kolbenheyer may have refused to involve himself in anything to do with a church, and Billy Reedy had been excommunicated since his unsanctioned second marriage in 1897. But George Johns had been pallbearer for John A. Dillon's funeral less than two years earlier, and at forty-seven he was athletically vigorous, gray-haired, with a "substantial girth" and a "cold blue eye trained to penetrate sham." He had also never commented publicly on *The Awakening*—and if he thought Chopin's critics were wrong, he never said so in print.)

Kate Chopin was buried in Section 17, Lot 47, along the Way of the Second Dolor, in a plot originally purchased by Mrs. C. F. Benoist (Oscar's grandmother). In the center of the plot was an obelisk dedicated to Marie Clémence Wood, Oscar's aunt, who had died in 1867; to the left of the obelisk were the graves of Emelie Hughes Chopin and her child, buried there the previous July (although the gravestone says June).

Kate Chopin's simple granite gravestone contains only her name and dates:

KATE CHOPIN

February 1851
August 1904

Later, Kate Chopin's children would be buried around her: They died in the same order they had been born.

A lilac bush, Kate Chopin's favorite flower, grew near her grave, its blossoms faintly shadowing her stone.

EPILOGUE

WITHIN A FEW YEARS AFTER
their mother's death, Kate Chopin's daughter and four bachelor sons all married. Lélia, already engaged while her mother was alive, was married eight
months later to Frederick Robert Hattersley, a son of the English-born flour
broker, on April 5, 1905, in her new home at 4122 Maryland Avenue. It was
a small, quiet ceremony, because she was still in mourning for her mother.

By 1910, Oscar C. Chopin, the *Post-Dispatch* cartoonist, had married Louise
Hinckley of St. Louis, also in a small ceremony, at the home of the bride's
mother. George Chopin, the physician, married Frances Gleeson; "Phil" (Felix) Chopin married "Lottie" (Charlotte) Smart—and Fred Chopin created
something of a scandal by marrying twice.

Fred's second marriage, performed hastily and secretly, became newspaper
headline news on September 1, 1914: F.H. CHOPIN WEDDED AGAIN IN ST. LOUIS/
DIVORCED MAN RETURNS FOR CEREMONY WITHOUT INFORMING FRIENDS AND REL-
ATIVES. Fred, identified as the "son of a former St. Louis woman author and
defendant in a sensational divorce suit four years ago," married Kathryn Quinn
of Morgan Street, in a ceremony performed by a justice of the peace. Fred
had been working in Minneapolis as a Diamond Match Company salesman, and did not tell anyone in the family that he would be returning to St.
Louis to marry "Kitty" Quinn, the daughter of a plumbing contractor. But a
St. Louis newspaper did not hesitate to recount the story of Fred's earlier
marriage:

397 ❖

Chopin's first wife, Mrs. Myrtle Chopin, filed suit for divorce and custody of their two children at Clayton in 1910. She accused him of intemperance, cruelty and non-support. In announcing her intention to file the suit, Mrs. Chopin told reporters of the shock that came to her when she awoke one morning and found her husband's friends sprawling around the floor of their home after a jollification lasting until after midnight.

Kate Chopin's children and grandchildren tended to be unconventional and talented—noted for their creativity, their flair for drama, their appreciation for the ridiculous. They also had their sad moments: Lélia's young husband died just four years after their wedding, leaving her with a small son, Robert. Like her mother, grandmother, great-grandmother, and great-great-grandmother, Lélia remained a widow for the rest of her life—and she lived that life with zest.

"Lil" Hattersley had grown up among card players: St. Louis women all belonged to card clubs, and Kate had called herself a "euchre fiend." In the ebullient 1920s, as professions opened to women, Lil became an expert bridge player and teacher who divided her time between New York and Palm Beach, and published six books on bridge and backgammon. From New York, Lil wrote articles on New York drama for the *St. Louis Globe-Democrat*, where she was cheered for her "literary attainments" and "engaging style" of writing. Her book on backgammon was praised by Frank Crowninshield, the editor of *Vanity Fair*, who claimed that backgammon was already a "social menace," a plague, "[a]nd when Mrs. Hattersley's book reaches the circulation which I predict for it, life in our smarter communities will become quite unbearable."

Lélia Chopin Hattersley was always dramatic: Her pictures show a dark, mysterious-looking woman, her eyes shadowed and dark-rimmed. She was nearly six feet tall, a large, flamboyant woman whose imperious style reminded her nieces and nephews of Margaret Dumont, the dowager in Marx Brothers films. "Aunt Lil" was a brilliant businesswoman who sometimes embarrassed her relatives by creating scenes in restaurants (poor service and canned orange juice especially enraged her)—but there was always an aura of excitement about her.

Lil promoted her mother's writings, and encouraged the critic Fred Lewis Pattee to reprint Kate Chopin's stories. Like her mother, Lil had a pioneering spirit and an individualistic streak: During a St. Louis visit, she lectured on bridge at the Racquet Club, where—according to the *Globe-Democrat*—"there is almost monastic exclusion of women."

Lil's artistic brother, the cartoonist Oscar C. Chopin, also left St. Louis a few years after his mother's death. Oscar moved to California, where he became cartoonist for the *San Francisco Examiner* and a friend of William Randolph Hearst, who later sent him to Baden-Baden to recover from what proved to be a terminal illness (probably tuberculosis). Oscar and Louise Chopin's daughter, named Kate for her grandmother, was a very gifted artist who died young, of cancer, in New York.

Fred Chopin, whose singing and piano playing had enlivened the gatherings of his fellow soldiers, attempted a career as a concert pianist, but eventually moved to California with his second wife and worked most of his life as a candy-company representative. His nieces and nephews remember him as a small, neat, precise man whose wife clipped his mustache for him; he was also nattily dressed, and wore straw sailor hats in the summer. He still played the piano, and on his tombstone was recorded what he evidently considered the best year of his life:

> Fred Chopin
> Pvt Btry A Mo Light Arty
> Sp Am War
> JAN 26 1876   FEB 6, 1953

"Phil" (Felix) Chopin remained in St. Louis, where he was an attorney: According to a biographical sketch in the 1906 *Book of St. Louisans*, Felix Chopin was a Democrat who enjoyed hunting, fishing, canoeing, and golf, and belonged to the Missouri Athletic Club. A few years later, Felix gave up his law practice, after the suicide of his partner, Billy Scullin, the Central High classmate who had lost his legs in a railroad accident not long after their graduation—but late in life Felix returned to work in St. Louis's domestic court. Like his mother and sister, he was also a dedicated card player. Like his brother Oscar, he had some artistic talent: With a mirror, he liked to sketch himself—although he also claimed, joshing to his nephews, that he was "the world's ugliest man." He was said to be the most devout of Kate Chopin's children, but he also had a spirit of adventure, and enjoyed taking his nephews on long automobile excursions.

Felix stayed in the same circles as his mother, and kept the same physician: Felix and Charlotte Chopin's son Tom was delivered by Dr. Frederick Kolbenheyer, who also continued his colorful career. In 1914, he headed a German-American committee that commissioned a black, larger-than-life voluptuous nude, called "The Naked Truth," for the Compton Heights Reservoir Park. (Neighborhood youngsters still sit on the statue's lap or fondle her breasts.) Kolbenheyer died in 1921 in Omaha.

Kate Chopin's physician son, George, settled in Baden, a German town in north St. Louis, where he had a medical practice for more than fifty years. "Doc"'s wife strongly disapproved of Kate Chopin (whom she had never known) because Kate "read herself out of the Catholic Church"—but Doc, said to have the keenest sense of humor in the family, sometimes said that Kate Chopin had been ahead of her time and "too darn smart" to be a Catholic. He adored her and often described her wicked playfulness: She delighted in taking out library books unsuitable for children to read and then leaving them about, temptingly, while cooing, "I find that book very boring, but you might like it." (After that, no one dared pick up the books.)

Kate Chopin's eldest son, Jean, who never recovered from his losses, worked as a traveling salesman in the Southwest for the Chicago Gas and Electric Fixture Manufacturing Company, and was staying at his brother Doc's home when he died of typhoid fever, in March 1911. (His will divided his estate between Doc and his sister, Lélia, and asked that the writings of his mother, Kate Chopin, be republished.) Oscar Chopin died in January 1933; Doc in February 1952; Fred in February 1953; Felix in June 1955; and Lélia in May 1962.

Kate Chopin's dozen grandchildren included, in St. Louis, a painter (Marjorie Chopin McCormick), a lawyer (George), a security and law-enforcement agent (Thomas), and an advertising copywriter (David)—who, when he was young, was sometimes the victim of his dramatic aunt Lélia's scathing comments about his written compositions. (Lélia's own son, Robert Chopin Hattersley of New York, was also in the advertising business.) Kate Chopin's granddaughter Lélia Chopin Conway (known as "Toots") published an appreciative article on her famous grandmother in *Maryville Magazine*, the journal of the Sacred Heart school in St. Louis—and "Toots"'s son edited and published a book and author magazine.

Among Kate Chopin's great-grandchildren—of whom there are more than two dozen—there are screenwriters (including another Kate Chopin, who has written a screenplay about the original Kate's life), stand-up comics, chemists, lawyers, farmers, athletes, artists, medical writers, and book editors. Lélia Chopin's granddaughter Grace Hattersley, a New York model, was in the news in 1987 as the companion of rock star Billy Idol: She was described as "a gorgeous model with Social Register connections," the daughter of a Wall Street executive and granddaughter of a bridge expert who was "the daughter of Kate Chopin, an author of Southern stories." On MTV, Grace Hattersley was identified as "a blue-blood brunette."

But none of Kate Chopin's descendants settled in Louisiana—where a different legacy continued. In New Orleans, Kate Chopin was largely forgotten—although as late as the 1960s, some literary clubwomen considered hers a scandalous name. ("I never thought I'd hear her name mentioned here," a member of Le Petit Salon told the writer-professor W. Kenneth Holditch of the University of New Orleans.) But in Cloutierville, in the Cane River country, people never ceased talking about the racy author with her fashionable clothes and flirtatious ways.

Albert Sampite remained in his adobe house in Cloutierville, still restlessly traveling when he could, drinking more than he should, and keeping company with his neighbor Maria Normand. When her granddaughter Ivy DeLouche, born in 1906, came to live with Maria, Albert Sampite considered her his special pet and neglected his own grandchildren: His grandson Albert was frightened of the large, silent, morose man who used to ride about at night on Fanny, his gray mare. (Sometimes his valet, Colton Gallion, would accompany him.)

But for the child Ivy, who called him "Nonky" ("Uncle"), Albert Sampite was a doting friend who ate supper with her and her grandmother and treated Ivy to brandied peaches and homemade vanilla ice cream. He was very good-looking and very generous to Ivy, who even then sensed that he was her grandmother Maria's lover, and "the mature love of her life": When he returned from trips, there would always be warm embraces and hugs with Maria. During one trip to New Orleans, despite a serious illness at the Hotel Dieu, Albert Sampite managed to write Ivy a loving letter in purple ink, and she considered him "a joy and a pleasure."

Not long afterward, in the house of his estranged wife, Loca, Albert Sampite died, on June 12, 1913. The world had also changed immeasurably since his youth as a Cane River country farmer, a Civil War soldier, and a lover of horses: On the day that he died, the newspapers were full of stories about automobiles, druggists who sold cocaine, and woman suffrage.

Because she was not his wife, Maria Normand did not attend his funeral, but stayed in bed, under the mosquito bar, weeping bitterly the entire day. Albert Sampite was buried between his parents in the Cloutierville cemetery, where his tombstone bears the message HE IS AT REST.

Afterward, too, there was a lawsuit. Albert's daughter, Marie Sampite Pollock, sued Maria Normand to recover a plot of land that Albert had given Maria—in exchange for the fine and beautiful sewing she did for him, Maria said. Kate Chopin's brother-in-law Phanor Breazeale was one of the attorneys in the case, and Cane River country people gossiped and scoffed about the "fine sewing."

The lawsuit was settled amicably, but Albert and Loca Sampite's daughter was never placated. Marie Sampite Pollock felt that Kate Chopin had ridiculed Cloutierville people in her stories, and all her life Marie believed, and passed on to her children, what she had heard in the early 1890s: "Kate Chopin broke up my parents' marriage."

Maria Normand lived until 1922, and Loca Sampite until 1926, years in which Kate Chopin was virtually forgotten outside the Cane River country. In the 1920s, Lesche Club drama students at the Louisiana Normal School (now Northwestern State University in Natchitoches) wrote plays based on Kate Chopin's short stories, among them "Ma'ame Pélagie," "In Sabine," "A No-Account Creole," and "A Lady of Bayou St. John." (One of the most active Lesche Club members, and the author of a dramatic version of "Désirée's Baby," was Marie Breazeale, daughter of Marie Chopin and Phanor Breazeale.) "The old Normal" also had one dormitory, Kate Chopin Hall, which existed until a fire destroyed it in the 1970s—but most of its residents did not know who Kate Chopin was, nor did they recognize her portrait.

Kate Chopin's lamp, the one that Albert Sampite had given to Maria Normand, was finally broken by a New Orleans handyman—but Kate's gaming table remains in the house where Albert Sampite died. It is now used as a kitchen table by his granddaughter, Leona Sampite.

In 1980, Albert and Loca Sampite's grandson, Joseph Sampite, was elected mayor of the town of Natchitoches.

A quarter-century after Kate Chopin's death, a first biographer investigated her life. Daniel Rankin, a red-haired New Orleanian who resembled the entertainer Arthur Godfrey, was a Marist priest who began following the trail of Kate Chopin in the early 1930s. Rankin, then a graduate student at the University of Pennsylvania, did some very selective interviewing, mostly with men: He claimed there were no women among the St. Louis acquaintances that Kate Chopin's children suggested he meet. Often Rankin did not indicate his sources, and later said that his notes had been accidentally lost.

With his 1932 dissertation, *Kate Chopin and Her Creole Stories*, Rankin published eleven Chopin short stories and transcribed much of her schoolgirl commonplace book and honeymoon diary. He also gathered priceless information through letters from Kate Chopin's childhood friend Kitty Garesché, then over eighty. (Mother Garesché, a Sacred Heart nun, died in 1940.) But Rankin was careless about many facts, and when he visited Louisiana, he did not talk with the Sampites in Natchitoches Parish, nor did he interview the younger Dr. Scruggs or any of Kate Chopin's Charleville and Benoist relatives. In fact, Rankin talked with very few people: Phanor Breazeale, it was said, deliberately sidetracked Rankin, whose main source proved to be Fannie Hertzog Chopin, Kate Chopin's sister-in-law. But Fannie Hertzog had been young enough to be Kate's daughter, and her memories were few, selective, and not always accurate.

In St. Louis, Rankin had visited Doc (George) Chopin's family, stayed with them for three weeks, and prevailed upon them to chauffeur him about for his research—but the book he wrote was, the family thought, not an accurate portrait of Kate Chopin. Lélia Chopin Hattersley, particularly incensed, called Rankin's study a whitewash and "a milquetoast"; she called him "that horrible man" and particularly objected to his suggesting that Dr. J. B. Chopin, Oscar's father, could have been the model for Harriet Beecher Stowe's Simon Legree. Other family members called Rankin a nice person but a "fat liar."

Afterward, Rankin became a professor of English at St. Mary's Manor in South Langhorne, Pennsylvania, and collaborated with Claire Quintal on a 1964 biography of Joan of Arc. Perhaps as punishment for his own biographical sins, Rankin was first reported deceased in May 1971, several years before his actual death. A month later, the University of Pennsylvania Alumni Office was informed that reports of his death had been greatly exaggerated: He was still alive and living in Worcester, Massachusetts.

Rankin did encourage the Chopin family to donate her manuscripts from their armoire to the Missouri Historical Society. (Before that, her grandchildren at Doc's house had played with them, leaving squiggles on some pages; they also played her music on their piano.) But except for Rankin, there had been little national interest in Kate Chopin between her death in 1904 and her rediscovery in the 1960s.

Kate Chopin was not quite forgotten in St. Louis. In 1910, her friend Vernon ("Bunnie") Knapp recalled her as "beyond doubt, the most brilliant, distinguished and interesting woman that has ever graced St. Louis," with "every grace and talent essential to the maintenance of a brilliant social circle: brilliant in the sense of mentality and wit. . . . More than one lady that has lived in St. Louis found her house a real home, where her friends and the friends of her children could at all times go and find entertainment, instruction and pleasure."

One of those children, George and Minne Johns's son Orrick, also praised Kate Chopin in a 1911 *Mirror* article as "the most individual feminine talent America has produced. There is none to compare with her." Johns mourned her loss: She "was persecuted for the candor of her novel 'The Awakening,'" and "her touch was not vulgar enough to please." Yet, he concluded, her time and place might come: "Had Kate Chopin written in French her books to-day would have been French classics."

But her contemporary Alexander DeMenil was still fighting the genteel battle, trying to force the late Kate Chopin into a mold not of her choosing. In 1920, he wrote that in Kate O'Flaherty's late teens and early twenties, "there was not a brighter, more gracious, and handsomer young woman in St. Louis"— but *The Awakening*, he reported, was "a novel with an unfortunate chapter that she agreed with me later on, should have been omitted."

The Awakening was reprinted in 1906, but was then unavailable for more than half a century. Of Kate Chopin's short stories, only "Désirée's Baby" re-mained consistently in print—largely through the efforts of the critic Fred Lewis Pattee, who continually anthologized the story and praised its merits.

In 1961, a Norwegian graduate student at Harvard took a course from the French professor Cyrille Arnavon, in which the class read *The Awakening*. Arnavon, who had published a French translation of *The Awakening (Edna)* in 1953, suggested that the student, Per Seyersted, write a paper on Kate Cho-pin—and Seyersted, fascinated, chose her as the subject of his doctoral disser-tation.

Seyersted spent seven years combing archives for manuscripts, letters, and scraps; he met with Father Daniel Rankin in Paris; and one day, on a layover at John F. Kennedy Airport in New York, Seyersted telephoned the only Hat-tersley in the phone book—and found Kate Chopin's grandson.

From his attic, Robert Hattersley retrieved a notebook of Kate Chopin's, containing her 1894 diary, several short stories and translations, and "The Storm." When Seyersted published *The Complete Works of Kate Chopin* in 1969, it was the first publication of "The Storm"—seventy-one years after Kate Chopin had composed that celebration of adultery and sensuality.

The Complete Works and Seyersted's *Kate Chopin: A Critical Biography* (also published in 1969) coincided with the growth of the women's movement in the United States. In 1972, *Redbook* reprinted *The Awakening*, billing it as a "classic underground novel"—and for readers whose feminist consciousness was growing, *The Awakening* was a stunning rediscovery, a piercing insight into American women's literary past.

Meanwhile, in Cloutierville, Louisiana, a lifelong resident named Mildred LaCaze McCoy had settled on a project that would inspire her for the rest of her life: the restoration of the Kate Chopin home.

Mildred McCoy, a widow, had always known about Kate Chopin, and es-pecially treasured "For Marse Chouchoute," in which a character is named Verchette: Mildred McCoy's mother had been a Vercher, a common name in the Cloutierville area. In 1964, Mildred McCoy bought the Chopin home, and turned it into the Bayou Folk Museum/Kate Chopin Home—a museum of life in the Cane River country, and a tribute to Kate Chopin.

The museum's treasures include a tinted picture of Kate Chopin from 1869, with her hair in an elaborate crown of braids, with a white sacque and cameo at her throat. She gave that picture to the younger Dr. Samuel Scruggs, whose daughter gave it to the museum—where there are also three forks that belonged to Kate Chopin, the sewing cabinet that belonged to Mrs. Scruggs, and many portraits, documents, and scrapbooks of Cane River country lore. The museum also displays two of the books from Kate Chopin's personal library: R. E. Lee

Gibson's 1901 *Sonnets and Lyrics,* including his sonnet "'To the Author of 'Bayou Folk,'" autographed by Gibson to Kate Chopin; and *Elizabeth and Her German Garden,* by Countess Elizabeth Mary Russell.

In 1970, the Louisiana Tourist Commission designated the Bayou Folk Museum/Kate Chopin Home as an official Louisiana Landmark, and in 1975 it was placed on the National Register of Historic Places. After Mildred McCoy's death in 1985, the museum's acting curator was Lucille Tinker Carnahan—who, as a schoolteacher in the late 1920s, had once boarded at the Kate Chopin house. In 1987, the museum was purchased by the Association for the Preservation of Historic Natchitoches.

The Awakening is now considered a major American novel, taught in universities and colleges everywhere. Kate Chopin is discussed at scholarly conferences and written about in journals and books; she is also the subject of lampoons at Harvard and graffiti in New Orleans. *The Awakening* has been translated into French, Italian, German, and most of the Scandinavian languages; in Poland it was an immediate best-seller; and films have been made of Kate Chopin's "The Story of an Hour" and *The Awakening.*

Robert Stone's 1986 novel *Children of Light* describes the filming of *The Awakening* in which the actress playing Edna Pontellier finds that the voice of the sea is still seductive, luring the soul to wander in abysses of solitude. The heroine, Lu Ann, ends her story much as Edna did. But in *The New York Times Book Review* in 1987, the novelist Jill McCorkle suggested a modern alternative:

> At the end of Kate Chopin's novel "The Awakening," Edna Pontellier, who is swimming out into the ocean with every intention of drowning, realizes she has made a terrible mistake. She thinks of her husband, and how dull and controlled her life with him has been; she thinks of Robert, her young lover, who awakened her sexually and then left with his brief "Goodbye—because I love you." What an easy line. She imagines the two of them discovering her drowned body. Her husband would say, "How could she have gone swimming without anything on? What will everyone say?"

> It is as if Edna is now, finally, again, really waking up. She doesn't want to die over those two. What a waste. She starts swimming back toward shore, thinking of all the things her new life will bring: a divorce, a job, birth control, single parenthood, shorter skirts. Edna, swimming with strong steady strokes, is convinced that she's on to something, and she would rather be a pioneer than dead.

All the attention would have heartened Kate Chopin, who was ambitious for fame and recognition—but as a reserved and self-contained person, she might have been less pleased to be the subject of a biography. (When she reviewed the edition of Edwin Booth's letters, she imagined him saying, "I shrink from the indelicacy.")

Yet Kate Chopin might also have recognized in herself an ideal subject, much like her characters who exercise a fascination because so much of them is unknown. Kate Chopin did not wrestle with her demons in public, nor did she seek to preach or persuade; she kept her own counsel, and her own secrets. Like Edna in *The Awakening*, Chopin resolved "never again to belong to another than herself," and she found her greatest strength in solitude.

Kate Chopin, like Edna Pontellier, was a modern woman in a still-Victorian world. Unlike other women writers of her era, she did not have the support of a political movement (as Charlotte Perkins Gilman did), or a writing family (as Alice James did), or a network of other writing women (as Sarah Orne Jewett did). As the mother of a large family with a small income, she did not have the cushion of wealth (as Edith Wharton did).

And so Kate Chopin created herself. Virtually alone among writers in her own time, she possessed that special spark that transcends time. She was, finally, what Edna could not be: "the artist with the courageous soul that dares and defies."

APPENDICES

I

CHRONOLOGY OF KATE CHOPIN'S LIFE

1850–MID-1870—ST. LOUIS

February 8, 1850—birth of Catherine O'Flaherty—first home: Eighth Street between Chouteau and Gratiot

Fall 1855—Kate O'Flaherty enrolls in Academy of the Sacred Heart (which she attends sporadically for the next thirteen years), becomes friends with Kitty Garesché

November 1, 1855—death of Thomas O'Flaherty (father) in railroad accident

January 16, 1863—death of Victoire Verdon Charleville (great-grandmother and teacher)

February 17, 1863—death of George O'Flaherty (half-brother), a Confederate soldier

1863—banishment of Kitty Garesché and her family

1865–1866—Kate's family moves to 1118 St. Ange Avenue

Fall 1865—Kate attends the Academy of the Visitation, then returns to Sacred Heart Academy

1867–1870—keeps commonplace book: diary, extracts from authors, original poem ("The Congé"), reactions to flirting and other social obligations

June 29, 1868—graduation from Sacred Heart Academy

1869—writes "Emancipation: a Life Fable," unpublished

March–May 1869—visits New Orleans

April 15, 1870—death of Julia Benoist Chopin, Oscar Chopin's mother

June 9, 1870—marriage to Oscar Chopin of Louisiana, Holy Angels Church, St. Louis

June–September 1870—European honeymoon, keeps honeymoon diary in commonplace book

MID-1870–MID-1879—NEW ORLEANS

New Orleans homes: 443 Magazine Street; northeast corner Pitt & Constantinople; 209
      (now 1413) Louisiana Avenue
November 14, 1870—death of Dr. J. B. Chopin.
May 22, 1871—son Jean Baptiste born in New Orleans, baptized in St. Louis in August
September 24, 1873—son Oscar Charles born in St. Louis, baptized in St. Louis
December 27, 1873—Thomas O'Flaherty (brother) killed in buggy accident, St. Louis
September 14, 1874—Oscar in Battle of Liberty Place, with White League and associ-
      ated companies, New Orleans
October 28, 1874—son George Francis born in St. Louis, baptized in St. Louis
January 26, 1876—son Frederick born in New Orleans (no baptismal record)
January 8, 1878—son Felix Andrew born in New Orleans (no baptismal record)

LATE 1879–MID-1884—CLOUTIERVILLE ("CLOOCHYVILLE") IN NATCHITOCHES "NAK-I-TUSH") PARISH, LOUISIANA

December 31, 1879—daughter Lélia born in Cloutierville, baptized Marie Laïza in
      Cloutierville
December 10, 1882—death of Oscar Chopin
—romance with Albert Sampite
mid-1884—Kate Chopin's return to St. Louis

MID-1884–1904—ST. LOUIS

1884–1885—lives at 1125 St. Ange Avenue, then 1122 St. Ange
June 28, 1885—death of Eliza O'Flaherty

1886—moves to 3317 Morgan Street (now Delmar)

June 1887—first Cloutierville visit since Oscar's death

1888—"Lilia. Polka for Piano" published

1888—writes first draft of what becomes "A No-Account Creole"

May 24, 1888—Loca Sampite leaves Albert Sampite

Sept. 24, 1888—Loca Sampite sues for legal separation from her husband

1888–1889—Chopin works on "Unfinished Story—Grand Isle"

January 10, 1889—first literary publication: "If It Might Be" (poem)

April 24, 1889—Kate brings Oscar's body back to St. Louis from Cloutierville

April 30, 1889—Loca Sampite's suit for separation dismissed

June 1889—Chopin writes "Wiser than a God"

July 5, 1889—begins writing *At Fault*

August, 1889—writes "A Point at Issue!"

October 27, 1889—first short-story publication: "A Point at Issue!" *St. Louis Post-Dispatch*

December 1889—"Wiser than a God" published in *Philadelphia Musical Journal*

September 1890—*At Fault* published at Chopin's expense

December 1890—becomes charter member of Wednesday Club

June 1891—John A. Dillon moves to New York

August 19, 1891—Loca Sampite's legal separation from Albert Sampite takes effect

August 20, 1891—"For Marse Chouchoute" (first Louisiana story) published in *Youth's Companion*

March 7, 1892—writes "Miss McEnders"

April 4, 1892—resigns from Wednesday Club

April 9–10, 1892—writes "Loka"

July 15–17, 1892—writes "At the 'Cadian Ball"

August 27, 1892—death of Cora Henry Chopin, sister-in-law

August 27–28, 1892—writes "Ma'ame Pélagie"

Oct. 22, 1892—"At the 'Cadian Ball" published in *Two Tales*

Nov. 24, 1892—writes "Désirée's Baby"

Jan. 14, 1893—*Vogue* publishes "Désirée's Baby"

May 1893—trip to New York and Boston

August 11, 1893—Houghton, Mifflin accepts *Bayou Folk*

October 1, 1893—hurricane of Chênière Caminada destroys much of the Grand Isle area that Chopin knew

October 21–23, 1893—writes "At Chênière Caminada"

March 24, 1894—Houghton Mifflin, publishes *Bayou Folk*

April 19, 1894—Chopin writes "The Story of an Hour" ("Dream of an Hour")

May 4, 1894—October 26, 1896—writes "Impressions" (Diary)

Late June, 1894—attends Indiana conference of Western Association of Writers

June 30, 1894—writes "The Western Association of Writers"

July 7, 1894—"Western Association of Writers" published in *Critic*

July 21–28, 1894—hostile responses to Chopin's "Western Association of Writers" in *Minneapolis Journal, Cincinnati Commercial Gazette*

August 1894—first national profile: William Schuyler's article in *The Writer*

December 6, 1894—"Dream of an Hour" published in *Vogue* with note about "Those Who Have Worked With Us"

March 1895—sends Maupassant translation collection to Houghton, Mifflin (rejected)

April 1895—"Cavanelle" published in *The American Jewess*

April 10–28, 1895—writes "Athénaïse"

January 27, 1897—grandmother Athénaïse Charleville Faris dies

February 3, 1897—meets Ruth McEnery Stuart

March 6, 1897—"Miss McEnders" by "La Tour" published in *St. Louis Criterion*

March 11, 1897—Reedy's *Mirror* reveals satirical truth about "Miss McEnders"

Mar. 1897—writes "The Locket," unpublished

June 1897 (?)—begins writing *The Awakening*

June 1897—John A. Dillon makes short trip to St. Louis

June 24—July 1, 1897–Kate Chopin visits Natchitoches Parish

November 1897—Way & Williams (Chicago) publishes *A Night in Acadie*

January 16, 1898—"Is Love Divine?" (*St. Louis Post-Dispatch*) quotes from novel-in-progress

January 21, 1898—finishes *The Awakening*

January 1898—Way & Williams accepts *The Awakening*

February 6, 1898—"Has High Society Struck the Pace That Kills?" (*St. Louis Post-Dispatch*)

March 1898—goes to Chicago, seeking literary agent

Spring–Summer 1898—son Frederick in Spanish-American War

July 19, 1898—writes "The Storm"

November 1898—books transferred from Way & Williams to Herbert S. Stone & Company

December 1898—visits Natchitoches Parish, sells Cloutierville house, visits New Orleans

March 1899—Lucy Monroe's favorable review of *The Awakening* in *Book News*

April 22, 1899—*The Awakening* published (no documentary evidence that it was ever banned)

July 1899—Chopin's statement on *The Awakening* published in *Book News*

October 1899—travels to Wisconsin lake country, where she receives English letters praising *The Awakening*

November 26, 1899—article in *St. Louis Post-Dispatch*: "On certain brisk, bright days," with "A St. Louis Woman Who Has Won Fame in Literature"

November 29, 1899—gives reading at Wednesday Club

1900—John A. Dillon in Chicago

February 1900—Herbert S. Stone returns (declines to publish) *A Vocation and a Voice*

December 9, 1900—publishes "Development of the Literary West: a Review" in *St. Louis Republic*'s Special Book Number

1900—appears in first edition of *Who's Who in America*

1901—is subject of sonnet "To the Author of 'Bayou Folk,'" by R. E. Lee Gibson

June 4, 1902—son Jean marries Emelie Hughes

July 3, 1902—"Polly" published in *Youth's Companion* (last publication)

October 15, 1902—John A. Dillon dies

December 1902—Chopin makes her will

1903—moves to 4232 McPherson Avenue

July 7, 1903—death of Emelie Chopin, Jean's wife

August 20, 1904—Chopin has cerebral hemorrhage after day at the St. Louis World's Fair

August 22, 1904—Chopin dies

August 24, 1904—burial of Kate Chopin

II

KATE CHOPIN'S
WRITINGS

This list, an adaptation and updating of Per Seyersted's bibliography, includes all of Kate Chopin's known writings, both published and unpublished. Also listed here are writings recorded in her manuscript account notebooks, but now destroyed or lost. The items are arranged in order of composition, with final title, date of composition, first appearance in print, and inclusion in collections. Where titles vary, I have listed variations. CW includes information about changes from manuscript to print versions, and KCPP includes transcriptions of Chopin's manuscript account notebooks.

ABBREVIATIONS

BF = Kate Chopin, *Bayou Folk* (Boston: Houghton, Mifflin, 1894).
CW = Per Seyersted, ed., *The Complete Works of Kate Chopin* (Baton Rouge: Louisiana State University, 1969).
DSR = Daniel S. Rankin, *Kate Chopin and Her Creole Stories* (Philadelphia: University of Pennsylvania, 1932).
ET = Emily Toth, *Kate Chopin* (New York: William Morrow, 1990).
KCM = Per Seyersted and Emily Toth, eds., *A Kate Chopin Miscellany* (Natchitoches and Oslo: Northwestern State University Press and Universitetsforlaget, 1979).
KCPP = Emily Toth and Per Seyersted, eds., *Kate Chopin's Private Papers* (Bloomington: Indiana University Press, forthcoming).
NA = Kate Chopin, *A Night in Acadie* (Chicago: Way & Williams, 1897).

PS1 = Per Seyersted, "Kate Chopin: an Important St. Louis Writer Reconsidered," *Missouri Historical Society Bulletin* 19 (January 1963), 89–114.

PS2 = Per Seyersted, "Kate Chopin's Wound: Two New Letters," *American Literary Realism* 20:1 (Fall 1987), 71–75.

SCB = Per Seyersted, *Kate Chopin: A Critical Biography* (Oslo and Baton Rouge: Universitetsforlaget and Louisiana State University, 1969).

TB = Thomas Bonner, Jr., *The Kate Chopin Companion, with Chopin's Translations from French Fiction* (Westport, CT: Greenwood, 1988).

Autograph book (with pictures, poems, brief comments by Kate O'Flaherty). 1860—.

"Katie O'Flaherty, St. Louis. 1867" (diary and commonplace book). 1867–1870. DSR (in part). KCM (in part). KCPP (in full).

"Emancipation. A Life Fable." Undated: late 1869 or early 1870. PS1. CW.

New Orleans diary. 1870—. Seen by Rankin; later lost.

Letter to Marie Breazeale. June 21, 1887. KCM. KCPP.

"Lilia. Polka for Piano." Undated. Published for the author by H. Rollman & Sons, St. Louis, 1888. KCM. KCPP.

"If It Might Be" (poem). Undated. *America* (Chicago) 1 (January 10, 1889), 9. CW.

("Euphrasie" (story). 1888. See "A No-Account Creole.")

Manuscript Account Books (2). 1888—. KCPP.

"Unfinished Story—Grand Isle." 1888–89. Destroyed.

"A Poor Girl" (story). May 1889. Destroyed.

"Wiser than a God" (story). June 1889. *Philadelphia Musical Journal* 4 (December 1889), 38–40. CW.

"A Point at Issue!" (story). August 1889. *St. Louis Post-Dispatch*, October 27, 1889. CW.

"Miss Witherwell's Mistake" (story). November 18, 1889. *Fashion and Fancy* (St. Louis) 5 (February 1891), 115–17. CW.

"With the Violin" (story). December 11, 1889. *Spectator* (St. Louis) 11 (December 6, 1890), 196. CW.

At Fault (novel). July 5, 1889–April 20, 1890. Published for the author by Nixon-Jones Printing Co., St. Louis, September, 1890. CW.

"Monsieur Pierre" (story; translation from Adrien Vely). April 1890. *St. Louis Post-Dispatch*, August 8, 1892. TB.

"Psyche's Lament" (poem). Undated; probably 1890. DSR. CW.

Letter to the *St. Louis Republic*. October 18, 1890. *St. Louis Republic*, October 25, 1890. KCM. KCPP.

Young Dr. Gosse (novel, also called *Young Dr. Gosse and Théo*). May 4–November 27, 1890. Destroyed.

"A Red Velvet Coat" (story). December 1–8, 1890. Destroyed or lost.

"At Fault. A Correction" (letter). December 11, 1890. *Natchitoches Enterprise*, December 18, 1890. ET. KCPP.

"Mrs. Mobry's Reason" (story). January 10, 1891. *New Orleans Times-Democrat*, April 23, 1893. CW.

"The Shape of the Head" (translation of an article listed in Chopin's account book as "A Study in Heads"). Undated. *St. Louis Post-Dispatch*, January 25, 1891. KCPP.

"A No-Account Creole" (story). 1888 (called "Euphrasie"); rewritten January 24, 1891–February 24, 1891. *Century* 47 (January 1894), 382–93. BF. CW.

"Octave Feuillet" (translation?). February 1891. Destroyed or lost.

"Roger and His Majesty" (story). March 1, 1891. Destroyed.

"Revival of Wrestling" (translation). Undated. *St. Louis Post-Dispatch*, March 8, 1891. KCPP.

"For Marse Chouchoute" (story). March 14, 1891. *Youth's Companion* 64 (August 20, 1891), 450–51. BF. CW.

"The Going and Coming of Liza Jane" (story). April 4, 1891. Syndicated, American Press Association, as "The Christ Light." December 1892. CW calls the story "The Going Away of Liza."

"The Maid of Saint Phillippe" (story). April 19, 1891. *Short Stories* (New York), 11 (November 1891), 257–64. CW.

"A Wizard from Gettysburg" (story). May 25, 1891. *Youth's Companion* 65 (July 7, 1892), 346–47. BF. CW.

Letter to the *Century*. May 28, 1891. KCM. KCPP.

"A Shameful Affair" (story). June 5, 7, 1891. *New Orleans Times-Democrat*, April 9, 1893.

Letter to R. W. Gilder. July 12, 1891. KCM. KCPP.

"A Rude Awakening" (story). July 13, 1891. *Youth's Companion* 66 (February 2, 1893), 54–55. BF. CW.

"A Harbinger" (story). September 11, 1891. *St. Louis Magazine* 12 (apparently November 1, 1891: No copies can be found). CW.

"Dr. Chevalier's Lie" (story). September 12, 1891. *Vogue* 2 (October 5, 1893), 174, 178. CW.

"A Very Fine Fiddle" (story). September 13, 1891. *Harper's Young People* 13 (November 24, 1891), 79. BF. CW.

"Boulôt and Boulotte" (story). September 20, 1891. *Harper's Young People* 13 (December 8, 1891), 112. BF. CW.

"Love on the Bon-Dieu" (story). October 3, 1891, as "Love and Easter." *Two Tales* (Boston) 2 (July 23, 1892), 148–56. BF. CW.

"An Embarrassing Position. Comedy in One Act (play)." October 15–22, 1891. *Mirror* (St. Louis) 5 (December 19, 1895), 9–11. CW.

"Beyond the Bayou" (story). November 7, 1891. *Youth's Companion* 66 (June 15, 1893), 302–3. BF. CW.

"Typical Forms of German Music (essay)." Paper read at the Wednesday Club, St. Louis, December 9, 1891. Possibly the same as "Typical German Composers," essay offered in 1899 to the *Atlantic*. Destroyed or lost.

"After the Winter" (story). December 31, 1891. *New Orleans Times-Democrat*, April 5, 1896. NA. CW.

"The Bênitous' Slave" (story). January 7, 1892. *Harper's Young People* 13 (February 16, 1892), 280. BF. CW.

"A Turkey Hunt" (story). January 8, 1892. *Harper's Young People* 13 (February 16, 1892), 287. BF. CW.

"Old Aunt Peggy" (story). January 8, 1892. BF. CW.

"The Lilies" (story). January 27–28, 1892. *Wide Awake* 36 (April 1893), 415–18. NA. CW.

"Mittens" (story). February 25, 1892. Destroyed or lost.

"Ripe Figs" (story). February 26, 1892. *Vogue* 2 (August 19, 1893), 90. NA. CW.

"Croque-Mitaine" (story). February 27, 1892. PS1. CW.

"A Trip to Portuguese Guinea" (translation?). February 27, 1892. Destroyed or lost.

"A Visit to the Planet Mars" (translation?). March 1892. Destroyed or lost.

"Transfusion of Goat's Blood" (translation?). March 1892. Destroyed or lost.

"Miss McEnders" (story). March 7, 1892. *Criterion* (St. Louis), 13 (March 6, 1897), 16–18, signed La Tour. CW.

"Cut Paper Figures" (also called "Manikins" and "How to Make Manikins": translation?). Undated. *St. Louis Post-Dispatch*, April 5, 1892. KCPP.

"Loka" (story). April 9–10, 1892. *Youth's Companion* 65 (December 22, 1892), 670–71. BF. CW.

"Bambo Pellier" (story). May (?) 1892. Destroyed or lost.

"At the 'Cadian Ball" (story). July 15–17, 1892. *Two Tales* (Boston) 3 (October 22, 1892), 145–52. BF. CW.

"A Visit to Avoyelles" (story). August 1, 1892. *Vogue* 1 (January 14, 1893), 74–75. BF. CW.

"Ma'ame Pélagie" (story). August 27–28, 1892. *New Orleans Times-Democrat*, December 24, 1893. BF. CW.

"A Fancy" (poem). Probably 1892. DSR. KCM. KCPP.

"Désirée's Baby" (story). November 24, 1892. *Vogue* 1 (January 14, 1893), 70–71, 74. BF. CW.

"Caline" (story). December 2, 1892. *Vogue* 1 (May 20, 1893), 324–25. NA. CW.

"The Return of Alcibiade" (story). December 5–6, 1892. *St. Louis Life* 7 (December 17, 1892), 6–8. BF. CW.

"In and Out of Old Natchitoches." (story). February 1–3, 1892. *Two Tales* 5 (April 8, 1893), 178–79. NA. CW.

"Mamouche" (story). February 24–25, 1893. *Youth's Companion* 67 (April 19, 1894), 178–79. NA. CW.

Letter to Marion A. Baker. May 4, 1893. KCM. KCPP.

Letter to R. W. Gilder. May 10, 1893. KCM. KCPP.

"Madame Célestin's Divorce" (story). May 24–25, 1893. BF. CW.

"The Song Everlasting" (poem). Before June 1893. Published in the program for the St. Louis Wednesday Club's "Reciprocity Day: An Afternoon with St. Louis Authors." November 29, 1899. CW.

"You and I" (poem). Before June 1893. Published in the program for the St. Louis Wednesday Club's "Reciprocity Day: An Afternoon with St. Louis Authors." November 29, 1899. CW.

"It Matters All" (poem). Before June 1893. DSR. CW.

"If the Woods Could Talk" (poem). Before June 1893. KCM. KCPP.

"A Sentimental Serenade" (poem). Before June 1893. KCM. KCPP.

"A Message" (poem). Before June 1893. KCM. KCPP.

"An Idle Fellow" (story). June 9, 1893. CW.

"A Matter of Prejudice" (story). June 17–18, 1893. *Youth's Companion* 68 (September 25, 1895), 450. NA. CW.

"Azélie" (story). July 22–23, 1893. *Century* 49 (December 1894), 282–87. NA. CW.

"A Lady of Bayou St. John" (story). August 24–25, 1893. *Vogue* 2 (September 21, 1893), 154, 156–58. BF. CW.

"La Belle Zoraïde" (story). September 21, 1893. *Vogue* 3 (January 4, 1894), 2, 4, 8–10. BF. CW.

"At Chênière Caminada" (story). October 21–23, 1893. *New Orleans Times-Democrat*, December 23, 1894. NA. CW.

"A Gentleman of Bayou Têche" (story). November 5–7, 1893. BF. CW.

"In Sabine" (story). November 20–22, 1893. BF. CW.

"A Respectable Woman" (story). January 20, 1894. *Vogue* 3 (February 15, 1894), 68–69, 72. NA. CW.

"Tante Cat'rinette" (story). February 23, 1894. *Atlantic Monthly* 74 (September 1894), 368–73. NA. CW.

"A Dresden Lady in Dixie" (story). March 6, 1894. *Catholic Home Journal* (March 3, 1895). NA. CW.

Bayou Folk (collected stories). Published March 1894, by Houghton, Mifflin, (Boston).

"The Story of an Hour" (story). April 19, 1894. *Vogue* 4 (December 6, 1894), 360. Written and first published as "The Dream of an Hour." CW.

"Impressions. 1894" (diary). May 4, 1894–October 26, 1896. Published in part in SCB. KCM (in full). KCPP (in full).

"Lilacs" (story). May 14–16, 1894. *New Orleans Times-Democrat*, December 20, 1896. CW.

"Good Night" (poem). Undated. *New Orleans Times-Democrat*, July 22, 1894. CW.

"The Western Association of Writers" (essay). June 30, 1894. *Critic* 22 (July 7, 1894), 15. CW.

"A Divorce Case" (story; translation from Guy de Maupassant). July 11, 1894. TB.

"A Scrap and a Sketch": "The Night Came Slowly" (story). July 24, 1894; "Juanita" (story). July 26, 1894. *Moods* (Philadelphia) 2 (July 1895), n.p. CW prints the two separately as "The Night Came Slowly" and "Juanita."

"Dorothea" (untitled story, possibly a real-life observation–not listed separately in manuscript account notebook, and not sent out separately for publication). July 25, 1894, in "Impressions. 1894." KCM. KCPP.

"Cavanelle" (story) July 31–August 6, 1894. *American Jewess* 1 (April 1895), 22–25. NA. CW.

"Mad?" (story; translation from Guy de Maupassant). September 4, 1894. TB.

Letter to Stone & Kimball. September 10, 1894. KCM. KCPP.

"Regret" (story). September 17, 1894. *Century* 50 (May 1895), 147–149. NA. CW.

"The Kiss" (story). September 19, 1894. *Vogue* 5 (January 17, 1895), 37. CW.

"Ozème's Holiday" (story). September 23–24, 1894. *Century* 52 (August 1896), 629–31. NA. CW.

" 'Crumbling Idols' By Hamlin Garland" (essay). Undated. *St. Louis Life* 10 (October 6, 1894), 13. CW.

Letter to Waitman Barbe. October 2, 1894. KCM. KCPP.

"The Real Edwin Booth" (essay). Undated. *St. Louis Life* 10 (October 13, 1894), 11. CW.

"Emile Zola's 'Lourdes' " (essay). Undated. *St. Louis Life* 10 (November 17, 1894), 5. CW.

"A Sentimental Soul" (story). November 18–22, 1894. *New Orleans Times-Democrat*, December 22, 1895. NA. CW.

"Her Letters" (story). November 29, 1894. *Vogue* 5 (April 11, 18, 1895), 228–30, 248. CW.

Letters to A. A. Hill. December 26, 1894; January 1, 11, 16, 1895. KCM. KCPP.

"Odalie Misses Mass" (story). January 28, 1895. *Shreveport Times*, July 1, 1895. NA. CW.

"It?" (story; translation from Guy de Maupassant). February 4, 1895. *St. Louis Life* 11 (February 23, 1895), 12–13. TB.

"Polydore" (story). February 17, 1895. *Youth's Companion* 70 (April 23, 1896), 214–215. NA. CW.

"Dead Men's Shoes" (story). February 21–22, 1895. *Independent* (New York) 49 (February 11, 1897), 194–95. NA. CW.

"Solitude" (story; translation from Guy de Maupassant). March 5, 1895. *St. Louis Life* 13 (December 28, 1895). 30. TB.

"Night" (story; translation from Guy de Maupassant). March 8, 1895. TB.

Letter to J. M. Stoddart. March 31, 1895. KCM. KCPP.

"Athénaïse" (story). April 10–28, 1895. *Atlantic Monthly* 78 (August, September, 1896), 232–241, 404–13. NA. CW.

"A Lady of Shifting Intentions" (story). May 4, 1895. Destroyed or lost; extant fragment in KCM, KCPP.

"Two Summers and Two Souls" (story). July 14, 1895. *Vogue* 6 (August 7, 1895), 84. CW.

"The Unexpected" (story). July 18, 1895. *Vogue* 6 (September 18, 1895), 180–81. CW.

"Two Portraits" ("The Nun and the Wanton") (story). August 4, 1895. DSR. CW.

"If Some Day" (poem). August 16, 1895. CW.

"Under My Lattice" (poem). August 18, 1895. KCM. KCPP.

"To Carrie B." (poem). Autumn 1895. CW.

"The Falling in Love of Fedora" (story). November 19, 1895. *Criterion* (St. Louis) 13 (February 20, 1897), 9, signed La Tour. Published in CW as "Fedora."

Letter to Cornelia F. Maury. December 3, 1895. KCM. KCPP.

"For Mrs. Ferris(s)" (poem). December 1895. KCM. KCPP.

"To Blanche" (poem). December 1895. KCM. KCPP.

"Vagabonds" (story). December (?) 1895. DSR. CW.

"Suicide" (story; translation from Guy de Maupassant). December 18, 1895. *St. Louis Republic*, June 5, 1898. TB.

"To Hider Schuyler—" (poem). Christmas 1895. CW.

"To 'Billy' with a Box of Cigars" (poem). Christmas 1895. CW.

Letter to Stone & Kimball. January 2, 1896. KCM. KCPP.

"Madame Martel's Christmas Eve" (story). January 16–18, 1896. CW.

"The Recovery" (story). February, 1896. *Vogue* 7 (May 21, 1896), 354–55. CW.

"A Night in Acadie" (story). March 1896. NA. CW.

"A Pair of Silk Stockings" (story). April, 1896. *Vogue* 10 (September 16, 1897), 191–92. CW.

"Nég Créol" (story). April, 1896. *Atlantic Monthly* 80 (July 1897), 135–38. NA. CW.

"Aunt Lympy's Interference" (story). June, 1896. *Youth's Companion* 71 (August 12, 1897), 373–74. CW.

"The Blind Man" (story). July, 1896. *Vogue* 9 (May 13, 1897), 303. CW.

"In the Confidence of a Story-Writer" (essay). October 1896. *Atlantic Monthly* 83 (January 1899), 137–39, published without an author's name. CW. (An earlier version, written September 1896 and entitled "Confidences," is also published in CW.)

"Ti Frère" (story). September 1896. KCM. KCPP.

"For Sale" (story; translation from Guy de Maupassant). October 26, 1896. TB.

"A Vocation and a Voice" (story). November 1896. *Mirror* (St. Louis) 12 (March 27, 1902), 18–24. CW.

"A Mental Suggestion" (story). December 1896. CW.

"To Mrs. R" (poem). Christmas 1896. CW.

"Let the Night Go" (poem). January 1, 1897. CW.

Letter to the *Century*. January 5, 1897. KCM. KCPP.

Inscription for Ruth McEnery Stuart. February 3, 1897. KCM. KCPP.

"Suzette" (story). February 1897. V*ogue* 10 (October 21, 1897), 262–63. CW.

"As You Like It" (a series of six essays). Undated, individual essay titles supplied by Per Seyersted. *Criterion* (St. Louis), p. 13:

    I. "I have a young friend . . ." February 13, 1897, 11. CW.

    II. "It has lately been . . ." February 20, 1897, 17. CW.

    III. "Several years ago . . ." February 27, 1897, 11. CW.

    IV. "A while ago . . ." March 13, 1897, 15–16. CW.

    V. "A good many of us . . ." March 20, 1897, 10. CW.

    IV. "We are told . . ." (March 27, 1897), 10. CW.

"The Locket" (story). March 1897. CW.

"A Morning Walk" (story). April 1897. Published as "An Easter Day Conversion." *Criterion* (St. Louis) 15 [sic] (April 17, 1897), 13–14. CW.

"An Egyptian Cigarette" (story). April 1897. V*ogue* 15 (April 19, 1900), 252–54. CW.

A *Night in Acadie* (collected stories). Published November 1897, by Way & Williams (Chicago).

The Awakening (novel). June (?), 1897–January 21, 1898, listed in Chopin's notebook as "A Solitary Soul." Published April 22, 1899, by Herbert S. Stone & Company (Chicago & New York). CW.

"A Family Affair" (story). December (?), 1897. Syndicated—American Press Association, January 1898. *Saturday Evening Post* 172 (September 9, 1899), 168–69. CW.

" 'Is Love Divine?' The Question Answered by Three Ladies Well Known in St. Louis Society" (interview). *St. Louis Post-Dispatch*, January 16, 1898, 17. ET. KCPP.

"Has High Society Struck the Pace That Kills?" (interview). *St. Louis Post-Dispatch*, February 6, 1898, 12. ET. KCPP.

Letter to Lydia Arms Avery Coonley Ward. March 21, 1898. PS2. KCPP.

"Elizabeth Stock's One Story" (story). March 1898. PS1. CW.

"A Horse Story" (story). Also called "Ti Démon." March 1898. KCM. KCPP.

"Father Amable" (story; translation from Guy de Maupassant). April 21, 1898. TB.

"There's Music Enough" (poem). May 1, 1898. DSR. CW.

"An Ecstasy of Madness" (poem). July 10, 1898. DSR. CW.

"The Roses" (poem). July 11, 1898. KCM. KCPP.

"The Storm" (story). July 19, 1898. CW.

"Lines to Him" (poem). July 31, 1898. KCM. KCPP.

"White Oaks" (poem). August 24, 1898. KCM. KCPP.

"Lines Suggested by Omar" (poem). August 1898. KCM. KCPP.

"The Lull of Summer Time" (poem). Undated, but probably August 1898. KCM. KCPP.

"To Henry One Evening Last Summer" (poem). October 21, 1898. KCM. KCPP.

"By The Meadow Gate" (poem). October 24, 1898. KCM. KCPP.

"Old Natchitoches" (poem). December 1898. KCM. KCPP.

"An Hour" (poem). Undated, but before January 1899. DSR. KCM. KCPP.

"In Spring" (poem). Undated, but before January 1899. *Century* 58 (July 1899), 361. KCM. KCPP.

"I Wanted God" (poem). Undated, but before February 1899. CW.

"My Lady Rose Pouts" (poem). Undated, but before February 1899. KCM. KCPP.

"Come to Me" (poem). Undated, but before February 1899. KCM. KCPP.

'O! Blessed Tavern" (poem). Undated, but before February 1899. KCM. KCPP.

"As Careless As the Summer Breeze" (poem). Undated, but before February 1899. KCM. KCPP.

"One Day" (poem). Undated, but before February 1899. KCM. KCPP.

"Ah! Magic Bird!" (poem). Undated, but before February 1899. KCM. KCPP.

"With a Violet-Wood Paper Knife" (poem). Undated, but before February 1899. KCM. KCPP.

"Because—" (poem). Undated, but probably 1899. CW.

"The Godmother" (story). January–February 6, 1899. *Mirror* (St. Louis) 11 (December 12, 1901), 9–13. CW.

"The Haunted Chamber" (poem). February 1899. CW.

Letter to the *Youth's Companion*. February 11, 1899. KCM. KCPP.

"A Little Country Girl" (story). February 11, 1899. CW.

"Life" (poem). May 10, 1899. DSR. CW.

Letter to Herbert S. Stone. May 21, 1899. KCM. KCPP.

Statement on *The Awakening*. May 28, 1899. *Book News* 17 (July 1899), 612. KCM. KCPP.

Letter to Herbert S. Stone. June 7, 1899. KCM. KCPP.

"A Little Day" (poem). Undated, but probably 1899. KCM. KCPP.

Inscription for Madison Cawein. August 17, 1899. KCM. KCPP.

Letter to Richard B. Shepard. August 24, 1899. KCM. KCPP.

Letter to Richard B. Shepard. November 8, 1899. PS2. KCPP.

"A Reflection" (story). November 1899. DSR. CW.

"On certain brisk, bright days" (untitled essay, title supplied by Per Seyersted). Undated, but undoubtedly November 1899. *St. Louis Post-Dispatch*, November 26, 1899. CW.

"Ti Démon" (story). November 1899. CW.

Letter to the *Century*. December 1, 1899. KCM. KCPP.

"A December Day in Dixie" (story). January 1900. DSR (in part), CW (in full).

"Alexandre's Wonderful Experience" (story). January 23, 1900. KCM. KCPP.

"The Gentleman from New Orleans" (story). February 6, 1900. CW.

Letter to the *Youth's Companion*. February 15, 1900. DSR. KCM. KCPP.

"Charlie" (story). April 1900. CW.

"The White Eagle" (story). May 9, 1900. *Vogue* 16 (July 12, 1900), 20, 22. CW.

"Alone" (poem). July 6, 1900. KCM. KCPP.

"To the Friend of My Youth: To Kitty" (poem). DSR (who dates it August 24, 1900). CW.

"Development of the Literary West: a Review" (essay). Undated. *St. Louis Republic*, December 9, 1900, p. 1. ET. KCPP.

Letter to R. E. Lee Gibson. October 13, 1901. KCM. KCPP.

"Millie's First Party" (story). Also called "Millie's First Ball." October 16, 1901. Destroyed or lost.

"The Wood-Choppers" (story). October 17, 1901. *Youth's Companion* 76 (May 29, 1902), 270–71. CW.

"Toots' Nurses" (story). October 18, 1901. Destroyed or lost.

"Polly" (story). January 14, 1902, as "Polly's Opportunity." *Youth's Companion* 76 (July 3, 1902), 334–35. CW.

Letter to Marie Breazeale. February 4, 1902. KCM. KCPP.

UNDATABLE MATERIALS:

Reminiscences about Kitty Garesché. Undated; 1885? DSR. KCM. KCPP.

"The Impossible Miss Meadows" (story). CW. Possibly a sketch for "The Falling in Love of Fedora."

Letter to Mrs. Tiffany. Undated. KCM. KCPP.

Letter to Professor Otto Heller (Washington University). December 26, no year. KCPP.

Letter to Mrs. Douglas. July 10, year unknown. KCM. KCPP.

III

THE ALLEGED
BANNING OF
THE AWAKENING

During the last two decades, thousands of readers have been told that *The Awakening* was banned. That has, in fact, been part of the novel's appeal—for few people can resist reading a banned book. "A Daring Writer Banned" is indeed the title for Chapter 8 in Per Seyersted's 1969 Kate Chopin biography, and Seyersted is the one most responsible for the rediscovery, and new appreciation, of Chopin's writing.

When *Redbook* reprinted *The Awakening* in November 1972 as "a classic underground novel," the magazine's introductory note claimed that "the Mercantile Library in St. Louis refused to handle it." As for Kate Chopin, according to *Redbook*, "the St. Louis Fine Arts Club expelled her as a member. Acquaintances cut her, friends deserted her."

As Seyersted had pointed out (but only in a footnote), there is no evidence that such a club existed. As his research also showed, Chopin did not lose her friends (or at least not all of them). They wrote her glowing fan letters about *The Awakening*; they invited her to read from her writings at the Wednesday Club, the most prestigious women's club in St. Louis.

But Seyersted's facts came too late to overcome the legend. The mythical, blackballing fine arts club still appears in notes about Chopin. Some critics even rename it the St. Louis Art Association or the St. Louis Arts Society. In fact the only organization with a similar name in Chopin's day, the St. Louis Artist's Guild, did enroll her as a member.

The book-banning story, too, has become a staple—yet there is no proof that *The Awakening* was ever banned. The alleged banning of *The Awakening* is a complex story that is difficult to disentangle.

Within a few years after Chopin's death in 1904, the myth was spread that she had been so hurt by the reception of *The Awakening* that she never wrote again.

The earliest source of that rumor seems to be the author's daughter, Lélia Chopin Hattersley, who wrote to the critic Leonidas Rutledge Whipple in 1907 that "my Mother

. . . never discussed the reception of *The Awakening* with me . . . But I know how deeply she was hurt by many facts, principally that she never wrote again." And so Whipple wrote in his essay on Kate Chopin for the *Library of Southern Literature* that "the unfriendly reception given *[The Awakening]* by certain narrow-minded critics struck deep at the author's heart, even killing her desire to write so that from about 1899 until her death in St. Louis, August, 1904, she produced nothing more."

It should be noted that Lélia Chopin Hattersley, a very dramatic person, was something of a storyteller and mythmaker herself, and virtually all of her memories that have appeared in print can be proven wrong. According to Lélia, her mother was a much-beloved Lady Bountiful in Cloutierville, but in fact Kate Chopin was notorious for her flamboyant fashions and her flirting. Lélia also claimed that her mother preferred to write in the sitting room, with children "swarming" about her—but Kate had had her own study throughout the 1890s while Lélia was living with her. The Chopin children were in fact young adults leading their own lives, as the society pages show. And since Lélia lived with her mother for her entire life, she undoubtedly knew that Kate did continue to write after *The Awakening*.

For a while, Lélia's version did prevail. Fred Lewis Pattee, who frequently reprinted "Désirée's Baby" and kept Chopin's reputation alive, nevertheless believed she had stopped writing. In his *American Literature Since 1870* (1915), Pattee wrote that ". . . five years before her death, discouraged by the reception of her novel *The Awakening*, Kate Chopin became silent."

Other informants closer to Chopin's time also reported that the criticism of *The Awakening* had killed her creative impulses. In a 1928 master's thesis at Tulane, for instance, Amy Elizabeth Taggart wrote that after the "storm of protest" over *The Awakening*, Kate Chopin stopped writing. Taggart had corresponded with the author's son Felix—whose memories were also unreliable. (He claimed, for instance, that *The Awakening* had been condemned because "a woman permits a man to kiss her on the neck"—but no such scene takes place.)

The myth of Kate Chopin's silence was continued by, among others, Dorothy Anne Dondore in her influential article on "Kate O'Flaherty Chopin" for the *Dictionary of American Biography*. Dondore wrote: "It is one of the tragedies of recent American literature that Mrs. Chopin should have written *The Awakening* two decades in advance of its time, that she should have been so grievously hurt by the attacks of provincial critics as to lay aside her pen."

But Daniel Rankin, investigating and restoring Chopin's works in the early 1930s, established that the earliest informants had been wrong. As her own manuscript account notebooks show, Chopin had both written and published stories after *The Awakening*: Among others, she published "The White Eagle" in *Vogue* in 1900 and "A Vocation and a Voice" in *Reedy's Mirror* (St. Louis) in 1902. At the time of her death, she expected to publish her third short story collection, *A Vocation and a Voice*, within a year. By rediscovering and publishing both her record of story writing and the texts of some of the stories, Rankin proved without a doubt that Kate Chopin had not stopped writing, despite the severe criticism of her novel.

But Rankin, who was often careless with his facts, introduced another myth: He wrote that *The Awakening* "was taken from circulation by order of the librarian of the St. Louis Mercantile Library. Kate Chopin was denied membership in the Fine Arts Club of the city." Rankin gave no source and later told Per Seyersted that his notes had been accidentally lost.

After Rankin, critics spread a sad tale: *The Awakening* had been removed from library shelves; Chopin had been shunned by her friends; and she had been denied membership in a fine arts club. All these charges appear, for instance, in a 1932 master's thesis by Nora Alice Norris, who had corresponded with Rankin. According to Norris, "It was the attitude of certain parts of St. Louis society, the withdrawal from circulation of her novel by the St. Louis Mercantile Library, and the refusal of admittance by the St. Louis Art Association which *did* hurt the sensitive writer."

Felix Chopin added to the legend of the banning of *The Awakening* in a 1949 interview with Charles van Ravenswaay, then director of the Missouri Historical Society. According to Felix, "Many newspapers and libraries treated the book as indecent. The Mercantile Library, among others, took it out of circulation, and Mother resigned her membership as a result. She was broken hearted at the reaction to the book."

Subsequent articles also reported that *The Awakening* had been banned and/or withdrawn from library circulation. For instance, Robert Cantwell wrote in 1956: "The book was banned from library circulation, and the author refused admittance to the St. Louis Arts Society." Said Kenneth Eble (1956): ". . . the book was taken from circulation at the Mercantile Library, and . . . she was now denied membership in the Fine Arts Club." Edmund Wilson continued the legend (1962): "It was taken out of circulation in the St. Louis Mercantile Library . . . and she was blackballed on being put up for membership in the St. Louis Fine Arts Club." Similar reports came from Stanley Kauffmann (1966): ". . . it was banned from libraries, . . ." and Larzer Ziff (1966): "In her own city of Saint Louis the libraries refused to circulate the book, and the Fine Arts Club denied her membership because of it."

With the publication of Per Seyersted's biography, the story of the banning of *The Awakening* became entrenched—and, indeed, it was part of the revival of the novel. Seyersted himself had little reason to doubt that the book had been banned. Rankin had said so, and so had Chopin's son, and library records from the St. Louis Public Library and the Mercantile Library were evidently not available. Further, a former director of the Mercantile Library, Clarence E. Miller, told Seyersted that Kate Chopin had once come to the library with a friend and been told that the library had taken the book from circulation.

Also, Kate Chopin's own words about her book—"The libraries? They don't keep it"—could be construed to mean "The book is banned." But more likely she was recording an exasperated reaction. People often do ask writers, "Where can I get your book?" rather than going to libraries or bookstores and finding it themselves.

After Seyersted's book, other scholars promulgated the story that *The Awakening* had been banned. For instance: George Spangler (1970): ". . . the book was withdrawn from the libraries in St. Louis, her native city, and she was denied membership in the St. Louis Fine Arts Club . . ." Bert Bender (1974): ". . . [she was] refused membership in the St. Louis Fine Arts Club, and the novel was quickly banned from the public libraries in St. Louis." Clement Eaton (1974): ". . . the book was banned from circulation in the St. Louis Library." In the 1980s, countless critics also reported that *The Awakening* had been banned—and professors usually begin their lectures on *The Awakening* with that "fact."

I came to doubt the banning story only because Beverly Bishop, former archivist at the Missouri Historical Society, once told me that Joan Mayerson Clatworthy, another Chopin researcher working in the late 1970s, had expressed doubts.

My inquiries showed that there is no documentary evidence for the banning. No contemporaries who opposed censorship railed against the suppression of *The Awakening* (as they did, for instance, over the hounding of Oscar Wilde, or the withdrawal of certain French novels from the public school libraries). The records now available from the St. Louis Mercantile Library and the St. Louis Public Library show that both libraries did indeed stock copies of *The Awakening*, and that they were not taken from the shelves until long after publication—when, presumably, the copies were worn out. Even Lélia Chopin Hattersley, eloquent in supporting her mother's work, apparently never claimed that the book had been banned.

Yet it is not hard to see why the belief that *The Awakening* was banned has become entrenched. Clarence E. Miller, the retired librarian who shared the story with Per Seyersted, was taking part in an American tradition: the mocking of our ancestors for their (alleged) pruderies. *The Awakening* was withdrawn, Miller told Seyersted, by "bigoted people on the book-committee." Available library committee reports show no withdrawal or banning—but Miller, speaking more than sixty years after the alleged banning, may have genuinely believed that it took place. Certainly there have been many other similar tales.

Americans do enjoy book-banning stories. We find them enticing, titillating. In the case of Grace Metalious's *Peyton Place* (1956), for instance, rumors that the book had been banned in all of Canada spurred sales in the United States; the story that her schoolteacher husband had been fired because of her book made *Peyton Place* an instant best seller. When, twenty-five years later, I wrote that he had *not* been fired, reviewers of my book generally ignored my denial. Most led off their reviews of my 1981 Metalious biography with some variety of the same "fact": "Teacher Fired for Wife's Book."

And so I suspect that most editors and reviewers will continue to proclaim that *The Awakening* was banned—regardless of my denials. Possibly the book-banning story will lead even more people to read the book, for Kate Chopin herself wrote about the appeal of banned books to a young person: "He has been led to believe that the work is dangerous and alluring. Failing to obtain it at the libraries he is quite convinced that it is pernicious and altogether delightful, whereupon he hurries, in some instances, to the nearest book store and spends his week's allowance in procuring it."

The fact that *The Awakening* was not (apparently) banned may matter less, in the end, than the fact that the book has been revived. The alleged banning of *The Awakening* did not aid book sales in Chopin's day—but the belief in the banning has enabled us to rediscover a lost literary treasure.

And so, long after her death, gossip has, at last, been good to Kate Chopin.

(The Notes to this Appendix are on p. 505–506.)

NOTES

Abbreviations used in Notes
BOOKS AND DOCUMENTS

CW = *The Complete Works of Kate Chopin*, ed. Per Seyersted. Baton Rouge: Louisiana State University Press, 1969.

DSR = Daniel S. Rankin, *Kate Chopin and Her Creole Stories*. Philadelphia: University of Pennsylvania, 1932.

ESM = Elizabeth Shown Mills, *Chauvin dit Charleville*. Cane River Creole Series. Mississippi State, Mississippi: Mississippi State University, 1976.

FELIX = "Statement on Kate Chopin," January 19, 1949, interview with Felix Chopin (Kate's son), notes taken by Charles van Ravenswaay of MHS. Reprinted in KCM, KCPP.

HSL = William Hyde and Howard L. Conard, eds., *Encyclopedia of the History of St. Louis*. New York, Louisville, St. Louis: Southern History Company, 1899.

KOCB = Kate O'Flaherty's commonplace book, 1868–70, which includes her honeymoon diary. Reprinted with mistakes in DSR; reprinted partially in KCM; reprinted completely in KCPP. Original at MHS.

KC94 = Kate Chopin's 1894 diary, in the notebook called "Impressions." Reprinted in KCM and KCPP. Original at MHS.

KCM = Per Seyersted and Emily Toth, eds., *A Kate Chopin Miscellany*. Natchitoches: Northwestern State University Press, and Oslo: Universitetsforlaget, 1979. Updated and superseded by KCPP.

KCPP = Emily Toth and Per Seyersted, eds., *Kate Chopin's Private Papers*. Bloomington: Indiana University Press, forthcoming. Updates and supersedes KCM.

MAB = Kate Chopin's manuscript account books, reprinted in KCPP. Originals at MHS.

OCUS = *Oscar Chopin, Executor, v. United States No. 592, French and American Claims Commission*, Files of the French and American Claims Commission, Diplomatic Archives, National Archives, Washington, D.C.

OJ = Orrick Johns, *Time of Our Lives* (New York: Stackpole, 1937).

SCB = Per Seyersted, *Kate Chopin: a Critical Biography*. Baton Rouge: Louisiana State University Press and Oslo: Universitetsforlaget, 1969.

Wilson = Maryhelen Wilson, "Kate Chopin's Family: Fallacies and Facts, Including Kate's True Birthdate," *Kate Chopin Newsletter* 2 (1976–77), 25–31.

WS = William Schuyler, "Kate Chopin," *The Writer* VII (August 1894), 115–17. Reprinted in KCM, KCPP.

NOTE: All of Kate Chopin's works are quoted from CW unless otherwise stated. With *The Awakening*, chapter numbers are cited.

LIBRARY COLLECTIONS

McCoy Collection = Collection of scrapbooks and other materials gathered by Mildred McCoy, NSU. Some of the scrapbooks have been microfilmed and are available on loan.

Melrose Collection = Collecton of scrapbooks and other materials gathered by Cammie G. Henry, NSU.

MHS = Missouri Historical Society, St. Louis.

NSU = Cammie G. Henry Research Center, Eugene P. Watson Memorial Library, Northwestern State University, Natchitoches, Louisiana.

INDIVIDUALS INTERVIEWED AND FREQUENTLY CITED

Carnahan = Lucille Tinker Carnahan, former curator of the Kate Chopin Home/Bayou Folk Museum, Cloutierville, interviews 1975–89. Lucille Tinker Carnahan also prepared for me several family trees and an invaluable map designating the houses in Cloutierville in the 1880s.

Cloutierville Group = joint interview, 1985, with Louise Rachal Barron, Lucille Tinker Carnahan, Emma Richter Masson, Louise Pollock, Albert Sampite, Leona Sampite. (Louise Pollock, Albert Sampite, and Leona Sampite are all grandchildren of Albert and Loca Sampite.)

DeLouche = the late Ivy DeLouche, former resident of Cloutierville, grandniece of Albert and Loca Sampite, interviews 1976, 1984, 1986.

McCoy = the late Mildred McCoy, founder of the Kate Chopin Home/Bayou Folk Museum, Cloutierville, interviews 1976–79

Sampite = Leona Sampite of Cloutierville, granddaughter of Albert and Loca Sampite, interviews 1984–89.

Waters = the late Julia ("July") Breazeale Waters, Kate Chopin's niece, interviews 1975, 1984.

Wells = Carol Wells, former archivist at NSU, interviews and letters 1984–89.

PROLOGUE:

19: "Provide yourself . . .": Lewis Ely's letter of May 13, 1899. KCM, KCPP, at MHS.

19: "Irish Beauty": Kitty Gareschè, cited in DSR, p. 52.

19: "Female loveliness": January 7, 1869, letter from J. H. Tighe of New York to James Murrin of St. Louis. KCPP.

19: "Amiability" and "cleverness": WS writes of her "amiability of character and her cleverness."

19: Air of marquise: SCB, p. 61.

19: "Mysterious fascination": SCB, p. 61, quoting DSR, p. 106.

19: "Rogue in porcelain": "Among the New Books," *St. Louis Post-Dispatch*, December 11, 1897, p. 4.

19: Romantic novels: WS.

19: "General spreeing" and "whose only talent lies in their feet," KOCB, reprinted in KCM, KCPP. KOCB also includes advice about flirting.

20: "Society swells" were a favorite target of criticism by Chopin's friend William Marion Reedy.

20: "A pink-red group of intellectuals" with "eccentric clothing": FELIX.

20: "Worthy critical faculty": KC94 entry for June 7, 1894.

20: "Seductive entreaties," *The Awakening*, chap. XXXI.

21: "Sex fiction": "Books of the Day," *Chicago Times-Herald*, June 1, 1899, p. 9.

21: "Notes from Bookland," *St. Louis Globe-Democrat*, May 13, 1899, p. 5.

21: Frances Porcher, "*The Awakening*," *St. Louis Mirror*, May 4, 1899, p. 6.

21: Sibert (Willa Cather), "Books and Magazines," *Pittsburgh Leader*, July 8, 1899, p. 6. Also discussed in Sharon O'Brien, "Sentiment, Local Color, and the New Woman Writer: Kate Chopin and Willa Cather," *Kate Chopin Newsletter* II:3 (Winter 1976–77), 16–24.

21: "Books of the Week," *Providence Sunday Journal,* June 4, 1899, p. 15.
21: G. B., "Kate Chopin's Novel," *St. Louis Post-Dispatch,* May 20, 1899, p. 6. DSR, 173n, incorrectly attributes this review to the *St. Louis Republic* for that date, and other critics have followed DSR. The review was discovered in the *Post-Dispatch* by Richard Arthur Martin, "The Fictive World of Kate Chopin," Ph.D. Thesis, Northwestern University, 1971, 189–90. Martin reprints the review on p. 194.
21: "The artist with the courageous soul that dares and defies": The passage from *The Awakening* is quoted by Sue V. Moore, May 1899 letter to Kate Chopin, KCM, KCPP. Original at MHS.
21: "More wisdom than the Holy Ghost": *The Awakening,* Chap. VI.

CHAPTER 1: A CURIOUS CHILD

23: 1855 photograph is in this volume.
23: Marie Therese: 1985 interview with Maryhelen Wilson, St. Louis genealogist. While reading St. Louis newspaper obituaries, Wilson found a reference (undated) to Marie Therese.
23: St. Louis living conditions: James Neal Primm, *Lion of the Valley: St. Louis, Missouri* (Boulder, CO: Pruett Publishing Company, 1981), pp. 162–64, 358, 474; Charles Van Ravenswaay, "Years of Turmoil, Years of Growth: St. Louis in the 1850's," *Missouri Historical Society Bulletin,* July 1967, pp. 303–324.
24: O'Flaherty household: "Ed. O'Flaherty, 25, surveyor" is listed at the O'Flahertys' house in the 1850 United States Census, but he does not appear in the 1860 United States Census. According to Wilson (1985 interview), Jane O'Flaherty probably died in 1856. She is buried in Calvary Cemetery under the name "Jennie O'Flaherty."
24: O'Flaherty slaves: 1855 Missouri Census Book, 1860 Missouri Census Slave Schedules. The 1855 Census Book lists four slaves, all unnamed, at the O'Flahertys' address: two females, between the ages of twenty-one and forty-five; one female between fifteen and twenty-one; and one male between twenty-one and forty-five.
24: George O'Flaherty's prizes: Information about academic awards appears in the *Catalogue of the Officers and Students of the St. Louis University, Missouri, 1855–1856* (St. Louis: Republican Book and Job Printing Office, 1856), pp. 2–26. I am indebted to Brian Forney, Head Reference Librarian, Pius XII Memorial Library, St. Louis University, for this information.
24: George O'Flaherty's letter: DSR, pp. 21–22.
24: "Wet, disagreeable day": *Missouri Republican,* February 8, 1850.
24: "Cath.": The 1850 United States Census lists "Cath. 7/12" with the O'Flahertys. According to census practice, "7/12" means seven months old, and the census taker noted the O'Flahertys in August 1850.
24: Women's fibbing about their ages: Wilson.
24: Baptismal record: Jean Bardot, *"L'influence française dans la vie et l'oeuvre de Kate Chopin." Thèse de doctorat,* Université de Paris-IV, 1985–1986, p. 18. The baptismal record, very misspelled, reads: *"L'an dix huit cent cinquante, le douze mai, Je soussigné,*

ai baptisé Catherine, fille de Thomas Oflohiatry et d'Elisa Fealis son épouse, née le huit février dernier. Le parrain est Charles Sanguinnet et la marraine est Jeanne Sanguinnet, qui one signé avec nous le présent acte. signé: O. Renaud, prêtre/ Charles Sanguinett/ Jane Sanguinett." (On May 12, 1850, Father O. Renaud baptized Catherine O'Flaherty, born the previous February 8, the daughter of Thomas O'Flaherty and his wife Eliza Faris.)

24: Jane Sanguinet or Sanguinette was Eliza O'Flaherty's sister; her husband, Charles, was a descendant of one of St. Louis's oldest French fur-trading families. Katie O'Flaherty, contrary to custom, was not named for her same-sex godparent.

24: "I am younger today . . . .": KC94.

24: Katie O'Flaherty's father . . . and Kate's early outing: DSR, pp. 29–31. Rankin attributes the story to a letter from Chopin's son Felix, but Rankin himself may have created some of the more colorful details, such as the description of the horses, footman, and carriage. Rankin's notes for his biography were accidentally lost: SCB, pp. 10–11.

25: Descriptions of the St. Louis levee (harbor) appear in Winston Churchill, *The Crisis* (New York: Macmillan, 1901), p. 3; Cyril Coniston Clemens, "The History of St. Louis, 1854–1860," M. A. Thesis, Washington University, 1949, p. 3; HSL, pp. 362, 898; Ernest Kirschten, *Catfish and Crystal* (Garden City, NY: Doubleday, 1960), p. 85; Primm, pp. 165, 167; Van Ravenswaay, p. 304.

25: Pickery: DSR, p. 94.

25: "Where no woman": *The Awakening*, Chap. X.

26: Eliza O'Flaherty's background: DSR, pp. 24–27, 105; Wilson and 1985 Wilson interview; ESM, pp. 51–54. Eliza Faris's birthdate was July 11, 1828, according to a handwritten genealogical chart at Oakland estate, supplied by Jeannine Cook.

26: Eliza and Thomas O'Flaherty's portrait is at MHS.

26–29: Thomas O'Flaherty's background: DSR, pp. 16–22. The O'Flaherty fury is mentioned in *Fodor's Ireland 1981* (New York: David McKay, 1981), pp. 184–85, but Rankin gives a different wording that he says became part of the Litany during Elizabethan times: "From the ferocious O'Flahertys, Good Lord, deliver us"—DSR, p. 16. Irish conditions: Edward Wakin, *Enter the Irish-American* (New York: Thomas Y. Crowell, 1976), pp. 7–11. Ireland is called the "most distressful country" in the song "The Wearin' of the Green."

28: Irish deaths in New Orleans canals: Wakin, p. 51.

28: Roger McAllister: His name is sometimes incorrectly given as Robert, but he signed himself as Roger.

28–29: Other sources for Thomas O'Flaherty's civic activity: Membership in Catholic Orphan Association: J. Thomas Scharf, *History of St. Louis City and County* (Philadelphia: Louis H. Everts & Co., 1883), p. 1759. Mercantile Library: Mercantile Library membership records, supplied by Robert Behra and John Neal Hoover. Firemen: SCB, p. 15; Scharf, pp. 795, 1828; McCune Gill, *St. Louis Story* (Hopkinsville, KY: St. Louis Historical Record Association, 1952), p. 245.

29: Thomas O'Flaherty's marriage: DSR, pp. 20–21. The Reilhe-O'Flaherty marriage notice (November 25, 1839) is reprinted in Lois Stanley, Maryhelen Wilson, and George F. Wilson, *Marriage Records of St. Charles County, Missouri, 1805–1844* (St. Louis: privately printed, 1970), p. 60. Catherine Reilhe O'Flaherty's death notice, from January 27, 1844, is reprinted in Lois Stanley, George F. Wilson, and Maryhelen Wilson, *Death Records of Pioneer Missouri Women, 1808–1849* (St. Louis: privately printed,

1981), p. 52. Catherine Reilhe O'Flaherty is buried in Calvary Cemetery next to her son George. DSR, p. 21 claims that Catherine Reilhe O'Flaherty died giving birth to George, but George's obituary and tombstone say that he was in his twenty-third year when he died in 1863, putting his birth in 1840 or 1841. Likewise, the United States Census lists him as nine years old in 1850 and nineteen in 1860. George was baptized in St. Francis Xavier Church on February 25, 1844 (1986 communication from Deacon Martin G. Towey, archivist, Archdiocese of St. Louis). Since George's baptism took place nearly a month after his mother's death, that may have given rise to the tradition that she died giving birth to him.

29: Ages of marriage in Eliza Faris's family: Wilson. Charleville background: ESM, pp. 50–55.

30: "Closing the portals," *The Awakening*, Chap. VII.

30: O'Flaherty home: DSR, pp. 11, 12, 37, 38; "A St. Louis Woman Who Has Won Fame in Literature," *St. Louis Post-Dispatch*, November 26, 1899, part 4, p. 1. The site of the O'Flahertys' home is now occupied by Ralston Purina, makers of Meow Mix, Puppy Chow, and other pet-food products.

30: Slaves: Louise is mentioned in Eliza O'Flaherty's March 10, 1864, letter to her uncle F. A. Charleville: KCM, KCPP, original at MHS. Male slave held Kate's pony: DSR, p. 37. WS says that Kate O'Flaherty "knew the faithful love of her negro 'mammy.'"

30: Neighbors: Deborah Isaacs, "Ante-Bellum Days in St. Louis," *Glimpses of the Past* V:10–12 (October–December, 1938), 139–155, esp. 152–53.

30: "Solid men of St. Louis": The 1864 St. Louis City Directory reprints (p. 97 ff.) the 1861 list of "solid men," and includes the widowed Eliza O'Flaherty. In the 1860 United States Census, Eliza O'Flaherty owned real estate valued at $150,000.

30–31: Descriptions of the Gasconade disaster: *Missouri Republican*, Nov. 1, Nov. 3, Nov. 5, 1855, and Scharf, pp. 1159–1160. Reverend Teasdale's last words: Margaret Haley Carpenter, *Sara Teasdale* (New York: Schulte, 1960), p. 10. Reverend Teasdale's granddaughter Sara, born nearly thirty years after the Gasconade disaster, grew up to be the greatest St. Louis poet of the generation after Kate Chopin's.

31: Louis A. Benoist: Elizabeth S. Benoist, *St. Louis Silhouettes* (St. Louis: Hawthorn Publishing, n.d.), pp. 143–45.

31: Erroneous death reports: "Mr. Moore," and "Erroneous Report," both *Missouri Republican*, November 5, 1855.

31–32: Thomas O'Flaherty's funeral: DSR, p. 31 and n.; *Missouri Republican*, November 6, 1855.

32: Kate O'Flaherty's tuition: Old City House Demi Pensionnat Pupils' Accounts, St. Louis Academy of the Sacred Heart, National Archives of the Society of the Sacred Heart, Villa Duchesne, St. Louis. I am indebted to Sisters Mary Cecelia Wheeler and Marie Louise Martinez for showing me these records.

32: Kitty's description of Eliza O'Flaherty: DSR, p. 35.

32: Worth of Eliza O'Flaherty's estate: 1861–64 St. Louis City Directory, p. 97ff.

32: "Story of an Hour": Kate Chopin called her story "The Dream of an Hour," and it was published under that title in *Vogue* in 1894. Per Seyersted, CW, called it "The Story of an Hour," and modern editors have followed his lead.

CHAPTER 2: TALES AT AN IMPRESSIONABLE AGE

Sources of information about Kate O'Flaherty's maternal ancestors: DSR, pp. 13–15, 22–28, 35–36; SCB, pp. 13–19; ESM, *passim*, and especially pp. 50–57; Elizabeth Shown Mills, "Colorful Characters from Kate's Past," *Kate Chopin Newsletter* 2:1 (Spring 1976), 7–12; Wilson; and Maryhelen Wilson, "Woman's Lib in Old St. Louis: 'La Verdon,' " *St. Louis Genealogical Society* 14:4 (n.d.), 139–40. As Mills and Wilson show, much of what Rankin alleged about Kate O'Flaherty Chopin's ancestry is incorrect.

34: "Temporal prosperity," ESM, p. 57.

34: Portrait of Madame Charleville: ESM, KCM.

34: Madame Charleville's birthdate: Her obituary, ESM, p. 57, indicates she was born in 1780, but her marriage entry lists her as the younger child in her family, making her birth no earlier than 1784 (ESM, p. 147, n4). According to Wilson, Victoire was sixteen when she married in 1797, making her birthdate 1781.

34: *L'Année du Grand Coup*: Described in Ernest Kirschten, *Catfish and Crystal* (Garden City, NY: Doubleday, 1960), pp. 62–68 and James Neal Primm, *Lion of the Valley: St. Louis, Missouri* (Boulder, CO: Pruett Publishing Company, 1981), p. 44. Madame Rigauche and her school: John Francis McDermott, *Private Libraries in Creole St. Louis* (Baltimore: Johns Hopkins University, 1938), p. 59. The massacre grew in retelling: Catherine Condé Benoist, the mother of the financier Louis A. Benoist, claimed to have seen one villager carrying the head, trunk, and members of her late husband, "ruthlessly murdered and barbarously mutilated by the savages." But Catherine Benoist, who was also Oscar Chopin's great-grandmother, was not born until 1781, fully a year after the massacre took place. See "Madame Catherine Benoist," 1859 obituary from the *St. Louis Evening Bulletin*, provided by Jeannine Cook, Oakland estate, Affton, Missouri.

34: Little formal education: In 1819, when the St. Louis Catholic families agreed to build a school, 51 of the 117 householders who pledged support signed with an X (Primm, p. 92). McDermott (p. 13, n) says that women were more likely than men to be able to write their names. Women's reading Madame Sévigné: Eugénie Berthold, *Glimpses of Creole Life in Old St. Louis* (St. Louis: Missouri Historical Society, 1933), p. 13. Catherine Condé Benoist's reading: "Madame Catherine Benoist."

35: The speech of Creole ladies: Berthold, p. 14.

35: Reisz playing Chopin: *The Awakening*, Chap. IX: "I have always said no one could play Chopin like Mademoiselle Reisz!"

36: Château d'Oléron is a small seaport on the Ile d'Oléron, off the coast of the French state of Charente Maritime; it was originally part of the old French state of Poitou. (Note from Elizabeth Shown Mills, McCoy Collection.) More recently, Mills has questioned whether the much-recopied documents for the Charleville family actually do trace them back to the Château d'Oléron of the bishopric of La Rochelle. Possibly the Charleville family comes from Oléron, on the Spanish border near Lourdes, or even from the Château of Orleans, which can easily be mistranscribed as Oléron (1985 Mills communication).

36: La Rochelle: I am indebted to André Prévos for information about La Rochelle as a Protestant center and site of *The Three Musketeers*. Peter Newman, *The Company of Adventurers* (Markham, Ont.: Penguin Books, 1985), p. 59, refers to La Rochelle as a Huguenot town in connection with trade in beaver hats. When the Charlevilles left the Old World, they shucked off their original last name, *Chauvin*—a Huguenot family name in the province of Anjou that translates into English as "baldie" (ESM, pp. ix, 14). The first New World arrivals called themselves "Chauvin *dit* Charleville," the *dit* indicating a nickname—but they soon dropped the slightly comical "baldie" forever.

37: Victoire Verdon's marriage and out-of-wedlock child: Elizabeth Shown Mills thinks the baby was the product of a brief reconciliation (ESM, p. 62), but Maryhelen Wilson believes that another man, whose name has been lost to the historical record, was responsible ("Women's Lib in St. Louis," p. 140).

37: Madam Charleville's suit against the Chouteau estate: Documents are in the Chouteau Collection, MHS.

37: Madame Charleville's marriage, early childbirth: According to Elizabeth Shown Mills ("Colorful Characters," pp. 8, 11 n9), 27 percent of first births for white American mothers in this period occurred either before marriage or within the first seven months of marriage. In *Hands and Hearts: A History of Courtship in America* (New York: Basic, 1984), Ellen K. Rothman shows that into the early nineteenth century, most courting couples did have sexual relations before marriage—but that changed with the advent of "Victorianism" by midcentury.

38: Life in early St. Louis: Berthold, pp. 9, 13–14; Primm, pp. 85, 94; Kirschten, p. 70; McDermott, p. 22; J. Thomas Scharf, *History of St. Louis City and County* (Philadelphia: Louis H. Everts, 1883), p. 298.

38–39: Madame Chouteau: HSL, p. 366; Kirschten, pp. 55–56; SCB, p. 226; Scharf, pp. 179–80; Primm, p. 14; Katharine T. Corbett, "Veuve Chouteau, a 250th Anniversary," *Gateway Heritage* 3:4 (Spring 1983), pp. 42–48.

39: Elizabeth de Volsay: De Volsay's will includes a sarcastic codicil, leaving his errant wife three coats, an embroidered waistcoat, and *five pairs of breeches* (Scharf, p. 176, emphasis Scharf's). Scharf and Kirschten both spell de Volsay with an A; McDermott spells it with an E.

39: Louis Dunois: Wilson; Cyprian Clamorgan, *The Colored Aristocracy of St. Louis* (St. Louis: 1858), p. 15.

40: St. Phillippe as first slave village in Illinois: HSL, p. 1976.

40: Madame Charleville moved: Exactly when Victoire Verdon Charleville joined the O'Flaherty household is unclear. The 1850 census lists her in the household of her daughter Henriette (also called Harriet) Hunt and Henriette's husband Daniel; the 1860 census places her in Eliza O'Flaherty's home.

41: Sacred Heart schooling records: The St. Louis Sacred Heart Academy first admitted day pupils in 1857. (The school was called by various names: St. Louis Sacred Heart Academy, Academy of the Sacred Heart, Convent of the Sacred Heart.) All the surviving Old City House records are in the National Archives of the Society of the Sacred Heart, Villa Duchesne, St. Louis.

41: Kitty Garesché's recollections: DSR, pp. 36–38.

41: Kitty Garesché's family: Dorothy Garesché Holland, *The Garesché, de Bauduy, and Des Chapelles Families: History and Genealogy* (St. Louis: Schneider Printing, 1963), passim. The French Gareschés were from La Rochelle, and had a distinctly Huguenot cast. Juliette McLane's father was also U.S. treasurer and secretary of state, and ambassador to England again under James K. Polk. One of her sisters married a son of Alexander Hamilton, another married the Civil War General Joe Johnston, and a third married into the Tiffany family in New York. Source: 1932 obituary for Lily Garesché, Kitty's sister, MHS.

41: Portrait of Kitty Garesché: Dorothy Garesché Holland, copy at Villa Duchesne archives.

42: Visiting and Tom O'Flaherty: Kitty Garesché remembered that Kate had "a brother who must have been younger than herself, for I recall only his name—Tom" (DSR, p. 38). Tom was actually two years older. Kate never mentions him in her surviving writings, and his absence from recollections and records is puzzling.

42–43: Mariquitta and Julius Garesché: Louis Garesché, *Biography of Lieutenant Colonel Julius P. Garesché* (Philadelphia: Lippincott, 1887), esp. pp. 75–84, 243, 311, 370. Because it was traditional among the French-raised to call the older generation "Uncle" and "Aunt," Kitty would have called Julius, Alexander, and Ferdinand Garesché her uncles—but they were actually her father's cousins. Death of Julius Garesché: Holland, p. 172.

43: Cavalry officer in *The Awakening*: Chaps. VII, XXXIX.

43: Tree climbing: DSR, pp. 37–38; fragment of reminiscences: KCM, KCPP. DSR (p. 42) dates the fragment from toward the end of Kate's life—but Seyersted, on handwriting evidence, dates it as the late 1880s (KCM, pp. 195, n2). Seyersted's attribution is also convincing on other grounds: By the late 1880s, Kate Chopin was beginning a literary career, and looking into her past for material was a logical exercise.

44: Sacred Heart schooling: The records of Kate O'Flaherty and Kitty Garesché's school enrollment and fees are in the "Old City House Demi-Pensionnat Pupils' Accounts 1840–1860," the "Old City House Pupils Accounts 1860–1861," and the "Old City House Demi Pensionnat Pupils' Accounts 1864–1872," all at the National Archives of the Society of the Sacred Heart, Villa Duchesne, outside St. Louis. Other record books were lost during moves or not kept during the Civil War. I am indebted to Sister Mary Cecelia Wheeler for aiding me with the records. Kate O'Flaherty and Kitty Garesché's enrollment records:

> September–November 1855—Kate was a boarder.
> October–December 1856—Kitty was a boarder.
> September–November 1857—Kate was a day student.
> September 1858–February 1959—Kate and Kitty were both boarders.
> February 1859–July 1859—Kitty was a boarder.
> September 1859–February 1860—Kate was a boarder.
> September 1860–May 1861—Kate and Kitty were both day students.

Sacred Heart ledgers show that both girls' families paid for books and stationery (school supplies), at a cost ranging from $1.50 to $5.00. Tuition was $12.50 per term; board was $25. Money does not seem to have been Kate's reason for not enrolling regularly: Her teenaged aunt, Josephine Faris, was also a Sacred Heart boarder in September 1858, and Josephine stayed for the entire school year, until July 1859. School attendance was not compulsory in Missouri until 1905.

As eight-year-old boarders in 1858–59, Kate and Kitty would have returned to school for *rentrée* (reopening) in the fall with their required provisions, as listed in Louise Callan, *Society of the Sacred Heart in North America* (New York: Longmans Green, 1937), p. 749:

> bedding (a mattress, a pillow, two pairs of sheets, two blankets and a coverlet);
> necessary clothing: changes of linen (underwear), stockings, neck and pocket handkerchiefs, a sun bonnet, a white muslin veil, two pairs of shoes, one pair of gloves;
> eating utensils: a silver spoon, knife and fork, a cup, two plates, a tumbler, a toothbrush;
> other items: combs, a bag for the linen; a trunk, a work basket (for needlework), six capes of cambric and one of black velvet, one cloak, six towels.

44: Sacred Heart dressing and bathing: According to the British novelist Antonia White, every Sacred Heart girl became adept at an intricate series of contortions, under her voluminous calico cloak, to protect herself from "the scandalising sight" of her own naked body—even during bathing. White, "Child of the Five Wounds," reprinted in *As Once in May: the Early Autobiography of Antonia White and Other Writings*, ed. Susan Chitty (London: Virago, 1983), p. 152. Sacred Heart rituals had scarcely changed since the founding of the order in the early nineteenth century: When White published *Frost in May*, an autobiographical novel about Sacred Heart school life, in 1933, she received letters from "old children" (graduates) who were convinced, from her descriptions, that she was their contemporary. But one of the children had left in 1883 and the other in 1927; White herself left in 1914.

45: Intrigue, rivalry: Mary McCarthy, *Memories of a Catholic Girlhood* (New York: Harcourt Brace Jovanovich, 1957), p. 92. The American novelist Agnes Repplier called Sacred Heart life a world of "adventures, and imaginings, and sweet absurdities," in *In Our Convent Days* (Boston and New York: Houghton Mifflin, 1905), p. viii. See also Carol Gelderman, *Mary McCarthy: a Life* (New York: St. Martin's, 1988), pp. 36–38.

45: Sleeping posture and last words: White, pp. 153, 155.

45–46: Sacred Heart curriculum: Callan, passim, and esp. pp. x, xii, 741, 742, 756–58; M. O'Leary, *Education with a Tradition: an Account of the Educational Work of the Society of the Sacred Heart* (New York: Longmans Green, 1936), passim and esp. pp. 153, 169.

46: Guardian angels: White, p. 156.

47: Curtsies: Repplier, p. 215; 1985 interview with Elizabeth Baer, Manhattanville student in the 1950s–early 1960s.

47–49: Kitty's descriptions: DSR, pp. 38–40.

47–48: Dr. Kane's Expedition is described in "Amusements," *Missouri Republican*, February 8, 1861.

48: Museum: "St. Louis Museum," *Missouri Republican*, July 13, 1856.

48: Parrots: Chopin recorded her dislike in KC94.

48–49: Tom Thumb: DSR, p. 40; Irving Wallace, *The Fabulous Showman: the Life and Times of P. T. Barnum* (New York: New American Library, 1959), pp. 83–84, 102. See also Neil Harris, *Humbug: the Art of P. T. Barnum* (Boston: Little, Brown, 1973).

49: Women in the news: "Another Frightful Infanticide—Diabolical Murder of a New Born Child," *Missouri Republican*, March 30, 1859. Mary Kennedy: "Female Vagrant," *Missouri Republican*, July 29, 1859. Advertisement: "Women Voting": *Missouri Republican*, January 13, 1859.

CHAPTER 3: SECRETS AND A SPECIAL FRIENDSHIP

51–54: Kitty and Kate's reading: DSR, p. 37.

51: Cecilia Mary Caddell, *Blind Agnese; or, the Little Spouse of the Blessed Sacrament* (Dublin: James Duffy, 1873), pp. 6, 157.

51–52: Bernardin de Saint Pierre, *Paul and Virginia* (Philadelphia: Porter & Coates, n.d.), time-telling by sugar canes, p. 83.

52: Margaret Oliphant, *Zaidee: a Romance* (London: Blackwood's, 1855). United States: *Littell's Living Age*, Vols. 44–48 (1855–56), quotations from p. 379.

52: About *The Wide Wide World*, *Queechy*, and other domestic novels Kate O'Flaherty read: Emily Toth, "That Outward Existence Which Conforms: Kate Chopin and Literary Convention," Ph.D. Thesis, Johns Hopkins University, 1975, esp. Chaps. II and III.

52: Departed husbands: What befell Kate's maternal grandfather is unknown. According to his tombstone, Wilson Faris died in 1845. The last Faris child, Josephine, was apparently born in 1843, but Maryhelen Wilson (1985 interview) believes that Wilson Faris abandoned his family earlier.

52–53: Ralph Waldo Emerson, "Woman," in *Miscellanies* (Boston: Houghton, Mifflin, 1904), pp. 406–7.

53: Edna and Emerson: *The Awakening*, Chap. XXIV.

53: "Unwholesome intellectual sweets": *At Fault*, CW, 798.

53: Reading Scott: Alexander N. DeMenil, "A Century of Missouri Literature," *Missouri Historical Review* 15:1 (October 1920), pp. 117–19.

53: "Mild, timid, and gentle": Sir Walter Scott, *Ivanhoe* (New York: New American Library, 1962), p. 229.

53–54: Grace Aguilar, *Days of Bruce* (New York: A. L. Burt, 1852), descriptions of Isoline (preface, iii); Agnes (preface, iii, 3); "What could be now the past" (p. 127); "Memory had awakened" (p. 127). In *The Awakening*: Descriptions of Adèle Ratignolle (Chap. IV) and Edna Pontellier (Chap. VII); "The past was nothing" and "impassioned, newly awakened being" (Chap. XV).

54: Kitty about slave sales: DSR, p. 35.

54–55: Descriptions of church: DSR, p. 40; J. Thomas Scharf, *History of St. Louis City and County* (Philadelphia: Louis H. Everts, 1883); HSL, p. 1945.

55: Secessionist speech: *Missouri Republican*, December 17, 1860.

55: Thomas O'Flaherty as unionist: M. Blair, et al., "Address to the Democracy of Missouri," St. Louis Mercantile Library, n.p., n.d. Librarian Robert Behra dates the document as between 1847 and 1850.

55ff: "Leaves of Affection," MHS, contents reprinted in KCPP. "Aunt Boyer," sixty-one in 1860, was the sister of Kate's grandmother Marie Athanaise (or Athénaïse—the spelling varies) Charleville Faris. Unlike most Charleville women, Pélagie had remarried after the death of her first husband. Henry Battie died when she was twenty-one; a year later, she married François Charles Boyer. ESM, p. 51.

55: Lovers in *The Awakening:* Chap. VIII.

56: "I love": Although I cannot identify the poem, I do not think it was composed by eleven-year-old Katie O'Flaherty.

56: "We have been friends together": In Caroline Elizabeth Sarah Norton, *The Undying One and Other Poems* (London: Henry Colburn and Richard Bentley, 1830), pp. 215–16. Norton's poem was reprinted among the "Famous Poems," *St. Louis Republic* magazine, January 27, 1901, n.p. Kitty's version of the poem, with her miscopyings (or editings), is reprinted in KCPP.

56: James Thomas, *From Tennessee Slave to St. Louis Entrepreneur: The Autobiography of James Thomas,* ed. Loren Schweninger (Columbia: University of Missouri, 1984), p. 155.

56–57: George: Although the 1860 census missed him, *Kennedy's St. Louis City Directory for 1860* lists "George O'Flaherty: Clerk, Union Insurance Company. Boards on the west side of Eighth street, between Gratiot and Chouteau." George's school records: Brian Forney, Head Reference Librarian, Pius XII Memorial Library, St. Louis University.

57: St. Louis Germans: In Germany, young men had fomented the 1848 revolution "to sweep away the horde of petty despots, and unite their pigmy Principalities and Duchies into a glorious and wide-ruling Germany. They were a generation too soon, however": John McElroy, *The Struggle for Missouri* (Washington, D.C.: National Tribune Company, 1909), pp. 14–15.

57: Slave loyalty: Eugénie Berthold, *Glimpses of Creole Life in Old St. Louis* (St. Louis: Missouri Historical Society, 1933), pp. 16, 17; James Neal Primm, *Lion of the Valley: St. Louis, Missouri* (Boulder, CO: Pruett Publishing Company, 1981), p. 187.

57: St. Louis slavery c. 1860: Galusha Anderson, *A Border City During the Civil War* (Boston: Little, Brown, 1908), p. 170; Primm, p. 187; Harrison Trexler, *Slavery in Missouri, 1804–1865* (Baltimore: Johns Hopkins Press, 1914), p. 19. Eliza O'Flaherty's slaves: 1860 Missouri Slave Schedules, p. 338.

58: Archbishop Kenrick's announcement: HSL, p. 2411. Threats against Sacred Heart convent: Louise Callan, *The Society of the Sacred Heart in North America* (New York: Longmans Green, 1937), pp. 532–34.

58: German horsemen: *Missouri Republican,* February 9, 1861.

58: Berthold mansion: Primm, p. 246; James Peckham, *General Nathaniel Lyon and Missouri in 1861* (New York: American News Company, 1866), p. 82. "Blew and blasphemed": Peckham, p. 98.

59: Communion: Kitty's description, DSR, p. 40. Children usually made their First Communions at eleven or twelve in the nineteenth century.

59–60: Camp Jackson, further events: Anderson, pp. 89–90, 107, 110–11; Peckham, pp. 158, 159; Bruce Catton, *The Coming Fury* (New York: Pocket Books, 1961), pp. 382, 383. For later generations, Camp Jackson was still talked about with terror and wonder: 1984 interview with Michael Riordan (born 1890).

60–61: Frémonts: Anderson, pp. 206–24; Primm, p. 255; HSL, p. 1366; Irving Stone, *Immortal Wife: the Biographical Novel of Jessie Benton Frémont* (Garden City, NY: Doubleday, 1944); David Nevin, *Dream West* (New York: Putnam, 1983); William E. Parrish, *A History of Missouri, Vol. 3, 1860–75* (Columbia: University of Missouri

Press, 1973), pp. 39–41; Winston Churchill, *The Crisis* (New York: Macmillan, 1901), pp. 355–57, 368–69, 390–91; Bruce Catton, *Terrible Swift Sword* (New York: Pocket Books, 1963), pp. 10–11, 22–23, 28–30.

61: Sacred Heart reopening: Callan, pp. 532–34.

61–62: Assessments: Parrish, pp. 44, 68–72; Churchill, pp. 373–83; Primm, pp. 261–62; HSL, p. 56; Scharf, pp. 416–17, 422–26, 433–34; W. Wayne Smith, "An Experiment in Counterinsurgency: The Assessment of Confederate Sympathizers in Missouri," *Journal of Southern History* 35 (August 1969), pp. 361–80. In 1866, "A List of the Disloyal and Disfranchised Persons in St. Louis County" was compiled from official documents and printed at the Missouri Democrat office. Janice Fox assisted me with the MHS copy.

62: McDowell's building: Parrish, p. 65; Scharf, pp. 417–18.

62: According to librarian Brian Forney (1985 letter), Thomas O'Flaherty received no student awards or distinctions.

CHAPTER 4: REBELLION AND SILENCE

63–64: Kate and the flag: Kitty Garesché, DSR, pp. 43–44.

63: Punishments for war sentiments: HSL, pp. 196, 713. Young ladies: "Local News," *Missouri Republican*, July 14 and 16, 1863. Nevertheless, some St. Louis women actively aided the Confederacy, among them a Mrs. McLure (HSL, pp. 1400–1401), Mrs. J. A. Coons (James Neal Primm, *Lion of the Valley: St. Louis, Missouri* [Boulder, CO: Pruett Publishing Company, 1981,] p. 262), and Mrs. Ada B. Haines (J. Thomas Scharf, *History of St. Louis City and County* [Philadelphia: Louis H. Everts, 1883], 449). Treatment of secessionists in St. Louis: G. B. Carson, "Secesh," *Missouri Historical Society Bulletin* (January 1967), pp. 119–45; Hannah Isabella Stagg, "Local Incidents of the Civil War," *Collections of MHS*, no. 4, pp. 63–72.

64: Dr. Stevens: Kitty Garesché (DSR, p. 43) did not name the "neighborly friend, an eminent physician and a strong Unionist" whose "kind, timely interference" saved Kate, but Dr. Stevens was the only physician in the area: In the 1864 city directory, he is at Gratiot between Eighth and Ninth Streets. About Dr. Stevens: HSL, pp. 695, 1270, 1421, 1424, 1427, 1529.

64: Chopin herself described the flag incident in her fifth "As You Like It" essay in the *St. Louis Criterion* (March 20, 1897): CW, p. 716. SCB about "Littlest Rebel": pp. 20, 202, n26.

64–65: George O'Flaherty as soldier: DSR, p. 45. His capture: "Local News," *Missouri Republican*, August 20 and 21, 1862. General Hindman's report, presumably dictated to George: Thomas C. Hindman, *Report of Major General Hindman of his Operations in the Trans-Mississippi District* (Richmond, VA: R. M. Smith, 1864).

64: Gratiot Street Prison: HSL, p. 1945; Scharf, pp. 418–19; William E. Parrish, *A History of Missouri, Vol. 3, 1860–75* (Columbia: University of Missouri, 1973), p. 66.

64: Kate and Kitty's flowers: Kate Chopin, "As You Like It," *St. Louis Criterion* (March 20, 1897), p. 716; DSR, p. 43.

65: Weather in January 1863: Carson, "Secesh," pp. 138–39.

65: Madame Charleville's obituary: ESM, p. 57, also in Landry Charleville entry in *Biographical and Historical Memoirs of Northwest Louisiana* (Nashville: Southern Publishing, 1890), pp. 333–35, and DSR, p. 46, but DSR misprints the death date. According to the obituary, Madame Charleville was eighty-two years and ten months old at her death. Calvary Cemetery records list Victoire Verdon Charleville as buried in Section 2, Lot 56, but her grave is unmarked.

65–66: George's death: The O'Flahertys' neighbor Anne Ewing Lane mentions learning about deaths from the newspapers: Carson, p. 126. HSL, p. 2445 describes George O'Flaherty and others who died for the Confederacy as "gallant and chosen spirits." Kate O'Flaherty, "The Early Dead": KOCB, reprinted in KCM, KCPP. The inscription on the pillar marking George O'Flaherty's and his father's graves says, "George, son of Thomas O'Flaherty, born in St. Louis, who died at Little Rock, Arkansas, February 17, 1863, aged 23 years."

66–67: All entries are copied verbatim from "Leaves of Affection," MHS, KCPP. Mary Elder may have been related to Laura Elder, a Confederate lady who used to visit Gratiot Street Prison and supply prisoners with "necessities." A family named Elder also lived on the same block as the O'Flahertys. Scharf, p. 419; Deborah Isaacs, "Ante-Bellum Days in St. Louis," *Glimpses of the Past* V:10–12 (October–December, 1938), p. 152.

67: Garesché banishment: Dorothy Garesché Holland, *The Garesché, de Bauduy, and Des Chapelles Families: History and Genealogy* (St. Louis: Schneider Printing Company, 1963), p. 169. New York move: Holland 169 and "Notice de la Mère Lily Stanislas Garesché," document at the National Archives of the Society of the Sacred Heart, Villa Duchesne, St. Louis.

67: Edna's school friend: *The Awakening*, Chap. VII.

67: Enrollment: Louise Callan, *Society of the Sacred Heart in North America* (New York: Longmans Green, 1937), p. 534.

67–68: Kate's attic reading: WS.

68: Neighbor about Shiloh: Carson, "Secesh," p. 129. The battle of Shiloh or Pittsburg Landing took place on April 6–7, 1862.

68: Charleville boys: Eliza O'Flaherty's March 10, 1864 letter, KCM, KCPP; original at MHS. Albert Sampite's military papers: Leona Sampite.

68–69: Vicksburg celebrations in St. Louis: HSL, pp. 1918–1919; Anne Ewing Lane's 1863 letter to her sister Sarah L. Glasgow in Wiesbaden, MHS. Eliza O'Flaherty's March 10, 1864 letter to F. A. Charleville: MHS, KCM, KCPP. Eliza's memories: Emma Perrier, one of the listening youngsters, used to tell the story to later residents of Cloutierville, Louisiana, including Lucille Tinker Carnahan and Leona Sampite.

69: Slaves: "Negro 'mammy,' " WS. Most household slaves were gone from St. Louis by 1862; some joined the armies in other states, but eight thousand black men also fought in the Union Army for Missouri. See Galusha Anderson, *A Border City During the Civil War* (Boston: Little, Brown, 1908), p. 62, and Harrison Trexler, *Slavery in Missouri, 1804–1865* (Baltimore: Johns Hopkins, 1914), pp. 19, 206–7. By June 1864, the *Canton Press* of eastern Missouri reported that slave escapes were complete: "The colored element in this place has about cleaned out" (Parrish, pp. 76, 104).

69: Charles Faris as clerk, and family romance: Eliza O'Flaherty's March 10, 1864 letter (MHS; KCM, KCPP).

CHAPTER 5: "A TELLER OF MARVELLOUS STORIES"

Quotations from Kate O'Flaherty in this chapter are from KOCB unless otherwise stated. KOCB is reprinted in full in KCPP.

71: Kate O'Flaherty as student: WS. Unserious: See, for instance, "On Certain Brisk, Bright Days," CW, pp. 721–23.

71: Sterling Price's invasion: J. Thomas Scharf, *History of St. Louis City and County* (Philadelphia: Louis H. Everts, 1883), pp. 441–43.

71: Booth as drunk: Sarah Jane Full Hill, *Mrs. Hill's Journal—Civil War Reminiscences*, ed. Mark M. Krug (Chicago: Lakeside Press, R. R. Donnelly & Sons, 1980), pp. 225, 230–31.

72: Kate O'Flaherty's adult portrait: MHS.

72ff.: Sisters Marie Louise Martinez and Mary Cecelia Wheeler (National Archives of the Society of the Sacred Heart, Villa Duchesne) and Sister Cecilia, V.H.M. (St. Louis Academy of the Visitation) provided me with Kate O'Flaherty's school records.

72: Eliza O'Flaherty's March 10, 1864 letter to F. A. Charleville: MHS; KCM, KCPP.

72: St. Ange Avenue: The city directory lists Eliza at Eighth Street for the last time in 1865. She had sold the property by 1870, according to Wilson. Amanda Faris and Roger McAllister had been married in September 1851; Zuma Tatum (according to Wilson) "artfully concealed" her own age. Nina and Marie McAllister attended the Sacred Heart Academy from September 1870–July 1871, according to the "Old City House Demi Pensionnat Pupils' Accounts 1864–1872." But Nina must have been there earlier: she appears in Kate's 1867 poem, "The Congé" (KOCB). Kate disparaged Nina as "a child" in KOCB.

72: According to Calvary Cemetery records, Tatum children were buried there on March 5, 1866, and June 16, 1866. The 1868 St. Louis city directory lists John Tatum as a steamboatman.

73: Visitandines' history: William Barnaby Faherty, S. J., *Deep Roots and Golden Wings: One Hundred and Fifty Years with the Visitation Sisters in the Archdiocese of St. Louis, 1833–1983* (St. Louis: River City Publishers, 1982). Faherty mentions Clémence Benoist's enrollment and describes the school (pp. 72, 73, 89, 90, 91). Visitation curriculum, tuition, uniforms, and amusements: Faherty, pp. 17, 87, 89, and prospectus and information sent by Sister Cecilia, V.H.M.

73: Kate Chopin as "the greatest public achiever": Faherty, p. 82, who also calls Chopin's *Bayou Folk* "a collection of stories of Louisiana folkways unexcelled in American letters in the category of local color." Kate Chopin's granddaughter, Marjorie Chopin McCormick, was graduated from the Academy of the Visitation in 1926, and her class set a record—perfect attendance—for their fiftieth reunion. Interview with Marjorie Chopin McCormick, 1985.

73: Kate's musical memory: DSR, pp. 37, 48, quoting Kitty Garesché. Visitandines and musical programs, lamps: Prospectus; Faherty, pp. 21, 28, 91.

73–74: Sacred Heart curriculum for older girls: Callan, p. 741. Sacred Heart students were required to learn to write well, as an inflexible rule stated, "The mistresses of the higher classes will assign each week two themes, or essays; one of these will always be a letter, the other alternately an essay, narrative or descriptive, and a literary analysis."

74: Records: The ledger of prizes awarded at the Sacred Heart school, along with most records from the Old City House, was lost in 1893, according to librarians at Villa Duchesne. Children of Mary information, including the Rules of the Congregation of the Blessed Virgin Mary: Sisters Mary Cecelia Wheeler and Marie Louise Martinez: Callan, pp. 218, 658, 670. Kate O'Flaherty's records as Child of Mary: Congregation of the Blessed Virgin Mary Sodality Book, Villa Duchesne. Kate Chopin's membership: According to a 1986 letter from Nancy Merz of the Jesuit Missouri Province Archives, Kate O'Flaherty Chopin paid dues in the Children of Mary Sodality from 1878–94 and then again until 1904, the year of her death.

75–76: Madam O'Meara as "much loved": KOCB. The term "Mother" is used for Sacred Heart nuns who teach—but the nuns are also known as "Madam" or "Madame," with their given names. About Madam O'Meara: Kitty Garesché, in DSR, p. 46; Callan, p. 662; and Virginia Dunn, "Gleanings from the Life of Mary Philomena O'Meara, R.C.S.J.," M.A. thesis St. Louis University, 1925, esp. pp. 3, 7, 14, 22, 23. Mary O'Meara was born on February 23, 1844.

76: Kate's "habit of looking on the amusing side": DSR, p. 35.

77: *Madame Swetchine: The Life and Letters of Madame Swetchine by Count De Falloux*, trans. H. W. Preston (Boston: Roberts Brothers, 1867), p. 37. "Naive zest": Kate O'Flaherty may have meant to write *"native* zest." She seems not to have proofread carefully. Madame Swetchine was sometimes assigned as punishment in Sacred Heart schools: During a retreat, Agnes Repplier reported, she saw a classmate raise her eyes "from the 'Pensées Chrétiennes' of Madame Swetchine (I recognized the crimson cover, having been recently obliged to translate three whole pages of it as a penance)." From *In Our Convent Days* (Boston and New York: Houghton, Mifflin, 1905), p. 86.

79: "The Early Dead": Kate O'Flaherty's handwriting is not always clear, and the last name could be Enninger or Ervinger. The 1866 cholera epidemic killed 3,527 people in St. Louis.

79: "Memories": Copied verbatim, with Kate O'Flaherty's misspellings and mispunctuations.

80: "Essays and poetic exercises": WS.

80: Children of Mary information appears in the Congregation of the Blessed Virgin Mary Sodality book, Villa Duchesne. Frank Blakely's formal first name is always listed as Francis, not Frances. Madam (Mary) Hamilton is listed as directress of the Children of Mary, but evidently by spring she was sharing the duties with Madam O'Meara. The name *Bulte* is sometimes recorded in the school ledgers as *Bultey*, and in 1864 Miss E. Bulte—evidently a young lady with wide and varied interests—paid extra tuition for lessons in music, piano, German, and drawing ("Old City House Demi Pensionnat Pupils' Accounts 1864–1872"). Lizzie Bulte appears under that name and spelling in the 1870 St. Louis census. Extra lab fees: Listed for February 1868 in "Old City House Demi Pensionnat Pupils' Accounts 1864–1872."

82: Madam O'Meara about women as intellectual companions: Dunn, p. 23.

83: "The dual life": *The Awakening*, Chap. VII.

84: Lilacs outside St. Louis convent: Callan, p. 666.

84: Sacred Heart graduation: "St. Louis Convents," *Missouri Republican*, June 30, 1868.

84: Kate as "acknowledged belle": WS.

84: Kitty Garesché: Dorothy Garesché Holland, *The Garesché, de Bauduy, and Des Chapelles Families: History and Genealogy* (St. Louis: Schneider Printing Company, 1963), pp. 174, 246. Bauduy Garesché, Kitty's father, died on November 21, 1868. It had taken a court battle, spearheaded by her uncle Alex J. P. Garesché, to overturn the required loyalty oath that Kitty's father refused to take.

CHAPTER 6: POPULARITY AND ITS PRICE

Quotations in this chapter from Kate O'Flaherty are from KOCB.

85: Kitty Garesché about Kate in 1868: DSR, p. 52. Kate's height: FELIX.

85: Description of Edna Pontellier: *The Awakening*, Chap. II.

86: St. Louis opera productions: William G. B. Carson, *St. Louis Goes to the Opera, 1837–1941* (St. Louis: Missouri Historical Society, 1946), p. 4.

86–87: Fashions: Kathryn Weibel, *Mirror Mirror: Images of Women Reflected in Popular Culture* (New York: Doubleday Anchor, 1977), 180–88. The 1869 portrait of Kate O'Flaherty: MHS.

88: Phoebe Couzins Collection: MHS. Mary Foote Henderson: HSL, p. 1017; Adele Sarpy Morrison: HSL, pp. 1570–71. In the 1890s, Morrison's salon rivaled Kate Chopin's, according to Vernon Knapp's "Is There an Interesting Woman in St. Louis?" *St. Louis Republic*, September 11, 1910, p. 1, KCM, KCPP.

88: Virginia Minor and suffrage struggle: St. Louis Womanhood Scrapbook VIII, 153 (MHS); Virginia Minor Collection, MHS; Sharon Brown, "Virginia Minor and Her Right to Vote," unpublished paper; William E. Parrish, *A History of Missouri, Vol. 3, 1860–75* (Columbia: University of Missouri, 1973), pp. 251–53. In 1872, Virginia Minor attempted to vote, but the registrar refused to allow it. Eventually her case, *Minor* v. *Happersett*, reached the Supreme Court—which, on March 29, 1875, ruled that states could set any restrictions on suffrage that they chose. Women in Missouri did not get the right to vote until 1919, twenty-five years after Virginia Minor's death. Necrology Scrapbook IIc, 79, MHS.

89: "Blue Stockings": Kate O'Flaherty's comments were inspired by the account of Mr. Stillingfleet's conversation and his blue stockings in Boswell's *Life of Samuel Johnson* (New York and Oxford: Oxford University Press, 1960), p. 1147, entry for Tuesday, 8 May 1781.

89–90: Kate O'Flaherty lists the author as "Miss Mulock," but Dinah Maria Mulock had married George Lillie Craik in 1864. Kate O'Flaherty's extracts from *The Woman's Kingdom* are undated, but entries before and after are dated February 24 and March 25. The suffragists' mission to Jefferson City took place in early February 1869. Parrish, p. 251.

90: Léonce Pontellier's household complaints appear particularly in Chapter XVII of *The Awakening*.

90: Biographical information about the Maffitts: HSL, pp. 1340–41. "Mrs. Maffitt's party": CW, 717.

92–93: Oscar Chopin: Information about the Benoists: documents at Oakland estate. A letter of Oscar's from September 12, 1866, shows that he was already working for Louis A. Benoist in St. Louis: Jean Bardot, "French Creole Portraits: The Chopin Family from Natchitoches Parish," unpublished paper. Oscar Chopin's full name and birthdate: Elizabeth Shown Mills Collection, NSU.

92–93: Oscar's years in France, his letters: Jean Bardot, *"L'influence française dans la vie et l'oeuvre de Kate Chopin."* *Thèse de doctorat,* Université de Paris-IV, 1985–1986, pp. 43–45, 286–287, 292–93, 298. Translations from Oscar Chopin's letters by Jean Bardot, reprinted with permission.

94: J. H. Tighe letter: January 7, 1869, letter to James Murrin of St. Louis, supplied by Jeannine Cook. KCPP.

94: Victor Hugo, "The Man Who Laughs; or, By the King's Command," *Appleton's Journal* (April 3, 1869), pp. 1–6. The novel is serialized in later issues.

94: New Orleans companions: Mrs. Mary Morton Sloan was the wife of a very prominent St. Louis citizen, Edwin C. Sloan; her daughter Mamie, a contemporary of Kate's, eventually married Sylvester A. Pratte, descended from one of the oldest families (and former mayors) of St. Louis. Mamie Sloan Pratte's son Sylvester, born in 1872, served in the Spanish-American War, as did Kate Chopin's son Fred, born in 1876. HSL, p. 1797. Rosie cannot be identified: She may have been a servant.

94: Mark Twain's *Life on the Mississippi* records the details of river travel, with some ironic humor. For a fictionalized version, see my own novel, *Daughters of New Orleans* (New York: Bantam, 1983), esp. Chaps. 16–18.

95: "Creoles": The term *Creole* has many meanings. Today in Louisiana, "Creole" most often means a person of mixed white and black ancestry, although such a person might also be called a "Creole of color." But Kate Chopin uses the word *Creole* in its earlier sense, to mean a white person of pure French or Spanish ancestry.

96: Lamartine: Lamartine was a romantic favorite of young ladies, as Kitty Garesché's uncle Julius noted: See Louis Garesché, *Biography of Lieutenant Colonel Julius P. Garesché* (Philadelphia: Lippincott, 1887), p. 311.

97: Learned to smoke: FELIX.

98: Oakland estate: I am indebted to Jeannine Cook for a 1984 tour and for pictures and papers.

98: Kitty's training: Described in M. O'Leary, *Education with a Tradition: an Account of the Educational Work of the Society of the Sacred Heart.* (New York: Longmans Green, 1936), p. 152.

98: Balls at Oakland: Described in Elizabeth S. Benoist, *St. Louis Silhouettes* (St. Louis: Hawthorn Publishing, n.d.), pp. 127–28.

98: Kate about when "love came to her heart": her son Felix, quoted in DSR, p. 58.

CHAPTER 7: A WRITER'S HONEYMOON

Quotations from Kate O'Flaherty Chopin are all from her honeymoon diary (KOCB, the same notebook as her commonplace book). The honeymoon diary is reproduced, with errors, in DSR, pp. 59–78; correctly, with notes, in KCM, pp. 67–87; and with fuller notes in KCPP.

100: About Holy Angels Church: J. Thomas Scharf, *History of St. Louis City and County* (Philadelphia: Louis H. Everts, 1883), p. 1665.

100: About Father Kielty: HSL, pp. 1172–73. In the 1890s, Father Kielty and Kate Chopin both wrote for St. Louis newspapers, and in 1894 he published an article asking, "Is Suicide a Sin?"

102: The Continental Hotel: Described by Eleanor Cohen Seixas in her diary, excerpted in Penelope Franklin, ed., *Private Pages: Diaries of American Women, 1830s–1970s* (New York: Ballantine, 1986), p. 319.

102: "Miss Clafflin": Per Seyersted (SCB, p. 33) believes that the Chopins met Victoria Woodhull, sometimes described as the "most spectacular figure" of the Gilded Age—but Kate's "Miss Clafflin" could just as easily have been Tennessee.

103: European travel: Curtis Guild, *Over the Ocean; or, Sights and Scenes in Foreign Lands* (Boston: Lee and Shepard, 1875). Guild was a Boston editor. Shipboard amusements: Mark Twain, *Innocents Abroad* (New York: New American Library, 1966), p. 31. The Rare Books Room of the Pattee Library, Pennsylvania State University, owns many handwritten and illustrated booklets by American travelers to Europe in the late nineteenth century.

105: "Princliest": I am reproducing Kate Chopin's diary as written, including spelling errors.

106: Vernon Knapp article: "Is There an Interesting Woman in St. Louis?" *St. Louis Republic*, September 11, 1910, part 5, p. 1. KCM, KCPP.

107: Cologne cathedral: In fact, the cathedral was completed in 1880, exactly ten years after the Chopins' visit.

108: American heiresses' marrying European royalty: For Jennie Jerome's story, see Ralph G. Martin, *Jennie: The Life of Lady Randolph Churchill* (Englewood Cliffs, NJ: Prentice-Hall, 1969). The best satirical view of heiresses in search of earls is Edith Wharton's *The Custom of the Country* (1913). Wharton, born Edith Newbold Jones of New York, was eight years old in 1870, the year of the Chopins' honeymoon.

109: Menstrual euphemisms and paraphernalia: Janice Delaney, Mary Jane Lupton, and Emily Toth, *The Curse: a Cultural History of Menstruation* (New York: Dutton, 1976; revised and updated edition, Urbana: University of Illinois Press, 1988).

110ff.: Tourist information: Heidelberg Castle: Guild, pp. 352–53, 355. Swiss mountain climbing: Guild, pp. 377–80. Dying lion: Guild, p. 389. Cathedral organ: Guild, pp. 386–88. Music and Edna: *The Awakening*, Chap. IX.

112: Lil Chouteau: Lilia (sic) Clemence Chouteau (1850–1932) eventually married John Still Winthrop (1848–1920), according to William C. Foley and C. David Rice, *The First Chouteaus: River Barons of Early St. Louis* (Urbana: University of Illinois, 1983), p. 213.

116: Siege of Paris: Robert Baldick, *The Siege of Paris* (New York: Macmillan, 1964), pp. 22–26; Melvin Kranzberg, *The Siege of Paris* (Ithaca, NY: Cornell University Press, 1950), pp. 4, 10–14, 23; Elizabeth Wormeley Latimer, *France in the Nineteenth Century, 1830–1890* (Chicago: A. C. McClurg, 1903), pp. 243, 246–76; Renée Winegarten, *The Double Life of George Sand* (New York: Basic Books, 1978), p. 312.

119: "The coming . . . wonderfully Frenchy": Twain, *Innocents Abroad*, p. 83.

CHAPTER 8: NEW ORLEANS AND MOTHERHOOD

OCUS, an extensive file of documents for Oscar Chopin's father's lawsuit against the United States for Civil War damages, includes Oscar's testimony in "The Memorial of Oscar Chopin," and many witnesses' depositions. I am indebted to Elizabeth Shown Mills for transcribing some of these materials (Mills Collection, Folder 7, NSU), and for directing me to the originals. Ron Swerczek of the National Archives located the file for me.

121: Description of Edna's house: *The Awakening*, Chap. XVII. Chopins' house as resembling Edna's: DSR, p. 79.

121–122: Chopins' first house: The house was renumbered 1431 Magazine when street numbers were changed in 1894. As late as 1964, the house still existed, but now the site is the paved playground for Jackson School. House information: *Insurance Map of New Orleans, LA.*, Vols. 1 and 4 (New York: Sanford Publ. Ltd., 1876), Southeastern Architectural Archive, Howard-Tilton Memorial Library, Tulane University. Geoffrey Kimball aided me with the archive materials. Photographs of surviving houses in the Chopins' block and architectural descriptions: Mary Louise Christovich, Roulhac Toledano and Betsy Swanson, eds., *New Orleans Architecture, Vol. 1, the Lower Garden District* (Gretna, LA: Friends of the Cabildo and Pelican Publishing Company, 1971), pp. 135–36.

122: J. B. Chopin and "A Matter of Prejudice": DSR, p. 82. Dr. J. B. Chopin's bad temper is still legendary in the Cloutierville area: Carnahan and other current residents.

122: Jean Baptiste Chopin's birth and background: OCUS (his birthplace was "commune of Jouaignes, Canton of Braine, arrondissement de Soissons, department of Aisne"). According to his church marriage record, Chopin was the son of Antoine Chopin and Marie Thérèse Everard, and a native of Jouaignes, department of L'Aisne, France (record reproduced in Elizabeth Shown Mills, *Natchitoches Church Marriages, 1818– 1850: Translated Abstracts from the Registers of St. François de Natchitoches, Louisiana* [Tuscaloosa, AL: Mills Historical Press, 1985], p. 123). OCUS lists his father's name as Nicolas Antoine Chopin (p. 1). According to the birth certificate copy in the Bayou Folk Museum, Dr. Chopin was born April 24, 1818 (DSR, p. 84 gives an incorrect date).

122: Dr. Chopin's setting out for Mexico: 1988 interview with Julie Chopin Cusachs (Kate Chopin's niece).

122: Natchitoches Parish: Louisiana has parishes rather than counties.

122: Julie Benoist: She was the second daughter of Louis A. Benoist's older brother Charles Francis, originally of St. Louis, and Suzette Rachal of Cloutierville. The Julie (or Julia) Benoist-J. B. Chopin marriage record is reprinted in Mills, p. 130 (DSR, p. 84 gives an incorrect date). According to Julie Chopin Cusachs (letter to Oakland estate), Julie Benoist was born in New Orleans September 26, 1826.

122–23: Dr. Chopin's cruelty: DSR, pp. 84–88, SCB, pp. 35–37. The late Lise DeLouche Charleville of Cloutierville often recounted stories of his cruelty (Carnahan). Simon Legree legend: McCoy Scrapbooks.

123: Julie Benoist Chopin's piano: OCUS.

123: Chopin children: OCUS and their gravestone markers, reprinted in Lucile Keator Prudhomme and Fern B. Christensen, comps., *The Natchitoches Cemeteries: Transcriptions of Gravestones from the 18th, 19th, and 20th Centuries in Northwest Louisiana* (New Orleans: Polyanthos, 1977). Oscar's sister Marie's tombstone lists her birth as April 1862, but she is also called "dau. Oscar Chopin."

123: J. B. Chopin's return visits during the war: OCUS, DSR, p. 86. Piano destroyed, J. B. Chopin's flight, his passport application: OCUS. J. B. Chopin's property inventory: Succession of J. B. Chopin and Suzette Benoist, Central District Court, New Orleans. I am indebted to Barbara Ewell for copying the succession documents for me.

123: French railroad stocks: DSR, pp. 86–87, Succession of J. B. Chopin and Suzette Benoist.

124: According to DSR, p. 87, the elder Chopins lived on Royal Street, between Conti and St. Louis Streets, in the French Quarter, but their names do not appear in city directories. "A fragile person": Lise DeLouche Charleville, recounted by Carnahan. Typhoid as cause of death: Waters.

124: New Orleans when Chopins arrived: Articles in *New Orleans Daily Picayune*, October 8, 1870.

124: Kate's charming J. B. Chopin: DSR, p. 84.

125: "Long and painful malady": OCUS. J. B. Chopin's hotel bill, in his Succession file, ends with November 14, 1870.

125: Creole mourning customs: Leonard V. Huber, "Reflections on the Colorful Customs of Latter-Day New Orleans Creoles," *Louisiana History* 21:3 (1980), 223–35.

125: Oscar's relatives (unnamed): DSR, pp. 78–82. According to Carnahan, Natchitoches Parish relatives would have been the first to want to meet and judge Kate.

125: Kate's walking: DSR, pp. 92–95. Her Cuban cigarettes: FELIX. Rankin claims that the confused character in Kate Chopin's story "Cavanelle" represents Chopin's own confusion about the mule cars in New Orleans. Another view of Chopin's New Orleans life: Emily Toth, "Kate Chopin's New Orleans Years." *New Orleans Review* 15:1 (Spring 1988), 53–60.

125: Kate Chopin's diary from the New Orleans years is lost (DSR, pp. 92–95). While I was writing this book, a Mrs. A. Rodriguez of New Orleans wrote me that she had a collection of letters written by Kate Chopin—but Mrs. Rodriguez did not include a return address. I have never been able to locate her.

126: Marie Chopin's staying with Kate and Oscar: Waters. Perhaps because her parents' early deaths shadowed her youth, Marie never talked about her childhood. Mrs. L. Tyler: DSR, p. 89.

126ff.: Mardi Gras: Charles L. Dufour and Leonard V. Huber, *If Ever I Cease to Love: One Hundred Years of Rex, 1872–1971* (New Orleans: Upton, 1970); Arthur Burton LaCour, with Stuart Omer Landry, *New Orleans Masquerade* (New Orleans: Pelican Publishing, 1952, 1957); Edwin L. Jewell, ed., *Jewell's Crescent City, Illustrated: Commercial, Social, Political and General History of New Orleans, Including Biographical Sketches of its Distinguished Citizens, Together with a Map and General Strangers' Guide* (New Orleans: Jewell, 1873); *New Orleans Daily Picayune*; Robert Tallant, *Mardi Gras* (Garden City, NY: Doubleday, 1948); Robert Tallant, *Romantic New Orleanians* (New York: Dutton, 1950).

126–127: Dr. Faget: Edward Larocque Tinker, *Creole City: Its Past and Its People* (New York: Longmans Green, 1953), pp. 152–53; John Wilds, *Crises, Clashes and*

Cures: A Century of Medicine in New Orleans (New Orleans: Orleans Parish Medical Society, 1978), p. 125. Wilds gives his name as Charles Jean; his publications list him as J. C., presumably Jean Charles. Faget's treating Chopin: J. B. Chopin's Succession shows a bill for two hundred dollars from Dr. C. Faget. According to Wilds's list (p. 185), J. C. Faget belonged to the Orleans Parish Medical Society from 1878 to 1899 (the year *The Awakening* was published)—but John Duffy, ed., *The Rudolph Matas History of Medicine in Louisiana*, Vol. 2 (Baton Rouge: Louisiana State University, 1962), says that Dr. Faget died in 1884 (p. 387). Dr. Faget's medical papers: J. C. Faget, M.D., "Type and Specific Character of True Yellow Fever" (New Orleans: Jas. A. Gresham, 1873) and "The Type of Specificity of Yellow Fever" (Paris: J. B. Ballière and New Orleans: Am. Lutton, 1875). Kate Chopin's "Dr. Chevalier's Lie" came from "an actual incident in the life of a physician of New Orleans" (DSR, p. 134).

127: Displacement of midwives: Barbara Ehrenreich and Deirdre English, *For Her Own Good: 150 Years of the Experts' Advice to Women* (Garden City, NY: Anchor Press/ Doubleday, 1979); Ehrenreich and English's *Witches, Midwives, and Nurses* (Oyster Bay, NY: Glass Mountain Pamphlets, n.d.); and Mary Poovey, " 'Scenes of an Indelicate Character': The Medical 'Treatment' of Victorian Women," *Representations* 14 (Spring 1986), 137–68. Chloroform: Adrienne Rich, *Of Woman Born: Motherhood as Experience and Institution* (New York: W. W. Norton, 1976), p. 169.

127–128: KC94. Reticence: See, for instance, Arvazine Cooper's journal, in Eve Merriam, ed., *Growing Up Female in America: Ten Lives* (New York: Dell, 1971), pp. 148–49. Edna's memories of childbirth: *The Awakening*, Chap. XXXVII.

128: Oscar Chopin's bills from the Grand Hôtel Bergère are in the papers for the Succession of Jean Baptiste Chopin.

128: The young Jean Baptiste Chopin was baptized in Holy Guardian Angels Church, St. Louis.

128–129: Children's birthdates: St. Louis did not yet keep birth certificates, but dates for young Oscar and George appear on baptismal records from Holy Guardian Angels Church. According to the 1900 United States Census, Oscar Charles Chopin was born September 1873, George Francis Chopin October 1874, and Lélia December 1879. But the same census also lists Kate Chopin's birthdate as February 1849, two years earlier than the usual date given. (DSR, pp. 88, 89, gives wrong dates for Frederick and Lélia.)

129: Portrait of Kate Chopin with four sons: SCB, photo at MHS. The portrait is so unflattering that Kate's granddaughter Marjorie Chopin McCormick—who points out that Kate never wore a cross in any other pictures—thinks it may not be Kate at all, but a servant. Oscar's picture: Mills Collection, NSU.

129: According to DSR, p. 95, Oscar opened his office in late 1870, but in that case it should have appeared in the 1871 city directory. An "O. Choppin, clk. Joseph Hay & Co. r. 36 Perdido" appears in the 1870 directory, but that is unlikely to be Oscar: He was in St. Louis and Europe for most of the year. Cotton factors' procedures: Thomas Knox, *Camp-Fire and Cotton-Field: Southern Adventure in Time of War* (New York: Blelock and Company, 1865), pp. 394–95. Degas: G. William Nott, "Giant in Art World Lived in New Orleans," *Item Tribune Magazine* (New Orleans), December 28, 1924, p. 15, Louisiana Scrapbook No. 2, Louisiana Collection, Howard-Tilton Memorial Library, Tulane University. According to Tallant, *Romantic New Orleanians*, p. 314, Degas was visiting relatives and painting them.

Among Oscar's clients was Albert Sampite of Cloutierville: The J. B. Chopin Succession papers include a December 8, 1872, document about a financial transaction involving Oscar, his brother Lamy, and Albert Sampite, for plantation-repair payments. 220–21: Oscar's lists: DSR, pp. 96–97. Oscar advertised his new Carondelet Street address in the October 8, 1873, edition of the "Business Directory of the Principal and Leading Houses and Firms," published in the *New Orleans Price Current, Commercial Intelligencer and Merchants Transcript*:

> CHOPIN, Oscar—Cotton Factor and Commission Merchant, No. 65 Carondelet St., New Orleans.

In the 1874 directory Oscar is listed as a "cotton factor and com. mer.," and from 1878–80 he is listed in city directories at 77 Carondelet. Kate's diary: DSR, pp. 94–95.

130: Chopins' addresses: According to DSR, p. 89, the Chopins moved to Constantinople and Pitt in late summer 1874, but Kate was in St. Louis then, expecting her third child. The New Orleans city directory lists the Chopins at the northeast corner of Pitt and Constantinople, but contemporary maps show no house on that corner (Southeastern Architectural Archive, Tulane). Louisiana Avenue house: *Atlas of the City of New Orleans, Louisiana* (New York: E. Robinson, 1883). The Louisiana Avenue house belongs to a women's historical association: I am grateful to Rosa Porter for allowing me to visit it.

130: Louisiana Avenue servants: In the 1880 census, Henry Kopman, a cotton weigher, his wife Anna, and three children occupied 209 Louisiana Avenue, together with two servants: Domininge Lessia and Estella Pias, both identified as twenty-three-year-old "mulatto" females. Since servants often stayed with the house, the two women had probably worked for the Chopins.

130–131: Mrs. L. Tyler: DSR, pp. 89–90. Rankin gives no other identification for Mrs. Tyler, who lived in Newark, New Jersey, when he interviewed her. She may have been related to Chauncey Tyler, listed in the city directories as a coal merchant with offices at 15 Carondelet and a home at 749 Magazine Street. A description of the Garden District's homes and gardens appears in Tallant, *Romantic New Orleanians*, p. 91.

131: Mrs. Tritle: SCB, p. 38. The Ratignolles: *The Awakening*, Chap. XVIII, DSR, p. 81.

131: Addresses of Kate's relatives: *Edwards' City Directories*, 1870, 1871, 1872; *Gould's Directory* for 1872–85. In 1877, one Elijah McAllister was also listed for 1125 St. Ange. By 1877, the McAllisters' son Andrew was listed separately in the city directory, as a Circuit Court clerk, and once as a conveyancer. (In the mid-1880s, he was listed as a roofer.)

131–132: Kolbenheyer: "Dr. Kolbenheyer's Body Brought Home," *St. Louis Post-Dispatch*, April 10, 1921, Necrology XI, 98, MHS. DSR, p. 89, about his friendship with Eliza O'Flaherty.

132: Jean's godparents: Baptismal records, Holy Guardian Angels Church, St. Louis. Young Thomas O'Flaherty is listed in the city directory only once: *Edwards' Directory* for 1872 says "bds. 1217 St. Ange." Directories mostly excluded anyone who was not head of a household. Tom's St. Louis University record: Brian Forney, head reference librarian, St. Louis University. Mercantile Library memberships: Robert Behra. Tom's death: Report provided by Maryhelen Wilson of St. Louis and printed as "Brother Tom's Final Ride," *Kate Chopin Newsletter* 3:1 (Spring 1977), 40.

133: Eads Bridge opening: DSR, pp. 17, 89; James Neal Primm, *Lion of the Valley: St. Louis, Missouri* (Boulder, CO: Pruett Publishing Company, 1981), p. 305.

133: George's baptismal record: Holy Guardian Angels Church, St. Louis.

133: Civil War in Louisiana: Robert Tallant, *Romantic New Orleanians* (New York: Dutton, 1950), p. 188; my novel, *Daughters of New Orleans* (New York: Bantam, 1983); John D. Winters, *Civil War in Louisiana* (Baton Rouge: Louisiana State University, 1963).

133ff.: Louisiana Reconstruction: Joy Jackson, *New Orleans in the Gilded Age: Politics and Urban Progress, 1880–1896* (Baton Rouge: Louisiana State University, 1969); Philip Matthew Mabe, "Racial Ideology in the New Orleans Press, 1862–1877," Ph.D. Thesis, University of Southwestern Louisiana, 1977; Geraldine Mary McTigue, "Forms of Racial Interaction in Louisiana, 1860–1880," Ph.D. Thesis, Yale, 1975; Joe Gray Taylor, *Louisiana Reconstructed, 1863–1877* (Baton Rouge: Louisiana State University, 1974); Edward Larocque Tinker, *Creole City: Its Past and Its People* (New York: Longmans Green, 1953); Ted Tunnell, *Crucible of Reconstruction: War, Radicalism and Race in Louisiana, 1862–1877* (Baton Rouge: Louisiana State University, 1984). Quote from Northerner: Stuart Omer Landry, *The Battle of Liberty Place: the Overthrow of Carpet-Bag Rule in New Orleans—September 14, 1874* (New Orleans: Pelican Publishing, 1955), p. 22. McTigue's apt summary of white fears: "When Negro slavery ended, mistresses and masters discovered several dismaying truths: the extent to which they had never really known their so-familiar human chattels at all; the attachment they had developed to the exercise of dominion over others; the magnitude of their dependency on black people; and the jealousy they felt when outsiders related to Negroes in roles traditionally reserved for white Southerners. Class divisions among Caucasians blurred into insignificance next to the imperatives of white supremacy" (p. 3).

134: Formation of White League and associated companies: *New Orleans Daily Picayune*, June 9, 1874, "The White League." Landry, p. 130, claims that League members all had military training; Tinker, p. 134, says that all members of the First Louisiana Regiment were ex-Confederates—but Oscar Chopin was not. One member of the elite Boston Club was Dr. Samuel Choppin, who was not related to Oscar, but who is mentioned in Kate Chopin's story, "A Sentimental Soul": "Mamzelle Fleurette saw Choppin's coupé pass clattering over the cobblestones and stop before the locksmith's door. She knew that with her class it was only in a case of extremity that the famous and expensive physician was summoned. For the first time she thought of death."

134: Angell's advertisements: *Daily Picayune*. About him: Landry, p. 203, Tunnell, p. 291; photograph, Landry facing, p. 181.

134: McGloin: *The City of New Orleans: The Book of the Chamber of Commerce and Industry of Louisiana and Other Public Bodies of the "Crescent City"* (New Orleans: George W. Engelhardt, 1894), p. 170. In 1871, the New Orleans City Directory lists his home as 109 Constance. "The Origin of May" (sic) appeared in the *Daily Picayune*, April 20, 1873. Later a court-of-appeals judge, McGloin edited a Catholic publication called *The Holy Family* and wrote novels, his most praised being a story of Southeast Asia called *Norodom: King of Cambodia* (Jackson, pp. 289–91).

135ff.: Battle of Liberty Place: Landry, esp. pp. 234–40. In Landry's lists of all participants, Company B includes both French and Anglo-Saxon names, and many occupations, including booksellers, doctors, dentists, attorneys, and ministers. Sources vary about deaths and casualties: Tunnell, p. 294, says the White League forces had twenty-one killed, nineteen wounded. Music: Landry, p. 180. The White League rose again after the 1876 election—but whether Oscar Chopin took part is unknown. Among the Liberty Place veterans dedicated to honoring their own exploits was Captain W. T. Vaudry, a White League founder who wrote to the newspapers about the soldiers' gallantry. In 1891—the year the Battle of Liberty Place monument was erected on Canal Street—Kate Chopin created a character named Captain Vaudry, in "The Maid of St. Phillippe." Vaudry is the French soldier who wants to take the wild, independent Marianne back to France with him and surround her with luxuries—but she refuses to be "the mother of slaves." Photo of monument: Landry, p. 213. Chiseled on the monument were the names of the White Leaguers killed.

In 1932, an inscription was given to the monument: "United States troops took over the state government and reinstated the usurpers but the national election in November 1876 recognized white supremacy and gave us our state." In 1974, a new plaque was added, repudiating the philosophy of white supremacy as repugnant to modern New Orleanians. In November 1989, the obelisk was moved from the foot of Canal Street as part of a streets project, but the federal Advisory Council on Historic Preservation ruled that the monument had to be restored within eighteen months and within two blocks of its previous location. "Whites protest at N. O. supremacy monument," *Baton Rouge Sunday Advocate*, October 15, 1989, p. 3B; " 'White supremacy monument' to be moved," *Baton Rouge Sunday Advocate*, November 12, 1989, p. 4B.

136: School integration struggles: Roger A. Fischer, *The Segregation Struggle in Louisiana, 1861–1877* (Urbana: University of Illinois, 1974). Landry, p. 73, discusses integration of saloons.

137: Mrs. Tyler's statement, DSR, p. 90, is the only evidence that Kate spent summers at Grand Isle. Edna's astonishment at absence of prudery: Chap. IV of *The Awakening*.

137ff.: Grand Isle: Sally Kittredge Evans, Frederick Stielow, and Betsy Swanson, *Grand Isle on the Gulf: an Early History* (Metairie, LA: Jefferson Parish Historical Commission, 1979); Frederick Stielow, "Grand Isle, Louisiana, and the 'New' Leisure, 1866–1893," *Louisiana History* 23:3 (Summer 1982), 239–57; Frederick Stielow, "Isolation and Development on a Louisiana Gulf Coast Island: Grand Isle, 1781–1962," Ph.D. Thesis, Indiana University 1977; Betsy Swanson, *Historic Jefferson Parish, from Shore to Shore* (Gretna, LA: Pelican Publishing, 1975).

137–138: Rockaway, birds, sea in *The Awakening*: Chap. III. According to Swanson, p. 161, the only transportation vehicles on Grand Isle were a mule cart and a mule-drawn train. Willoz building: Stielow, "Grand Isle," p. 243. Lebruns' place: *The Awakening*, Chap. VII. A photograph of a typical galleried Creole cottage on Grand Isle appears in Swanson, p. 143. Krantz Hotel: Stielow, "Grand Isle," p. 244; Swanson, p. 161. Edna's key: *The Awakening*, Chap. VII, Stielow, "Grand Isle," p. 247. Grand Isle as tropical paradise: Stielow, "Grand Isle," pp. 249–50; DSR, pp. 90–91; *The Awakening*, Chap. V. Robert's tales: *The Awakening*, Chaps. X, XII. Madame Antoine also tells Edna and Robert about "the whispering voices of dead men and the click of muffled gold" (Chap. XIII).

138: Bathing suits: See, for instance, "August Fashions: Bathing Dresses," *New Orleans Daily Picayune*, August 3, 1873. Fashions changed: In a painting by John Genin of surf bathers at Grand Isle toward the end of the century, some of the bathers have bare arms (Swanson, p. 160).

138: Farivals twins' playing: The "Poet and Peasant Overture" had been performed for Kate O'Flaherty's graduation from the Sacred Heart Academy.

138: Grand Terre, Fort Livingston: Swanson, pp. 153, 155–59; *The Awakening*, Chap. XII. The old fort survived the 1893 hurricane that destroyed most of Grand Isle as Kate Chopin knew it, but the hurricane of 1915 demolished the gulf face of the fort. The pirate Jean Lafitte had also built a fort on Grand Terre, evidently in the shape of a martello tower, but whether it existed in Kate Chopin's day—and whether it is the old fort Robert mentions to Edna—is unknown. See Swanson, p. 151.

138: No Grand Isle church: Swanson, pp. 165–66. Kate and Oscar Chopin and their children had already left New Orleans by the time a priest did arrive on Grand Isle, in December of 1882. Insisting that they did not want or need a priest, the island inhabitants sent him to the nearby peninsula, the Chênière Caminada—where, in 1884, he managed to build Our Lady of Lourdes, the church Edna attends (and runs away from) in *The Awakening*, Chap. XIII.

139: "Unfinished Story": MAB.

139: 1893 hurricane: Stielow, "Grand Isle," pp. 255–56.

139: Grand Isle resort: Grand Isle is still advertised as a vacation spot, especially for fishing: Local oil rigs seem to attract big fish. But swimming is strongly discouraged, because of the treacherous undertow. Tourist brochures still advertise the "mysterious old Fort Livingston on Grand Terre Island, waiting to be explored" and "the exotic swamplands of Barataria Bay, where the ghost of the pirate Jean Lafitte still lingers." "Grand Isle Louisiana—'Finest Fishing Anywhere.' " Grand Isle Tourist Commission, Inc., n.d.

139: Yellow fever and Chopins: Oscar's grandfather Charles Francis Benoist had died of it in the epidemic of 1853.

139: Oscar Chopin's debts: Benoist and Chopin Business Papers, 1870–1880s, E. P. Watson Collection, NSU. Oscar's buying land: The documents for Oscar Chopin's land purchases in 1876 and 1879 are in the family papers now belonging to Leona Sampite of Cloutierville, Louisiana. Why her grandfather Albert Sampite had the papers is unknown—and intriguing.

CHAPTER 9: THE GOSSIP IN CLOUTIERVILLE

140: Pronunciation of town name: McCoy Scrapbook gives "Clewchie-ville" as the pronunciation; most current residents say "Cloochyville." Waters, who grew up in Natchitoches in the 1890s, used to say "Cloochay-ville" or "Cloocher-ville."

140: Travels of Cloutierville natives: Carnahan, Waters.

140–141: Cloutierville autumn: Journalist "Catharine Cole" (Martha Field) so described Natchitoches Parish in the 1888 *New Orleans Daily Picayune*. Melrose Scrapbooks 70 (14), 71 (86), NSU.

141: Riding astride: Carnahan, reporting memories of Cloutierville residents Margaret Owen, Mrs. Armstrong Charleville, and Ida Masson; Wells, reporting memories of residents Frank Majers and Carmen Breazeale. According to McCoy, Kate Chopin rode both sidesaddle and Western style.

141: Alexis Cloutier: Carnahan, McCoy. DSR, p. 99, mentions Cloutier's hopes, but calls him (incorrectly) "Alexander." The original Cloutier arrived in Quebec from France in 1642; Alexis Cloutier's father was among the Acadians expelled by the conquering British in 1753 (Carnahan).

141: Chopin's clothes: DSR, p. 103, Carnahan, McCoy. Memories of Lise DeLouche Charleville and Emma Perrier: Carnahan. Promenading on horseback: Carnahan, Cloutierville Group, McCoy.

142: Kate Chopin's Charleville relatives: ESM, pp. 101–12.

142: Description of Lamy Chopin: Waters. Lamy Chopin and Cora Henry were married January 16, 1878, according to "Lamy Chopin," *Biographical and Historical Memoirs of Northwest Louisiana* (Nashville and Chicago: Southern Publishing, 1890), pp. 334–35. According to her gravestone, Marie Eugénie Chopin (known as "Nini" in the family) was born October 5, 1879.

142: Resentment against nonsoldiers: Carnahan, Cloutierville Group. Charles Bertrand earned money for J. B. Chopin while the Chopins were in France. Plundering and war: OCUS; Elizabeth Shown Mills and Gary B. Mills, *Tales of Old Natchitoches* (Natchitoches: Association for the Preservation of Historic Natchitoches, 1978), pp. 108–10; Felix Pierre Poché, *A Louisiana Confederate: Diary of Felix Pierre Poché*, ed. Edwin C. Bearss and trans. Eugenie Watson Somdal (Natchitoches: Louisiana Studies Institute, Northwestern State University, 1972), pp. 105–10.

142: Slaves: Disappearance with Yankees: Gary B. Mills, *The Forgotten People: Cane River's Creoles of Color* (Baton Rouge: Louisiana State University, 1977), p. 119. Slaves owned by J. B. Chopin and his mother-in-law, Suzette Rachal Benoist, in 1862: *Biographical and Historical Memoirs of Northwest Louisiana*, p. 298. By the end of the war: OCUS.

143: Dr. Scruggs: Carnahan, McCoy. Biographical sketch: Mildred McCoy, "Uncle Tom's Cabin Revisited," *Alexandria Daily Town Talk* (May 1, 1972), McCoy Scrapbook. As Union supporter: McCoy article; Mills and Mills, pp. 108–12. Virginia-born: McCoy and United States Census for 1870 (but Poché, p. 264, n20, says he was born in Connecticut, as does the 1860 census). Scruggs was born about 1821 (1880 census) and died February 17, 1886 (McCoy article). Wealth: His worth in the 1860 census was listed at seventy-three thousand dollars (McCoy Scrapbook). As Mason: *Biographical and Historical Memoirs of Louisiana* (Chicago: Goodspeed, 1892), Vol. 2, pp. 170–71; McCoy article. Arrest and acquittal: Mills and Mills, pp. 119, 121–22; *Biographical and Historical Memoirs of Northwest Louisiana*, p. 304; Marguerite T. Leach, "The Aftermath of Reconstruction in Louisiana," *Louisiana Historical Quarterly* 32 (July 1949), pp. 663, 666. *Uncle Tom's Cabin* story: Carnahan, McCoy, McCoy Scrapbook.

143: Religious: The Chopins' prie-dieu eventually passed to Gustine Weaver, a friend of Cammie G. Henry, patron and collector of Cane River artifacts. Henry's Melrose Scrapbook Number 210, NSU (Cab. 21, 33) has an April 2, 1937, letter from Weaver to Henry about the prie-dieu, including a poem by Weaver:

On My Prie-Dieu

Working—Has been My Prayer;
Made up of vital breath!
Majestic Secrets I have found—
Key to The Gates of Death!

Wiiling—Has been My Prayer
Made up of marks and dots!
My Life—Has been My Manusciipt—
"Dear Lord! Excuse the blots!"

143: French nuns and priests: Sister Dorothy Olga McCants, ed. and trans., *They Came to Louisiana: Letters of a Catholic Mission, 1854–1882* (Baton Rouge: Louisiana State University, 1970), pp. 33, 134–35. According to Elizabeth Shown Mills's investigations (1985 communication), Oscar was born September 30, 1844, and baptized August 17, 1845. His godparents were Oscar Roubieu and Roselia Sompayrac. Missionary's 1861 objections: McCants, p. 135.

143. Birth and baptism of Marie Chopin: McCoy.

143–144: Lélia: The baptismal records of St. John the Baptist Catholic Church in Cloutierville are on Microfilm, NSU: Lélia's record is on Reel 7. Her baptismal record is also available in *Baptisms, 1872–1894, No. 4*, Church of St. John the Baptist, Cloutierville, Louisiana, p. 87: A copy of the church register was supplied to me by Elizabeth Shown Mills. In French, Father Jean Marie Beaulieu recorded, "In the year 1880 on the 29th of February I baptized Marie Laïza, born on the 31st of December and the legitimate daughter of Oscar Chopin and Catherine O'Flaherty. Godfather: Jh Henry. Godmother: Mrs. O'Flaherty." The godfather's name, written as "Jh Henry" with a quotation mark under the *h*, could be Joseph Henry or his son John Henry, but most likely it was Joseph, the husband of Oscar's sister Eugénie.

Lélia's name: The name *Laïza* is not a saint's name: As Barbara Ewell has discovered, it does not appear in Donald Attwater's *Penguin Dictionary of Saints* (Baltimore: Penguin, 1965). Popularity of the name *Lélia*: Elizabeth Shown Mills (1985 communication) notes that there were at least two other Cane River country Lélias (Brosset and Cockfield) born around the same time as Lélia Chopin. Lélia Cockfield's mother was a first cousin of Oscar Chopin's mother. Lélia as named after the Sand character: SCB, p. 65, and further discussion in Emily Toth, "That Outward Existence Which Conforms: Kate Chopin and Literary Convention," Ph.D. Thesis, Johns Hopkins University, 1975, p. 288.

Kate O'Flaherty and Lil Chouteau: In their graduation year (1868), Kate won highest honors as a Child of Mary at the Sacred Heart Academy—while at the Academy of the Visitation, Lil was awarded first premiums in virtually all her subjects (English, Christian Doctrine, Book-Keeping, French, Instrumental Music, Composition and Rhetoric, and Ornamental Work and Housekeeping). "The Academy of Visitation," *Missouri Republican*, June 30, 1868.

The adult Lélia Chopin may have created the story that a packet boat operated by Captain Teal, *The Lélia*, was named after herself: SCB, p. 45, Elizabeth Shown Mills 1985 communication. The packet boat is mentioned in *Biographical and Historical Memoirs of Northwest Louisiana*, p. 315.

144: Chopins' house: At a sheriff's sale on May 20, 1876, the house and property consisting of 135 arpents were sold to Oscar for $4,099, according to documents at the Bayou Folk Museum. Descriptions and history of the house: Carnahan, McCoy, Bayou Folk Museum information sheets—but Mills and Mills say the home was built in 1806 (p. 46). "*Briqueté*" and "*bousillage*" are both explained more fully in Mills, *Forgotten People*, p. 179. The house was not comfortable: When schoolteachers Lucille Tinker (later Carnahan) and Emma Richter (later Masson) lived there in 1928, the house walls used to sweat and run water—and Mrs. LaCaze, the mother of Mildred McCoy, also complained of the dampness when she lived there (Carnahan, McCoy).

145: Cow milking: Carnahan, McCoy. The cow milking appears in Lucille Carnahan's original play, *Our Town and Its Oldest Citizen*, performed March 8, 1967, for Emma Perrier's one-hundredth birthday. Perrier died May 29, 1969; the play is in the McCoy Collection. In other versions of the incident, Kate milked the cow with her mother, or with her mother and Emma Perrier.

145: Gazing: Cloutierville Group; Emma Perrier used to mention Kate Chopin's gazing. DSR, p. 100.

145: Natchitoches Parish weather: According to Waters, born in Natchitoches in 1895, the Cane River frequently froze in winter, and there was snow every year. A McCoy Scrapbook photo shows snow on the Cane River in January 1904, the year Kate Chopin died in St. Louis. In the 1850s, there might be frost as late as March 19 in Natchitoches Parish, according to Lestant Prudhomme's diary in Lyle Saxon's *Old Louisiana* (New York and London: Century, 1929), p. 189. There were heavy frosts in late February, 1880, around the time of Lélia's baptism—but by Kate Chopin's first March in Natchitoches Parish, in 1880, people were already outdoors in shirt sleeves, and the new corn was growing ("Local Gleanings," February 21, 1880, and "Weather Items," *Natchitoches People's Vindicator*, March 6 and March 20, 1880). Natchitoches Parish is cooler and less humid than New Orleans.

145ff.: Oscar's store: Carnahan, McCoy, Waters, and DSR, p. 100, agree that Oscar was not a successful businessman. Description of store: DSR, p. 100. A similar store appears in Lyle Saxon's *Children of Strangers* (London: Bodley Head, 1937), pp. 13, 20–21: Saxon lived and wrote at Melrose Plantation in the Cane River country. Lagniappe: Emma Perrier, recalled by Carnahan, McCoy. Saturday sales: Carnahan. Chinese in the Cane River country: Lucy M. Cohen, *Chinese in the Post-Civil War South: a People Without a History* (Baton Rouge: Louisiana State University, 1984), esp. pp. 53–56, 133.

146: "Lady Bountiful": Lélia Chopin Hattersley letter to Leonidas Rutledge Whipple, November 12, 1907, DSR, p. 102. Beautiful and charitable: Cloutierville Group. Age: The 1880 census lists Kate Chopin as twenty-seven-years old in 1880, but she was twenty-nine by the official census date, in June. Whether she lied or the census taker erred cannot be determined. The Bussys: I am indebted to Elizabeth Shown Mills (1985 communication) for pointing out that Kate Chopin was godmother only once, for the Bussys. "Simple people": Lélia Chopin Hattersley's letter to Whipple, DSR, p. 102.

147ff.: Father Beaulieu: Photo in Bayou Folk Museum and KCM; McCants, pp. ix, 27, 33, 41, 45, 46, 134–35; *Biographical and Historical Memoirs of Northwest Louisiana*, p. 322; DSR, p. 100; SCB, p. 103; Mildred McCoy, "Bayou Folk Musings," *Natchitoches Times*, July 27, 1972, McCoy Scrapbook; Roger Baudier, *The Catholic Church in Louisiana* (New Orleans: A. W. Hyatt Printers, 1939), p. 405; Carnahan. Marriage sermon: Father Beaulieu gave his sermons in French; the one quoted here is translated by Eve Mouton, typescript in McCoy Scrapbook. When the Cloutierville church was virtually destroyed by fire on June 21, 1985, the cross on Father Beaulieu's grave was one of few surviving artifacts (Carnahan).

147: Kate's imitations: SCB, p. 204, n14.

148: Example of intricate kinships: During Kate and Oscar Chopin's first January in Cloutierville, Anna Newton Sers was married to Jack C. Johnson; four months later, her older sister Marie Marguerite "Daisy" Sers married Thomas Jefferson ("T. J.") Flanner. The brides were Kate's second cousins, the daughters of Melanie Eugénie ("Ginny") Charleville, Eliza O'Flaherty's cousin. The second groom, T. J. Flanner, was related to Oscar, whose godfather had been Flanner's uncle Oscar Roubieu. Young Flanner's grandfather had married the sister of Oscar's grandmother, Suzette Rachal Benoist, and another Roubieu had been the first wife of Joseph Henry, whose second wife was Oscar's sister Eugénie. ESM, pp. 2, 103, 110, 111.

149–150: Lovy Charleville: ESM, pp. 102, 109. According to the Rules of the Congregation of the Blessed Virgin Mary, Kate Chopin had an obligation to say certain prayers for another Child of Mary; she may also have written Lovy's obituary, reprinted in ESM. Rules: National Archives of the Society of the Sacred Heart, Villa Duchesne, St. Louis. "Flaming, outspoken revolt": *The Awakening*, Chap. XXXVII. Louis "Chouchoute" Sers, Lovy's widower, was the stepbrother of Albert Sampite: Alphonse Sampite had married the widowed Ginny Charleville Sers. ESM, p. 103.

150: William Robinson and Aurore Charleville: ESM, pp. 103–4. Aurore Charleville, born in 1840, was one of the older Sacred Heart girls when Kate O'Flaherty was first enrolled.

151: Maria Normand and Sylvère DeLouche: DeLouche. Fine linen suit: 1989 interview with Mary DeLouche. Sylvère DeLouche did not gain wisdom as he aged: As an old man, he broke his hip chasing a girl around a table, and had to go about on crutches—whereupon his daughter called him "that old fool." Mary DeLouche, 1989 interview.

CHAPTER 10: "A CERTAIN LIGHT WAS BEGINNING TO DAWN"

152: *Branles*: A *branle* is on display at the Bayou Folk Museum/Kate Chopin Home in Cloutierville. Child rearing: 1984 interview with Emma Richter Masson.

152: Children's schooling: Cloutierville Group. No direct information is available about the early schooling of Jean, Oscar C., George, Frederick, Felix, and Lélia Chopin. But Clémence Benoist, a cousin the same age as Oscar C., attended the small village school across from the Chopins' house, as did Dr. Scruggs's son Samuel. Both teachers were young: According to the census of 1880, Sallie Griffin was twenty-three and her sister Blanche twenty-one. Sallie Griffin took over the school from her sister in 1882 (Carnahan). Clémence Benoist describes her education in her school notebook, in the Melrose Collection, Folder 1053, NSU.

152: Kate's reading: WS.

153–154: Entertainments and feasts: Carnahan. First electric lights: Mrs. S. H. Scruggs (the former Corinne Masson, daughter-in-law of Dr. Scruggs), recounted by Carnahan. A *veillée* appears in Kate Chopin's story "Ti Frère," KCM, KCPP. Mrs. Scruggs's name is variously written as Lise Anne, Lisa Anne, Lisa or Lise (Carnahan, DeLouche, census).

153: Forks: Three of Kate Chopin's forks were donated by Robert Hattersley, Kate Chopin's grandson, to the Bayou Folk Museum/Kate Chopin Home in Cloutierville. The Chopins' gaming table is the kitchen table in Leona Sampite's Cloutierville home.

154: Kate Chopin's amusements: Carnahan, Cloutierville Group, DeLouche. Expensive clothes from New Orleans: McCoy Collection includes large bills for hats, ordered between May 12 and September 1, 1882, from stores on Magazine Street and Gravier Street in New Orleans. Visiting: Carnahan. Afternoon naps: DeLouche. Smoking: Harnett Kane wrote that Chopin was ostracized for smoking, but he may have exaggerated (McCoy Scrapbook). "Some people thought she was quite risque because she smoked cigarettes in public," according to a paper by Eunice Elaine McGraw Dawson for Social Studies 103 at Northwestern State University (McCoy Collection). Relatives' embarrassment: Carnahan.

154: Dressing, powerful, aggressive: DeLouche. More popular with men: Cloutierville Group and Emma Perrier, reported by Leona Sampite.

154: Edna's consciousness: *The Awakening*, Chap. VI.

154: Long rides after dark: Cloutierville Group.

154–155: Léonce as good husband: *The Awakening*, Chap. III. "Warm feeling": Waters—but Lélia was not quite three when her father died. Raffish world: In Chopin's unpublished story, "Ti Frère," KCM, KCPP. Edna's questioning: *The Awakening*, Chap. VI. 270–72: Seasons: Lyle Saxon, *Children of Strangers* (London: Bodley Head, 1937), pp. 82, 92, 107–8, 110, 154, 209, 244–45. The cycle of cotton growing: Joe Gray Taylor, *Louisiana Reconstructed, 1863–1877* (Baton Rouge: Louisiana State University, 1974), p. 372. Chopin's preference for four o'clocks: Carnahan. Chopin's descriptions of night, nature, and seasons: such stories as "After the Winter," "Loka," "The Return of Alcibiade," "Croque-Mitaine," and "Ti Frère." "All the same. . . .": "Vagabonds." SCB, p. 217, n4, says "Vagabonds" is autobiographical, about Kate Chopin as a Cloutierville widow.

156: Halloween in *At Fault*: CW, pp. 813, 819.

156ff.: "Swamp fever": DSR, p. 104, is the source for the diagnosis of "swamp fever." Natchitoches Parish residents differ as to whether "swamp fever" meant malaria or yellow fever: Carnahan, DeLouche, Sampite, Waters. The late Arthur Watson, a Natchitoches attorney, believed it was a general name for any serious fever (1984 interview). About yellow fever and malaria: John Duffy, ed., *The Rudolph Matas History of Medicine in Louisiana*, Vol. II (Baton Rouge: Louisiana State University, 1962); Gordon Harrison, *Mosquitoes, Malaria and Man: A History of the Hostilities Since 1880* (London: John Murray, 1978); J. Livingston, *The Cause of, and Remedy for, Yellow Fever* (New Orleans: A. M. Hyatt, 1879); Edwina Walls, "Observations on the New Orleans Yellow-Fever Epidemic, 1878," *Louisiana History* 23:1 (Winter 1982), 60–67; John Wilds, *Crises, Clashes and Cures: a Century of Medicine in New Orleans* (New Orleans: Orleans Parish Medical Society, 1978); Greer Williams, *The Plague Killers* (New York: Scribner, 1969). Patsy Copeland, librarian at the Matas Medical Library at Tulane University, assisted me.

156ff.: Doctors' visits and treatment: Bills from Drs. Scruggs and Griffin to Oscar's estate. Copies at the Bayou Folk Museum and in McCoy Collection.

157: Petroleum: Harrison, p. 126, and Williams, p. 109, call this the "oiling of stagnant pools." Petroleum, mosquito netting, and sleeping on the second floor—as the Chopins did, because mosquitoes do not fly high—were all suggested public-health measures by the early twentieth century, once mosquitoes were established as the cause of disease.

157: Dr. Faget's papers: "Type and Specific Character of True Yellow Fever as Shown by Observations Taken with the Assistance of the Thermometer and Second-Hand Watch" (New Orleans, 1873), and "The Type and Specificity of Yellow Fever Established with the Aid of the Watch and Thermometer" (Paris and New Orleans, 1875).

157: Malaria as ever-present threat: Taylor, p. 431. Whether someone died of malaria also depended on the type and strain of plasmodia attacking the blood—but that was unknown in the Chopins' day (Williams, p. 104). Quinine: Alfred Goodman Gilman, Louis S. Goodman, and Alfred Gilman, eds., *Goodman and Gilman's Pharmacological Basis of Therapeutics*, pp. 1054–57. I am indebted to Erik Senuty for supplying this reference.

158: Oscar's Hot Springs trip: "Personal," *The People's Vindicator*, September 3, 1881. Also according to "Society Gossip," *The People's Vindicator*, October 8, 1881: "Mrs. Oscar Chopin, who lives in Cloutierville, is visiting relatives in St. Louis. She expects to remain several months in that city." Clippings: Wells.

158: According to Williams, p. 102, the spleen, which is just under the ribs to the left of the stomach, would be swollen enough for a doctor to feel it with his fingers, if a person had or recently had had malaria. An enlarged spleen was a classic sign of malaria: Hippocrates identified enlargement of the spleen with people who lived in damp, hot lowlands. Because nineteenth-century doctors had little training—some had no more than a year of a few casual classes and courses of reading—they might not easily be able to distinguish the liver from the spleen. Country doctors' lack of thermometers: Duffy, pp. 338–40.

158: November 17 bill: McCoy Collection.

159: Ten grains as standard dose of quinine: Wilds, pp. 2–3; Williams, p. 116. Twenty grains is a standard dosage today, according to pharmacist Erik Senuty.

159: Oscar's death: Necrology Scrapbook IIC, p. 5, MHS, contains a newspaper clipping with no other identification: "CHOPIN—On the 10th inst., at Cloutierville, La., after a short illness, Oscar Chopin, aged 38 years, a nephew of the late Louis A. Benoist. New Orleans papers please copy." (Oscar was actually a great-nephew of Louis A. Benoist, whose brother was Oscar's grandfather Charles F. Benoist.)

There has been a great deal of confusion about Oscar's death date. According to his brother-in-law Joseph Henry's testimony in Dr. J. B. Chopin's lawsuit for war damages (OCUS), Oscar died on December 17, 1882; according to the recollections of Charles Bertrand, the son of the storekeeper Kate and Oscar knew, Oscar died on December 2 (Melrose Collection, folder 198). Chopin's two previous biographers differ: October, 1882 (DSR, p. 104) and January 10, 1883 (SCB, p. 46). But the coffin order dated December 10, the newspaper clipping, and a letter from Calvary Cemetery—in "The Misdated Death of Oscar Chopin," listed below—are conclusive evidence that he died on December 10, 1882. Lack of church death record: May 5, 1976, letter from Mildred McCoy to Elizabeth Shown Mills, McCoy Scrapbook. See also Emily Toth, "The Misdated Death of Oscar Chopin," *Kate Chopin Newsletter* 1:2 (Fall 1975), p. 34 and "The Practical Side of Oscar Chopin's Death," *Kate Chopin Newsletter* 1:3 (Winter 1975–76), p. 29.

159: Coffin order is at the Bayou Folk Museum (McCoy Collection).

159: Funeral practices: Carnahan, Waters.

160: Widowhood in *At Fault*: p. 741.

160ff.: Oscar's financial affairs: McCoy Collection includes Oscar's bills, lists of debts, correspondence, and tax assessments, together with records of Kate Chopin's payments.

Leona Sampite also has some receipts for money Kate Chopin advanced to local workers (most of whom signed with an X).

161: Kate's legal petitions: McCoy Collection.

CHAPTER 11: SCANDAL

In these notes, "DeLouche" means Ivy DeLouche, unless otherwise stated.

163: Chopin's widowhood stories: "The Dream of an Hour" (now called "The Story of an Hour"), "A Lady of Bayou St. John," "A Sentimental Soul."

163: Widowhood and work: WS.

164: SCB, p. 217, n4, about *Vagabonds*: "As the MS at MHS of this latter sketch indicates, it describes an actual incident in the life of Kate Chopin, the Cloutierville widow." Crossed-out passages in "Vagabonds" ms.: CW, p. 1026.

164: Men's wanting to help Kate: Cloutierville Group; Carnahan, quoting Lise DeLouche Charleville and Corinne Masson Scruggs, who used to say that "naturally the young woman did not know how to run a store, nor how to handle a plantation— and so she had several young men in the village who were quite willing to help her." "Snooty . . . dirty": Perrier, as told to Leona Sampite. "Sweet on Kate": Carnahan, DeLouche, Emma Richter Masson, Louise Pollock.

165: Pronunciation: Some announcers in Natchitoches Parish incorrectly pronounce the name "Sam-petey." The unusual last name may be from the French "*sans pitié*," or "without pity."

165ff.: I am indebted to Leona Sampite for sharing documents and traditions about the Sampite family. Her collection includes census records, military records, a marriage certificate for J. A. Sampite and Lodoiska Deslouches (the original is in the Court House, Natchitoches) and a handwritten note by Lodoiska Deslouches Sampite, stating, "Loca Delouche born September 6th, 1843—I had six children four dead two living Doctor J. A. Sampite born July 21, 1879. Mrs. Marie Lise Sampite (Mrs. Pollock) born October 9, 1876" (KCPP). According to his tombstone, Alphonse Sampite (Albert's father) was born May 8, 1808, and died February 28, 1871; his wife Lise DesLouches or DesBoves (the carving is worn away) was born February 28, 1810, and died October 9, 1861. Eight years after his wife's death, Alphonse Sampite married Melanie Eugenie Charleville Sers, a first cousin of Eliza O'Flaherty's (ESM, p. 103).

According to family tradition, the elder Sampites were born in France, but another source says the Sampite family was known in Cloutierville in the eighteenth century: Lucille Tinker Carnahan, "Cloutierville," in Germaine Portré-Bobinski and Clara Mildred Smith, *Natchitoches: the Up-to-Date Oldest Town in Louisiana* (New Orleans: Dameron-Pierson, 1936), p. 205. The 1850 United States Census lists the elder Sampites with three children, all born in France, and none named Albert (the closest is "Valsin"). His possible education in France: Cloutierville Group. The only evidence for Albert Sampite's birthdate is his tombstone, and tombstones are often unreliable evidence.

The family name of Albert Sampite's wife was evidently Deslouches, also written as

DesLouches, Delouche, and DeLouche (which I will use for consistency). Source: DeLouche. Often the whim of census takers or clerks determined the spelling.

165: Sampite slaves: Melrose Collection, Folder 192 includes a December 23, 1856 document recording the sale of a "mulatto (griffe) slave named Moses" to Alphonse Sampite by Lucien Condet, a free man of color. Sixteen slaves in 1862: *Biographical and Historical Memoirs of Northwest Louisiana* (Nashville and Chicago: Southern Publishing, 1890), p. 298. In the same record, Dr. Scruggs owned twenty-seven slaves; Dr. J. B. Chopin, forty-two; and Joseph Henry (Oscar Chopin's future brother-in-law), fifty-six.

165: Albert Sampite's military records owned by Leona Sampite: Number cards; certificate after capture at Vicksburg, July 8, 1863; certificate after surrender of the Sixth Louisiana Field Battery Light Artillery on May 26, 1865, then paroled June 6, 1865. He is listed with the 26th Louisiana Infantry in Andrew B. Booth, comp., *Records of Louisiana Confederate Soliders and Louisiana Confederate Commands*, Vol. III–Book 2 (New Orleans, 1920), p. 437. Company G of the 26th Louisiana Infantry was known as the Prudhomme Guards, commanded by Octave Metoyer, and they spent most of their time on picket duty in Mississippi or Louisiana, according to Arthur W. Bergeron, Jr., *Guide to Louisiana Confederate Military Units, 1861–1865* (Baton Rouge: Louisiana State University, 1989), pp. 134–36. Another source suggested by Bergeron, p. 136: Winchester Hall, *The Story of the 26th Louisiana Infantry*, n.p., 1890?. Walk from Vicksburg: Cloutierville Group.

165: Sampite hands in 1880: 1880 census. Wealth: Albert's tax records (owned by Leona Sampite) show that his land grew more and more valuable: In 1880, his property was assessed at $3,895; by 1884, it was $6,090; by 1888, it was $9,825. Leona Sampite's collection also includes land documents from Akron, Washington County, Colorado.

165: Albert's appearance: Photograph reproduced in this book, by permission of Leona Sampite. (According to Don Sepulvado of the Photography Lab at Northwestern State University, the original was a tintype, which was then photographed and touched up.) Albert's treatment of workers: DeLouche—who recalled that only one worker, Nanco, dared answer him back. Literary description of Creole planters: "The brow and cheek of this man were darkened by outdoor exposure, but they were not weather-beaten. His shapely, bronzed hand was no harder or rougher than was due to the use of the bridle-rein and the gunstock. His eye was the eye of a steed; his neck—the same. His manner was military; his sentiments were antique; and his clothing was of broadcloth; his boots were neat; and his hat was soft, broad, and slouched a little to show its fineness." (Lillian Bankston, "The Louisiana Plantation as Seen Through Literature," M.A. Thesis 1934, Louisiana State University, pp. 14–15—also in Melrose, bound volume number 1).

166: Ladies' men in Sampite family: Carnahan, Cloutierville Group. Quotation from descendant: Carnahan (the descendant did not want her name used).

166: Sampites with little in common: Cloutierville Group. But according to one descendant, Loca was not an exceptional homemaker: she knew only one cake recipe (interview with Mary DeLouche, 1989). Albert's travels: DeLouche. Among Albert's lawsuits: In May of 1881, he sued William Roberson for money owed him ($110.40, borrowed in 1876); on the same date Albert sued J. C. Johnson for $460.75 for goods Albert had sold him, including whiskey, shoes, nails, candy, envelopes, seed, calico, buttons, thread, sardines, sugar, and coffee—evidently all bought at one of the Sampite plantation commissaries. The suit was dismissed. Lodoiska's name: Carnahan, DeLouche.

166: Mrs. Scruggs was Loca's mother. Loca's father, J. B. Sylvère DeLouche, had died in the yellow fever epidemic of 1853. His widow, Lise Ann, married Dr. Samuel Oglesby Scruggs, and their son, Samuel H. Scruggs, also became a physician.

167: Loca's romantic past and war doings: Carnahan, from Louise Pollock. The best-known school in Bardstown, Kentucky, was Nazareth Female Academy, and an 1859 graduation program from Nazareth is among Leona Sampite's family papers. But the program does not list any DeLouches as Nazareth students, and according to Sister Agnes Geraldine McGann of the Sisters of Charity of Nazareth Mother House, no DeLouches appear in any school enrollment records. Personal communication, 1989.

167: Records of land given to Loca: Leona Sampite family papers. Dowries were not uncommon in nineteenth-century marriages among propertied people in Louisiana.

167: Intersecting land: The Succession of Oscar Chopin mentions this land, sold at auction after Oscar's death: "The former interest of Julien Anty in the Louis B. Rachal Plantation on the left bank of Cane River descending bounded above by lands of Raoul Rachal, below by lands of J. A. Sampite, in rear by lands of Mrs. W. P. Rabalais, adjudicated to Antoine Marinovich, as the highest bidder therefore at the sum of $100." (Succession of Oscar Chopin, p. 2, McCoy Collection). Possible meetings and meeting places: Carnahan, Cloutierville Group, DeLouche, Sampite. Everyone in Cloutierville had horses and buggies, and according to Ivy DeLouche, "When it's dark, it's really dark . . . those men had facilities."

167–168: Kate Chopin's financial papers: in Leona Sampite's collection.

168: Romance while Oscar alive: Leona Sampite always heard that the affair was going on before Oscar's death; Mildred McCoy thought it possible that Oscar "accepted Kate's liberal ways"; but Lucille Carnahan doubts it.

169: Kate Chopin, "I had loved . . .": KC94.

169: Rumors: Lise DeLouche Charleville (born in 1873, married in 1905) was Loca Sampite's niece, and reticent about people she had known. Grandchildren who heard the stories: Eleanor Sampite Dimmick, Leona Sampite, Louise Pollock, Albert Sampite, and Corinne Scruggs Carnahan (Dr. Scruggs's granddaughter). Sources: Carnahan, Cloutierville Group, DeLouche, Sampite, Waters. Arthur Watson, Kate Chopin's grandnephew in Natchitoches, had not heard of the affair (1984 interview). Marie Sampite Pollock said the affair destroyed her parents' marriage: Cloutierville Group.

169: Albert Sampite's drinking: DeLouche.

170: Descriptions of Alcée Arobin in *The Awakening*: Chaps. XXV, XXVII.

170: Oscar's father's lawsuit: OCUS.

170: Louisiana divorce law: George Elliott Howard, *A History of Matrimonial Institutions* (Chicago: University of Chicago, 1904, rpt. New York: Humanities Press, 1964), Vol. 3, pp. 69–70, 83–84. In 1870, Louisiana passed an omnibus divorce clause, allowing complete dissolution of wedlock "for any such misconduct repugnant to the marriage covenant as permanently destroys the happiness of the petitioner"—but this was repealed in 1877.

171: *At Fault*, CW, p. 808.

171: Whipping Landry Charleville: According to Mildred McCoy's version, Kate Chopin called Landry Charleville out of his store and threatened him with a riding crop for gossiping about her. Lucille Tinker Carnahan and Emma Richter Masson heard that Kate Chopin raised her whip as if to strike him, but Charleville backed away. Elizabeth

Shown Mills heard that Landry Charleville once took a whip to Kate Chopin, allegedly over her behavior with Albert Sampite (1985 communication). Biographical sketches of Landry Charleville appear in ESM 101–2, and *Biographical and Historical Memoirs of Northwest Louisiana*, pp. 333–34. By the time he confronted Kate Chopin, Landry Charleville was an embittered man: He and his wife had outlived all five of their children.
171: Leather strap: Loca Sampite cited the beatings with a leather strap in her 1888 petition for legal separation: Mrs. A. Sampite vs. J. A. Sampite, no. 10283. Judgment filed April 3, 1889. Villagers' claims about wife beating by Frenchmen and Alexis Cloutier: Carnahan. Kate Chopin may have been thinking of Alexis Cloutier for her story "Athénaïse," in which the title character shudders at the thought of her husband's "ugly bare feet—washing them in my tub, befo' my very eyes, ugh!" Albert's drinking and haughtiness: Cloutierville Group, DeLouche.
172: "The general talk": Carnahan.
172: Leaving boys behind: Carnahan, Emma Richter Masson, Arthur Watson. No one knows which boys Kate left behind, but one was probably young Oscar, who had close ties around Natchitoches Parish: When Kate visited Louisiana again in December 1891, eighteen-year-old Oscar remained for several months. Young Oscar had attended school irregularly, if at all, and he was a poor speller—which caused some embarrassment later in life when he became a newspaper cartoonist and his misspellings were circulated all over St. Louis. His school attendance: 1984 interview with George Chopin, his nephew.
172: Dresser for Emma Perrier: Carnahan, McCoy. As of 1989, the dresser was still in the Perriers' old house, part of a legal dispute, although Emma Perrier had died in 1969. Filigree bottles: 1989 interview with Mary DeLouche.
172: Items Kate left to Albert: Sampite. Gaming table: Carnahan, Sampite. Oil lamp: Cloutierville Group, DeLouche, McCoy. Albert gave the lamp to his sister-in-law Maria Normand, and eventually it passed to Ivy DeLouche, Maria Normand's granddaughter and Albert Sampite's grandniece. Ivy DeLouche told me (1975 interview) that she gave the lamp to a handyman to repair, and he destroyed it—but Mildred McCoy believed that Ivy DeLouche had sold the lamp (1975 communication). See Emily Toth, "Kate Chopin Remembered," *Kate Chopin Newsletter* 1:3 (Winter 1975–76), pp. 21–27. Albert's lantern late at night: Cloutierville Group. "Psyche" poem: Seyersted (CW) dates it 1890. Lamp in *The Awakening*: Chap. XXXVIII.
173: Death of Roger McAllister: The 1880 St. Louis city directory is the first to list Amanda as "wid." Eliza O'Flaherty: DSR, p. 105.
173: Lise DeLouche Charleville once wrote a history of Cloutierville education (Carnahan).
174: Central High curriculum: James Neal Primm, *Lion of the Valley: St. Louis, Missouri* (Boulder, CO: Pruett Publishing Company, 1981), pp. 332, 335–42. Felix as quarterback: 1986 interview with Tom Chopin, Felix's son. Condé Nast: Caroline Seebohm, *The Man Who Was Vogue: The Life and Times of Condé Nast* (New York: Viking, 1982), pp. 21–22 for Nast's schooling. Condé Nast was related to Oscar and Kate Chopin: His grandfather, Louis A. Benoist, was the brother of Oscar's grandfather; Condé's half-sister Clémence had married Kate's uncle Charles Faris.
174–175: Kolbenheyer's persuasions, swindler: DSR, pp. 106–7.
174: "Prostrate with grief": DSR, p. 105.

CHAPTER 12: AT FAULT

Kate Chopin's story lists, manuscript submissions, acceptances, rejections, sales, and earnings are all recorded in MAB, reprinted in KCPP.

176: The Morgan Street house no longer exists; City Hall does not have its architectural plan. No more church: DSR, p. 106.

176: Marie Chopin's romance: Waters, 1984. Waters did not recall Buddy Henry's given name, but said he had gone to Yale. Sources on Phanor Breazeale: Waters; Henry E. Chambers, *A History of Louisiana* (Chicago and New York: American Historical Society, 1925,) Vol. 3, p. 290; *The Convention of '98* (New Orleans: William E. Myers, 1898), pp. 36–37; "The Personnel of the Louisiana Constitutional Convention," *Men and Matters* (June 1898), pp. 34–35; obituaries in Melrose Scrapbook no. 73, pp. 128–29. Breazeale's gravestone lists his dates as 1858–1934, but Waters said he was born in 1859 or 1860, and that there were always arguments about whether he was born December 31 or January 1 (1984 interview). Stuffing ballot boxes: Breazeale's own "Statement on Reconstruction Natchitoches": KCM, KCPP, original at NSU.

177: Kate Chopin letter to Marie Breazeale: KCM, KCPP, original at MHS.

178: Loca Sampite's petition for legal separation is D. C. no. 10283, bundle 470, March 1889, in the Court House in Natchitoches. "A leather strap": The words "a leather strap" are lightly crossed out on the court papers. But since the papers were—and still are—open to the public, the words may not have been crossed out originally. "Acquets" is a Louisiana legal term.

179: Clémence Benoist's notebook: Melrose Collection, Folder 1053. Clémence Benoist was the daughter of Oscar Chopin's uncle Victor Benoist.

180: About *America* magazine: Hugh Dalziel Duncan, *The Rise of Chicago as a Literary Center from 1885 to 1920: a Sociological Essay in American Culture* (Totowa, NJ: Bedminster Press, 1964), pp. 58–59.

180: Kate Chopin's 1889 visit: All of Chopin's Louisiana visits reported here are documented either by letters, Natchitoches newspaper notices, or interviews. Her 1889 visit and Casimir Perrier's making the casket were reported by Emma Perrier to Emma Richter Masson, according to Lucille Tinker Carnahan. No Natchitoches newspapers survive from that time.

180: Oscar Chopin's grave (unmarked) is in Section 3, Lot 9 of Calvary Cemetery, according to the cemetery maps.

181: "Lilia" polka: KCM, KCPP.

182: Felix's recollections: FELIX. Descendants: 1985 interviews with David and George Chopin and Marjorie Chopin McCormick.

183: Children's stories: "A Red Velvet Coat," a children's story Chopin wrote in December of 1890, was accepted by *Youth's Companion* but never published (MAB).

183: Idle women: *At Fault*, CW, p. 781. Thorstein Veblen's classic discussion, *The Theory of the Leisure Class: an Economic Study of Institutions*, was first published in 1899.

183ff.: New Women sources: Papers of Thekla Bernays, Susan Blow, Phoebe Couzins, and Florence Hayward, all at MHS. Also useful, although it contains errors, is Mrs. Charles P. (Anne) Johnson, ed., *Notable Women of St. Louis, 1914* (St. Louis: Woodward, 1914), MHS. I am also indebted to Susan Koppelman for information in connection with her short-story collection *Old Maids: Short Stories by Nineteenth Century U.S. Women Writers* (Boston and London: Pandora Press—Routledge & Kegan Paul, 1984).

183–184: Virginia Minor: Virginia Minor's papers are at MHS.

184: "A lone wolf": FELIX. According to newspaperman William A. Kelsoe, men who favored woman suffrage were seldom heard in public: *St. Louis Reference Record* (St. Louis: Von Hoffman, 1928), p. 165. According to Michael Riordan, born in St. Louis in 1890, local men claimed to be against suffrage, on the grounds that women wouldn't know enough about politics (1984 interview).

185: Thérèse's appearance: AF, pp. 741, 743. Fanny's weight gain: AF, p. 839. Beauty standards: Clarence Day wrote of himself and other Yale students in the 1880s that they considered Lillian Russell "a voluptuous beauty, and there was plenty of her to see. We liked that. Our tastes were not thin or ethereal." Quoted in Lois Banner, *American Beauty* (New York: Knopf, 1983), p. 136. Description of David Hosmer: AF, p. 743.

185: "Act of a coward": AF, p. 769; "Reading of morbid literature": AF, p. 779.

185: Kate Chopin's wig: interview with Carmen Breazeale, 1975, reported in Emily Toth, "Kate Chopin Remembered," *Kate Chopin Newsletter* 1:3 (Winter 1975–76), pp. 21–27.

185: Anna Sneed Cairns and Harriet Worthington: HSL, p. 295; "Anna Sneed Cairns," *Missouri Historical Review* 25 (January 1931), pp. 356–57. Cairns (1841–1930) opened her Forest Park University in 1891, and operated it until 1925.

185: Melicent at euchre party: AF, p. 855.

186: Denton Snider: HSL, pp. 2089–90; Max Putzel, *The Man in the Mirror: William Marion Reedy and His Magazine* (Cambridge, MA: Harvard University Press, 1963), p. 58. Worthington's and Snider's projects also resemble the life's work of Edwin Casaubon, the dry-as-dust pedant in George Eliot's *Middlemarch*, who is putting together a "Key to All Mythologies."

186: Mr. Worthington: AF, p. 846.

186: Kate Chopin's Sodality membership: 1986 letter from Nancy Merz.

186: Lucilla and Sacred Heart: AF, pp. 838, 841–42, 846–48.

186–187: Hosmer remarriage in *At Fault*, p. 784. Information about the various Hosmers appears in HSL, pp. 50, 154, and 1344, and in Joan Mayerson Clatworthy, *Kate Chopin: the Inward Life Which Questions*, Ph.D. Thesis, State University of New York at Buffalo, 1979, pp. 106, 107, 109. Clatworthy appears to be confusing Frederick and J. K. Hosmer (she says that J. K. was a minister), and she gives no source for the information that J. K. Hosmer had a daughter named Melicent, born in St. Louis on January 16, 1884. A St. Louis Hosmerologist is needed.

187: Kate Chopin as indulgent mother: 1985 interviews with David Chopin, George Chopin, and Marjorie Chopin McCormick, 1985; Martha Wheelock's 1984 interview with Robert Hattersley.

187: "Tragic mulatto" convention in AF: Emily Toth, "That Outward Existence Which Conforms: Kate Chopin and Literary Convention," Ph.D. Thesis, Johns Hopkins University, 1975, Chap. VI.

188: AF quotes; Melicent in Cane River country: AF, pp. 753, 755, 770–71. Melicent and Grégoire's visit: AF, pp. 751, 771–72. Grégoire as lover: AF, p. 800.

188: *Uncle Tom's Cabin* controversy: The belief that Harriet Beecher Stowe visited the Cane River country is discussed fully in D. B. Corley, A *Visit to Uncle Tom's Cabin* (Chicago: Baird and Lee, 1892), and in many items in the McCoy and Melrose Scrapbooks. The late Arthur Chopin Watson, grandson of Lamy Chopin, gave me a copy of Corley's book, which features his mother, Eugénie ("Nini"), as a kind of Little Eva character. Kate Chopin's "McFarlane" is named after the real-life Robert McAlpin, whose land had been purchased by J. B. Chopin, Oscar's father.

189: "Monsieur Pierre": In the *Post-Dispatch*, "Monsieur Pierre" was subtitled "How François Lost His Life and His Wife by the Same Shot. From the French of Adrien Vely, by Kate Chopin." Kate Chopin's translation is reprinted, for the first time since its original publication, in Thomas Bonner, Jr., ed., *The Kate Chopin Companion* (Westport, CT.: Greenwood Press, 1988), pp. 175–78.

189: "Very strongest work": WS.

189: *At Fault* appearance: There are copies in the libraries at Washington University and Yale, and in the Library of Congress.

189–190: Sending out copies: MAB.

190: Review of *At Fault*. *Spectator* X (October 4, 1890), p. 55. Noted in Marlene Springer, *Edith Wharton and Kate Chopin: a Reference Guide* (Boston: G. K. Hall, 1976), p. 177.

190: Dillon and "A Poor Girl": SCB, p. 52. Review: "A St. Louis Novelist: 'At Fault,' Mrs. Kate Chopin's New Novel," *St. Louis Post-Dispatch*, October 5, 1890, p. 31.

190: *St. Louis Life* plans: "Announcement," *St. Louis Life*, December 14, 1889, p. 4.

190: "People We Know," *St. Louis Life*, October 11, 1890, p. 8. I assume that Sue V. Moore is the author of this sketch: Editors generally wrote most of the unsigned material in their periodicals.

190–191: "Literary News," *St. Louis Republic*, October 18, 1890, p. 10. Chopin's reply: "Literary News," *St. Louis Republic*, October 25, 1890, p. 10. Reprinted KCM, KCPP.

191–192: Chopin's admiration of Howells: SCB, p. 53, citing DSR, p. 129, and interview with Rankin.

192: Changes in A *Modern Instance* from magazine to book form appear in footnotes in *A Modern Instance*, ed. William M. Gibson (Boston: Houghton, Mifflin, 1957).

192: *Fashion and Fancy* review: Quoted in Anthony Paul Garitta, "The Critical Reputation of Kate Chopin," Ph.D. Thesis, University of North Carolina at Greensboro, 1978, p. 77. Garitta's dissertation is an excellent survey of reviews of Chopin's work.

192: "Recent Publications," *New Orleans Daily Picayune*, October 12, 1890, p. 15.

192–193: "Recent Fiction," *The Nation*, October 1, 1891, pp. 263–64. Discussed in Garitta, p. 78.

193–194: Flora, "Review of Mrs. Kate Chopin's Novel 'At Fault,' " *Natchitoches Enterprise*, December 4, 1890, p. 1. The *Enterprise* was a weekly, published every Thursday morning. I am grateful to Evelyn Stallings and Carol Wells for finding this review for me, together with Kate Chopin's answer.

193–195: Kate Chopin, "At Fault. A Correction," *Natchitoches Enterprise*, December 18, 1890, p. 3.

195: "Hotel Arrivals": *Natchitoches Enterprise*, December 18, 1890, p. 3.

195: Sampite separation: Albert and Loca Sampite signed an informal separation agreement on December 27, 1890. *Mrs. L. Sampite* v. *J. A. Sampité*, typed document, in the possession of Leona Sampite of Cloutierville. The separation was made permanent in the same document, with a judgment signed June 20, 1891, and ratified by both parties on August 19, 1891. Reprinted in KCPP.

CHAPTER 13: A PROFESSIONAL WRITER

Story submissions, rejections, earnings: MAB.

Diary entries quoted in this chapter: KC94.

197: Kate Chopin's *Post-Dispatch* translations: "The Shape of the Head" (January 25, 1891); "The Revival of Wrestling" (March 8, 1891); "How to Make Manikins" (April 5, 1891). The last is probably the same piece listed in MAB as "Cut-Paper Figures."

198: Unpublished pieces: In MAB, Chopin listed "Roger and His Majesty," a nine-hundred-word story, as having been rejected by Book Syndicate, *Once a Week*, and *Argonaut*, and then "Destroyed." "Octave Feuillet," twelve-hundred words, was sent to *Belford's* in February 1891, rejected in October, and then sent to the *Post-Dispatch*. It may have been a translation.

198: Ibsen publications and performances: According to Susan Wolstenholme (1985 communication), Chopin could have read *Ghosts* and *A Doll's House* in Henrietta Frances Lord's translation, published by Lily in Chicago and Appleton in New York in 1890. See also Wolstenholme's article, "Kate Chopin's Sources for 'Mrs. Mobry's Reason,'" *American Literature* 51:4 (January 1980), pp. 540–43—although Wolstenholme assumes, without evidence, that Ibsen and Wagner were Kate Chopin's sources. I know of no American literary works from the 1890s dealing with venereal disease—but such works may have existed.

198: "St. Louis Experiment": John C. Burnham, "The Social Evil Ordinance—A Social Experiment in Nineteenth Century St. Louis," *Missouri Historical Society Bulletin*, April 1971, pp. 203–17.

198: Charlotte Eliot, *William Greenleaf Eliot—Minister, Educator, Philanthropist* (Boston: Houghton, Mifflin, 1904).

198–199: Diary re *Heavenly Twins*: KCM, KCPP. "Sarah Grand" was a pseudonym for Frances Clark McFall (1862–1943), an Irish-born writer who published her first novel, *Ideala*, in 1888 and parodied masculine literary critics by describing a literary journal she called *The Patriarch*. Elaine Showalter, *A Literature of Their Own* (Princeton: Princeton University Press, 1977), pp. 31, 342. Thekla Bernays, a Wednesday Club member with Kate Chopin, reviewed *The Heavenly Twins* in "Currents of Literature," *St. Louis Daily Globe-Democrat*, April 25, 1894, Thekla Bernays Scrapbook, MHS, pp. 24–25.

199: Chopin's changing characters' names: See CW notes. "Azélie" had several names, including Amélite and Mélanie; the protagonist in "Regret" was sometimes called Angela or Aurélia, before Chopin settled on Aurélie. The ms. for "Mrs. Mobry's Reason" no longer exists.

199: Meramec country: The Meramec Highlands were a beautiful resort area in St. Louis County fifteen miles west of the city, accessible by two lines of electric railway, and also by the Missouri Pacific Railroad. See HSL, p. 1441. Chopin's letters: KCM, KCPP.

200: "The Going and Coming of Liza Jane" was Chopin's title for the story, reprinted in CW as "The Going Away of Liza." An earlier title was "A Woman Comes and Goes" (MAB).

200: "Life's delirium": *The Awakening*, Chap. XVIII.

201: Chopin on historical fiction: "In the Confidence of a Story Writer," CW, p. 704. Chopin wrote the essay in 1896, but it was not published in *The Atlantic* until January 1899.

202: Chopin's using real people: Kate Chopin occasionally called Cloutierville "Centre-ville," "Centerville," or "Orville" in her stories, but the details easily identify the actual town. Some characters' names are close to their originals, including Madame Verchette in "For Marse Chouchoute," likely inspired by the Vercher family of Cloutierville, and Dicey in "A Gentleman of Bayou Têche," based on a real-life servant (McCoy). For other similarities, see Chapter 15. But possibly as a form of disguise, Chopin gave many of her Cane River country characters Acadian French names—such as Ozéina, Eu-phrasie, and Odalie—that were much more common in South Louisiana. Northwest Louisiana people, including Cloutierville residents, generally had more ordinary names, such as Marie, Joseph, Lise, and Albert. (I am indebted to Barbara Ewell for noting the South Louisiana names, and to Lucille Tinker Carnahan for providing an explanation.)

359–60: Loca Sampite's separation: (Manuscript) Mrs. L. Sampite v. J. A. Sampite, No. 10.8 & 9, Natchitoches, June 20, 1891; and (typescript) *Mrs. L. Sampite* v. *J. A. Sampite*, December 27, 1890; June 20, 1891; and August 21, 1891 (documents owned by Leona Sampite). According to the typescript, Loca and Albert Sampite had agreed informally on a division of property on December 27, 1890. Their agreement was noted in a judgment on June 20, 1891, and then permanently ratified by both parties on August 19, 1891. In the settlement, Loca Sampite received their house and land surrounding it, including the 215 acres designated as the "Chopin" tract (pur-chased from Oscar's sister, Marie Chopin Breazeale). Loca Sampite also received farm equipment, corn, potatoes, farm animals, chickens, and "turkies," as well as the piano, furniture, and one thousand dollars in cash. The rest of their joint possessions belonged to Albert Sampite, and their entire community property was valued at sixteen thousand dollars.

202: Maria Normand DeLouche, Sylvère DeLouche, and Albert Sampite: DeLouche. The lamp: DeLouche; McCoy. Exactly when Albert Sampite and Maria Normand DeLouche became romantically involved cannot be pinpointed. She and Sylvère DeLouche were not legally separated until February 20, 1904, after twenty-three years of marriage, but their estrangement had been long-lasting. The DeLouche separation document is Marie E. Delouche v. Sylvère DeLouche, no. 13096, Bundle 617, Feb-ruary 1904 (Natchitoches Court House). The DeLouche name is spelled "Deslouche" in the document itself, which declares that the community's assets will be divided, and that Maria DeLouche will keep her property "free from the control and interference of the said defendant." (The last name has also been spelled "DesLouche," "DeyLouche," "Del'Ouche," "Dalouche," and "Delucie," according to Louis Raphael Nardini, Sr., *My Historic Natchitoches, Louisiana and Its Environment* [Natchitoches: Nardini Pub-lishing Company, 1963], p. 203.) The uncommonness of the name Sylvère is also evident in legal papers and public documents: It is often written as "Sylveste" or "Silver."

203: Chopin-Gilder correspondence: KCM, KCPP. Gilder's creed is described in SCB, pp. 68–69 and in Arthur John, *The Best Years of the* Century: *Richard Watson Gilder,*

Scribner's Monthly, and Century Magazine, 1870-1909 (Urbana: University of Illinois, 1981), passim.

204: Natchitoches trip: "Personal," *Natchitoches Enterprise*, December 10, 1891, p. 3. I am indebted to Evelyn Stallings for finding this item.

204: Emma Perrier: Miss Emma—known as *Nénaine* to Albert Sampite's grandchildren—loved to talk about Kate Chopin (Cloutierville Group).

205: Chopin on Maupassant: CW, pp. 700-701 reprints the ms. version of Chopin's essay. In the published version, "In the Confidence of a Story Writer" (*Atlantic*, January 1899), Chopin's references to Guy de Maupassant were dropped.

206: Chopin's work habits: Her extant story manuscripts are at MHS. In CW notes, Per Seyersted compares the manuscript versions—where available—with the printed versions of Chopin's short stories, poems, and essays, and finds few changes. The manuscripts are, however, final copies: Chopin may have destroyed earlier drafts. Mss. for *At Fault* and *The Awakening* do not exist. Felix's memories (letter of August 11, 1925): Amy Elizabeth Taggart, "Mrs. Kate O'Flaherty Chopin: Her Life and Writing." M.A. Thesis, Tulane, 1928, p. 11. (This is the only piece of original biographical information in Taggart's thesis.) Harrison Clark, "Writers and Books Of Note that Have Come out of St. Louis," *St. Louis Republic* (December 9, 1900), special book number, n.p. Chopin on writing habits: "On Certain Brisk, Bright Days," CW, pp. 721–22, originally in *St. Louis Post-Dispatch*, November 26, 1899. Schuyler: WS.

207: "A Fancy," KCM, KCPP. Seyersted dates it 1892 on the basis of the handwriting.

207–208: Chopin as charter member of the Wednesday Club: 1985 communication from Mrs. Richard W. Maxwell of the Wednesday Club. The Wednesday Club records are now at MHS. Wednesday Club history, written by Martha S. Kayser, appears in HSL, pp. 2052, 2479–84. See also "The Wednesday Club," from the *Criterion*, Thekla Bernays Scrapbook, p. 39, MHS.

208: "Commercial instinct": KC94.

208: Margaret Barber Stone and her husband Charles H. Stone: HSL, p. 2200. The Stones appeared frequently in the society pages, which recorded their card parties, their daughter's marriage, and Professor Stone's camping trips. See, for instance, *St. Louis Post-Dispatch* society columns for December 21, 1890, and August 14, 1892. Modern Novel Club: HSL, p. 1555. Mrs. C. H. Stone, *The Problem of Domestic Service* (St. Louis: Nelson Printing Company, 1892), esp. pp. 7, 10. I am indebted to Marilyn Bonnell for the analysis of this pamphlet.

209: According to Mrs. Maxwell (1985), Kate Chopin's essay was scheduled for December 23 but delivered on December 9. According to the day's program, "the vocal part being rendered by Mrs. Herf with Mrs. Benjamin Taussig at the piano:

    1st Choral by Bach with Passion music according to St. John
    2, The Fugue, Handel's Amen Fugue in the Messiah
    3, Bach's Aria from the Passion Music according to St. Mathew
    4, Mozart's Aria from Figaro
    5, Parts of Hayden's and Beethoven's Sonatas
    6, Schubert's song from "Die Schone Mullioin" (sic)

(The program was transcribed for me by Mrs. Maxwell.)
209: "Confidences," CW, p. 704.

210: Albert not parlor person: Surviving letters (owned by Leona Sampite) from Albert Sampite to his children show that he wrote brusque prose and was not always grammatical. KCPP.

210: Chopin's resignation: Wednesday Club minutes, sent to me by Mrs. Maxwell (1985), now at MHS. After the announcement of Kate Chopin's resignation, the minutes read, "On motion of Miss Wall, the President was authorized to request at the next club meeting all members who had not joined one of the sections to stand and later to report to secretary."

CHAPTER 14: LOUISIANA INSPIRATION, ST. LOUIS AMBITION

Records of Kate Chopin's writings, payments: MAB. Diary entries: KC94.

211: June 1892 Natchitoches Parish flood: Mentioned in Albert Sampite's letter to his son Alphonse, June 14, 1892; also in an unattributed letter to Loca Sampite, June 19, 1892. Both letters are in Leona Sampite's papers and KCPP. Kate Chopin wrote "At the 'Cadian Ball" on July 15–17, 1892.

212: Albert's land: DeLouche. In 1890, according to documents in Leona Sampite's collection, Albert Sampite acquired land in Akron, Washington County, Colorado.

212: The Normands, a very colorful family, were descended from Dr. François Normand, an aristocratic graduate of a French university who emigrated to the Cane River country in 1824. He began a bitter feud with the Creole General François Gaiennie— and before their feud ended, a dozen people were killed. Dr. Normand's Paris-educated son, Jules Honorat, was an inveterate dabbler who in 1855 moved himself and his family to an international colony, Cuba, where they sat out the Civil War. Jules Normand, a sometime planter and hospital manager, also ran a photography business that was probably a cover for subversive political activity. After the war, the family returned to Louisiana with a crew of Chinese laborers from Cuba: Normand hoped to use them to pick cotton. Although the experiment failed, thirty-three Chinese men were still living in Natchitoches Parish when Kate and Oscar Chopin arrived in late 1879. Jules Normand became a merchant and a Natchitoches innkeeper, and persuaded Kate's enterprising brother-in-law, Lamy, to invest in an oily patent medicine called "Normand's Miraculous Balm," which Jules's father had started.

   Sources about Jules Normand: DeLouche; *Biographical and Historical Memoirs of Northwestern Louisiana* (Nashville: Southern Publishing, 1890), pp. 304, 362; Elizabeth Shown Mills and Gary Mills, *Tales of Old Natchitoches* (Natchitoches: Association for the Preservation of Historic Natchitoches, 1978), pp. 67–70. The Bayou Folk Museum has a picture of Jules Normand and his brother. Chinese workers: DeLouche; Lucy M. Cohen, *Chinese in the Post-Civil War South: A People Without a History* (Baton Rouge: Louisiana State University, 1984), pp. 53–56, 133; Joe Gray Taylor, *Louisiana Reconstructed, 1863–1877* (Baton Rouge: Louisiana State University, 1974), p. 391.

212–213: About Maria Normand DeLouche: DeLouche. Ivy DeLouche also owned the *Faust* sheet music that Gaspar Hernandez had given Maria Normand, and photographs of both of them and Sylvère DeLouche. The photographs are now owned by Mary

DeLouche. Duplicates are to be placed in the Bayou Folk Museum. Maria Normand was born in 1853, and she and Sylvère DeLouche were married on Kate Chopin's thirty-first birthday: February 8, 1881.

213: Sylvère DeLouche's behavior, refusal to work: DeLouche. Maria Normand, who raised cattle on the back of her property and sold them, was considered very industrious, while Sylvère was said to "live it up on family money" (Mary DeLouche interview, 1989).

213: Albert Sampite's house: DeLouche; Albert Sampite's grandchildren Louise Pollock, Albert Sampite, and Leona Sampite. Mrs. Scruggs's land: Sampite grandchildren. Albert Sampite's 1892 letter: Leona Sampite. Albert wrote affectionate letters to his children, inquiring after their health, describing his own health and farming problems, and making sure new pants were delivered to his son (letters owned by Leona Sampite, KCPP). He wrote quickly in pencil, and evidently spoke English as a second language: He uses such expressions as "since a few days" (a translation of the French *"depuis quelques jours"*) rather than "a few days ago." He was of the generation that grew up speaking French.

On February 20, 1891, the *Natchitoches Enterprise* reported that "Miss Marie Sampite, the beautiful daughter of Mr. J. A. Sampite, of Cloutierville, is spending several days in our city as the guest of Miss Maria Dufilho." In May 1891, the Sampites rented a Shreveport cottage for Marie, who had finished her schooling at the Sacred Heart Academy at Grand Coteau (document owned by Leona Sampite). The papers for Loca Sampite's December 1893 lawsuit (documents numbered 10849 or 11849, *Mrs. L. Sampite v. J. A. Sampite*) are missing from the Natchitoches Court House. Bullwhip: Leona Sampite.

213: Albert Sampite photograph: Leona Sampite. Sylvère DeLouche photographs: Mary DeLouche collection. About Charlie: DeLouche.

214: Death of Cora Henry Chopin: *Natchitoches Enterprise*, September 1, 1892. A week later, Kate Chopin's story "For Marse Chouchoute" was reprinted in the *Enterprise*, taking up virtually the entire front page.

214: Names in "Ma'ame Pélagie": Kate probably gave the name Félix to the dead soldier in honor of her son. Her "Aunt Boyer," who had given her the autograph book she circulated at the Sacred Heart Academy, was named Pélagie.

214: Sources for Magnolia Plantation: 1986 interview with Betty Hertzog, current owner of Magnolia Plantation; "A 'Big House' Still Cherished," *Baton Rouge Advocate Magazine*, March 12, 1989, p. 20; *Biographical and Historical Memoirs of Northwestern Louisiana*, p. 319; "Magnolia Plantation—A Proud Tradition," *Natchitoches Times*, August 6, 1978, pp. 1, 6A, 7, article supplied by Lucille Tinker Carnahan; François Mignon, "Cane River Memo: Cane River, The Lower Reaches," September 1971, McCoy Scrapbook; Gary B. Mills, *Forgotten People: the Cane River's Creoles of Color* (Baton Rouge: Louisiana State University, 1977), p. 237; Lyle Saxon, *Old Louisiana* (New York: Century, 1929), p. 365; Bonnie Warren, "The Magnolia of Cane River," *Louisiana Life* 10:1 (March–April, 1990), 24–27.

The new "Magnolia"—named, like the old one, for its setting in a magnolia grove— was a gray brick house. The "Ma'ame Pélagie" house was red brick—but both the real-life and fictional houses stand at the end of an avenue of live-oaks. The new Magnolia house (like the new house in "Ma'ame Pélagie") was made of less splendid materials than the old, with wood replacing brick in places where the change would not show.

About Fannie Hertzog Chopin: Lucille Tinker Carnahan; Julie Chopin Cusachs (Fannie

Hertzog Chopin's daughter); J. Fair Hardin, *Northwestern Louisiana: a History of the Watershed of the Red River, 1714–1937* (Shreveport and Louisville: Historical Record Assn., n.d.), Vol. III, pp. 69–70. According to her gravestone, Frances Hertzog was born in 1865, but the 1900 census says 1869, and J. Fair Hardin says 1871. Fannie Chopin was one of Rankin's principal sources, and he claims (p. 102) that there was a close friendship between Kate Chopin and Fannie Hertzog Chopin, but the fifteen- to twenty-year age difference and their differing attitudes toward literary production makes that doubtful. Fannie Chopin, educated at St. Mary of the Woods in Indiana, wrote such poems as "Ode to Natchitoches," "A Rosebud in the Garden of Melrose," "Somewhere Up There," and "Fifty Years at the Foot of the Cross," dedicated to a Natchitoches priest.

215: House rental to Dr. Colvin: Mildred McCoy, "Bayou Folk Musings," *Natchitoches Times*, June 22, 1972, McCoy Scrapbook.

216: Letter to Baker: KCM, KCPP, original at American Antiquarian Society.

216: Financial panic: "Industrials Were Hard Hit" and "Financial and Commercial," *New York Times*, May 4, 1893, pp. 1, 10. "Lizzie Borden Arraigned," *New York Times*, May 9, 1893, p. 2.

217: Chopin letter to Gilder: KCM, KCPP, original at New York Public Library. Gilder's offices and evenings: Arthur John, *The Best Years of the* Century: *Richard Watson Gilder*, Scribner's Monthly, *and* Century *Magazine, 1870–1909* (Urbana: University of Illinois, 1981), pp. 1–2, 140.

217: Boston trip: DSR, p. 31. SCB, p. 207, n25, says DSR probably garbled the time, and meant an 1893 trip: *Bayou Folk* was published in 1894. I agree with Seyersted.

218: Chopin's admirers: DSR, pp. 106, 107; Waters; McCoy, with information from Marjorie Chopin McCormick. Both Mildred McCoy and Marjorie McCormick suffered incapacitating strokes before I could verify this information with them. Mildred McCoy died in 1986 and July Breazeale Waters in 1989. In SCB (pp. 178 and 225, n37), Rankin quotes Dillon about *The Awakening*, giving the impression that he interviewed Dillon—but Rankin was only seven years old when Dillon died in 1902. Sources about John Alvarez Dillon and Blanche Valle Dillon: untitled clip, Necrology, I, p. 47, MHS; "John A. Dillon Dies at Bar Harbor, Me.", Necrology IIB, p. 15, MHS; "Jno. A. Dillon Dies at Bar Harbor," Necrology IIP, p. 23, MHS; "Journal of Clara Billon," Billon Papers, MHS, pp. 82–91. Dillon and Pulitzer: James Wyman Barrett, *Joseph Pulitzer and His World* (New York: Vanguard, 1941), pp. 49–50; HSL, p. 1635; Julian S. Rammelkamp, *Pulitzer's Post-Dispatch, 1878–1883* (Princeton: Princeton University Press, 1967), pp. 2, 4, 9, 13–15, 88–90; Don C. Seitz, *Joseph Pulitzer: His Life and Letters* (New York: Simon & Schuster, 1924), pp. 104, 184; Harry Wilensky, *The Story of the St. Louis Post-Dispatch* (St. Louis: St. Louis Post-Dispatch, 1981), pp. 6, 12. Rammelkamp's book includes a portrait of Dillon, opposite p. 16. Dillon, daughters and women's equality: Rammelkamp, pp. 14n–15n, 294. I am indebted to Daniel Pfaff of Pennsylvania State University for informing me that scarcely anything about John Dillon appears in Pulitzer's papers.

220: MAB shows that *Vogue* retained "It Matters All," then rejected it.

221: Visit from Lamy and Fannie Chopin: I am indebted to Carol Wells for finding this item: "Mr. and Mrs. L. Chopin returned on Monday night from an extended bridal tour which besides some delightful days at the World's Fair included a visit to some of the principal northern cities" ("Personal," *Natchitoches Enterprise*, November 2, 1893).

Uncle Tom's Cabin: DSR, p. 120; Lyle Saxon, *Old Louisiana*, pp. 254–64; clippings in Melrose and McCoy Scrapbooks. The D. B. Corley book, *A Visit to Uncle Tom's Cabin* (Chicago: Laird & Lee Publishers, 1892), contains affidavits from local people, including Landry Charleville, about the authenticity of Lamy Chopin's cabin. Lamy's Uncle Tom's Cabin was actually outside the fair grounds, in the enclosure of the Libby Prison War Museum, with other questionable projects not sanctioned by the fair. After the fair's end, the cabin disappeared.

221: Kate Chopin and women at the fair: Whether Kate Chopin attended the 1893 fair is unknown. Most likely she visited it during one of these 1893 periods in which she did not write anything: June 27–July 22; July 23–August 24; August 25–September 21; September 21–October 21. The suggestion that Madame Ratignolle resembles a Mary Cassatt figure was made to me by Charlotte Goodman. The black women's protest appears in Paula Giddings, *When and Where I Enter: the Impact of Black Women on Race and Sex in America* (New York: Bantam, 1984), pp. 85–87; Gerda Lerner, ed., *Black Women in White America: A Documentary History* (New York: Vintage, 1972), pp. 164–65; James Loewenberg and Ruth Bogin, eds., *Black Women in Nineteenth-Century American Life* (University Park: Pennsylvania State University, 1976), pp. 263–79.

221–222: "La Belle Zoraïde": For a longer discussion, see Emily Toth, "That Outward Existence Which Conforms: Kate Chopin and Literary Convention," Ph.D. Thesis, Johns Hopkins University, 1975, pp. 209–20. The dance scene in Chopin's story has some similarity to George W. Cable's *The Dance in Place Congo and Creole Slave Songs*, originally published in the *Century* magazine for February and April, 1886 (rpt. New Orleans: Faruk von Turk, 1974). "The Congo Dance," a long description, appeared in the *New Orleans Daily Picayune* on October 12, 1879. Congo Square, later renamed Beauregard Square, is now Louis Armstrong Park.

222: Last mass at Old City House: Louise Callan, *The Society of the Sacred Heart in North America* (New York: Longmans Green, 1937), p. 667.

CHAPTER 15: BAYOU FOLK

Diary entries quoted here are in KC94.

223: Houghton, Mifflin advertisement in *Publishers Weekly* 1155 (March 17, 1894), p. 450.

223: *Cottage Hearth* notice: Quoted in Anthony Paul Garitta, "The Critical Reputation of Kate Chopin," Ph.D. Thesis, University of North Carolina at Greensboro, 1978, p. 95.

223: *Bayou Folk* contains most of the Louisiana stories Kate Chopin had written through the end of 1893. Nine had been published for children, in *Youth's Companion* ("For Marse Chouchoute," "A Wizard from Gettysburg," "A Rude Awakening," "Beyond the Bayou," and "Loka") or *Harper's Young People* ("A Very Fine Fiddle," "Boulôt and Boulotte," "The Bênitous' Slave," and "A Turkey Hunt"). Of the adult stories, four had appeared in *Vogue* ("A Visit to Avoyelles," "Désirée's Baby," "A Lady of Bayou St. John," and "La Belle Zoraïde"), and three in *Two Tales* ("Love on the Bon-Dieu," "At the 'Cadian Ball," and "In and Out of Old Natchitoches"). One each had been published in the *Century* ("A No-Account Creole"), in the *New Orleans Times-Democrat* ("Ma'ame Pélagie"), and in *St. Louis Life* ("The Return of Alcibiade").

Of the other Louisiana stories Kate Chopin wrote through the end of 1893, seven would appear in *A Night in Acadie*: "The Lilies," "Mamouche," "A Matter of Prejudice," "Azélic," "At Chênière Caminada," "Ripe Figs," and "Caline." Of her other Louisiana stories from that period, she destroyed one ("Unfinished Story—Grand Isle"); published another one later ("After the Winter"); and tried and failed to publish two more ("Croque-Mitaine" and "A Little Free-Mulatto"). One more Louisiana story, "Dr. Chevalier's Lie," was published in *Vogue* but not reprinted in *Bayou Folk* or *A Night in Acadie*. Its subject—the death of a prostitute—may have made it seem unsuitable.

224: Houghton, Mifflin's request: December 19, 1893, letter to Kate Chopin, KCM, KCPP; original at Houghton Library, Harvard.

224: Lucille Tinker Carnahan, who first moved to Cloutierville in 1928, praises the accuracy of Kate Chopin's dialect renderings. Joan Lally discusses the levels of dialect (four black, six white) that Chopin uses to distinguish characters in *At Fault*. See Lally's "Kate Chopin: Four Studies," Ph.D. Thesis, University of Utah, 1973, esp. p. 19.

224: Real-life parallels: "For Marse Chouchoute" and Dicey: McCoy. Chopin's Houghton, Mifflin contract made her liable in any libel suits, but evidently she was never sued. The September 11, 1893, contract is in the Houghton Library, Harvard University.

225–226: "Living Tales from Acadian Life," *New York Times*, April 1, 1894, p. 23. As Garitta notes (p. 84), this is the earliest review that has been discovered—but there is no index to nineteenth-century book reviews.

225: Historian Elizabeth Shown Mills says she has never found a Cajun in the Cane River country (1985 communication). Local residents called themselves "French."

225: The word *bayou*: In "Beyond the Bayou," Kate Chopin refers to the bayou as "a stream." Désirée of "Désirée's Baby" does disappear "among the reeds and willows that grew thick along the banks of the deep, sluggish bayou"—but she is in the Cane River country, far from the Mississippi.

226: Reviews, all cited by Sue V. Moore in "Mrs. Kate Chopin," *St. Louis Life* 10 (June 9, 1894), pp. 11–12, KCM, KCPP. [title unknown]. *Portland Transcript.* "Literary Notes: New Publications." *Argonaut*, April 16, 1894, p. 8. "Bayou Folk," *Boston Beacon*, May 5, 1894, p. 3. "Literary Notices: Recent Fiction," *Hartford Daily Courant*, April 19, 1894, p. 10.

226: "Bayou Folk," *The Critic*, May 5, 1894, pp. 299–300.

226–227: "Recent Fiction," *Atlantic Monthly*, April 1894, pp. 558–59.

227: Other reviews: "Bayou Folk," *Public Opinion* 17:2 (April 12, 1894), p. 35; "The New Books," *New Orleans Daily Picayune*, April 15, 1894, p. 14; "Bayou Folk," *New Orleans Times-Democrat*, May 27, 1894, p. 26; "Fiction," *Review of Reviews*, May 1894, p. 625; *Pittsburgh Bulletin*, mentioned by Moore (I could not locate this review); "Recent Novels," *The Nation* 58:1513 (June 28, 1894), p. 488; "Fiction: Bayou Folk," *The Literary World*, April 21, 1894, p. 121.

227—228: St. Louis reviews: "Reflections," *Sunday Mirror*, April 15, 1894, p. 4; "Some Late Books," *St. Louis Republic*, May 20, 1894, p. 16. William A. Kelsoe's memoirs help explain the superficiality of many reviews, including his own. Kate Chopin, Kelsoe recalled more than twenty-five years later, had been "the author of several successful novels, one of which, 'Bayou Folk,' I read when I was the Republic's book-reviewer. I thought well of the book and said as much in our weekly column of book notices. Book reviewing was a side issue with me on the Republic. The paper could spare only a column a week then for its book reviews and put them on the editorial page. . . . [Meanwhile] each of us was expected to turn in a column and a half of editorial matter every day, so many long and so many short editorials, besides a few paragraphs." W. A. Kelsoe, *St. Louis Reference Record* (St. Louis: Von Hoffman Press, 1928), p. 277. "The Book Table," *St. Louis Post-Dispatch*, April 8, 1894, p. 32.

229–230: The Western Association's history appears in James L. Weygand, *Winona Holiday, The Story of the Western Association of Writers* (Nappanee, IA: 1948). *Indianapolis Journal* quotation is from Marybelle Burch, manuscripts librarian, Indiana State Library (1987 communication). Burch also provided a copy of the convention program and an article called "The Western Writers," by "A Teacher," published in *The Pen Magazine* 6:2 (July–September 1898), pp. 69–70.

229–230: Anderson, Indiana and Mrs. Sawyer: KC94 and convention program.

230: "Cultivated, varied, and gossipy": Garitta, p. 93.

230–231: Reprints of Chopin's article: Marybelle Burch supplied me with this information. Attacks on Kate Chopin: "Books and Authors," *Minneapolis Journal*, July 21, 1894; *Cincinnati Commercial Gazette*, July 28, 1894.

231–232: Meditation, "Dorothea," and "Juanita": KC94. SCB, p. 217, n4, says "Juanita" is based on a true story.

233: "The Dream of an Hour" is now called "The Story of an Hour."

233: "Impressions" is the title for KC94. When the notebook was discovered in Chopin's grandson Robert Hattersley's attic seventy years later, a round rat hole had been gnawed in the cover. Besides journal entries and poems, the diary contains essays ("The Western Association of Writers," "The Night Came Slowly"); translations from Guy de Maupassant ("A Divorce Case," "Mad," and "For Sale"); and four stories ("Juanita," "Cavanelle," "Regret," and "Ozème's Holiday"). Seyersted does not classify Chopin's diary entry about "Dorothea" as a short story.

234: Duodecimo Club: *Mirror*, April 15, 1894, p. 5.

234: Satirical exchange: *Mirror*, April 15, 1894, p. 5.

235: "Society," *St. Louis Life*, January 6, 1894, p. 11.

235: Letter from H. E. Scudder: November 7, 1893, KCM, KCPP. Original in Houghton Library, Harvard University.

235: Agnes Repplier about the *Atlantic*: George Stewart Stokes, *Agnes Repplier: Lady of Letters* (Philadelphia: University of Pennsylvania, 1949), p. 77.

235: Chopin's *Atlantic* acceptances and rejections: MAB. The eleven rejected stories were "A Dresden Lady in Dixie," "Lilacs," "Cavanelle," "A Sentimental Soul," "Odalie Misses Mass," "A Vocation and a Voice," "Elizabeth Stock's One Story," "Ti Démon" (twice), "Typical German Composers" (an essay), and "The Unwritten Law" (later called "The Godmother"). Virtually all the rejected stories have characters who violate accepted moral standards: They lie, break job rules, abandon religion, revel in sensuality, or rejoice in the deaths of others.

236: Chopin's translations of the Guy de Maupassant stories are reprinted in Thomas Bonner, Jr., *The Kate Chopin Companion* (Westport, CT: Greenwood Press, 1988).

236: Mrs. Hull (May 4, 1894 entry): The Hulls lived at 3335 Morgan (Kate was at 3317), and Lizzie Chambers Hull was the wife of Edward B. Hull, coal merchant, of the Hull Coal Company. According to the 1900 census, Mrs. Hull was born in 1842 in Missouri; her mother had been born in Kentucky and her father in Pennsylvania. Her children were all born in Missouri.

237: Parrot: A parrot misbehaves in *The Awakening*, Chap. IX. Blanche: Blanche Bordley was a daughter of Virginia Charleville Lynch, the sister of Kate's grandmother. Blanche married the millionaire Daniel Bordley, a director of the Liggett & Myers Tobacco Company, and considered herself the reincarnation of Marie Antoinette (Maryhelen Wilson, 1976 communication). Blanche Bordley died April 23, 1930, and her obituary is in Necrology, XV, pp. 62–63, MHS.

237: "The incomparable James Lane Allen": Kate Chopin, "Development of the Literary West: a Review," *St. Louis Republic*, special book number, December 1900, p. 1.

237: Poem to Blanche: MHS; KCM, KCPP. "Dispise" is Chopin's spelling.

238: In 1872, Kitty had pronounced her vows, and in 1877 she made her profession.

CHAPTER 16: LITERARY CELEBRITY

242: "Brief Comment," Providence *Sunday Journal*, April 15, 1894, p. 13. Chopin's name: The Western Association of Writers' supporter had called her "Kate Chapin." Even after *The Awakening* was published, Chopin's name appeared in quotation marks, as if a pseudonym, in Lady Janet Scammon Young's letter: KCM, KCPP.

242–243: Sue V. Moore, "Mrs. Kate Chopin," *St. Louis Life* 10 (June 9, 1894), pp. 11–12. Rpt. in full in KCM, KCPP; with some omissions in "General Gossip of Authors and Writers," *Current Literature* 16 (August 1894), p. 106 and "Mrs. Kate Chopin," *Book News*, September 1895, pp. 5–6. No author's name is given, but editor Moore is the likely author.

243–245: Schuyler: WS. Montgomery Schuyler: Galusha Anderson, *A Border City During the Civil War* (Boston: Little, Brown, 1908), p. 121, and in HSL, p. 156, 2025–27. Montgomery Schuyler was dean of Christ Church Cathedral and author of "The Church, Its Ministry and Worship" and "The Pioneer Church." William Schuyler (1855–1914); OJ pp. 88, 209, 222, 233–34; Fannie Hurst, *Anatomy of Me: A Wonderer in Search of Herself* (Garden City, NY: Doubleday, 1958), pp. 50–52, 54, 62–63, 66, 69; and Hurst's reminiscences on the fiftieth anniversary of Central High School, quoted in Susan Koppelman, "The Educations of Fannie Hurst," *Women's Studies International Forum* 10:5 (1987), p. 508. "To Hider Schuyler": KCM, KCPP.

244: Mrs. Humphry Ward, *Marcella* review: "Marcella," *Providence Sunday Journal*, April 15, 1894, p. 13. About Mrs. Humphry Ward: Elaine Showalter, *A Literature of Their Own* (Princeton: Princeton University Press, 1977), pp. 110, 227–31, 238, 338–39.

245: Letter to Waitman Barbe: KCM, KCPP, original at West Virginia University.

245–246: *Young Doctor Gosse*: Chopin's correspondence with Stone & Kimball, Joseph Marshall Stoddart: KCM, KCPP, originals at Newberry Library, Harvard, or owned by Per Seyersted. *Young Doctor Gosse* may have contained bits of other Chopin doctor characters, such as Dr. John-Luis of "Mamouche," Dr. Chevalier of "Dr. Chevalier's Lie," and Dr. Mandelet of *The Awakening*. Gosse was a well-known literary name: Edmund Gosse, the British man of letters, was a prolific reviewer and friend of Thomas

Hardy, Henry James, Robert Louis Stevenson, and many other literary men. But Chopin had no apparent reason to use Gosse's name in a novel.

A more likely inspiration for Kate's Young Doctor Gosse is "Young Dr. Scruggs," as he was always called, in Cloutierville. (The younger Samuel Scruggs had been just twenty-one when the Chopins moved back to St. Louis.) Kate Chopin frequently used similar names as mnemonic devices (such as *Chartrand* for the storekeeper Charles Bertrand), and *Gosse* borders on an anagram for *Scruggs*. Possibly *Young Dr. Gosse* included Cane River stories told by the younger Dr. Scruggs, a noted raconteur. Chopin may finally have destroyed the manuscript because it was too close to real life: Young Dr. Scruggs was also the half-brother of Loca Sampite. Dr. Scruggs as raconteur: Carnahan.

246: Acceptances and rejections: Most likely Kate Chopin sent "A Dresden Lady in Dixie" to the *Catholic Home Journal* because it had been rejected by other, better-known periodicals: *The Atlantic, Century, Scribner's, Harper's, Youth's Companion*, and *Cosmopolitan*. "Cavanelle" had been rejected by the *Century, The Atlantic, Harper's*, the *Chap-Book*, and *Scribner's* before Chopin sent it to *The American Jewess* on February 13, 1895. MAB.

246ff.: Rosa Sonneschein: Writers about the Sonnescheins usually misspell the name. It was SONNE-schein, without an *n* in the second syllable. Virtually the only reliable article on Rosa Sonneschein is Jack Nusan Porter's "Rosa Sonneschein and *The American Jewess* Revisited: New Historical Information on an Early American Zionist and Jewish Feminist," *American Jewish Archives* 32:2 (November 1980), pp. 125–31. Porter's article quotes information from Sonneschein's grandson and corrects previous sources, including his own "Rosa Sonneschein and *The American Jewess*: the First Independent English Language Jewish Women's Journal in the United States," *American Jewish History*, September 1978, pp. 57–63. I am indebted to Jack Nusan Porter for sending me his articles. Rabbi Sonneschein's dismissal from Shaare Emeth under "murky circumstances": Susan Koppelman's unpublished interviews with members of the St. Louis Jewish community.

246ff.: "Cavanelle," *The American Jewess* 1:1 (April 1895), p. 22. The manuscript is at MHS, and comparisons with the ms. and final version appear in CW, pp. 1019–21. Sonneschein added clarifying conjunctions, omitted clutter and repetition, and translated some French expressions into English. "Crudities": "On Certain Brisk, Bright Days," CW, p. 722. First languages of *American Jewess* readers: Porter's first article, p. 61, suggests that subscribers were German and Sephardic Jews, because the ads were for products that poor, East European Jews could not afford.

247–248: Sonneschein's editorial: "Editor's Desk," *The American Jewess* 1:1 (April 1895), p. 47. Chopin's photograph appears on p. 22 of the same issue. Quotations about *The American Jewess*: "Press Greetings," *The American Jewess* 1:2 (May 1895), pp. 99–100 and 1:3 (June 1895), pp. 152, 156.

248–250: Chopin's *St. Louis Life* reviews: " 'Crumbling Idols' by Hamlin Garland," October 6, 1894; "The Real Edwin Booth," October 13, 1894; "Emile Zola's 'Lourdes,' " November 17, 1894: All CW. Garland's "A Branch Road"; *Main-Travelled Roads* (New York: Harper & Brothers, 1891), p. 23. See Peggy Skaggs, " 'The Man-Instinct of Possession': A Persistent Theme in Kate Chopin's Stories." *Louisiana Studies* 14 (Fall 1975), pp. 277–85—phrase appears in CW, p. 401. Mollie E. Moore Davis, "A Bamboula": *An Elephant's Track and Other Stories* (New York: Harper, 1897).

Chopin did not mention that Garland was also one of her competitors: Three of his

Crumbling Idols articles had previously appeared in *Arena* magazine, which had never accepted a Chopin story. The most she had managed with the Arena Publishing Company was their offer to publish *Young Doctor Gosse* at her own expense. Garland had also had a story published by *Century* magazine as early as 1890, four years before Kate Chopin achieved that goal.

250: Reisz's lace and dyed hair: *The Awakening*, Chaps. IX, XVI.

251: For a woman, "moral" means "chaste": point also made by Kate Chopin's contemporary Charlotte Perkins Gilman, in her *Women and Economics*, published 1899.

454–56: The Blackmans: According to the 1900 census, George Blackman was born in September 1854, and Carrie Blackman in April 1856. I am indebted to Susan Koppelman for checking the census. Egeria quotation: OJ. The Blackmans' daughter Caroline later married Orrick Johns, son of Kate Chopin's friend George Johns. In a severe postpartum depression (and an eerie reenactment of *The Awakening*), Caroline Johns tried to drown herself—and then, in a sanitarium, she starved herself to death (OJ, pp. 312–16, 344). "To Carrie B.": KCM, KCPP. Carrie Blackman's portrait of a young woman reading a letter: "Pointedly Personal," *St. Louis Republic*, May 1, 1898, p. 9. The *Republic* does not say when Blackman painted her picture: Possibly it was inspired by Chopin's "Her Letters" (*Vogue*, April 11 and 18, 1895).

253: Editors' refusing "The Story of an Hour": SCB, p. 68, speculates that Richard Watson Gilder of *Century* magazine rejected the story as unethical.

CHAPTER 17: A ST. LOUIS SALON

254: St. Louis salons: (Vernon Knapp), "Is There an Interesting Woman in St. Louis?" *St. Louis Republic* (September 11, 1910), part 5, p. 1, KCM, KCPP. Seyersted attributes the unsigned piece to Knapp. Mrs. Otto Forster, Chopin children: "Reflections," *Mirror*, July 8, 1897, p. 5; "Folks in Society," *Mirror*, May 23, 1899, p. 10. Kate Chopin and Mrs. Otto Forster sometimes attended the same parties, such as "Miss Espenschied's Debut," *St. Louis Post-Dispatch*, December 5, 1897, p. 19.

254: A copy of *Bayou Folk* illustrated with sketches by Kate Chopin's son Oscar is in Special Collections at the Olin Library, Washington University, St. Louis.

254: The Blackmans' gatherings: OJ, pp. 181–83. According to the *St. Louis Post-Dispatch* ("St. Louis Artists' Guild," December 4, 1897, p. 2), the guild had been in existence nine years; its club rooms were at 1830 Locust Street. (The *Post-Dispatch* gives the club's name as "Artists'," but OJ calls it "Artist's.") A later guild member was Roger Baldwin, founder of the American Civil Liberties Union, who arrived in St. Louis just after Kate Chopin's death. Chopin as "beautiful and exquisite": OJ; p. 88.

254: George Johns's note to William Vincent Byars: Byars Collection, MHS. The letter is dated 1896 in pencil, but that date is crossed out and 1897 written in. The book mentioned is probably *New Songs to Old Tunes*. KCM, KCPP.

255: Al fresco suppers: FELIX.

255: William Vincent Byars, Byars family: Mary Warner Byars (William's daughter), "Reminiscences of William Vincent Byars," September 1949, Byars Collection, MHS; Alexander DeMenil, "A Century of Missouri Literature," *Missouri Historical Review*

15 (October 1920), 117; August 6, 1895, letter from George Julius to William Schuyler about William Vincent Byars, Byars collection, MHS; OJ, pp. 122, 208–9; William A. Kelsoe, ed., "William Vincent Byars," *St. Louis Reference Record:* Appendix (St. Louis: Von Hoffmann Press, 1928), p. 290.

255: Chopin's "nice American home": Knapp. Hepzibah Home: "Reflections," *Mirror,* July 8, 1897, pp. 4–5. Chopin, "I like to look": "As You Like It," February 13, 1897, essay in *St. Louis Criterion,* CW, p. 706. Chopin's neighbors: 1900 United States Census (the 1890 census was destroyed in a fire). Number 3315 Morgan was a boardinghouse kept by Lou Hoskins, a Kentucky-born widow; on the other side, at 3325, the Chopins' next-door neighbors were the E. C. Chases, a Vermont-born dentist with a wife, a daughter, three sons, and his mother. The daughter, Augusta, was seven years younger than Lélia Chopin, her traveling companion to a Minnesota resort in the summer of 1899.

255–256: Calling rituals, card: "Society Calling: A Much Needed Reform Being Adopted by the Ladies," *St. Louis Post-Dispatch,* December 14, 1890, p. 14; "Visiting Cards." *St. Louis Globe-Democrat,* January 28, 1898, p. 36. (Chopin finished writing *The Awakening* on January 21, 1898). According to I. H. Lionberger, *Glimpses of People and Manners in St. Louis, 1870–1920,* "Calling in the evening was an established custom, the more the merrier" (MHS typescript, p. 63). Chopin's day was Thursday: 1899 letter from Sue V. Moore: "If nothing prevents I think I'll drop in on you tomorrow 'Thursday' evening a little while" (letter at MHS:KCM, KCPP). "Clever woman writer": *St. Louis Life,* January 21, 1893, p. 4. During Chopin's 1893 visit to New York, a society writer suggested signature reproductions as calling cards: "Her Point of View," *New York Times,* May 7, 1893, p. 12. In *The Awakening,* Tuesday is Edna Pontellier's "day" for New Orleans callers—and Tuesday evening is her husband's time to berate her for her social failings.

256ff.: Chopin's salon: "Kate Chopin loved cards": DSR, p. 141. Grate fire and day bed: FELIX. Byars's groans: Mary Warner Byars. Schuyler's performances: OJ, p. 209. Vernon Knapp, "Is There an Interesting Woman in St. Louis?" Chopin's salon and opinions from Felix and George: 1984 interview with David, Ann, George, and Marie Chopin; 1985 interview with Tom and Rose Chopin. "I can hear you": May 10, 1899, letter from Lizzie L., MHS (KCM, KCPP). Chopin's listening to secrets: SCB, p. 60, from DSR (interview) and Mrs. Tritle.

257: Ferrisses: Evidently Mr. and Mrs. Franklin Ferriss, whose son Hugh became a noted architect. OJ about Ferriss: pp. 129, 168, 178, 179, 212–13, 258. Fannie Hurst "inordinately admired" Hugh Ferriss: (*Anatomy of Me* [Garden City, NY: Doubleday, 1958], p. 92). Mrs. Ferriss received a verse from Kate Chopin for Christmas 1895:

For Mrs. Ferris

> Five little robbins in a row.
> I wonder what they mean!
> For now a-days as well we know
> Things are seldom what they seem.
> Then let each bird a blessing be
> That's surely come to stay;
> That growling fates, as well we see,
> Can never drive away.

(MHS; KCM, KCPP).

257–258: Charles L. Deyo: The 1895 St. Louis city directory lists Deyo as "Exchange Editor." Later he was listed as "editorial writer." Deyo does not appear in standard biographical sketches or obituaries kept at MHS. There is no way to determine what Kate Chopin meant by his ill health: Whatever ailed him, he continued to work for the *Post-Dispatch* for the rest of Chopin's lifetime. According to HSL, p. 2071, Charles L. Deyo was one of the founders of the Single Tax League, with Hamlin Russell, a journalist; James A. Hill, a railroad master mechanic; and John G. Hummell, a tobacconist. The organization took the name "St. Louis Single Tax League" on August 12, 1888.

258ff.: Frederick Kolbenheyer: The spelling of Kolbenheyer's first name varies. Rosa Sonneschein called him Friedrich; Don Seitz wrote Frederich, a hybrid of the American Frederick and the German Friedrich (Seitz, *Joseph Pulitzer*, [New York: Simon & Schuster, 1924], pp. 57, 104). St. Louis city directories give the name as Frederick, but the 1900 census has Fredrich. DSR, p. 89, says that Kate Chopin's son Frederick, born in 1876 in New Orleans, was named for Kolbenheyer, who assisted at the birth of her older sons Oscar and George in St. Louis in 1873 and 1874. "Bomb thrower": 1984 interview with David Chopin; "great learning," FELIX. Biographical sketch: "Dr. Kolbenheyer's Body Brought Home," *St. Louis Post-Dispatch*, April 10, 1921, in Necrology XI, p. 98, MHS; frightening children, 1985 interview with Tom Chopin. A photograph of Kolbenheyer appeared in *The American Jewess* 4:1 (October 1896), p. 9. Rosa Sonneschein about Kolbenheyer: "Book Brieflets," *American Jewess* 4:1 (October 1896), pp. 46–47. Roeslein bookstore: Seitz, p. 57. Germania Club: HSL, pp. 888–89; J. Thomas Scharf, *History of St. Louis City and County* (Philadelphia: Louis H. Everts, 1883), p. 1819. MHS has a Germania Club file, but most items were missing when I inquired in 1984. The club's elegant and expensive house was located on the corner of Eighth Street and Gratiot, near the site of Kate O'Flaherty's childhood home.

Kolbenheyers' address: The 1900 census shows Fredrich Kolbenheyer, born May 1843, living at 2006 Lafayette Avenue with his wife, Agnes Kolbenheyer, born December 1848 in Austria; Lizzie Rehg, their servant, was born in Illinois in January 1866. Kolbenheyer's obituary (noted above) lists his daughter as Mrs. William Koenig of Omaha, probably the same as the Elsie Kolbenheier (sic) who belonged to the J. S. G. Euchre Club of the South Side in 1890: "Society News," *St. Louis Globe-Democrat*, December 21, 1890, p. 28. There were no other Kolbenheyers or Kolbenheiers in the city directory.

Chopin on "old fashioned mechanism and stage trapping": "Confidences," CW, p. 700. DSR about Kolbenheyer: pp. 89, 106; see also SCB, p. 48. "Viennese sweetheart": "Dr. Kolbenheyer's Body." "Kolby had eyes": 1985 interview with Tom Chopin. Kate Chopin's granddaughter Marjorie Chopin McCormick was delivered by Dr. Kolbenheyer, and does not think there was an affair between Kate Chopin and the doctor (1985 interview).

261ff.: Kate Chopin and Johns family: "The most individual feminine talent": Orrick Johns, "The 'Cadians," *Mirror* 20 (July 20, 1911), pp. 5–6—KCM, KCPP. George and Minne (Minnehaha) Johns: OJ, passim; "G. S. Johns Is Dead: St. Louis Editor, 83," *New York Times*, July 17, 1941, p. 19. Minne's cigarettes with Chopin and Florence Hayward: OJ, p. 201. Kate Chopin and bathtub cigar: SCB, p. 208, n47. O. K. Bovard at Chopin's salon: 1984 interview with David and George Chopin. About Bovard: OJ, p. 139; James W. Markham, *Bovard of the Post-Dispatch* (Baton Rouge: Louisiana State University, 1954), esp. pp. 10, 15, 20, 30, 56, 59, 61, 62. George Johns's salary: OJ,

p. 93, says his father earned fifty dollars a week, but Markham (*Bovard of the Post-Dispatch* 71) says that *Post-Dispatch*ers ordinarily earned twenty-five dollars a week. "If her own culture": Orrick Johns, "The 'Cadians." Julia Breazeale: Waters. Kate Chopin, "Then Wouldst Thou Know": CW, p. 730. She wrote the poem August 16, 1895, and it was not published in her lifetime. Pulitzer about George Johns: OJ p. 162 (evidently something Johns told his son). Regretting uncommitted sins: OJ, p. 289. Born four years before the Civil War, George Johns died just four months before Pearl Harbor.

George and Minne Johns's son Orrick grew up to be a poet, mystery writer, and radical who wrote for Reedy's *Mirror* and later for *New Masses*, but he outlived his father by only five years: Despondent and drinking heavily in 1946, living with his fourth wife, Orrick Johns put poison in beer and took his own life. Necrology, XXIII, p. 47, MHS.

265ff.: William Marion Reedy: Max Putzel, *The Man in the Mirror: William Marion Reedy and His Magazine* (Cambridge: Harvard University Press, 1963); Fred Wilhelm Wolf, "William Marion Reedy: a Critical Biography," Ph.D. Thesis, Vanderbilt University, 1951; Ethel King, *Reflections of Reedy: a Biography of William Marion Reedy of* Reedy's Mirror (Brooklyn, NY: Gerald J. Rickard, 1961).

Reedy reprinted "Désirée's Baby" in the September 30, 1894, issue of the *Mirror*. (The paper was known variously as the *St. Louis Mirror*, the *Mirror*, and finally as *Reedy's Mirror*. Issues are on file at the St. Louis Mercantile Library and the St. Louis Public Library.) Kate Chopin's poem "To 'Billy' ": I assume that the poem is to Reedy, the only "Billy" evident in Chopin's life. Chopin as "leader of a literary set": "Has High Society Struck the Pace That Kills?" *St. Louis Post-Dispatch*, February 6, 1898, p. 12. "Two Belles," "Female Immortals: an Interesting Communication," *Mirror*, June 3, 1897, p. 2. In the June 17 issue, Reedy asked that the "Two Belles" identify themselves, so that he could forward to them a great stack of mail he had received for them: "Reflections," *Mirror*, June 17, 1897, p. 8. Reedy, "An American Academy," *Mirror*, January 8, 1898, p. 7. On Sallie Britton Spottiswood Mackin, *A Society Woman on Two Continents* (New York and London: Continental Publishing Company, 1897): Chopin's "As You Like It," *St. Louis Criterion*, March 20, 1897, CW, pp. 715–17; "Arbaces McFudd" (William Marion Reedy), "Mrs. Mackin's Book," *Mirror*, March 11, 1897, p. 8.

268ff.: Kate Chopin and Ruth McEnery Stuart: Chopin's account appeared in her February 27, 1897, "As You Like It" column in the *St. Louis Criterion*, CW, pp. 711–13. Stuart's visiting with Mrs. E. C. Sterling: "Folks in Society," *Mirror*, February 4, 1897, p. 10. About Ruth McEnery Stuart: John Bassett, "Ruth McEnery Stuart," in *Southern Writers: A Biographical Dictionary*, eds. Robert Bain, Joseph M. Flora, and Louis D. Rubin, Jr. (Baton Rouge: Louisiana State University, 1979), pp. 437–39; R. R. K., "Ruth McEnery Stuart," *Dictionary of American Biography*, Vol. XVIII, ed. Dumas Malone (New York: Scribner, 1936), pp. 177–78; Carmen Meriwether Lindig, "The Woman's Movement in Louisiana, 1879–1920," Ph.D. Thesis, North Texas State University, 1982, pp. 109–12; Ethel C. Simpson, "Ruth McEnery Stuart: the Innocent Grotesque," paper delivered at the Louisiana Women Writers Conference, Loyola University of New Orleans, 1986. Chopin/Stuart influences: "La Belle Zoraïde" was published in *Vogue* in January 1894, and "The Unlived Life of Little Mary Ellen" in Stuart's *In Simpkinsville: Character Tales* in 1897. Chopin's "Nég Créol," written in April 1896, appeared in *The Atlantic* in July 1897; Stuart's "Caesar" had been published in Stuart's *Carlotta's Intended and Other Stories* in 1894. Chopin and Stuart's works are compared in Emily Toth, "That Outward Existence Which Conforms: Kate Chopin and Literary Convention," Ph.D. Thesis, Johns Hopkins University, 1975, pp. 145–69. Ruth McEnery Stuart's autographed copy of *Bayou Folk* is in the Ruth McEnery Stuart Collection at the Howard-Tilton Memorial Library, Tulane University—inscription reprinted in KCM, KCPP. According to SCB, p. 210, n72, Stuart does not seem to have mentioned Kate Chopin in her writings, not even in her article about Louisiana writers: Ruth McEnery Stuart, "American Backgrounds for Fiction, VI—Arkansas, Louisiana, and the Gulf Country," *Bookman* XXXIX (August 1914), pp. 620–30.

271: Chopin and other women: The papers of Bernays, Eliot, and Hayward are all at MHS. Children's list of friends: SCB, p. 209, n55. Waters said that she had never heard of "Aunt Kate's" having any close women friends.

CHAPTER 18: INTIMATE AND UNTIDY STORIES

272ff.: Kate Chopin's translations from Guy de Maupassant are reprinted in Thomas Bonner, Jr., *The Kate Chopin Companion* (Westport, CT: Greenwood, 1988). Chopin translated "A Divorce Case," July 11, 1894, not published; "Mad?" September 4, 1894, not published; "It?" February 4, 1895, published February 23, 1895, in *St. Louis Life*, pp. 12–13; "Solitude," March 5, 1895, published December 28, 1895, in *St. Louis Life*, p. 30; "Night," March 8, 1895, not published; "Suicide," December 18, 1895, published June 5, 1898, in *St. Louis Republic*; "For Sale," October 26, 1896, not published. "Father Amable," translated April 21, 1898, is incomplete and unpublished (and largely illegible to the naked eye—but Bonner has successfully transcribed it for his edition). Translation mss.: MHS.

273: Chopin's letters to Stoddart and Houghton, Mifflin, March 1895: KCM, KCPP.

273: Withdrawal of anticlerical books: Erik Stocker, Rare Books Librarian at the St. Louis Public Library, 1985 interview. Zola, Maupassant, Flaubert, kept out of American public libraries: Esther Jane Carrier, *Fiction in Public Libraries, 1876–1900* (New York and London: Scarecrow Press, 1965), p. 135. I am grateful to Barbara White for directing me to Carrier's book.

274: "Athénaïse" and Chopin's grandmother: Kate Chopin wrote "Athénaïse" between April 10–28, 1895. Her grandmother, Athénaïse Charleville Faris, was living with her son, Charles Faris, and her youngest daughter, Kate's aunt Josephine Faris Wilson. Grandmother Faris's sister, Harriet Charleville Hunt, lived with Kate's aunt Amanda McAllister on St. Ange Street. Scudder's acceptance letter: KCM, KCPP, original at Houghton Library, Harvard. "A Family Affair": The American Press Association had already syndicated Chopin's "The Christ Light" ("The Going and Coming of Liza-Jane"), and "In Sabine" and "In and Out of Old Natchitoches" after they appeared in *Bayou Folk*. "A Family Affair" was also reprinted in the *Saturday Evening Post* in September 1899—probably to take advantage of the fame Kate had achieved as author of *The Awakening*, published that April.

276: Chopin's opposing rules: "Confidences," CW, pp. 700–702, revised as "In the Confidence of a Story Writer," CW, pp. 703–5. The essay was slated for the January

1897 *Atlantic*, according to a letter to Kate Chopin from Walter Hines Page: KCM, KCPP). Why it was postponed for two years is unknown.

276: Chopin's card playing: "Pointedly Personal," *St. Louis Republic*, November 12, 1897, p. 13.

276: Most popular books: Winston Churchill was a St. Louis–bred novelist who, in his day, was better known than the British member of Parliament who later became the prime minister. In early 1898, the most-circulated novel at the St. Louis Public Library was Alexandre Dumas's *Count of Monte Cristo*, followed by Victor Hugo's *Les Misérables*, F. Marion Crawford's *Mr. Isaacs*, E. P. Roe's *He Fell in Love with His Wife*, and Eugène Sue's *The Wandering Jew*. St. Louis educators and churchmen deplored the popularity of the *Count of Monte Cristo*, believing it frivolous, sensational, and inappropriate for children: "Comparative Popularity of Novels Issued from the Public Library" and "The Most Popular Novel with St. Louis Readers," *St. Louis Post-Dispatch*, February 13, 1898, p. 10.

276ff: Chopin about censorship: "As You Like It," *St. Louis Criterion*, March 13, 1897, CW, pp. 713–15. Byars: See Notes to Chapter 17. The St. Louis Public Library records that would show whether *Jude the Obscure* was banned are not now available: 1987 interview with Erik Stocker. Reviewers around the United States did call *Jude the Obscure* coarse, obscene, and morbid: Quoted in Carrier, pp. 326–32. Edna Pontellier's damnation: Kate Chopin's Statement on *The Awakening*, *Books News* 17 (July 1899), p. 612 (KCM, KCPP).

278: Reedy about censorship: Max Putzel, *The Man in the Mirror: William Marion Reedy and His Magazine* (Cambridge: Harvard University Press, 1963), pp. 45, 71. Reedy's statements on censorship: "Thomas Hardy's Art," *Mirror*, June 25, 1896, p. 13; on *The Triumph of Death*: "Reflections," *Mirror*, March 11, 1897, p. 2; on *Les Misérables*: "Reflections," *Mirror*, October 14, 1987, p. 3. On Prévost and "wifely infidelity": "Reflections," *Mirror*, November 25, 1897, pp. 7–8; on elemental literature: March 24, 1898, quoted in Fred Wilhelm Wolf, *William Marion Reedy: a Critical Biography*, Ph.D. Thesis, Vanderbilt University, 1951, p. 80. Reedy fought censorship and suppression all his life. He was the first editor to print Edgar Lee Masters's *Spoon River Anthology*; he denounced the Society for the Suppression of Vice's attack on Theodore Dreiser's *The Genius*; he protested the denial of the mails to *The Masses*.

278: William Dean Howells, *Criticism and Fiction* (New York: Hill and Wang, 1967), pp. 128, 153, 159.

279ff.: Chopin and *Vogue*: "Those Who Have Worked With Us," *Vogue*, December 6, 1894, p. 359 for pictures, p. 380 for text. Chopin stories published in *Vogue* 1895–1897: "Two Summers and Two Souls," "The Unexpected," "The Recovery," "A Pair of Silk Stockings," "The Blind Man," "Suzette," and "An Egyptian Cigarette." All except "A Pair of Silk Stockings" were intended for her third short-story collection, *A Vocation and a Voice*: SCB, p. 210, n74. "The Anglo-Saxon novelist": *Vogue* 4:22 (November 29, 1894), p. 342.

280: Josephine Redding: Frank Luther Mott, *A History of American Magazines*, Vol. 4 (Cambridge: Harvard University, 1938–68), pp. 756n, 758–59. According to Caroline Seebohm, Redding was "a square little person given to wearing sensible shoes and a large hat" (*The Man Who Was Vogue: the Life and Times of Condé Nast* (New York: Viking, 1982)), pp. 42–43, 47.

281–282: "Curious psychic experience": FELIX.

282: "Mental energy,": "As You Like It," *St. Louis Criterion*, March 27, 1897, CW, pp. 718–20. Robert Fitzsimmons won the undisputed heavyweight championship from James J. Corbett on March 17, 1897. Charles Guiteau, President Garfield's assassin, had been hanged in 1882, while the Chopins were in Cloutierville.

282: War stories: Reedy praised *The Red Badge of Courage* (Putzel, p. 67, Wolf, p. 236), but some librarians objected to it (Carrier, pp. 332–35). Rejections of "The Locket" (MAB): *Youth's Companion,* the *Century, Polyglot, New Orleans Times-Democrat,* American Press Association (for syndication), the *Independent,* the *Chap-Book, St. Louis Republic,* and *Saturday Evening Post.* Oddly, Chopin did not send her story to Reedy's *Mirror.*

283: "Ti Frère": KCM, KCPP.

283: "A Night in Acadie": Chopin's correspondence with Gilder: SCB, pp. 68–69; KCM, KCPP; originals at New York Public Library. The story's original ending does not exist in ms. Barbara Ewell suggests that "A Night in Acadie" is a parody of a romance: *Kate Chopin* (New York: Ungar, 1986), pp. 117–18.

CHAPTER 19: MAKING ENEMIES

284ff.: Chopin's six essays from the *Criterion,* published between February 13 and March 27, 1897, are in CW, pp. 706–20. They appeared under the general heading "As You Like It": Per Seyersted created individual essay titles for clarity in CW.

284: *Criterion's* replacing *St. Louis Life:* "stately and mysterious": Joseph I. C. Clarke, *My Life and Memories* (New York: Dodd Mead, 1925), p. 257. On Henri Dumay: William Marion Reedy, "Reflections," March 11, 1897, p. 2, and September 23, 1897, p. 4; Clarke, p. 258; Thomas Beer, *The Mauve Decade,* quoted in Frank Luther Mott, *History of American Magazines,* Vol. 4 (Cambridge: Harvard University Press, 1957), p. 66. According to Mott (p. 100, n76), Sue V. Moore (whom Reedy, unaccountably, calls "Sallie") was editor and publisher of *St. Louis Life* from 1889 to 1891. In 1892, W. D. Alexander was publisher, and Ballard Turner was editor. In 1896, Mrs. Grace L. Davidson bought the magazine, changed its name to *Criterion,* and the next year moved it to New York. According to SCB, p. 208, n46, Dumay was fired from the *Criterion* in 1898, and went to work at the *New York World* (where his editor would have been Kate Chopin's friend John A. Dillon).

284: "Story of an Hour": Dumay's translation, *"Rêve d'une heure,"* is at MHS, with a note at the bottom in Kate Chopin's handwriting: "Translated by Henri Dumay K. Chopin Dream of an Hour." Chopin's inscription is further evidence that she called the story "The Dream of an Hour," not "The Story of an Hour," as it is called today. Dumay also changed the name of the husband's friend from *Richards* to *Richard.*

285: Reedy on "exalted aestheticism": "Reflections," September 23, 1897, p. 4.

285: Robert's talk: *The Awakening,* Chap. II.

287: Alexander Kielland, *Tales of Two Countries,* trans. William Archer with an introduction by H. H. Boyesen (New York: Harper & Brothers, 1891).

289: Jean Chopin in society: "Julie Chatard Keeps Lent By Being Gayer than Ever," *St. Louis Post-Dispatch,* February 27, 1898, p. 27. High Jean story: "Julie Chatard

Goes Into Ecstasies Over the Costumes at the Borden-Papin Wedding," *St. Louis Post-Dispatch,* February 20, 1898, n.p. in microfilm.

289: Florence Hayward's correspondence (Hayward Collection, MHS) reveals her curmudgeonly side—and her affection for her younger sister.

289: Readers who see "The Falling in Love of Fedora" as a lesbian story should consult Carroll Smith-Rosenberg, "The Female World of Love and Ritual: Relations Between Women in Nineteenth-Century America," *SIGNS* 1:1 (Autumn 1975), 1–29; Lillian Faderman, *Surpassing the Love of Men: Romantic Friendship and Love Between Women from the Renaissance to the Present* (New York: Morrow, Quill, 1981), esp. Part IIA: "Loving Friends." See also John D'Emilio and Estelle B. Freedman, *Intimate Matters: a History of Sexuality in America* (New York: Harper & Row, 1988).

290: *New England Magazine:* Chopin mentions that rejection in an 1893 letter to editor Marion A. Baker of the *New Orleans Times-Democrat:* KCM, KCPP, original at American Antiquarian Society. Other "Miss McEnders" rejections: MAB.

291ff.: Reedy on *The Criterion* and "Miss McEnders": "Reflections," March 11, 1897, p. 2. Whisky Ring: Jim Allee Hart, *A History of the St. Louis Globe-Democrat* (Columbia: University of Missouri, 1961), pp. 120–35; HSL, p. 2497; James Neal Primm, *Lion of the Valley: St. Louis, Missouri* (Boulder, CO: Pruett Publishing Company, 1981), pp. 318–20. William McKee photo: Opposite p. 131, Hart. At McKee's trial, one character witness was former St. Louis mayor James Britton—whose daughter Sallie, Kate O'Flaherty's schoolmate, grew up to be the self-promoting Sallie Britton Mackin, author of *A Society Woman on Two Continents,* the book satirized by Kate Chopin and Billy Reedy. (The *St. Louis Globe-Democrat,* still in the McKee-Britton camp, gave the book three columns of extravagant praise.) McKee at the Eads Bridge: Hart, pp. 120–21; Britton's testimony, Hart, p. 129. Ellen McKee's obituary: Necrology IIX, p. 204, MHS. William McKee's: O. W. Collet Scrapbook, MHS, pp 125–27. Ellen McKee's lack of jewelry, family's simple tastes: Hart, pp. 46, 82, 128, 169. Reedy on ghosts: "Reflections," September 23, 1897, p. 4, and September 30, 1897, p. 8. Clarke, pp. 257–64 about his editing *The Criterion* and the secrets of its financing.

CHAPTER 20: A NIGHT IN ACADIE: "IS LOVE DIVINE?"

Chopin's correspondence with Houghton, Mifflin and *The Atlantic* is in the Houghton Library, Harvard. Her communications with Stone & Kimball, Herbert Stone, or the *Chap-Book* are in several collections: Newberry Library, Houghton Library, University of Virginia. KCM, KCPP

294: Chopin's second collection: *A Night in Acadie* (Chicago: Way & Williams, 1897).

294–295: Versions of Chopin's *Atlantic* essay: "Confidences" and "In the Confidence of a Story-Writer," CW, pp. 700–705.

295: *Bayou Folk* printing: SCB, p. 210, n74. Royalties in MAB: $1.75 in 1895, $6.37 and $2.25 in 1896, $4.50 in 1897, $7.88 in 1898, $3.12 in 1899, $3.25 and $1.37 in 1900, $2.13 in 1901, and $3.35 in 1902. Chopin did not record royalties for 1903 and 1904, the last two years of her life.

296: Stone & Kimball: Sidney Kramer, *A History of Stone & Kimball and Herbert S.*

Stone & Co., with a Bibliography of Their Publications, 1893–1905 (Chicago: University of Chicago Press, 1940), esp. pp. 19, 27, 31, 38, 40, 46, 51, 98. According to MAB, Stone & Kimball declined "An Idle Fellow," "Athénaïse," "Vagabonds," "The Dream of an Hour," "Lilacs," "The Nun, the Wife & the Wanton," "Cavanelle," "The Locket," and "An Egyptian Cigarette." The two rejected poems were not published in Kate Chopin's lifetime: "Under My Lattice" (KCM, KCPP) and "Then Wouldst Thou Know" (under the title "If Some Day," CW, p. 730).

296: Way & Williams: Kramer, pp. 16, 65, 114, 115.

297–298: James Lane Allen: William K. Bottorff, *James Lane Allen* (New York: Twayne, 1964). "Repression": John Wilson Townsend, *James Lane Allen: a Personal Note* (Louisville, KY: Courier-Journal Job Printing Company, 1928), p. 85. "Romeo and Juliet," Townsend, p. 33. Changes from *Cosmopolitan* magazine ("Butterflies") to book version (*Summer in Arcady*—New York: Macmillan, 1896) are noted in Grant C. Knight, *James Lane Allen and the Genteel Tradition* (Chapel Hill: University of North Carolina, 1935), p. 128. From *Summer in Arcady*: "Laughing round-breasted girls" (p. 29); "Nature is lashing . . . rolling shoreward" (pp. 86–87, 137). Reviews: L. W. Payne, Jr., "The Stories of James Lane Allen," *Sewanee Review* 8 (January 1900), 1:45–55; Ghost, "Views and Reviews: James Lane Allen and the Problem Novel," *Vogue* 9 (February 25, 1897), p. 126. In the review, "Ghost" (obviously a pen name) did not distinguish between adultery and fornication.

299ff.: *A Night in Acadie* reviews: The only survey of reviews of *A Night in Acadie* is in Anthony Paul Garitta, "The Critical Reputation of Kate Chopin," Ph.D. Thesis, University of North Carolina at Greensboro, 1978, pp. 104–13. As there is no index to nineteenth-century book reviews, Garitta was able to find only seven reviews of the collection. I have located others (all noted here) from St. Louis, but there seem to have been few national notices. *A Night in Acadie* is also still neglected in Kate Chopin scholarship.

A Night in Acadie reviews outside St. Louis: "A Night in Acadie," *The Independent* 22 (December 16, 1897), p. 1662; "A Night in Acadie," *New Orleans Daily Picayune*, December 26, 1897, p. 9 (subject-verb agreement error is in the original); "More Novels," *The Nation* 66:1719 (June 9, 1898), pp. 446–47 (the awkward sentence about "thought too heavy" is as written); "Mrs. Chopin's 'Night in Acadie,' " *The Critic* 32:843 (April 16, 1898), p. 266.

St. Louis reviews: William Marion Reedy, "Reflections," *Mirror*, November 25, 1897, pp. 5–6; "The Newest Books," *St. Louis Post-Dispatch*, November 27, 1897, p. 4; "Two Romantic Stories by St. Louis Women," *St. Louis Republic*, November 28, 1897, book section, p. 9; "Literature," *St. Louis Globe-Democrat*, November 28, 1897, p. 35; "Among the New Books," *St. Louis Post-Dispatch*, December 11, 1897, p. 4. Earlier the *Republic* had claimed that Chopin's new book was coming out with Houghton Mifflin: "Pointedly Personal," *St. Louis Republic*, November 7, 1897, p. 13. About Alexander DeMenil and *The Hesperian*: HSL, pp. 522, 1344–47; William A. Kelsoe, *St. Louis Reference Record* (St. Louis: Von Hoffman, 1928), p. 184. "High tone magazine": "Some Late Books," *St. Louis Republic*, May 13, 1894, p. 16; William Marion Reedy, "Reflections," *Mirror*, July 29, 1897, p. 12. DeMenil's review: "Current Literary Topics: Kate Chopin's New Book," *The Hesperian* 2:4 (January–March 1898), pp. 171–72. Copies of *The Hesperian* are in the Rare Books section of the St. Louis Public Library.

305: Kate Chopin's correspondence with Richard Watson Gilder: KCM, KCPP. Originals at New York Public Library.

305–306: Chopin's visit to Chicago, meeting Mrs. Ward: Per Seyersted, "Kate Chopin's Wound: Two New Letters," *American Literary Realism* 20:1 (Fall 1987), pp. 71–75. About Chicago's literary life: Bernard Duffey, *The Chicago Renaissance in American Letters: a Critical History* (Ann Arbor: Michigan State College Press, 1956), esp. p. 55; Hugh Dalziel Duncan, *The Rise of Chicago as a Literary Center from 1885 to 1920: a Sociological Essay in American Culture* (Totowa, NJ: Bedminster Press, 1964), pp. 65, 104–5; Harriet Monroe, *A Poet's Life: Seventy Years in a Changing World* (New York: Macmillan, 1938), esp. p. 197.

306: Reading at St. Georges Guild: MAB.

306: Rejections of *A Vocation and a Voice*: MAB.

306–307: Chopin's letter to Professor Otto Heller about missing a Washington University lecture by a Dr. Pearses: Otto Heller Papers, Archives, Washington University, St. Louis, KCPP. The letter is dated December 26, but without a year. I am indebted to Beryl H. Manne, Washington University archivist, for a copy of this letter. Undated letter to Mrs. Tiffany: KCM, KCPP. Mrs. Tiffany's son was in a Spanish-American War company with Kate Chopin's son Felix. (The letter, undated, was pasted inside a now-lost copy of *A Night in Acadie* owned by Mrs. Dachine Rainer, who shared the contents with Per Seyersted.) Letter to Cornelia Maury, December 3, 1895 (MHS): KCM, KCPP.

307: John Devoy, comp. and publ., *A History of the City of St. Louis & Vicinity* (St. Louis: John Devoy, 1898), p. 211, for "Mrs. Margaret A. E. M'Lure," p. 220 for "Kate Chopin." Devoy recounted Kate Chopin's ancestry and reported accurately the dates of her Sacred Heart graduation, her marriage, and her husband's death—but wrote that *At Fault* was published in 1891, an error that Kate Chopin herself committed later on, in at least one letter (to Richard B. Shepard) and in her entry for *Who's Who in America* (1900). *At Fault* was actually published in 1890, and reviewed that year. Shepard letter (August 24, 1899): KCM, KCPP; Robert Hattersley shared the letter with Per Seyersted.

307ff.: Chopin and family in society: According to "Folks in Society," *Mirror*, February 13, 1896, p. 11: "A beautiful reception was given on last Thursday afternoon by Mrs. George W. Chadbourne, Miss Lydia Chadbourne and Mrs. Will M. Houser, when these ladies were assisted by Mrs. Will Aderton, Mrs. Henry Clover and Mrs. Kate Chopin, with Mrs. Josephine Papin and Mrs. George Hoblitzelle dispensing the cafe frappe. . . . The suite of three rooms were all decorated in pink carnations and roses. Several hundred ladies were present and partook of Mrs. Chadbourne's hospitality." Lélia at the theater: "Late Society News," *St. Louis Republic*, December 19, 1897, microfilmed p. no. unreadable. Lélia as handsome: "Folks in Society," *Mirror*, January 2, 1896, p. 11. "Miss Espenschied's Debut," *St. Louis Post-Dispatch*, December 5, 1897, p. 19. Bordley tea: "Folks in Society," *Mirror*, January 27, 1898, p. 11; "Society," *St. Louis Post-Dispatch*, January 30, 1898, p. 17; "The Polite World," *St. Louis Republic*, January 30, 1898, p. 13. Virginia ("Jenny") Lynch Donovan's husband, Francis (Frank) Donovan, had been a St. Louis lawyer, a partner of J. F. Conroy at the time George Chopin was born in 1874. Blanche Bordley was younger than Kate: Maryhelen Wilson, "Kate Chopin's Family: Fallacies and Facts, Including Kate's True Birthdate," *Kate Chopin Newsletter* 2 (Winter 1976–77), p. 26.

Social events for Chopin sons; George as handsomest: 1985 interview with David and

Ann Chopin and Marjorie Chopin McCormick. Medical training at Missouri Medical College: Robert James Terry, M.D., "Memories of a Long Life in St. Louis: Vol. IV. Medical and Anatomical Training," *Missouri Historical Society Bulletin*, January 1957, pp. 135–55. George Chopin is mentioned as one of the "cubs" on pp. 147–48. Forster gathering, for George and Jean: "Society," *St. Louis Post-Dispatch*, January 30, 1898, p. 17. Jean's Dutch supper: "Society," *St. Louis Post-Dispatch*, January 30, 1898, p. 17. Kate Chopin's gatherings: "Mrs. Huntington Smith's reception," *St. Louis Post-Dispatch*, February 13, 1898, p. 19; "Chart Club News," *St. Louis Post-Dispatch*, February 20, 1898, microfilm p. no. torn off.

308: William Marion Reedy, "Wives and Husbands," *Mirror*, January 13, 1898, p. 1.

309ff.: *St. Louis Post-Dispatch* interview series: "What Is the Unforgivable Sin in Society?" *Post-Dispatch*, January 30, 1898, p. 16; " 'Is Love Divine?' The Question Answered by Three Ladies Well Known in St. Louis Society," *Post-Dispatch*, January 16, 1898, p. 17. Mrs. Tudor Brooks lived at 3330 Morgan Street and was president of the Golden Chain Humane Society. "Women's Clubs," *St. Louis Globe Democrat*, March 7, 1897, p. 36. "The Killing Pace," *St. Louis Post-Dispatch*, January 23, 1898, p. 4. "Has High Society Struck the Pace That Kills?" *St. Louis Post-Dispatch*, February 6, 1898, p. 12.

312: Kate Chopin's ancestor Pélagie: ESM, p. 63, gives the husband's name as Bernard Moline, from Spain. According to Wilson, Pélagie disappeared from family history.

312ff: Spanish-American War: A useful short history is H. Wayne Morgan, *America's Road to Empire: The War with Spain and Overseas Expansion* (New York: John Wiley, 1965). I am indebted to Marilyn Bonnell for calling this book to my attention. Yellow journalism and war fever: Morgan, pp. 13, 53, 65. Reedy's cigar supply; "zanies"; circulation; attitude toward imperialism: Max Putzel, *The Man in the Mirror: William Marion Reedy and IIis Magazine* (Cambridge: Harvard University Press, 1963), pp. 80, 87, 90. William Marion Reedy, "Some Papers and the War," *Mirror*, June 2, 1898, p. 2.

313: Felix Chopin: 1985 interview with Tom and Rose Chopin. According to the April 1896 issue of the Central High School *High School News* (p. 4), Felix Chopin was elected president of the Athletic Association. The June 1896 issue, p. 1, reports Felix's victories at hurdles and pole vaulting; the October 1897 issue, p. 6, reports his being chosen as end and manager of the football team; by December 1897, p. 13, he was the first-string quarterback. Issues of the *High School News* are at MHS.

313ff.: Battery A: Valentine Mott Porter, "A History of Battery 'A' of St. Louis: with an Account of the Early Artillery Companies from Which It is Descended," paper read for MHS on February 11, 1904, reprinted in *MHS Collections* 4:2 (1905). Fred Chopin and Battery A soldiers: "Society in Battery A," *St. Louis Republic*, May 15, 1898, magazine section, p. 3; "Pointedly Personal," *St. Louis Republic*, May 15, 1898, magazine section, p. 4; "Departure of Battery A," *St. Louis Republic*, May 22, 1898, p. 2; "Society in Battery A," *St. Louis Republic*, May 22, 1898, p. 9; Tommy Atkins, "Our 'Sojer' Boys," *Mirror*, June 2, 1898, pp. 3–14 ("darkey story teller"); Tommy Atkins, "Our Soldier Darlings," *Mirror*, June 9, 1898, p. 12 (piano); Tommy Atkins, "From the Camp," *Mirror*, June 23, 1898, p. 13 (mentions death of a St. Louis soldier, his mother present when he died); Tommy Atkins, "News of Our Soldiers," *Mirror*, July 7, 1898, p. 13 (piano arrived); Tommy Atkins, "Battery Boys," *Mirror*, July 14, 1898, p. 13 (Chattanooga).

314. Benefit for Battery A: "Society," *St. Louis Republic,* June 19, 1898, p. 4.
314–315: Timetable of war events for Battery A: HSL, p. 1284. St. Louisans' contributions to the war: HSL, pp. 2446–48. "Sight of real food": Porter, p. 44.
315: "A Horse Story": KCM, KCPP. Chopin at first called the story "Ti Démon," and the *Century* rejected it. Later, she wrote a second story, under the same name, and sent it to the *Century* in December 1899: It was also rejected. See MAB, correspondence in KCM, KCPP. Harte's "Postmistress of Laurel Run": Bret Harte, *The First Family of Tasahara and Other Tales* (Boston: Houghton, Mifflin, 1896), pp. 188–208. Chopin's rejections: MAB.
315: Chopin's poems from 1898, according to Seyersted's datings: "There's Music Enough," "An Ecstasy of Madness," "The Roses," "Lines to Him," "White Oaks," "Lines Suggested by Omar," "The Lull of Summer Time," "To Henry One Evening Last Summer," "By the Meadow Gate," "Old Natchitoches," and probably "An Hour" and "In Spring." Some appear in KCM and KCPP; others are in CW, pp. 732–33. Chopin did not clearly date her poems, and there are multiple versions of several. The "live-oaks" version of the White Oaks poem is in a copy of *Bayou Folk* now belonging to Barbara Sims of Louisiana State University. I am grateful to Barbara Sims for sharing the version with me.

CHAPTER 21: "THE STORM" AND *THE AWAKENING*

317–318: Visit to Natchitoches: "Personals" column, *Natchitoches Enterprise,* June 24, 1897. For clippings about Kate Chopin's visits to Natchitoches, I am indebted to Carol Wells and Evelyn Stallings, NSU. Father Beaulieu performed his last wedding ceremony August 5, 1897, a month after Kate Chopin's visit, according to Mildred McCoy, "Bayou Folk Musings," *Natchitoches Times,* July 27, 1972, n.p. (McCoy Collection).
317: Flanners: T. J. Flanner had married Daisy Sers (whose mother was a Charleville) in 1880 in Cloutierville, while the Chopins lived there (ESM, pp. 110–11). "I remember Kate Chopin quite well, she spent some time with us," Florian Flanner wrote years later to Cammie G. Henry, the Cane River country antiquarian. "I have an autographed copy of 'A Night in Acadia' [sic] which she presented to me with a lovely little note." Flanner letter: Melrose Collection, Folder 64, KCPP.
317: Albert Sampite as grandfather: Loca and Albert Sampite's prettily dressed, convent-educated daughter, Marie, had married the charming and reckless John Pollock of New Orleans in January 1896 in Loca's parlor, after a whirlwind courtship. Their first child, a daughter with the un-French name Edith, was born that December (1900 United States Census; Leona Sampite; DeLouche; NSU microfilmed copy of marriage records of St. John the Baptist Catholic Church in Cloutierville; Cloutierville Group). Albert Sampite's traveling, Maria Normand's garden: DeLouche. Bullwhip: Leona Sampite. Cane River country descriptions: Chopin's "Beyond the Bayou," "Croque-Mitaine," and "Vagabonds." Albert Sampite's surviving letters to his estranged wife and children: KCPP. Alphonse Sampite attended Tulane University 1897–1901, after graduating from

the Bowling Green, Kentucky, College of Business and Finance: "Dr. J. A. Sampite of Natchitoches Parish Dies Here," *New Orleans Times-Picayune*, October 11, 1938, n.p., clipping supplied by Leona Sampite.

318: Chopin's departure: "Personals" column, *Natchitoches Enterprise*, July 1, 1897, p. 3, in citation file, NSU.

318ff.: Maria Normand's appearance: As a young woman, she set her ringlets by winding them around a malacca cane, but later wore her hair in a twist, according to De-Louche, who also reported Maria's cheering Cuban victories. The 1900 census entry on Sylvère DeLouche, difficult to decipher, shows him as forty-eight years old, and his occupation was either "Stock Driver" or "Grower." Maria and Sylvère DeLouche's children were named Marie and Samuel. Albert's giving Maria the lamp: McCoy, De-Louche. The lamp eventually passed to Maria Normand DeLouche's granddaughter, Ivy DeLouche (see note for Chap. 11, above).

319: Sewing machine, embroidery, Gaspar Hernandez: DeLouche. Mrs. Scruggs was still living in 1898. Gaspar Hernandez also gave Maria Normand two lovingly inscribed photographs, now in the possession of Mary DeLouche, who allowed me to copy them. The Bayou Folk Museum has Mrs. Scruggs's sewing machine cabinet.

320: Taboos: The Cather story was "Coming, Eden Bower!" later collected in *Youth and the Bright Medusa*. See Marilyn Arnold, "Coming, Willa Cather!" *Women's Studies: an Interdisciplinary Journal* 11:3 (1984), p. 247. According to SCB, p. 166, Guy de Maupassant was never so explicit as Kate Chopin. James Lane Allen's "borderland of mystery and reality": *Summer in Arcady* (New York: Macmillan, 1896), p. 215.

Women writers were rarely involved in the struggle for more open heterosexual expression in literature. In Clarence Gohdes's chapter on "The Facts of Life Versus Pleasant Reading," in Arthur Hobson Quinn, et al., *The Literature of the American People* (New York: Appleton-Century-Crofts, 1951), pp. 737–62, Kate Chopin is the only woman author cited as an proponent of a "sterner realism." Gohdes mentions the popular writer Amélie Rives, who, he says, presented a case of nymphomania in her 1888 novel, *The Quick or the Dead?*—but he cites no other women writers who sought to write more freely about physical sexuality. Both Larzer Ziff, in *The American 1890s* (New York: Viking, 1966), and Van Wyck Brooks, in *The Confident Years: 1885–1915* (New York: Dutton, 1952), mention only male authors as fighters against sexual taboos.

My informal surveys of newspaper book reviews in the 1890s have turned up few women writers whose work was termed "coarse" or "unpleasant," as *The Awakening* was: Those who were given such labels were all British. Among the British women writers considered immoral was the novelist Ouida, about whom one reviewer wrote: "It is difficult for the American reader, educated in reverence for women, to conceive of a member of that sex deliberately sitting down to portray the sin and shame of her own sisters, with an enthusiasm and a minuteness of detail possible only to one thoroughly initiated." Quoted in Esther Jane Carrier, *Fiction in Public Libraries, 1876–1900* (New York and London: Scarecrow Press, 1965), p. 306.

322: Changes in publisher: The entangled histories of Way & Williams and Stone & Kimball are discussed in Sidney Kramer, *History of Stone & Kimball and Herbert S. Stone & Company* (Chicago: University of Chicago Press, 1940). According to MAB, *A Vocation and a Voice* was transferred to Stone in November 1898; *The Awakening*, accepted by Way & Williams on January 21, 1898, was transferred to Stone in November 1898, then accepted by Stone in January 1899. According to Kramer (p. 121), in 1900 the books published by Way & Williams went to Doubleday—which apparently had no interest in reissuing *A Night in Acadie*, the only book Kate Chopin had published with Way & Williams.

322ff.: Kate Chopin's 1898 Natchitoches visit: "Personals" column, *Natchitoches Enterprise*, December 15, 1898; "The Gay Nineties," *New Orleans Times-Democrat*, Melrose Scrapbook, pp. 69, 90. Marie Chopin's husband, Phanor Breazeale, had clerked for the late A. H. Walmsley in the 1870s (see *The Convention of '98* [New Orleans: William E. Myers, 1898], p. 36). Lucy Walmsley had been Marie Chopin's close childhood friend in Natchitoches (Waters).

322–323: Camilla Lachs Breazeale: Interviews with Carmen Breazeale (1973 taped interview, NSU tape collection; 1975 interview); Arthur and Gene Watson (1984 interview); Waters; *Biographical and Historical Memoirs of Northwestern Louisiana* (Nashville: Southern Publishing, 1890), p. 325. Women's limited voting right: Carmen Meriwether Lindig, "The Woman's Movement in Louisiana: 1879–1920," Ph.D. Thesis, North Texas State University, 1982, p. 172. After women won the full voting right in 1920, Camilla Lachs Breazeale's niece Gladys—the daughter of Marie and Phanor Breazeale—became the first woman to carry the Louisiana vote to Washington: Melrose Scrapbook, pp. 70, 135.

323: Carmen Breazeale's story: 1973 NSU tape; my interview 1975; McCoy; Emily Toth, "Kate Chopin Remembered," *Kate Chopin Newsletter* 1 (Winter 1975–76), pp. 21–27. Also Sue Eakin, "Back Tracking: Spirit of Writer Kate Chopin Brought Back to Cloutierville," *Alexandria-Pineville Town Talk* (December 3, 1978), p. A-12, article supplied to me by Lucille Tinker Carnahan. Carmen Breazeale was born in 1889. Carmen Breazeale's grandmother also objected to the columnist Dorothy Dix, who was far more genteel in manner than Kate Chopin—although Dix did support many of the same values: She criticized the ideal of self-sacrifice for women, and advocated women's courage, strength, and financial independence. But by 1900 "Dorothy Dix" (Elizabeth Meriwether Gilmer of the *New Orleans Daily Picayune*), had moved to New York City. Sources: Dorothy Dix, "Are Women Growing Selfish?" in Margaret Culley, ed., *The Awakening by Kate Chopin* (New York: Norton, 1976), pp. 127–29; Margaret Culley, "Sob-Sisterhood: Dorothy Dix and the Feminist Origins of the Advice Column," *Southern Studies* 16:2 (1977), pp. 201–10; Carol Reuss, unpublished paper. Dorothy Dix's manner: Gene Watson and Rosa Bernard, 1984 interview.

323ff.: Breazeales: Waters. Breazeale daughters are mentioned in Henry E. Chambers, *A History of Louisiana* (Chicago and New York: American History Society, 1925), Vol. 3, p. 290. "Gracious, dignified hostess": Obituary for Mrs. Phanor (Marie) Breazeale: Melrose Scrapbook, pp. 71, 125. Euchre party: "The Gay Nineties," *New Orleans Times-Democrat*, December 25, 1898, Melrose Scrapbook, pp. 69, 91. Example of Phanor Breazeale's Reconstruction tales: "Statement on Reconstruction Natchitoches," KCM, KCPP.

In June 1898, Phanor Breazeale was a leader in the Louisiana Constitutional Convention, with a particular interest in railroads; he was a law partner of T. P. Chaplin; he had been appointed to the school board and elected district attorney. He was "a strong speaker, full of sarcasm and double meaning," who usually got his way. See *The Convention of '98*, pp. 36, 37; "Memoirs of James W. Jones Jr.," Folder 72, Jones Collection, NSU; Melrose Scrapbook, pp. 71, 105 and 116; Waters; 1984 interview with Arthur Watson. *Awakening* from French Quarter story: DSR, p. 92. "Haunted

Chamber": Seyersted's note (CW, p. 1032) says "tremulous" might be "tremendous." Waters (born 1895) died in 1989, leaving Julie Chopin Cusachs of Baton Rouge as probably the only living person who knew Kate Chopin. Cusachs, the daughter of Lamy and Fannie Hertzog Chopin, was born in 1898.

325: Chopin house: Pierre Rosenthal soon sold the home to Mr. and Mrs. John B. Culbertson, who occupied it until 1918 and moved the side stairway to the front of the house (a photograph is in the Bayou Folk Museum). In 1901, Rosenthal's daughter Clara, a thirty-six-year-old schoolteacher, married Kate Chopin's twenty-five-year-old cousin, F. A. Charleville (who was the first Cloutiervillian to have a telephone and an automobile—ESM, p. 112).

325: Chopin's leaving Cloutierville: "Personals" column, December 22, 1898, *Natchitoches Enterprise.*

325: Plagiarism of "Boulôt and Boulotte": DSR, p. 299. The plagiarized version does move the story from Natchitoches to St. Landry Parish, and some sentences are switched around. But Thomas Bonner, Jr. (1989 interview), says that the story of the two children who carry their new shoes rather than wearing them is a standard bit of southern folklore, which he was told as a child.

325–326: Mollie E. Moore Davis's salon: MEM. Davis, *Keren-Happuch and I* (no place or publisher listed, copy is marked 1907 in the card catalog at Hill Memorial Library, Louisiana State University). References to Kate Chopin and Davis's "Fridays": Part Second, "We Gather Up the Golden Threads," pp. 9–14. I am indebted to Rosan Jordan for pointing out this reference to me, and for informing me about the records of the New Orleans Quarante Club, which show that Davis lived at 406 Royal Street and that ghost stories were popular amusements at her parties. According to an unpublished paper, "Mollie Moore Davis: a Literary Life," by Patricia Brady of the Historic New Orleans Collection, Davis's books were all published by Houghton, Mifflin (Kate Chopin's publisher for *Bayou Folk*), but with larger printings—and Davis's short stories appeared in many of the same magazines.

326: Chopin's leaving New Orleans: Melrose Scrapbook, pp. 69, 91.

326: Dillon's July 1897 trip: Don C. Seitz, *Joseph Pulitzer: His Life and Letters* (New York: Simon & Schuster, 1924), p. 233.

326: Chopin's poems: "An Hour"—KCM, KCPP. "I Opened All the Portals Wide": the *Century* 58 (July 1899), p. 361, and discussed in William L. Andrews, "An Addition to Kate Chopin's Poetry," *American Notes & Queries* 13:8 (April 1975), pp. 117–18. According to MAB, Chopin sold a poem called "Abide with Me" to *Century* magazine for five dollars: Evidently the *Century* changed its title.

327: Weather: "Says Blizzard Is Due Today," *St. Louis Republic*, February 4, 1899, p. 1; "New Weather Record Made," *St. Louis Republic*, February 10, 1899, p. 1. Re "The Godmother": A family named LaCaze lived in Cloutierville, and more than sixty years later, Mildred LaCaze McCoy would create the Bayou Folk Museum in Kate Chopin's old home—but if Chopin based Gabriel Lucaze on any of the LaCazes, the original inspiration is lost.

327: "A Little Country Girl" to *Youth's Companion*: MAB.

328: R. E. Lee Gibson letter of February 26, 1899: KCM, KCPP, original at MHS. Gibson mentions "the Doctor," whom I take to be Kolbenheyer, since Chopin called him that in KC94.

328ff.: Lucy Monroe: Her review, in full:

A remarkable novel will come out of the West about the first of March, a novel so keen in its analysis of character, so subtle in its presentation of emotional effects that it seems to reveal life as well as to represent it. In reading it you have the impression of being in the very heart of things, you feel the throb of the machinery, you see and understand the slight transitions of thought, the momentary impulses, the quick sensations of the hardness of life, which govern so much of our action. It is an intimate thing, which in studying the nature of one woman reveals something which brings her in touch with all women—something larger than herself. This it is which justifies the audacity of "The Awakening" and makes it big enough to be true. The author has shown herself an artist in the manipulation of a complex character, and faulty as the woman is, she has the magnetism which is essential to the charm of a novel. It is a quality hard to analyze, for it does not seem to be in what she says or does; it is rather, as in life, in what she is. The novel pictures, too, with extraordinary vividness, the kind of silent sympathy which is sometimes the expression of the love that goes deep. The men in the book are capital, with the exception, perhaps of Robert, who is a bit wooden; and Edna's husband especially is drawn to the life. In construction, in the management of movements and climaxes, the thing shows a very subtle and a brilliant kind of art. The action takes place in and around New Orleans and the character of the novel as a whole is southern. Mrs. Kate Chopin, of St. Louis, is the author, and though she has published another book, called "A Night in Acadie," it has not the grasp of this. Messrs. Herbert S. Stone and Company are the publishers. (Lucy Monroe, "Chicago's New Books," *Book News* XVII, (March 1899), p. 387, reprinted in Richard Arthur Martin, "The Fictive World of Kate Chopin," Ph.D. Thesis, Northwestern University, 1971, p. 193.)

Martin notes on pp. 216–17, n1, that Monroe was first a secretary and literary adviser at Stone & Company, but became "chief reader and literary editor" when Harrison Rhodes left the company in July 1898. Lucy Monroe may have persuaded Stone & Company to publish *The Awakening*: Stone received the book in December 1898, and accepted it for publication in January 1899.

Other sources about Lucy Monroe: Daniel J. Cahill, *Harriet Monroe* (New York: Twayne, 1973), p. 23. Bernard Duffey, *The Chicago Renaissance in American Letters: a Critical History* (Ann Arbor: Michigan State College Press, 1956), pp. 53, 56. Harriet Monroe, *A Poet's Life: Seventy Years in a Changing World* (New York: Macmillan, 1938), pp. 56, 82, 87, 89, 90, 97, 108, 109, 144, 146, 148, 162, 163, 197.

329: Early *Awakening* notices: "The Rambler," *The Book Buyer* 18 (April 1899), p. 186; "News and Gossip about Forthcoming Books," *St. Louis Republic*, March 25, 1899. Both notices seem to be condensed paraphrases of Lucy Monroe's review: Possibly the book itself was not yet available.

330ff.: *The Awakening* passages: "As if some power," Chap. X; "the regal woman," Chap. XXX; "first kiss," Chap. XXVII; "dull pang of regret," Chap. XXIX; "voluptuous sting," Chap. XXXVI; "scene of torture," Chap. XXXVII; "there was no one thing," Chap. XXXIX; "mother-woman," "condition," "absence of prudery," "inborn and unmistakable," "harrowing story," all Chap. IV; "ecstasy of pain," Chap. XXXVII; "youth is given up," Chap. XXXVIII; "remember the children" (Madame Ratignolle actually says, "Think of the children, Edna. Oh think of the children! Remember them!" Chap. XXXVII).

Social background for *The Awakening*: Swimming was a popular recreation in St. Louis in the late 1890s, and a natatorium on Catalpa Street, between Chouteau and Gratiot—Kate Chopin's childhood neighborhood—was the favorite swimming place for upper-class women. See Peggy, "Society Swimmers," *Mirror*, July 21, 1898, p. 14. Flirtations between older married women and younger men—Robert is two years younger than Edna—were common in the 1890s, and regarded as an achievement for the older woman: Lois Banner, *American Beauty* (New York: Knopf, 1983), p. 192. The etiquette of calling cards is described in Arthur Meier Schlesinger, *Learning How to Behave: a Historical Study of American Etiquette Books* (New York: Macmillan, 1946), cited in Banner, p. 132. Calling-card etiquette: Elizabeth L. Connell, "Pasteboard Politeness: Calling Cards and the Rituals of Calling in Nineteenth-Century America," paper given at the 1984 Southeastern Nineteenth Century Studies Conference.

331: Only novel to describe a pregnant woman: My inquiries among scholars of late nineteenth-century American fiction have turned up no other examples—but I am willing to be corrected. *Esther Waters*: Kramer, pp. 118–19. To my knowledge, *The Awakening* is also unique among American novels in the 1890s for its candid treatment of a woman's adultery.

333: Robert's Vera Cruz romance: In the 1890s, the women of Jalapa (Vera Cruz) were noted for their beauty, according to Ziff, p. 5. This was, of course, also part of the double standard by which poor women and women of color were considered fair game for wealthy white American men.

334: Reedy on society romance: "Reflections," *Mirror*, September 16, 1897, p. 3.

334: *The Awakening*'s official publication date and description: Kramer, p. 297. The book's copyright date, according to Kramer, was April 24, but it was ready on April 22, according to *Publishers Weekly*.

335: "St. Louis Literature," *Mirror*, April 13, 1899, p. 4.

335: DeMenil party: "Social Affairs and Some Personal Notes," *St. Louis Republic*, April 21, 1899, p. 8; "Folks in Society," *Mirror*, April 27, 1899, p. 10.

CHAPTER 22: "THE STORY OF A LADY MOST FOOLISH"

336ff.: "Mrs. Chopin's New Book Is the Story of a Lady Most Foolish," *St. Louis Republic*, April 30, 1899, Part IV (magazine), p. 11. I am indebted to Robert Behra of the St. Louis Mercantile Library for locating this review.

337ff.: Letters to Kate Chopin from R. E. Lee Gibson, Lewis Ely, Sue V. Moore: KCM, KCPP, originals at MHS.

338ff.: Frances Porcher: Mrs. Charles P. (Anne) Johnson, *Notable Women of St. Louis: 1914* (St. Louis: Woodward, 1914), pp. 187–92. The sketch does not give Porcher's age. Porcher's name changes suggest that she may have been married more than twice: See "Frances Barnett Roper," William A. Kelsoe, *St. Louis Reference Record* (St. Louis: Von Hoffman, 1928), p. 117. The MHS catalog calls her Frances Smith Cannon Porcher, for *Mr. Perryman's Christmas Eve: The Story of a Life of Faithful Service* (Chicago:

Reilly & Britton, 1912). Porcher's writings: In her "Maurice Latimer, Gentleman" (*The American Jewess* 2:4 (January 1896), pp. 181–84), an old gentleman is run over by a streetcar. In "The Blind Man," which Kate Chopin wrote six months later, she ended her story the same way. Porcher, "A Queer Suicide Club," *Mirror*, January 7, 1897, pp. 5–6; "What Maisie Knew," *Mirror*, December 23, 1897, p. 7; "The Awakening: Kate Chopin's Novel," *Mirror*, May 4, 1899, p. 6.

629–37: Reviews and notices: "The Newest Books," *St. Louis Post-Dispatch*, May 6, 1899, p. 4; *Natchitoches Enterprise*, May 11, 1899, p. 2; "Weekly Record of New Publications," *Publishers Weekly*, May 13, 1899, p. 772; "Notes from Bookland," *St. Louis Globe-Democrat*, May 13, 1899, p. 5; C. L. Deyo, "The Newest Books," *St. Louis Post-Dispatch*, May 20, 1899, p. 4; G. B., "Kate Chopin's Novel," *St. Louis Post-Dispatch*, May 21, 1899, p. 6. Lewis Ely's note: KCM, KCPP, original at MHS.

DSR, p. 173, quotes from G. B.'s review ("Too strong drink for moral babes . . ."), but attributes the review to the May 20, 1899, *St. Louis Republic*—an error that has created much frustration among Chopin scholars. The review was found in the *Post-Dispatch* by Richard Arthur Martin, "The Fictive World of Kate Chopin," Ph.D. Thesis, Northwestern University, 1971, p. 194. Martin interprets the closing sentence of the review not as as a moral judgment but as a "conservative warning that the book is adult material."

344: Kate Chopin's photograph: The portrait and its accompanying article appear in "The Lounger," *The Critic* 35:866 (August 1899), p. 677, KCPP. The photograph is also on the jacket of Barbara Ewell's *Kate Chopin* (New York: Ungar, 1986). St. Louis society pages in 1899 note the appearance of prominent women without hats. Chopin's letters (May 21, June 7) to Herbert Stone: KCM, KCPP; her June 7 note also quoted in Sidney Kramer, *History of Stone & Kimball and Herbert S. Stone & Company* (Chicago: University of Chicago, 1940), p. 297. *Book News*: Chopin's statement in "Aims and Autographs of Authors," July 1899, p. 612; KCM, KCPP.

345–346: Chopin's correspondents: Lizzie L.'s letter: KCM, KCPP, original at MHS. Lizzie may have been Lizzie Bulte, a Sacred Heart schoolmate. "L.," whose address appears to be 1201 Equitable Building, is unknown. Original at MHS; KCM, KCPP.

347ff.: National reviews of *The Awakening*: Ten contemporary reviews are excerpted in Margaret Culley, ed., *The Awakening by Kate Chopin* (New York: Norton, 1976), pp. 145–55. Reviews quoted here: "Books of the Day," *Chicago Times-Herald*, June 1, 1899, p. 9; "Novels and Tales," *The Outlook*, June 3, 1899, p. 314; "Books of the Week," *Providence Sunday Journal*, June 4, 1899, p. 15; "New Publications," *New Orleans Times-Democrat*, June 18, 1899, pp. 14–15; "Book Reviews," *Public Opinion* XXVI (June 22, 1899), p. 794. Culley (pp. 151–52) reprints a review entitled "Fiction," attributed to *Literature* 4 (June 23, 1899), p. 570, but there is no issue with that date. "Books and Authors," *Boston Beacon*, June 24, 1899, p. 4; "100 Books for Summer Reading," *New York Times Saturday Review*, June 24, 1899, p. 408; "Fresh Literature," *Los Angeles Times*, June 25, 1899, p. 12.

349ff.: Anna L. Moss's letter: KCM, KCPP, at MHS. Mrs. Moss's prose, somewhat incoherent, is reproduced verbatim. Unknown correspondent: KCM, KCPP, at MHS. Seduction story cannot be identified.

352: Cather review: Sibert, "Books and Magazines," *Pittsburgh Leader*, July 8, 1899, p. 6, reprinted in Culley, pp. 153–55 and William M. Curtin, ed., *The World and the Parish: Willa Cather's Articles and Reviews, 1893–1902* (Lincoln: University of Nebraska Press, 1970), Vol. 2, pp. 693–94. The review was printed in the August 26 issue of the Lincoln *Courier*, according to Anthony Paul Garitta, "The Critical Reputation of Kate Chopin," Ph.D. Thesis, University of North Carolina at Greensboro, 1978, p. 134. See also Sharon O'Brien, "The Limits of Passion: Willa Cather's Review of *The Awakening*," *Women and Literature* 3 (Fall 1975), pp. 10–20.

CHAPTER 23: PRIVATE PRAISE AND PUBLIC CENSURE

353: Kate Chopin, "I Opened All the Portals Wide," *Century Magazine*, 58:3 (July, 1899), p. 361, reprinted in KCM, KCPP.

353: "The Lounger": see note for Chap. 22, above. KCPP.

354: Never discussed, never wrote again: DSR, p. 185. See also Appendix III.

354: Chopin's children: Fred as pallbearer: "Private Whittlesey Buried with Honors," *St. Louis Republic*, April 10, 1899, p. 2. Felix at Central High Dance: "Society," *St. Louis Republic*, May 14, 1899, p. 6. Scullin's accident: "Alumni," *High School News*, May–June 1899, p. 15. Young Oscar Chopin, who does not appear in society columns, may have been in Louisiana, or may have preferred to spend his time drawing: Within a year, he would become a *Post-Dispatch* cartoonist. Kate's rivalry with Lélia, Lélia's scenes: 1985 interview with Marjorie Chopin McCormick. Domino dance: "Current Happenings in the Social World," *St. Louis Republic*, January 5, 1899, p. 6. Philharmonic concert: "Social Affairs and Some Personal Notes," *St. Louis Republic*, April 5, 1899, p. 8. "Apollo Club Concert and Other Affairs," *St. Louis Republic*, April 19, 1899, p. 8. R. Park Von Wedelstaedt's rushing Lélia: Marcella, "The Inside of Society," *Mirror*, April 12, 1900, p. 18. Sulphur Springs: "Society Gossip," *St. Louis Post-Dispatch*, May 7, 1899, magazine, n.p. Lake Minnetonka: "Society," *Mirror*, July 6, 1899, p. 11. Excelsior: "Society," *Mirror*, July 20, 1899, p. 12. Thimble bee: "Society," *Mirror*, August 3, 1899, p. 10. Flower german: "Society," *Mirror*, August 10, 1899, p. 10. Spanish gitana: "Society," *Mirror*, September 7, 1899, p. 11. Lélia's return: "Society," *Mirror*, September 14, 1899, p. 10.

355ff.: Further *Awakening* reviews: William Morton Payne, "Recent Fiction," *The Dial* 37 (August 1, 1899), p. 75; "Recent Novels," *The Nation*, August 3, 1899, p. 96; "Current Literature," *Boston Herald*, August 12, 1899, p. 7; "Recent Publications," *Indianapolis Journal*, August 14, 1899, p. 4. "Literature," *The Congregationalist*, August 24, 1899, p. 256.

I could not locate the *Boston Times* review mentioned by Daniel Rankin in a personal letter to Nora Alice Norris (February 24, 1932). According to Rankin, the *Boston Times* called *The Awakening* "immoral" and "off-color," and said that if it had been printed in Paris instead of Chicago, it "would be pronounced very Frenchy." Rankin is quoted in Norris's "Kate Chopin," M.A. Thesis, Louisiana State University, 1932, p. 89.

355: Shepard letter: KCM, KCPP, original owned by Robert Hattersley.

356–357: Gibson letter: KCM, KCPP, at MHS. Cawein's letter praising *The Awakening* is reprinted in Otto A. Rothert, *The Story of a Poet: Madison Cawein* (Louisville, KY: John P. Morton, 1921), p. 212, and KCPP. Cawein's letter is dated March 30, but *The Awakening* was not officially published until April 22. Cawein's copy of *The Awakening* (now lost from the Harvard Library) was given to him by Gibson and autographed

May 16, 1899 (KCM, p. 198, n43). Cawein's letter of August 18, 1899, to Jenny Loring Robbins of Louisville about meeting Kate Chopin: Rothert 214, KCPP; original can no longer be located. Cawein himself was prematurely gray and looked much older than his years: Rothert, pp. 106, 136. Cawein as pantheist, spiritualist, believer in ghosts and fairies: Rothert, p. 129. The 1900 St. Louis City Directory lists a Minnie Cawein at 3315 Morgan, next door to Kate Chopin, but Rothert does not mention a Minnie Cawein. Chopin's "Ti Frère": KCM, KCPP. Madison Cawein, "Hoodoo," in *Weeds by the Wall* (Louisville, KY: John P. Morton & Company, 1901), pp. 90–91. Biographical sketch: Lawrence S. Thompson, "Madison Julius Cawein," in Robert Bain, Joseph M. Flora, and Louis D. Rubin, Jr., *Southern Writers: a Biographical Dictionary* (Baton Rouge: Louisiana State University Press, 1979), pp. 72–74.

357: Popular novels: "St. Louis Librarians Talk about Books That Are Popular Here Right Now," *St. Louis Republic*, May 7, 1899, p. 10.

358: T. A. Meysenburg membership: "Women's Clubs," *St. Louis Republic*, January 29, 1899, section 2, p. 5.

358ff.: Janet Scammon Young and Dunrobin Thomson letters: KCM, KCPP, at MHS. Chopin's showing letters to friends: SCB, p. 179. About whether the Londoners existed: SCB, pp. 179, 225, n38, n39.

360–361: Florence Hayward, "Advanced literary ladies"; OJ, p. 201. Hayward's memorabilia and letters, including four letters from Mark Twain, are in the Florence Hayward Collection, MHS. I have not been able to obtain copies of her books, both copyrighted 1886. Hayward had been a journalist since the 1880s, when she wrote society news (and acid commentaries) for the *St. Louis Spectator*, a weekly magazine, under the pseudonym "ECHO." She was particularly critical of men who "talk to a woman as a woman would to a child . . . Men have caused it to be distinctly understood that there is only one kind of woman that they dislike more than a very stupid one, and that is a very bright one": "ECHO," "Social Salad," *St. Louis Spectator*, February 21, 1885, p. 387, Hayward Collection, MHS. Hayward was also a founder of the St. Louis Artist's Guild, according to Mrs. Charles P. (Anne) Johnson, *Notable Women of St. Louis, 1914* (St. Louis: Woodward, 1914), pp. 88–89. See also Marguerite Martyn, "Most Advanced of St. Louis Women Calls Man's Advanced Views of Marriage 'Criminal': Miss Florence Hayward, Who 'Invented' Artist's Guild, Explains Difference between True and False Bohemianism," *St. Louis Post-Dispatch*, May 15, 1908, Hayward Scrapbook, 1899–1913, Hayward Collection, MHS.

As foreign correspondent: Hayward was the highest-paid writer for both the *Globe-Democrat* and the *Republic*, according to her bosses: Hayward Collection, October 1, 1901, letters to McClure, Phillips & Company from Henry King (*Globe-Democrat*) and the *Republic* managing editor (unreadable signature). Death rumors exaggerated: The London death notice, stating that Florence Hayward died "suddenly of heart disease," is in the Hayward Scrapbook; Hayward's rebuttal is "Florence Hayward's Letter," *St. Louis Globe-Democrat*, May 14, 1899, pt. 4, p. 8.

Suffragist dinners: Hayward Collection includes a program for the July 3, 1899, dinner of the "Society of American Women in London," which Hayward attended with Charlotte Perkins Stetson (later Gilman), Susan B. Anthony, Mrs. Humphry Ward, Sarah Grand, and others. Hayward sat across from Mrs. Stephen Crane. Appearance: Hayward Scrapbook includes many pictures of Florence Hayward, among them photographs and caricatures from her stint as the first woman ever to be a World's Fair commissioner (for the 1904 St. Louis Fair). Confederate background: Hayward Collection includes documents from the Daughters of the American Revolution and the North Carolina Colonial Dames; Hayward's father, later a Confederate colonel, had served in the Mexican War, after which the family settled in the New Mexico territory, where Florence was born in 1855 (she died in 1925). See Johnson, pp. 89, 92. Independent spinster: Hayward was noted for an address called "The Unimportant Spinster," reprinted in the *St. Louis Globe-Democrat*, June 15, 1901, p. 5.

Hayward's recent return: "Society," *Mirror*, November 30, 1899, p. 10. Joking pseud-·onyms: Hayward Collection letters show that Florence Hayward addressed friends as "chick-a-biddy" and called her mother "muzza," while her London friends gave themselves grandiose titles and took the names of popular palmists. One called himself "Count." J. Young Scammon is mentioned in James Neal Primm, *Lion of the Valley: St. Louis, Missouri* (Boulder, CO: Pruett Publishing Company, 1981), p. 234. Emma Scammon at Western Association of Writers: 1987 communication from Marybelle Burch, manuscripts librarian, Indiana State Library (noted in my Chap. 15, above). Laura E. Scammon, President of the Missouri Federation of Women's Clubs, is mentioned in St. Louis newspaper society pages in January 1898.

361: William Marion Reedy, "St. Louis Writers," *Mirror*, October 19, 1899, p. 2.

361: Shepard letter: Per Seyersted, "Kate Chopin's Wound: Two New Letters," *American Literary Realism* 20:1 (Fall 1987), pp. 71–75. Seyersted points out inconsistencies: Kate Chopin's previous letter to Shepard was in August, not July, and to our knowledge, Shepard had written her only one letter, not "letters." Seyersted believes that Kate Chopin was distraught.

362: The first "Ti Démon," which Chopin wrote in March 1898: KCM, KCPP. Chopin renamed it "A Horse Story." New "Ti Démon": CW, pp. 623–27. Correspondence, rejections: MAB, KCM, KCPP. Originals at Houghton Library, Harvard; New York Public Library.

362: Léonce about the procession: *The Awakening*, Chap. XVII; "grotesque pandemonium," Chap. XIX.

363: Social events: "In Honor of His Daughter," *St. Louis Post-Dispatch*, November 26, 1899, part 3, p. 33; "Junior Club Ball," *St. Louis Post-Dispatch*, November 26, 1899, part 3, p. 33.

363ff.: *Post-Dispatch* article: "St. Louis Woman Who Has Won Fame in Literature," *St. Louis Post-Dispatch*, November 26, 1899, pt. 4, p. 1, rpt. KCPP. Chopin's article: CW, pp. 721–23. Mrs. R_____, nowhere else identified, could have been Lalitte Bauduy Reedy. Wednesday Club membership list for 1899 includes ten married women with last names beginning with R: "Women's Clubs," *St. Louis Republic*, January 29, 1899, section 2, p. 5.

The *Post-Dispatch* article, showing Kate Chopin's workroom, proves wrong Lélia Chopin Hattersley's 1907 letter about her mother to Leonidas Rutledge Whipple: "She did not have a study or any place where she ever really shut herself off from the household. I know now that she often desired to do this when writing, but on the other hand, she never wished to shut us children out of her presence, and with the natural selfishness of children, we never tried to keep her undisturbed as she should have been." Quoted in DSR, p. 116. Lélia was not always accurate about her mother's career especially after *The Awakening*: See *Appendix III*. Chopin's study was also described as "quite a unique little den" with important periodicals and tomes: *St. Louis Republic*, August 11, 1895, quoted in Joan Mayerson Clatworthy, *Kate Chopin: The Inward Life Which Questions*, Ph.D. Thesis, State University of New York at Buffalo, 1979, p. 60, n. 22.

Smoking: Felix's disapproval of women's smoking: 1985 interview with Tom and Rose Chopin. Robert's comment, *The Awakening*, Chap. II. Cigarettes improper for men: *St. Louis Post-Dispatch* editorial for March 7, 1892: "When Oscar Wilde 'sassed' the critics he was smoking a cigarette; when the German Emperor defied the mob, he too was smoking a cigarette. The fearlessness of these two brave fellows is admirable" (p. 4). McKinley: "President's Smoking Causes Ill Health," *St. Louis Republic*, May 11, 1899, p. 8. Tobacco, lung damage: Lois Banner, *American Beauty* (New York: Knopf, 1983), p. 241. Florence Hayward on half of writers: Scrapbook, 1898 clipping. Kate's putting out cigarette if offensive: her son George (1984 interview with David and Ann Chopin).

367: *Awakening* royalties: MAB.

367ff.: Alleged removal of *The Awakening* from circulation: DSR, p. 173; FELIX; Felix's later interview: "Books and Authors: St. Louis to Paris Twice," *St. Louis Post-Dispatch*, July 5, 1953, p. 4-C. Chopin's children were not always accurate sources: One son once asked to see her grave in New Orleans, although her funeral and burial had taken place in St. Louis, where he lived (1984 interview with David and Ann Chopin). Lélia Chopin, who lived with her mother for her entire life, claimed that Kate Chopin did no more writing after *The Awakening* (DSR, p. 185), but Kate in fact produced over a dozen stories, essays, and poems—and Lélia was writing just three years after her mother's death.

Clarence E. Miller: SCB, pp. 175, 224, n27, and Seyersted, personal communications. Miller retired in 1958 and died in 1964, according to St. Louis newspaper clippings provided to me by Robert Behra, cataloguer, and John Neal Hoover, rare books librarian, of the St. Louis Mercantile Library. The Mercantile Library's head librarian at the time *The Awakening* was published was Horace Kephart, profiled by Charles E. Brown, reference librarian, in "Moments in Mercantile History: Horace Kephart: A Calling for Books and the Wilderness," *News of Note* (publication of the St. Louis Mercantile Library Association) 1:3 (Spring 1987), p. 19. Robert Behra and John Neal Hoover provided me with records of the O'Flaherty library memberships.

Controversy about fiction in libraries: "Librarian Crunden Has 'Worn Out' Oliver Optic," *St. Louis Post-Dispatch*, November 28, 1897, p. 17; "St. Louis Librarians Talk About Books That Are Popular Here Just Now," *St. Louis Republic*, May 7, 1899, p. 10. Collection of Duplicates: Erik Stocker, Rare Books Librarian at the St. Louis Public Library, and *Annual Report of the St. Louis Public School Library, 1874–1875* (St. Louis: Globe-Democrat Job Printing Company, 1876), pp. 22–23.

The Awakening accession records: St. Louis Public Library: Erik Stocker, Mercantile Library: Accession Book 110,001–120,000: Robert Behra, John Neal Hoover, and Charles Brown.

Book bannings and restrictions: Anti-Irish books included two 1906 books by Michael McCarthy—*Priests and People in Ireland* and *Irish Land and Irish Liberty*—bearing stickers saying "Withdrawn at the request of Judge Ryan." Information about these books, stickers, and bookplates: 1985 interview with Erik Stocker.

Reedy and Johns on censorship: "Uncle Fuller" (William Marion Reedy), "Reflections," *Mirror*, November 25, 1897, pp. 7–8; OJ mentions opposition to *Sister Carrie* (p. 170). Erik Stocker checked the *Annual Report of the Board of Directors of the St. Louis Public (Free) Library, 1898 through 1901* (St. Louis: Freegard Press, 1902).

DSR, p. 173 says Chopin was denied membership in the St. Louis Fine Arts Club, but SCB, p. 224, n29, can find no evidence that such a club existed. Chopin did belong to the St. Louis Artist's Guild, according to OJ. Men friends: Waters. Scandalous in New Orleans: 1984 interview with W. Kenneth Holditch.

See also Appendix III: "The Alleged Banning of The Awakening."

369: Wednesday Club; $15 for reading: MAB. Sources on the Wednesday Club: Wednesday Club of St. Louis, Constitution and By-Laws, List of Officers and Members, Programmes, MHS; Elizabeth Schmidt, "Charlotte Rumbold and the Wider Citizenship," unpublished paper; "Social Affairs and Some Personal Notes," St. Louis Republic, May 9, 1899, p. 8. The club's study topics: "Among the Women's Clubs," St. Louis Post-Dispatch, November 26, 1899, part III, p. 32. I am indebted to Mrs. Richard (Dorothea) Maxwell of St. Louis for supplying me with executive board records of the Wednesday Club, 1899–1900 and with a Record of Regular Meetings of the Wednesday Club, 1899–1900. Anna Louise Moss: 1898–1899 and 1899–1900 Year Books of the Wednesday Club: On March 7, 1899 Mrs. Moss presented an essay on "The Sonnet in English Literature"; on February 6, 1900, she spoke on Rudyard Kipling.

Kate Chopin's appearance at the club: Club program at MHS. According to SCB, p. 225, n42, "In Spring" was published in 1913 as "The Joy of Spring," with music by C. B. Hawley (New York and Cincinnati: John Church Company). Chopin's outfit: St. Louis Post-Dispatch for November 30, 1899 (p. 11), cited in Heather Kirk Thomas, " 'What are the prospects for the book?': Re-writing a Woman's Life," unpublished paper. Re Lillie Langtry: Florence Hayward had urged society matrons to "stand for decency and social purity; and to give Langtry a turndown. They did it, to a woman," and Langtry's concert was called off: "The Inside of Society," Mirror, April 12, 1900, p. 17.

371–372: Lélia's début: "Society," Mirror, November 30, 1899, p. 10, and December 7, 1899, p. 10. Clémence Benoist: Jeannine Cook, Oakland estate. Lélia in society: "This Week in Society," St. Louis Post-Dispatch, January 14, 1900, p. 18; January 21, 1900, p. 18; February 11, 1900, p. 18; March 11, 1900, p. 18; March 18, 1900, p. 18. "Reception to Mr. Irving and Miss Terry at University Club," St. Louis Republic, February 9, 1900, p. 6. Chopin's diary: KOCB, reprinted KCM, KCPP.

372: "The Youth's Companion Announcements: The Best of Reading for Girls," Youth's Companion, October 19, 1899, p. 511. "The Youth's Companion for 1898," St. Louis Republic, November 20, 1897, p. 8.

372–373: New writings and sales: MAB. "Alexandre's Wonderful Experience": KCM, KCPP. "Entertainment": "This Week in Society," St. Louis Post-Dispatch, February 11, 1900, p. 18. I have found no other mentions of Mrs. Walthew and Mrs. Calhoun; they were not members of the Wednesday Club. Lucy Monroe, the promoter of The Awakening, married a William J. Calhoun, but not until 1904. "A December Day in Dixie": correspondence in KCM, KCPP; MHS. The "dear old lady" in the story cannot be identified.

373: Cancellation of A Vocation and a Voice: Kramer, p. 298, SCB, pp. 182 and 226, n47. According to Seyersted, Stone & Company gave Kate Chopin no reason for their cancellation. Of the Vocation and a Voice stories, the eight already published in Vogue were "The Dream of an Hour," "Two Summers and Two Souls," "The Unexpected," "Her Letters," "The Kiss," "Suzette," "Recovery," and "The Blind Man." "The Falling in Love of Fedora" and "A Morning Walk" had already appeared in the St. Louis Criterion; "The Night Came Slowly" and "Juanita" in Moods; and "Lilacs" in the New Orleans Times-Democrat. Five were not published during Chopin's lifetime: "Elizabeth

Stock's One Story," "Two Portraits," "An Idle Fellow," "A Mental Suggestion," and "Ti Démon." Story list: DSR, p. 195, but the list is from a later time, since Chopin had not yet written "The White Eagle" when Stone rejected A *Vocation and a Voice*.

A *Vocation and a Voice* will be published as a collection for the first time in 1991, in a Viking Penguin edition that I am editing.
374: Royalties: MAB.

CHAPTER 24: IN DECLINE AND MELANCHOLY

375: United States Census, Gould's city directories. The 1901 *Gould's St. Louis Directory* lists George Chopin at both 3317 Morgan and 8118 N. Broadway, but all the other Chopins are listed at home.
376: "Ellis Glenn Is Not a Man," *St. Louis Post-Dispatch*, November 26, 1899, p. 1; "Brother of Ellis Glenn Appears," *St. Louis Republic*, February 7, 1900, p. 12. Glenn claimed to have a twin brother with whom she had changed identities, but no one believed her, and she was accused of being a Mrs. Cora Alice Cunningham-Rader of West Virginia. But the following February, a "brother of Ellis Glenn" did appear, and Elbert Glenn said he would take his sister's place in prison, if need be. "Eccentric clothing": FELIX, KCM, KCPP.
377: Death of Nina McAllister: Kate Chopin's letter to Marie Chopin Breazeale: KCM, KCPP, at MHS. Burial: Calvary Cemetery records.
378: "Alone": KCM, KCPP. SCB, p. 226, n50, points out that although "Alone" is among Chopin's manuscripts, it is not in her handwriting. Its doggerel rhyme is also uncharacteristic of her poetry.
378: "Kitty" poem: DSR, p. 42, gives the poem its title and date (CW, p. 1032). Since Kate Chopin was careless about keeping track of her poems, there may have been others after "Kitty," but none have been found.
378: Chopin children in society: "Society," *Mirror*, December 6, 1900, p. 11; "Society," *Mirror*, January 3, 1901, p. 11; "Society," *St. Louis Post-Dispatch*, April 3, 1904, p. 4-B.
379: Chopin's land sales: Heather Kirk Thomas, " 'What Are the Prospects for the Book?': Re-Writing a Woman's Life," unpublished paper.
379: *Who's Who in America*, ed. John W. Leonard (Chicago: A. N. Marquis & Company, 1903–1905), p. 265. The abbreviations, such as A7, all refer to the names of publishers.
379ff.: *Republic* advertisement: *St. Louis Republic*, December 8, 1900, p. 8. Florence Hayward, "The Way We Read. An Opinion," and Harrison Clark, "Writers and Books That Have Come Out of St. Louis," both in *St. Louis Republic*, December 9, 1900, Special Book Number, n.p.
380ff.: Kate Chopin, "Development of the Literary West: a Review," *St. Louis Republic*, December 9, 1900, Special Book Number, p. 1, KCPP. I am quoting the entire article here, since it is not available. Payment: MAB. F. A. Charleville: ESM, p. 112. Hamlin Garland, "The Land of the Straddle-Bug," *Chap-Book*, Vol. 2, in eight installments, November 1894–May 1895. The story was reprinted, with minor changes, under

the title *The Moccasin Ranch* (New York: Harper & Brothers, 1909). Mary Wilkins's "A Solitary" is in *A New England Nun and Other Stories* (New York: Harper & Brothers, 1891), pp. 215–33. Reedy and *Sister Carrie*: Max Putzel, *The Man in the Mirror: William Marion Reedy and His Magazine* (Cambridge: Harvard University Press, 1963), pp. 124–25.

385: R. E. Lee Gibson's *Sonnets and Lyrics* (Louisville, KY: John P. Morton and Company, 1901), autographed by Kate Chopin, is in the Kate Chopin Home/Bayou Folk Museum in Cloutierville, donated by David Chopin. Gibson's autograph is dated October 10, 1901. Chopin's letter to Gibson: KCM, KCPP, at MHS. DeMenil letter (November 29, 1901) to Gibson, Gibson Papers, MHS, KCPP. Gibson's *Bayou Folk* sonnet: *Sonnets and Lyrics*, p. 15.

386: Payments: MAB. "Millie's First Party": also called "Millie's First Ball" in MAB. A Kate Chopin granddaughter, her son George's daughter Lélia, was known by the nickname "Toots"—but she was born after her grandmother's death.

There is also an undated Chopin story called "The Impossible Miss Meadows," about a shabby young woman who visits a Wisconsin summer resort, where the good-looking and popular young people dislike her intensely. The mother tries to cheer up Miss Meadows, but the sons groan and slink away—whereupon the story ends, incomplete. "The Impossible Miss Meadows" may have been a draft for "The Falling in Love of Fedora," which it resembles: Kate Chopin did not list "The Impossible Miss Meadows" in MAB. Seyersted (CW, p. 1029) thinks Chopin wrote "The Impossible Miss Meadows" in 1903, but the ms. at MHS is undated.

386: Lamy's chartered trains: ESM, p. 114. Kate and Lélia's stomping baby chicks to death: Jean Bardot, 1988 interview, from Julie Chopin Cusachs, born just before Christmas in 1898. Kate's letter to Marie Breazeale: MHS, KCM, KCPP. Eugénie Chopin Henry's gravestone lists March 11, 1902, as her death date. French Benevolent Society event: Joan Maycrson Clatworthy, *Kate Chopin: The Inward Life Which Questions,* Ph.D. Thesis, State University of New York at Buffalo, 1979, p. 108.

388: Jean's wedding: *Globe-Democrat* clipping, dated June 19, 1902, in Sprague Scrapbook, Vol. 1, p. 22, MHS; "Society," *Mirror*, May 29, 1902, p. 11. Jean's wife's name is variously given as "Emelia," "Emelie," and "Emilie." Her tombstone and obituary both say "Emelie."

388–389: "Death List of a Day: John A. Dillon," *New York Times*, October 16, 1902, p. 9; "Jno. A Dillon Dies at Bar Harbor," Necrology IIP, p. 23, MHS; clipping in Necrology I, p. 47, MHS. Dillon on *The Awakening*: SCB, pp. 178–79, quoting from Seyersted's interview with Rankin, in the 1960s. Rankin's secondhand reports on what Dillon thought should be considered questionable: Dillon had died in 1902, when Rankin was seven years old, and Rankin was often careless about dates, facts, and quotations. *The Awakening* was never reviewed in extant issues of the *New York World*, where John A. Dillon was editor. Chopin and a married man: McCoy, who received the information from Marjorie Chopin McCormick. Fashionable church: SCB, p. 185.

389: Last Will and Testament of Kate Chopin, Missouri Circuit Court, 22nd Judicial Circuit, Probate Division, St. Louis City. Ailing: SCB, p. 185. Diabetes often correlates with stoutness and eye trouble: Chopin mentions an eye problem in an 1897 essay ("As You Like It," CW, p. 708), and the 1900 *Republic* sketch of her shows her wearing spectacles. Emphysema, one of many diseases associated with cigarette smoking and foul air: Chopin had been smoking unfiltered cigarettes for thirty-five years, ever since her trip to New Orleans in 1869, and St. Louis's air was famous for its filth.

There are no extant medical records for Kate Chopin. "I hope I will die first", SCB, p. 185, from interviews with Robert Hattersley and Marjorie Chopin McCormick.
389: Move to McPherson: The McDonalds lived at 4251. Land sales: In October 1902, Kate Chopin had granted powers of attorney for herself and her heirs to Phanor Breazeale and Lamy Chopin, her brothers-in-law in Louisiana (Heather Kirk Thomas, unpublished paper). Earnings: MAB. Jean and Emelie Chopin's street, Berlin, was renamed Pershing during the World War I wave of anti-German sentiment.
390: Chopin house: In February 1986, 4232 McPherson was listed on the National Register of Historic Places, as the last residence of Kate Chopin. (Now a private home belonging to John Bordeaux, it is not open to the public.) The original stairway and Victorian front parlor remain from Kate Chopin's day. The campaign for landmark status for the house: Susan Mowris, "If These Walls Could Speak," *St. Louis Home Magazine*, July 1985, p. 45; Charlene Prost, "7 Sites Advance Toward Historic Status," *St. Louis Post-Dispatch*, July 29, 1985, p. 3A; Emily Toth, "Crisis Alert: Kate Chopin House in St. Louis," *Legacy*, Spring 1985, p. 13; Elaine Viets, "Author's House Still Has Spirit," *St. Louis Post-Dispatch*, March 7, 1985, p. 1-F. The house's history and description are from the application for the National Register of Historic Places, prepared for the Landmarks Association of St. Louis, Inc. by Carolyn Toft and Maureen Jones. Esley Hamilton, Laura Moore, and Marcy Rosenthal were also helpful in gaining landmark status for the house. Number of rooms: I am relying on the house plan that I obtained from St. Louis City Hall—but the plan comes from a later date, and there have been many renovations. I am also indebted to John Bordeaux, Delores Lindsey, and Roberta Lindsey for a tour of the house. Oscar's drawing: 1984 interview with George Chopin.
390: Lélia: "Reign of the Veiled Prophet Is Near," *St. Louis Post-Dispatch*, October 4, 1903, Part I, p. 7. The "Weather Bird," created by Harry Martin, still exists in today's *Post-Dispatch*. Creation of Weather Bird: James W. Markham, *Bovard of the Post-Dispatch* (Baton Rouge: Louisiana State University Press, 1954), p. 14. Oscar Chopin's *Post-Dispatch* cartoons: April 4, 1904, p. 1; April 3, 1904, part 2, p. 1; Teddy Roosevelt and Panama: January 3, 1904, part 3, p. 3; minstrel show: March 1, 1903, p. 1; "A Post-Dispatch Cartoonist's Impressions of the Opening of the Baseball Season," April 3, 1904, part 5, p. 1.
391: "Mrs. Emelie Chopin Dead," *St. Louis Post-Dispatch*, July 8, 1903, p. 2. Emelie Hughes Chopin's gravestone lists her death date, incorrectly, as *June* 7, 1903; the Calvary Cemetery burial records list her as being buried *July* 9. Jean's breakdown: 1984 and 1985 interviews with David, Ann, George, and Marie Chopin, and Marjorie Chopin McCormick. According to Nora Alice Norris ("Kate Chopin," M.A. Thesis, Louisiana State University, 1932): "From 1902 to 1904, Mrs. Chopin's time was filled mostly in caring for her invalid son. She was planning upon resuming her writing at the time of her death in 1904" (p. 115).
391: Lélia as bridesmaid: "Society," *St. Louis Post-Dispatch*, April 3, 1904, p. 4-B. Lélia's engagement and visit, Breazeale plans to visit the fair: Waters.
391ff.: Chopin's fair visits: DSR, pp. 195–96, SCB, p. 185. Going alone: 1985 interview with Marjorie Chopin McCormick. About the fair: Margaret Johanson Witherspoon, *Remembering the St. Louis World's Fair* (St. Louis: Comfort Printing, 1973), passim. Mark Twain: Frances Hurd Stadler. Water: When Jean Chopin died in 1911 of typhoid, a waterborne disease, most likely it was from drinking water. (George O'Flaherty, Kate's half-brother and Jean's half-uncle, had died of typhoid during the

Civil War: It was one of the war's chief causes of death.) Chopin's honeymoon diary: KOCB. " 'Hats Off,' Sang Out Miss Florence Hayward," *St. Louis Post-Dispatch*, May 1, 1904, p. 9-A. No Women's Building: "Department for Women Not Wanted," *St. Louis Republic*, January 12, 1901, p. 1. Oscar Chopin drawings, "Some Types of Americans Chopin Thinks He Met at the Fair Yesterday," *St. Louis Post-Dispatch*, May 1, 1904, p. 1-D.

393: Charles A. Faris's tombstone lists his death date as May 21, 1904. His widow, fourteen years his junior, outlived him by forty years and died October 24, 1944. Their son, the Right Reverend Monsignor Charleville Benoist Faris, was born in 1895 and died in 1963, a year after Lélia. Small inheritance: Heather Kirk Thomas, unpublished paper.

393: Humidity and other problems for the fair: An excellent survey of the fair's negative sides is Susan M. Gray, "St. Louis Views the World's Fair: Some Negative Reactions to a Positive Event," paper given at the Midwest Popular Culture Association Convention in 1987.

393: Pennsylvania Day and other events: *St. Louis Post-Dispatch* articles, esp. "World's Congress of the Deaf Meets at the Big Fair" (August 20, 1904, p. 3); "Saturday Afternoon's World's Fair Program" (August 20, 1904, p. 3); "Pennsylvania Made Gorgeous Showing" (August 21, 1904, p. 2). Also David R. Francis, *The Universal Exposition of 1904* (St. Louis: Louisiana Purchase Exposition Company, 1913), pp. 262–63.

393ff.: Death reports and obituaries: DSR, p. 196, SCB, p. 185. "Mrs. Kate Chopin, the St. Louis Authoress, Dead," *St. Louis Globe-Democrat*, August 23, 1904, p. 13. (This is the only information about Chopin's third volume of short stories, presumably *A Vocation and a Voice*.) "Attractive mental attributes": "Death Comes to Mrs. Kate Chopin," *St. Louis Post-Dispatch*, August 22, 1904, p. 1. Also "Mrs. Kate Chopin. Well-Known Authoress Succumbed to Sudden Attack of Hemorrhage of the Brain." Necrology IIC, p. 191, MHS clipping file, probably from the *New Orleans States*. Notice from *New Orleans Times-Democrat*: reprinted in Amy Elizabeth Taggart, "Mrs. Kate O'Flaherty Chopin: Her Life and Writing," M.A. Thesis, Tulane University, 1928, p. 37. "Mrs. Kate Chopin, Who Died Suddenly Today," St. Louis Scrapbook, 1889–1906, p. 100, MHS; "Recent Deaths: Mrs. Kate Chopin's Career," *Boston Evening Transcript*, August 24, 1899, p. 5; Alexander DeMenil, "Current Literature: Kate Chopin," *The Hesperian*, October–December 1904, 383–84; William Marion Reedy, "Reflections: Death of Mrs. Chopin," *Mirror*, August 25, 1904, p. 1.

Late in his life, Kate Chopin's son George—known as "Doc" to everyone—used to talk about how much she enjoyed the fair, and he speculated that she had high blood pressure: 1985 interview with David Chopin and Marjorie Chopin McCormick.

396: Absent friends: George Johns in 1904: described in OJ, pp. 159–60.

EPILOGUE

Chopin interviews = 1984 and 1985 interviews with Kate Chopin's granddaughter, grandsons, and wives: Marjorie Chopin McCormick, David and Ann Chopin, George and Marie Chopin, Tom and Rose Chopin.

397ff.: Chopin's children's marriages: Lélia: Sprague Scrapbook, Vol. 1, p. 51, MHS;

Lélia's father-in-law: "Frederick Hattersley," Necrology Microfilm XV, p. 23, MHS. Oscar C. Chopin: "Miss Fannie Louise Hinckley," undated clipping in Sprague Scrapbook Vol. 1, p. 53, MHS; she was known as Louise. George ("Doc") Chopin: "Chopin-Gleeson," Sprague Scrapbook, Vol. 1, p. 51, MHS. Lil's calling Felix "Phil": Chopin interviews. Fred's remarriage: "F. H. Chopin Wedded Again in St. Louis," September 1, 1914, Biography Scrapbooks, MHS.

398: Lélia: "St. Louis Author Explains Bridge in Latest Book," MHS clipping from March 12, 1927, about Lélia Hattersley's publishing *Auction and Contract Bridge Clarified*; "Former St. Louisan Writes on Latest Craze—Backgammon," MHS clipping from September 18, 1930, about Lélia's latest book, *How to Play the New Backgammon*. According to the *National Union Catalog*, Lélia Hattersley's other books were *Contract and Auction Bridge Clarified* (a second edition of *Auction and Contract Bridge Clarified*), *Contract Developments*, *How to Play the Culbertson System*, and *Up to the Minute Contract*. Lélia's behavior, descriptions: Chopin interviews.

Promoting her mother's work: Lélia C. Hattersley letter to Fred Lewis Pattee, March 17, 1925, in the Fred Lewis Pattee Collection in the Fred Lewis Pattee Library, Pennsylvania State University, KCPP. Philip Skrainka, a New York friend of Lélia's who had also known Kate Chopin, corresponded with Pattee in 1923 about republishing a selection of Chopin's Louisiana stories, but nothing came of the venture. Skrainka's letters are also in the Fred Lewis Pattee Collection, and I am grateful to Charles Mann, Chief of the Rare Books and Special Collections, for calling these letters to my attention. Lélia Chopin Hattersley's son Robert preferred not to be interviewed for this book.

398–399: Oscar Chopin: Chopin interviews. His daughter: "Miss Kate Chopin, Artist, Dies After Long Illness," Necrology XXIII, p. 49, MHS, clipping from *St. Louis Post-Dispatch*, August 30, 1946.

399: Fred Chopin: "Frederic Chopin, 74, Former Resident, Dies," Necrology, XXIV, pp. 92, 93, from the *St. Louis Globe-Democrat*, February 7, 13, 1953, MHS. Fred, who had worked in the wholesale candy business, died in Oakland of a cerebral hemorrhage. Dress and manner: Chopin interviews.

399: Felix Chopin: Chopin interviews; "Felix Andrew Chopin," *Book of St. Louisans* (St. Louis: St. Louis Republic, 1906), pp. 118–19; "Felix André Chopin," Walter Stevens, *St. Louis, History of the Fourth City, 1763–1909* (Chicago: S. J. Clarke, 1909), Vol. 2, pp. 1001–2. Chopin's children and religion: According to Tom Chopin (1985 interview), Fred, Oscar, and Lélia were not practicing Catholics, but Felix was very devout. "Doc" was believed to be quite devout, but often missed mass because of medical emergencies—and some of his children have doubts about his faith.

399: Kolbenheyer: 1985 interview with Tom Chopin. Dr. Kolbenheyer delivered several of Kate Chopin's grandchildren, including George ("Doc")'s daughter Marjorie. The "Naked Truth" statue: Paul F. Guenther, "The *Westliche Post* of St. Louis," unpublished paper. A letter to Dr. Kolbenheyer from a sculptor about statue specifications is in the Cramer Family Papers, Box 2-2, MHS. "Dr. Kolbenheyer's Body Brought Home," *St. Louis Post-Dispatch*, April 10, 1921, in Necrology XI, p. 98, MHS. Dr. Kolbenheyer and his wife had gone to live with their daughter, Mrs. William H. Koenig, in Omaha, three years before his death. Kate Chopin, seven years younger than her outspoken friend, had gently laughed at Kolbenheyer's obsession with aging—but he outlived her by seventeen years.

399–400: George Chopin: Chopin interviews. "Dr. George F. Chopin Dies: Physician Here 50 Years," Medical III, 127, *St. Louis Post-Dispatch*, February 27, 1952, MHS.

"Frances Chopin Dies at Age 83," Necrology XXVII, p. 103, *Globe-Democrat* clipping marked March 19, 1965, MHS.

400: Jean Chopin: Waters remembered her cousin Jean as not seeming to have a job, since he would visit Louisiana for months at a time. "Jean B. Chopin Is Dead," Necrology II, p. 34, MHS, *Globe-Democrat* clipping dated March 21, 1911. "Chopin Will Favors Two Kin" (death notice for Jean B. Chopin), Necrology IIC, p. 251, MHS.

400: Kate Chopin's children and their children: Jean, none; Oscar, 1 (Kate); George, 6 (Frances, Marjorie, George, Dorothy, Lelia, David); Fred, 3 (2 from first marriage and Fred); Felix, 2 (Rosemary and Tom); Lélia, 1 (Robert Hattersley). A clipping about Robert Hattersley's marriage, untitled, is in Sprague Scrapbook, Vol. 1, p. 241, MHS. According to the obituary for "Doc"'s wife ("Frances Chopin" above), they had twenty-one grandchildren. Chopin interviews. Lelia Chopin (later Conway), "Kate Chopin," *Maryville Magazine* 8 (May 1933), pp. 24–26 (the article has numerous errors).

400: Grace Hattersley: Gene Ruffini and Mike Pearl, "Billy's Gal's Idol Hours in the Slammer," *New York Post*, February 20, 1987, p. 3. I am grateful to Robert Rosenblum for calling this to my attention. MTV, undated tape.

400: Le Petit Salon: 1984 interview with W. Kenneth Holditch.

401: Albert Sampite: DeLouche; Cloutierville Group. Louise Rachal Barron, 1985 interview, described Albert Sampite as a quiet man who didn't talk much and didn't worry about talking to everybody. He was a "lovely person and a good friend if you knew him. My daddy liked him so much."

402: Lesche Club: Lucille Tinker Carnahan; Waters; McCoy Scrapbooks, NSU. According to Carnahan, a portrait of Kate Chopin used to hang in Chopin Hall. Lamp: DeLouche. Gaming table: Sampite. Mayor Sampite: Joseph Sampite is the adopted son of Bathilde Guillot Sampite and her husband, Albert Sampite's son Dr. Alphonse Sampite, who died of a spider bite in 1938. Dr. and Mrs. Sampite raised a dozen children, and their pictures appear in the Bayou Folk Museum's doctor's office. Mayor Sampite has been reelected twice and likes to claim that his ancestors were "kicked out of France" (1989 interview).

402–403: About Rankin: Chopin interviews; interviews with Per Seyersted, Waters; biographical sketch, University of Pennsylvania Library Archives. Cited men as friends, lost his notes: SCB, 209, n55, pp. 10–11. Phanor Breazeale's sidetracking Rankin: McCoy. Fannie Hertzog as Rankin's source: Lucille Tinker Carnahan. Marjorie Chopin McCormick and Frances Gleeson Chopin gave Kate Chopin's manuscripts to MHS.

According to Nora Alice Norris ("Kate Chopin," M.A. Thesis, Louisiana State University, 1932), Rankin first became interested in Kate Chopin "when he heard a professor in a theological school in Paris acclaim her as the best short-story writer of the United States" (p. 11). It was later said that Rankin became interested in Kate Chopin when he met her granddaughter, Marjorie McCormick, while playing tennis in Atlanta—but Marjorie McCormick said in 1985 that she had never met Rankin.

403: Vernon Knapp, "Is There an Interesting Woman in St. Louis?" *St. Louis Republic*, September 11, 1910, part 5, p. 1: KCM, KCPP. Orrick Johns, "The 'Cadians," *Mirror* XX (July 20, 1911), pp. 5–6; KCM, KCPP. Alexander N. DeMenil, excerpt from "A Century of Missouri Literature," *Missouri Historical Review* 15:1 (October 1920), pp. 117–19: KCM, KCPP.

404: About Seyersted's research: Interviews with Seyersted; SCB, p. 189.

404: *Redbook* reprint of *The Awakening*: November 1972.

404–405: The McCoy Scrapbooks, NSU, record Mildred McCoy's tireless efforts in creating and promoting the Bayou Folk Museum/Kate Chopin Home. *Elizabeth and Her German Garden*, the only book remaining from Kate Chopin's personal library, was originally published anonymously. According to Rankin (interview, cited in SCB, p. 206, n16), Kate Chopin's private library consisted mostly of works of fiction, including many by William Dean Howells. She also had copies of the *Yellow Book*. The most recent director of the Association for the Preservation of Historic Natchitoches is Maxine Southerland.

405: Lampoons and graffiti: "Study Technique: How to Write the Harvard Five-Page Paper." *Harvard Lampoon* 158 (November 1973), pp. 54–55; Jan Gilbert, "Kate Chopin Up Against the Wall." *Kate Chopin Newsletter* 2 (Fall 1976), p. 46. Robert Stone, *Children of Light* (New York: Knopf, 1986). Jill McCorkle's suggestion: "Twisting the Tale at the End: a Symposium," *New York Times Book Review*, December 6, 1987, p. 52.

406: "I shrink from the indelicacy": "The Real Edwin Booth," CW, p. 695.

406: "Never again to belong": *The Awakening*, Chap. XXVI; "Courageous soul," Chap. XXXIX.

APPENDIX III: THE ALLEGED BANNING OF *THE AWAKENING*

422: "A Daring Writer Banned": SCB, pp. 164–185.

422: Introduction to *The Awakening: Redbook* magazine, November 1972, p. 199.

422: Nonexistent fine arts club: SCB, p. 224 n. 29. Chopin's friends' letters are in MHS and are reprinted in KCM and KCPP.

422: St. Louis Artist's Guild (sometimes spelled Artists or Artists'): SCB, p. 224, n. 29. Orrick Johns listed Kate Chopin as a Guild member: OJ, Vol. LXXXVIII, pp. 181–83.

422–423: Lélia Chopin Hattersley: quoted in DSR, pp. 185–86; the ellipses are Rankin's, and the letter no longer exists. Leonidas Rutledge Whipple, "Kate Chopin (1851–1904)" in Edwin Anderson Alderman and Joel Chandler Harris, eds., *Library of Southern Literature* (New Orleans: Martin & Hoyt, 1909), p. 864.

423: Lélia about Lady Bountiful: DSR, p. 102. Chopin and swarming children: DSR, p. 116. Lélia's false recollections all appear in her letter to Leonidas Rutledge Whipple: Apparently she was shaping an image of Kate Chopin for the critic. Chopin's study appears in a sketch by her son Oscar in the *St. Louis Post-Dispatch* for November 26, 1899, pt. 4, p. 1. Her study ("quite a unique little den . . . with bookshelves filled with volumes of no flippant order . . .") was also described in an 11 August 1895 article in the *St. Louis Republic*. That article is quoted in Joan Mayerson Clatworthy, "Kate Chopin: the Inward Life Which Questions," Ph.D. Thesis, State University of New York at Buffalo, 1979, p. 60 n. 22.

423: Critics on Chopin's silence: Fred Lewis Pattee, *American Literature Since 1870* (New York: Century Company, 1915), p. 364; Amy Elizabeth Taggart, "Mrs. Kate O'Flaherty Chopin," M. A. Thesis, Tulane University, 1928, p. 7; FELIX; Dorothy A. Dondore, "Kate O'Flaherty Chopin," *Dictionary of American Biography*, Vol. IV, ed. Allen Johnson (New York: Charles Scribner's Sons, 1930), pp. 90–91.

423: Chopin's continuing to write and publish: DSR, pp. 185–86; MAB, in KCPP. A *Vocation and a Voice*, edited by Emily Toth, is scheduled for publication as a collection for the first time in 1991.

423: *Awakening* taken from circulation, Chopin barred from fine arts club: DSR, p. 173. Rankin's lost notes: SCB, pp. 10–11.

424: Nora Alice Norris, "Mrs. Kate Chopin," M.A. Thesis, Louisiana State University, 1932, p. 8.

424: Felix Chopin's recollections: FELIX.

424: Sources about banning: Robert Cantwell, *"The Awakening* by Kate Chopin," *Georgia Review*, Vol. X (Winter 1956), p. 494; Kenneth Eble, "A Forgotten Novel: Kate Chopin's *The Awakening*," *Western Humanities Review*, Vol. X (Summer 1956), p. 261; Edmund Wilson, *Patriotic Gore: Studies in the Literature of the American Civil War* (New York: Oxford University Press, 1962), p. 591; Stanley Kauffmann, "The Really Lost Generation," *New Republic*, Vol. CLV (December 3, 1966), p. 37; Larzer Ziff, *The American 1890s: Life and Times of a Lost Generation* (New York: Viking, 1966), p. 305.

424: Clarence E. Miller's recollection: SCB, p. 175.

424: Chopin on libraries: "On Certain Brisk, Bright Days," *St. Louis Post-Dispatch*, November 26, 1899, pt. 4, p. 1, CW.

424: Sources about the banning: George Spangler, "Kate Chopin's *The Awakening*: A Partial Dissent," *Novel: A Forum on Fiction*, Vol. III (Spring 1970), p. 255; Bert Bender, "Kate Chopin's Lyrical Short Stories," *Studies in Short Fiction*, Vol. II (Summer 1974), p. 258; Clement Eaton, "Breaking a Path for the Liberation of Women in the South," *Georgia Review*, Vol. CXXVIII (Summer 1974), p. 194; Judith Fryer, *The Faces of Eve: Women in the Nineteenth Century American Novel* (New York: Oxford University Press, 1976), p. 207; Beverly Bishop, 1984 interview; Clatworthy, "Kate Chopin."

425: St. Louis library information: see Chapter 23; Miller on book-committee: SCB, pp. 175 and 224, n. 27.

425: *Peyton Place*: Emily Toth, *Inside Peyton Place: The Life of Grace Metalious* (Garden City, N.Y.: Doubleday, 1981), esp. chs. 9 and 10.

425: Dangerous, alluring books: Kate Chopin, "As You Like It," CW, pp. 714–715.

SELECT
BIBLIOGRAPHY OF
WORKS RELATED
TO KATE CHOPIN

In recent years, countless articles on Kate Chopin have appeared—many of them, unfortunately, marred by biographical inaccuracies. Listed here are the published works and archival materials that have been most useful to me. These items should be of value to anyone studying Kate Chopin and her milieu, including folklore and gossip as well as strictly factual data.

Items from the *Kate Chopin Newsletter* may be obtained at a nominal charge from the Penn State Room, Fred Lewis Pattee Library, Pennsylvania State University, University Park, PA 16802.

I expect to be donating notes and materials from my own research to the Hill Memorial Library, Louisiana State University.

BOOKS AND BOOK-LENGTH STUDIES

Arner, Robert. "Kate Chopin." *Louisiana Studies* (Spring 1975). Entire issue devoted to Kate Chopin.

Bardot, Jean. "*L'influence française dans la vie et l'oeuvre de Kate Chopin.*" *Thèse de doctorat*, Université de Paris-IV, 1985–86.

Bonner, Thomas, Jr. *The Kate Chopin Companion, with Chopin's Translations from French Fiction.* Westport, CT: Greenwood Press, 1988.

Culley, Margaret, ed., *The Awakening: An Authoritative Text, Contexts, Criticism.* New York: W. W. Norton, 1976.

Ewell, Barbara C. *Kate Chopin.* New York: Ungar, 1986.

Garitta, Anthony Paul. "The Critical Reputation of Kate Chopin," Ph.D. Thesis, University of North Carolina at Greensboro, 1978.

Koloski, Bernard J., ed. *Approaches to Teaching Kate Chopin's "The Awakening"*. New York: Modern Language Association of America, 1988.

Rankin, Daniel. *Kate Chopin and Her Creole Stories*. Philadelphia: University of Pennsylvania Press, 1932.

Seyersted, Per. *Kate Chopin: a Critical Biography*. Baton Rouge: Louisiana State University Press, and Oslo: Universitetsforlaget, 1969.

Seyersted, Per, and Emily Toth, eds. *A Kate Chopin Miscellany*. Oslo and Natchitoches: Universitetsforlaget and Northwestern State University Press of Louisiana, 1979. Abbreviated as KCM.

Skaggs, Peggy. *Kate Chopin*. Boston: G. K. Hall, 1985.

Toth, Emily and Per Seyersted, eds., *Kate Chopin's Private Papers*. Bloomington: Indiana University Press, forthcoming. Abbreviated as KCPP.

Toth, Emily. "That Outward Existence Which Conforms: Kate Chopin and Literary Convention," Ph.D. Thesis, Johns Hopkins University, 1975.

BIBLIOGRAPHIES

Bonner, Thomas, Jr. "Kate Chopin: An Annotated Bibliography." *Bulletin of Bibliography* 32 (July–September 1975), pp. 101–5.

Gannon, Barbara C. "Kate Chopin. A Secondary Bibliography." *American Literary Realism* 27:1 (Spring 1984), pp. 124–29.

Inge, Tonette Bond. "Kate Chopin." In Maurice Duke, Jackson R. Bryer, and M. Thomas Inge, eds., *American Women Writers: Bibliographical Essays*. Westport, CT.: Greenwood Press, 1983, pp. 47–69.

Potter, Richard. "Kate Chopin and Her Critics: An Annotated Checklist." *Missouri Historical Society Bulletin* 26 (July 1970), pp. 306–17.

Seyersted, Per, and Emily Toth, eds. *A Kate Chopin Miscellany*. Oslo and Natchitoches: Universitetsforlaget and Northwestern State University Press, 1979, pp. 201–61.

Springer, Marlene. *Edith Wharton and Kate Chopin: A Reference Guide*. Boston: G. K. Hall, 1976.

Springer, Marlene. "Kate Chopin: A Reference Guide Updated." *Resources for American Literary Study,* 11 (1981), pp. 25–42.

ST. LOUIS BACKGROUNDS

Anderson, Galusha. A *Border City During the Civil War*. Boston: Little, Brown, 1908.

Berthold, Eugénie. *Glimpses of Creole Life in Old St. Louis*. St. Louis: Missouri Historical Society, 1933.

Churchill, Winston. *The Crisis*. New York: Macmillan, 1901.

Clark, Harrison. "Writers and Books That Have Come Out of St. Louis." *St. Louis Republic*, December 9, 1900, Special Book Number, n.p.

Clemens, Cyril Coniston. "The History of St. Louis, 1854–1860," M.A. Thesis, Washington University, 1949.

Devoy, John, comp. and publ. A *History of the City of St. Louis & Vicinity*. St. Louis: John Devoy, 1898.

Gill, McCune. *St. Louis Story*. Hopkinsville, KY: St. Louis Historical Record Association, 1952.

Holland, Dorothy Garesché. *The Garesché, de Bauduy, and Des Chapelles Families: History and Genealogy*. St. Louis: Schneider Printing, 1963.

Hyde, William, and Howard L. Conard, eds. *Encyclopedia of the History of St. Louis*. New York, Louisville, St. Louis: Southern History, 1899.

Johns, Orrick. *The Time of Our Lives: the Story of My Father and Myself*. New York: Stackpole, 1937.

Johnson, Mrs. Charles P. (Anne), ed. *Notable Women of St. Louis, 1914*. St. Louis: Woodward, 1914.

Kelsoe, William A., ed. *St. Louis Reference Record*. St. Louis: Von Hoffman, 1928.

Kirschten, Ernest. *Catfish and Crystal*. Garden City, NY: Doubleday, 1960.

Necrology Scrapbooks, Missouri Historical Society, St. Louis.

Primm, James Neal. *Lion of the Valley: St. Louis, Missouri*. Boulder, CO: Pruett Publishing Company, 1981.

Putzel, Max. *The Man in the Mirror: William Marion Reedy and His Magazine*. Cambridge: Harvard University Press, 1963.

St. Louis Womanhood Scrapbooks, Missouri Historical Society, St. Louis.

Scharf, J. Thomas. *History of St. Louis City and County*. Philadelphia: Louis H. Everts, 1883.

Society Scrapbooks, Missouri Historical Society, St. Louis.

Stadler, Frances Hurd. *St. Louis: A History of the City from Its Founding to the Eve of Its Two-Hundredth Anniversary*. St. Louis: Post-Dispatch, 1962.

Thomas, James. *From Tennessee Slave to St. Louis Entrepreneur: The Autobiography of James Thomas*, ed. Loren Schweninger. Columbia: University of Missouri, 1984.

Wednesday Club of St. Louis, Constitution and By-Laws, List of Officers and Members, Programmes. Missouri Historical Society.

Wolf, Fred Wilhelm. *William Marion Reedy: a Critical Biography*, Ph.D. Thesis, Vanderbilt University, 1951.

SACRED HEART SCHOOLING

Callan, Louise. *Society of the Sacred Heart in North America*. New York: Longmans Green, 1937.

Gelderman, Carol. *Mary McCarthy: A Life*. New York: St. Martin's, 1988.

McCarthy, Mary. *Memories of a Catholic Girlhood*. New York: Harcourt Brace Jovanovich, 1957.

National Archives of the Society of the Sacred Heart, Villa Duchesne, St. Louis.

O'Leary, M. *Education with a Tradition: an Account of the Educational Work of the Society of the Sacred Heart*. New York: Longmans Green, 1936.

Repplier, Agnes. *In Our Convent Days*. Boston and New York: Houghton, Mifflin, 1905.

White, Antonia. *As Once in May: the Early Autobiography of Antonia White and Other Writings*, ed. Susan Chitty. London: Virago, 1983.

LOUISIANA BACKGROUNDS

Biographical and Historical Memoirs of Louisiana. Chicago: Goodspeed, 1892.

Biographical and Historical Memoirs of Northwestern Louisiana. Nashville and Chicago: Southern Publishing, 1890.

Carnahan, Lucille Tinker. "Cloutierville." In Germaine Portré-Bobinski and Clara Mildred Smith, *Natchitoches: the Up-to-Date Oldest Town in Louisiana*. New Orleans: Dameron-Pierson, 1936.

Chopin, J. B. and Suzette Benoist. Succession Papers. Central District Court, New Orleans.

Chopin, Oscar, Executor, v. the United States No. 592, French and American Claims Commission, Files of the French and American Claims Commission, Diplomatic Archives, National Archives, Washington, D. C. Excerpted in Mills Collection.

Chopin, Oscar. Succession Papers. McCoy Collection.

Corley, D. B. *A Visit to Uncle Tom's Cabin*. Chicago: Baird and Lee, 1892.

Evans, Sally Kittredge; Frederick Stielow; and Betsy Swanson. *Grand Isle on the*

Gulf: an Early History. Metairie, Louisiana: Jefferson Parish Historical Commission, 1979.

Hardin, J. Fair. *Northwestern Louisiana: a History of the Watershed of the Red River, 1714–1937*. Shreveport and Louisville: Historical Record Assn., n.d.

Holditch, W. Kenneth, ed., *In Old New Orleans*. Jackson: University Press of Mississippi, 1983.

Insurance Map of New Orleans, LA., Vols. 1 and 4. New York: Sanford Publ. Ltd., 1876.

Jackson, Joy. *New Orleans in the Gilded Age: Politics and Urban Progress, 1880–1896*. Baton Rouge: Louisiana State University, 1969.

Jones, Anne Goodwyn. *Tomorrow Is Another Day: The Woman Writer in the South, 1859–1936*. Baton Rouge: Louisiana State University, 1981.

Landry, Stuart Omer. *The Battle of Liberty Place: the Overthrow of Carpet-Bag Rule in New Orleans—September 14, 1874*. New Orleans: Pelican Publishing, 1955.

Lindig, Carmen Meriwether. "The Woman's Movement in Louisiana, 1879–1920." Ph.D. Thesis, North Texas State University, 1982.

May, John R. "Local Color in *The Awakening*." *Southern Review* 6 (1970): pp. 1031–1040.

McCants, Sister Dorothy Olga, ed. and trans. *They Came to Louisiana: Letters of a Catholic Mission, 1854–1882*. Baton Rouge: Louisiana State University, 1970.

McCoy Collection: Scrapbooks and other materials gathered by Mildred McCoy. Cammie G. Henry Research Center, Eugene P. Watson Memorial Library, Northwestern State University, Natchitoches, Louisiana.

McVoy, Lizzie Carter, ed. *Louisiana in the Short Story*. University, Louisiana: Louisiana State University, 1940.

Melrose Collection: Scrapbooks and other materials gathered by Cammie G. Henry. Cammie G. Henry Research Center, Eugene P. Watson Memorial Library, Northwestern State University, Natchitoches, Louisiana.

Mills Collection: Photographs, letters, and other materials gathered by Elizabeth Shown Mills. Cammie G. Henry Research Center, Eugene P. Watson Memorial Library, Northwestern State University, Natchitoches, Louisiana.

Mills, Elizabeth Shown. *Chauvin dit Charleville*. Cane River Creole Series. Mississippi State: Mississippi State University, 1976.

Mills, Elizabeth Shown, and Gary B. Mills, *Tales of Old Natchitoches*. Natchitoches: Association for the Preservation of Historic Natchitoches, 1978.

Mills, Gary B. *The Forgotten People: Cane River's Creoles of Color*. Baton Rouge: Louisiana State University, 1977.

Poché, Felix Pierre. *A Louisiana Confederate: Diary of Felix Pierre Poché*, ed. Edwin C. Bearss and trans. Eugenie Watson Somdal. Natchitoches: Louisiana Studies Institute, Northwestern State University, 1972.

Prudhomme, Lucile Keator, and Fern B. Christensen, comps. *The Natchitoches Cemeteries: Transcriptions of Gravestones from the 18th, 19th, and 20th Centuries in Northwest Louisiana*. New Orleans: Polyanthos, 1977.

Saxon, Lyle. *Children of Strangers*. London: Bodley Head, 1937.

Saxon, Lyle. *Old Louisiana*. New York and London: Century, 1929.

Swanson, Betsy, *Historic Jefferson Parish, from Shore to Shore*. Gretna, LA: Pelican Publishing, 1975.

Tallant, Robert. *Mardi Gras*. Garden City, NY: Doubleday, 1948.

Tallant, Robert. *The Romantic New Orleanians*. New York: Dutton, 1950.

Taylor, Joe Gray. *Louisiana Reconstructed, 1863–1877*. Baton Rouge: Louisiana State University, 1974.

Tinker, Edward Larocque. *Creole City: Its Past and Its People*. New York: Longmans Green, 1953.

Toth, Emily. *Daughters of New Orleans*. New York: Bantam, 1983.

Tunnell, Ted. *Crucible of Reconstruction: War, Radicalism and Race in Louisiana, 1862–1877*. Baton Rouge: Louisiana State University, 1984.

Wilds, John. *Crises, Clashes and Cures: a Century of Medicine in New Orleans*. New Orleans: Orleans Parish Medical Society, 1978.

Winters, John D. *Civil War in Louisiana*. Baton Rouge: Louisiana State University, 1963.

BIOGRAPHICAL ARTICLES

Chopin, Felix. "Statement on Kate Chopin," January 19, 1949, interview with Felix Chopin (Kate's son), notes taken by Charles van Ravenswaay of the Missouri Historical Society. Reprinted in KCM, KCPP.

DeMenil, Alexander. Excerpt from "A Century of Missouri Literature," *Missouri Historical Review* 15:1 (October 1920), pp. 117–119. Reprinted in KCM, KCPP.

Dondore, Dorothy A. "Kate O'Flaherty Chopin." *Dictionary of American Biography*. New York: Scribner, 1930, pp. 90–91.

Gremmels, Marion. "After Seyersted: Limitations of Chopin Biography." Unpublished paper, presented at the Mid-America American Studies Association meeting, 1984.

Johns, Orrick. "The 'Cadians." *Mirror* XX (July 20, 1911), pp. 5–6. Reprinted in KCM, KCPP.

(Knapp, Vernon.) "Is There an Interesting Woman in St. Louis?" *St. Louis Republic*, September 11, 1910, part 5, p. 1. Reprinted in KCM, KCPP.

"The Lounger." *The Critic* 35:866 (August 1899), p. 677. Reprinted in KCPP.

Mills, Elizabeth Shown. "Colorful Characters from Kate's Past." *Kate Chopin Newsletter* 2:1 (Spring 1976), pp. 7–12.

Moore, Sue V. "Mrs. Kate Chopin." *St. Louis Life* 10 (June 9, 1894), pp. 11–12. Reprinted in KCM, KCPP.

Norris, Nora Alice. "Kate Chopin," M.A. Thesis, Louisiana State University, 1932.

"The Practical Side of Oscar Chopin's Death." *Kate Chopin Newsletter* 1:3 (Winter 1975–76), p. 29.

Schuyler, William. "Kate Chopin." *The Writer* VII (August 1894), pp. 115–17. Reprinted in KCM, KCPP.

Seyersted, Per. "Kate Chopin: an Important St. Louis Writer Reconsidered." *Missouri Historical Society Bulletin* 19 (January 1963), pp. 89–114.

Seyersted, Per. "Kate Chopin's Wound: Two New Letters." *American Literary Realism* 20:1 (Fall 1987), pp. 71–75.

Toth, Emily. "The Independent Woman and 'Free' Love." *Massachusetts Review* 16 (Autumn 1975), pp. 647–64.

Toth, Emily. "Kate Chopin and Literary Convention: 'Désirée's Baby.' " *Southern Studies* 20:2 (Summer 1981), pp. 201–8.

Toth, Emily. "Kate Chopin Remembered." *Kate Chopin Newsletter* 1:3 (Winter 1975–76), pp. 21–27.

Toth, Emily. "Kate Chopin's New Orleans Years." *New Orleans Review* 15:1 (Spring 1988), pp. 53–60.

Toth, Emily. "Kate Chopin's *The Awakening* as Feminist Criticism." *Louisiana Studies* 15 (Fall 1976), pp. 241–51.

Toth, Emily. "The Misdated Death of Oscar Chopin." *Kate Chopin Newsletter* 1:2 (Fall 1975), p. 34.

Toth, Emily. "A New Biographical Approach." In *Approaches to Teaching Kate Chopin's "The Awakening"*, ed. Bernard J. Koloski. New York: Modern Language Association of America, 1988, pp. 60–66.

Toth, Emily. "St. Louis and the Fiction of Kate Chopin." *Missouri Historical Society Bulletin* 32 (October 1975), pp. 33–50.

Toth, Emily. "The Shadow of the First Biographer: The Case of Kate Chopin." *Southern Review*, 26 (April 1990), pp. 285–292.

Toth, Emily. "Timely and Timeless: the Treatment of Time in *The Awakening* and *Sister Carrie*." *Southern Studies* 16 (Fall 1977), pp. 271–76.

Wilson, Maryhelen. "Kate Chopin's Family: Fallacies and Facts, Including Kate's True Birthdate." *Kate Chopin Newsletter* 2 (Winter 1976–77), pp. 25–31.

Wilson, Maryhelen. "Woman's Lib in Old St. Louis: 'La Verdon,' " *St. Louis Genealogical Society* 14:4 (n.d.), pp. 139–40.

INDEX